RENAISSANCE
HUMANISM ❧
Volume 1

RENAISSANCE HUMANISM

FOUNDATIONS, FORMS, AND LEGACY

VOLUME 1 · HUMANISM IN ITALY

Edited by Albert Rabil, Jr.

UNIVERSITY OF PENNSYLVANIA PRESS

PHILADELPHIA 1988

Library of Congress Cataloging-in-Publication Data

Renaissance humanism.
    Bibliography: p.
    Includes index.
    Contents: v. 1. Humanism in Italy—v. 2. Humanism
beyond Italy—v. 3. Humanism and the disciplines.
    1. Humanism. 2. Renaissance—Italy. I. Rabil, Albert.
B778.R43   1988   001.1'094   87-13928
ISBN 0-8122-8066-0 (SET)
ISBN 0-8122-8063-6 (V. 1)
ISBN 0-8122-8064-4 (V. 2)
ISBN 0-8122-8065-2 (V. 3)

To

MARISTELLA LORCH

Catalyst Among Scholars
Whose Initial Idea Has Developed into These Volumes

CONTENTS

VOLUME 2 ❧ HUMANISM BEYOND ITALY

PART III • HUMANISM BEYOND ITALY

VOLUME 3 ❧ HUMANISM AND THE DISCIPLINES

PART V • THE LEGACY OF HUMANISM

PREFACE

The study of Renaissance humanism became a recognized scholarly enterprise after the publication of Georg Voigt's *The Revival of Classical Antiquity or the First Century of Humanism* (1859) and, more significantly, of Jacob Burckhardt's *The Civilization of the Renaissance in Italy* (1860). Both writers maintained that the Italian Renaissance gave rise to a new personality type, one who had a thirst for fame and adopted a naturalistic attitude toward the world. Burckhardt called this new person a "spiritual individual," which meant, variously, a self-centered person, one who embodied a new kind of moral autonomy or emancipation from traditional religious standards and political authorities, or one always seeking to give full expression to his personality. Accordingly, for a long period the great debate was over the nature and cultural significance of the new kind of consciousness embodied by the humanists. Wilhelm Dilthey, Giovanni Gentile, and Ernst Cassirer, writing during the earlier decades of the twentieth century, regarded humanism as a new philosophy of human values, the chief among which were those values of individualism, secularism, and moral autonomy which had been identified by Burckhardt. The implication of this view was that humanism was hostile to Christianity and, indeed, initiated the development of modern paganism. This view was challenged in 1952 by Giuseppe Toffanin, who argued that far from being pagan and heterodox, Renaissance humanism was the champion of the authentic Latin-Catholic tradition against late medieval Aristotelian science.

These parameters of interpretation have largely been supplanted by the work of Paul Oskar Kristeller during the past generation. On the basis of the most comprehensive study of its sources ever undertaken, Kristeller has effectively established the claim that humanism is part of a rhetorical tradition that has been a continuous aspect of western civilization since classical antiquity. Moreover, humanism has specific roots in the medieval culture from which it arose, notably in the theory and practice of letter and speech writing, the study of classical poetry, prose, and grammar in the cathedral schools of France, and the study of Greek. That the humanists belong to a rhetorical tradition is now generally accepted, though different constructions are placed on what this means. Kristeller has gone on to argue that a study of the humanists' works leads one away from the conclusion that they were professional philosophers. They have no consistent philosophical position and are not concerned with philosophy in the traditional sense. Their preoccupations were those of the rhetorical tradition from which they emerged: grammar, poetry, history, rhetoric, and moral philosophy. Kristeller's formulations constitute the most widely accepted paradigm of humanist studies today. Most of the essays in these volumes reflect adherence to it in one way or another. This paradigm has had a profound impact on the earlier debates about the nature of humanism. The idea that humanism is either a radical departure from the past or a radical defense of traditional values has given way to more mediate studies, which have attempted to reveal the specific relations of the humanists to institutions and their specific ideas on particular issues. This more nuanced discussion of their relationships and ideas is reflected in many of the essays collected here.

Among Kristeller's generation of scholars, his definition of humanism has been challenged by the leading Italian scholar in the field, Eugenio Garin, who regards Renaissance philosophy (for example, Platonism and Aristotelianism) as integral to humanism and treats the philosophers as part of the humanist tradition. While widely respected, Garin's views have not found general acceptance; the writings of the humanists in their various forms and locations bear out to most interpreters the general applicability of Kristeller's paradigm, as the great majority of the essays in these volumes make clear.

Garin has exercised more influence in incorporating the notion of "civic humanism"—first formulated by Hans Baron to designate a specific historical situation in early Quattrocento Florence—into a broader view of humanism and Renaissance thought. He began with the questions: What inspired the humanists to turn from medieval rhetoric to the classical tradition? What motivated their commitment to the disciplines in which they were most interested? Both Garin and Baron believe that humanism as a cultural movement cannot be understood apart from the social and political conditions under which it arose. Their exploration of these conditions, especially in medieval and Renaissance Florence, has led to the recognition of a greater variety within the humanist movement than was previously suspected. Civic humanism, which is explored in these volumes, does not, however, replace Kristeller's paradigm, inasmuch as it applies only to a small group of humanists largely in one location and for a limited period. But it is an important contribution to our understanding of humanism itself and, equally important, to its legacy.

* * *

The initial idea for these volumes grew from a course on "Renaissance Humanism" taught at Barnard College/Columbia University by Professor Maristella Lorch and me in the spring of 1979, one of several courses developed through an institutional grant from the National Endowment for the Humanities. We used funds made available through that grant to invite a number of distinguished scholars in Renaissance humanist studies to participate in the course. Professor Lorch suggested the idea of a textbook based on the course, and her initial idea has developed, through several permutations, into the present collection.

We believe we have produced something unique and uniquely valuable for students of the Renaissance at all levels. During the past generation our knowledge of Renaissance humanism in its particular manifestations has grown so vast and at such a rate that the kinds of syntheses mentioned earlier by scholars of a past generation would be much more difficult today, especially if humanism is conceived as a Europe-wide movement interacting with other major movements and institutions. What we have done here is to bring specialists together to accomplish what no one scholar working alone could have achieved.

Each writer, a close student of the field about which he or she writes, was instructed to synthesize the state of the field on the assigned topic. In some cases this task involved a study of what other scholars have discovered, in others an attempt to create a synthesis that has not existed or been perceived before. In a number of cases the articles here represent condensations of book-length studies, which are themselves the major statements of the topics in those areas, for example, the articles by Marianna D. Birnbaum, John F. D'Amico on Rome, Margaret L. King on Venice, Claude V. Palisca, Mario Santoro, Retha M. Warnicke, and Ronald G. Witt. With five exceptions, the forty-one essays published here were written explicitly for these volumes. The five exceptions are Kristeller's essay on humanism and moral philosophy, King's on women and humanism in Italy, and the essays by Deno J. Geanakoplos, Anthony Grafton, and David B. Ruderman. Three of these (King, Geanakoplos, Ruderman) are not readily available; one has been expanded (Ruderman), and in all five the notes have been updated. In very large part, then, this is an originally conceived and executed collaborative scholarly project.

Each essay is addressed to a wide audience. Undergraduates studying in this field for the first time will find here the closest approximation to a textbook that is available in the field. The various essays will introduce a student to any topic that might be addressed in a course on humanism and to the various contemporary interpretations of humanism. The volumes should be of equal or greater value to advanced students, including college and university teachers, whether scholars in the field or not, who want to introduce themselves and their students to Renaissance humanism. We have tried to ensure that all essays are clear, and to this end all quotations have been translated into English. At the same time, all studies relevant to a topic have been included in each essay, regardless of the language in which they were written; many of these are repeated in several essays, and all, both books and articles, have been included in the bibliography located at the end of Volume 3.

A word should be said about the title of these volumes and the scope they promise. The "foundations" and "forms" of humanism are treated in comprehensive fashion. In the "foundations" section, classical, patristic, and medieval backgrounds to humanism are dealt with, and Petrarch, the "father" of humanism, is treated in relation to his ties to all three backgrounds. The forms of humanism have been divided into two frames of reference, geographical (Volumes 1 and 2) and disciplinary (Volume 3). The geographical is further divided into Italian (Volume 1) and European outside Italy (Volume 2). These proceed in chronological fashion, the essays on Italian humanism focusing primarily on the Quattrocento and those on humanism in other countries including the fifteenth century but also extending into and often proceeding to the end of the sixteenth. The disciplinary frame of reference cuts across geographical regions, and each essay proceeds in chronological order, sometimes up to 1700.

The section on the "legacy" of humanism is confined to one essay by Kristeller, a general overview. Actually, the legacy of humanism may be said to involve in part its impact on art, law, music, science, and theology, topics addressed in the final sections of the disciplinary treatment of humanism. It also involves, of course, the impact of humanism on the development of classical scholarship and of the disciplines central to the *studia humanitatis,* all of which are treated in the section on disciplines and institutions. The legacy has thus been more broadly confronted than the one essay in the "legacy" section implies. At the same time, the focus has been placed deliberately on humanism itself, tracing its development as long as it is discernible as a movement in European culture. To trace the impact of humanism after it merged into the broader currents of European culture is a very large task, perhaps as large as the task undertaken here. All readers should therefore be aware that although the legacy of humanism is addressed in various ways in these volumes, the topic itself is not systematically analyzed to the same extent as the foundations and forms of humanism.

* * *

Editing these volumes has been at times a trying, but at times also, and ultimately, a rewarding experience. I would like to thank the National Endowment for the Humanities, which provided not only the institutional grant through which this project was initiated but also a personal research fellowship during 1981 and 1982, which enabled me to complete an initial draft of several essays I have contributed, to edit essays in hand, and to enlist many new contributors.

I would like to thank two secretaries at the State University College at Old Westbury: Marion Pensabene, who typed about half of the essays in their final form, and Rosemary Smith, who entered the bibliography in its various phases into a computer; and a colleague, Professor Michael Taves, for help in generating the index on a computer. In addition, I would like to thank the College at Old Westbury for extensive support with respect to the copying and mailing costs involved in bringing the manuscript to its completed form. Most especially, I owe a deep debt of gratitude to Selby Hickey, the college's academic vice-president, through whose efforts the college has contributed toward underwriting the costs of producing these volumes. An underwriting grant has also been received from the Center for International Scholarly Exchange at Barnard College/Columbia University, whose help is here gratefully acknowledged. In addition, several individuals have contributed significantly toward underwriting the costs of publication, and to all of them I extend a deepfelt thanks.

My greatest debt of gratitude is to Paul Oskar Kristeller. These volumes themselves are in an important way a tribute to his scholarship. But in a more personal sense, I am grateful for his constant counsel through letters and (more frequently) telephone conversations. In addition to helping frame the general outline of these volumes, he assisted in the solicitation of contributors—especially during the early stages of the project—and he has read a number of the essays. His graciousness to younger scholars working in the field has become legendary in his own time; this project is certainly a wonderful instance of it.

The volumes are dedicated to Maristella Lorch, the initiator of the original course and the instigator of the idea that has now become this anthology. As the concept of the project matured, we have tried it out together in subsequent incarnations of our initial course on humanism. Without her patient and enduring goodwill and her genius for bringing people together this project would never have been begun, let alone completed.

ALBERT RABIL, JR.

RENAISSANCE HUMANISM☙

Volume 1

PART I

FOUNDATIONS OF HUMANISM

A THE CLASSICAL AND MEDIEVAL ANTECEDENTS OF HUMANISM

B PETRARCH AND THE HUMANIST TRADITIONS

A ❧ THE CLASSICAL AND MEDIEVAL ANTECEDENTS OF HUMANISM

1 ❧ RENAISSANCE HUMANISM AND CLASSICAL ANTIQUITY
Paul Oskar Kristeller

I SHALL NOT TRY TO DEFINE THE RENAISSANCE OR HUMANISM. There is a whole literature on that subject, and I have stated my views on it more than once in print.[1] I shall try instead to describe briefly what the humanists of the Renaissance, mainly in Italy and during the fourteenth and fifteenth centuries, did for the study of classical antiquity, especially of pagan antiquity, and how this study affected their other studies and those of their contemporaries, for the classical studies of the humanists had a profound impact on Renaissance civilization as a whole.

I would like to make a sharp distinction between the study of Roman antiquity and the study of Greek antiquity, for the contributions of the humanists to these two areas of classical antiquity were quite different in nature and significance. I shall begin with Roman antiquity and with classical Latin literature, and speak afterward about the study of Greek antiquity.[2]

*　　*　　*

The interest in Roman antiquity and in classical Latin literature was of wider and more immediate concern to the humanists and their contemporaries than was the study of Greek. There was a much greater temporal continuity, for Latin had been used continually throughout the Middle Ages as a language of the church and of diplomacy, of instruction, of science and learning, and also of literature; and it served as an important vehicle of intellectual expression. Moreover, at least some of the classical Latin authors were commonly known, read, and studied during the Middle Ages, and it would be quite wrong to assume that the average medieval scholar was unfamiliar with them. It is clear from the manuscript tradition, from the quotations and imitations in medieval literature, and from the documents of the medieval schools that many ancient Latin writings were widely read and known, including Vergil, Ovid, Seneca, and at least some of the works of Cicero. Moreover, it was well known that Roman civilization had flourished on the very territory of western Europe; had founded most of the cities, especially in Italy, that were still flourishing; and had left behind many buildings and other monuments that attracted the curiosity and admiration of later centuries. Roman law and institutions continued to exercise a direct influence, and at least the Italians looked on the ancient Romans as their direct ancestors. Whereas the French, English, and Germans tended to sympathize with the native inhabitants of their countries rather than with the Romans, there was for the Italians a patriotic quality in the study and admiration of the Romans, and this attitude is quite apparent in Petrarch, Valla, and many other Italian humanists.

We must now try to understand what the humanists contributed to the study of Roman antiquity and literature, and in what manner they went beyond their medieval predecessors. First of all, they collected the classical Latin texts scattered in different libraries; in doing so, they discovered some important texts that had been practically unknown to their predecessors. Some medievalists have tried to debunk the humanist discoveries by saying that a text that we discover must have been there in the first place before it could be discovered. By this token, no text can ever be discovered unless it is forged. What I mean by humanist discoveries is something else. The texts were there, to be sure, but they survived only in one or two places, and they were read and copied only by very few scholars, who happened to have access to these places. When a humanist discovered a text, the text became generally known and was read, copied, and studied more widely. Some of the newly discovered texts were quite important: Lucretius, Cicero's letters and some of his orations, Catullus, Propertius, and Tacitus. All of these texts were not generally known to medieval scholars and became now, thanks to the humanist discoveries, generally accessible to western readers. Cicero's *De oratore* was very little known during the Middle Ages, whereas his *De inventione* was widely used as a textbook of rhetoric. The statements often made that Cicero was either well known or unknown during the Middle Ages are both wrong. Some of his works were well known, and others were unknown; in order to make correct statements, we must study the history of each text. This study has been begun by Remigio Sabbadini and other scholars, but many pertinent facts are still in need of much further investigation.

Apart from discovering new authors, the humanists also discovered older and better manuscripts for some of the authors who had been well known before. A famous example is Quintilian, whose work was widely accessible in an incomplete version, whereas the humanists discovered a better and more complete text.

An important activity of the humanists consisted in the copying of classical texts. Prior to the invention of printing—that is, before the middle of the fifteenth century—all texts were copied by hand and circulated in manuscript books. The humanists were very active as copyists and scribes, and the great diffusion of classical Latin literature during the early Renaissance is reflected in the large number of manuscript copies made during the fifteenth century. I venture to think that for any ancient Latin writer, the number of extant fifteenth-century manuscripts is greater than the copies from all previous centuries taken together. This fact is usually overlooked, because classical scholars have traditionally paid attention only to the older manuscripts, and in the past have pretty much ignored and despised the copies made during the fifteenth century. More recently, greater attention has been given to the later manuscripts, and whenever a census of the extant manuscripts of a classical Latin author is attempted, the very large number of fifteenth-century copies becomes apparent.

The diffusion and accessibility of classical Latin texts may also be studied from the content of the major libraries founded during the Renaissance period. They usually included all the classical authors that were known at that time. An early example is the library of Petrarch, which has been reconstructed by modern scholars, mainly by Pierre de Nolhac and Giuseppe Billanovich.[3] Many of these manuscripts have been identified. Most of them are now in Paris, while others are scattered or lost. Some of the manuscripts were written in Petrarch's own hand, others were copied for him by secretaries, and many were given to him or bought by him at different times of his life. Petrarch annotated many of these manuscripts, and it is apparent that he owned most of the classical Latin authors, including some of the church fathers, which he mentions or cites in his own writings.

We know of a number of other libraries formed in the fifteenth century that included a large number of classical Latin texts. These libraries belonged to princes or scholars. Some of them are extant, such as the Urbino collection now in the Vatican, the Laurenziana collection in Florence, or the Malatestiana in Cesena, while others are now dispersed but have been reconstructed, such as the Visconti and Sforza libraries in Milan, the Aragon library in Naples, or the library of King Matthias Corvinus in Budapest.[4]

As professional scribes and copyists, the humanists adopted two new forms of handwriting that were different from the Gothic script of the preceding period, and this change brought about a reform of handwriting. One was the regular humanist script, which was believed to be an imitation of the ancient Roman script but was in fact based on the Carolingian script. Slightly later, around the middle of the fifteenth century, the humanists developed another type of script, which is called the humanist cursive and which is the ancestor of our Italic script.[5] These two scripts dominated the later history of handwriting and that of printing up to the present day; and one might say that the humanist reform of handwriting is the most lasting achievement of the humanists. Thanks to the humanists, we still write a kind of Roman or Italic hand and find the Gothic script they rejected harder to read. This humanist script is still familiar to us, and it is likely to persist until somebody tries a revival of the Gothic script or develops yet another.

Another important contribution by the humanists to classical studies was the practice and development of textual criticism. They collated different manuscripts of the same texts, studied their variant readings, and tried to identify and follow the oldest and best manuscripts of a particular text. They also tried to emend the text and correct the readings of the manuscripts with the help of their own knowledge and ingenuity. In initiating the technique of textual criticism, the humanists were the ancestors of modern classical philologists, who in later centuries developed and refined this technique to a much higher degree.

When printing was invented in Germany around the middle of the fifteenth century and was brought to Italy in 1467, the classical Latin texts were soon published in printed editions, and many well-trained humanists acted as editors of these editions. Practically all early editions of the Latin classics from the late fifteenth and the sixteenth centuries were edited by humanist scholars, often quite carefully and on the basis of some well-selected manuscripts.

The humanists not only copied and edited the texts of the classical Latin writers, they also wrote many commentaries on them, usually on the basis of class lectures. Continuing the practice of the medieval grammarians, the humanists gave courses on ancient authors in a school or university, read the texts with their students, and added their explanations. These commentaries were written down either by the teachers or by their students, and they often found their way into print. The commentaries on classical Latin authors, medieval as well as humanistic, represent a very large body of literature, which has just begun to be explored. We are still far from a complete bibliographic record of the commentaries written on individual Latin texts and authors. The method used by the humanists in their commentaries—the knowledge and understanding that they show of the text, its language, and the historical and literary problems it presents as compared with their late ancient and medieval predecessors and their modern successors—is an important task for future research, for which we lack even the basic premises at this time.

Another area in which the humanists were active was the translation of classical texts into Tuscan and other Italian dialects, and also into French and other vernacular languages. The purpose of these vernacular translations, which steadily increased from the fourteenth century to the sixteenth, was to make the classical Latin writers accessible to a reading public that did not know enough Latin to read them in the original.

The study of the classical texts led the humanists into other problems and subjects. They tried to understand the correct spelling and prosody, the vocabulary and metrics, the style and composition of the ancient Latin language, which they admired and tried to imitate. For they considered the medieval Latin language and literature, as far as it had departed from classical usage, to be a change for the worse, and in their effort to emulate classical Latin they tried to avoid, not always successfully, the peculiar features of medieval Latin.

The humanists did not limit their study of Roman antiquity to the literary sources. They were much interested in ancient inscriptions, medals, and works of art, and initiated such disciplines as epigraphy, numismatics, and archaeology. This side of the humanists' activity has recently been treated by Roberto Weiss.[6] They also studied ancient history and classical mythology, Roman and provincial topography, and the knowledge thus acquired was of great help for a better understanding of ancient literature.

But the humanists were not only scholars, the predecessors of modern historians and philologists, they were also writers. The study of the ancient authors was in part an exercise for imitating them. As a writer, the humanist followed the ancient authors as his models, and he was convinced that the successful imitation of the classics was the best way to become a good writer. The manner and extent of this imitation varied from case to case and was even the subject of some controversies. There was difference of opinion over whether one should imitate Cicero alone or might imitate other ancient authors, and whether one should imitate the ancient writers in all respects or might combine imitation of the classics with some novelty of expression appropriate to the different realities and ideas of the contemporary world. But nobody doubted that a study of the ancient authors, and a certain degree of imitation, was useful and even essential.

The humanists tried above all to follow and recapture the correct usage of classical Latin. Though not completely successful, they attained a good command of ancient orthography, vocabulary, and syntax, and, to a lesser extent, of ancient prosody and metrics. They also tended to imitate the chief literary genres of the ancient Romans. In prose, they produced an extensive literature of orations and letters (both public and private), of dialogues, and of histories, whereas in verse they composed an impressive number of elegies and epigrams, and a somewhat smaller body of odes and eclogues, epic and didactic poems and plays. In their treatises, they dealt extensively with educational, moral, and political problems.

This voluminous literature of the humanists, some of it still unpublished, reflects clearly the intellectual life and activity of the period. Most of it is written in Latin, which was evidently still a living language, at least for those who had enjoyed a humanist education. But we should not underestimate the impact of their work on the vernacular literature of the same period. For a long time, the vernacular was only used in daily speech and in certain forms of popular poetry and literature. If the vernacular language were to treat learned subjects, to deal in prose with any topic whatsoever, and to take over all the functions previously reserved for Latin, it had to be transformed and, as it were, educated after the model of Latin. It had to be standardized and regularized in grammar, vocabulary, and syntax; and this actually happened during the Renaissance period, culminating in the sixteenth century.

*   *   *

Passing from the Latin to the Greek studies of the humanists, we must take note of a number of significant differences. The study of Greek began much later than the study of Latin, and it affected fewer persons. It had far fewer precedents in the Middle Ages, and it built instead on the traditions of the Byzantine East. Petrarch, who belongs to the early period of humanism, knew very little Greek. He took some beginner's lessons and owned a couple of Greek manuscripts, but he did not know enough to read an ancient Greek author in the original text. There are no Greek quotations in his writings, and in this respect he did not equal his model Cicero, who knew Greek extremely well and whose letters are full of Greek phrases. Cicero felt that the Greek language had many specific terms and phrases, especially in philosophy, for which there was no precise equivalent in Latin, and where he did not attempt to coin a Latin term that would render the Greek adequately, he retained the Greek word unchanged. Petrarch envisaged the importance of Greek, but he did not master the language, and the real study of Greek among western humanists began after his time, at the very end of the fourteenth century.

It made significant progress during the fifteenth and sixteenth centuries but was never as widely diffused among students and scholars as was Latin. There were many humanist scholars who had an excellent mastery of the Latin language and literature but who had little or no Greek. Thus we can understand why even in the sixteenth century the major Greek authors were often printed in bilingual editions of Greek and Latin. These editions were the sixteenth-century equivalents of our Loeb Library, which prints the classical Greek (and Latin) texts on the left and the English translation on the right. Many people buy and use these editions and pretend to read the left page, while in fact they only read the right page. This was probably also true of the Greek and Latin editions of the sixteenth century.

The study of Greek in the West had few precedents in the Middle Ages. Medieval western scholars were familiar with the Latin language and with some Latin classical authors, though perhaps not as thoroughly as were the humanists. But there was no tradition of Greek scholarship in the Latin West during the Middle Ages. There were few Greek texts in western libraries, no regular courses of Greek in the schools or universities. There were a number of Latin translations from the Greek, but they were limited to specific authors and subjects, such as the church fathers, Aristotelian philosophy, mathematics, and medicine, and the quality of these translations was quite uneven. With few exceptions, the great scholars of the Middle Ages knew no Greek.[7]

The Greek studies of the humanists had their precedents, however, in the Byzantine East, where the study of classical Greek language and literature had never been interrupted and where the texts of the ancient Greek writers were preserved and copied.[8] The close contacts between western and Byzantine scholars began during the fourteenth and early fifteenth centuries, while the Byzantine Empire still existed. Many western, and especially Italian, scholars went to Constantinople and other Byzantine centers to learn the Greek language and to study ancient Greek literature. Likewise, Byzantine scholars came to the West and began to teach their language and literature in Italy and elsewhere. Petrarch's teacher of Greek was a southern Italian, Barlaam of Calabria, who had been trained in Constantinople, and there was another southern Italian trained in the East, Leontius Pilatus, who was a protégé of Boccaccio and taught for a short while in Florence, not only in Boccaccio's home but also at the university. He made the first Latin translation of Homer, using a Greek manuscript that had been sent to Petrarch by a Byzantine friend.

Much more influential was Manuel Chrysoloras, who came to teach Greek at the University of Florence in the 1390s, at the suggestion of

Coluccio Salutati, and had many prominent Italian humanists among his students. His example was followed by many Byzantine and Italian scholars, and by the end of the fifteenth century the study of Greek had become well established at a number of universities and even in a few secondary schools.

The Byzantine scholars and their western pupils and successors taught Greek as a literary language that was relatively close to the classical Greek of late antiquity and quite different from the popular dialects spoken in Byzantine Greece during the later Middle Ages. There was a tradition of textbooks on Greek grammar that were used to instruct Byzantine schoolboys in classical Greek, and these textbooks were revised to serve the needs of western students.

Along with the study of the language went the process of collecting manuscripts of the Greek classical writers and of laying in the West the foundation for libraries of Greek manuscripts. A few classical texts were found in southern Italy, where Greek was still alive as a spoken language. But most of the Greek manuscripts were brought from the East by western students and by Byzantine scholars. After the middle of the fifteenth century, when many Byzantine scholars emigrated to the West following the Turkish conquest of Constantinople (1453), many Greek classical texts were copied in the West from older manuscripts by Byzantine scholars and by their western pupils.

After 1490, and during the sixteenth century, most of the Greek classical texts came to be printed, first in Italy and later in France and other countries. Through these printed editions, classical Greek literature became available all over Europe, and this fact in turn helped to encourage and promote the study of Greek.

The methods that the humanists applied in their study of Latin they also practiced in their study of Greek, though perhaps less extensively. The humanists copied and edited the texts of the classical Greek authors, and they applied to it their tested methods of textual criticism. They also produced learned commentaries intended to explain the difficult passages of their authors to readers and students. The Byzantine scholars who came to the West continued to write in Greek, though some of them learned Latin fairly well. However, few western humanists mastered Greek well enough to write it. Leonardo Bruni wrote a treatise on the constitution of Florence in Greek; several scholars were able to write Greek letters, and leading Hellenists such as Francesco Filelfo or Angelo Poliziano even composed Greek poetry. But these are few exceptions, and on the whole it is evident that the study of Greek aimed primarily at the reading and understanding of classical Greek literature, whereas the study of Latin continued to be affected by the practical concern for writing Latin well and fluently, in prose and in verse, and after the model of the ancient Roman authors.

At the same time, there was a vast activity of translating classical Greek texts into Latin. Thus a large body of important Greek literature that had previously been unknown or inaccessible was introduced to the West for the first time. This literature included all of Greek poetry, that is, Homer, Hesiod, Pindar, the tragedians, and Aristophanes; all of Greek historiography such as Herodotus, Thucydides, Polybius, and many later writers; and all of Greek oratory such as Lysias, Isocrates, and Demosthenes. Of the Greek patristic writings, many had been translated in late ancient or medieval times, but many more were translated for the first time during the fifteenth and sixteenth centuries. The new translations also included some advanced mathematical writers such as Pappus and Diophantus. Philosophers such as Plutarch and Lucian, who had been practically unknown before, were to become extremely popular during the Renaissance and afterward. Among the major philosophers, Aristotle had been well known during the Middle Ages, but a few writings of the Aristotelian corpus, the works of Theophrastus, and many of the Greek commentaries on Aristotle were added by the humanist translators. They also added most of the sources of non-Aristotelian Greek philosophy: most of the writings of Plato, Plotinus, and the other Neoplatonists; the Stoic writers Epictetus and Marcus Aurelius; the Skeptic philosopher Sextus Empiricus; and the *Lives of the Philosophers* by Diogenes Laertius, a work that contained much information on all of Greek philosophy, and especially on Epicurus and his school.

As I mentioned earlier, a limited number of Greek authors had been known in Latin versions during the Middle Ages, such as Aristotle and the church fathers, and also many writers on mathematics, astronomy, and medicine. Many of these works were retranslated with different criteria and in a different context, and additional works of the same writers such as Hippocrates, Galen, and Archimedes were now added as well.

The details of this translation process are still being investigated, and many of the basic bibliographic facts are not yet known. There are many high-sounding generalizations on the matter in the handbooks, but we are not yet able to say with precision which works of Hippocrates or Galen were known during the Middle Ages and how many of them were known only during the Renaissance, or how the various medieval and humanist translations of the same Greek texts differ from one another in method, accuracy, and clarity. But it remains one of the most important contributions of Renaissance humanism that practically the entire body of classical Greek literature became available to the West, both through editions of the original texts and in accurate Latin and vernacular translations.

*   *   *

This newly available source material had a stimulating and fermenting effect on all areas of literature, the arts, the sciences, and learning. In literature humanist Latin poetry marked in many ways—in style, themes, and literary genres—the transition from medieval to early modern poetry. In philosophy, Aristotle began to be understood on the basis of the Greek text and the ancient Greek commentators rather than from medieval Latin translations and commentaries that were less reliable. Plato and Neoplatonism became completely known for the first time, for the Middle Ages knew only some of the works of Plato and Proclus, and none of Plotinus. To be sure, Augustine read a Latin translation of Plotinus, but we do not know how much it contained, and it completely disappeared after his time. Some of the teachings of Stoicism, Epicureanism, and Skepticism had been known through Cicero and Seneca, but the newly translated Greek sources and the newly found text of Lucretius made these doctrines much more accessible. These alternative ancient doctrines were widely discussed, and they prepared the way for new and more original philosophical ideas in the sixteenth century.

In mathematics and astronomy, the whole body of Greek science was absorbed, and thus the way was prepared for further progress in the late sixteenth and the seventeenth centuries, which went beyond the limits of ancient Greek science. The main sources of Greek geography, Ptolemy and Strabo, were translated for the first time in the fifteenth century, and some scholars have argued that these texts played a role in the geographical discoveries of the late fifteenth and the sixteenth centuries. We know, for example, that Columbus owned a copy of Ptolemy's *Geography* in Latin, which is preserved in the Biblioteca Colombina in Seville.

Students of medicine now had access to the entire corpus of Greek medical literature, which had previously been known only in part and in less reliable translations. Just as in the case of mathematics, its lessons had to be digested before new progress beyond the limits of the ancients could be made.

The study of the Greek New Testament and of the Hebrew Old Testament, as well as of many Greek patristic writings, had a great impact on religious and theological scholarship.[9]

Even legal thought and practice were thoroughly influenced by a more precise and more historical study of the *Corpus iuris civilis,* at a time when Roman law was still the foundation of legal practice in Italy and parts of France, and even extended its territory and authority into Germany.

Renaissance architects studied and imitated ancient monuments and treatises, and many sculptors were impressed with the ancient statues and sarcophagi that had been known for a long time or that were newly excavated. The painters, who had few ancient models to imitate, turned increasingly to the representation of ancient historical and mythological subjects or tried to recreate examples of ancient paintings known from literary descriptions, such as the calumny of Apelles described by Lucian.[10]

Even the theorists and practitioners of music, who had no ancient models and no usable ancient literature, attempted to revive ancient music and produced in this attempt important results—for example, the opera—although the relationship to antiquity was not as authentic as they believed.

We must realize that the imitation of antiquity includes the apocryphal as well as the authentic, as we saw also in the case of humanist script. Many works admired in the Renaissance as works of classical antiquity are considered by modern scholars either as medieval forgeries or as forgeries of late antiquity that were supposed to be of a much earlier age. The *Centiloquium* attributed to Ptolemy has recently been recognized as a medieval Arabic composition subsequently translated into Greek and Latin. The treatise *De spiritu et anima,* cited and used as a work of St. Augustine by Pier Candido Decembrio in his treatise on immortality, has turned out to be the work of a twelfth-century Cistercian writer. The Chaldaic oracles attributed to Zoroaster, the writings that go under the name of Hermes Trismegistus, the Symbols and Golden Words attributed to Pythagoras are all forgeries of late antiquity pretending to be of a much earlier age, and they were all admired by Platonists and other Renaissance thinkers as monuments of very early wisdom.[11] The letters of Phalaris were among the most popular writings during the fifteenth and sixteenth centuries until the English philologist Richard Bentley proved in the early eighteenth century that they were a forgery of late antiquity.

All this is but a part of a very broad and interesting picture, which has not yet been completely or sufficiently explored or studied. Many sources remain to be discovered, and the *fortuna* of many ancient Greek and Latin authors is still imperfectly known. Any new question we ask cannot be settled with a ready-made answer from a handbook or dictionary, but it may lead to a completely new investigation and even to a new bibliography.

NOTES

1. W. K. Ferguson, *The Renaissance in Historical Thought* (Cambridge, MA, 1948); P. O. Kristeller, *Renaissance Thought and Its Sources*, ed. M. Mooney (New York, 1979).

2. R. Sabbadini, *Le scoperte dei codici latini e greci ne' secoli XIV e XV*, 2 vols. (Florence, 1905–14); *Catalogus Translationum et Commentariorum, Mediaeval and Renaissance Latin Translations and Commentaries*, ed. P. O. Kristeller, F. E. Cranz, and V. Brown, 6 vols. to date (Washington, DC, 1960–86).

3. P. de Nolhac, *Pétrarque et l'humanisme* (Paris, 2d ed., 1907); G. Billanovich, "Petrarch and the Textual Tradition of Livy," *Journal of the Warburg and Courtauld Institutes* 14 (1951): 137–208.

4. E. Pellegrin, *La bibliothèque des Visconti et des Sforza* (Paris, 1955); T. de Marinis, *La biblioteca napoletana dei re d'Aragona*, 4 vols. (Milan, 1947–52), *Supplemento*, 2 vols. (Verona, 1969); C. Csapody and K. Csapodi Gardonyi, *Bibliotheca Corviniana* (New York, 1969; 2d ed., 1978).

5. B. L. Ullman, *The Origin and Development of Humanistic Script* (Rome, 1960); A. de la Mare, *The Handwriting of Italian Humanists*, vol. 1 (Oxford, 1973).

6. R. Weiss, *The Renaissance Discovery of Classical Antiquity* (Oxford, 1969).

7. W. Berschin, *Griechisch-lateinisches Mittelalter* (Bern, 1980).

8. D. J. Geanakoplos, *Byzantine East and Latin West* (Oxford, 1966).

9. See, in these volumes, Chapter 2, the three essays on humanism and theology (Chapters 35–37), and the essay on Erasmus (Chapter 23).

10. D. Cast, *The Calumny of Apelles: A Study in the Humanist Tradition* (New Haven, 1981).

11. F. A. Yates, *Giordano Bruno and the Hermetic Tradition* (London, 1964).

2 ❧ THE RENAISSANCE IDEA OF CHRISTIAN ANTIQUITY: HUMANIST PATRISTIC SCHOLARSHIP
Eugene F. Rice, Jr.

THE PHRASE "CHRISTIAN ANTIQUITY" REFERS TO THE EARLY church and to the literature produced by Christian writers of the first six centuries. Because of the sanctity, learning, knowledge of Scripture, theological insight, and antiquity of these writers, later generations called them "fathers" and "doctors": *sancti antiqui patres, doctores defensoresque ecclesiae* (the holy ancient fathers, teachers, and defenders of the church). Among the Greek fathers Origen (ca. 185–ca. 254), Eusebius of Caesarea (ca. 260–ca. 340), Basil the Great (ca. 330–ca. 379), Gregory Nazianzus (329–389) and his younger brother Gregory of Nyssa (ca. 330–ca. 395), and St. John Chrysostom (ca. 347–407) are outstanding. In the West four Latin fathers were singled out from an early date as preeminent: saints Ambrose (ca. 339–397), Jerome (ca. 345–420), Augustine (354–430), and Gregory the Great (ca. 540–604). Medieval authors paired these four fathers with the four evangelists, compared them to the four rivers of paradise, and called them "mouths of the Lord." In 1295 Pope Boniface VIII commanded that they be venerated with the same solemnity as the apostles.

Renaissance humanists searched for manuscripts of patristic works in the older monastic and cathedral libraries of Italy and the North as indefatigably as they hunted the pagan classics; and their self-congratulation at discovering works of the fathers "rotting away in mouldy obscurity," "covered in dust and filth," or "abandoned to roaches and worms," as they invariably and often inaccurately put it, was as warm as their jubilation at finding a little-known codex of Plautus or Tacitus. Such enthusiasm should not occasion surprise. There were no atheists in the Renaissance. No humanist was a pagan. From the beginning of the "revival of antiquity," enthusiasm for ancient pagan literature was inseparable from an enthusiasm for ancient Christian literature. The discovery, rediscovery, and reevaluation of Christian antiquity was an integral part of the more general humanist rediscovery and reevaluation of ancient art and letters.

The most important and original achievement of humanist patristic scholarship in the Renaissance was the reappropriation by the Latin West of the early church's Greek literature. The chronology of the reception of Greek pagan literature is well known. The astonishing fact is that Homer, the lyric poets, the tragedians, Herodotus and Thucydides, Aristophanes, the mathematicians (with the exception of Euclid), the later medical authors (Oribasius and Paul of Aegina), Plato's *Dialogues* (with the exception of the *Timaeus*), Aristotle's *Poetics* (Aristotle's other major works were well known to the philosophers and theologians of the thirteenth century)—in short most of the masterpieces of Greek literature that have survived—were read in Europe, first in Latin translation, then in the original Greek, and by more than a handful of people, only after 1400. Less widely appreciated is the equally important fact that the reception of Greek patristic literature followed the same pattern. With the exception of works already translated into Latin in antiquity (notable among these are treatises and commentaries by Origen and John Chrysostom's *Homilies on Matthew*), a few works translated in the sixth century in Cassiodorus's monastery of Vivarium in southern Italy, and a very few others translated in the Middle Ages (the most important example is the pseudo-Dionysian corpus, writings attributed to Dionysius, the disciple of St. Paul, but in reality the work of an anonymous author active in Syria in the sixth century), the bulk of Greek patristic literature was first made readily available to European intellectuals during the fifteenth and early sixteenth centuries, principally in Italy, by western humanist scholars and Greek émigrés.

The fortune of the Latin fathers was different. Generally speaking, their works were available, admired, read, and used throughout the Middle Ages, as any count of manuscripts will show. What is characteristic of the humanist reappropriation of the Latin fathers is, therefore, not so much the discovery or rediscovery of works previously unread or little read as it was the fact that familiar works were read with a new kind of historical and critical sense and judgment. The initial results of reading familiar texts with new eyes were principally three: first, the identification and elimination of the very large number of spurious works, which over the centuries ignorance, credulity, and pious fraud had attributed to the most respected and authoritative of the fathers; second, the successful subjection to skeptical scrutiny of the legends with which their biographies had become entwined; and, third, the diffusion of improved texts of their works in editions constructed on the scholarly principles of the new philology.

＊　　　＊　　　＊

What happened to St. Jerome is a good example of these processes. By the end of the fourteenth century knowledge of his life was clouded by errors of fact and a disordered chronology. Many commentaries, sermons, and treatises circulated under the false authority of his name. The busy fancy of hagiographers had woven into the historical narrative the legendary episodes that were to become the sources of his identifying attributes in the visual arts, the faithful lion and cardinal's hat. Apocryphal letters, circulating under the names of St. Augustine, St. Cyril of Jerusalem, and Eusebius of Cremona (Jerome's alleged successor as abbot of the monastery Jerome had founded in Bethlehem), exaggerated his virtues and multiplied the miracles attributed to the power of his name and relics in order to promote him to the position of premier Christian saint, equal in holiness and glory to St. John the Baptist. About 1345 a professor of canon law at the University of Bologna wrote a book in his praise so influential that it laid the foundation of a new devotion, a popular religious cult that spread rapidly through Italy and beyond, into Spain, France, Switzerland, the Netherlands, and Germany. Devotees of this cult founded new religious orders in Italy and Spain dedicated to his name. In short, a generalized and balanced respect for a great doctor of the church narrowed and intensified to the veneration of an ascetic virtuoso and miracle worker. It is against this background that we can best grasp the originality and principles of humanist patristic scholarship.

The outstanding student of St. Jerome among the humanists was Erasmus. From early youth, Erasmus had admired Jerome's Latin style, erudition, and piety; and he worked for many years preparing an annotated edition of Jerome's letters, which appeared in 1516. He prefaced the second volume with a life of his favorite father. It is the first critical biography of the saint, and it marks in method and result the cleanest possible break with the past. Erasmus stated his critical principles with devastating simplicity: he would allow as sources only Jerome's own authentic works or the works of contemporaries; and he established the canon of what were in fact the authentic works and letters with breathtaking penetration and flair. He attacked the letters about Jerome attributed to Eusebius of Cremona, St. Augustine, and St. Cyril of Jerusalem with indignant irony. The author is unlearned and his style barbarous, so stupid he would rob even the truth itself of plausibility, the impudent purveyor of fables that contradict every rule of historical credibility. And so Jerome lost his cardinal's hat, his lion, his virginity, his knowledge of Arabic, his most picturesque austerities, and his miracles. Miracles, said Erasmus, are confected by fabulists to bamboozle the vulgar. Saints should be portrayed as they are, as human beings, as men and women alive in history; they should not have the uniqueness of their personalities blurred by conventional fictions or falsified with tales of sackcloth, scourges, prodigious fasts, and incredible vigils. We should write about the saints in the spirit of early Christian piety. "The truth," said Erasmus, "has a force of its own more potent than any fiction. . . . Let anyone who wants miracles read Jerome's authentic works; they themselves are wonderful enough and contain almost as many miracles as they have sentences."[1]

Erasmus's work on the text of the letters was less happy. His extraordinary command of Latin and the sensitivity of his ear to nuances of style and usage produced a host of inspired guesses; time after time his conjectural emendations of corrupt passages are still accepted. But he worked too fast and he lacked system. So it is not surprising that his successors found much to criticize. Mariano Vittori, a distinguished scholar and linguist (he wrote a grammar of the Ethiopian language), began to reedit Jerome soon after the middle of the century. With the help of monks in Florence, Bologna, Brescia, Rome, the abbey of Monte Cassino, and the Dominican convent in Naples, he collated twenty manuscripts of Jerome's letters with the text of Erasmus's edition in 1516. He boasted that he was able to correct or improve Erasmus's text in more than fifteen hundred places. To be sure, it was Erasmus who had laid the foundation; while the important points illustrated by improved editions like Vittori's are that the humanists had invented and were gradually perfecting a method for restoring texts from the remoter past to something approaching their original integrity, and that scholarship itself, with the indispensable help of printing, was becoming a cooperative, cumulative enterprise.

* * *

Reading the fathers with new eyes could, of course, mean more than reading them with historical perspective and critical sophistication. Humanists often admired the fathers for reasons different from those of their medieval predecessors, and often used them in different ways and for different purposes.

The grounds of their admiration were as various as their own needs and aspirations, as many-sided as patristic literature itself. Everyone praised the eloquence of the fathers. Humanists considered the fathers ancient men of letters, who had themselves been poets, orators, and the friends of philosophers and who wrote, as one of them put it, before "Roman eloquence began to totter with the tottering Roman Empire."[2] They pointed out that their own ideal of eloquence was that of the fathers also. "To enable us to make effective use of what we know," wrote Leonardo Bruni, "we must add to our knowledge the power of expression. . . . Proficiency in literary form, not accompanied by broad acquaintance with facts and truths, is a barren attainment; while information, however vast, which lacks all grace of expression, would seem to be partly thrown away. . . . But where this double capacity exists—breadth of learning and grace of style—we allow the highest title to distinction and abiding fame."[3] Bruni then lists the great ancient authors who have joined knowledge and eloquence in this way: Plato, Aristotle, Cicero, Seneca, Augustine, Jerome, and Lactantius, four pagans and three fathers of the Latin church. Toward the middle of the fifteenth century, Lorenzo Valla, in the proem to book 4 of his *Elegancies of the Latin Language,* argued, in defense of the study of classical rhetoric, that all the Latin and Greek fathers—he named Jerome, Hilary, Ambrose, Augustine, Lactantius, Basil, Gregory, and John Chrysostom—"clothed the precious gems of their divine discourse with the gold and silver of eloquence," and went on to remark that "anyone ignorant of eloquence is entirely unworthy to discuss theology."[4]

Not only was patristic literature itself eloquent and a model of the proper union of style and content; the example of the fathers was used to justify the reading of the pagan classics and the cycle of studies based on the classics that had come to be known by the end of the fourteenth century as the *studia humanitatis.* Coluccio Salutati stressed the dependence of the fathers on the pagan poets and orators for their eloquence. Unless Jerome had studied the classics, he would never have been able to translate the Bible into moving Latin. If Augustine had been ignorant of the poets, especially Vergil, he would not have been able so eloquently to defend Christ against the false beliefs of the Gentiles. Leonardo Bruni translated St. Basil's *Ad adolescentes,* a warm defense of secular learning, because, he said, "through the authority of such a man I wished to put an end to the ignorant perversity of those who attack the *studia humanitatis* and regard them as wholly abhorrent."[5] Shallow churchmen, wrote Aeneas Silvius, later Pope Pius II, tell us that reading the poets corrupts morals. Yet "the fathers themselves, Jerome, Cyprian, Augustine, did not hesitate to draw illustrations from heathen poetry and so sanctioned its study."[6]

A close look at the patristic scholarship of a single humanist—Zanobi Acciaiuoli, Florentine poet, Dominican friar, and prefect of the Vatican Library under Pope Leo X—will uncover other, sometimes unexpected, reasons why humanists admired the fathers and how they used them. Between 1500 and 1519 Zanobi translated four patristic works from the Greek. The first was *In Hieroclem* by Eusebius of Caesarea, an attack on a certain Hierocles, governor of Bithynia under Diocletian. Hierocles had written a book to show that the Neopythagorean wise man and magus Apollonius of Tyana, who had died aged almost one hundred during the reign of Nerva, was a great sage, as remarkable a worker of miracles and as potent an exorcist as Jesus Christ. The second work translated by Zanobi was a commentary on the apocryphal Old Testament book of Ecclesiasticus by Olympiodorus, a sixth-century deacon of Alexandria. Finally, he translated two works by Theodoret, bishop of Cyrus, near Antioch, from 423 to 466: a treatise *On Providence* and a work entitled *A Cure for Pagan Maladies or the Truth of the Gospels Proved from Greek Philosophy.*

None of these works had been translated into Latin before, and Zanobi seems to have translated them as they were called to his attention by his friends or as he came across them in the Medici and Vatican collections. They do have certain things in common, however. With the partial exception of Olympiodorus's commentary, all have some philosophical content—Eusebius's *Against Hierocles,* for example, ends with a long and eloquent defense of human freedom and responsibility. All contain a good deal of information about pagan literature, thought, and religion, some of it especially precious because unobtainable elsewhere— Theodoret in the *Curatio* quotes more than one hundred pagan philosophers, poets, and historians in about 340 different passages. All, in Zanobi's opinion, are eloquent and elegantly written, an elegance he disingenuously despairs of matching in his translation. All of them, finally, are apologies, that is, their purpose is to attack paganism and defend the Christian faith.

Zanobi especially emphasized the last point. He has selected these works for translation, he tells us, because they are necessary and useful antidotes to particular intellectual poisons. "A few years ago," he writes in his preface to Theodoret's *Curatio,*

> when the *Life of Apollonius of Tyana* by Philostratus was published in Latin, I decided to translate Eusebius's *In Hieroclem* . . . as an antidote to Philostratus's poison, in order that no one should be deluded by his legendary story and think like the Pythagorean Hierocles that Apollonius was the equal of Jesus Christ, but rather recognize him as the poisonous imposter he really was. I now hear that the Greek text of Plato has appeared [Zanobi refers to the edition of Marcus Musurus and Aldus, published in Venice in 1513, the *editio princeps* of Plato], a philosopher whose eloquence is incomparable but some of whose doctrines have always been perniciously harmful to the Christian church. In these circumstances I think it useful to translate this book of Theodoret into Latin, for he shows how contradictory are Plato's teachings and those of

many other philosophers on the most important matters and how shameful their morals. From it our contemporaries may learn to avoid what is harmful in the philosophers and to devote themselves with renewed piety and ardor to reading sacred literature.[7]

Zanobi's purpose, in short, was to counter the errors of Hellenism. Through the *Curatio* of Theodoret he warned his contemporaries against Plato's community of wives and his foolish notions about the transmigration of souls and showed them that Socrates, whom all proclaimed "the best of the Greek philosophers," was an irascible and libidinous old man who went to the gymnasium to look at handsome boys, got drunk with Aristophanes and Alcibiades, had two wives at once, and frequented prostitutes as well. He hoped that Eusebius's *Against Hierocles* would alert the attentive reader to the diabolical traps hidden in contemporary as well as in ancient Neopythagoreanism. He considered Theodoret's *On Providence* an antidote to Epicurus and Democritus, "who say that our lives are ruled by chance and fortune rather than providence,"[8] and to the Aristotelian teaching that God is indifferent to what happens in the sublunar world, a doctrine commonly discussed by the secular Aristotelians of the Italian universities in Zanobi's own day. In passing he gives the Stoics a pat on the back for their more acceptable teachings about providence, but shows in the end how only the Hebrew and Christian fathers knew and spoke the truth, the Hebrews through a glass darkly, the Christians clearly and plainly.

Patristic works, then, were admired and used because they were treasure houses of new facts about ancient history and society, philosophy and religion, pagan and Christian, and of quotations from classical texts now lost; and because excellent arguments to counter and refute pagan philosophical doctrines that contradicted Christian revelation could be found there as well. At the same time, humanists found in the fathers philosophical doctrines that seemed to support their own generally optimistic view of human nature. The Greek fathers as a group put a more generous emphasis on the doctrine of free will than did the theological tradition of the Latin West. Anyone trying to defend the freedom of the will had at hand probing arguments from the Greek fathers. Humanists tended to stress moral freedom, a preference closely related to their educational interests and the central position of moral philosophy in the *studia humanitatis*. It is wholly unsurprising, therefore, to find Erasmus relying on a single Greek patristic authority, namely Origen, when at last he attacked Luther in 1524 in *De libero arbitrio*.

Even more striking is the influence of several Greek patristic works in developing the idea of the dignity of man. Several Greek fathers had

developed at length the themes of man as the link between the physical
and intellectual worlds, of macrocosm and microcosm, of the soul as a
separate spiritual substance ruling the body, and of free choice, always a
constituent notion of the idea of the *dignitas hominis:* that man is
a largely autonomous moral agent, containing in his own nature the possibility of the most varied development, who can, by free choice, become
akin to any being, become like a rock or plant or beast if he turn toward
evil, like the angels if he turn toward good. This cluster of ideas in the
later fifteenth- and sixteenth-century formulation had as its nourishing
sources pages of Gregory of Nyssa and Nemesius of Emesa's *On the
Nature of Man* (ca. 390). A remarkable encomium of man occurs at the
end of the first chapter of Nemesius's treatise, a passage derived directly
from Origen's *Commentary on Genesis* (of which only fragments survive) in which he had mingled Christian themes with themes from Pos-
idonius's *Hymn to Man* (partially preserved in Cicero's *De natura
deorum*) to forge an important link in that tradition which extends from
the celebrated chorus in Sophocles's *Antigone* to Pico della Mirandola's
Oration:

> Who can fittingly admire the dignity of man, who joins in himself
> the mortal and immortal, the rational and irrational; who bears in
> his own nature the image of the whole creation (and for this reason
> is called a microcosm or little world); who is God's special care
> and for whose sake God made all things and Himself became
> man. . . . Who can enumerate the excellence and ornaments of the
> nature of man! He crosses the seas, he penetrates the heavens with
> the eye of the mind, he understands the course of the stars and
> their intervals and sizes; . . . no science, art or doctrine escapes his
> penetration; . . . he foresees the future; he rules over all, he domi-
> nates all, enjoys all; speaks with angels and with God; commands
> at his pleasure all other creatures; subjugates the demons;
> learnedly investigates the natural world and the essence of God,
> becomes a house and a temple of God and achieves all this by piety
> and virtue.[9]

Patristic works could be put to more practical and more convenient
purposes: for example, to inspire young monks, to refute arguments
against monastic life, and to defend the superiority of chastity to marriage. Here is Ambrogio Traversari, general of the Camaldolensian Order
and the earliest important humanist translator of Greek patristic works,
dedicating to Pope Eugenius IV in 1434 a Greek treatise on virginity that
he believed to be by Basil the Great: "With such diligence does this de-

fender set forth, depict and praise the glory of virgin chastity, with such care does he safeguard, arm and fortify it, and in short with such vigilance does he reveal and lay bare all snares and guard against them, that in my judgment no one has ever dealt more diligently with this matter." [10] Another motive of Traversari's patristic scholarship was to show that the Greek Orthodox church was in error, especially on the matter of the Procession of the Holy Spirit. Thus when Cardinal Cesarini began to prepare the Latin case before the meeting of the Council of Ferrara–Florence, called to negotiate the reunion of the Greek and Latin churches, he asked Ambrogio to translate Basil's *Adversus Eunomium* because he believed it to support the Latin position on the doctrinal points at issue, that is, he wished to refute the Greeks out of their own mouths by citing Greek patristic authority. This episode foreshadows the unprecedented use of the fathers in the sixteenth century in partisan theological controversy.

Even more intimate was the relation of patristic study to efforts at church reform. Increasingly in the fifteenth century and universally in the sixteenth, the apostolic and patristic church, the primitive and ancient church, became a model for reform, while reform itself came to be understood as the effort to restore the church to the image of its ancient holiness. Humanists frequently used the early church as a historical exemplar by which to measure the condition of the contemporary church, while at the same time deploring the decadence of the present day, the many abuses in the church, the clergy's worldliness and ignorance, the tepidness of monastic observance. If we are to reform the church in head and members, they said, we must imitate the examples of the noble ancients; not pagan heroes, but the apostles, Anthony the hermit, Jerome and Augustine, Basil, Pachomius, and Benedict, who composed rules of monastic life.

But humanist intellectuals admired the fathers above all because they found in their works—or thought they did—a normative style of piety and religious sensibility, one distilled in the Petrarchan phrase *docta pietas* (learned piety), and in the formula used by many humanists to describe their religious program: the union of wisdom and piety with eloquence. This is why humanists used the fathers as polemical rods with which to beat the scholastics, the professional theologians in university faculties of theology. For not only was the style of these theologians said to be barbarous and therefore incapable of persuading men and women to love God and their neighbors, but the vast summas in which they ordered theology were thought to be unnecessarily dry and complex. When scholastic theologians (as was their wont) raised knotty difficulties, opposed authorities *sic et non*, probed *quaestiones* in disputations

and reconciled them by a subtle logic, they were pandering—so humanists believed—to their own dialectical pride rather than serving the faith;
indeed they contaminated theology with profane philosophy. Humanists
pictured themselves as paladins of simplicity, as Hercules vanquishing the
Hydra or Alexander cutting the Gordian knot. To the theology of the
schoolmen they opposed the "old and true theology" of the fathers
(which they conveniently claimed to have prefigured their own) and
which they understood to be simpler, more pure, more personal and
emotional, more humbly and accurately dependent on the divine text,
directed less to the presumptuous and inevitably disputatious goal of
trying to know God in his fullness than toward the more human and
possible aim of ardently loving him, more persuasively concerned with
moral teaching, closer to the source of truth. The scholastics had sought
to make theology a science, a *scientia* in the Aristotelian sense, that is, to
establish a systematically ordered body of true and certain knowledge
derived from the certain but undemonstrable principles of revelation.
This effort, too, humanists typically attacked as misguided, arrogant,
and dangerous because it produced only sophistry, arid intellectualism,
emotional poverty, and lack of charity. The learned and eloquent piety
of the fathers, by contrast, was not a science but a positive wisdom, a
holy rhetoric derived from the holy page of Scripture. The simple evangelical, scriptural faith Renaissance humanists attributed to the fathers
justified their own aversion to scholastic method, their insistence on a
return to the sources in the original languages, the normally exegetical
form of their own theological work, and the end they sought—an eloquent and warm personal piety joined to moral probity, an evangelical
and scriptural faith consciously tailored to give spiritual and moral guidance to an educated laity.

The fathers, therefore, wrote no summas. As the most orthodox possible soldiers of Christian truth, they wrote polemics against heretics or
commentaries on Scripture, making the blinding illumination of the sacred text accessible to the fragile eyes of the human mind. We come to
the fathers depressed with worldly cares. We leave them hungry and
thirsty for the page of Scripture. The Christianity that compels men's
hearts is the eloquently preached Word of Scripture, not the subtle analysis of doctrine. Love is more important than knowledge, concord than
debate, virtuous action than nicety of belief.

Ultimately, the correctness of patristic methods, and so the purity
and truth of their theological results, was due to the fact that they rested
on the techniques of textual criticism. The scriptural page was central,
and the fathers had made every effort to reach its true meaning. Origen
and Jerome had read the Bible in its original Hebrew and Greek; they

had developed the critical techniques necessary to maintain an uncontaminated transmission of the holy text; they had prepared new translations and corrected older ones against the original. The biblical studies of the fathers thus became a model for an important part of the humanist program: the call for a return to the sources, the learning of Greek and Hebrew, and the critical examination and correction of the Vulgate, the Latin translation of the Bible commonly read in the western church, most of it the work of St. Jerome. Italian humanists were relatively little interested in the critical study of the text of the Bible, the most notable exception being Lorenzo Valla, whose *Annotations on the New Testament* were published by Erasmus and stimulated Erasmus's own much more ambitious and successful program of biblical study. Erasmus, in turn, became the model of a host of humanistically trained sixteenth-century scholars, both Catholic and Protestant.

The fathers, then, offered humanists a Christian vision of antiquity, a Christian eloquence, a Christian philosophy, and a pristine theology, ancient and true, a moving union of piety and wisdom with eloquence, which seemed necessarily to reconcile the tensions between Christianity and the ideals of classical culture and to prove that such a reconciliation continued to be possible. This perceived reconciliation seemed consequently to solve one of their central problems: the proper relation between an enthusiasm for the antique and a firm commitment to Christian values. Salutati put it very well at the end of his life: "The *studia humanitatis* and the *studia divinitatis* are so interconnected that true and complete knowledge of the one cannot be had without the other."[11]

NOTES

For orientation in the literature on humanist patristic scholarship and the humanist idea of Christian antiquity, see E. Garin, "La *dignitas hominis* e la letteratura patristica," *La Rinascita* 1 (1938): 102–46; D. Gorce, "La patristique dans la réforme d'Erasme," *Festgabe Joseph Lortz*, ed. E. Iserloh and P. Manns, 2 vols. (Baden-Baden, 1958), 1:233–76; H. H. Gray, "Valla's *Encomium of St. Thomas Aquinas* and the Humanist Conception of Christian Antiquity," in *Essays in History and Literature Presented by Fellows of the Newberry Library to Stanley Pargellis*, ed. H. Bluhm (Chicago, 1965), 37–51; P. O. Kristeller, "Augustine and the Early Renaissance," in *Studies in Renaissance Thought and Letters*, 2 vols. (Rome, 1956–85), 1:355–72; E. F. Rice, Jr., "The Humanist Idea of Christian Antiquity: Lefèvre d'Etaples and His Circle," *Studies in the Renaissance* 9 (1962): 126–60; and C. L. Stinger, *Humanism and the Church Fathers: Ambrogio Traversari (1386–1439) and Christian Antiquity in the Italian Renaissance* (Albany, NY, 1976).

    1. *Eximii doctoris Hieronymi Stridonensis vita ex ipsius potissimum litteris contexta per Desiderium Erasmum Roterodamum*, ed. W. K. Ferguson, *Erasmi opuscula* (The Hague, 1933), 139.

2. *The Prefatory Epistles of Jacques Lefèvre d'Etaples and Related Texts,* ed. E. F. Rice, Jr. (New York, 1972), 240.

3. *Leonardo Bruni Aretino. Humanistisch-philosophische Schriften,* ed. H. Baron (Leipzig, 1928), 6–7, 19.

4. *In quartum librum Elegantiarum praefatio,* ed. E. Garin, *Prosatori latini del Quattrocento* (Turin, 1976), 612–22.

5. *Bruni Schriften,* ed. Baron, 99–100.

6. *Aeneae Silvii de liberorum educatione,* ed. J. S. Nelson (Washington, DC, 1940), 176–77.

7. *Theodoriti Cyrensis episcopi de curatione Graecarum affectionum libri duodecim Zenobio Acciaolo interprete* (Paris, 1519), sig. a, ij, v; Biblioteca Apostolica Vaticana, Ottob. lat. 1404, fols. lv–2.

8. Ottob. lat. 1404, fols. 155v–156.

9. *Patrologia graeca,* ed. J.-P. Migne (Paris, 1858), 40, cols. 532C–533B.

10. Stinger, *Humanism and the Church Fathers,* 170–207, 215–17.

11. *Epistolario di Coluccio Salutati,* ed. F. Novati, 5 vols. (Rome, 1891–1911), 4: 184–85.

3 ❧ MEDIEVAL ITALIAN CULTURE AND THE ORIGINS OF HUMANISM AS A STYLISTIC IDEAL
Ronald G. Witt

THE ITALIAN HUMANISTS, LIKE THE MEDIEVAL RHETORICIANS OR *dictatores* before them, were essentially literary men, seekers of eloquence. What distinguished them from their predecessors was a stylistic ideal, the imitation of ancient Latin models. Enthusiastically seeking the key to recapturing the style of the ancient pagan authors, they turned with a passion to the ancient texts and gradually honed their own philological skills and the very process of their thinking. Although a wide range of other factors favored the Italians in their efforts to understand and learn from the ancient past, their success derived immediately from their commitment to ancient Latin style. Through mastery of style they attained mastery of a culture, with the creative consequences for western civilization that ensued. Any effort to explore the origins of Italian humanism entails, therefore, answering two questions: What was the origin of the new taste for ancient style? and: How did that taste initially manifest itself?

The problem of the first historical manifestations of classical imitation is a relatively easy one. The fourteenth century already acknowledged the founder of the new literary movement to have been Lovato dei Lovati of Padua (ca. 1240–1309), and subsequent research has produced nothing to undercut his priority. Lovato's claim to the pioneering role in the establishment of classical standards of style, however, rests solely on his poetry. His earliest extant poetic writing, two Latin letters to a friend, dates from about 1268.[1] Taking ancient poets as his models, Lovato clearly strives in the letters to match vocabulary, meter, and tone with those of his source of inspiration. Judged as a whole, his surviving poetry occasionally displays a weakness for wordplay, assonance, and rhythms characteristic of medieval poets, but such unevenness is to be expected.[2] His contribution lies primarily in aspiration rather than in accomplishment.

Lovato's prose provides a striking contrast to his poetry. Because of their official nature one would not, of course, expect to find him trying to classicize the legal language of his notarial documents. Lovato might also have considered it inappropriate to experiment with prose in a treatise explaining the meter in Seneca's tragedies. But his *Dictamina*, a short collection of twenty-one periods specifically designed as rhetorical exercises, would seem to have been ideal for such a purpose. Yet, despite the occasional borrowing of a word or phrase from some ancient author, the elaborate and often obscure lines offer not the slightest ring of ancient prose.[3] It is not that he failed to achieve the effect but rather that he never intended to do so.

This bifurcation in Lovato's work, that is, between a reformed poetry and an unreformed prose, is characteristic of the literary movement he pioneered for the first forty years. A reformed Latin prose made its appearance only about 1308–1313 with the composition of Riccobaldo of Ferrara's *Historiae*, soon to be followed by Albertino Mussato's *De gestis Henrici VII Caesaris*, which was completed about 1315.[4] Although disparity in chronology is to be expected in that poetic models are much easier to imitate than those of prose, nevertheless, the fact that humanist style first appeared in poetry is fundamental to defining the problem of the origins of the new taste. It suggests that, in view of the traditional assignment of poetry to grammar, we are in pursuit of the origins of a literary movement with a strong grammatical component.[5] To determine these it is necessary to investigate the literary history of Italy in the centuries preceding Lovato, particularly the role of grammar, and—because the two are inextricably linked—of rhetoric in Italian cultural life.

*   *   *

As historically defined in western Europe, grammar and rhetoric constituted two very different centers around which to organize education and ultimately a way of life. The different character and tendencies present in the disciplines of grammar and rhetoric emerged with the formation of the two disciplines in the Greco-Roman system of education. As it existed in the golden days of the Roman Empire in the first century B.C. and first century of the Christian era, the curriculum of the schools made rhetoric the superior discipline in the educational hierarchy. The task of the grammarian was to prepare the student to pass on to the school of rhetoric, where he could learn the subject that would enable him to participate fully in the political life of the state. Though subordinate, grammatical studies provided students with skills that extended beyond the requirements for entering the school of rhetoric; in this way the grammarian managed to promote some of his own interests.[6]

The grammarian began his educational program on the assumption that his charges had learned the elements of reading and writing from the *magister ludi*. His own task was to give the student a good understanding of Latin grammar, an appreciation of literature, and initial training in the art of composition. At the outset detailed study was devoted to the letters of the alphabet, the syllables, and the parts of speech. Selections from the poets served as the basis for a minute examination of syntax and provided the students with an introduction to literary analysis. In the course of a line-by-line study of a poem, the grammarian discussed the author's biography, the historical and mythological references found in the work, together with the metric, the etymology of the vocabulary, and the various figures used by the poet. He taught the student to search for truth hidden beneath a veil of imagery. Close study of the text incidentally revealed discrepancies in different copies and easily encouraged the grammarian to engage in textual criticism.

The student left the grammar school with some experience in reciting poetry and composing short pieces of prose, but delivery and prose composition were to be the main objectives of his training from then on. The rhetor set his students to imitating the great prose writers of the culture, especially the orators. Students learned to declaim, to debate, and to deliver orations of their own making. Success at these assignments augured well for their future standing in society.

Obviously there was continuity between the grammar-school teaching and that of the rhetorical school. The rhetor presupposed grammatical training in his students: the rules of prosody learned earlier facilitated the mastering of prose metric required in orations, and appropriate citations from the poets proved a vital ingredient in making an impressive speech. The grammarian, by contrast, utilized some prose texts in his instruction; interpretation of the poets could not have been made without help of the *colores rhetorici* borrowed from the rhetor. The figures of thought and style, the tropes and commonplaces were employed to make the poetry at both the outer and inner level clear to the students.

The grammarian's dependence on devices of rhetoric to accomplish his ends suggests the need for a threefold meaning of rhetoric.[7] "Primary rhetoric" is the art of speechmaking and develops out of the needs of public life. It includes speeches, impromptu and written, as well—at least in the ancient and medieval period—as public letters that were delivered orally and in this way classify as speeches.

"Secondary rhetoric" involves all other literary genres, for example, history, private correspondence, poetry, and philosophical discussion when it has literary pretensions. In this wider area rhetoric relates to invention, arrangement, and especially to style, in other words, to the particular selection of words and their order chosen by the author regardless of subject matter.

To these two, however, should be added a tertiary meaning of rhetoric, that of rhetoric as a way of thought that seeks conclusions by inference rather than by demonstration, whose weapon is more often the enthymeme than the syllogism. As such, rhetoric not only contrasts with Aristotelian dialectic but also with the grammarian's reliance on etymology, glossing of texts, and allegory to produce truth.

While interdependence must be acknowledged, it is meaningful to see the grammarian-poet and the rhetorician-orator as representing two poles of attraction, one or the other of which characterizes the dominant tendencies operative in many individual writers and movements. This contrast between the grammarian and the rhetorician (in the primary and tertiary senses) highlights two different approaches to knowledge and two potentially contrasting ways of life.

Outside the classroom, the grammarian in his own work remains a student of texts, a philologist, a specialist in mythology. He finds pleasure in treating the smallest details of a poem, eager to find there a word or phrase that could raise him to a general truth of natural, moral, or theological import. He delights in allegory. Since all poetry is erudite, the poet is himself a grammarian who feels the need to express the movements of his emotions and thoughts through his own sets of images. Whether as creative artist or as philologist, the grammarian requires the quiet of the study or of solitary places. He leads a private life, a *vita contemplativa*, and the audience for his work is a narrow elite of specialists or like-minded men.

By contrast, the life of the rhetorician is the *vita activa*, aimed ideally at the achievement of practical public ends. The rhetorician's objectives are best realized in the marketplace, where his audience is the general public. Unlike the grammarian, the orator knows no "right" way to express an idea because one's words have to be adjusted to the particular audience at the particular moment. Moreover, he has no time for obscure meanings or hidden messages: his concern is clarity and his goal is action.

Now both in the system of education and in the rewards given by the society, the rhetorician or orator of the first century B.C. and first century of the Christian era was superior in standing to the grammarian, and that hierarchy endured in ancient culture long after the political institutions that justified it had vanished. However, with the collapse of the empire and the disappearance of an extensive public capable of understanding an oration delivered in ancient Latin, the rhetorician lost his preeminence and the grammarian stepped out of his shadow. The concern for rhetoric by no means disappeared. If not for composing orations, the ancient speech manuals—especially the work of Cicero's youth, the *De inventione*—provided training in composition applicable to all forms of literary expression. But more than this, the Middle Ages inherited particularly from the late empire an interest in rhetoric as a way of thinking and in its relationship to the various divisions of logic, such as dialectic and sophistic argument. Considered in this context, rhetoric would become a part of the study of logic in Europe after the tenth century.

The Carolingian Renaissance of the late eighth and early ninth centuries, directed by a monarch bent on raising the educational level of his people, represented a triumph for the grammarian. For Alcuin, the so-called schoolmaster of the empire, grammar was doubtless the queen of the trivium: "Grammar is the science of letters and the guardian of right speech and writing." The art embraced not merely the letters, syllables, words, and parts of speech but also things like figures of speech, prosody, poetry, stories, and history.[8] While theology was the supreme wisdom, nonetheless, preoccupied as it was with the etymology of terms and analyses of allegories, the grammatical orientation of its methodology becomes evident.

The limited number of those who knew Latin necessarily restricted the role of primary rhetoric in Carolingian society. Accounts of school curricula indicate no serious training either in speechwriting or delivery. Sermons appear to have been largely repetitions of patristic homilies.[9] Admittedly, Alcuin felt called on to compose a dialogue on the art of rhetoric, *Dialogus de rhetorica et virtutibus,* 80 percent of which derived from *De inventione*.[10] With Charlemagne as narrator, Alcuin presents a curious account of rhetoric almost entirely focused on judicial oratory. The extent to which Latin pleading was useful in a legal system based on custom is questionable, as is the level of priority it would have had even for clerics. Very likely, in the absence of conditions fostering Latin oratory in the society generally, Alcuin, anxious to cover this art of the trivium with a manual as he did the other two and lacking an orientation dictated by contemporary needs, merely took over Cicero's focus on judicial oratory in making his exposition.

Because letter writing plays such an important part in the discussion of *ars dictaminis* below, a brief word about this literary genre, especially the private letter, is in order. Clearly the grammatical character of Carolingian learning is demonstrated by the letters the society produced. The rich collections of correspondence we encounter in the late eighth and the ninth centuries are the productions of scholars steeped in the writing of the ancient poets and prose writers as well as in the Bible and in works of early Christian writers. Like the ancients they accept the conception of the letter as a kind of conversation, even though they are usually either incapable of manipulating the language to attain an informal tone or do not understand what that tone would be. The wealth of classical citations in prose and poetry, the echoes of ancient authors even in their own prose, suggest the grammarian's point of view to letter writing.[11]

Although the Carolingian Renaissance lost its impetus by the middle years of the ninth century with the breakdown of the empire, the structure of education, oriented as it was around grammar, continued to dominate the schools of Europe for at least two more centuries.[12] From the late tenth century, however, the ascendancy of grammar, primarily in northern Europe, ultimately came to be rivaled by a new passion for the study of logic, which was taught for the first time in a systematic fashion by Gerbert at Rheims in the last quarter of the century.[13] Along with the intensive study of the works of the *logica vetus* went that of later imperial writers like Victorinus and Martianus Capella, and these writings taken together insistently raised questions as to the place of rhetoric as a species of reasoning in relationship to logic as the genus.[14] Consequently, the fortune of rhetoric insofar as it was tied to logic tended to improve.

The *Metalogicon* of John of Salisbury, written in the 1150s, illustrates in a striking way the role of rhetoric in northern European education by the twelfth century. John writes approvingly of the method of Bernard of Chartres, who, essentially a grammarian, taught both poetry and prose to his students. Within the context of Bernard's program, rhetoric was understood primarily in a secondary sense as the art of composition. Despite his own stylistic gifts, John himself in the *Metalogicon* concentrates on rhetoric as a division of logic, with little or no relationship to the art of writing.[15]

In the light of the situation in Italy it is important to note that the Carolingian tradition of letter writing throve in the North until the end of the twelfth century. The private letter remained the vehicle for the expression of personal feelings by learned men, who with varying degrees of success interpreted their thoughts and experiences against the backdrop of their education in ancient and early Christian literature. Indeed, with their facility for writing Latin and their deep self-awareness, twelfth-century writers like Peter the Venerable, John of Salisbury, and Peter of Blois produced in their letters some of the finest literary works of the Middle Ages.[16]

Although they wrote a correct, fluent, and often eloquent Latin prose, twelfth-century northern writers seem uninterested in imitating ancient prose style. At the same time, much learned Latin poetry in the North contrasts in its penchant for elaborate ornamentation with the poetry of the classical period. Yet a few poets at times composed works imitating major traits of ancient poetry in vocabulary, diction, theme, and control of rhetorical devices. Although he enjoys using different styles and an underlying mannerism pervades his work generally, Hildebert of Lavardin is one of these. Marcus Valerius, an otherwise unknown twelfth-century poet, perhaps even captures ancient style in his bucolic poetry, but even for him classical style enjoyed no privileged position.[17]

*　　*　　*

In comparison with northern Europe, in Italy the passing of the Carolingian curriculum came early, at least in the area north of Rome, where humanism eventually arose. Only with reservations, in fact, can one speak of Italian participation in that cultural movement. True, in the late eighth century certain Italians—Paul the Deacon, Fardolfo, Peter of Pisa, and Paolino of Aquilea—were instrumental in constructing the Carolingian program of education itself in the circle around Charlemagne; but there were no central or nothern Italians of stature to take their place after 800, so humiliating had been the Lombard defeat.[18] Direction for the cultural revival came from Frankish bishops in key sees, assisted by Frankish and immigrant Irish scholars like Hilderic, Dungal, and others.[19] We can identify a few Italians such as Pacificus, the archdeacon of Verona, who copied more than two hundred manuscripts himself, but they were not directing the movement.[20]

While there is ample evidence of active scriptoria in a number of Italian cities, little survives in the way of poetry, letters, and religious work when compared to the lands beyond the Alps. Two mid-tenth-century series of episcopal decrees suggest by implication that at least four different types of schools were available in the Italian kingdom— cathedral, parish, monastic, and private schools—yet these documents come from a time that an Italian-directed intellectual revival was underway and can only be applied to the previous century with caution.[21] Of the existence of cathedral schools, the basis of a great deal of scholarly discussion, we have little in the way of solid evidence for the ninth century. The copying efforts of the episcopal scriptorium in Lucca by 800 point to the existence of a school of liberal studies in the area of the cathedral.[22] At Verona not only the rich production of the scriptorium under Pacificus in the first half of the ninth century but also the presence of a *scholasticus* among the canons make the existence of a school certain.[23] Nevertheless, it would be difficult to make a case for other areas.

On the whole, however, the level of intellectual life and the educational infrastructure must have undergone some enhancement over the century in order to explain the developments in the next. Unambiguous indications of economic, political, and demographic revivals seem to come too late in the century to be associated as causes with this development, but there is still much to be learned in this area. In any case, beginning with the appearance in a document of a *grammaticus Sapiens* as a canon in the cathedral chapter of Arezzo in 933–36, the references to *magischole* and *magistri* increase to become widespread throughout northern and central Italy in the first sixty years of the eleventh century.[24] More than this, in the middle decades of the tenth century there emerge a few Italians, scholars like Atto of Vercelli and Liudprand of Cremona, whose works indicate an intellectual and cultural level matching that of anyone in contemporary northern Europe.[25] This truly Italian-dominated revival drew its inspiration from the Carolingian cultural program centered on grammar, however, and the guiding model for education remained, as in the previous century, the learned bishop.

The style of much of the writing in this period is heavily ornate, often obscure, reflecting a concern for dazzling an audience at the risk of impeding communication. In 965 Gunzo of Novara in his *Epistola augiensis,* written to the monks of Reichenau, took the exceptional step of using a Ciceronian judicial oration as model for his defense of a particular grammatical usage.[26] With his complicated language and interminable listing of authorities in typical Carolingian fashion, Gunzo's audience in the refectory, where presumably the letter was read aloud, would have been unable to follow the argument, but they would scarcely have believed that a man with such learning could be wrong on a point of grammar.

Italian intellectual life, however, cannot be adequately described unless this culture dealing with books is taken in conjunction with that concerned with documents. The written word as documentation for human interaction was far more common in Italy than in northern Europe in the ninth century, and the extent to which laymen were brought into contact with writing was correspondingly greater. Not coincidentally, with one exception (802), all of Charlemagne's capitularies referring to written law seem to have been intended for application only to Italy.[27]

The mass of written evidence remaining from these centuries suggests that elementary Latin literacy was widespread.[28] These semiliterate, some from the highest level of society, would lack sufficient training to be able to work their way through a text of Vergil, but self-interest forced them to understand the charters and other legal documents that played a role in their daily lives. Thus beneath the educational level of the culture of the book lay that of the document.

The classic literate layman in this latter culture was the notary, who usually learned his trade through apprenticeship; but not all notaries had limited intellectual horizons.[29] The *notarii sacri palatii* connected with the royal palace at Pavia, first under the Lombard kings and then under the Carolingians, were in the course of the ninth century applying large portions of the *Corpus iuris civilis* in selective fashion to cover situations on which Lombard law was silent.[30] Outside of Pavia there was a large group of men, whose autograph signatures appear in witness lists, who define themselves simply as *judices*. Important men locally, they exercised consultative or decision-making functions at trials and, if not necessarily literate, some would have had the ability to read the documents that very often served as the essential proof in deciding a case.[31] Among the semiliterate we must also count most of the clerics, who could read a charter more easily than the Psalter.

Just as the tenth century witnessed a rise in the level of book culture, so the culture of the document became more sophisticated. By the end of the century the overwhelming percentage of surviving documents indicate that they were drawn up by notaries. The same century exhibited a tendency toward greater homogeneity in the form and content of documents, at least in the northern third of Italy, with Pavia appearing as the most influential center.[32] Furthermore, notaries other than those of Pavia began to assume titles like the Pisan notary, Urso, who in 927 signed himself simply as *notarius* and in 934 claimed to be *notarius et iudex dominorum reghum*.[33] In Parma in 953, a *notarius dominorum regum* appears for the first time, and in Padua the next year, a *notarius et iudex dominorum nostrum regum*.[34] By the end of the century 90 percent of the notaries in Lombardy had these kinds of titles.[35] There seems to have been a vigorous effort on the part of central authorities to privilege notarized documents as evidence and to regulate notarial practices in general.[36]

Already decades before 1000 the renewal of Italian intellectual vigor and the strengthening and regularization of the Italian notariate began to draw strength from an economic, political, and demographic revival that favored urbanization. These material developments were Europe-wide in scope, but their specific effects varied depending on the area. In northern Europe the expansion of the economy and the serious attempt to concentrate political power led to a proliferation of chanceries at the secondary level, encouraging ambitious young clerics to get the kind of education that would ultimately be profitable.[37]

The Carolingian curriculum had been designed largely to provide the student with the aristocratic cultural background expected of high aulic officials and future princes of the church. In the course of the eleventh century the northern cathedral schools expanded their curriculum to meet the demands of the more intensive intellectual life, especially increasing the study of dialectic; but no need was felt to sever continuity with the past.[38] The clergy continued to be the carriers of an elite culture, except that the level of training rose and students graduated with better control over the Latin idiom. The new chanceries stood ready to provide clerics with increasing opportunities to earn a lucrative income in some lord's service.

In Italy by 1000, by contrast, lay notaries easily had a monopoly on work, even in many episcopal chanceries. By the early twelfth century, with the exception of the tradition-bound archbishopric of Ravenna, they seem everywhere to have triumphed in the ecclesiastical centers.[39] The diffusion of the institution of the count-bishop, to the extent that it intensified supervision in the diocese, further enhanced opportunities for laymen with skills of literacy and knowledge of law, as did the establishment of the communes from the last part of the eleventh century. Culturally this was of great significance in that the ecclesiastical chanceries of northern Europe were usually closely linked with the cathedral library and the school, providing employment for an intellectual elite of clerics. In Italy, because of lay penetration of the chanceries, these connections were broken.

The presence of a relatively large class of literate or, more accurately, semiliterate individuals, lured by the expanding opportunities after 1000, had a detrimental effect in the long run on the traditional grammatically oriented school curriculum. The demand for rhetorical-legal studies that emerged in the eleventh century rode on the crest of a buoyant documentary culture eager to see its sons advance their economic and political position in an expanding world through access to the books of the law. The response to the pressure amounted to a reorientation of the educational program by 1100.

*   *   *

Whereas in eleventh-century northern Europe Aristotle and his commentator Boethius offered the key structural principles for intellectual life, in Italy that role was played by Cicero. The ancient Roman, of course, had his own dialectic, but in it the syllogism played a minor role, while stress was placed on inference, on a consideration of consequences, and on a fortiori arguments. At the same time, the power of the syllogism to demonstrate a "truth" could at times serve the orator even when arguing a practical point because of the conviction syllogistic demonstration commanded.[40] Put simply, while in France rhetoric as a form of reasoning was auxiliary to dialectic, in Italy the reverse was true.

There was some diffusion of the texts of Gerbert's logic curriculum south of the Alps but they are difficult to trace. Papias, the learned lexicographer of Lombardy, about 1045 drew on some of them for his definitions of words pertaining to logic, but they have little effect on his basically Ciceronian approach to logic.[41] The only teacher of the new dialectic so far identified in eleventh-century Italy was Drogo, who taught at Parma in the 1030s and 1040s but left no writings. His student, Anselm of Besate, however, in his *Rhetorimachia* dedicated originally to his master and composed in 1047–48, gives us some idea of the effect the Aristotelian-Boethian logic had on an Italian student. Intended as a judicial oration to illustrate the rules of rhetoric, the work professes to seek only verisimilitude in proving its incredible charges against the author's own relative, Rotilando.[42] The dialectical arguments do little to move the case along and function more as *colores rhetorici*.

Contemporary writings on dialectic in northern Europe had perhaps not yet moved far beyond Anselm of Besate's puerile games, but the sights of dialecticians there were higher, and by the last quarter of the century a breakthrough in theology occurred. A brilliant young legist like Lanfranc of Pavia, unable to satisfy his desire for instruction in dialectic with a higher purpose in Italy, became the first known Italian to move to France for that reason. Leaving Italy in the 1030s, he eventually created a leading center for that art at Bec.[43] Other Italians, such an Anselm of Lucca and Anselm of Aosta, came to study with him in the next decades.[44]

In Italy, at the same time, rhetoric and law, part of rhetoric's own being, held the field. Peter Damian (ca. 1007–1072) depicted the "roaring of the crowds" in the marketplace and courts and, as archbishop of Ravenna, complained that he could neither contemplate nor write because of the continual disputes about property and other matters involving the archdiocese.[45] He blamed the heads of churches for neglecting their duties "and like laymen" studying "not sacred writings but the decrees of the law and court litigation. . . . The Scripture is shut, and through the mouths of the clerical order run the civil laws."[46] Writing to Henry III in 1041, the German ecclesiastic Wipo advised the emperor to compel the German nobility to study law as did the Italian nobility, so they could defend themselves in court.[47]

Despite the fact that we know that cathedral schools blossomed in the early eleventh century, it is difficult to establish a clear link between their curriculum and the craze for legal studies. Clearly both Anselm of Besate and Peter Damian had been beautifully trained in the poets before embarking on rhetorical studies, which in Peter's case led to legal training. As for Anselm, he tells his former teacher Drogo in the *Rhetorimachia* that, after leaving him, he had spent time studying with another of Drogo's former students, Sichelmo, at the cathedral school at Reggio, and he praises the latter as skilled both in rhetoric and law.[48] Yet in the *Rhetorimachia* the few references to the law have a decorative function and indicate nothing as to whether or not Sichelmo actually taught law.

If law was in fact being taught in the cathedral school of Reggio, the method of legal instruction at Ravenna seems to have been the more common. At Ravenna, according to a description of Peter Damian in 1046, law was not taught in the cathedral school, but rather lawyers running private schools instructed students in the art of arguing cases and perhaps gave some instruction in drawing up documents.[49] The most advanced center for legal studies in the eleventh century was Pavia, where immediately after the turn of the century lawyers began to manifest a new grasp of the texts of Roman law and of the need to resolve apparent contradictions both between that law and the Lombard law and between elements of the Roman law itself.[50] Nevertheless, there is no sign of a cathedral school in the city and at least one lawyer active there, Bonfigli, seems to have been training students.[51] Incidentally, until the middle decades of the century, these lawyers of Pavia were also engaged in notarizing acts, which suggests a continuity between the documentary culture of earlier centuries and the *jurisperiti* of the eleventh.[52]

Like Pavia, Bologna in this century showed no sign of having a cathedral school, yet Bologna was to take the lead in legal studies from the first decades of the twelfth. We can also identify a private law school in operation there in the 1070s and 1080s. The teaching of Pepo, moreover, seems to have had almost immediate repercussions on notarial practice in the city. In the next generation Irnerius, Pepo's great successor, is said to have produced as his first legal work a set of model notarial documents.[53]

The temptation is great to see the development of legal instruction as an outgrowth of notarial schools in the eleventh century, but there is no strong evidence for the existence of such schools in northern or central Italy. My sense is that the ways of coming to legal studies were various. The cathedral schools with their libraries were probably the most important centers for teaching grammar, but they had no monopoly on legal education, which made fewer demands on the supply of books. Consequently, much teaching was probably in the hands of private individuals, themselves practicing lawyers. While students went to these schools to become lawyers, they would also have had some experience with constructing notarial documents. In cities like Pavia and Bologna a legal culture developed where notaries trained by apprenticeship lived in close contact with the more highly trained lawyers, and advances in legal scholarship easily passed into reform of notarial practice.[54]

Although courtroom oratory is known only through occasional

summaries, we can affirm that, aside from short bursts of eloquence, there was probably not much. Even the humanists in the fifteenth century were unable to develop judicial oratory, so powerful was the tradition of interrupting the discourse with references to particular passages from the Roman law. The flood of eloquence unleashed by the burning issue of church reform in the second half of the eleventh century, however, provides ample evidence of the vigor of primary rhetoric outside the courtroom.

Peter Damian could easily count as the greatest preacher since late antiquity and Pope Gregory VII as the most eloquent writer of official correspondence. Intended, as such correspondence usually was, to be read aloud, either by or to the recipient, Gregory introduced into his papal letters a series of rhetorical questions, occasional interjections, and expressions designed to convey pathos.[55] Of great power as well was the long letter addressed to Henry IV by Peter Crassus, apparently a lawyer from Ravenna, which expresses a novel viewpoint in opposition to the Gregorian reform program.[56] Unlike the ornate writers of the tenth century, these writers lived in the midst of intense public debate; they employed simple vocabulary and sentence structure; their aim was to persuade their audience by appealing to authority, reason, and emotion.

A major casualty of the reform program was the cathedral school, that institution in which the grammatical curriculum of northern and central Italy thrived. Within the last twenty-five years of the century cathedral chapters were riven by disputes over aspects of reform like clerical marriage and lay investiture. The diocese of Bergamo for years had an imperial bishop in the city and a reformed clergy in the country. At Mantua the canons seem for more than fifty years to have lost their collective life.[57] At Milan one hears no more of the splendid school described by Landulph Senior in mid-century.[58] The chronicle of Landulph Junior, composed early in the next century, depicts a clergy that did its advanced study in France at places like Paris and Laon.[59] Cathedral schools like those at Lucca survived as centers of liberal-arts training, but as an institution the cathedral school lost its leading role in Italian education after 1100.[60] With it went the traditional educational program going back to the Carolingian period.

As the eleventh century advanced and the numbers of laymen seeking literacy increased, the elite variety of education fostered by the cathedral schools became in any case irrelevant for most students. Whereas the dominant educational model of Italy to the early eleventh century had been a Carolingian one of the learned bishop, from the late eleventh century a new model, that of the Roman lawyer—and later that of the lawyer of both Roman and canon law—replaced it. The majority of students, who could not aspire to such heights, sought as a minimum the communication skills adequate for writing a letter and, possibly beyond that, the ability to draw up legal documents. This growing market of students created a demand for manuals dealing with letter writing (*ars dictaminis*) and collections of legal documents.

The most flexible kind of institution in the new age was that of the private school run by a single teacher, often an itinerant like Adalbertus of Samaria, who moved from town to town in the early twelfth century contracting with groups of students for a term of his services.[61] Traveling light, these individuals had to make do without cathedral libraries; but, in any case, the new popular market they served did not demand a widely read teacher or extensive reading assignments. The principal tool of instruction was the manual.

After an elementary education in a parish or private school, the student was ready for a course in *ars dictaminis*. The student might then go on to an apprenticeship with a notary or even to a school of law, which would give him training presumably in rhetoric and dialectic as well as in Roman law. Some students surely came to legal studies with broader backgrounds, but the general tendency was toward a spare, efficient program of education, aiming at producing lawyers, notaries, and *dictatores,* that is, notaries with notarial and letter-writing skills employed in chanceries or in teaching these skills.

Masters in cathedral schools might try to respond to the new clientele by advertising writing courses based on the practical *ars dictaminis* method, as did Hugo, canon of the cathedral of Bologna in the 1120s; but the average lay student had little need for the rest of the cathedral curriculum.[62] Given the unambiguous focus of educational interest, the private teacher could easily compete with the great establishments. The documentary culture of Italy had by 1100 impressed its stamp on the culture of the book.

By 1150 the common practice was for Italian scholars interested in grammatical studies, Aristotelian dialectic, and theology to go to France, and for French students of Roman law to come south to Bologna. Within a few decades more canon-law studies at Bologna, feeding on the advances made in Roman law, would have a parallel power of attracting students.[63] In Italy dialectic stood captive to rhetoric and to legal studies, and rhetoric enjoyed a full life both in its tertiary sense as logic and in its primary function as oral eloquence, not only in courtroom speeches and public letters but, as will be shown, in private correspondence as well.

* * *

The rapid spread of *ars dictaminis* manuals after 1100 resulted in standardization of letter-writing style at a relatively low level. Because of the importance of skills in composing public letters, instruction in writing this kind of letter with its orientation to oral delivery enjoyed priority. Quite naturally, individuals writing to public powers could be expected to observe the same rules of official rhetoric. At the same time, because political power was tied into a wide variety of social functions and individuals were often difficult to separate from office, *dictatores* were easily encouraged to impose the same rules on what earlier ages had considered personal letters. Consequently, with the official letter as model, the writers of manuals tended to think of formulating rules for effectively stating a message communicated in the form of a speech or oration, and they standardized letters accordingly.

There had been some discussion concerning the art of letter writing prior to the composition of the *Flores rhetorici dictaminis* by Alberico of Monte Cassino about 1075, but he deserves credit for being the first to develop a manual for letter composition. In it he proposes to treat "the rhetorical division of every speech, that is, the *exordium* or *proemium*, the *narratio*, the *argumentatio*, and the *conclusio*," rubrics borrowed from Isidore of Seville. To these he adds a fifth, the *salutatio*.[64] While briefly touching on the role of the *narratio*, the *argumentatio*, and the *conclusio*, the author devotes several lengthy paragraphs to both the *salutatio* and the *exordium*. Alberico reflects well the tendency to assimilate the letter to a speech when he characterizes the task of the *exordium* as rendering the reader "attentive, kindly disposed, and docile" and illustrates his whole discussion of epistolary theory by giving among other examples a passage based on a speech in Sallust. Reflecting the grammatical background from which he came, Alberico conceived of his instruction on letter writing as only part of an extensive program in training students to write, one founded on a thorough training in the Latin authors.

While most of Alberico's northern and central Italian successors and imitators tended to sever the connection between letter writing and a broad grammatical education, they reflected a similar tendency to refer to letters as speeches. Under pressure from friends, Adalbertus of Samaria consents to give advice to those wishing to create prose orations (*prosaicas orationes*) and urges writers to adapt their style to the social level of the recipient, just as is done in public assemblies.[65] An anonymous Bolognese *dictator*, writing about 1140, defines the letter simply as "a speech (*oratio*) consisting of parts, harmoniously and clearly written, fully expressing the feeling of the sender."[66]

Although none of the early *dictatores* can be accused of considering the letter identical to a written speech, the oration remained in important respects the model for the letter. Just as the oration had six parts, so the letter was strictly divided into distinct parts. Frequently the manuals supplied a choice of words or phrases appropriate for introducing each division.[67] Like the speech, the letter normally had an *exordium* designed to render the listener compliant.[68] This use of the *exordium* best exemplified the oratorical character of the letter. The tone of letters, even when they were supposedly personal communications, was formal and consciously crafted to evoke the desired response. Both the speech and the letter had concern for efficiency, with no allowance made for digressions that did not serve the central object of the composition. This was a "modern" style with almost no classical quotations and few biblical ones.

Letters conceived on such impersonal lines suited the bureaucratic purposes of political organizations well. Diplomacy particularly requires an elaborate protocol by which subtle changes in formulas or structure constitute signals of altered attitudes and situations. The early humanists in the fourteenth century had the good sense to realize this and to make concessions to established practices. But at the same time *dictamen*'s tyranny of stylistic prescriptions discouraged spontaneity and that direct expression of thought and feeling which gave the public letters of Gregory VII and the personal ones of Peter Damian their character. Furthermore, the demands of *brevitas* meant that *dictatores* had little space for the philosophical ruminations and anecdotal meanderings especially found in the private letters of other periods.

These straightforward, brief letters, almost always bare of quotations, were written in what the age called the *stilus humilis*. Easy to compose, they could be whipped off by a talented notary in a few minutes when writing under the pressure of business in the office. This humble style was identical with *ars dictaminis* style in the twelfth century. Moreover, when early in the thirteenth century speech manuals began to appear, there was little to distinguish the examples they give of speeches from those of letters.[69] By the same period as well *dictatores* were starting to write prose histories of contemporary events, and these too were marked by the *stilus humilis* adapted from the letter.[70] In other words, *ars dictaminis* by the early thirteenth century in northern and central Italy exerted a determining influence on most literary prose composition, and its basic style was *stilus humilis*.

*   *   *

By the last decade of the twelfth century northern and central Italy would appear to have been the least likely territory in Europe to host an elitist literary movement based on imitation of ancient authors.[71] In these same years, however, this practical rhetorical culture, whose highest intellectual achievements were in legal studies and whose most significant trait was its widespread literacy, experienced something like a cultural invasion from the North, primarily from France. From the last decades of the twelfth century, three major foreign sources of influence become apparent: late twelfth-century French treatises on *dictamen;* the French development of preaching; and manuals on poetry and grammar along with French Latin poetry.

In the field of *dictamen* France until the 1180s had been primarily on the receiving end. The first French-authored manual of *dictamen* so far identified is the *Ars dictandi aureliensis,* dated convincingly as around 1180.[72] The last decades of the century, however, saw the production of at least three important French manuals, that ascribed commonly to Peter of Blois written about 1185, Geoffrey of Vinsauf's *Summa de arte dictandi* written in 1188, and the manual of Bernard of Meun, which dates perhaps from the early 1190s.[73]

At the same time France changed from an importer into an exporter of *dictamen* theories. At least in the late 1180s Geoffrey was installed as teacher of *dictamen* in Bologna, and by the mid-1190s the Bolognese professor of *dictamen,* Boncompagno, gave expression in his *Tractatus virtutum* to what he felt was a direct threat to the Italian *stilus humilis* tradition. He saw the *stilus aureliensis* (style of Orleans) as a menace to the simple, direct Latin style, which, as we have seen, had been characteristic of Italian *ars dictaminis* since the late eleventh century. For Boncompagno the French approached letter writing as grammarians and not as rhetoricians. They pursued literary expression in their letters at the expense of efficiency, and this meant, in fact, that they preferred obscurity to clarity.[74] French letters were products of the study, not of the busy world of the marketplace and the chancery. For this reason the general literary interests of the French threatened to distort the letter as a form of communication.

His *Boncompagnus* or *Rhetorica antiqua,* extant in its second edition, published in 1226 or 1227, recalls an event in the 1190s in which Boncompagno, for purposes of ridiculing the current rage for the style of Orleans, circulated a letter purporting to have been written by a certain Robert of France. Although he doubtless exaggerated the style, Boncompagno intended the letter to be taken seriously by his readers, so it could not have been too grotesque a parody. Robert's letter simply bristles with neologisms and is tortured and pretentious in its language and construction. It reflects a decided effort to communicate a simple affair as if it were a matter of universal truth.[75] Such a letter would certainly have required hours to compose and demanded talent beyond that possessed by the typical student Boncompagno was trying to train.

By the first decades of the thirteenth century the menace to the *stilus humilis* seems to have diminished. Boncompagno made his most strident criticisms of the French in the *Tractatus virtutum* and the *Palma,* works of 1197 and 1198. His references to the conflict in his later works have a retrospective character. In the two *dictamen* treatises of another Bolognese *dictator,* Bene of Florence, the *Summa dictaminis* (after 1199) and the *Candelabrum* (1220–26), the author, despite his clear preference for the Italian style, was able to define the *stilus aureliensis* with calm objectivity.[76] Indeed, the *stilus humilis* was to remain the basic style of *dictamen* used in Italian chanceries north of Rome into the fifteenth century. Nevertheless, the French "grammatical" conception, as we shall see, contributed to engendering a number of elite styles of letter writing in the period 1200–50.

While Italy had been precocious in the *ars dictaminis,* northern Europe had the advantage in developing the *ars praedicandi,* which dates in the manual format at least from the early thirteenth century. From the time of the Investiture Conflict down to the early thirteenth century Italian rhetorical interests had been focused on secular rather than religious eloquence, while preaching languished.[77] But in the North, twelfth-century preachers developed the art of popular preaching in their battles against heretics and in their efforts to arouse popular enthusiasm for the crusades.[78] Maurice de Sully, bishop of Paris 1160–96, himself a famous preacher, stood at the center of a group of men devoted to developing the art that at various times included Peter the Chanter, Robert of Courçon, and Stephen Langton.[79] In all probability Innocent III, who studied at Paris in this period and knew members of de Sully's following, derived much of the zeal he displayed for preaching during his pontificate (1198–1216) from his French experience.[80] This emphasis reached its culmination in the tenth canon of the Fourth Lateran Council in 1215, which commanded bishops everywhere to provide for regular preaching in their dioceses.[81]

In view of the expectation that preaching was to be done widely, not merely by a group of experts, it was only natural that manuals of *ars praedicandi,* prescribing the rules for organizing and giving a sermon, would be developed.[82] These *artes praedicandi* vary widely in their contents: some offer lists of themes, exempla, and other references to aid the preacher in preparing his sermons. Most, however, present mainly the techniques of preparing the sermon itself. One begins with a theme taken from the Old or the New Testament, which will form the subject of the sermon. After the first enunciation of the theme, one introduces a pro-theme (or exordium), essentially a prayer of exhortation. In the early *artes* the theme would then be repeated and developed by use of examples and authorities with a conclusion and final formulas. But in the course of the thirteenth century the organization became more elaborate, with the exordium receiving its own commentary and the discussion of the theme being broken down into divisions and subdivisions.[83] The influence of dialectic on the format becomes, therefore, increasingly prominent.[84]

Not surprisingly, until the late thirteenth century all such manuals identified by author appear to be of French or other northern origin. These foreign manuals, nevertheless, enjoyed an enormous popularity in Italy and governed preaching style into the fifteenth century.[85] Significantly, the chronology of the creation of northern *artes praedicandi* roughly paralleled that of the *artes arengandi,* manuals, as we have seen, authored in Italy, giving instruction to a wide public on the preparation and delivery of secular speeches.

At this stage of research it is difficult to do more than suggest a causal link between the rich diversity of Italian styles of *dictamen* found in the period 1200 to 1250 on the one hand, and the French "grammatical" approach to *dictamen* and the new importance of preaching on the other. Besides the *stilus humilis,* dominant through the century, three new styles developed. The most imposing of the three, the style preferred by the papal *dictatores* for the most important correspondence from the pontificate of Honorius III (1217–27) and by the imperial chancery from about 1221, was the *stilus rhetoricus.*[86] Conceived unambiguously as "oratorical," the letter in *stilus rhetoricus* was marked by frequent interjections and interrogatives, creating the impression of deep feeling. The masters of the style displayed an attraction for rhymed prose, strongly reminiscent of the Vulgate, while echoes and actual quotations of biblical passages were ubiquitous.

One senses the beginnings of the style in the diction of Innocent III with its measured expressions of pathos, often captured and reinforced by biblical quotations.[87] The flowering of the style, however, came only after his death and reached its height in the 1240s. The papal chancery had produced nothing like this since Gregory VII, but that pope's correspondence lacked the formal structure, grammatical correctness, and standard phraseology necessary in diplomatic letters by 1200.

Just as the papal letters of Gregory had been connected with a period of great preaching, so it may be that a similar connection existed with the more formalized *stilus rhetoricus* of the thirteenth century. Having developed its form in France, the sermon in Italy caused *dictatores* to realize the aural potential of the letter to the fullest. Initially drawing force for their compositions from biblical associations, by midcentury *dictatores* with new literary interests, as we shall see, began to introduce references to and quotations from ancient authors to strengthen their arguments. Although the Latin remained medieval, the letter in *stilus rhetoricus* hence assumed something of a classical rather than a Christian ring.[88]

A second new style, and one closely associated with the *stilus rhetoricus,* was the *stilus obscurus.* A *dictator* like Piero della Vigna tended to use *stilus rhetoricus* in his official capacity in the imperial chancery and the *obscurus* in his private writings.[89] Whereas the *rhetoricus* made extensive use of the *colores rhetorici,* the message was generally communicated in a simple vocabulary without complicated syntax. In his own letters, however, Peter often limited oratorical effects while indulging in very complex sentence structure and rich figurative language replete with neologisms. While these traits suggest a relationship to French literary influence, the heavy reliance on echoes of the Psalms and the Song of Solomon both in vocabulary and imagery derived from associations with the sermon.

By contrast, a third style remains closely related to the *humilis* in its straightforward quality of sentence construction. At the same time it is similar to the *obscurus* in its reliance on a rich vocabulary and in the use of figurative language, especially its frequent borrowing of biblical images. Just as there was a tendency for the *obscurus* to serve as the private counterpart for writers of the *stilus rhetoricus,* so this style acted in the same capacity for authors in the *stilus humilis.*

Paradoxically, Boncompagno was the first to employ this last style, in the preface to the *Palma* of 1197, and it reappeared in some of his letters, his *Rota veneris, Liber amicitiae,* and the introduction to his law treatises such as *Oliva.*[90] Similarly, Bene of Florence prefaced his *Candelabrum* with a short introduction replete with biblical echoes.[91] Guido Faba indicated a similar preference for this new style in composing his prefaces.[92]

A bitter enemy of the school of Orleans and its literary treatment of the letter, Boncompagno seems here to have been an innovator moved to borrow some of the weapons of his enemies and to have been awake as well to the possibilities for eloquence created by the new preaching. Nonetheless, he was cautious. While displaying his rhetorical powers in key places in his works, he did not encourage his students to emulate him but rather urged them to cultivate a simple style by which they could earn their livelihood. In any case, by at least 1270 all these innovative styles had become rare. When they reappear, the writer is an exceptionally skilled one like Brunetto Latini, Dante, or, much later, the Florentine humanist Coluccio Salutati in his official letters as chancellor of the Florentine Republic.[93]

A third and final French influence affecting Italy's intellectual life dominated by legal studies and *ars dictaminis* came from the abundant production of Latin poetry in twelfth-century France, the treatises on *ars poetria* and grammar manuals composed into the thirteenth century. The brilliant development of Italian *volgare* poetry from the middle decades of the thirteenth century, culminating in the poetry of Dante, has long obscured a striking fact about Italian literary life in the Middle Ages. From the Carolingian revival until the beginnings of *volgare* poetry, southern Italy produced little Latin poetry, compared with France, and the area north of Rome less still.

Generally speaking, two subjects preoccupied Italian Latin poets: political-civil poetry dealing with battles, rules, and cities, and ascetic or political-religious poetry focusing on religious piety and church politics. There was almost no poetry dealing with love, ancient fables, biblical events, or scientific or philosophical subjects.[94] Yet paradoxically it was in northern and central Italy, even poorer in the production of Latin poetry than the south, that the new style of poetry was born after 1260.

Despite an influx of French poetic works in Latin from the late twelfth century, Italians did not derive much inspiration for writing Latin poetry on their own. French Goliardic poetry made almost no impression on Italian writers, while their mannerist colleagues did only a little better.[95] The high tide of their effect came in 1193 when the Bolognese-trained Henry of Settimella published his *Elegia,* a work manifesting the direct inspiration of the most popular French poets of the epoch: Matthew of Vendôme, Alan of Lille, and Walter of Châtillon. The communication between France and Bologna must have been relatively intense in these years, because Walter's *Alexandreis,* from which Henry borrowed generously for stylistic purposes, had been composed only about a decade before the *Elegia* itself.[96] In his turn Henry joined the French poets in influencing a second Italian writer, Stefanardo di Vimercate, whose *De controversia hominis et fortuna* reflects both the mannerist poetic style and French philosophical concerns.[97] With only Henry and Stefanardo (d. 1297), one can hardly speak of a literary movement.

The effects of French treatises on *ars poetria,* like those of Matthew of Vendôme, Geoffrey of Vinsauf, and John of Garland, are more difficult to assess. Bene of Florence was among the first to indicate acquaintance with the French theorists in his *Candelabrum,* a kind of summa on *dictamen.* Bene principally used the treatises of Matthew and Geoffrey, themselves written in poetry, as sources for illustrations for his discussion of *colores rhetorici* in the eighth book; but references and echoes abound in other parts of the discussion.[98] The fact that they are found in a work devoted to prose composition, however, indicates that the traditional Italian concern with prose writing remained intact.

The *Doctrinale novum* of Master Sion of Vercelli, dated between 1244 and 1268, made a fuller use of these French poetry manuals. In his broad work dealing with spelling, grammar, classical meter, rime, and *dictamen*, Master Sion, apparently inspired by Matthew, Geoffrey, and John of Garland, prescribed rules not only for a *dictamen prosaicum* but also a *dictamen ritmicum*.[99] He would seem to be returning to a conception of rhetoric that had not been seen in Italy since Alberico of Monte Cassino, who developed the manual of *ars dictaminis* as only one aspect of a larger vision of the art of composition.

The *Doctrinale novum,* in its sections dealing with grammar, furthermore, clearly depends at points on Alexander of Villedieu's *Doctrinale,* a work published about 1200.[100] This dependence is important in that it reflects the penetration of French methods of teaching grammar at the elementary level by midcentury. Already Bene of Florence in his *Summa gramatice,* written at the turn of the thirteenth century, provides evidence of the influence recent French grammarians like Peter Helias were having on the advanced teaching of the subject. Bono of Lucca, Bene's student, followed his master's lead in composing his own summa, decades later.[101]

Even if French influence did not have the effect of reversing the centuries-old tradition of indifference to poetic creation, the popularity of French manuals of grammar and poetry indicates a renewed interest in these areas. As for prose writing, while their *dictamen* style remained unaltered, aulic *dictatores* like Peter of Pressa and Henry of Isernia in the south were using citations from pagan writers to convey their own ideas and sentiments.[102] Around 1260 in Padua another *dictator,* Rolandinus of Padua, demonstrated a fairly wide knowledge of ancient texts in his *Chronica in factis et circa facta Marchie trivixane,* a history of the career of Ezzelino da Romano.[103]

Although pagan literature became incorporated comfortably into works composed in traditional *dictamen,* nonetheless, this period witnesses expressions of heightened respect for these writings. Latini's efforts to interpret Cicero's rhetorical teachings in *volgare* to his own generation in the 1260s signify his need to reinforce the rules of *ars dictaminis* with the sanction of ancient authority.[104] After 150 years of largely turning away from its ancient past, guided by the French, Italians in central and northern Italy were entering upon a period of its rediscovery.

If we leave aside sociological explanations like a growing hierarchical tendency within thirteenth-century society, it seems clear that the rising tide of grammatical interest in Italy occurred in close connection with the growing institutionalization of Italian education. While the organization of communal *studia* at the upper level of education did not eliminate the private teacher, it gave a more rational structure to the whole process of education, presumably leading to a greater degree of specialization.[105] The consequence would have been an intensification of training at each level and a gradual raising of the intellectual level of courses.

The change in the program of rhetoric in Bologna is clear. There exists little proof, despite their repeated claims to be relying on Cicero's *De inventione* in their manuals, that the twelfth-century *dictatores* really paid much attention to that work. By the end of the century, however, Boncompagno seems to have been lecturing on Cicero, and in the thirteenth century this work formed a part of instruction in rhetoric at Bologna.[106] At least by the 1260s a course on the *Ad Herennium* was introduced.[107]

The increased demands made on the student by these works meant that they had to come to the study of rhetoric with better training in grammar. French treatises of *ars grammatica* and *ars poetria* may have helped to meet the new teaching needs in some classrooms, but the general effect of the pressure was probably to intensify study of ancient Latin writers.

Nonetheless, as far as Latin style is concerned, Latini's detailed study of Cicero's *De inventione* merely served to endorse the basic assumptions inherent in *ars dictaminis* style, and the teaching of his work in conjunction with *dictamen* contributed to forestalling the advent of classicizing oratory for at least a century. In introducing frequent references to ancient authors, Peter of Pressa, Henry of Isernia, and Rolandino were simply following centuries-old northern practices. Lovato was the first to strike out on a new path, breaking with medieval Latin style.

*   *   *

As noted at the outset of this analysis, by the last quarter of the thirteenth century, a new literary movement was developing in northern Italian cities such as Padua, Verona, and Vicenza. Initially expressing themselves in poetry and subsequently in prose as well, an elite developed that in time became known as the humanists. Although Mussato's play inspired by Seneca, the *Ecerinis*, was presented with great success in the public square of Padua in 1315, only a handful of people in the audience could probably have followed the difficult language.[108] As far as prose is concerned, one of Mussato's histories, a work written in uncharacteristically simple style, explicitly represents a concession by the author to the Society of Notaries of Padua, the educated laymen of the city. After Mussato had written so many works of history for learned men, they petitioned him to compose something about their city that notaries and humble clerics could understand.[109]

In their scholarly and poetic interests members of this new literary movement were similar first to the Carolingian writers and then to the literary scholars of France, England, and southern Germany in the eleventh and twelfth centuries, who carried on, while greatly enriching, the Carolingian grammatical tradition. Nevertheless, in contrast to a few northern poets in these previous centuries who at times produced classicizing poetry, these Italian writers were committed to writing consistently in ancient style. As poets none of them before Petrarch attained a level of poetic expression equal to the best classicizing work of Hildebert of Lavardin, but what makes their poetry significant is that they were working not as isolated individuals but as members of a growing movement motivated by a common aesthetic ideal. The Italians' devotion to classicizing prose from the early fourteenth century was unmatched in any of the twelfth-century French writers.

Two major questions arise at this point: Why did the classicizing grammatical revival begin when it did? and: Why was this group of scholars led to pursue a consistently classicizing expression first in poetry and then in prose not found in the northern writers in the twelfth century? We already have part of the answer in the general grammatical revival just discussed as occurring in part as a result of French influence and institutional changes in education. The vitality of *volgare* poetry throughout the peninsula, however, must also be counted as a cause. While Latin poetry in Italy languished, as we have seen, poetry in the vernacular was evolving from the opening decades of the thirteenth century, and it seems probable that by the 1260s this development was encouraging a poet to begin writing Latin poetry in an effort to rival accomplishments in the mother tongue.

More puzzling, however, is the problem of why this new poetry was so consistently classicizing. Part of the answer lies in the very fact that Italians had such a weak medieval Latin poetic tradition of their own. Once they began to write Latin poetry, they could receive inspiration directly from the ancient poets they read. The French, Germans, and English were, by contrast, hindered by their own rich medieval background in writing such poetry.

A broader level of explanation for its classicizing form can be found in the environment peculiar to Italy in which the movement occurred. Products of an urban culture marked by a high degree of secularism and a city-state experience, Italians of the thirteenth century were in a better position to appreciate classical culture than any other European group. Italy was also unparalleled in the numbers of physical reminders of the society's Roman roots. The popular enthusiasm created in the 1280s, when Lovato identified a newly discovered body as the remains of the Trojan founder of Padua, Antenor, illustrates the depth of admiration felt by the multitude for an ancient society that was part of their cultural mythology.[110] The passionate reception of Mussato's *Ecerinis* by a populace that could grasp almost nothing of the text furnishes another example of the popular support provided for humanistic endeavors. Once assimilation of the poetic style was attained, this welter of associations with the ancient past obviously served to push scholars forward to seek understanding of the ancient culture as a whole.

Furthermore, of all Europeans the Italians were most like the ancient Romans in the rhetorical orientation of their thought processes. The differing fate of dialectic in eleventh-century France and Italy provides dramatic evidence of the hold that Ciceronian rhetoric as a form of logic held on the Italian mind. The leading intellectual discipline in the society—law—perfectly reflected this cast of mind comfortable with arguments of verisimilitude and proofs by inference, the usual proofs available in the world of practical affairs. Italians, therefore, instinctively appreciated the ancient Roman mentality and, once absorbed in the writings of the Romans, could go further than any other people in grasping the particular formation of their phrases and thoughts.

While explanations are still conjectural, the progress of humanism is clear. Beginning in poetry, the learned classicism invaded one field of secondary rhetoric after another. The first advance beyond poetry occurred in the field of history early in the fourteenth century.[111] By the late 1320s, with Geri d'Arezzo, the first truly personal letters begin to appear, and with Petrarch's letters emerges the conscious principle, inspired by the ancients, that the private letter was a conversation.[112] The spread of humanism in these decades did not mean, however, that the domain of *ars dictaminis* had suffered serious inroads. Petrarch and Boccaccio, together with humanists in the next generation, continued to write official letters and make speeches in *ars dictaminis* style, or, in the case of Petrarch, in the medieval style of *ars arengandi* and *ars praedicandi*. Classicizing Latin was employed for personal writings while *ars dictandi* served official purposes. Petrarch and Boccaccio were private scholars and did not write very much in the latter area, but in the case of others who worked as professional *dictatores*, like Giovanni del Virgilio in the early part of the century and Coluccio Salutati in the last half, there was a significant difference between their professional writings and their pri-

vate ones. Giovanni del Virgilio in poetry endeavored to imitate the ancients, whereas his existing manual of *ars dictaminis* suggests that he
continued to write and teach medieval prose style.[113] As chancellor of
Florence, Salutati exhibited marvelous talent in applying *stilus rhetoricus*
to the official correspondence of the Florentine Republic, while in his
private life he embraced a classicizing style imitative of Seneca. His surviving orations, like those of Petrarch, follow medieval models.[114] Consequently, it can be said that throughout the fourteenth century, primary
rhetoric remained largely governed by traditional styles, while classicizing tendencies moved out from poetry to influence other fields of secondary rhetoric. This truncated grammatical orientation characterized the
first century of humanism.

The oration, the prime area for the rhetorician, did not undergo
humanist reforms until the last few years of the fourteenth century, and
Vergerio the Elder was the first to use classical form in a speech.[115] From
this point on, humanism became enriched by an oratorical component.[116]
At the same time, public letters, fettered by rigid rules, continued to be
written according to the prescriptions of *ars dictaminis* throughout the
fifteenth century, and humanists realistically followed the custom in this
highly formalized area of communication.

Admittedly, as was said at the outset of this analysis, the distinction
between grammar and rhetoric in reality was more muddled than the
models of the two disciplines would suggest. Certainly the early humanists, emulating Cicero, frequently referred to themselves as orators or
rhetoricians. Notwithstanding, humanism in Italy undeniably began in
poetry, the bastion of the grammarians, and for more than a hundred
years neglected to annex the area of primary rhetoric, leaving it the preserve of the *ars dictaminis*. Fourteenth-century humanists like Giovanni
del Virgilio, Petrarch, and Salutati, led double lives, using classicizing
style or *ars dictaminis* and *ars praedicandi*, depending on the public or
private character of the apparent audience.

The progressively expanding endeavor of early humanists to shape
their own writings in accord with ancient precedents in time wrought a
profound intellectual change. The grammarian's tireless study of ancient
vocabulary and syntax as found in the classical authors gradually produced "a reorganization of consciousness," habits of expressing ideas
with precision and nuances that both unlocked the mentality of the classical authors and allowed the humanists themselves to approach their
own world with that perspective.[117] Although the underlying structure of
their prose remained as in the Middle Ages essentially paratactic[118]—
they were self-conscious when writing periodic style—nonetheless, the
growing mastery of ancient syntactical forms like the subjunctive per-

mitted them to grasp concepts and differentiate emotions as *dictatores* of previous centuries had never done.

Furthermore, that mastery of style provided a key to understanding content can hardly be doubted in a case like that of the evolution of republican thought. The new focus of attention on ancient oratory in the 1390s, first by Vergerio, served to inspire a fresh appreciation of the republican themes found in the orations of Cicero and a number of Greek counterparts. In his *Laudatio urbis florentinae* published in 1402–3, Leonardo Bruni articulated for the first time in fifteen hundred years a systematic republican interpretation of history and politics.[119] Already in the 1370s Salutati as Florentine chancellor had expressed, in scattered official letters written in splendid *ars dictaminis* style, elements of the republican vision; but his presentation was fragmentary and accorded ill with the underlying concept of his own thought on politics.[120] Bruni's consistent republicanism after 1402–3 owes much, of course, to his life experience,[121] yet his obviously intensive study of the oratorical genre permitted him to integrate his experiences with those of ancient republicans and to speak forth unambiguously as a republican.

Paradoxically, humanism was born in an area that had been among all those counted as part of western culture the least concerned for its ancient literary inheritance. Living in the very shadow of the tremendous monuments of the pagan world, Italians of the twelfth and early thirteenth centuries were too busy developing their own political organization and their economic order to pay much heed to the potential guidance ancient culture could provide, except in the two practical subjects of law and medicine. Yet in actual fact no western culture was closer in mentality, economic, political, and social life to the ancient Romans. The significance of French influence on Italian intellectual life in the first half of the thirteenth century appears to have been enormous, but once the passion to reclaim their ancient heritage was kindled, the Italians were led independently to its assimilation.

NOTES

1. Guido Billanovich, "Il preumanesimo padovano," in *Storia della cultura veneta. II: Il Trecento* (Vicenza, 1976), 33. Billanovich's work provides the most complete account of bibliography on Lovato. See as well R. Weiss, "Lovato Lovati (1241–1309)," *Italian Studies* 6 (1951): 3–28.
2. He generally avoids the "mannerism" characteristic of much medieval poetry. J. Martin, in her pioneering article "Classicism and Style in Latin Literature," in *Renaissance and Renewal in the Twelfth Century*, ed. R. L. Benson, G. Constable, and C. D. Lanham (Cambridge, MA, 1982), 550, defines medieval mannerism as follows: "Medieval mannerism, which exaggerates qualities found already in the stylistic theory and practice of

classical Latin, is manifested particularly in elaboration and exaggeration of the traditional *ornatus* (embellishment) recommended by ancient theory. Thus hyperbaton, the separation of words belonging together grammatically, is a normal feature of literary Latin; but its exaggerated use becomes manneristic." Weiss, "Lovato Lovati," 20, however, in discussing a set of poems exchanged between Lovato and a group of his friends, characterizes Lovato's contribution as belonging "linguisticamente alla letteratura latina del primo umanesimo, ma spiritualmente a quella in volgare." He then adds, "Non c'è dubbio che un tale giudizio avrebbe colmato d'orrore il buon Lovato."

3. Billanovich, "Il preumanesimo," 2:38–40.
4. On Riccobaldo of Ferrara see A. Campana, "Riccobaldo da Ferrara," in *Enciclopedia dantesca* (Rome, 1973), 3:908–10; A. T. Hankey, "Riccobaldo of Ferrara, Boccaccio and Domenico di Bandino," *Journal of the Warburg and Courtauld Institutes* 31 (1958): 208–26; Giuseppe Billanovich, *La tradizione del testo di Livio e le origini dell'Umanesimo*, vol. 1, *Tradizione e fortuna di Livio tra medioevo e umanesimo*, pt. 1 (Padua, 1981), 18–33. Riccobaldo's *Pomerium Ravennatis ecclesie*, composed in 1297, while clearly reflecting the author's use of Livy, does not yet manifest stylistic reform. For partial editions of this work, see A. T. Hankey's recent edition of Riccobaldo's *Compendium romanae historiae: Ricobaldi Ferrariensis Compendium romanae historiae*, 2. vols. (Rome, 1984), ix–x. Even in the later works, however, when Riccobaldo is not able to follow Livy, he proves unable to maintain the level of diction.
5. Those acquainted with P. O. Kristeller's many works on *dictamen* and humanism cannot fail to recognize the formative influence they have had on this analysis. His *Eight Philosophers of the Italian Renaissance* (Stanford, 1964), 160–62, identifies a strong grammatical component in Italian humanism and suggests the medieval French grammatical tradition as one of the movement's sources. He particularly stresses the role of the French practice of textual commentary. I will not, however, discuss this particular topic here, in that my concern is to explore the origins of a stylistic ideal, which itself would explain why, when the Italians adopted French techniques of textual analysis, the consequences were very different. Admittedly, as Italian scholars advanced in their philological endeavors, their ability to realize their stylistic models increased.
6. S. F. Bonner, *Education in Ancient Rome: From the Elder Cato to the Younger Pliny* (Berkeley, 1977), 189ff., especially 250. See also H. I. Marrou, *A History of Education in Antiquity*, trans. G. Lamb (New York, 1956), 223–42, 267–81. Bonner, 218–19, suggests that ancient grammarians may have used prose works to provide students with initial exercises in composition, but that they did not indulge in the detailed analysis of these works as they did for poetry. G. A. Kennedy, *The Art of Persuasion in Greece* (Princeton, 1963), 269, acknowledges some overlap but considers the study of poets to have belonged principally to the school of grammar and that of the prose writers to the school of rhetoric.

7. G. A. Kennedy, *Classical Rhetoric and Its Christian and Secular Tradition from Ancient to Modern Times* (Chapel Hill, 1980), 4–5, establishes the distinction between primary and secondary rhetoric.

8. Alcuin of York, *Opusculum primum: Grammatica*, in *Patrologia latina*, ed. J. P. Migne (Paris, 1863), 101, cols. 857d–58a.

9. J. Longère, *La prédication médiévale* (Paris, 1983), 35–54, discusses Carolingian reliance on homilies constructed by piecing together texts from the fathers. There is, however, evidence of occasional originality. Cf. H. Barré, *Les homéliaires carolingiens de l'école d'Auxerre* (Vatican City, 1962).

10. *Rhetores latini minores*, ed. K. Halm (Leipzig, 1863), 525–50.

11. Collections of Carolingian correspondence are edited in *Monumenta Germaniae historica* (hereafter MGH), *Epistolae*. See for example vol. 6, pt. 1 (Berlin, 1902), 127–206. For Lupus Servatus's correspondence, see the edition of L. Levillain, 2 vols. (Paris, 1927–35).

12. On the role of the cathedral and monastic schools in France from the ninth to twelfth centuries, see J. Chatillon, "Les écoles de Chartres et de Saint-Victor," *La scuola nell'Occidente latino del alto medioevo* 2 (1972): 795–839; G. Paré, A. Brunet, and P. Tremblay, *La renaissance au XIIe siècle: Les écoles et l'enseignement* (Paris and Ottawa, 1933); L. Maître, *Les écoles épiscopales et monastiques en Occident avant les universités (768–1180)* (Paris, 2d ed., 1924); E. Lesne, *Les livres, "scriptoria" et bibliothèques du commencement du VIIIe à la fin du XIe siècle: Historie de la propriété ecclésiastique en France*, 6 vols. (fasc. 19, 30, 34, 44, 46, 50, 53) (Lille, 1910–43), see vol. 4; R. R. Bezzola, *La société féodale et la transformation de la littérature de cour: Les origines et la formation de la littérature courtoise en Occident (500–1200)* (Paris, 1960), pt. 2.1, 19–45; P. Riché, *Les écoles et l'enseignement dans l'Occident chrétien de la fin du Ve siècle au milieu du XIe siècle* (Paris, 1979), 141–47 and 179–84.

13. R. W. Southern, *The Making of the Middle Ages* (New Haven, 1953), 175ff. As late as Anselm, however, argumentation was so closely dependent on grammar that M. Colish, "Eleventh-Century Grammar in the Thought of St. Anselm," in *Arts libéraux et philosophie au Moyen Âge* (Montreal and Paris, 1969), 789, describes logic in this century as "Aristotelianized grammar."

14. R. McKeon, "Rhetoric in the Middle Ages," *Speculum* 17 (1942): 15ff. Carolingian writers had occasionally treated rhetoric as a part of logic, but the new concern with logic from the late tenth century brought the nature of the relationship to the fore. McKeon (12 and 14–15) also notes the tendency of rhetoric to be tied to theology as "the art of stating truths certified by theology" (15).

15. *Metalogicon*, ed. C. I. Webb (Oxford, 1929), 1.24, 53–57, for Bernard. For John's position on rhetoric as part of logic, see M. B. Ryan, "John of Salisbury on the Arts of Language in the Trivium" (Ph.D. diss., Catholic University of America, Washington, DC, 1958), 137ff.

16. For the continuity of eleventh-century letter writing with Carolingian tradition, see the bibliography and analyses in C. Erdmann, *Studien zur*

Briefliteratur Deutschlands im elften Jahrhunderts, MGH, Schriften des Reichsinstituts für ältere deutsche Geschichtskunde 1 (Leipzig, 1938). Peter the Venerable's letters are found in *The Letters of Peter the Venerable,* ed. G. Constable, 2 vols. (Cambridge, MA, 1967); those of John in *Letters,* ed., W. J. Millor and H. E. Butler, rev. C. N. L. Brooke, 2 vols. (London and New York, 1955–79); and Peter of Blois's correspondence is located in *Patrologia latina* 207, cols. 1–560. By the second half of the twelfth century *ars dictaminis* was becoming important in France as well as in Italy, but the French adapted it to fit their own more grammatical orientation: see my "Boncompagno on Grammar and Rhetoric," *Journal of Medieval and Renaissance Studies* 16 (1986): 1–31, and below.

17. Abundant evidence exists to show that medieval scholars knew of a number of disparities between their Latin and that of the ancients: see, for example, Martin, "Classicism and Style," 557–65. To an extent, at least, medieval writers consciously followed an independent path: they did not feel limited by ancient stylistic models. On Hildebert and Valerius see ibid., 551–54 and 556–57. Valerius's "mannerist" preface, designed to highlight the Vergilian poems to follow, tends to give them the character of set pieces. Walter of Châtillon also captured a good deal of the flavor of ancient epic in his *Alexandreis,* but the corpus of his works reflects his enthusiasm for rime and other devices dear to medieval poetry: F. J. E. Raby, *A History of Secular Latin Poetry in the Middle Ages* (Oxford, 2d ed., 1957), 2:190–204. Although, as has been suggested, Lovato's style was uneven, nonetheless his production of verse reflects a consistent effort to reform.

18. R. R. Bezzola, *La tradition impériale de la fin de l'antiquité au XIᵉ siècle: Les origines et la formation de la littérature courtoise en Occident (500–1200)* (Paris, 1958), pt. 1.1, 30–33 and 138.

19. On Dungal, see M. Ferrari, " 'In Papia conveniant ad Dungalum' (Tav. I–III)," *Italia medioevale e umanistica* 15 (1972): 1–52. On his Spanish religious opponent, see idem, "Note su Claudio di Torino 'Episcopus ab ecclesia damnatus,' " *Italia medioevale e umanistica* 16 (1973): 291–308. On Hilderic as a central figure in the compilation of key manuscripts: G. Billanovich, "Terenzio, Ildemaro, Petrarca (Tav. I–VII)," *Italia medioevale e umanistica* 17 (1974): 1–60; C. Villa, " 'Denique Terenti dultia legimus acta . . . ': Una 'lectura Terenti' a S. Faustino di Brescia nel secolo IX," *Italia medioevale e umanistica* 22 (1979): 1–44; idem, "A Brescia e a Milano," in C. Villa and G. C. Alessio, "Tra commedia e Comedía," *Italia medioevale e umanistica* 24 (1981): 1–17; and subsequent issues of this learned journal.

20. R. Avesani, "La cultura veronese dal secolo ix al secolo xii," in *Storia della cultura veneta* (Vicenza, 1976), 1:251–57, summarizes his career and the culture of Verona under four Frankish bishops.

21. Ratherius (d. 974), bishop of Verona, in his *Synodica,* 13, warns that no cleric shall be promoted unless he shall have studied "either in our city, or in some monastery, or with some wise man *(apud quemlibet sapientem)*": *Patrologia latina* 136, col. 564. His fellow bishop, Atto of Vercelli (d. 960), in his *Capitulare* 41 *(Patrologia latina* 134, col. 40) orders clerics in the

rural districts to take only what parents offer in payment for teaching their children.

22. L. Schiaparelli, *Il codice 490 della Biblioteca capitolare di Lucca e la scuola scrittoria lucchese (sec. viii–ix)* (Rome, 1924), 60.

23. A. Campana, "Il carteggio di Vitale e Pacifico di Verona," *Atti del congresso internazionale di diritto romano e di storia del diritto, Verona 27–28–29-ix-1948*, 4 vols. (Milan, 1951–53), 1:272–73. As contrasted with northern Europe and southern Italy, monasteries in this area made only a minor contribution to scholarship in the ninth century, with the possible exception of Bobbio. See, however, P. Engelbert, "Zur Frühgeschichte des Bobbieser Skriptoriums," *Revue bénédictine* 78 (1968): 220–60.

24. D. A. Bullough, "Le scuole cattedrali e la cultura dell'Italia settentrionale prima dei comuni," *Vescovi e diocesi in Italia nel medioevo (sec. IX–XIII)* (Padua, 1964), 133–34. Listings of references to cathedral schools from the ninth to the twelfth century are found in A. Dresdner, *Kultur und Sittengeschichte der italienischen Geistlichkeit im 10. und 11. Jahrhundert* (Breslau, 1890), 234–56; and G. Manacorda, *Storia della scuola in Italia*, 1 vol. in 2 pts. (Milan, 1913), 1:2:283–337. This information, however, is to be used with great caution.

25. Bullough, "Le scuole," 132–33. S. F. Wemple, *Atto of Vercelli: Church, State and Christian Society in Tenth Century Italy* (Rome, 1979), 35, questions Atto's knowledge of the classics, however, because he calls Socrates, Plato, Aristotle, and Zeno, along with Vergil, Ovid, and others "poets."

26. *Gunzo: Epistola ad Augienses und Anselm von Besate: Rhetorimachia*, ed. K. Manitius, MGH, Quellen zur Geistesgeschichte des Mittelalters, 2 (Weimar, 1958), 19–57.

27. G. Theuerkauf, "Burchard von Worms und die Rechtskunde seiner Zeit," *Frühmittelalterliche Studien* 2 (1968): 145.

28. For some statistics on lay and clerical literacy in the eighth century in Italy, see A. Petrucci, "Libro, scritture e scuole," *La scuola nell'Occidente latino dell'alto medioevo* 19 (1972): 323–25. See also G. C. Fissore, "Cultura grafica e scuola in Asti nei secoli ix e x," *Bullettino dell'Istituto italiano per il medioevo* 85 (1974–75): 17–51. Recently, B. Stock, *The Implications of Literacy* (Princeton, 1983), 41, has stressed the importance of the Italian notariate in these centuries, but within the context of his general discussion Italian precedence in literacy plays no particular role. See the brief observation on literacy and semiliteracy in J. Le Goff, "Alle origini del lavoro intellettuale in Italia: I problemi del rapporto fra la letteratura, l'università e le professioni," *Letteratura italiana*, vol. 1, *Il letterato e le istituzioni* (Turin, 1982), 651–52.

29. There is no firm evidence for the existence of schools of *ars notaria* before the twelfth century. The assumption is that notaries received training through apprenticeship as did notaries in rural areas even in the fourteenth century. See my *Hercules at the Crossroads: The Life, Works, and Thought of Coluccio Salutati* (Durham, NC, 1983), 30–31.

30. On the school of Pavia the work of G. Mengozzi, *Ricerche sull'attività della*

On the school of Pavia the work of G. Mengozzi, *Ricerche sull'attività della scuola da Pavia nell'alto medioevo* (Pavia, 1924), is still valuable, but see now C. Radding, *A World Made by Men: Cognition and Society 400–1200* (Chapel Hill, 1985), 173–86. The approach of the legal men to the Roman law in this period was piecemeal: U. Gualazzini, "La scuola pavese, con particulare riguardo all'insegnamento del diritto," *Atti del 4° congresso internazionale di studi sull'alto medio evo* (Spoleto, 1969), 35–73, at 71–72. Some *notarii sacri palatii* from 874 began to use the title *judex sacri palatii* as well, which may mean a change in their status but as against C. Manaresi, *I placiti del regum italicum* (Rome, 1955), xvii, not necessarily the existence of a "scuola per i giudici." We await the study of Prof. Radding, *The Origin of Medieval Jurisprudence*, which will deal with the Pavese legal tradition from the ninth to the twelfth century.

31. J. Fried, *Der Entstehung des Juristenstandes im 12. Jahrhundert. Zur sozialen Stellung und politischen Bedeutung gelehrter Juristen in Bologna und Modena* (Cologne and Vienna, 1974), 30.

32. G. Costamagna, "Parte secondo: L'alto medioevo," in M. Amelotti and G. Costamagna, *Alle origini del notariato italiano* (Rome, 1975), 212–20; P. S. Leicht, "Documenti toscani del secoli XI–XII," *Bullettino senese di storia patria* 16 (1909): 174–90, at 180.

33. Urso, *Regesta della chiesa di Pisa*, ed. N. Caturegli (Rome, 1938), 21–22.

34. *Le carte degli archivi parmensi dei sec. X–XII*, ed. G. Drei, 3 vols. (Parma, 1924–50), 1:188; and *Codice diplomatico padovano dal secolo sesto a tutto l'undecimo*, ed. A. Gloria (Padua, 1877), 64.

35. Costamagna, "Parte secondo," 200.

36. Ibid., 201.

37. On the growth of chanceries, see my "Medieval *Ars Dictaminis* and the Beginnings of Humanism: A New Construction of the Problem," *Renaissance Quarterly* 35 (1982): 4–5, nn. 6 and 7.

38. J. W. Baldwin, "Masters at Paris from 1179 to 1215: A Social Perspective," in *Renaissance and Renewal*, 151–58, provides statistics proving the link between promotion in the church and in government service and the possession of advanced education during the twelfth and thirteenth centuries.

39. The generalizations in these two sentences of the text are based in part on an examination of published documents for the tenth to the twelfth century from eight northern and central Italian areas and in part on the studies listed subsequently. For the collections, besides those listed in notes 33 and 34 above for Pisa, Parma, and Padua, there are the following: *Registro della chiesa cattedrale di Modena*, ed. E. P. Vicini, Regesta chartarum Italiae 16 (Rome, 1931) and 21 (Rome, 1936); *Codex diplomaticus langobardiae* (Turin, 1873); *Registro mantovano*, ed. P. Torelli (Rome, 1914); *Documenti per la storia della città di Arezzo nel medio evo*, vol. 1 (650–1180), ed. U. Pasqui (Florence, 1899); *Le carte degli archivi reggiani fino al 1050*, ed. P. Torelli (Reggio, nell'Emilia, 1921). For Bologna, see the key article by G. Cencetti, "Note di diplomatica vescovile bolognese dei secoli XI–XIII," *Scritti di paleografia e diplomatica in onore di Vincenzo Federigi* (Florence,

1944), 159–223. On Ravenna, see G. Buzzi, *La curia arcivescovile e la curia cittadina di Ravenna del 850–1118* (Rome, 1915). For Milan in the twelfth century, see *Antiqui diplomi degli arcivescovi di Milano e cenni di diplomatica episcopale*, ed. G. C. Bascapè (Florence, 1937).

40. On Cicero's "dialectic," see A. Cantin, *Les sciences séculières et la foi: Les deux visages de la science au jugement de S. Pierre Damien (1007–1072)* (Spoleto, 1975), 383–84.

41. In his *Elementarium*, Papias, under "syllogismis" ([Milan, 1476], fol. 219), writes that "not only rhetors use [syllogisms], but especially dialecticians," thus implying that his audience would first think of their usefulness for rhetoricians. Cf. Cantin, *Les sciences séculières*, 397, n. 69. For the dating of this work, see V. de Angelis, *Papiae elementarium: Littera A* (Milan, 1977). The author criticizes (iv–v), however, the accepted Italian origin of Papias, which is based on that author's concentration on Italian geography and special focus on Lombardy. In view of the sources for the lexicon, de Angelis believes that such concentration on Italy says nothing of Papias himself. The extensive treatment of Lombardy and his phrase "terra amata" are drawn from Paul the Deacon and Isidore of Seville, respectively. In my view, even if the phrases on Lombardy are borrowed, the link of Papias with the area determined that he chose to make this focus.

42. On Drogo, see Manitius's preface to edition of *Rhetorimachia* (cited above, n. 26), p. 64. For date of work, see C. Violante, "Anselmo da Besate," *Dizionario biografico degli italiani* (Rome, 1974), 18:408. In his work Anselm states clearly that he seeks *verisimilitudinem* and not *veritatem* (103) and thus will use *hypotheses* rather than *theses* (105), because he is writing a judicial oration (177).

43. On Lanfranc, see M. T. Gibson, *Lanfranc of Bec* (Oxford, 1978), especially 4–15; for his correspondence, *The Letters of Lanfranc Archbishop of Canterbury*, ed. H. Clover and M. Gibson (Oxford, 1979). Radding, *A World Made by Men*, 199, implies that we should not overestimate the accomplishments of the earliest eleventh-century logicians like Berengar.

44. On Anselm of Lucca's French studies, see C. Violante, "Anselmo da Baggio," *Dizionario biografico degli italiani* (Rome, 1974), 18:399. On those of Anselm of Lucca, see F. S. Schmitt, "Anselmo d'Aosta," ibid., 18:387.

45. *Patrologia latina* 145, col. 198; and *Patrologia latina* 144, col. 225. Papias (*Elementarium*, fol. 201v) emphasizes the link between rhetoric and the law when under "rhetorica" he writes: "Rhetorica est ratio dicendi et iurisperitorum. . . ."

46. *Patrologia latina* 144, col. 227.

47. *Tetralogus, Die Werke Wipos*, ed. H. Bresslau (Hanover, 3d ed., 1915), 81.

48. Despite Peter's attack on secular learning in later life, his writings contain frequent references to ancient literature: F. Dressler, *Petrus Damiani: Leben und Werk* (Rome, 1954), 187. On his knowledge of law: Cantin, *Les sciences séculières*, 505–10. Much of what he knew about logic came from Cicero, but he probably knew one work from the Aristotelian-Boethian corpus, the latter's commentary on Aristotle's *De interpretatione*: ibid.,

378–79. Anselm refers to Sichelmo as "our Cicero" and as "a Justinian above all others in his imperial edicts and legal decisions": *Rhetorimachia*, 99.

49. In 1046 he argued with the assembled legal men of the city over the issue of the forbidden degrees of consanguinity for marriage: *Patrologia latina* 145, cols. 191–204. For the date of letter, G. Lucchesi, *Per una vita di san Pier Damiani: Componenti cronologiche e topografiche*, 2 vols. in 1 (Cesena, 1972), 2:157. From the text it seems clear that these men were both practicing lawyers and teachers. He advises them (200): "You who are responsible for imposing discipline in the classroom amidst the crowds of students (*clientium*) should not fear to submit to the discipline of the church; and to you, who like wise men plead cases in the courts, it should suffice to hear the words of one teaching in Christ's house of prayer." Peter's contemporary biographer and friend used the term *clientes* in the sense of students when he wrote of Peter himself (*Patrologia latina* 144, col. 117): "mox alios erudire, clientium turba ad doctrinae ipsius famam undique confluente, studiossime coepit."

50. G. Diurni, *L'Expositio ad librum papiensem e la scienza giuridica preirneriana* (Rome, 1976), 124–64; and Radding, *A World Made by Men*, 173–86.

51. Diurni, *L'Expositio*, 195. The author of the *Expositio* attributes *Discipuli* to him.

52. Prof. Radding has informed me that at least as late as 1077 *judices sacri palatii* were also signing as *notarii sacri palatii*.

53. G. Arnaldi, "Alle origini dello Studio di Bologna," in *Le sedi della cultura nell'Emilia Romagna: L'età comunale* (Milan, 1984), 105–7. The close connection between the *ars notaria* and Roman law studies in the late eleventh and early twelfth centuries led G. Cencetti, "Studium fuit Bononie," *Studi medievali* 3d ser. 7 (1966): 781–833, to see the law school of Bologna as an outgrowth of a notarial school. See as well his earlier "Sulle origini dello studio di Bologna," *Rivista storica italiana* ser. 6.5 (1940):250.

54. See Arnaldi, "Alle origini," 108.

55. The sermons of Peter have recently been reedited: *Sancti Petri Damiani Sermones*, ed. I. Lucchesi (Turnhout, 1983). The letters of Gregory are published by E. Caspar, *Das Register Gregors VII*, MGH, *Epistolae Selectae* 2.1–2 (Berlin, 1920–23). H. Hoffman, "Zum Register und den Briefen Papst Gregors VII," *Deutsches Archiv* 32 (1976): 86–130, discusses problems connected with the origins of the present collection of letters. Gregory VII had allegedly been taught by one of the great scholars of his day, Laurence of Amalfi: W. Holtzmann, "Laurentius von Amalfi, ein Lehrer Hildebrands," *Studi gregoriani* 1 (1947): 207–36; republished in *Beiträge zur Reichs- und Papstgeschichte des hohen Mittelalters* (Bonn, 1957): 9–33. On his style see V. Ussani, "Gregorio VII scrittore nella sua corrispondenza e nei suoi dettati," *Studi gregoriani* 2 (1947): 341–59. Official letters were doubtless read aloud as a rule, but the extent to which other correspondence was delivered orally cannot be determined. On oral reading of writ-

ings, see R. Crosby, "Oral Delivery in the Middle Ages," *Speculum* 2 (1936): 88–110; and G. Constable, *Letters and Letter-Collections* (Turnhout, 1976), 53–54. Also see *Letters of Peter the Venerable*, 2:27, n. 115.

56. The letter is published as *Petri Crassi defensio Heinrici IV regis*, ed. L. de Heinemann, MGH, *Libelli de lite* 1 (Hanover, 1891), 433–53. I. S. Robinson, *Authority and Resistance in the Investiture Contest: The Polemical Literature of the Late Eleventh Century* (Manchester, 1978), 75–83, questions the attribution of the work to Peter Crassus. For present purposes, however, the important point is that the author was Italian.

57. On Bergamo, see E. Cattaneo, "Le riforme del secolo XI e XII," *Archivio storico lombardo* 87 (1960): 26–27. Parma at least for four years (1102–1106) had two bishops: R. Schumann, *Authority and the Commune, Parma 833–1133* (*Impero e comune, Parma 833–1133*) (Parma, 1973), 330–31. G. Fasoli, "Ancora un'ipotesi sull'inizio dell'insegnamento di Pepone e Irnerio," in *Scritti di storia medievale* (Bologna, 1974), 567–81, introduces the divisive character of the investiture reform program to explain how the teaching of law evolved outside the cathedral of Bologna, first with Pepo and then with Irnerius. In Mantua between 1086 and 1140 the canons seem not to have existed as a collective entity: A. Montecchio, "Cenni storici sulla canonica cattedrale di Mantova nei secoli XI e XII," in *La vita comune del clero nei secoli XI e XII*, 2 vols. (Milan, 1962), 2:179.

58. *Landulphi Senioris Mediolanensis historiae libri quatuor*, ed. A. Cutolo (Bologna, 1942), 76–77.

59. Although he mentions an Arnaldus *magister* as *scholarum magister*, Landulph Junior (*Landulfi de Sancto Paulo Historia mediolanensis*, ed. L. Bethmann and P. Jaffé, MGH, *Scriptores* 20 [Hanover, 1868]), 22, received his own early education with an uncle and his advanced training in France, as did the others whose education he mentions.

60. F. Gastaldelli has published both on liberal arts and on theology at Lucca. See his "Note sul codice 619 della Biblioteca capitolare di Lucca e sulle edizione del *De arithmetica compendiose tractata* e della *Summa dialectice artis*," *Salesianum* 39 (1977): 693–702, at 696–97. It is highly improbable that there was a thriving cathedral school at Cremona as V. Tirelli argues in "Gli inventari della biblioteca della cattedrale di Cremona (sec. X–XIII) e un frammento di glossario latino del secolo X," *Italia medioevale e umanistica* 7 (1964): 1–76, at 18ff. Without other evidence the use of the presence of *magistri* in the list of cathedral canons from the late twelfth century (p. 30) probably means only that these individuals have advanced university training: R. W. Southern, "The Schools of Paris and the School of Chartres," in *Renaissance and Renewal*, 134–35. When in 1185, moreover, the chapter guarantees that those "qui in scholis fuerint" are assured of their full share of the clothing ration just like those "canonicorum ecclesiae deserventium" (34), this almost certainly does not point to the existence of a school in the cathedral. Rather, it suggests that Cremona was one of the centers that, by the late twelfth century, was not penalizing canons who studied theology at some center of learning. After 1219 this practice became

the rule of the church by papal command: H. Denifle, *Die Entstehung der Universitäten des Mittelalters bis 1400* (Berlin, 1885; reprinted Graz, 1936), 746–47.

61. In an exchange of letters with a prospective student in Cremona who promised him fifty students if he came to teach in their city, Adalbertus promised to do so after his contract in Bologna expired: W. Holtzmann, "Eine oberitalienische *ars dictandi*," *Neues Archiv* 46 (1926): 34–52, at 38. A letter contained in the collection attributed to Henry Francigena (B. Odebrecht, "Die Briefmuster des Henricus Francigena," *Archiv für Urkundenforschung* 14 [1936]: 231–61, at 247) may also be the work of another itinerant teacher, a certain W. de Saramando, who writes a prospective student that he has desired his friendship "since the beginning of my arrival in this land."

P. F. Gehl, "From Monastic Rhetoric to *Ars Dictaminis:* Traditionalism and Innovation in the Schools of Twelfth-Century Italy," *American Benedictine Review* 34 (1983): 33–47, insists on the role of the monasteries in propagating *ars dictaminis* in the twelfth century. It is not clear, however, why they would begin to play a role in Italian education they did not seem to play in the previous century. Monte Cassino would be an exception. Although Gehl's position cannot be lightly dismissed, his major proof for monastic activity is that many of the surviving manuscripts of the manuals from the twelfth century come from monastic sources. As he himself points out (36), however, schoolbooks were the most easily worn out. Private teachers without institutional support would not be likely to have their libraries preserved. The monastic origin of texts, consequently, merely shows that monks continued their interest in *ars dictaminis* in the twelfth century, but says nothing about monastic leadership in the movement. Apart from Paul of Camaldoli it would be difficult to identify Italian *dictatores* of certain monastic origin in the period.

62. *Rationes dictandi prosaice,* ed. L. Rockinger, in *Briefsteller und Formelbücher des eilften bis vierzehnten Jahrhunderts* (Munich, 1863), 53–94.

63. The emergence of Bologna as the leading center of legal studies was perhaps initially connected with the dependence of the powerful house of Canossa from the late eleventh century on the legists of the city for help in governing the family's vast territories: Arnaldi, "Alle origini," 108–15. That one of the earliest Bolognese jurists was Irnerius also greatly contributed to the attraction of the city for students. Furthermore, Bologna was located in a fertile region capable of feeding a large student population and geographically at the center of an area where in the eleventh century there had been a number of cathedral schools. Finally, because Bologna does not seem to have had a cathedral school, or at least one of any importance, the bishop of the city would probably have felt less threatened by the growth of independent schools than would the bishops of cities like Parma and Milan where there were active cathedral schools. The parallel between the rise of Bologna and that of Paris is obvious and certainly some of the same factors can be used to explain the two phenomena. Cf. R. W. Southern, "Schools of Paris," 114–21. The differences in the specialties and character of the

teaching personnel of the two centers, however, can be explained by the cultural contexts in which they evolved.

64. Alberico de Monte Cassino, *Flores rhetorici,* ed. D. M. Inguanez and H. M. Willard (Monte Cassino, 1938), 36–38. See the bibliography in A. Lentini, "Alberico," *Dizionario biografico degli italiani* (Rome, 1960), 1:646. Alberico drew his description of the parts of the oration most immediately not from Cicero, but from Isidore of Seville, *Etymologiae,* 2.7. The division *salutatio* may derive from Victorinus. See *Flores,* 25, n. 1.

65. Adalbertus Samaritanus, *Praecepta dictaminum,* ed. F.-J. Schmale, MGH, Quellen zur Geistegeschichte des Mittelalters, 3 (Weimar, 1961), 30 and 34.

66. *Rationes dictandi,* ed. Rockinger, *Briefsteller,* 1:10. For the false attribution of this work to Alberico, see Schmale's edition of *Praecepta dictaminium,* 2, and bibliography, 2, n. 2. Schmale dates the work about 1140. H. Bloch, "Monte Cassino's Teachers and Library in the High Middle Ages," in *La scuola nell'Occidente latino dell'alto medioevo* (Spoleto, 1972), 563–605, assigns a date after 1137 (588–89).

67. While *dictatores* were relatively flexible in allowing the nature of the material to dictate the number of parts, still there was controversy over the number suitable for the normal letter. Conrad von Mure, *Die Summa de arte prosandi des Konrad von Mure,* ed. W. Kronbichler (Zurich, 1968), 31, refers to a debate among *dictatores* as to whether the letter has three or five parts. However, one early thirteenth-century *dictator,* a certain William by name, maintained that the letter had six parts. See C. Samaran, "Une *summa grammaticalis* du XIIIe siècle avec gloses provençales," *Archivum latinitatis medii aevi* 31 (1961): 215b. William defends the very six-part organization (*salutatio, captatio, proverbium, narratio, petitio,* and *conclusio*) that Boncompagno in his *Palma* regards as long ago abandoned. See C. Sutter, *Aus Leben und Schriften des Magisters Boncompagno* (Freiburg i.B., 1894), 109. Boncompagno puts *exordium* for *proverbium.*

On vocabulary for introducing parts of letters, see, for example, Guido Faba, *Summa dictaminis,* ed. A. Gaudenzi, *Il Propugnatore* n.s. 3.2 (1890), 348–49; Thomas of Capua's treatment of linking words in *Die Ars dictandi des Thomas von Capua,* ed. E. Heller (Heidelberg, 1928–29), 40–41. Significantly, set phrases and a commonly accepted vocabulary of transition are characteristics of oral literature. See Crosby, "Oral Delivery," 106ff.

68. Even Boncompagno, who did not regard the *exordium* as a principal part of the letter, devoted treatises to its composition. Although the *Isagoge* remains unpublished, the *Breviloquium* is found in *Breviloquium di Boncompagno da Signa,* ed. G. Vecchi (Bologna, 1954). The most complete treatment of Boncompagno's conception of the *exordium* is found in J. R. Banker's "Giovanni di Bonandrea's *Ars dictaminis* Treatise and the Doctrine of Invention in the Italian Rhetorical Tradition of the Thirteenth and Early Fourteenth Centuries," (Ph.D. diss., University of Rochester, 1972), 145ff.

69. For a brief summary and sources on speech manuals, see G. Vecchi, "Le Arenge di Guido Faba e l'eloquenza d'arte civile e politica duecentesca," *Quadrivium* 4 (1960): 65–69; and P. O. Kristeller, *Renaissance Thought*

and Its Sources, ed. M. Mooney (New York, 1979), 237–38 and 320–21. Although following ancient theory medieval rhetoricians distinguished three levels of style (the simple, medium, and high styles), in practice they used only two, the simple and the high, which were characterized variously as *sermo simplex–sermo figuratus, ornatus facilis–ornatus difficilis, stilus humilis–stilus altus,* etc.: E. R. Curtius, "Die Lehre von den drei Stilen in Altertum und Mittelalter," *Romanische Forschungen* 64 (1952): 66–69. H. M. Schaller, "Die Kanzlei Kaiser Friedrichs II," *Archiv für Diplomatik, Schriftengeschichte, Siegel- und Wappenkunde* 4 (1958): 269, describes the *stilus altus* as a genus of *elocutio* relying for effect on rhetorical figures, tropes, and topoi, while the *humilus* depends on rhythm. Also see the detailed study of the *stilus humilis* in the early Middle Ages by E. Auerbach, "Sermo humilis," *Romanische Forschungen* 64 (1952): 304–64, and 66 (1954): 1–64. As a matter of fact, rhetoricians in the thirteenth and fourteenth centuries combined to varying degrees these rhetorical devices and rhythm.

70. Boncompagno's *Liber de obsidione Ancone (a. 1173),* ed. G. C. Zimolo, in Muratori, *Rerum italicarum scriptores* n.s. 6.3 (Bologna, 1937) was an early example of the use of the style in writing history.

71. Occasionally in the twelfth century, of course, one encounters instances of some knowledge of the ancient writers in northern and central Italy. Paul of Camaldoli's *Introductiones* written in the last half of the century (V. Sivo, "Le *Introductiones dictandi* di Paolo Camaldolese," in *Studi e ricerche dall'Istituto di Latina* 3 [Geneva, 1980], 69–100) indicates Paul's acquaintance with the standard Latin poets. For a twelfth-century Italian commentary on the *De inventione* see C. Alessio, "Brunetto Latini e Cicerone (e i dettatori)," *Italia medioevale e umanistica* 22 (1979): 123–69, at 125–26.

72. *Ars dictandi aureliensis,* ed. L. Rockinger, *Briefsteller,* 103–14.

73. See especially for bibliography A. Dalzell, "The *Forma Dictandi* Attributed to Albert of Morra and Related Texts," *Mediaeval Studies* 39 (1977): 440–65. Also see my "On Bene of Florence's Conception of the French and Roman Cursus," *Rhetorica* 3 (1985): 77–98 (pagination confused, pp. 84–87).

74. See my "Boncompagno on Grammar."

75. The letter is published in C. Sutter, *Aus Leben und Schriften,* 42–43; see also *Multiplices epistole que diversis et variis negotiis utiliter possunt accomodari,* ed. V. Pini (Bologna, 1969). For a dating of Boncompagno's writings see G. Vecchi, "Boncompagno," *Dizionario biografico degli italiani* (Rome, 1969), 11:722–25.

76. Witt, "On Bene of Florence's Conception," 81–82. Bene's *Candelabrum* has recently been published in a superb edition: *Bene Florentini Candelabrum,* ed. G. C. Alessio (Padua, 1983).

77. R. Rusconi, *Predicazione e vita religiosa nella società italiana da Carlo Magno alla controriforma* (Turin, 1981), 22–23.

78. B. Smalley, *The Study of the Bible in the Middle Ages* (Oxford, 2d ed., 1952), 244, stresses the rise of popular preaching in the twelfth century and

the application of allegory to the sermon: "allegory could be used for instructing the laity, for presenting to them the Church and her sacraments in a concrete and intelligible form." Cf. P. B. Roberts, *Stephanus de Lingua-Tonante: Studies in the Sermons of Stephen Langton* (Toronto, 1981), 41–43.

79. Roberts, *Stephanus de Lingua-Tonante*, 44–45. Stephen is known to have preached in Italy (18). On this circle, see as well J. Longère, *Oeuvres oratoires de maîtres Parisiens au XIIe siècle*, 2 vols. (Paris, 1973), 1:14–29.

80. Roberts, *Stephanus de Lingua-Tonante*, 2 and 42.

81. Ibid., 42.

82. For lists of manuals, see the following: H. Caplan, *Mediaeval "Ars Praedicandi"* (Ithaca, 1934); and idem, *Mediaeval "Artes Praedicandi": A Supplementary Handlist* (Ithaca, 1936); T. M. Charland, *Artes praedicandi: Contribution à l'histoire de la rhétorique au Moyen Âge* (Paris and Ottawa, 1936), 21–106; H. Caplan and H. H. King, "Latin Tractates on Preaching: A Book-List," *Harvard Theological Review* 42 (1949): 185–206; J. J. Murphy, *Medieval Rhetoric: A Select Bibliography* (Toronto, 1971), 71–81; M. Jennings, "Monks and the *Artes Praedicandi* in the time of Ranulph Higden," *Revue bénédictine* 86 (1976): 119–28; and S. Gallick, "*Artes Praedicandi:* Early Printed Editions," *Mediaeval Studies* 39 (1977): 477–89.

83. Roberts, *Stephanus de Lingua-Tonante*, 77–79.

84. Charland, *Artes praedicandi*, 9.

85. Charland, ibid., 33, suggests on the basis of P. E. Longpré, "Les *distinctiones* de Fr. Thomas de Pavia, O.F.M.," *Archivum Franciscanum Historicum* 16 (1923): 3–33, at 14, n. 4, that the tract on preaching ascribed to Pseudo-Bonaventura may be by Thomas of Pavia (fl. 1249–56). J. J. Murphy, *Rhetoric in the Middle Ages: A History of Rhetorical Theory from Saint Augustine to the Renaissance* (Berkeley, 1974), 310–26, suggests that the first manuals were English. Nonetheless, there is little question that the form came into Italy through the French.

86. The letters of Honorius III are found in *Epistolae saec. XIII e regestis pontificum romanorum selectae*, ed. C. Rodenberg, MGH *Epistolae* 1 (Berlin, 1883). The new style seems to affect imperial letters beginning with those of 10 February 1221: J. L. A. Huillard-Bréholles, *Historia diplomatica Friderici secundi*, 6 vols. (Paris, 1852–61), 2:1:123–27. For bibliography on the style, see my "Medieval *Ars Dictaminis*," 14–15, n. 32.

87. Schaller, "Die Kanzlei," 279–80.

88. See below in this essay.

89. See examples of private style in J. L. A. Huillard-Bréholles, *Vie et correspondance de Pierre de la Vigne* (Paris, 1865), 289ff. Though more stylistically restrained than those of della Vigna, the letters sent out by Thomas of Capua in his own name differ from those dispatched in that of the popes he served. For Thomas's letters, see E. Heller, "Der kuriale Geschäftsgang in den Briefen des Thomas von Capua," *Archiv für Urkundenforschung* 13 (1935): 198–318. See as well, *Collectio monumentorum veterum et recentium ineditorum*, ed. S. F. Halm, 2 vols. (Brunswick, 1724–26), 1:279ff.

The culmination of the biblical-allegorical *stilus obscurus* is certainly the exchange of letters published by P. Sambin, *Un certame dettatorio tra due notai pontifici (1260): Lettere inedite di Giordano da Terracina e di Giovanni da Capua* (Rome, 1955).

90. Sutter, *Aus Leben, (Palma)* 106, *(Rota Veneris)* 81–82, *(De amicitia)* 75–77, and *(Oliva)* 67–68.

91. *Candelabrum*, 3.

92. See E. Kantorowicz, "An Autobiography of Guido Faba," *Medieval and Renaissance Studies* 1 (1943): 253–80. Republished in idem, *Selected Studies* (Locust Valley, NY, 1965), 210–12.

93. See my *Coluccio Salutati and His Public Letters* (Geneva, 1976), 32–33, for Latini's one surviving public letter. On Dante's correspondence, see A. Vallone, "Il latino di Dante," *Rivista di cultura classica e medioevale* 8 (1966): 184–92. For Salutati, see generally my *Coluccio Salutati*, and D. de Rosa, *Coluccio Salutati: Il cancelliere e il pensatore politico* (Florence, 1980), 13ff.

94. U. Ronca, *Cultura medioevale e poesia latina d'Italia nei secoli XI e XII*, 2 vols. (Rome, 1892), 1:245ff.

95. On the Goliards in Italy, see G. Bertoni, *Il duecento* (Milan, 1930), 235–39. Enrico da Settimello, *Elegia*, ed. G. Cremaschi (Bergamo, 1949).

96. Enrico da Settimello, *Elegia*. For the date of the *Alexandreis: Galteri de Castellione, Alexandreis*, ed. M. L. Colker (Padua, 1978), xv, where date of 1182 is given.

97. G. Cremaschi, *Stefanardo da Vimercate: Contributo per la storia della cultura in Lombardia nel sec. XIII* (Milan, 1950), 39–40.

98. *Candelabrum*, 247–90, constitutes the eighth book, but see also the detailed notes to each book for references. Perhaps the earliest mention of this twelfth-century French literature occurs in Paul of Camaldoli's *Introductiones dictandi:* V. Sivo, "Le *Introductiones dictandi*," 72.

99. G. Capello, "Maestro Manfredo e maestro Sion: Grammatici vercellesi del Duecento," *Aevum* 17 (1943): 61–70, especially 68. *Candelabrum*, lxix–lxx, provides the date.

100. Capello, "Maestro Manfredo," 65–66 and 68.

101. The location of manuscripts of Bono de Lucca's *Summa* can be found in the alphabetical index to G. L. Bursill–Hall, *A Census of Medieval Latin Grammatical Manuscripts* (Stuttgart, 1981), 362. The *Census* makes no mention of Bene's grammar. I have used the Marc. Lat. xiii, 7, for study of the work. The development of grammatical studies in Italy in the thirteenth century has to this time received little attention, and much remains to be done.

102. E. Müller, *Peter von Prezza, ein Publizist der Zeit des Interregnums* (Heidelberg, 1913), publishes the letters of Peter of Pressa, while those of Henry of Isernia are found in *Regesta diplomatica nec non epistolaria Bohemiae et Moraviae*, ed. J. Emler, 2 (Prague, 1882), and in K. Hampe, *Beiträge zur Geschichte der letzten Staufer* (Leipzig, 1910). On Peter, see also R. M. Kloos, "Petrus de Prece und Konradin," *Quellen und Forschungen aus italienischen Archiven und Bibliotheken* 34 (1954): 88–108. H. Wieru-

szowski, *Culture and Politics in Medieval Spain and Italy* (Rome, 1971), 609–10, discusses their interest in the Latin classics.

103. The *Chronica,* ed. A. Bonardi, is published in Muratori, RIS, 8, n.s. 1 (Città di Castello, 1905–06). Although he obviously admired and read ancient literature, his style does not impress me as an attempt to imitate the great Latin authors, as Wieruszowski maintains in *Politics and Culture,* 614–15. The *Chronica* has been translated by J. R. Berrigan with the title *The Chronicles of the Trevisan March* (Lawrence, KS, 1980).

104. See my "Brunetto Latini and the Italian Tradition of *Ars Dictaminis,*" *Stanford Italian Review* 3 (1983): 5–24.

105. On the thirteenth century *studia,* see H. Rashdall, *The Universities of Europe in the Middle Ages,* ed. F. M. Powicke and A. B. Emden, 3 vols. (Oxford, 1936), 2:1–62; Manacorda, *Storia della scuola in Italia,* 1.1:165–262; U. Gualazzini, *Ricerche sulle scuole pre-universitarie del medioevo* (Milan, 1943), 305–75.

106. See my "Boncompagno and the Defense of Rhetoric," 17–18.

107. See my "Medieval *Ars Dictaminis,*" 20, n. 47.

108. The text of Mussato's play is found in *Ecerinide,* ed. L. Padrin (Bologna, 1900). The *Ecerenis* brought Mussato immediate success, and it was decreed that the play would be presented annually as a reminder to the Paduans of the dangers of tyranny: G. Carducci, "Della Ecerinide e di Albertino Mussato," in ibid., 254–55.

109. The *De obsidione Patavii* in Muratori, *Rerum italicarum scriptores* 10 (Milan, 1727), represented for Mussato an awkward attempt to write in a style comprehensible to those outside his narrow circle. The introduction to the work (687) sets forth his motive for the composition. The notaries seek that, just as he has treated the events dealing with the lord of Verona, Cangrande della Scala, in his prose histories, so now he should treat them "in a kind of harmonious meter for your delight and that of our fellow citizens. And you [the notaries] add to your request that whatever the meter is, the language should not be lofty, like tragedy, but sweet and close to the understanding of the people; and just as in a higher manner our *History* with its elevated style served more learned men, this metric work, bent to the service of an easier muse, would be of charm to notaries and the average cleric." On the style of the *De obsidione,* see M. Dazzi, *Il Mussato preumanista, 1261–1329: L'ambiente e l'opera* (Venice, 1964), 97–98.

110. Weiss, "Lovato Lovati," 20–21.

111. For Riccobaldo see above. For Mussato's historical writings, see M. Dazzi, "Il Mussato storico," *Archivio veneto* 6 (1929): 359–471. Giovanni da Cermenate's *Historia,* which antedates Mussato's historical work by only a few years, indicates another kind of approach to writing classicizing prose: *Historia Iohannis de Cermenate (sec. XIV),* ed. L. A. Ferrai (Rome, 1889).

112. The letters of Geri are published by Weiss, *Il primo secolo,* 53–66 and 105–32. The prose letters are found on 109–15, 120–25, and 133. In contrast with the first five, the sixth letter reflects Geri's skill at composing in *dictamen.* In his letter of dedication to his first letter collection, Petrarch states

his conception of the letter as an informal conversation: *Le familiari,* ed. V. Rossi, 4 vols. (Florence, 1934), 1:3–14. See discussion and bibliography in my "Medieval *Ars Dictaminis,*" 27–31.

113. For bibliography on Giovanni del Virgilio, see G. Billanovich, "Giovanni del Virgilio, Pietro da Moglio, Francesco da Fiano," *Italia medioevale e umanistica* 6 (1963): 206; and especially P. O. Kristeller, "Un *Ars dictaminis* di Giovanni del Virgilio," *Italia medioevale e umanistica* 4 (1961): 181–200.

114. See my "Medieval *Ars Dictaminis,*" 24, n. 51.

115. On Vergerio's contribution to the rebirth of classicizing oratory, see J. M. McManamon, "Innovation in Early Humanist Rhetoric: The Oratory of Pier Paolo Vergerio (the Elder)," *Rinascimento* 22 (1982): 3–32. See also his "Pier Paolo Vergerio (the Elder) and the Beginnings of the Humanist Cult of Jerome," *Catholic Historical Review* 71 (1985): 353–71.

116. The distinction between the concerns and interests of the grammarian and those of the rhetorician in the fifteenth and sixteenth centuries is brilliantly developed by J. W. O'Malley in two articles: "Grammar and Rhetoric in the Spirituality of Erasmus," *Paideia: Special Renaissance Issue* (in press); and "Egidio de Viterbo, O. S. A. e il suo tempo," *Studia augustiniana historica* 9 (1983): 68–84. This conflict could also be conceived in terms of the conflict between poet and orator. See O. B. Hardison, "The Orator and the Poet: The Dilemma of Humanist Literature," *Journal of Medieval and Renaissance Studies* 1 (1971): 33–44.

117. M. Baxandall, *Giotto and the Orators* (Oxford, 1971), 6 and 8ff.

118. Although the ancients themselves recognized the need at times to employ paratactic structures based on everyday speech (*oratio perpetua*), the period was the normal form used in good writing and oratory. The humanists tended to prefer less intricate subordination and followed the structure of popular language to a much greater degree. This and other important differences between ancient and Renaissance Latin are treated by R. Spongano, "Un capitolo di storia della nostra prosa d'arte," in *Due saggi sull'umanesimo* (Florence, 1964), 39–78.

119. The work is edited by H. Baron, *From Petrarch to Leonardo Bruni* (Chicago, 1968), 232–63. C. T. Davis, *Dante's Italy and Other Essays* (Philadelphia, 1984), 254–89, however, shows that all the elements for such an exposition were already under discussion by the early fourteenth century. Cf. my *Coluccio Salutati,* 77–79.

120. Witt, *Coluccio Salutati,* 53–56.

121. Bruni's civic humanism has been defined and analyzed by H. Baron in a variety of works but most notably in *The Crisis of the Early Italian Renaissance,* 2 vols. in 1 (Princeton, rev. ed. 1966). Among others, Florentine humanists like Poggio and Palmieri deserve the title of orator for their achievements.

B 🙰 PETRARCH AND THE HUMANIST TRADITIONS

4 🙰 PETRARCH, CICERO, AND THE CLASSICAL PAGAN TRADITION

Maristella Lorch

CICERO'S INFLUENCE NEVER DIED IN ROME OR IN THE WEST. IN the first century after Christ his message was clarified and emphasized by Quintilian, a professional teacher of rhetoric who believed with equal enthusiasm in language as the highest expresson of the human being and in the art of speaking and writing as the most personal form of *humanitas*. Cicero, induced by his love of eloquence, had in his rhetorical works considered philosophy an ancilla of eloquence. But he had devoted the last years of his life to making Greek philosophy familiar to the Romans and had preferred to be called a "philosopher." He had opened the problem of the relation of philosophy to rhetoric but had not provided a satisfactory solution to it. Quintilian can be regarded as the restorer of philosophical rhetoric. In an era of highly specialized culture, he attempted to reinstate general culture and education. He did so within his profession by trying to give to the art of eloquence, which had decayed into a technique practiced by professional *declamatores*, the breadth and the nobility of a universal science.

Cicero presents rhetoric as a practical science essential to the welfare of the Roman state. Quintilian presents it as a systematic body of knowledge, leaving no detail undiscussed. What Quintilian offers is thus the end result of the Ciceronian theory of language and its use as an expression of *humanitas*. Valla, at the height of the movement we call humanism, takes the most original view of the relation between Cicero and Quintilian:

> Here is what I think of these two authors. Nobody can know Quintilian if he does not know Cicero more than well. Nor can one follow Cicero faithfully if he does not let himself be guided by Quintilian. . . . Nor was there after Quintilian anybody expert in

eloquence, anybody who devoted himself for his educational formation to Quintilian's art with the intention of imitating him. I
place myself ahead of anyone who did not follow this method, no
matter how good he was in the art of rhetoric.[1]

For Petrarch the discovery of Quintilian's *Institutiones oratoriae* in 1350
did not bring the immeasurable joy that the discovery of a text by Cicero
usually did. He was, however, among the first to look at Quintilian with
a new interest—due to his interest in Cicero—and with a new perspective. He admired in Quintilian the *rhetor* who in ancient Rome had res-
urrected Cicero and placed his work in correct perspective after a century
of neglect. "I had no taste for anything but Cicero, especially after I read
the *Oratorical Institutes* of Quintilian."[2] After all, was he not now at the
threshold of an era that he regarded as different from the dark preceding
age, performing a role analogous to that of Cicero?

Although Cicero's influence declined in Rome after Quintilian, it
was eventually revived by Christianity. Tertullian was the implacable
enemy of all aspects of pagan civilization and preached against all forms
of contact: "Beware of those who have devised a Stoic, a Platonic, or a
dialectical Christianity." Nonetheless, Cicero became the spiritual guide
of many Latin Christian fathers after the vogue of the so-called "new
Latin" or *elocutio novella,* which found in Apuleius its most prominent
representative. His Christian counterparts were Minucius Felix, Arnob-
ius, and especially Lactantius (a friend of Emperor Constantine), who
took pride in being called "the Christian Cicero." Yet Lactantius did not
turn to Cicero only as a master of style but also as the pagan writer who
anticipated Christianity; he pointed to *De republica,* book 3, as an example of this fact. Ambrose, the bishop of Milan, recognized the Christian quality of the Ciceronian concept of *humanitas.*[3] And Jerome's
attraction to Cicero is legendary. A sick Jerome one day saw himself
before God at the Last Judgment being asked: "Who are you?" To his
answer that he was a Christian came the reproach: "No, you are not a
Christian but a Ciceronian. Where your treasure is, there your heart is
also." He swore then that he would never again touch a pagan book (an
oath he did not keep). Jerome's decision in the first centuries of Christianity could be taken as a symbol of the persistent influence of Ciceronian prose on the curial, literary culture of the Middle Ages. It is also an
indication that in a Christian world Cicero's survival could not be identified exclusively with his style, even though the latter was regarded as
the best paradigm of Latin prose writing.

It is probably owing to the Latin Christian fathers that the rhythm
of Ciceronian prose was still to be felt in the official prose of the high

Middle Ages. Indeed, during the twelfth and thirteenth centuries, at the court of Pope Innocent III and at the chancellery of King Frederick II of Swabia, Ciceronian prose was the model. Its survival is all the more striking in view of the fact that the medieval *artes dictandi* do not reflect the explicit influence of Cicero.

Apart from the influence of his style, Cicero himself was the type of virtuous pagan who was nonetheless excluded from the Christian paradise because he did not know the Redeemer. In this respect a transformation in attitude toward Cicero (and other ancient pagan writers) is discernible between Dante (d. 1321) on the one side and Petrarch (d. 1374) on the other. Dante still recognized a radical break between pagan and Christian worlds; Petrarch affirmed their continuity. In *De ignorantia*, Petrarch treats Cicero as a visionary who, while speaking of the nature of the gods in *De natura deorum*, intuited, before the birth of Christ, the existence of *one* God. He also pointed to his constant reading of Cicero as proof of his true Christianity, against the hypocritical Christianity of his enemies who were admirers of Aristotle. Among the fathers his favorite is Augustine who admitted, in an oft-quoted passage of his *Confessions*, that Cicero's *Hortensius* had been instrumental in his conversion to Christianity:

> By the ordinary course of study I fell upon a certain book of one Cicero, whose tongue almost every man admires, though not so his heart. This book of his contains an exhortation to philosophy and it is called *Hortensius*. Now this book quite altered my affection, turned my prayers to thyself, Lord, and made me have entirely other purposes and desires. All my vain hopes I henceforth slighted; and . . . I thirsted after the immortality of wisdom.[4]

Together with Augustine, Ambrose, Lactantius, and Jerome are the direct predecessors of Petrarch in his relation with Cicero. Yet, after a millennium, due to the fact that Petrarch, though deeply and sincerely a Christian, was motivated mainly by cultural needs and interests, Cicero's attraction was to take a special form that, in turn, influenced his humanist successors.

*   *   *

Cicero reigns supreme in Petrarch's world. There exists between the two a personal relationship inspired by a commonly shared faith in *humanitas*, that is, in the possibility of realizing man's noblest tendencies through the exercise of the liberal arts, which—for those who are naturally gifted—should bring about a union of thought and word, mind and verbal expression. Cicero's *humanitas* helps establish peace between Petrarch and the world, provides a stimulus for his writing, and inspires in him a hope of a continuing form of earthly life beyond physical death. Thus time and space are canceled in what can only be called a friendship; and friendship is, of all human affections, the one Petrarch most cherishes. For this reason, throughout his life he searched relentlessly for Cicero's books, took great joy in discovering a new one, and experienced pain comparable to the loss of a friend when a copy he has loaned to someone else disappears.

Petrarch's dialogue with Cicero, which lasts uninterruptedly from his early years—when his father put Cicero's rhetorical books in his hands—to the year of his death, marks the climax of the history of Cicero's *fortuna* in the western world. Never did Cicero speak more directly than he did to the Tuscan poet at the threshold of the Renaissance. Never was his influence more constructive and, ideologically speaking, more inspiring.[5] Humanism, in the most creative forms it takes in shaping its relationship with classical antiquity, owes much to the Petrarch–Cicero dialogue, which ignored the time between and made the written word of a nonreligious text live as the carrier of an "immortal" message. The presupposition for this dialogue was that the written word—literature, the *litterae humanae*—makes history, and that philology, as the study of a text and reflection of man's ever-changing life, is the truest form of philosophy.

Petrarch's and Cicero's biographies do not have much in common. Neither did Petrarch, especially after discovering and reading Cicero's letters to Atticus, accept Cicero's personal behavior as exemplary. But Petrarch accepted Cicero the man and the writer, the orator and the politician, to a much greater extent than anyone either before or since in the western evaluation of Cicero. For Petrarch, Cicero's sublime style was the man, the *homo* in his frailty but also in his unflagging pursuit of an ideal form of *humanitas*. Petrarch accepted Cicero's relentless drive toward human perfection as akin to his own. The warmth of the style reflected this drive, which he felt to be present in all of Cicero's writings, the orations as well as the rhetorical works, the letters as well as the philosophical dialogues. Cicero longed—as did Petrarch—to share this drive for moral perfection with others around him. Thus while in search of a culture for a group of specialists (the orators), he came to establish a general culture.

Cicero's concepts of *honestas* and *virtus,* the Stoic aspects of his thought, are the focus of Petrarch's admiration. *Honestas* is the pure good desirable per se and, in the service of others, uncontaminated by any selfish purpose; *virtus* is the human effort to reach it. Cicero's *virtus* is first of all *fortitudo* or moral strength, paradigmatically represented by Regulus who voluntarily returned to the Carthaginians knowing that he would be tortured and killed, by Mucius who burned his hand to prove his point, by Lucretia who committed suicide for the shame of having been violated, and by Epicurus who called himself happy on the last day of his life—though suffering great physical pain—because he was at peace with himself. This kind of *virtus* is *justitia*, because it keeps society together; *prudentia*, the deep knowledge of truth, but which allows us to distinguish between good and evil, the source of all virtues; and finally *temperantia* or *constantia* or *modestia*, inseparable from *honestum* or pure good, because it suggests the decorous in every circumstance, the measure or harmony to which every act should conform. Like Ambrose before him, Petrarch received this message from Cicero's *De officiis*, a dialogue written for his son on the duties of the Roman citizen. But he also felt it as a leitmotif in all of Cicero's writings.[6]

Petrarch's interpretation of the Ciceronian concept of *virtus* is an original contribution to the reading of Cicero that was to bear its fruit among the humanists. There were those—especially Coluccio Salutati and Leonardo Bruni among the Florentines—who exploited this human quality in its unselfish aspect of *fortitudo* as self-sacrifice for society, especially for one's own country.[7] Others—the majority—developed the concept of virtue as moral strength, which allows man to conquer difficulties and tame *fortuna*. Among these, the last and most prominent defender of *virtù* was Machiavelli, who defined Fortune as a woman who needs to be trampled on and crushed under man's *virtù*.[8]

This implication of the Ciceronian *virtus* had been intuited and exploited in Augustine's time by Pelagius and his followers. Pelagius believed virtue to be the result of human effort rather than of divine grace, each man consequently responsible for his own actions, human nature good rather than evil, and man gifted with free will. Augustine successfully counterposed to Pelagius's human virtues the three theological virtues of faith, hope, and love. The Pelagians were the last of the early Christians to appeal directly to Cicero, celebrating him like Christ. Petrarch, an intense reader and admirer of Augustine as well as of Cicero,[9] was deeply torn by the conflict inherent in the concept of *virtus*.

Among the interpreters of the Ciceronian *virtus* descended from Petrarch, there were those, finally, who would reverse the judgment and reject the human quality of virile strength in favor of a deeper nonrational instinct of self-preservation that involved both self-love and containment of self-love to allow man to live in society. Basically, this nonrational instinct is love for life and for God who is the origin of all forms of life. Lorenza Valla, who best represents this point of view, calls this instinct *voluptas*, pleasure, a word Cicero hated because it brought into prominence that most despicable human tendency to live on the basis of one's own self-interest. Valla's celebration of *voluptas* implies a ruthless attack on the Ciceronian *virtus* so dear to Petrarch. In Valla, almost a century after Petrarch, the reign of Cicero was reaching its end.

*   *   *

Between 1966 and 1978 five biographies of Cicero in English alone were published. But if there appears to be a renewed interest in Cicero, the history of Cicero's *fortuna* from the sixteenth to the twentieth centuries indicates that it was not always so.

Erasmus, in his *Ciceronianus* (1528), seeks to combat precisely a form of idiotic "Ciceronianism" that marks the end of Cicero's constructive influence. Annibal Caro in Italy was warning the Italians against an empty imitation of Petrarch (known as Petrarchism) at the same time as Erasmus was warning humanists against an empty imitation of Cicero.[10] It is more than a coincidence—it was a crisis in the humanist movement and a symptom of its decline—that both Cicero and Petrarch were misunderstood at the moment that humanism reached its highest development.

When, with German Romanticism, the most violent anti-Latin and anti-Roman revolt broke loose, Cicero became the center of the polemic. The reason might simply have been that for a long time the Petrarchan way of reading Cicero in his entirety and dialoguing with him had decayed into an imitation of the beauty of his Latin style, as if style per se had not been declared by Cicero a purely empty crust when it did not reflect a strong, warm, active, humane personality. In 1870 the great German historian Theodor Mommsen condemned Cicero to death, so to speak, for his weak and contradictory ideology and for his private life. There were defenders, for example Gaston Boissier in France.[11] But it was in Germany, in the period after World War I, that Cicero was rediscovered as the perfect interpreter of that miracle of assimilation, fusion, and creation which constitutes the true glory of Roman civilization. Richard Reitzenstein, in a famous lecture at Göttingen, "Romanity in Cicero and Horace," pointed out that Cicero had regarded it as the obligation of Rome, as a dominating power, to rule its subjects with honesty and to discourage factions when the party in power advocated the peace of the community. Conscious that Rome was the heir of Greek culture, Cicero exhorted the Romans to establish a fraternity of spirits, and he formulated a concept of *patria* as the community to which each man brings the noblest part of himself. This position is once again close to Petrarch's evaluation of Cicero.

*   *   *

Even a superficial glance at Cicero's biography convinces us that he is a man very difficult to judge because of the impulsive nature of his contrasting passions. He was indeed more a *homo* than a *vir*,[12] showing in himself the good and the bad in humanity with a constant desire to pursue the good, even if he could not always successfully achieve it. The same was true also of Petrarch. Moreover, both Cicero and Petrarch came from cultured middle-class families, were born in the provinces, had fathers who cherished intellectual values, and lived in the city while loving the seclusion of the country. With respect to this last point, however, there was a significant difference between the two: Petrarch's constant longing was for *otium* or seclusion as the essential condition for his studies, while Cicero, on the contrary, longed for *negotium* or public involvement. An analysis of these different longings can tell us much about what attracted Petrarch to Cicero and what he made of him.

Otium means "leisure, vacant time, freedom from business."[13] In the case of Cicero it means primarily "literary activity" and "literary occupation,"[14] freedom from public affairs. An *otiosus* is a private person, one not in official life.[15] *Negotium*, from *nec-otium*, means precisely the negation of *otium*: business, employment, occupation. Cicero was all his life heavily involved in *forensia negotia*.[16] A *negotiosus* is thus a busy person, one full of business, as in "troublesome and busy employment."[17] I cannot here explore fully the significance of these two concepts for either Cicero or Petrarch. I shall limit myself to some observations relevant to the relationship between Petrarch and Cicero.

Cicero was so heavily involved in *negotium* that his letters to Atticus have been defined as a political history of his own time, which he could describe in intimate personal terms because he participated so actively in it.[18] At the same time, no one appreciated more than Cicero the necessity of *otium* for the full realization of man's *humanitas*. *Otium* must be married to *negotium*. The myth of the birth of civilization through the marriage of *sapientia* and *eloquentia* indicates how deeply rooted this conviction was in Cicero. Cicero's mature life began in the public forum, where he tried to realize the ideal of a great orator and accomplished jurist. But then in 79 B.C. he traveled to Greece, where he spent two years studying not only rhetoric, poetry, and art, but also philosophy. He says of himself that he came back from the orient *prope mutatus*, another man. He had discovered himself. Comparing himself to other orators in the *Brutus*, he finds them regrettably deprived of literary culture,

ignorant of philosophy—the matrix of all noble actions, of jurisprudence, and of Roman history. Handicapped by these deficiencies in their
own profession, they were incapable of moving from attack to pleasant
wit, from analysis to synthesis.[19]

Yet *negotium* triumphed in Cicero's life. His fifty-eight orations reflect the tumultuous last years of the Roman Republic. He remains
throughout, from the Verrine to the Catilinarian orations (which earned
him the title "father of his country") and finally to the Philippics (which
portray the end of the drama), sincerely devoted to his ideals of public
responsibility. In politics he is an idealist who lives with the nostalgia of
a past Roman greatness, a moral greatness equal to the political greatness of a free republic. The two are inseparable. Consequently he remains attached, throughout his life, to those who seem to him *boni,* good
in the old sense, no matter to what party they belonged. Here—we can
judge from our distance—he commits, at times, some serious errors.

Finally, during the last ten years of his life, embittered by public and
personal tragedies (his break with Caesar, divorce from his wife Terentia,
marriage followed by divorce from a young woman, the death of his
beloved daughter Tullia, and the rise to power of his archenemy Antony)
he withdrew completely into the seclusion of an *otium* that reveals him
more active than ever before, this time in writing. He longs to tear away
from Greece the glory of philosophy and give it to Rome. With the loss
of freedom, he fears that the death of eloquence is imminent. Writing in
a new idiom, substantially his own creation, he labors over twenty or so
philosophical works.[20] His aim is now clearly to open to the Romans the
road to acquiring the moral ideal that was the glory of the Greeks.

Far from betraying his devotion to *negotium* in this latter period, he
complements it by trying to create what makes the *vir vere romanus*
(truly Roman man). With the exceptions of the *Academica,* dedicated to
the problem of knowledge, and the *De natura deorum, De divinatione,*
and *De fato,* which deal with theological matters, Cicero's philosophical
works develop a practical philosophy, inspired by a deep concern for
defining the duties of the citizen toward his country and of man toward
himself as *homo,* partaking of a common *humanitas.* They seek to provide solace for pain and death and to instill faith in the immortality of
the soul. His themes are therefore the highest good, human happiness,
justice, and duty. The center of his attention is always his beloved *respublica* in which he sees, like the historian Polybius, a perfect fusion of
the three forms of government. As in politics, so in ethics, Cicero is motivated by a deeply felt need to refrain from abstractions and utopian
dreams. It is primarily in the *De officiis* that his ideal of *homo humanus*
achieves its most convincing and passionate expression. He transfers into

the Roman world the noble ideas of the Stoic Panaetius, who belonged to that Scipionic circle to which Cicero owes so much. Rome, he believes, should aspire to a universal ethical ideal beyond its political power.

The fusion of *otium* and *negotium* is most evident in Cicero's oratorical works. They reflect an alternation of reasoning or argumentation with a direct "speaking to the soul," as Cicero says in the *Brutus*.[21] The most mature of these is the *De oratore,* whose interlocutors all belong to the past. The scene is Cicero's villa in Tusculum. The subject: What is the substance of eloquence? The answer: *Humanitas.* The ideal orator combines the Greek ideal of *paideia* (education) with the Roman practical political spirit. This concept is at the heart of the humanists' attraction to Cicero. Two years after *De oratore,* in 46 B.C., in the midst of dark political turmoil, Cicero wrote a complementary treatise, *Orator,* the subject of which is the beauty of the word, the great variation of oratorical styles necessary if the orator wants to persuade and to conquer, and the importance of rhythm even in prose. The trilogy is completed by the *Brutus,* a chronological presentation of the history of eloquence. The book closes with an intellectual self-portrait, the first of its kind in classical antiquity.[22] In all these works, taken singly and as a whole, we find a writer who believed that political life provided the best means of self-expression and a political man who found in literature the expression of his deepest *humanitas.*

While the Rome of his time is the substance of his work, one cannot escape the conviction that the principal character in the play is Cicero himself, with an uninterrupted faith in his ability and achievements and a corresponding indignation at seeing unworthy people placed ahead of him. His desire for glory is the inexhaustible stimulus to his action—a glory characterized by virtue or honesty and uprightness, but still a desire for glory. Cicero feels this glory coming to him by virtue of his political ideals and the expression he was capable of giving to them through his eloquence.

The only literary expression in which Cicero reveals himself in his everyday clothing are his letters. This explains the surprise, not to mention the intense pleasure, of Petrarch when he discovered in Verona in 1345 Cicero's *Letters to Atticus, Quintus, and Brutus.*[23] With his discovery Petrarch, who had until then intensely admired the great official Cicero, was suddenly allowed to live near him as a *homo* torn by personal dilemmas due to weaknesses he does not always recognize. That Petrarch should have continued to love and admire Cicero after having seen him in all his frailty is fundamental to understanding the kind of relationship he had with Cicero. Petrarch saw his faults and wished Cicero had been different, but forgave him.

Like Cicero, Petrarch was and remained politically a conservative incapable of accepting innovations. Also like Cicero, he was inclined to all sorts of sacrifices for the sake of peace. He was thus led to analyze critically the relation between Cicero and Caesar. Why did Cicero, after long hesitation, finally break with Caesar, who represented a future of peace and strength, and turn to a defeated and weak Pompey? Petrarch interpreted his decision not as a heroic loyalty to his moral principles but as a stubborn incapacity to give in to what was best for peace.[24]

Petrarch decided to collect and make public his own letters in a period of intense literary activity and also of a certain political involvement between 1353 and 1361. Cicero was obviously his inspiration. His motivation remained, however, that of a person who seeks *otium* and hates *negotium*. In the preface to his *Letters on Familiar Matters* he characterizes his style as similar to Cicero's but defines very differently from Cicero his attitude toward *negotium:*

> In his orations [Cicero] displayed an extraordinary force, pouring forth a bright and rapid flood of eloquence. Cicero used this manner very often in defense of his friends and often against his political enemies . . . and forty-four times for himself. But I am inexpert in this kind of thing, for I have avoided public responsibilities and while no doubt I have been pricked by vague anonymous murmurings and whisperings, I have never till now suffered any legal injury that I had to counter or evade; and it is not my practice to intervene in the case of others' wrongs. For I have not learned to frequent the law-courts and to lend my tongue to others. My nature is averse and reluctant to this sort of thing. It has made me a lover of silence and solitude, an enemy of the courts, a despiser of money. It is fortunate that I haven't had to practice that lawyer-craft; I might have done it very badly.
>
> So I have rejected the oratorical style which I don't need and which I don't do naturally. (Even if it overflowed in me I have no occasion to use it.)[25]

It follows that Petrarch's letters, unlike Cicero's, are not a reflection of his era's living political life, but also that Petrarch saw clearly the basic difference between himself and his admired friend and teacher. He was born for cultivating *otium;* a full-time dedication to the study of literature was his *negotium,* and he was never asked to take up any other form. His political involvement, when it took place, was a willful act on his part, as in the case of his support of Cola di Rienzo.

Politically, Petrarch leaned toward those who, like the Visconti of

Milan or the Venetian aristocrats, assured his freedom to study.[26] Indeed, during the last twenty years of his life Petrarch tried to find for himself that ideal setting which would allow him complete intellectual independence. In an invective written in 1355 against the nephew of Pope John XXII, Petrarch defended himself against his Florentine friends who had accused him of betraying his republican political ideals by accepting the hospitality of the Visconti despots of Milan. Not so, declared Petrarch. All he wanted from them was a guarantee of intellectual independence, "leisure, silence, serenity, and freedom."

Political leaders in Italy found a scholar as renowned as Petrarch an ornament for their courts, which added to their prestige and credibility. For this reason, Petrarch was able to obtain for himself a social status that few intellectuals have enjoyed in any age. Interestingly, Petrarch could, as he did in a letter to Guido Setto in 1355, dramatically contrast the political condition of Italy to his own, describing the condition of Italy as miserable but his own as satisfactory.

Petrarch's expressed need for *otium* was sincere. A minimum of security that allowed him to live without worry, the possibility of seclusion from the hoi polloi whom he despised, were the essential requirements of his *negotium*. Acquisition of knowledge that would help humanity and lead to discovery of the true self required peace. In this respect, Petrarch felt a kinship with Cicero, who needed *otium* for the same purpose during the last years of his life.

The *otium* desired by Petrarch was different from that of the religious. The layman dedicated to *otium*, says Petrarch, "spends his life praising God and liberal studies, invents new things and remembers those discovered by the ancients, takes a necessary rest and enjoys a few honest pleasures and thus loses a little or nothing of his day."[27] Here, indeed, we are close to the world of Epicurus, whom Cicero could not but praise as an individual, but whose doctrine he considered deleterious for humanity because of its aloofness from political and social responsibilities. But there is a second, more important difference between Petrarch's *otium* and that of the religious. For Petrarch *otium* offered the possibility of achieving fame. And that is precisely what his writing meant to him. In the *Secretum*, in which he has himself questioned by Augustine on the causes of his unhappiness with the world and with himself, he agrees with Augustine that he will renounce many things, including his love for Laura; but he will not agree to renounce fame. At the end of the dialogue Augustine asks Petrarch to abandon his Latin poem *Africa*, from which he expected the greatest recognition, and his work on Roman history, *De viris illustribus*, in order to devote all his time to his own soul. Cicero is quoted in support of Augustine's point, saying that a wise man's life is a preparation for death. Yet Petrarch stubbornly insists that even if he wanted to do differently he could not. And the two part with Augustine declaring: "Well, so it must be, if it cannot be otherwise."

Fame, however, is the reputation that comes from the expression of noble thoughts. Writing is a way of making humanity better. This is the essential point of contact between Petrarch and Cicero. What Petrarch enthusiastically embraces in Cicero and feels deeply congenial to his own needs is the concept of *humanitas* with all its lofty moral and aristocratic implications. Through literature, the *litterae humanae,* man actualizes the loftiest part of himself. To be a *literatus* in this sense is to achieve the noblest thing possible in any profession, and one can rightly expect public recognition from it. For Petrarch, as for Cicero, glory is something real and legitimately desirable.[28]

Finally, however, Petrarch would like to be able to read the *humanitas Romana* in light of the *humanitas Christiana.* In *De ignorantia* he says the following about Cicero:

> Of all the writings of Cicero, those from which I often received the most powerful inspiration are the three books which . . . he entitled *On the Nature of the Gods.* There the great genius speaks of the gods and often ridicules and despises them—not too seriously, it is true. It may be that he was afraid of capital punishment. . . . When I read these passages, I often have compassion for his fate and grieve in silent sorrow that this man did not know the true God. He died only a few years before the birth of Christ. . . . When the same Cicero in his later years, in the books he wrote *About the Gods*—not about God—gains control of himself, how he is lifted up by the wings of genius! At times you would think you were hearing not a pagan philosopher but an Apostle.[29]

Petrarch sought to use Cicero in such a way as to gain a wisdom that is finally beyond knowledge and can contribute to a *humanitas Christiana.*

* * *

It is difficult to summarize Petrarch's *De ignorantia,* which he defines as invective, a genre he resurrects from antiquity. Its focus is on the purpose of learning, a recurrent theme in Petrarch's writings and one close to his heart. He regards learning for learning's sake as totally useless, if not damaging, and especially—as Cicero says—if it is done "in confused and undisciplined order and with much frivolity and vain boasting."[30] The learning of facts is equally pointless unless they are directed towards a better knowledge of the self. "What is the use, I beseech you, of knowing the nature of quadrupeds, fowl, fishes and serpents and not knowing or even neglecting man's nature, the purpose for which we are born, and whence and whereto we travel." [31]

With irony and sarcasm Petrarch tries to prove that the four learned men who accuse him of ignorance are actually the ignorant ones. As for himself, he is happy to believe in God rather than in Plato, Aristotle, Varro, and Cicero who, with all their knowledge, did not know the true God. Petrarch is calling here for the theological virtues (faith, hope, and love) to replace or complement the cardinal virtues (fortitude, justice, temperance or continence, and prudence), which are the quintessence of Cicero's uprightness (*honestum*). *Humanitas* for Cicero implied the exercise of these virtues. But in his now lost *Hortensius*, Cicero expressed himself, at least in Augustine's interpretation, in such a way as to allow room for love and hope, if not faith. Petrarch exploits this ambiguity in Cicero. Hence his continual references to Cicero throughout the invective for support of his own thesis. This thesis can be summarized in his own words:

> Sorrowfully and tacitly I recognize my ignorance, when I consider how much I lack of what my mind in its craving for knowledge is sighing for. But until the end of the present exile has come and terminated this our imperfection by which we know in part (1 Cor. 13:9) I console myself with the consideration that this belongs to our common nature. . . . How infinitely small, I beseech you, is the greatest amount of knowledge granted to one single mind.[32]

It is the old motif, "I know this one thing, that I know nothing." At the same time, however, and with an ever greater strength, Petrarch insists on an element hardly Ciceronian: "My portion shall be humility and ignorance, knowledge of my own weakness and contempt for nothing except the world and myself and . . . furthermore, distrust in myself and hope in Thee."[33] Cicero did not conceive in any way of this kind of *docta ignorantia* or learned ignorance as it was to be expressed during the Quattrocento by Nicholas of Cusa. But the notion is a leitmotif in the *De ignorantia.*

Nonetheless, Cicero, at least in Petrarch's interpretation of him, was much closer to a Christian understanding of learning than Aristotle, for unlike Aristotle, who taught us what it means to be good, Cicero inspires us to be good through the words that sting and move to action:

> I have read all of Aristotle's moral books. . . . Sometimes I have perhaps become more learned through them when I went home,

but not better, not so good as I ought to be; and I often complained to myself, occasionally to others too, that by no facts was
the promise fulfilled which the philosopher makes at the beginning
of the first book of his Ethics, namely, that "we learn this part of
philosophy not with the purpose of gaining knowledge but of becoming better." I see virtue, and all that is peculiar to vice as well
as to virtue, egregiously defined and distinguished by him and
treated with penetrating insight. When I learn all this, I know a
little bit more than I knew before, but mind and will remain the
same as they were, and I myself remain the same. It is one thing to
know, another to love; one thing to understand, another to will.
He teaches what virtue is, I do not deny that; but his lesson lacks
the words that sting and set afire and urge toward love of virtue
and hatred of vice or, at any rate, does not have enough of such
power. He who looks for that will find it in our Latin writers, especially in Cicero and Seneca, and, what may be astonishing to hear,
in Horace, a poet somewhat rough in style but most pleasing in his
maxims.
    . . . Aristotle was a man who ridiculed Socrates, the father of this
kind of philosophy, calling him—to use his own words—"a ped-
dler in morals," and despised him, if we believe Cicero. . . . No
wonder he is slow in rousing the mind and lifting it up to virtue.
However, everyone who has become thoroughly familiar with our
Latin authors knows that they stamp and drive deep into the heart
the sharpest and most ardent stings of speech, by which the lazy
are startled, the ailing are kindled, and the sleepy aroused, the sick
healed, and the prostrate raised, and those who stick to the ground
lifted up to the highest thoughts and to honest desire.[34]

Petrarch rejects the cardinal virtues as expressed by Aristotle, but he
is ready to accept them again in the Latin authors, especially Cicero,
because of the power of words that sting and arouse. Thus the *humanitas
Romana* of Cicero is accepted by Petrarch in the sense supported by the
myth that the origin of civilization lay in the marriage of wisdom and
eloquence, that is, in the power of the word when it is fed by noble
thoughts. "The highest thoughts and the noblest desires" are the aims of
Cicero's *humanitas*, but they cannot be transmitted to man except
through the word that stings and arouses, heals and lifts up. For this
reason Cicero is the principal author with whom Petrarch dialogues in
De ignorantia. "I still read the works of poets and philosophers, particularly those of Cicero," he says, "with whose genius and style I have been
particularly delighted since my early youth. I find much eloquence in
them and . . . power of words."[35] Genius and style, mind and words,

eloquence and philosophy are, for Petrarch as for Cicero, conceived together.

It is in this respect that Petrarch sees an affinity between Cicero and
Christianity, for Christianity also not only teaches us what the good is
but seeks to arouse us to do the good. He almost coopts Cicero into a
Christian frame of reference, as indicated in the quotation at the end of
the preceding section; but he finally draws back, quoting Lactantius in
criticism of Cicero's notion of the gods. But his desire to claim Cicero for
the same reasons that he claims Christianity are evident later in the invective, when he discusses Cicero's *Hortensius*. For here the emphasis is
almost wholly on the question of willing virtue. And those who teach us
to will the good are close indeed to Christianity, even though they may
not be Christian:

> For though our ultimate goal does not lie in virtue, where the phi-
> losophers locate it, it is through the virtues that the direct way
> leads to the place where it does lie; and these virtues, I must add,
> must be not merely known but loved. Therefore, the true moral
> philosophers and useful teachers of the virtues are those whose first
> and last intention is to make hearer and reader good, those who do
> not merely teach what virtue and vice are but . . . sow into our
> hearts love of the best and eager desire for it and at the same time
> hatred of the worst and how to flee it. It is safer to strive for a
> good and pious will than for a capable and clear intellect. The ob-
> ject of the will . . . is to be good; that of the intellect is truth. It is
> better to will the good than to know the truth. . . . Therefore, those
> are far wrong who consume their time in learning to know virtue
> instead of acquiring it, and, in a still higher degree, those whose
> time is spent in learning to know God instead of loving Him. . . .
> Things that are absolutely unknown are not loved; but, for those
> to whom more is not granted, it is sufficient to know God and vir-
> tue so far as to know that He is the most lucid, the most fragrant,
> the most delectable, the inexhaustible source of all that is good,
> from which, through which, and in which we are as good as we
> are, and to know that virtue is the best thing next to God Him-
> self.[36]

The *humanitas Christiana* of love and hope here complements the *humanitas Romana* of Cicero in which virtue for virtue's sake reigns supreme. Once again, Petrarch professes to be a Ciceronian in the sense
that he admires Cicero, but a Christian in the object of his truth and
happiness. He believes, however, "that Cicero himself would have been
a Christian if he had been able to see Christ and to comprehend his

doctrine."[37] Banking heavily on the authority of Augustine, who says the same of Plato, he asks himself: "If this fundament stands, in what way is Ciceronian eloquence opposed to Christian dogma? Or how is it harmful to consult Cicero's writings?"[38] This is no rhetorical question but the logical conclusion of Petrarch's premises.

A number of conclusions can be drawn from the preceding analysis. First, by rejecting moral imitation of pagan classics Petrarch establishes a world of his own, quite distinct from the authors whom he considers so close to him in spirit, though not in time, thus revealing a remarkable historical sense. Second, the real basis of Petrarch's love for Cicero is Cicero's eloquence; but eloquence does not involve words alone, it involves also an ethical theory. It follows further that for Petrarch, to be a Ciceronian means to emulate Cicero's eloquence. But while, as regards rhetorical theory, he agrees wholly with Cicero, as regards ethical theory, he is enriched by a Christian perspective that goes beyond earthly virtue to embrace faith, hope, and love. But the two worlds—pagan and Christian—are not now so much opposed as they are complementary to one another.

In arriving at this standpoint Petrarch went through a considerable development. In his early youth he focused primarily on the classics, and his admiration for classical authors was unbounded. Then around 1340 he began reading Christian authors, most notably Augustine, and a crisis ensued that was reflected in the *Secretum* and in much of his poetry. The crisis cannot be identified simply as a conflict between pagan and Christian values. Rather, the dilemma that tortured Petrarch throughout his life was more a conflict between his intense desire for inwardness and the demands of the external world, which—in the form of his love for Laura and for glory—pressed strongly upon him. Petrarch's letters to and about Cicero are part of his inward life, and an analysis of them will clarify the role Cicero plays in Petrarch's basic conflict.

*   *   *

What induced Petrarch to collect his letters? "What is to keep me from looking back, like a weary traveler from a height at the end of a long journey, and reviewing the stages of my early progress?" Thus he writes in 1350 in the letter that serves as a preface to his collected *Letters on Familiar Matters* or *Familiares*.[39] From this epistle we learn why he collected his correspondence and how he views his life.

Petrarch has a tragic concept of life. Time flees inexorably. "Time has slipped through our fingers" stands at the opening of the letter as its motivation. Death is present in every instant. "The remembrance of life's brevity assails me."[40] He sees himself as a knight errant, spurred on from adventure to adventure by his own anguish. "Compare my wanderings with those of Ulysses," he says, reminding the reader that, as the son of a Florentine exile, he had from childhood "experienced perils and fears in his wandering life," and had never been allowed "to cast anchor in any harbor." His purpose here, however, is to attribute his many correspondents to his mobility and, by contrast, to indicate why Cicero and Seneca, his great masters in letter writing, had only a few. Thus his style is different. But the issue gives him the opportunity to hint at his moral restlessness.

One of the causes of embarrassment in collecting his letters is making known his own moral weaknesses. In 1350, after the great plague had created a physical vacuum around him and had reinforced his ascetic tendencies, his letters reflect in their language a weakness "filled with unmanly whinings." "Was I indeed a man in youth, to become a boy in old age?"[41] Since his earlier letters reflect greater fortitude, he would like to change the order of the letters to conceal his recent weakness. He reflects, however, that he is now beginning to feel stronger, so that perhaps the letters demonstrating his weakness will be followed by still others in which his strength will reassert itself.

Petrarch collects his letters as part of his never-ending desire for fame—the same reason he collected his poems: "Naturally I was drawn by no small affection for my own inventions." "I wondered," he writes, "what foundations I had laid, what would remain of all my toils and vigils."[42] Looking through the material in 1350, he experiences a sensation not unlike the sensation of looking down from the top of Mont Ventoux after the painful ascent. He sees from a point of arrival in his own life how he had lived his life. He hardly recognizes some of his letters and poems because his point of view has altered so greatly. His style has changed with life itself. Thus the lack of coherence in style is only apparent: his style reflects his life at various stages, and through every stage he writes. Petrarch's life is writing. "When I stop writing," he says, "I think I'll stop living."[43] He lives his life by mirroring it in his own writings.

In his introductory letter we discover also why Petrarch was moved to the rather strange choice—as he admits himself—of writing to people long dead. His best correspondents, he says, share with him his concept of life as eternally changing, the conviction that the flow can be stopped only for an instant and then only through the pen, the feeling that we must fight for a continual improvement of ourselves, and the belief that the *literatus* reflects in his writings his own life and the lives of others as he sees them. But where among his contemporaries can he find these attitudes? He feels isolated in his own age and finds in the past those who share his views. Cicero is his principal guide. "Seneca crammed into his letters all the moral system of his books, while Cicero treats philosophical matters in his books and puts domestic news and timely gossip in his letters."[44] Petrarch agrees with Cicero's procedure, regarding his letters as "delightful reading" which "relax from concentration on difficult subjects," and he shares Cicero's conviction that "the proper aim of the letter is to tell the addressee something he doesn't know."[45]

Petrarch addressed two letters to Cicero and discussed Cicero in a number of others. What do they reveal? A letter written at the end of Petrarch's life (March or April 1374) constitutes the epitome of what Cicero meant to him.[46] Petrarch says in the letter that "from my very childhood . . . I fell in love with Cicero's work whether by natural instinct or at my father's urging."[47] The consequence of this love is evident in the judgment Petrarch passes on his father: he might have become a great scholar had life given him a chance. We can deduce from this judgment that Cicero is the best possible guide for one who would become a scholar. Cicero's writings possess that inner spark which spurs one on to understand better what one is reading. The proof of this Petrarch finds in the fact that even as an old man his feelings in relation to Cicero are those he nourished as a young boy. "It is remarkable that while I didn't understand anything, I already felt exactly what I feel today, when after all I do understand something, little though it be."[48]

Petrarch's humanistic studies were interrupted by the study of law—a lost seven years in his view. His father, who pushed him in this direction, also burned his "classics" when he discovered that Petrarch still studied them secretly. Responding to Petrarch's tears on the occasion, however, he pulled out of the fire Vergil and Cicero's *Rhetoric*, telling his son that he could read the first to relax his mind and the other to assist him in his law studies. Thus Cicero became—as he desired to be—a guide in practical life.

After the death of his father, Petrarch turned away from the study of law, and Cicero became his principal guide in studies as well as in life. He describes his relentless search for Cicero's works and his sole preoccupation with them, a prejudice confirmed by his reading of Quintilian who, like Petrarch, preferred Cicero to Seneca. Great was his joy when he discovered a new work by Cicero or even obtained defective copies of works he already possessed. But great also was his sorrow when he lost any work by Cicero, as happened in the case of some he loaned to his old teacher, Convenevole da Prato, who had pawned them out of economic necessity. Petrarch sought diligently to locate the pawned works of Cicero—caring nothing about the other books he had lost—but to no avail. Interestingly, Petrarch says that at this time he "never touched any sacred writings." Although he was later to do so, Cicero was the most formative influence in his early development.

Petrarch felt isolated in his own time, because few around him shared his conviction that education is the process of self-understanding. His writing was an escape from the isolation in which he lived: "I am forever talking, forever writing, not so much to benefit our times, which have fallen to such a sad state, as to discharge my mind and myself of my thoughts by writing them down."[49] It is for the same reason that he quotes the ancients so abundantly: "I write for myself and while I am writing I eagerly converse with our predecessors in the only way I can; and I gladly dismiss from mind the men with whom I am forced by an unkind fate to live."[50] The sight of his contemporaries offends him but that of the ancients inspires him, for in them he finds magnificent deeds and glorious names, which fill him with unspeakable joy, and none more so than Cicero.

The solitude and seclusion of his country home in the Vaucluse is ideal for the creation of a republic of letters that does not obey the laws of time and space. In a letter written from there in 1352, he describes his relation with Cicero in such intimate, but at the same time concrete, terms as to make a reader ignorant of history believe that Cicero lived in Provence around 1350. "Escaping lately, as it is my custom, the noise of the hateful city, I took refuge in my transalpine Helicon, and with me came your Cicero. He was amazed by the place." Together they "spent ten tranquil leisurely days together, and I think he enjoyed his stay and my company."[51] Cicero brought with him many noble companions, all of whom became Petrarch's intimates:

> Cicero was accompanied by many eminent superior men. Not to mention the Greeks, there were Brutus, Atticus, and Herennius whom Cicero has made famous. There was the most learned Marcus Varro, with whom Cicero likes to stroll in the academic groves. There were Cotta Velleius and Lucilius Balbo with whom Cicero made keen examinations of the nature of the gods. There were Nigidius and Cratippus with whom he sought out the secrets of nature and essence of the world. There was his brother Quintus Cicero . . . and his son Marcus Cicero. . . . The orator Hortensius was there and Epicurus. . . . With Laelius and Scipio he defined true friendship and the proper form of the republic. And not to prolong this endlessly, foreign kings mingled with the Roman citizens and with them Cicero expounded his views on matters of the

highest moment with truly divine utterances. And, my friend . . .
Milo was defended, Lateranus reprehended, Sulla excused, and
Pompey praised.[52]

This description of a party of illustrious men marks the birth of humanism as a dialogue with antiquity. The Greeks are left respectfully aside.
They are for the time being hardly known. And the Romans are chosen
among those whom Cicero immortalized in his dialogues. One or two
generatons after Petrarch, his successors—Poggio, Bruni, Valla—rees-
tablished with contemporary persons a full-fledged Ciceronian dialogue.

The purpose of dialogue is not imitation but emulation. In a letter
written in 1360,[53] Petrarch declares that while in the past he placed his
trust solely in the ancients, now he places it also in himself. As a young
man he trusted what he read, as an older man he trusts what he knows
through his own experience. Now, he says, "I need no authority of poet
or philosopher. I am my own witness, my own author."[54] Real love—as
his love for Cicero—sets him free to be himself. This, in the final analysis, is the purpose of a liberal education.

The development of this attitude is evident in an incident that took
place nine years before the letter above was written.[55] Petrarch was returning home with some friends one evening and the conversation turned
to Cicero. He discovered in the group a man who loved Cicero even more
than he did—at least the man upbraided him for having criticized Cicero
in letters Petrarch had addressed to him. Petrarch uses the occasion to
affirm that Cicero had his faults, which he himself recognized and be-
wailed, but that he nonetheless rose above these in his works. Petrarch
says that he wrote letters to Cicero initially because he found in him
much to admire but also some things that disturbed him. Perhaps today,
he says, I would not have written them. They were products of a younger
enthusiasm. It is time for us to look at these two letters.

The first one Petrarch wrote from Verona on 16 June 1345, shortly
after he had discovered Cicero's familiar letters.[56] "I could hear your
voice, Marcus Tullius, confessing much, complaining of much." Much
that Petrarch read he did not approve:

Why did you choose to involve yourself in so many vain conten-
tions? . . . Why did you abandon the retirement proper to your
age, profession, and fortune? . . . What tempted you to dealings
that brought you to a death unworthy of a philosopher? Alas you
forgot your own advice to your brother Quintus. . . . I omit your
treatment of Julius Caesar whose well-tested clemency set free even
those who assailed him. . . . I am filled with shame and distress for

your errors. . . . What avails it to instruct others . . . to be forever
talking in elegant phrases if you do not listen to your own words?
. . . How much better it would have been for you the philosopher
to have grown old in country peace, meditating, as you yourself
write somewhere, on eternal life, not on transitory existence!

In the history of Cicero's *fortuna* this letter stands as a landmark because
it presupposes a unity of the man and the writer, criticizing the man
because he did not live up to the nobility evident in the writer. Lorenzo
Valla later criticized Cicero for the opposite: for not having behaved in
his writings sufficiently as an orator, but rather having given himself over
to the abstractions of the philosophers. Petrarch identifies with the humanity of Cicero—his weak and noble sides and his inability to unify
the two.

The second letter to Cicero, written six months later, adopts a different tone. "If you are offended, let this letter mollify you and prove that
the truth is not always hateful. . . . It was your life that I censured, not
your mind and your tongue. I admire your mind, I am bewitched by your
tongue. . . . I am sorry for your life."[57] The letter, from beginning to end,
is a touching testimony to the concrete substance of dialogue with the
ancient writers so characteristic of humanism in Petrarch and after:

> O great father of Roman eloquence, I thank you, as do all who
> bedeck themselves with the flowers of the Latin language. It is
> from your fount that we draw the waters that bathe our fields. We
> are sustained by your leadership, by your words of encouragement,
> by the light that illumines our simplicity. It is by your presence in
> spirit that we have gained whatever art and principles in writing
> we may possess.[58]

It is because of Cicero's great value in this respect that Petrarch bemoans
once again the loss or corruption of Cicero's works—as well as those of
other great writers—through time. He bewails also the state of Rome
itself, which, if Cicero could know it, would bring tears to his eyes. The
two are, however, united in the values of Roman culture, their separation
in time notwithstanding.

Petrarch often regrets the loss of learning that has resulted from the
perishing of manuscripts, the fact that "books that are naturally obscure
have become totally unintelligible . . . and have perished utterly. Thus
our time has lost bit by bit some of the sweetest fruits of literature,
wasted the toils and vigils of our most superior intellects, and squan-
dered, I venture to say, the most excellent products of our world."[59] It is

for this reason that "I put my weary fingers and my frayed and well-worn pen to the task," and he sees himself, in so doing, as performing a service to humanity. When he discovered that Cicero himself had copied down the orations of others, his joy was complete. "I was so stirred by this experience that I was confirmed in my purpose."[60] "If ever anything can emerge from my darkness to increase the splendor of his celestial eloquence," he concludes, "it will perhaps be due chiefly to this fact, that I was so captured by his indescribable sweetness that I performed the naturally tedious work of writing with so much eagerness that I was hardly aware of it."[61]

The relationship Petrarch entertains with Cicero is so intimate that he can even afford to joke about it. "Listen," he says, "to the trick Cicero played on me—Cicero whom I have loved and cherished since boyhood! I have a great volume of his letters, which I wrote out some time ago with my own hand, since it was too hard for the scribes."[62] This book, he tells his correspondent, was placed standing on the library floor and, caught by the edge of Petrarch's gown, fell more than once and wounded his leg. The wound became swollen and infected and caused him great trouble. Perhaps, he jokes, Cicero was angry at being placed on the floor and wanted to be placed higher up.

Cicero's voice remained always with Petrarch, exhorting him to live with humanity. Even if Petrarch rejected the humanity of his time, indeed precisely for this reason, Cicero's voice was an incitement to live life as a *homo,* learning how to cope with human frailty, treasuring the joy of his mission to transmit human values currently neglected from a glorious past to future generations. Renaissance humanism found one of its most authentic reflections in Petrarch's encounter with Cicero.

NOTES

1. Valla, *Antidotum in Poggium,* 1, quoted in S. Camporeale, *L. Valla, Umanesimo e teologia* (Florence, 1972), 94.
2. *Letters from Petrarch,* ed. and trans. M. Bishop (Bloomington, IN, 1966), 295.
3. See R. J. Deferrari, "St. Ambrose and Cicero," *Philological Quarterly* 1 (1922): 142.
4. Augustine, *Confessions* 3.4, trans. W. Watts (Cambridge, MA, 1919).
5. See J. E. Seigel, *Rhetoric and Philosophy in Renaissance Humanism: The Union of Eloquence and Wisdom, Petrarch to Valla* (Princeton, 1968), esp. chaps. 1–2.
6. Cicero, *Tusculan Disputations* and *On Duties.* See also M. Liscu, *Etude sur la philosophie morale chez Ciceron* (Paris, 1950), 229–71; P. M. Valente, *L'Ethique stoicienne chez Ciceron* (Paris, 1956), chaps. 2–4. See now, M. Lorch, *Valla's Defense of Life: A Theory of Pleasure* (Munich, 1985).

7. See Chapter 7, below in this volume.

8. Machiavelli, *The Prince and the Discourses*, intro. M. Lerner (New York, 1950), *Prince*, chap. 25.

9. See Chapter 5, below in this volume, and C. Trinkaus, *In Our Image and Likeness: Humanity and Divinity in Italian Humanist Thought*, 2 vols. (Chicago, 1970), vol. 1, chap. 1; and J. H. Whitfield, *Petrarch and the Renascence* (New York, 1965), chap. 3.

10. See E. Paratore, "Cicerone attraverso i secoli," in *Marco Tullio Cicerone* (Florence, 1961), 235–53.

11. See G. Boissier, *Ciceron et ses amis* (Paris, 13th ed. 1905).

12. *Homo* is the human being, understood generically. *Vir* is the person of virtue, superior to other animals because of reason.

13. C. T. Lewis and C. Short, eds., *A Latin Dictionary* (Oxford, 1879, repr. 1962), 1285.

14. Cicero uses the phrases "oti moderati atque honesti" (*Brutus*, 2.8); "otii ad scribendum" (*De oratore*, 1.1.3); "Tusculani requiem atque otium" (ibid., 1.52.224); "otium suum consumpsit in historia scribenda" (ibid., 2.13.57); "otio literato" (*Tusc.*, 5.36.105).

15. Cicero, *De officiis*, 1.21.70.

16. See Cicero, *De oratore*, 2.6.23.

17. Cicero, *Pro Murena*, 8.18.

18. Cornelius Nepos, *Atticus*, 16.3. Similarly G. Leopardi, *Zibaldone di pensieri*, ed. F. Flora (Milan, 1937; 7th ed., 1967), vol. 1, pt. 3, 144, 380; and *Marco Tullio Cicerone*, 35.

19. Cicero, *Brutus*, 93.322.

20. He lists them in *De divinatione*, 2.1.1–4.

21. Cicero, *Brutus*, 23.89.

22. See G. Misch, *Autobiographie in Altertum* (Leipzig, 1907), 196ff.

23. Cicero gathered his letters (which were always dictated and vary from formal dispatches and pamphlets to hurried notes) in two great collections. The first includes the *Epistolae ad Atticum* in sixteen books, never edited by Cicero and covering the period from 67 to 44 B.C.; and the *Familiares*, also in sixteen books, which contain replies as well and were published after Claudius's rule. Two smaller collections of letters include the three books to his brother Quintus from 60 to 54 B.C. and the two books to and from Brutus covering the last year of Cicero's life.

24. On Petrarch's changing interpretations of Caesar, see H. Baron, "The Evolution of Petrarch's Thought: Reflections on the State of Petrarch Studies," in *From Petrarch to Leonardo Bruni* (Chicago, 1968), 7–50, esp. 34–41.

25. *Letters from Petrarch*, 17.

26. In a short treatise in 1373, *De republica administranda*, and in a letter to Francesco da Carrara, Petrarch celebrates the ideal prince who is just and enlightened because he generously supports intellectual work. The letter to Francesco da Carrara has been translated in *The Earthly Republic: Italian Humanists on Government and Society*, ed. B. G. Kohl and R. G. Witt with E. B. Welles (Philadelphia, 1978), 35–78. In another letter (*Familiares*,

12.2) to Niccolò Acciaiuoli he defines an *institutio regia*. See further the introductory essay by Kohl in *Earthly Republic,* 25–34; and R. Amaturo, *Francesco Petrarca* (Rome, 1980).

27. U. Bosco, *F. Petrarca* (Milan, 1956), 110.
28. See Cicero, *Tusc.,* 3.2.
29. Translated in *The Renaissance Philosophy of Man,* ed. E. Cassirer, P. O. Kristeller, and J. H. Randall, Jr. (Chicago, 1948), 79–80.
30. *Tusc.,* 2.4.12, quoted in *Renaissance Philosophy of Man,* 56.
31. *Renaissance Philosophy of Man,* 58–59.
32. Ibid., 66–67.
33. Ibid., 65.
34. Ibid., 103–4.
35. Ibid., 78.
36. Ibid., 105–6.
37. Ibid., 115.
38. Ibid.
39. *Letters from Petrarch,* 15–23.
40. Ibid., 16.
41. Ibid., 21.
42. Ibid., 16.
43. Ibid., 22.
44. Ibid., 20.
45. Ibid.
46. Ibid., 292–99.
47. Ibid., 292.
48. Ibid., 292–93.
49. Ibid., 68.
50. Ibid.
51. Ibid., 109.
52. Ibid., 110.
53. Ibid., 200–203.
54. Ibid., 202.
55. Ibid., 203–6.
56. Ibid., 206–7.
57. Ibid., 208–10, at 208.
58. Ibid., 208.
59. Ibid., 154–56 at 154.
60. Ibid., 155.
61. Ibid.
62. Ibid., 215–16, at 215.

5 &. PETRARCH, AUGUSTINE, AND THE CLASSICAL CHRISTIAN TRADITION
Albert Rabil, Jr.

IN 1896 A MANUSCRIPT OWNED BY PETRARCH WAS DISCOVERED that contained, on the flyleaf at the end, a list of books in Petrarch's handwriting. Petrarch labeled them "my specially prized books. To the others I usually resort not as a deserter but as a scout."[1] This list is, in fact, three lists, the first and third of which were written at the same time and earlier than the second.

Not surprisingly, at the head of the first list are a number of the philosophical works of Cicero, under the heading of *Moralia*. Below these are listed several rhetorical works, though these were added later, as is evident from the fact that Cicero's name appears opposite the philosophical titles at the center point of that list. The *Tusculan Disputations*, second on the list, is the most cited work of Cicero's in Petrarch's *Familiares* (more than six hundred citations). After Cicero comes Seneca—his letters (often cited by Petrarch), moral essays, and tragedies (not often cited). Seneca's *De remediis fortuitarum*, third on the list, became the basis for Petrarch's *De remediis utriusque fortunae*.[2] Aristotle's *Nicomachean Ethics* is squeezed in between Cicero and Seneca but was not written in at the same time as the original list.[3] Then come Boethius, eight historians (among whom Livy was his favorite), three exempla, the poets (headed, of course, by Vergil), grammarians with Priscian heading the list, one dialectical work and several astrological treatises.

The third list, written at the same time, contains only four works. All are by St. Augustine, though neither author nor subject is mentioned. The first is the *City of God*, by far the most often cited. Petrarch bought a copy of it in 1325; it is the earliest of Petrarch's known autographs yet to have been discovered.[4] The *Confessions* are next, known to have been in Petrarch's possession from 1333 and perhaps earlier, also frequently cited by him. The two other works mentioned are the *Soliloquies* and a letter to Proba, *On the Speaking God* (epistle 130).

The second list repeats some of the items from the first list: several of Cicero's philosophical works, Seneca's letters and tragedies, Boethius, several historians and poets. In addition, the list includes the book in which the list itself was written, a manuscript containing Cassiodorus's *On the Soul* and Augustine's *On True Religion*.

Petrarch owned many more books than those contained in these lists. It is impossible to date the lists by noting what is missing and when he obtained the works of missing authors or titles. Many of those missing are missing because they were not as avidly read and were not as important to him.[5] All the more striking, then, is the inclusion of St. Augustine, the only theological writer on either list. Striking also is Petrarch's testimony in his spiritual autobiography, begun when he was forty-three. Speaking to Augustine, his guide, he says, "from my youth upwards, I have had the increasing conviction that if in any matter I was inclined to think differently from yourself I was certain to be wrong."[6] What influence on Petrarch's intellectual development is discernible from his readings of these "favorite books" by Augustine?

*   *   *

Petrarch felt himself a stranger in the intellectual world in which he actually lived. It is unnecessary to cite his love for Cicero to account for his sense of estrangement. Appeal can be made equally well to the works of Augustine, and first of all to the *City of God*. In that treatise, written between 413 and 426 in the wake of the Roman Empire's collapse (Rome was sacked in 410), Augustine attempted to answer the charge of a number of pagan writers that Christianity was responsible for its collapse. In the first ten of the *City of God's* twenty-two books, Augustine pointed out that Rome's misfortunes antedated Christianity. He argued, too, that Rome was indeed crumbling and that it was due to the aim of Rome itself. Communities, he said, are defined in terms of what they love. There are two possibilities: the love of God and the love of earthly things. Those who love God belong to the City of God, and their reward is eternal. Those who love earthly things belong to the City of Man and are rewarded with earthly things. Now Rome sought temporal glory and achieved it. But since temporal glory is ephemeral, Rome was also ephemeral and was bound to crumble. There is nowhere in Augustine the lament of his contemporary, Jerome, that in the fall of Rome a world had collapsed, because for Augustine the world had not collapsed. Even as Rome was falling, he saw the Christian church building a new world on its ruins.

In the last twelve books Augustine presents the origin (books 11–14), history (books 15–18), and destiny (books 19–22) of the two cities. Their origin, as already recounted, is found in what each loves. The history of the two cities involves Augustine in a comparative analysis of Babylonian and Roman history on the one side and the history of the

Hebrews on the other. He does not, however, identify the City of God with the Bible: for although Abel, Noah, and Abraham represent the City of God, Cain, Esau, and Ishmael represent the City of Man. The jurisdictions of the two cities are overlapping. The real difference between the two is that the City of God is made up of people from all over the world; it is no respecter of geographical boundaries, as are earthly empires. The destinies of the two cities are also different. For Augustine the end is not like the beginning. The earthly city ends in destruction, the heavenly city in the Kingdom of God, of which no one can have a perfect vision in this life but only in the life to come.

There were three important ideas bequeathed by the *City of God* to the Middle Ages. First, Augustine's presentation of history was noneschatological. Many early Christians had believed (as Jesus probably also believed) that the world would end very soon. The fact that it did not posed a problem for Christian theology. Augustine's solution to this problem was that history may go on for a very long time but that Christian purposes are being worked out in it, no matter how long it lasts. Christians can stop worrying about when the world will end and build the City of God on earth (as far as this is possible). Second, Augustine presented a vision of Christianity as a universal phenomenon. It cut across all geographical boundaries, languages, cultures. Whereas politics presented a picture of a fragmented world, Christianity was a force for universal unity. The latter became the ideological underpinning for the development of the medieval papacy, which ended, in reality, just about the time Petrarch was born. Finally, Augustine made it clear that Christians are sojourners on this earth, that their true home is in heaven, and that while they are on earth their minds are nonetheless fastened on God. The otherworldliness of the Middle Ages, while it did not originate with Augustine, was powerfully reinforced by him and became one hallmark of medieval civilization.

Petrarch was not interested in eschatology, ecclesiastical ideology, or otherworldliness. Rather, what seeped into his consciousness from the *City of God* was Augustine's contrast, reiterated time and again, between the greatness of Rome and the fact that no earthly glory endures. This contrast led him to realize the futility of human life and the fleeting character of fame, even though, as we shall see, he refused in his *Secret* to give up his quest for earthly glory. This tension between detachment from and attachment to this world is exemplified in Petrarch's *dissidio,* or sadness of soul.[7]

Much attention has been given to Petrarch's *dissidio* in recent years, and though there are many differences in the way interpreters of Petrarch characterize it, there are some underlying similarities as well. Jerrold Seigel regards Petrarch's conflict as a function of the shift in intellectual center of gravity from philosophy to rhetoric.[8] Philosophy means here the search for what is true (in other words, wisdom), rhetoric the attempt to inspire men to action through persuasion. Philosophy thus aims at certainty and is contemplative; rhetoric cannot aspire to certainty inasmuch as its arena is the marketplace or the active lives of men. Cicero recognized the split between the two and refused to follow Aristotle in making rhetoric part of philosophy. Cicero's solution was to adopt alternately the more rigorous ethical position of the Stoics, according to which virtue is the only good, and the less rigorous ethical position of the Peripatetics, according to which there are several kinds of goods. The Stoics are closer to the truth but less relevant to life in the world, the Peripatetics more relevant to life in the world but further from wisdom. Petrarch rediscovered the Ciceronian model of the relation between rhetoric and philosophy and with it Cicero's conflict. Petrarch firmly believed that philosophy and rhetoric (eloquence) needed each other. Wisdom, he believed, could only be pursued in solitude, and he criticized the rhetorical ideal of the outward in favor of the inward life, using Augustine as his guide. But the full realization of the inward life is impossible and is removed from life in the world, to which rhetoric is much closer. Petrarch's *dissidio* was based on his striving for an ideal he could not attain; it represented the internal psychological conflict between his human nature and his divine vision. His union of the two came through his acceptance (following Cicero) of skepticism: the use of whatever philosophies were helpful.

Charles Trinkaus finds that Petrarch's "double consciousness" belongs to a long tradition traceable to Plato in the *Theaetetus;* it is the conflict between goodness and truth, or between will and intellect.[9] According to the Stoics there is an innate knowledge of the good within us, enabling us to know the good. Augustine draws on this tradition, developing the idea that there are two forms of knowledge, one derived from sense perception and another from inferior illumination. But for Augustine both forms of knowledge are controlled by the will. Trinkaus says that for Augustine the will "has become the deepest and most energetic part of the self, which has grown through attachment to customary ways and even more importantly through an innate joy in and love for the truth. Thus the will can be torn in opposite directions."[10] Reason cannot overcome the contradictions within the self because these lie deeper than reason, in the will. Conflict of will can be healed only through grace. "Insight concerning the self is not enough, either for Augustine or Petrarch, but insight concerning the self was a needed preliminary to the possibility of grace."[11] Petrarch found in Augustine one who had experienced the conflicts he was experiencing and who had also experienced the solution that he sought.[12]

As Trinkaus points out in an earlier study, Petrarch's solution was not very different from that of the Ockhamists, who also argued for the limitations of the intellect and placed the struggle for faith in the will. Petrarch rejected their solution, as he did also that of the Thomists, because the form of scholastic thought was incomprehensible and the content (dialectics and natural philosophy) irrelevant.[13] He was not indifferent to philosophy, but it was moral philosophy as practiced by Cicero and Augustine that represented the kind of philosophy relevant to his needs.[14]

The conflict that Trinkaus finds both in classical antiquity and in the medieval thought against which Petrarch reacted, William Bouwsma has found running through the thought of all Renaissance humanists, beginning with Petrarch.[15] One side of this conflict is represented by the Stoics who stand for a rational world view, in which human nature is derived from a view of the cosmos. Human nature thus tends to be viewed in relation to an intellectual approach to life—idealistically and impersonally. Stoicism emphasizes the contemplative quality—commensurate with the life of the mind—and the inwardness of freedom; it has little to say about active life, bodily existence, or the limitations of the will. Augustinianism, by contrast, stands for a voluntaristic world view in which the cosmos is understood in relation to human nature. Thus human nature tends to be treated personalistically. It is instructive that Dante omitted Augustine from the group of theologians answering questions in the *Paradiso*, while Petrarch invoked him in the *Secret* as one whose struggles had been similar to his own and to whose experience he could appeal. Augustinian humanism is thus realistic, focusing on the problems of concrete existence, the active life. Freedom is not only inward but also outward; hence there is a conflict between will and fortune that must be faced. Problems cannot be resolved simply by appeal to reason; recourse must be had to grace. The will is thus more primary in the living of life than the intellect, and God is known primarily through revelation and faith rather than through reason.

All of these interpretations recognize a conflict that became acute in Petrarch's time and that had its precedents in both classical antiquity and the Middle Ages, as well as a subsequent history, in part the heritage of the humanist movement stemming from Petrarch. Certainly it is possible to say that Pietro Paolo Gerosa is incorrect in asserting that the inward conflict described by Petrarch is Christian, a transformation of pagan consciousness in which the conflict was always external, outside the self.[16] It is also clear that the formulation of the conflict in Petrarch's life and work owes a great deal to his intimate associations with Cicero and Augustine. What concerns us here is Augustine's role in this conflict and its resolution.

✳   ✳   ✳

Many interpreters have noted Petrarch's affinity with Augustine's *Confessions,* as opposed to what Bouwsma calls the structural and doctrinal writings of Augustine.[17] We know that Petrarch obtained in 1333 from the Augustinian monk Dionigi da Borgo San Sepolcro a pocket-sized copy of Augustine's *Confessions* that he carried on his person until the last year of his life. He may have owned another copy even earlier. There exists nothing like this work in Greek literature. Plato and Aristotle both suggested that moral development is rational, but Augustine suggested that it is introspective and personal. Inward reflection leads to sadness, indeed, is united with it. And this sadness is what we find both in Augustine's *Confessions* and in Petrarch.[18]

Petrarch relates his *dissidio* to Augustine in a letter he wrote in December 1336. The attitude expressed in it is one Petrarch had lived with for some time:

> You say that to someone like me who even now continues to wallow in things philosophic the words of Augustine must appear almost like a dream. It would have been better had you said that as I reread all those things, my entire life should have seemed nothing more than a dream and a fleeting apparition. Sometimes while reading them I am aroused as if from a very heavy sleep, but because of the oppressive burden of mortality my eyes close again and again, and I arouse myself and continue falling asleep over and over again. My wishes fluctuate and my desires are discordant and, being so, they tear me to pieces. Thus does the external part of man battle against the internal.[19]

Several months later, on 26 April 1337, Petrarch wrote the letter recording his ascent on that day of Mont Ventoux to the same Dionigi da Borgo San Sepolcro who had given him his pocket-sized copy of the *Confessions.*[20] In it, the feelings expressed in the letter of the preceding December came to a crisis point. He looked about for a proper companion with whom to make the ascent, settling finally on his brother. As they began the ascent, an aged shepherd tried to dissuade them, arguing the difficulty of the attempt. Unable to do so, he traveled with them a short distance, showing them the best routes. While his brother attacked the steepest but shortest routes directly, Petrarch sought an easier one through the valleys, but failed miserably. When he finally caught up with his brother, the latter had been waiting for him for some time. The same thing happened a second time before he finally reached the summit. He was overwhelmed by the view, especially the vision—in his mind's eye—of his native Italy. Then he remembered that this day of his ascent marked the completion of the tenth year since he had abandoned his study of law in Bologna. He was led to reflect on the greatness of the changes he had undergone since then and cites a passage from the *Confessions:* "Let me remember my past mean acts and the carnal corruption of my soul, not that I love them, but that I may love Thee, my God" (2.1.1). On this passage Petrarch comments:

> Many dubious and troublesome things are still in store for me. What I used to love, I love no longer. But I lie: I love it still, but less passionately. Again have I lied: I love it, but more timidly, more sadly. Now at last I have told the truth; for thus it is: I love, but what I should love not to love, what I should wish to hate. Nevertheless I love it, but against my will, under compulsion and in sorrow and mourning.[21]

He reflected that if he made as much progress during the coming decade as he had made during the past two years he might be ready to face death with equanimity by his fortieth year. But he wept over his imperfection. Then he thought it time to take another good look around, since he must soon depart. He admired every detail of what he saw, and then decided to open his copy of Augustine's *Confessions.* His intention was to read whatever first came to his attention. The passage he chose was, "And men go to admire the high mountains, the vast floods of the sea, the huge streams of the rivers, the circumference of the ocean and the revolutions of the stars—and desert themselves" (10.8.15). It was as if he had been struck by a bolt of lightning:

> I was stunned, I confess. I bade my brother, who wanted to hear more, not to molest me, and closed the book, angry with myself that I still admired earthly things. Long since I ought to have learned even from pagan philosophers that "nothing is admirable besides the mind; compared to its greatness nothing is great." (Seneca, *Ep.* 8.5) I was completely satisfied with what I had seen of the mountain and turned my inner eye toward myself. From this hour nobody heard me say a word until we arrived at the bottom.[22]

But while he did not speak, he reflected. He was convinced that the words he had read had been addressed to him and to no one else, just as

Augustine believed he had been addressed by Paul just prior to his own conversion. The analogy suggests the impact Petrarch believed this event to have had on his life. He added:

> as Augustine, having read the other passage, proceeded no further, the end of all my reading was the few words I have already set down. Silently I thought over how greatly mortal men lack counsel who, neglecting the noblest part of themselves in empty parading, look without for what can be found within. I admired the nobility of the mind, had it not voluntarily degenerated and strayed from the primordial state of its origin, converting into disgrace what God had given to be its honor.[23]

On the impact of this experience on Petrarch Professor Kristeller has written: "The return from nature to man, which is so characteristic of Petrarch, and the whole emphasis on man which became so important throughout the Renaissance, is here, in its origin, connected with the name and doctrine of Augustine."[24]

*   *   *

The *dissidio* was also reinforced by Petrarch's reading of *On True Religion*, listed in his catalog of favorite books and owned by him at least from 1335. Central to that treatise is the idea that unity cannot be found in temporal things. The beautiful aspect of temporal things is their multitude, but it breaks down also into many affects, and this multitude of affects becomes a multitude of sufferings. For the soul seeks unity but finds multiplicity. Love is perpetual but is faced with discordant passions that come and go, leaving the soul in indecision, disquietude, inertia.[25]

On True Religion (390) differs from the *Confessions* (397) and the *City of God* (413–26) in emphasizing less the grace of God and more the importance of human will. At the conclusion of *On True Religion* Augustine writes that God "grudges nothing to any, for he has given to all the possibility to be good, and has given to all the power to abide in the good as far as they would or could."[26] He would never have written these words in his later works, especially after his conflict with Pelagius, contemporary with the writing of the *City of God*.

Petrarch was much guided by Augustine's *On True Religion* in his own version of Augustine's *Confessions*, his *Secret*, in which Augustine urges that if Petrarch only has the will he may change. The *Secret*, set in 1342–43 on the occasion of his brother's becoming a Carthusian monk, but actually written—as has recently been proved—in 1347, 1349, and 1353, with marginal notes added in 1358,[27] represents, in part, the de-

velopment that took place as a result of the experience on Mont Ventoux.[28] Augustine was his guide in both. In his preface, Petrarch says that
while he was meditating on death, Truth appeared to him in the form of
a beautiful virgin, and with her was an aged man, St. Augustine. Truth
addresses St. Augustine as follows:

> Augustine, dear to me above a thousand others, you know how de-
> voted to yourself this man is, and you are aware also with how
> dangerous and long a malady he is stricken, and that he is so much
> nearer to Death as he knows not the gravity of his disease. It is
> needful, then, that one take thought for this man's life forthwith,
> and who is so fit to undertake the pious work as yourself? He has
> ever been deeply attached to your name and person; and all good
> doctrine is wont more easily to enter the mind of the disciple when
> he already starts with loving the Master from whom he is to
> learn.[29]

Truth reminds Augustine that he also was once shut up in a mortal body
and subject to the same temptations as Petrarch. Always obedient to
Truth, and professing his love as well for "this sick man," Augustine
agrees to speak to Petrarch.

In the first of their three dialogues Petrarch and Augustine confront
immediately the problem of will, which Augustine regards as the source
of Petrarch's *dissidio*. Augustine tells Petrarch that he who has discovered
that he is miserable will desire to be so no longer, that he who has this
desire will seek to realize it, and that he who seeks to realize it will be
able to reach what he wishes. It is this latter point that disturbs Petrarch,
who points out that many realize their misery and desire to overcome it
but will never reach the end they seek. His examples, however, all relate
to external factors preventing fulfillment. Augustine, following the
Stoics, says that none of these things can make one happy or unhappy;
only virtue can do that. So, then, Petrarch lacks virtue or something essential to it. Augustine reiterates that to sin or not to sin is a human
choice. At this point Petrarch reminds Augustine that he himself had had
the same problem: "as often as I read the book of your *Confessions*, and
am made partaker of your conflict between two contrary emotions, between hope and fear (and weep as I read), I seem to be hearing the story
of my own self, the story not of another's wandering, but of my own."[30]
He has chosen Augustine as his guide because the two share the *dissidio*
that once plagued Augustine and now plagues Petrarch. The way to overcome it, Augustine counsels, is to govern the passions with reason. If
reason will only meditate on death, feel its sting, then there will be a

change of will. Petrarch wonders why such meditation does him so little good. Augustine responds as he had in the *City of God* and *On True Religion:* the many impressions of the body will never give us rest; the soul must seek unity beyond the multiplicity of corporeal life.

> Of a truth the countless forms and images of things visible, that one by one are brought into the soul by the senses of the body, gather there in the inner center in a mass, and the soul, not being akin to these or capable of learning them, they weigh it down and overwhelm it with their contrariety. Hence that plague of too many impressions tears apart and wounds the thinking faculty of the soul, and with its fatal, distracting complexity bars the way of clear meditation, whereby it would mount up to the threshold of the One Chief Good.[31]

Petrarch responds: "You have spoken admirably of that plague in many places, and especially in your book *On True Religion* (with which it is, indeed, quite incompatible). It was but the other day that I lighted on that work of yours in one of my digressions from the study of philosophy and poetry, and it was with very great eagerness that I began to peruse it."[32]

In the midst of his discussion of those attitudes that block unity, Augustine says in *On True Religion:* "In sum three classes of men are thus distinguished: for lust of the flesh means those who love the lower pleasures, lust of the eyes means the curious, and ambition of this world denotes the proud."[33] In the second and third dialogues Petrarch adapts these observations to his own spiritual dilemma and explores with Augustine those things that block his own quest for unity.

A number of sins are examined in the second dialogue: Petrarch's pride in knowledge and in his physical appearance, his pride in scorning others, his desire for temporal things, and his ambition, earthly anxieties, search for honor, lust, and melancholy. One of these, his love for glory or honor, is mentioned but not discussed (Augustine raises it in dialogue three as one of Petrarch's principal sins). Of the sins discussed here Petrarch denies each but Augustine often has the last word, suggesting that Petrarch tacitly admits some guilt in every case. Three sins are discussed at some length. The first is Petrarch's desire for temporal goods, the discussion of which suggests his sojourn to Milan. Petrarch was evidently troubled by this weakness, inasmuch as he had earlier prided himself on a life of poverty. In this passage he defends his moderation—a change of attitude brought on by the opulence of the court of Milan. Augustine points out that when one begins piling up goods, there are never enough.

It is another source of a *dissidio* that, far from leaving Petrarch, continues to pursue him throughout his life—as the conclusion of the *Secret* also suggests. To the sin of lust Petrarch readily confesses and says that it alternately rises and falls; he prays, like Augustine in the *Confessions*, that he may be saved from it but not yet.[34] Melancholy, the last sin discussed in the second dialogue, is the feeling produced by the *dissidio* that Petrarch cannot shake. It appears to reside in his desire to be financially independent and intellectually superior, in short, completely autonomous. Augustine counsels him to think with Seneca that when he sees how many are ahead of him, he should look also at how many are behind. More importantly, he should remember that few men have lived the lives they wanted to live. Petrarch has come closer to this goal than many, a consideration that leads Petrarch to say he will never again complain of his poverty and will give up his melancholy.

Two sins are left for the third dialogue, Petrarch's love for Laura and his desire for earthly glory. These are the sins Augustine believes may bring Petrarch to ruin. Petrarch, by contrast, regards them not as chains but as treasures. Laura, for example, brought out the best in him and made him more than he was. Augustine responds that Laura made him less. His love for her coincided with the period in his life when his lusts were least under control. She caused him to lose sleep, neglect his friends, and face the danger of going to Rome for the laurel crown. Laura had, in short, turned him away from God. Augustine suggests that Petrarch prepare his soul to flee. Three remedies offered by Cicero are considered: satiety, shame, and reflection. The first is passed over as impossible and unsuitable to Petrarch's condition. The second, shame, amounts to a constant reminder that the body grows old and decays; one should act in a way becoming to one's age. Finally, turn to reason instead (to which Augustine had devoted much attention in *On True Religion*): think about more worthy tasks that claim attention.

Finally, there is Petrarch's overriding ambition. You seek too eagerly the praises of men and an enduring name, Augustine chides him. What is glory but gossip by some people about others? Petrarch, who often scorns the common crowd, should not be attracted by such plaudits. He need not give up all ambition, but he should put virtue before glory; if he does so glory will take care of itself. He should, however, abandon his poem *Africa* and take up meditation. Petrarch responds that he wishes Augustine had told him all this before he undertook his studies, for now that he has begun them he cannot put them altogether aside. Augustine's last response is to remind Petrarch that "we are falling into our old controversy. Want of will you call want of power. Well, so it must be, if it cannot be otherwise. I pray God that He will go with you where you go, and that He will order your steps, even though they wander, into the way of truth."[35]

∗   ∗   ∗

Although Augustine was his guide, Petrarch did not reach the same point in his *Secret* that Augustine had reached in his *Confessions*. Augustine's will was transformed and his old habits abandoned once and for all; Petrarch carried his *dissidio* with him throughout his life.[36] Why, guided by Augustine's example, did the peace Augustine achieved escape Petrarch? It has already been suggested that Petrarch suffered from a conflict between the demands of philosophy and the demands of rhetoric, or between intellect and will. I would generalize this conflict further by suggesting yet another variation: that while Augustine sought the peace of God in otherworldliness, Petrarch sought peace in this world and found his conflict precisely in the various dimensions of his worldliness.

The insights of David Marsh in his recent study of the development of the dialogue form among Quattrocento humanists tend, I think, to corroborate this interpretation. Petrarch's *Secret*, he writes, "marks the beginning of the revival of the classical dialogue by breaking with the dogmatism of the medieval dialogue and by asserting the Ciceronian notion of free discussion."[37] Augustine, following his conversion, had rejected the dialogue for the soliloquy—a conversation between the soul and God.[38] It is instructive to note the differences between the historical Augustine and Petrarch's representation of him, not in terms of Augustine's Stoicism in the dialogue but in relation to the idea of dialogue itself. In book 2, when Augustine says that one learns truth from reason and from authority, Petrarch, in responding, adds experience.[39] Moreover, Augustine is made to challenge his own authority (as church father rather than as author of the *Confessions*) in encouraging Petrarch to search for the truth. Very early in the first dialogue there is the following exchange:

> FR.: I don't dare say that I think the opposite, for my estimation of you since my youth has grown so great that if I should hold any opinion other than yours, I may know that I have erred.
> AUG.: Refrain from flattery, please. Rather, since I perceive that you have agreed with my words not so much from judgment as from awe, I grant you the freedom to say whatever you may think.[40]

Augustine is even made to say, a little further on, that "a moderate contention often leads to the truth."[41] Moreover, the two debate various ideas throughout their three dialogues without finally coming to an agreement. Each is left free to hold his own views. Thus, unlike Augustine's soliloquies, Petrarch's dialogue is a conversation with a friend and guide, that is, a social relationship with another human being who has experienced what Petrarch is experiencing rather than a relationship with God. In dialoguing with Augustine the way he does, Petrarch is restoring the social character of discourse abandoned by Augustine in his attempt to attain a direct link between the soul and God.[42]

Marsh's view implies that Petrarch's movement back to Augustine is, paradoxically, a movement away from Augustine and the civilization he fostered and into the future. Instead of the dogmatic certainty of the church in which the historical Augustine finally found refuge, Petrarch asserts the ideal of freedom of inquiry, the confrontation of opposing points of view, the relativity and multiplicity of truths at the level of experience, and finally, the social character of dialogue as a conversation between friends rather than as a soliloquy of the soul seeking God.

On the basis of the preceding analysis, it would perhaps not be too presumptuous to conclude that in Augustine we see a triumphant church arising on the ruins of empire, while in Petrarch we see the loss of religious hegemony and the beginning of the search for a more constructive worldliness. Be that as it may, the *dissidio* reflected in the reading of Augustine during his formative years remained with Petrarch all his life and is reflected throughout his letters, poems, biographies, and treatises. In this respect, Petrarch is unique among the humanists; other humanists were decisively influenced by him, but no other was so decisively influenced by Augustine.

*   *   *

In some respects, however, other humanists as well as Petrarch were indebted to Augustine. Augustine's works comprise the first systematic presentation of philosophy, ethics, and culture from within a Christian frame of reference by a Latin father.[43] Petrarch was attracted to Augustine in part for this reason. He was scornful of scholastic philosophy, as is evident from his criticisms in the *Secret*,[44] criticisms he repeated and expanded in his old age. Its predominance was one reason Petrarch believed he had been born into the wrong age. And as he sought to return to classical Roman culture, so also he sought to return to classical Christian culture. Augustine was the greatest representative of classical Christianity, living as he did prior to the fall of the Roman Empire and incorporating the pagan Roman culture he inherited into a Christian frame of reference.[45] The fact that Augustine was listed among Petrarch's "favorite books" along with his beloved Roman writers indicates that for him Augustine was a "classic." Together with the other fathers of the church (whom Petrarch read later in Milan),[46] he represented a classical Christian tradition parallel to the classical pagan tradition. He could, in this way, be studied as a literary figure. And among the humanists, the study of Scripture and the fathers became the study of "sacred literature," a much broader genre than theology.[47]

Petrarch, in particular, constantly cited his two favorite classical figures—Augustine and Cicero—together. In this way he united the two classical traditions and distinguished them from his own contemporary culture. For example, in the letter of 1336 cited earlier to indicate the *dissidio* that resulted from his reading of Augustine, Petrarch writes in the immediately preceding passage:

> You say that I have been fooling not only the stupid multitude with my fictions but heaven itself. You maintain, then, that I have embraced Augustine and his books with a certain amount of feigned goodwill, but in truth have not torn myself away from the poets and philosophers. Why should I tear asunder what I know Augustine himself clung to? If this were not so, he would never have based his *City of God*, not to mention other books of his, on so large a foundation of philosophers and poets, nor would he have adorned them with so many colors of orators and historians. And indeed my Augustine was never dragged to the tribunal of the eternal judge in his sleep, as happened to your Jerome, he was never accused of being a Ciceronian, a name which was leveled against Jerome and caused him to swear that he would no longer touch any pagan book, and you know how diligently he avoided all of them and especially those of Cicero. But Augustine, who had received no interdiction in his sleep, not only was unashamed to make ready use of them but openly confessed that he had found in the books of the Platonists a great part of our faith, and that from the book of Cicero entitled *Hortensius* through a wonderful internal change had felt himself turned away from deceitful hopes and from the useless strife of quarreling sects and toward the study of the one truth. And inflamed by his reading of that book he began to soar higher as a result of his change in feelings and abandonment of passions. O worthy man and beyond mention great, whom Cicero himself would have praised from the rostrum, and publicly thanked, you are indeed fortunate because among so many ingrates one at least wanted to be most grateful! O magnificently humble and humbly lofty man, you do not abuse writers through the use of the pens of others, but rather, steering the floating ship of the

Christian religion among the reefs of heretics and conscious of your present greatness, without arrogance recall the truths of your origin and the early beginnings of your youth. And so great a doctor of the church does not blush at having first followed the man from Arpino [Cicero] who held a different view! And why should he blush? No leader should be scorned who shows the world the way to salvation. What obstacle does either Plato or Cicero place in the way of the study of truth if the school of the former not only does not contradict the true faith but teaches it and proclaims it, while the solid books of the latter deal with the road leading to it?[48]

In his *Secret* more than a decade later, when Petrarch refers to *On True Religion* at the end of the first dialogue, he has Augustine add immediately thereafter:

And yet in that book, allowing for a difference of phraseology such as becomes a teacher of catholic truth, you will find a large part of its doctrine is drawn from philosophers, more especially from those of the Platonist and Socratic school. And, to keep nothing from you, I may say that what especially moved me to undertake that work was a word of your favorite Cicero. . . . It was the passage where in a certain book [*Tusc.* 1.16.38] Cicero says, by way of expressing his detestation of the errors of his time: "They could look at nothing with their mind, but judged everything by the sight of their eyes; yet a man of any greatness of understanding is known by his detaching his thought from objects of sense and his meditations from the ordinary track in which others move." This, then, I took as my foundation, and built upon it the work which you say has given you pleasure.[49]

Augustine does not say these words, and Cicero's work is not quoted in *On True Religion*. But it is significant that Petrarch read Augustine in relation to his favorite Cicero. Both here are allied as "classics" over against the "barbarians" of Petrarch's own generation.

The affinities Petrarch sees between his favorite "classics" are not only acknowledged by Augustine but also developed in his ethical standpoint. For Augustine's knowledge of Platonism—like Petrarch's—was derived principally from the accounts of it in Cicero's works. And his own ethics bears the strong stamp of Cicero's and Seneca's Stoicism. "The gulf between Stoicism and Christianity considered as ethical systems," one modern critic has written, "is far wider than that between the attitude and language of Augustine and the Latin Stoics. . . . Men who sought to reconcile Christ and Chrysippus would scarcely remark the incompatibility of Augustine and Seneca."[50] It required no unnatural leap for Petrarch to see both Christian and pagan classical moral philosophy as closely united in aim in the sources read often by him.

Augustine could borrow as freely as he did from pagan culture because, as a Christian, he saw no conflict between his Roman past and his Christianity. Rather, he believed that everything good in the past could simply be taken over and used to serve the ends of a Christian civilization. The conflicts that beset his contemporaries over the relation between paganism and Christianity did not bother him at all. Ambrose, the bishop of Milan and the person most responsible for Augustine's conversion, could only adopt the pagan past he had abandoned by believing that what was good in it had already been said by Moses and therefore antedated the pagan tradition. Jerome, Augustine's illustrious contemporary, certainly the greatest scholar produced by the early church in the West, was deeply immersed in pagan literature, but he always felt guilty about it. Once God appeared to him in a dream and told him that he was no Christian but a Ciceronian. Jerome never ceased to be a Ciceronian, but he could also never quite forgive himself for this aberration. There was none of this uncertainty in Augustine. On the contrary, Augustine exults that he was brought to Christianity through the pagan tradition. He writes in his *Confessions:*

> If I had first been formed by your Sacred Scriptures and if you had grown sweet to me by my familiar use of them, and I had afterwards happened on those other volumes, they might have drawn me away from the solid foundation of religion. Or else, even if I had persisted in those salutary dispositions which I had drunk in, I might have thought that if a man studied those books alone, he could conceive the same thoughts from them.[51]

Instead, having been converted to Christianity after his exposure to pagan literature, he developed the attitude that a Christian could make any use of the pagan tradition that would enhance his Christian faith. In *On Christian Doctrine* he writes:

> When the Christian separates himself in spirit from their miserable society, he should take this treasure with him for the just use of teaching the gospel. And their clothing, which is made up of those human institutions which are accommodated to human society and

necessary to the conduct of life, should be seized and held to be converted to Christian uses.[52]

On Christian Doctrine was among the works of the fathers Petrarch read after he went to Milan in 1353. It served him well in his defense of himself as both a humanist and a Christian, as it did generations of humanists after him. For Petrarch found in this little treatise—one of the most important in the history of education—a means of gaining the criteria by which to reconcile learning with religion.[53]

In the first of the four books of *On Christian Doctrine* Augustine argues that there are two kinds of things: those to be enjoyed and those to be used. Only God is to be enjoyed; all other things are to be used so that we might enjoy God. Things to be used are signs, and these are of two kinds. Some contain what they signify in themselves, for example, smoke signaling fire. Others, conventional signs, signify other things because human beings have decided that they shall. Among the most important conventional signs are books, and of course the most important book is Scripture. Books do not interpret themselves; their meanings are available only to those who can read the signs properly. Some things are unknown, others ambiguous. Some signs are given to us literally, others figuratively.

Book 2, from which the passage quoted above was taken, was very important to Petrarch. In it Augustine discusses unknown figurative signs. To interpret these signs, he says, we need a knowledge of languages, of the natures of animals, stones, and plants, of numbers (but not of astrology or magic), and of music. Knowledge of art and other forms of imitation, as well as of institutions of dress, adornment, sex, and class are also useful. A knowledge of history, of the science of disputation, and of the rules of eloquence is indispensable. A knowledge of astronomy, however, is dispensable. Augustine thus includes, as useful for a Christian to know, all three of Aristotle's categories of knowledge: theoretical, practical, and productive. It is not difficult to see why this particular book so attracted Petrarch. For it justified his taking from the pagans what was useful in them without giving up his Christianity. The arguments he used, following Augustine, became those of the humanists after him in dealing with men who would separate classical and Christian. Boccaccio's arguments, in the first famous defense of their union,[54] are taken from Petrarch—and ultimately from book 2 of *On Christian Doctrine*.[55]

In book 4 Augustine deals with persuasion, a subject close to the hearts of all humanists and particularly close to Petrarch. For the purpose of persuasion eloquence suited to the occasion is necessary. In speaking we should always seek to be clear and to say those things that will persuade others. Augustine cites Cicero's delineation of three forms of speaking: subdued, moderate, and grand. A teacher should use each as the occasion demands (subdued when teaching, moderate when condemning or praising, grand when persuading). But he who cannot speak both eloquently and wisely does better to speak wisely without eloquence than to speak foolish eloquence.

Humanists could find in this treatise not only many reasons for learning pagan literature but also a justification of their interests in the recovery and editing of texts and the need for persuasion in moral philosophy. All these tendencies, present in Petrarch—in significant measure through his reading of Augustine—culminated in Erasmus, not only the most eloquent moral philosopher and defender of the study of classical pagan literature among the humanists but also the editor of Scripture and of the fathers. It is not too much to conclude that the encounter between Petrarch and Augustine, though in some respects unique among the humanists, brought into being the idea of Christian classical antiquity, an idea that, on the one side, enlarged humanism and, on the other, subjected the Christian tradition to the same kind of critical analysis that was applied to the pagan tradition. Both innovations were to bear a rich harvest in the immediate as well as in the more distant future.

NOTES

1. This is the interpretation of B. L. Ullman, "Petrarch's Favorite Books," in *Studies in the Italian Renaissance* (Rome, 2d ed., 1973), 113–33 at 114–15. Ullman has reinterpreted the material gathered by P. de Nolhac, *Pétrarque et l'humanisme* (Paris, 2d ed., 1907; reprint, 1965), 2:189–206.

2. C. Trinkaus, *The Poet as Philosopher: Petrarch and the Formation of Renaissance Consciousness* (New Haven, 1979), 23.

3. Ullman, "Petrarch's Favorite Books," 121.

4. Ibid., 125.

5. Ibid., 130–32.

6. Petrarch, *Secret*, trans. W. H. Draper (London, 1911), 14.

7. P. P. Gerosa, *Umanesimo cristiano del Petrarca: Influenza agostiniana attinenze medievali* (Turin, 1966), is the most thorough and penetrating study of Augustine's influence on Petrarch. But see also the works cited in the following notes.

8. J. E. Seigel, *Rhetoric and Philosophy in Renaissance Humanism* (Princeton, 1968), chaps. 1–2.

9. Trinkaus, *Poet as Philosopher*, chap. 2.

10. Ibid., 48.

11. Ibid.
12. C. Trinkaus, *In Our Image and Likeness: Humanity and Divinity in Italian Humanist Thought*, 2 vols. (Chicago, 1970), 1:40ff.
13. Ibid., 1:23–25.
14. Ibid., 1:25ff.
15. W. J. Bouwsma, "The Two Faces of Humanism: Stoicism and Augustinianism in Renaissance Thought," in *Itinerarium Italicum: The Profile of the Italian Renaissance in the Mirror of Its European Transformations*, ed. H. A. Oberman and T. A. Brady, Jr. (Leiden, 1975), 3–50.
16. Gerosa, *Umanesimo cristiano*, chap. 5.
17. Bouwsma, "Two Faces," 13–14; Trinkaus, *In Our Image*, 1:18; D. Marsh, *The Quattrocento Dialogue* (Cambridge, MA, 1980), 20.
18. Gerosa, *Umanesimo cristiano*, 81.
19. *Familiares*, 2.9, in *Rerum familiarum libri I–VIII*, trans. A. S. Bernardo (Albany, NY, 1975), 101.
20. The letter has been translated a number of times. See *The Renaissance Philosophy of Man*, ed. E. Cassirer, P. O. Kristeller, and J. H. Randall, Jr. (Chicago, 1948), 36–46.
21. Ibid., 42.
22. Ibid., 44.
23. Ibid., 45.
24. P. O. Kristeller, "Augustine and the Early Renaissance," in *Studies in Renaissance Thought and Letters*, 2 vols. (Rome, 1956–85), 1:355–72, at 362.
25. Gerosa, *Umanesimo cristiano*, 90–91.
26. Augustine, *On True Religion*, 55.113, in *Augustine: Earlier Writings*, ed. and trans. J. H. S. Burleigh (Philadelphia, 1958), 225–83 at 282.
27. F. Rico, *Vida u obra de Petrarca: Lectura del "Secretum"* (Chapel Hill, NC, 1974), 7–16, 468–71. See also his "Precisazioni di cronologia Petrarchesca: Le 'Familiares' VIII.ii–v, e i rifacimenti del 'Secretum,'" *Giornale storico della letteratura italiana* 105 (1978): 481–525.
28. Gerosa, *Umanesimo cristiana*, 97.
29. Petrarch, *Secret*, 4.
30. Ibid., 21.
31. Ibid., 43.
32. Ibid.
33. *On True Religion*, 38.69, p. 261.
34. Petrarch, *Secret*, 79–80; Augustine, *Confessions*, 8.7.17, trans. J. K. Ryan (Garden City, NY, 1960).
35. Petrarch, *Secret*, 192.
36. Gerosa, *Umanesimo cristiano*, chaps. 3 and 6.
37. Marsh, *Quattrocento Dialogue*, 16.
38. Marsh suggests that there is some symmetry in the fact that Petrarch wrote his *Secret* in Milan, the city in which Augustine had been converted to Christianity. Thus the city that marked the death of the dialogue was also the place of its rebirth one thousand years later. Ibid., 17.

39. *Secret*, 78; Marsh, *Quattrocento Dialogue*, 19.

40. *Secret*, 14–15; Marsh, *Quattrocento Dialogue*, 21 (the trans. is Marsh's).

41. Quoted Marsh, *Quattrocento Dialogue*, 21; see *Secret*, 21.

42. Marsh, *Quattrocento Dialogue*, 22–23.

43. See N. Abercrombie, *St. Augustine and Classical French Thought* (Oxford, 1938), 1–17.

44. *Secret*, 29–30.

45. On this topic, see J. -B. Reeves, O.P., "St. Augustine and Humanism," in *A Monument to St. Augustine*, ed. M. C. D'Arcy (London, 1930), 123–51.

46. de Nolhac, *Pétrarque et l'humanisme*, 2:206ff.; Gerosa, *Umanesimo cristiano*, chap. 10.

47. Kristeller, "Augustine and the Early Renaissance," 362–63.

48. *Rerum familiarium libri I–VIII*, 99–100. In a passage from his *De ignorantia* (in *Renaissance Philosophy of Man*, 47–133), written near the end of his life, in which he is extolling Ciceronian moral philosophy in relation to Aristotelian scholasticism, Petrarch reminds his readers once again that Augustine was turned to his quest for wisdom in part by reading Cicero's *Hortensius* (see p. 105).

49. *Secret*, 44.

50. Abercrombie, *St. Augustine*, 6.

51. *Confessions*, 7.20.26 (p. 179).

52. Augustine, *On Christian Doctrine*, 2.40.60, trans. D. W. Robertson (New York, 1958), 75.

53. Gerosa, *Umanesimo cristiano*, 168 and n. 61.

54. Boccaccio, *On Poetry: Being the Preface and the Fourteenth and Fifteenth Books of Boccaccio's "Genealogia Deorum gentilium,"* trans. C. G. Osgood (Indianapolis, 1956).

55. Gerosa, *Umanesimo cristiano*, chap. 14. Book 3, omitted in the discussion here, deals with the clarification of ambiguous signs in interpreting Scripture. Rules put forward by Augustine here had been followed by patristic writers and continued to be followed by medieval and Renaissance writers.

6 ♛ PETRARCH, DANTE, AND THE MEDIEVAL TRADITION
Aldo S. Bernardo

I T IS GENERALLY CONCEDED THAT ITALIAN LITERATURE BEGINS WITH three giants—Dante, Petrarch, and Boccaccio—whose greatness and influence are practically indisputable even today. Interestingly, during and shortly after their own lives they ranked just as highly, and were often judged equal or superior to any and all writers, whether contemporary or ancient. Even the writers themselves sensed their own greatness and expressed it in some form in their own works.[1] Why should this curious phenomenon of a sudden triple bulge in the evolution of literature have occurred at this particular time? One reason doubtless was that in the works of these three giants the great synthesis between classical and Christian values for the first time achieves near perfection. Although each attained a different mix in the synthesis, their extraordinary awareness of the manner in which the two civilizations complemented each other and their dramatic conveyance of such an awareness in vernacular masterpieces could not within a very short time fail to appear a giant step forward in the history of ideas and culture.

Since St. Augustine, and even earlier, serious western writers and thinkers had tacitly or openly agreed that classical civilization could not simply be cast aside and relegated to extinction because of its paganism. However, in 1 Corinthians 7:31 St. Paul had solemnly proclaimed that with the birth of Christ the world as man had known it until that moment was "passing away" and a new world and a new humanity were taking its place. But during the succeeding dozen centuries an inexorable fusion of classical and Christian values had continued unabated in practically all areas of thought, despite the eclipse of Rome, the "barbarian" Dark Ages, and the Holy Roman Empire. Ironically, the great synthesis burst forth magnificently in the works of our three writers almost at the very moment that the great medium of classical expression, the Latin language, was losing its pristine form and was evolving into new forms of expression, the Romance languages. If ever there were a threshold in the history of culture, the three hundred years between the tenth and fourteenth centuries, with the rise of modern languages, certainly formed a major one. The further fact that Italian, the vernacular that had been slowest in developing, produced the three literary giants who were to influence the development of most western literatures so profoundly, should not prove too surprising. By inheriting the experience of other already developed vernacular literatures, the natural genius of what have been called the Three Crowns of Florence had enabled them to achieve an amalgamation of the very best qualities of the two great traditions, the classical and the Christian.

Each of the three writers acknowledged that antiquity had already shown the way to unveiling human potential; each was fully aware that the Christian ethic was superior to any developed by any preceding civilization; each had mastered to an astounding degree the two main currents and felt perfectly at ease with both; and all three had come at the end of a long line of writers and thinkers who had so digested and integrated the classical and the Christian heritages that by the fourteenth century the original classical texts had been lost or misplaced in some monastic or private library and had been practically rewritten by commentators. By the fourteenth century the idea and concept of Rome required such a double focus that in art ancient heroes often wore medieval garb, while in literature Petrarch felt comfortable addressing several personal letters to a number of ancient writers. By this time Italian social, cultural, and historical conditions had reached a kind of ideal high point that allowed Dante, Petrarch, and Boccaccio to achieve in literature the first clearly great syntheses of the classical and Christian heritages. What these writers accomplished is in many ways the essence of humanism. The so-called search for and rediscovery of ancient texts that marked most of the fifteenth century began when the church cautiously started to acknowledge that such works were not harmful to believers and actually encouraged monastic libraries to collaborate in such a search. The essence of humanism, and for that matter of the Renaissance, lay not so much in the "rediscovery" of the ancients as in a new appreciation and acceptance of their accomplishments. What was basically involved in the great synthesis was an attitude toward reality that paralleled that of the ancients but within the Christian framework. Ultimately it represented an attempt to establish humans as truly "free" creatures. However, the real novelty of this concept was one of degree rather than of kind, since "freedom" was also an important component of the Christian ethic.

*　　*　　*

Before turning to Petrarch, we must take a moment to examine a dimension of Dante's *Divine Comedy* that will serve to delineate more clearly Petrarch's role in the synthesis. Anyone familiar with the *Comedy* is aware of the enormous number of figures taken from antiquity who populate all three realms. Indeed, no one who was anyone in ancient Greece or Rome seems to be missing. However, it is not in the profusion of names that Dante contributes to the synthesis. It is rather in his clear awareness of and respect for the sharp contrast between the classical and Christian views of universal history.

A few years ago John Freccero tried to show that the Ulysses episode in the *Comedy* reflected Dante's Christianized view of history.[2] For the ancients, history seemed to be made in the very image of man. Like men, civilizations succeeded one another according to the life cycle. Time seemed to move in an eternal circle, with repetition its only rationale. In the face of an inexorable destiny, the only human hope for a kind of permanence resided in an aspiration to worldly glory and human reason.

It was St. Augustine who first pointed out in his *City of God* that with the birth of Christ a new view of universal history had begun. In his words appearing in the twelfth book of that work, "the circles have been shattered." Christ seemed to cut through the circle of time and to establish a fixed point, thereby substituting a linear progression for the circular flux. Time finally appeared to be moving toward its consummation, the fullness of time, which in retrospect gave to all history a clear meaning, just as a target gives meaning to the flight of the arrow. In addition to universal history, Christ seemed also to have wrought a change in the history of the individual soul, whose story could no longer be reduced to the curve extending from birth to death, but rather was a continuing trajectory toward a death that would give meaning to life. We thus have a new linear conception of time, which inevitably came to represent a logically opposite pole of narrative art insofar as it reflected a picture of human existence. The journey of Homer's Ulysses with its eventual return to the starting point was the archetype of the circular concept of time in narrative. In a sense the *Aeneid* also showed how Aeneas, for Vergil, was but the initiator of a circle within circles intended to reflect the inevitable eternity of Rome.

The formal Christian view, however, may be seen in Dante's handling of the Ulysses story, which also regards the journey as an emblem of human time, but with a distinct glossing from a linear, Christian viewpoint, namely, the perspective of death. As Dante's earliest commentators attest, even unlearned people of the time knew that Homer's hero returned safely to Ithaca. Despite this, Dante has him die within sight of the Mount of Purgatory. What we have, then, is a Christian critique from beyond the grave of earthly heroism. The questions asked by Dante's Vergil of Ulysses deal primarily with where and why he died rather than with details of his journey. This was what ultimately mattered with the Christian ethic. Death is no longer the end; rather the meaning of death for the medieval mind had to do with salvation or damnation.

*   *   *

Among my first interests in dealing with Petrarch was his puzzling attitude toward Dante, as well as Boccaccio's desperate attempts to influence Petrarch's disturbing coolness.[3] After these many years I am still convinced that it was primarily Petrarch's special brand of humanism that kept him from grasping the great merits of the *Comedy*. To put it rather crudely, Petrarch had "digested" his favorite ancients in a way far different from Dante. He learned to live with them through their writings in a kind of fraternal communion, either, as Guido Martellotti has shown, to extract rules for living for himself and for others, or to use ancient exemplars to justify or excuse personal weaknesses.[4] Indeed the recurring comparisons of himself with the ancients (or vice-versa) endows his Latin works with a confessional tone that has much in common with that of the *Canzoniere*. The sense of timelessness reflected in such comparisons is intensified by the fact that, while most of the Latin works have opening dates, they have no closing dates. Petrarch's use of the ancients, according to Martellotti, seemed to reflect a desire to rest his thought in values that appeared eternal, thereby allowing him to flee for the moment the anguished sense of transiency and death that so permeated his Italian poetry. As Martellotti also observes, the examples offered by the beloved *auctores* "seem as solid as reefs in the eternal flux of time."

In fact it is not uncommon to find Petrarch expressing his preference for something classical over something Christian. For instance, in saying that life can be viewed as a living death, he makes reference to "Cicero whom I almost trust more regarding this matter than the majority of Catholic writers." Or again, he expresses his preference for the Stoic definition of virtue above any other. Or finally, he offers his agonizing account of trying to pay no heed to the multitude's ridicule of his studies, but he is even more disturbed by the fact that "I sometimes scarcely approve of my own studies and vigils; and I feel I would be acting more wisely if I abandoned everything for which I labor and waste such valuable time in order to begin doing the one thing I have long meditated, for which alone I came into this short and wretched life." He goes on to confess, however, that "often another thought follows upon this excuse: that my studies are in no way harmful to that purpose and are perhaps even useful. . . . May truth find a place amidst these alternating mental deliberations!"[5]

For Petrarch, imitation of great writers and thinkers of the past was perfectly acceptable provided that one imitated only subjects and thoughts, not words. Like a bee, a writer may cull from the flower of a past great, but the honey he then produces must be his own.[6] This process led to an attitude considerably different from Dante's. For Dante the most admired greats from antiquity, including even Aristotle and Plato, had to submit to the inexorable doctrine that, despite and perhaps because of their keen minds, they had been incapable of truly foreseeing the Word made Flesh and had spent their lives in a kind of existential limbo.[7] For Petrarch such a view appeared simplistic and unacceptable. Any real or pseudo-ancients from whom he had learned had become part of himself. When this process of gestation was over, his personal stance vis-à-vis the human condition was just as classical as it was Christian. His faith was firm, but its foundations were different from Dante's.

Dante's substructure was what might be called biblical linearity, and any knowledge that strayed from such linearity was admirable but incomplete. Whence the eerily lit but elaborate Noble Castle of Wisdom or Fame in his Limbo, surrounded by the walls of the cardinal and speculative virtues and with its seven gates of the liberal arts and inhabitants representing the great intellectual pre-Christ spirits. The total of their human knowledge could not compare with that contained in the Scriptures whose primary termini were Creation, Revelation, and Redemption, viewed through the eyes of the theological rather than the cardinal virtues.

It was otherwise for Petrarch, the Christian humanist. The human intellect had reached its zenith in classical times, and while Christian salvation may indeed have eluded the writers and heroes of those times, the products of their minds and actions could well be viewed as attesting to the greater glory of God. Petrarch simply could not accept Augustine's shattering of the circles that had enclosed the ancients.[8]

The contrast between Petrarch's and Dante's views of Vergil may serve to dramatize the distinction in the humanistic spirit of the two great poets. In an article written many years ago I tried to justify Pierre de Nolhac's view that unlike most scholars or writers who preceded him, Petrarch "most certainly read Vergil as a poet more often than he studied him as a moralist." While for Dante Vergil's greatness resided in what he had written, for Petrarch it also resided in how he had written. For Petrarch Vergil's appeal is primarily intellectual; for Dante, spiritual and moral. Petrarch judged Vergil a great poet without reservation; Dante implies a reservation in Vergil's fate in the *Comedy* despite the special role he assigns to him in the poem.[9] Indeed, Dante's placing of Aeneas in Limbo, Achilles in the circle of the lustful, and Ulysses among fraudulent counselors could only have contributed to Petrarch's coolness toward the

Comedy. The classical-type hero, though bereft of Christian grace, still appealed to Petrarch. He was the first and last great Italian poet to dedicate a large portion of his life to a Roman hero in an epic in Latin following classical norms, and to be crowned for it even though it was incomplete. Indeed, according to his own account, two great centers of Christianity, the University of Paris through its chancellor and Rome through her senate, presumably vied to bestow the crown.

Like Dante he too believed that the primary function of literature was to promote virtue. His definition of virtue, however, as borrowed from the ancient Stoics, was to "feel rightly about God and to act rightly among men."[10] What Dante attempts to accomplish in his religious epic, according to his *De vulgari eloquentia,* is to fill what he considered a serious lacuna in vernacular literature: a great poem about rectitude, spiritual uprightness, Christian doctrine. For Petrarch, great poetry conveyed the uprightness of all great human deeds and creativity, both of which he tried to depict in the *Africa.*

Vergil indirectly plays a central role in the famous letter with which Petrarch forwards his first eclogue to his monastic brother.[11] In the second section of his letter Petrarch provides a thorough gloss of the eclogue, explaining that the two shepherd protagonists, Silvius and Monicus, are really he and his brother. In the allegory, Monicus, having left the fields and his flock, enjoys a peaceful existence in the shade of a cave while his brother, Silvius, is forever attempting to climb steep hills. Monicus tries to convince his brother to cease his useless wandering and labors and seek instead refuge in his cave, where the songs he will hear will be even sweeter than those he is trying to emulate. But Silvius considers the poet in his brother's cave inferior to the two shepherds in whose footsteps he is following. When Silvius notes that he has offended his brother, he promises to return another time to hear the sweetness of his poet's song. He must meanwhile hasten away in order to complete a work in praise of a famous man to whom no one had previously given due recognition. As he departs, Monicus reminds him of the dangers inherent in postponing such resolutions.

The two shepherds in whose footsteps Silvius follows are Homer and Vergil. The singer favored by Monicus is David, while the famous man Silvius must celebrate in Homeric and Vergilian strains is Scipio Africanus, conqueror of Hannibal. Of particular interest is the manner in which Petrarch, as Silvius, contrasts the poetry of David with that of Vergil and Homer. What he finds displeasing in David is that he "makes excessive reference to the citizens and walls of the little Jerusalem and never strays from there, and is always ready with tears and breathes hoarsely in his breast." On the contrary, his preferred classical poets have a different song:

> [They] sing of Rome, Troy, the battle of kings; the power of grief and love and wrath; the spirit that rules the waves and the winds and the stars. With varying images they depict the rulers, chosen by lot, of the Triple Realm, brothers all three: Jove, the loftiest, sceptered, with a serene countenance; in the center position, armed with a trident and with curly locks, the ruler of the deep; and lastly, the god of shadows, flanked by a surly mate; and the black boatman of the Tartarean Marsh who makes round trips through the tarry waters; the sisters, who, in accordance with immutable law, work the moral threads with merciless hands. And they also sing the eternal night of the Stygian shades, the snaky-haired Furies, the temple and the forum; they sing of the woods and fields, arms and heroes, and depict the entire world with lofty verses.

In his defense of David, Monicus maintains that the Psalmist sings of truth:

> [He] sings instead of one God who caused the vanquished throng of the gods to tremble; who governs the bountiful heavens with his nod; who holds the liquid ether in equilibrium and spreads heaps of dew and cold snow; who draws out from a propitious cloud the rains badly needed by the dry fields; who thunders and shakes the agitated heavens with streaking flame; who assigns age to the movement of the stars and seeds the earth; who compels the sea to move in waves and the mountains to be still; who gave us our body and soul to which he added the innumerable other skills by perfecting the original double gift; who, by showing us the alternating of life and death, taught us the best road that leads tired men above the stars and brings us back to it by warnings. This is the God that my shepherd sings; so I beg you not to call him hoarse; powerful is his voice that penetrates souls with a mysterious sweetness.

By implication David's poetry was for Petrarch too similar to Dante's, which also contained too much wailing and gnashing of teeth. In short, it possessed too much linearity toward a single goal and was excessively concerned with the human demise on earth rather than with potential human immortality. Not that eschatology or this-worldliness are in themselves good or bad; basically, the one-eyed Monicus and the sylvan poet (actually called Silvius by his friends) are really extremes between which the true poet lies. If the poet never wanders from the walls of the little Jerusalem, he is, like David and Dante, more a theologian than a poet. If he limits himself to things of this world, he is like a pagan poet who sees man as a victim of recurring cycles in a closed universe. The great poet sings of heroes whose true greatness no God or gods can call into question.[12] Elsewhere Petrarch discourages a local ruler from entering the religious life because his services to his people can also lead to his salvation. "No one," he explains, "who participates in honorable activity may be excluded from this path. It has also been established, according to the opinion of Plotinus, that one becomes blessed and is cleansed not only through the penitential virtues but also through the political ones. To speak of a Christian example, Martha's active solitude is not to be scorned even though Mary's contemplation may be superior." [13]

As was recently pointed out, for Petrarch philosophy ought to be not only a *meditatio mortis* but also *ars vitae*.[14] It is in this fusion that we may see most clearly the essence of Petrarch's humanism. He was capable of seeing the ancients as human beings possessing all those qualities with which God had endowed his creatures except, perhaps, a Christian awareness. He felt this in both the active and the contemplative life of the ancients. In his last article before his untimely death, Guido Martellotti uses a phrase from *De vita solitaria* to define Petrarch's concept of what was truly distinctive in the ancients' pursuit of excellence. After having shown, in a particular section of this work, how Christianity in his day was retreating on all fronts, Petrarch states his conviction that were Julius Caesar to return, his *animi vis et acrimonia* (strength of mind and energy) would prompt him to undertake the liberation of the sepulcher of Christ. It is this quality, "so badly needed in our time," that Petrarch exalts in his history of great men (*De viris illustribus*), especially in its expanded version, where he alludes to Adam as man's "bitter and harsh origin" but then proceeds, with Jacob and Joseph, to a true celebration of human virtues. The *animi vis et acrimonia* possessed in one form or another by the privileged few throughout history could still, for Petrarch, be of great value in his own day for the good of humanity and country.[15]

Petrarch's conviction that the wisdom of the ancients derived from minds possessing an uncanny ability to deal with an objective and legitimate moral order may be seen in an incident also reported by Martellotti. A well-known classical philologist of the eighteenth century inserted the famed Mago episode of Petrarch's *Africa* into the text of the *Punica* of Silius Italicus, whom Petrarch knew and admired as a classical writer. The philologist insisted that it was a lost fragment of the late classical poem, and when he was confronted with Petrarch's authorship, he accused him of plagiarism.

This incident, according to Martellotti, would have proved flattering to Petrarch not only because a piece of his writing was confused with that of an ancient *auctor*, but also, and perhaps primarily, because he would have viewed the error as justification against the critics of his own day who for years had accused him of having placed Christian sentiments on the lips of a pagan, Mago. A similar fate eventually befell other samples of his writings (many of his philological conjectures were later taken as genuine lessons in modern editions of Livy and Cicero, while his *De gestis Cesaris* was considered the work of an unknown ancient down to the nineteenth century); but what befell the Mago episode represents perhaps the clearest vindication or reflection of Petrarch's global humanism.[16]

In a letter to Boccaccio he defends the episode in strictly human terms. He first staunchly denies that Mago was too young to utter his famous last words, and then declares that the feelings expressed in those words are so naturally human that to call them Christian is a sign of a sterile and ignorant intellect. He writes: "For I ask in the name of Christ, what is in those words that is Christian and not rather human and common to all people? What is there if not grief and groaning and repentance at the last moment. . . . A man who is not a Christian can also recognize his error and sin."[17]

Petrarch was also able to adopt the reverse perspective. He would view a key biblical figure such as David as both human and divinely inspired. This perspective may best be seen in the *Triumphs*. In the later form of chapter 3 of the Triumph of Glory after his avowed "rediscovery" of church writers,[18] Petrarch placed David after Homer and Vergil for having sung a "canzon vera e non finta." But in the earlier and finished version of the same chapter, not a single biblical writer appears among the men of letters. David, for example, is placed in the second chapter among the men of action, at the head of the biblical contingent. Petrarch's incredible awareness of his ambivalence emerges most directly where he asserts: "I seem to be able to love both (classical and Christian models) at once, one in the matter of style, and preferring not to ignore the other in matters of wisdom."[19]

Petrarch's letter to Boccaccio,[20] therefore, is a document that establishes his distinctive humanism on foundations that are totally different from those used by the church fathers. Instead of basing his reconciliation of Christianity and paganism on the linear or providential argument used by church writers, he bases it on a fundamental sameness and equality of the human spirit. In fact, from this perspective Christianity becomes for Petrarch the one religion that best responded to human needs and aspirations that are felt in similar ways by the human race in different places and times.

*   *   *

Amazingly similar situations recur at the critical final moments of most of Petrarch's masterpieces, both Latin and Italian. They are found in the last pages of the *Secretum, Africa, De vita solitaria,* the two collections of letters, the *Canzoniere,* and the *Triumphs,* not to mention the Coronation Oration, which defines his classical poetics. Each instance reveals a Petrarch who at least for the moment feels the pull of greatness in the classical sense, a greatness in which, as Freccero noted, "the only hope for permanence . . . resided in the aspiration to worldly glory and human renown," but at the same time a Petrarch who simultaneously tries to tone down his stance by confessing his Christian awareness of final things. He is, in many ways, like Dante's wayfarer in the last scene of the *Comedy,* who sees the need to "square the circle" but knows it cannot be done. Petrarch somehow feels that he would prefer to retain both geometrical figures in their pure form as long as possible. He is extremely sensitive to what will be called "the Renaissance sense of limit" and had indeed written numerous pages on the inexorableness of death, but he resists the temptation to adopt the Christian perspective completely. This hesitation or ambivalence is at the heart not only of Petrarch's humanism, but of his lyricism as well. Let us briefly see how it emerges.

As was seen earlier, in the ending of the first eclogue (the writing of which Wilkins places between 1345 and 1347) Petrarch agrees someday to listen to his brother's poet, David, after he has completed his epic celebrating Scipio Africanus (which remained unfinished). The desire to help Scipio's name live on is in keeping with his position that human greatness must be given its due regardless of when it occurs. For Petrarch it was perfectly natural that a Christian writer living almost fifteen hundred years after the exploits of a great and unsung Roman hero should undertake his glorification for posterity. In fact, around 1347–49 he assumes the same position in the *Secretum* in which, in the presence of Lady Truth, he debates against a view he assigns to St. Augustine that has been called a *de contemptu mundi.* In book 3, he refuses to accede to the charge of an excessive love of earthly glory as seen in the two works he was working on at the time, *De viris illustribus* and *Africa.* For Petrarch's Augustine, such time-consuming works may lead to eternal damnation since they distract him from the narrow path of his own salvation. Petrarch's rebuttal rings clear and strong: "Oh, no! You must come forth with something more persuasive than that if you can, for I have found that (argument) expedient rather than effective. I am not contemplating becoming a god in order to achieve eternity or to embrace heaven and earth. Human glory is sufficient for me; only this do I long for, and, mortal that I am, I desire only mortal things." The *Secretum*, like the first eclogue, thus ends in a staunch defense not only of classical exempla and studies, but of those works by Petrarch that deal most directly with subject matter drawn from classical antiquity. Yet, at the very end he does express an intention to turn eventually to spiritual concerns.[21]

In my book on Petrarch's *Africa* I point out three factors that attracted his attention to Scipio Africanus in such an extraordinary way.[22] The first was the incredible account of a historian—Livy. The second was the still more amazing dream account of a philosopher and orator—Cicero. The third was the manner in which Cicero's account had been made into a compendium of knowledge and philosophy by a late Roman commentator—Macrobius. Cicero's surprising passage that appears at the end of the sixth book of *De republica* had drawn the attention of Christian and non-Christian commentators alike, as an isolated extract bearing the title of the *Somnium Scipionis*. Macrobius's commentary not only links it with Platonic thought, but concludes that the two thinkers had ended their respective works on the establishment and function of the state with a "fable" for reasons that doubtless appealed greatly to Petrarch. In the view of Macrobius, Plato's myth of Er shows that "in order to implant . . . fondness for justice in an individual nothing was quite as effective as the assurance that one's enjoyment did not terminate with death." Cicero's *Somnium* had intended "to teach us that the souls of those who serve the state well are returned to the heavens after death and there enjoy everlasting blessedness."[23] That such great minds could have seen in Scipio's deeds matter that qualified him to have an experience so close to Christian revelation was a primary reason why Scipio became a nearly perfect hero in Petrarch's mind.

It was this process of transforming "the solid foundations" of history into the exciting fabric of which poetry and philosophy are made that also marked Petrarch's peculiar brand of humanism. For him the matter of history and philosophy achieves its greatest potential when it is molded into meaningful patterns through the agency of poetry. De Nolhac noted this point very early when he wrote: "Petrarch dreams and composes as a poet even when he considers himself destined to restore and reproduce in his books the knowledge of the ancients."[24] By crossing Livy with Cicero and Macrobius he came to conceive Scipio as an ideal living symbol of what history and philosophy teach us man should strive to be. What he saw of particular significance in Scipio was not so much his saving of Rome in her darkest hour, but a degree of virtue that had enabled him to reach into the future and incite his adopted grandson to the final destruction of the archenemy, Carthage, by appearing to him in a dream that had all the marks of divine intervention. Whether the dream was based on fact did not really matter. What mattered was that a great Roman *auctor* such as Cicero made the dream culminate his arguments on the constitution of a republic, that a later *auctor* had made the vital connection with the conclusion of Plato's masterpiece, and that down to his own day the dream had served as a model for so many other "auctorial" moments, not excluding Dante's. As he clearly implies in the *Canzoniere,*[25] Scipio is Achilles, Odysseus, and Aeneas rolled into one, and perhaps even superior to them, since he rested on unquestionably historical foundations. As with the other heroes, Scipio's mysterious role in perpetuating the central importance of Rome for mankind and for Christianity had to take precedence over his possible damnation in the Christian scheme of things. For this reason he deserved to be celebrated in the grand manner of Vergil, and for this reason Petrarch felt deserving of the first laurel crown awarded by the Roman senate on the Capitoline since ancient times. And yet even in this symbolic ceremony Petrarch carefully picked the days of Christ's passion and resurrection for the three-day affair.

As I and others have shown in detail, Petrarch's Coronation Oration is a celebration of the poetic art's values as practiced by the ancients, especially by Vergil.[26] The Oration is in fact a commentary on these two verses from Vergil's *Georgics* (3.291–92): "But a sweet longing urges me upward over the lonely slopes of Parnassus." In the first section of his commentary Petrarch addresses the qualities that a poet must possess. The second deals with the "nature of the profession of poetry," while the third speaks of the nature of the poet's reward. Among the best rewards enjoyed by the great poet is his ability to give immortality to the names of great men of valor. Indeed, it is precisely for this reason the laurel crown is the most fitting reward for both caesars and poets. Each in his way acquires immortality, a basic quality of the laurel, through achievements worthy of glory. There are two ways of attaining such glory, namely, the way of bodily strength and the way of the mind or spirit. The laurel crown is an appropriate reward for both. What is ultimately involved in Petrarch's view is "the immortality of fame sought through warfare or through genius." Thus both in his coronation and in his oration Petrarch seemed to be touching and experiencing a moment of eternity that was basically classical but skillfully staged so that it could not be called pagan. The moment reached its dramatic climax in reality when

Petrarch, dressed in robes lent to him by King Robert of Naples, solemnly marched, followed by the entire Roman senate, at high noon on Easter Sunday 1341 to St. Peter's, where he deposited his laurel crown on the high altar. This highly symbolic act epitomized Petrarch's Christian humanism and could be viewed as a benchmark of formal humanism.

Something similar occurs in *De vita solitaria*. The main body of the work is devoted primarily to the defense of a solitude as practiced not by the religious mystic but by a scholar intent upon serious studies and seeking kindred minds. Toward the end of the work he repeats: "Whether our desire is to serve God, which is the only freedom and the only felicity, or by virtuous practice to develop our mind, which is the next best application of our labor, or through reflection and writing to leave our remembrance to posterity and so arrest the flight of the days and extend the all too brief duration of our life, or whether it is our aim to achieve all these things together, let us, I pray you, make our escape at length and spend in solitude what little time remains." Finally, in the closing paragraph he once again defines his ambivalence: "Differing here from the practice of the ancients whom I follow in many things, I found it grateful in this unassuming book of mine often to insert the sacred and glorious name of Christ." This, however, remains but a Christian homage, as he proceeds to indicate how near the ancients had come to intuiting ultimate Christian truth: "If this had been done by those early guides of our intellectual life, if they had added the spark of divinity to their human eloquence, though great the pleasure which they now afford, it would then have been still greater."[27] Yet, a perusal of the work shows that the solitary life was as useful for the great man of antiquity as it was for the great saints and fathers of the church.

Petrarch's two collections of Latin letters, the *Familiares* and the *Seniles*, likewise seem to reflect a surprisingly circular rather than linear concept of time. The first collection, containing letters of his younger years, ends with a book of letters that, looking backward, are directed to those Petrarch considered the greatest thinkers and authors of antiquity as if they were contemporaries. They include Cicero, Seneca, Varro, Livy, Gnaeus Pollio, Horace, Vergil, and Homer. Interestingly, the introductory letter to this last book is on the subject of life's brevity and gives a brief autobiographical sketch. During the course of his account, however, at the very point he proclaims the Augustinian doctrine that life is a continual dying, he adds, "until such time as we are allowed to prepare for ourselves through some work of virtue the road that leads to the true life in which no one ever dies but all live eternally." Whereupon he makes a shocking assertion that anticipates the Triumph of Eternity: "In that place what once pleased will please forever, and forever one will enjoy an ineffable joy which is never altered and which will never come to an end."[28]

The *Seniles,* the second collection of letters containing letters of his later years, end with the famous and unfinished Letter to Posterity. In it he bequeathes to future generations his personal legacy of a lifelong search for truth regardless of where it lies, whether in pre- or post-Christian times—a legacy he symbolizes in an extended description of his coronation and in his attempts to complete *Africa.* The message to posterity is that it must be a new antiquity but with the insights of Christianity—a distinctly circular rather than linear perspective.[29]

The *Canzoniere* likewise reflects a similar ambivalence between classical and Christian, notable in the poet's endless playing with the name of his beloved. In my analysis of the several forms undergone by the collection, I show the manner in which the image of Laura evolves from one containing heavily classical tones to one that attempts to incorporate clearly Christian ones.[30] In the first form of the collection, Laura's image seems to be projected against a complex background of classical mythology and history that reflects a wide spectrum of meaning, as symbolized primarily in the myth of Apollo and Daphne.

The second form, put together a year or so prior to Laura's death, included the two poems that were eventually to open the two parts of the collection. The first one introduces the entire work as a series of vain experiences that the poet now presumably recants, while the second declares such recantation to be virtually impossible.[31]

The third form contains the conversion of Laura's image from the Daphnean myth of earthly beauty, love, and art to a lady guide to the Christian God and the Christian heaven. This vision remains blurred, however, and becomes clarified only with the fourth form. With this form, Laura is not completely spiritualized, but the theme of a lady guide to heaven where human qualities are not viewed disparagingly is clearly present.

The last poem of the fifth form shows the old, "live" laurel that death had overthrown, replaced by a new one to which the poet feels attached not only through love but through the Muses. Despite Laura's transformation from flesh to spirit, she still partakes of classical elements. While eternally enjoying the sight of the Christian God, she has left behind as legacy her desires for such human ideals and aspirations as fame, honor, virtue, loveliness, chaste beauty in celestial garb. One critic sees in the form and meter of the poem Petrarch's obvious pleasure in recalling classical images and recollections, as well as his strong awareness of having raised vernacular love poetry to classical heights.

The very last poems added by Petrarch to the ninth and final form[32] are intended to round out the first part of the *Canzoniere*. One[33] judges Laura's beauty as superior to that of the greatest classical models, including Helen and Lucretia. The last poem that closes the first part[34] returns to the Laura-laurel motif in its first verse: "Victorious triumphal tree, honor of emperors and of poets. . . ." Yet the reordering of the *Canzoniere*'s last thirty poems, along with the retention of the very last hymn to the Virgin as the final poem from the moment it was first introduced in 1370 echoes the same classical-Christian ambivalence that has been visible elsewhere.

In the *Triumphs* Petrarch came closest to resolving his dilemma. The title itself, together with its Latin subtitles and the use of terza rima, reflect the poet's last serious effort to reestablish, though with considerable vagueness, a concept of human time that, while not entirely circular, insisted on an eternity in which human merit, human virtue, and human glory also represented a kind of salvation. There is little question that the work was intended as an alternative to Dante's *Comedy*. The attempt to reorder the last thirty poems in the *Canzoniere* in order to reflect a true recantation for his earthly love as well as a Christian conversion was, of course, in keeping with the traditional formula. But the fact that during the very period of his reordering he was also trying to put the finishing touches on the *Triumph of Eternity*, which he called his *ultimus cantus* and in which he worked so diligently to save his Daphnean Laura, once again reveals his lifelong wavering. In the last triumph Laura as myth, representative of the loftiest human ideals, appears not to clash with Laura as living Christian witness. What seems to happen, indeed, is that instead of discarding the myth, Petrarch revives it with a vengeance but adds a seemingly Christian dimension.

The poet had already expressed in the two *canzoni* preceding the last hymn to the Virgin a view of Laura that coincides with the Laura of the final Triumph. In a dream vision,[35] he has Laura define the means he should have employed to continue pursuing their love after her death. They consisted in "plucking palm and laurel branches" that she draws from her bosom and which signified victory over worldly attachments and pursuit of true merit, respectively. He ought, she says, to have "weighed with an accurate balance mortal things and these deceptive chatterings of yours . . . plucking at last one of these branches." He seems already to have plucked the laurel of glory by honoring her with his pen. He must now pluck the palm of renunciation. And Petrarch had literally acted out this moment when he had deposited his laurel crown on the altar of St. Peter's.

Similarly, the penultimate *canzone* describes a debate between the poet and Love in which Love exculpates himself for Laura's death and proceeds to prove how the poet through Laura had not only risen above the multitude but would have been afforded a ladder to the First Cause if only he had been able to recognize the incomparable virtues inherent in Laura. In short, even his beloved epitomized the same basic ambivalence.

The highly erudite *Triumphs* may actually be viewed as a continual "plucking of the palm and laurel," for once the dreaming poet sees the great number of kindred spirits provided by history in man's battle against cupidity, he realizes why his Laura can truly be representative of "the clear germ of virtue" and of the force (*animi vis et acrimonia*) that had incited great men of all past ages to triumph over death, false glory, and time. However, only those who recognized the intrinsic purity and beauty of such a legacy could partake of it and thereby be worthy of fame beyond time. It was this great lesson that Laura had tried to teach him from the very beginning of their love, and that he had struggled so long and so unsuccessfully to try to define. In the first part of the *Canzoniere* he had restricted himself to a kind of Cupid–Venus, Apollo–Daphne relationship. In the second part, after Laura's death, he had slowly developed a lady guide to heaven, who eventually partook excessively of the tradition of Beatrice.

In the *Triumphs,* if my thesis is correct, he makes a daring leap and provides a lady guide who descends from the female figure of Philologia, the heroine of Martianus Capella's *De nuptiis Philologiae et Mercurii.* As the spirit and unity of all knowledge, Philologia was viewed primarily as Sapientia agreeing to marry Mercury, a symbol of Eloquentia, through the intervention of Apollo, the god of knowledge and learning (and also the central figure in the Daphne myth). As the figure of Philologia evolves in the long work of Martianus, she, too, like Laura, paves the way to Olympus for great heroes and thinkers whose achievements have made them deserving of heavenly reward. By becoming a sort of Pallas of the Muses, Philologia is able to reveal divine teachings to men, for, as one critic observes, she "possesses the power of the Word of God because she is the Word."[36] Unlike Boethius's Lady Philosophy, Laura of the *Triumphs,* like Philologia, is as much at home with the Muses and the Graces as with Lady Philosophy and the Virtues. As such she can lead mortals to a heaven that is at least not incompatible with Christian doctrine. She is Chastity and Beauty occupying the Glorified Body of Sapientia. She is indeed, as Capella's Philologia had been called, a "reductio omnium artium ad Philologiam (Lauream)."

Ultimately in his *Triumphs* Petrarch could be said to be juxtaposing, if not fusing, Mount Parnassus and Calvary. Indeed Parnassus, Helicon,

Olympus, the Capitoline, and Calvary could all be viewed as the same, for they testified to the legacy of creativity and of potential divinity bestowed by God upon his favorite creature, the human being. At the summit of each, he seems to be saying, is something at once too beautifully human and too beautifully divine for these qualities to be mutually exclusive. And this something is the power of creativity, for which a person is crowned with a crown of laurel and God with a crown of thorns. This conclusion perhaps explains Petrarch's near obsession with Good Friday, Christ's passion and resurrection, moments that seem so inextricably bound with his very existence and especially with his love of Laura and his coronation.

*   *   *

It is no wonder, then, that both of Petrarch's attempts at epic, the *Triumphs* in Italian and the *Africa* in Latin, are reserved for the select few. The *mondo novo* of the Triumph of Eternity will be inhabited only by

> . . . those who merited illustrious fame
> That time had quenched, and countenance fair
> Made pale and wan by Time and bitter Death,
> Becoming still more beauteous than before
> Will leave to raging Death and thieving Time
> Oblivion, and aspects dark and sad.
> In the full flower of youth they shall possess
> Immortal beauty and eternal fame.[37]

As for his *Africa*, it will be understood, according to Petrarch, only if and when a new breed of men, who have qualities similar to the ancients, will once again inhabit the earth. Addressing his poem, the poet exclaims:

> But if you, as is my wish
> and ardent hope, shall live on after me,
> a more propitious age will come again:
> this Lethean stupor surely can't endure
> forever. Our posterity, perchance,
> when the dark clouds are lifted, may enjoy
> once more the radiance the ancients knew.
> Then shall you see on Helicon's green slope
> new growth arise, the sacred laurel bear
> new leaves, and talents will spring up renewed,

and gentle spirits in whose hearts the zeal
for learning will be joined with the old love
for all the Muses will come forth again.
Among such men my life will be more sweet
and my fame will deride the sepulchre.[38]

Perhaps the most illuminating words written by Petrarch in this vein
occur in the letter that kept Boccaccio from leaving the republic of letters.[39] In it he declares that while the journey to salvation may be a
blessed experience for all, "that journey is more glorious that achieves
the summit accompanied by the loveliest light; whence the piety of an
ignorant but pious man is inferior to the piety of a man of letters."

Only when the ancient republic of letters, knowledge, selfless
achievement, and beauty are seen as consonant with Christian doctrine
can humankind be said to have truly grasped the real meaning of salvation. The incredible procession marking the Triumph of Eternity, in
which we see Laura leading the supreme heroes of all time toward an
eternity of fame and beauty in a heaven representing a continuum for an
idealized humanity, reveals a vision that is far more daring than Dante's
(including his procession at the summit of Purgatory). If I am correct in
surmising that the procession of figures headed by Laura is for the most
part the same as is depicted in the Triumph of Fame, the inclusion of
Ulysses and Diomedes seems to be a direct challenge to Dante's disposition of the great Homeric heroes. We thus have Petrarch seemingly asserting that while the Christian and Dantean linear perspective, which
focuses on rewards and punishments after death, may well apply to those
who had been graced with the Christian faith, supreme human achievement that had clearly benefited humankind could not be excluded from
the rewards assigned by a God whose essence was Charity as defined by
St. Augustine. For Petrarch the linear concept of time, which had resulted
from Christ's "breaking" of the ancient circular pattern, did not apply to
the recurring spirals of greatness marking human potential, for these
only served the greater glory of God. It was this brand of humanism
rather than Dante's that eventually led to the Neoplatonism of Ficino
and others, which was essentially a kind of Christian apotheosis of Plato,
the pagan philosopher who must have known, Augustine believed, the
writings of the Hebrew prophets if not the prophets themselves, and who
incidentally was the originator of the cyclical concept of existence.[40] Petrarch had clearly inherited Augustine's outlook, but unlike Augustine
and Dante he was incapable of fully accepting the concept of Christ's
birth marking a point in time that eternally locked the gate of salvation

to the truly great writers and leaders of antiquity. This was to become and to remain the great dilemma of the humanistic movement.[41]

NOTES

1. In *Familiares* 13.7 Petrarch seems to realize that his example may be turning young people's minds to the study of letters in a way that may prove dangerous, since it is only for the few. (Petrarch, *Letters on Familiar Matters, IX–XVI*, trans. A. S. Bernardo [Baltimore, 1982], 199–203.) In *Paradiso* 1.24–26 and 25.1–12 Dante likewise expresses an awareness of his own greatness. Around 1364, in *Seniles* 5.2 to Boccaccio, Petrarch ascribes Boccaccio's desire to destroy his own works in the vernacular to the fact that they were inferior to his, and he gallantly offers to relinquish first place to Boccaccio if that is indeed what he seeks. In his letter to Jacopo Pizzinghe, Boccaccio eulogizes both Dante and Petrarch, pointing out that Petrarch "cleansed the fount of Helicon, swampy with mud and rushes, restoring its waters to their former purity, and reopened the Castalian cave which was overgrown with the entwining of wild vines. Clearing the laurel grove of briars, he restored Apollo to this ancient temple and brought back the Muses, soiled by rusticity, to their pristine beauty. Then he ascended to the topmost peaks of Parnassus" (*Opere minori*, ed. A. F. Massèra [Bari, 1928], 195–96). Finally, in 1346 Leonardo Bruni eulogizes all three in his "Vita di Messer Francesco Petrarca": see P. Villani, *Liber de civitatis Florentinae famosis civibus*, ed. G. C. Galleti (Florence, 1847). The passage appears in translation in *The Portable Renaissance Reader*, ed. J. B. Ross and M. McLaughlin (New York, 1953), 130.

It is generally recognized that Petrarch's humanism underwent two and perhaps three phases of development. In the first phase the younger Petrarch was engrossed in the recovery and restoration of ancient texts for their own sake. In the second phase the dominant note was an increasing awareness of the many similarities existing between classical and Christian thought. There is, however, what might be called an intermediate phase in which Petrarch discovered, prior to his turning his full attention to Christian writers, that classical thought was in itself directly applicable to his own day. The *Africa* (begun 1338), the early versions of *De viris illustribus* (begun 1338), and the *Rerum memorandarum libri* (begun 1343) marked the first phase; *De vita solitaria* (1346–71) and *De otio religioso* (1347–57) together with the *Secretum* (1342–58) marked the second; while *De remediis utriusque fortunae* (1354–66) marked the intermediate phase.

The following bibliographic listing is neither exhaustive nor faultless, and is intended simply as a convenient classification of varying interpretations of Petrarch's humanism.

General studies include H. Baron, "The Evolution of Petrarch's Thought: Reflections on the State of Petrarch Studies," in *From Petrarch to Leonardo Bruni* (Chicago, 1968), 7–50; C. Calcaterra, "Il Petrarca e il Petrarchismo," in *Problemi ed orientamenti critici di lingua e di letteratura italiana,* ed. A. Momigliano (Milan, 1949), 3:167–273; U. Dotti, "La formazione dell'umanesimo nel Petrarca," *Belfagor* 33 (1968): 532–63; E. Garin, *Italian Humanism: Philosophy and Civic Life in the Renaissance,* trans. P. Munz (New York, 1965), 19–27; P. O. Kristeller, *Eight Philosophers of the Italian Renaissance* (Stanford, 1964); *Petrarch, the First Modern Scholar and Man of Letters,* ed. J. H. Robinson and H. W. Rolfe (New York, 1914); E. H. R. Tatham, *Francesco Petrarca, the First Modern Man of Letters: His Life and Correspondence,* 2 vols. (London, 1925–26); C. Trinkaus, *In Our Image and Likeness: Humanity and Divinity in Italian Humanist Thought,* 2 vols. (Chicago, 1970), 1:3–50; and idem, *The Poet as Philosopher: Petrarch and the Formation of Renaissance Consciousness* (New Haven, 1979).

Phase 1 is studied in G. Billanovich, *Petrarca letterato,* vol. 1, *Lo scrittoio del Petrarca* (Rome, 1947); idem, "Dalle prime alle ultime letture del Petrarca," *Il Petrarca ad Arquà,* ed. G. Billanovich and G. Frasso (Padua, 1975), 13–50; idem, "Petrarca e gli storici romani," *Francesco Petrarca, Citizen of the World,* ed. A. S. Bernardo (Padua and Albany, 1980), 100–14. A. Bobbio, "Seneca e la formazione spirituale e culturale del Petrarca," *La bibliofilia* 43 (1941): 224–91. M. Boni, "Note ai *Rerum memorandarum libri,*" *Studi petrarcheschi* 2 (1949): 167–81. R. T. Bruère, "Lucan and Petrarch's *Africa,*" *Classical Philology* 56 (1961): 83–99. M. Cottino-Jones, "The Myth of Apollo and Daphne in Petrarch's *Canzoniere,*" *Francis Petrarch, Six Centuries Later,* ed. A. Scaglione (Chapel Hill and Chicago, 1975), 152–76. G. Crevatin, "Scipione e la fortuna del Petrarca nell'umanesimo," *Rinascimento* 17 (1977): 3–30. M. Feo, "Il sogno di Cerere e la morte del lauro petrarchesco," *Il Petrarca ad Arquà,* 117–48. N. Festa, "L'*Africa* poema della grandezza di Roma nella storia e nella visione profetica di Francesco Petrarca," *Annali della cattedra petrarchesca* 2 (1931): 39–67. G. Martellotti, "Sulla composizione del *De viris* e dell'*Africa,*" *Annali della R. Scuola Superiore di Pisa* 10 (1941): 247–62; idem, "Petrarca e Cesare," ibid. 16 (1942): 149ff.; idem, "La 'Collatio inter Scipionem, Alexandrum, Hanibalem, et Pyrrum,' un inedito del Petrarca nella biblioteca della University of Pennsylvania," *Classical, Medieval and Renaissance Studies in Honor of B. L. Ullman,* ed. C. Henderson, 2 vols. (Rome, 1964), 2:145–68; idem, "L'umanesimo del Petrarca," *Il veltro* 14.1–2 (1980): 71–82. N. Mann, "Petrarchism and Humanism: The Paradox of Posterity," in *Francesco Petrarca, Citizen of the World,* 287–300. E. Raimondi, "Alcune pagine del Petrarca sulla dignità umana," *Convivium* 19 (1947): 376–93. M. Waller, *Petrarch's Poetics and Literary Theory* (Amherst, 1980). J. H. Whitfield, *Petrarch and the Renascence* (Rome, 1953). R. M. Wilhelm, "Vergil's Dido and Petrarch's Sophonisba," *Studies in Language and Literature,* ed. C. Nelson (Richmond, KY, 1976), 585–91.

Phase 2 is treated in A. S. Bernardo, *Petrarch, Scipio and the "Africa": The Birth of Humanism's Dream* (Baltimore, 1962); idem, *Petrarch, Laura and the "Triumphs"* (Albany, 1974); idem, "La laura umanistica del Petrarca," in *Il Petrarca ad Arquà*, 7–12. K. Foster, *Petrarch: Poet and Humanist* (Edinburgh, 1984). K. Heitmann, "Insegnamenti agostiniani nel *Secretum*," *Bibliothèque d'humanisme et Renaissance* 22 (1960): 34–43. The intermediate phase is discussed in H. Baron, "Petrarch's *Secretum*: Was It Revised, Why?" in *From Petrarch to Leonardo Bruni*, 51–101. G. Billanovich, "Da Livio di Raterio al Livio del Petrarca," *Italia medioevale e umanistica* 2 (1959): 103–78. C. Calcaterra, "La concezione storica del Petrarca," in *Nella selva del Petrarca* (Bologna, 1942), 415–43; "Dedalus," ibid., 119–44. U. Dotti, "Aspetti della tematica petrarchesca, I: Umanesimo e poesia in Petrarca," *Letterature moderne* 9 (1959): 582–90. E. Faenzi, "Dall'*Africa* al *Secretum*, nuove ipotesi sul *Sogno di Scipione* e sulla composizione del poema," in *Il Petrarca ad Arquà*, 60–115. G. Martellotti, "Linee di sviluppo dell'umanesimo petrarchesco," *Studi petrarcheschi* 2 (1949): 51–82; idem, "In margine ai *Trionfi* e al *De viris*," ibid., 95–99. T. Mommsen, "Petrarch and the Decoration of the Sala virorum illustrium in Padua," *Art Bulletin* (1952): 95–116. *The Three Crowns of Florence: Humanist Assessments of Dante, Petrarca, and Boccaccio*, ed. and trans. D. Thompson and A. F. Nagel (New York, 1972). C. Trinkaus, "Petrarca and Classical Philosophy," in *Francesco Petrarca, Citizen of the World*, 249–74; idem, *Poet as Philosopher;* idem, *In Our Image*. F. X. Murphy, "Petrarch and the Christian Philosophy," in *Francesco Petrarca, Citizen of the World*, 223–47. J. Petrie, *Petrarch: The Augustan Poets, the Italian Tradition and the Canzoniere* (Dublin, 1983). S. Sturm-Maddox, *Petrarch's Metamorphoses: Text and Subtext in the "Rime Sparse"* (Columbia, MO, 1985).

2. "Dante's Ulysses, From Epic to Novel," in *Concepts of the Hero in the Middle Ages and the Renaissance* (Albany, NY, 1975), 101–19. A portion of what follows is included, from a different perspective, in my forthcoming essay, "Petrarch's Autobiography: Circularity Revisited," scheduled to appear in the autumn 1986 issue of *Annali d'italianistica*.

3. "Petrarch's Attitude Toward Dante," *PMLA* 70 (1955):488–517.

4. Martellotti, "L'umanesimo del Petrarca."

5. *Familiares* 10.5; 11.3; and 14.8, respectively (*Letters on Familiar Matters IX–XVI*, 79, 89–92, 247).

6. *Familiares* 1.8 (*Letters on Familiar Matters, I–VIII*, trans. A. S. Bernardo [Albany, NY, 1975], 41–46).

7. Indeed, God's grace allows them to retain their intellect in the "nobile castello" of Limbo:
    L'onrata nominanza,
    Che di lor suona su ne la tua vita,
    Grazia acquista nel ciel che sì li avanza. (*Inferno* 4:76–78)

8. Despite the controversy surrounding the ending of the *Secretum* there is little question that in it Petrarch clearly and consciously states an obligation to complete his transmittal of the classics to posterity, even at the risk of compromising his salvation. See my *Petrarch, Laura and the "Triumphs,"* 81; also my "Petrarch's Attitude Toward Dante," 499.

9. "Petrarch's Attitude Toward Dante," 495–500.

10. *Familiares* 11.3 (*Letters on Familiar Matters, IX–XVI,* 90).
11. *Familiares* 10.4 (ibid., 69–75).
12. See also my *Petrarch, Laura and the "Triumphs,"* 81–82.
13. *Familiares* 3.12 (*Letters on Familiar Matters, I–VIII,* 146).
14. This in essence is the message contained in Garin's brief section on Petrarch in his *Italian Humanism,* which has since been repeated in most subsequent studies on the subject. Cf. Dotti, "La formazione," 532–46.
15. "L'umanesimo del Petrarca," 78.
16. Ibid., 71–72.
17. *Seniles* 2.1.
18. See *Familiares* 22.10; *Seniles* 16.1.
19. *Familiares* 22.10.
20. See *Seniles* 2.1.
21. For differing views, see O. Giuliano, *Allegoria, retorica e poetica nel "Secretum" del Petrarca* (Bologna, 1977); F. Rico, *Vida u obra de Petrarca: Lectura del "Secretum"* (Chapel Hill, NC, 1974); F. Tateo, *Dialogo interiore e polemica ideologica nel "Secretum" del Petrarca* (Florence, 1965).
22. Petrarch, *Scipio and the "Africa."*
23. Macrobius, *Commentary on the Dream of Scipio,* trans. W. H. Stahl (New York, 1952), 82, 92.
24. *Pétrarque et l'humanisme* (Paris, 2d ed., 1907), 1:12.
25. *Canzoniere,* 186, in *Petrarch: Selected Sonnets, Odes, and Letters,* ed. and trans. T. G. Bergin (New York, 1966).
26. C. Calcaterra, *Nella selva del Petrarca,* 109–18; E. H. Wilkins, *The Making of the "Canzoniere" and Other Petrarchan Studies* (Rome, 1951), 9–69; Bernardo, *Petrarch, Laura and the "Triumphs,"* 75–77. For an English translation of the oration, see Wilkins, *Studies in the Life and Works of Petrarch* (Cambridge, MA, 1955), 300–13.
27. *The Life of Solitude,* trans. J. Zeitlin (Urbana, IL, 1924), 301, 316.
28. *Familiares* 24.1, lines 224–55.
29. Francesco Petrarca, *Prose,* ed. G. Martellotti et al. (Milan, 1955), 3–19.
30. Bernardo, *Petrarch, Laura, and the "Triumphs,"* 26–63.
31. *Canzoniere,* 264.
32. *Canzoniere,* 259–63: 259, 260, and 262 (pp. 90–91).
33. Ibid., 260 (p. 91).
34. Ibid., 263.
35. Ibid., 359.
36. P. Ferrarino, "La prima, e l'unica, 'Reductio omnium artium ad philologiam': Il 'De nuptiis Philologiae et Mercurii' di Marziano Capella e l'apoteosi della filologia," *Italia medioevale e umanistica* 12 (1969): 5.
37. *The Triumphs of Petrarch,* trans. E. H. Wilkins (Chicago, 1962), 112.
38. *Petrarch's "Africa,"* trans. T. G. Bergin and A. S. Wilson (New Haven, 1977), 239–40.
39. *Seniles* 1.5.
40. Freccero, "Dante's Ulysses," 102.

41. It is interesting to note that Martellotti divides the evolution of Petrarch's humanism into two phases. He calls the first "intransigent" and "receptive," consisting of the period in which Petrarch's discovery and readings of the ancients seemed to absorb his entire being. It was with the *De remediis* that this attachment was subordinated to the possible fruits and benefits to be derived from ancient authors by his own day. Indeed, he considered this work a manual for living, being convinced that the examples offered by the ancients and transmitted by writers could and must serve as a norm for everyday life. We thus move from a profound contemplation of the ancient world (almost an escape from reality) to a preoccupation with contemporary interests as served by the wisdom of the ancient world. This view may perhaps best be seen in his letters, which represent a happy fusion of humanity and literature.

Martellotti sees the second phase of Petrarch's humanism in his attempt to reconcile classical culture and Christian doctrine. His exclusive love for the Roman world is complemented by other reasonable voices, starting with St. Augustine in the *Secretum*. With *De vita solitaria* (ca. 1345) we see the two cultures side by side, while in the concept of *otium* as defined in the *De otio religioso* Petrarch thought he had found a real point of contact between pagan wisdom and Christian spirituality. It was, in fact, shortly after *De vita solitaria* that he decided to expand the original design of *De viris illustribus* to include not only the Romans but all great men, starting with Adam, as found in both sacred and profane history. As a result, even in the relatively late *De ignorantia* (1365–70) Cicero's sayings are compared to those of the apostles. See Petrarch, *Prose, 729.*

PART II

ITALIAN HUMANISM

A　HUMANISM IN THE MAJOR CITY-STATES OF QUATTROCENTO ITALY

B　ITALY'S LEADING HUMANIST

C　HUMANIST CULTURE AND THE MARGINS OF SOCIETY

A & HUMANISM IN THE MAJOR CITY-STATES OF QUATTROCENTO ITALY

7 & THE SIGNIFICANCE OF "CIVIC HUMANISM" IN THE INTERPRETATION OF THE ITALIAN RENAISSANCE
Albert Rabil, Jr.

I N HIS STILL CLASSIC ANALYSIS OF THE RENAISSANCE, JACOB BURCK-hardt asserted that both republics and despotic states indifferently produced "the individual" who emerged for the first time in four-teenth-century Italy:[1] for these men were characterized above all else by their learning, their indifference to politics, and their cosmopolitanism. The class of men known as humanists, intended by this description, were devoted above all to classical—Greek and Latin—languages and litera-ture. In classical culture they found all they needed for the expression of their many-sided personalities. Burckhardt admitted that it was above all others the Florentines "who made antiquarian interests one of the chief objectives of their lives" and that "they were of peculiar significance dur-ing the period of transition at the beginning of the fifteenth century, since it was in them that humanism first showed itself practically as an indis-pensable element in daily life."[2]

For several generations after Burckhardt, interpretation of Renais-sance humanism emphasized it as an antiquarian movement more or less diffused throughout Italy. The fact that it first expressed itself most force-fully in Florence around the turn of the fifteenth century and that Flor-ence was a republic rather than a princely state did not lead anyone to raise the question of whether there might be some connection between humanism and Florentine polity and, if so, whether the definition of hu-manism as a movement indifferent to politics might not need to be mod-ified. No one did so, that is, until Eugenio Garin in Italy, and Hans Baron, first in Germany and after the rise of Hitler in the United States, made this question their point of departure. The conclusions they reached have had a profound effect on the interpretation of Renaissance humanism.

*   *   *

Eugenio Garin has argued most forcefully that "early humanism was a glorification of civic life and of the construction of an earthly city by man"[3] and that in this respect it represents a much more radical break with the Middle Ages than the Middle Ages with classical antiquity.[4] The most powerful representatives of civic humanism belong to Florence, which was the cradle of humanism and its most brilliant light throughout the period of humanism's ascendancy.[5] But the spirit evoked by civic humanism was not confined to Florence. It spread with the humanist movement throughout the cities and courts of Italy, breathing a new ethos into an old world.

The new spirit began with Petrarch and continued until the rise of Platonism (roughly from 1350 until 1475), when it was replaced by new impulses—the Florence of Savonarola was not at all the Florence of Leonardo Bruni. But even as humanist culture and the conditions that had given rise to it were dying, the spirit it had generated continued to be diffused. In the fifteenth century it found expression in art, history, and education. In the sixteenth, it flowered in science and religion.

What does the glorification of civic life and the construction of an earthly city by man mean? It means the validation of human activity of all kinds and, with this validation, the belief that activity takes precedence over contemplation inasmuch as it keeps human beings rooted in practical human concerns. Garin finds this new attitude most perfectly expressed in the prologue of Leon Battista Alberti's *Della famiglia*. Alberti asks the question whether human failure or success depends on fortune or on human character. His answer is unequivocal: fortune triumphs only over those who submit to it. The Romans, he argues, did not triumph over many barbarous nations by luck but by the strength of their own virtues. These virtues were, primarily, concern to do good works and keep the traditions of their fatherland, and "as long as they possessed lofty and pious spirits, grave and mature counsel, perfect faith and loyalty toward the fatherland—as long as concern for the public good outweighed with them the pursuit of private ends, as long as the will of the state overruled the individual's desires"—so long did Rome prosper. But "as soon as unjust desires counted for more in Italy than good laws and the hallowed habits of restraint, the Latin empire grew weak and bloodless."[6] Fortune cannot rob us of our character, and as long as we possess nobility of soul we can ascend to the highest peaks of human achievement and glory. Alberti goes on to say that what is true of empires is true also of families, and he wishes to exhort his own kinsmen to maintain the traditions that enabled the family to rise to greatness in the past.

Individual greatness is part of cultural greatness. And cultural greatness is the product of many generations working always with the future in view. Matteo Palmieri says in this connection: "It is not possible to say whence a man comes; but it is certain that there is in our hearts a longing for future centuries which compels us to seek eternal fame, a happy condition for our country and enduring health for those who are about to descend from us."[7] Human beings achieve personal greatness by having in mind the greatness of the community of which they are a part.

The source of this new attitude was the *studia humanitatis*. Through their labors in philological criticism, humanists for the first time discovered a distance between the past and the present. It was this humanist discovery that brought to awareness the fact that a break had occurred and gave rise to the need to define the present as against the past. The sense of separation created the need to build anew—on the past but differently from the past. When Pier Paolo Vergerio writes of education, he "seeks to show how *litterae*, through their ability to further the conversation between minds across the ages, make the soul capable of absorbing a richer and more all-embracing kind of *humanitas*. 'What is there more beautiful than reading and writing and to get to know the ancient world and to converse with those who will live after us and to appropriate all ages, the past as well as the present?' Thanks to *litterae* the mind unfolds and enlarges itself. And while it enriches itself with untold treasures, it learns to respect the value of other minds and to live in human society. Wisdom, far from incarcerating itself in an ivory tower 'lives in cities, flees solitude and longs to be of help to as many men as possible.'"[8]

Garin, then, argues that humanism is much more than an antiquarian movement, that it represents an alliance between the man of thought and the man of action, that this alliance finds its fullest expression in Florence where scholarship was joined with a republican civic spirit, that this civic humanism spread throughout the cities and courts of Italy during the Quattrocento, and that as it did so it profoundly affected attitudes and developments in the arts and sciences. Although Garin's analysis moves largely within the framework of the history of ideas, he affirms a concrete connection between ideas and their social and political context, a connection that created new ideas (in relation to the Middle Ages) and influenced politics in new directions.

*   *   *

Hans Baron has made the question of civic humanism the central preoccupation of his scholarly career.[9] Although his interpretation is similar to Garin's,[10] it involves a thesis much more sharply defined. And it is Baron's formulation that has been so widely discussed in the interpretation of Renaissance humanism during the past generation.

Baron begins with two important assumptions. First, as he says, "we have learnt to interpret the coming of the early Renaissance also as a fundamental transformation in *Weltanschauung*."[11] This view, articulated in a general way by Wilhelm Dilthey, reinforces Burckhardt's contention that there is a fundamental discontinuity between the Middle Ages and the Renaissance. Something must therefore account for it. Second, as Vasari long ago recognized, there were two Renaissances in art, but only the second of them, in early Quattrocento Florence, established the new Renaissance *Weltanschauung*.[12] But if the Renaissance really began in Florence at the beginning of the Quattrocento there must be some connection between this beginning and humanism.

Baron discovered the connection in "civic humanism," which appears in his earliest writings in German and English. In his edition of Bruni's works in 1928[13] he argued that from Salutati to Ficino humanists in Florence were identified with the wealthy ruling families, shared their interests, and developed a positive evaluation of social activity. Such a development was only possible in a republic; humanists who patronized the courts of despots were contemptuous of the business enterprises of the Florentine burgher and extolled the life of leisure. Thus civic humanism cannot be separated from Florence's republican political tradition, for it could have developed in no other environment.

The actual transition he traces in two articles published in English in 1938. In one, entitled "Franciscan Poverty and Civic Wealth as Factors in the Rise of Humanistic Thought,"[14] he demonstrates that in the thought of all Trecento humanists—above all in Petrarch, but also in his Florentine disciples—the attitude toward wealth and the active political life is ambivalent. Petrarch extolled poverty when he lived at Vaucluse but not after he moved to the court of Milan. Petrarch cites Cicero and Seneca in whose writings the Stoic wise man eschews riches in favor of a life of solitude and independence, and he finds these views echoed in writer after writer. Such an attitude was out of step with the feeling of the Florentine citizens, who could not be reconciled to a humanism of this kind. In fact a new view emerged in 1415 in Francesco Barbaro's treatise *On Wifely Duties*, "the first time that we meet with expressions of the genuine civic spirit in humanistic literature."[15] In it he describes possessions as useful for many purposes, especially for our descendants. Shortly afterward, Bruni's apology for wealth rediscovered the civic character of Aristotle's *Politics* and the positive evaluation of wealth in Aristotle's *Ethics*. Humanists in Florence and elsewhere began to echo these views, to rediscover Xenophon's *Oeconomicus*—the most kindly disposed of all classical works toward the acquisition of wealth—and to discover more positive attitudes in Seneca and Cicero as well.

In another article, "Cicero and the Roman Civic Spirit in the Middle Ages and the Early Renaissance,"[16] Baron examines still another side of the attitude toward Cicero that helps to mark the transition. In the Middle Ages Cicero was seen as the Stoic sage removed from the world (corroborated by the medieval view of Cicero's attitude toward wealth), a perspective affirmed in part by Petrarch, who was repelled by his discovery (in 1345 in the *Letters to Atticus*) of Cicero the political figure. The civic humanists of the early Quattrocento, by contrast, found in Cicero's combination of literary and political activity a view of him congenial to themselves.

Baron thus established his thesis that the transformation we call the Renaissance that occurred in early Quattrocento Florence applied not only to the history of art but also to the humanist movement. But the question remains: What caused the transformation? Why was there suddenly a new appreciation for the positive values of wealth and of Cicero the philosopher-statesman? Whence arose civic humanism? In his major work on the subject, published in 1955,[17] Baron ascribed the cause to Florence's conflict with Milan, culminating in a war fought between 1400 and 1402 in which Florence avoided Milanese conquest.

The possibility of conquest by Milan posed a threat to Florentine autonomy almost continually after 1350. Milan was ruled by Ghibellines, men who had been appointed by the emperors and who made themselves tyrants when Hohenstaufen rule came to an end (1254 in Germany, 1266 in Sicily). The leading force against the Ghibellines was the papacy, now in exile at Avignon, allied with Guelf (bourgeois) cities like Florence. More often than not (though not consistently) Florence saw itself as a defender of the church and supporter of its policies. In 1377, however, the papacy, preparing to return to Rome from its extended exile at Avignon, sent legates ahead to assert strong leadership (in effect tyrannies) in the areas surrounding Rome. Florence soon found itself at the head of a central-Italian league fighting in the "War of the Eight Saints" against the dangers of attack from the papal state. The outcome of this war was to strengthen the tendency of the Florentines to regard themselves as the leaders of the free city-states.

During the 1380s Milan continued to expand southward and to incorporate smaller city-states into its orbit of power. Neither Rome nor Venice would aid Florence but were content to let Florence bear the burden of opposition to Milan. Florence did so—between 1390 and 1392 and again between 1397 and 1398. The latter struggle ended in a treaty that did not, however, guarantee the safety of the city-states allied with Florence, and within two years Milan had annexed them all. In 1400, therefore, Florence was isolated; only Bologna stood as a buffer between Milan and Florence. With a sense of desperation, Florence hired a mercenary army of German knights, led by Rupert of the Palatinate, the newly elected pretender to the imperial throne. The Visconti, however, defeated Rupert in October 1401, before he could make his way very far into Italy. Milan was now at the height of its power, and Florence seemed doomed. In the spring of 1402 (when the armies could once again campaign), the Milanese entered Bologna. By June nothing lay between the Milanese army and Florence. The Florentines expected to see the enemy before the gates any day. Yet the signal for attack was not given, probably because the Visconti had defeated its other enemies by a show of might and by propaganda, waiting for treachery and defection to undermine a city. But the moment came and went. For the plague erupted in northern Italy, carrying off the Milanese tyrant, Giangaleazzo Visconti, on 3 September. Milanese expansion was altogether halted, at least for a time, by his death.

The Florentines "credited their almost miraculous salvation more to the brave stand which they alone had made than to the sudden removal of the tyrant from the scene."[18] The fact that Florence had met the crisis alone was decisive for the climate of that city. "When the crisis had passed, the real issue of the Florentine–Milanese contest stood revealed: out of the struggle had come the decision that the road was to remain open to the civic freedom and the system of independent states which became a part of the culture of the Italian Renaissance."[19]

The effects of this event on the humanists were immediate and decisive. In a *History of Florence, 1380–1406*, written in 1407, Gregorio Dati asserted that "all the freedom of Italy lay in the hands of the Florentines alone, that every other power had deserted them."[20] To the humanists, Florence had become the city of freedom. This view is nowhere more evident than in Leonardo Bruni's *Panegyric to the City of Florence* (which Baron dates 1403–4 rather than, as previously believed, 1400) and his second *Dialogue to Peter Paul Vergerius* (which Baron dates 1405 rather than 1401).[21] In the latter he raised for the first time questions about Dante's interpretation of Caesar and his assassins Brutus and Cassius. Dante had placed Caesar in limbo and his assassins in the depths of hell. Now Dante had long been the pride of Florence, but his monarchical views were contrary to the republican sentiments of those who had just lived through a crisis threatening their liberty. Bruni sought a solution that would both exalt republican sentiments and save Dante. He argued that Dante had used historical figures only to serve the ends of his poetical imagination without actually taking sides with Caesar's tyranny against the last defenders of civic freedom in Rome. This new republican view of Dante had been unknown during the Trecento. So congenial was it to the feeling of the humanists that it was repeated by humanists throughout the century.

Bruni also argued in dialogue 2 that the republic had given rise to men of great talent in many fields but that "after the republic had been subjected to the power of one man, those brilliant minds vanished as Cornelius Tacitus says."[22] This judgment was new, both because no one had consistently maintained it in the past and because it rested on a new historian, Tacitus, who had only recently been rediscovered through the manuscript at Monte Cassino brought to Florence by Boccaccio. In Tacitus himself the judgment quoted by Bruni had been a secondary one, for he had accepted the imperial monarchy as a historical necessity and, indeed, became a guide for monarchical publicists in the sixteenth and seventeenth centuries. Bruni selected a facet of Tacitus congenial to his new point of view.

In his *Panegyric* Bruni maintained further, following the lead of Salutati, that Florence had been founded during the days of the Roman Republic, before the corruption of the empire had set in. It was the Roman army under Sulla in the first century B.C. that founded Florence. By the time Bruni came to write his history of Florence some years later, he added to his arsenal of reasons for Florence's establishment during the Roman Republic the discovery of the part the Etruscan city-states played in pre-Roman times. Thus Florence had originally been a city with free blood running in its veins. To the argument that Vergil, Horace, and other great writers lived during the reign of Augustus, Bruni replied that they had been raised under the Republic. (Poggio was to make the same reply to Guarino during the next generation in the same dispute.) Finally, the freedom of these city-states was stifled by the Roman Empire and reemerged after its fall. Thus the resurgence of Florence in contemporary times has its roots in the earlier energy of the city in republican Rome. Machiavelli developed this conception of Bruni's that a wealth of human energies had been stifled by the Roman Empire but came to the fore again with the rise of free city-republics.[23] Not until the triumph of monarchic absolutism in the latter part of the sixteenth century was this republican interpretation of Roman history in Florence challenged.

Baron argues further that this change in political preference from monarchy to republic involved at the same time a deeper underlying change in intellectual vision (part 4), in other words, that the humanism that emerged in Florence could only have emerged under the conditions of a free city-state. Not only so, but this new civic humanism became determinative for the whole of humanism during the Quattrocento (part 5): the essence of Italian humanism in general during the Quattrocento was Florentine civic humanism.

In order to appreciate these larger claims, the nature of the change in consciousness must first be explored. Baron sees it preeminently in Bruni's *Dialogues*. In dialogue 1 Bruni argues, through Niccolò Niccoli, that classical learning is dead in his own time (Salutati excepted) and that this fact is reflected in the myriad deficiencies of the "three crowns of Florence," Dante, Petrarch, and Boccaccio. Dialogue 2 rehabilitates the three Florentine writers and asserts that far from being dead, learning is everywhere being revived. The reversal of historical judgment is profound. Instead of seeing the classical past as something to which the present can never measure up, it is regarded as something to be equaled and surpassed. In other words, the classical ideal is no longer to be viewed only as an intellectual tradition but is fused with civic aspirations. Civic humanism is the result of this fusion.

Baron finds evidence of this new civic humanism in the transformation of humanist attitudes toward the vernacular. In 1435 a debate took place between Bruni, Biondo, and other humanists working in the Roman curia, which was exiled at the time in Florence. Biondo argued that the Italian vernacular had been created by a fusion of Latin with the languages of the Germanic invaders of the Roman Empire. Bruni opposed Biondo's view, contending that there had always existed both a popular and a learned way of speaking and that popular speech was the Italian vernacular, even in the days of Terence and Cicero. Biondo's theory is the more historically correct and was judged so even by his contemporaries. But Bruni may not have been affirming a rigid classicism that finds no value in the vernacular, as previous interpreters have largely maintained. Indeed, in Biondo's account of the debate itself, it is evident that he regarded the vernacular as inferior. Bruni instead may have been attributing a higher value to the vernacular, and so giving a higher status to popular culture. This interpretation is suggested more strongly by his *Life of Dante* written during the following year (1436) in which he asserted that *every* language has its own perfection, even its own way of speaking scientifically, thus explicitly placing the vernacular on a level with Latin and Greek. This judgment coincides with the earliest use of the vernacular as a literary language by humanists in the 1430s, notably by Palmieri and Alberti. After Bruni, one finds in Alberti, Lorenzo de' Medici, and Cristoforo Landino affirmations of the equality of the vernacular with the classical languages. This alliance indicates a new type of classicism, one "willing to employ the ancient model as a guide in building a new literature with a new language in a new nation."[24]

The fusion between the civic spirit and Christianity is evident in a different way. In the Trecento there had been a tendency to fuse pagan and Christian literature. The tendency is evident in Petrarch and Boccaccio; Petrarch had argued that the pagan poets were really monotheists and Boccaccio that they were the first theologians. Salutati did not at first accept this position, apologizing in a letter of 1378 for reading pagan poets in spite of their errors. But in the late 1390s he developed the earlier position of his predecessors, maintaining that the pagan poets were genuine seekers after piety. Thereafter he used this idea as a key to interpreting classical mythology. He did not, for all that, identify pagan gods with Christian saints. But a number of humanists were led to make this identification. Francesco da Fiano, for example, a Roman humanist writing at the turn of the century, argued in his enthusiasm for antiquity, that even theologically there was little difference between paganism and Christianity. Salutati was drawn back from this tendency by the emergence of civic humanism. In other words, civic humanism arrested the movement of humanism toward paganism and brought it closer to Christianity.[25] No longer glorifying classical culture as an ideal, humanists were free to use their classicism in the interest of elevating their own culture without confusing the two.

As one would expect, civic humanists assumed different attitudes toward their own world. Both Petrarch and Boccaccio extolled the ideal of the aloofness of the sage and expressed contempt for marriage and civic responsibility. In his *Life of Dante* Boccaccio viewed Dante's family life and his worries about administration of the city-state as the causes of his unhappiness. This attitude persisted among a number of Quattrocento humanists. The most outstanding example among many who could be cited is Niccolò Niccoli, Bruni's spokesman in his *Dialogues*. He sought neither marriage nor public office, but lived solely for his studies, as his eulogists said after his death. Baron characterizes him as "the type of citizen turned socially irresponsible man of letters," and cites in this connection Niccoli's opposition to Florentine efforts to resist tyranny.[26] A purely scholarly attitude that seeks to avoid identification with civic life—exemplified chiefly in marriage and service to the state—was a strong tendency among *literati*, which the emergence of civic humanism in Florence short-circuited.

These new attitudes, Baron believes, were not confined to Florence. When, in the 1420s, Milanese expansion once again brought Florence into conflict with the Visconti, Florence was badly defeated on the battlefield and was saved from being overrun only by the intervention of

Venice. Venetian humanists, deeply influenced by Florentine civic humanism after 1402, spoke of themselves as protectors of Italy's liberty. Their hope for permanent cooperation between the "free peoples" of Italy became an inspiring political ideal among Venetians as well as among Florentines.[27] Other, smaller city-states were subsequently added to this alliance. Genoa broke away from Milan in 1435–36 and joined Florence and Venice. Lucca followed suit in 1438. All four were then joined in an alliance of the "free peoples" of Italy. It was in this atmosphere that the Florentine Poggio Bracciolini (in 1435) and the Venetian Pietro del Monte (in 1440) defended the "Respublica Romana" against Caesar.

The high point of this republican sentiment was reached in the late 1440s. In 1447 the last Visconti died and the Milanese proclaimed a "Respublica Ambrosiana." Because of its lack of republican tradition, Milan was unable to establish a firm republican regime. Instead, in the ensuing chaos, Venice was persuaded to take over some of the smaller city-states formerly under Milan. This event led Milan to turn once again to dictatorship, this time to the Sforzas. The ensuing Treaty of Lodi pitted Florence in an alliance with Milan against Venice and Naples. The absence of a republican tradition in Milan halted the progress of republicanism and hence also of civic humanism. Neoplatonism replaced humanism as the dominant thought current in Florence. But by then the civic spirit had left its place of birth and had spread throughout Italy. Baron summarizes this period as follows:

> Humanism, as molded by the Florentine crisis, produced a pattern
> of conduct and thought which was not to remain limited to Floren
> tine humanists. From that time on there would exist a kind of Hu
> manism which endeavored to educate a man as a member of his
> society and state; a Humanism which refused to follow the medie
> val precedent of looking upon the Rome of the emperors as the di
> vinely guided preparation for a Christian 'Holy Empire' and the
> center of all interest in the ancient world; a Humanism which
> sought to learn from antiquity by looking upon it not melancholi
> cally as a golden age never again to be realized, but as an exem
> plary parallel to the present, encouraging the moderns to seek to
> rival antiquity in their vernacular languages and literatures and in
> many other fields. Whereas such an approach to the past and to
> the present had nowhere been found before 1400, it became insep
> arable from the growth of Humanism during the Renaissance.[28]

These qualities of civic humanism became the chief contributions of humanism to the subsequent development of the West. Baron continues,

"Renaissance Humanism would by no means occupy the place in the growth of the modern world that is rightly attributed to it had those traits ever disappeared again after they had emerged from the early-Quattrocento crisis." For "although this type of socially engaged, historically-minded, and increasingly vernacular Humanism far from exhausts the rich variety of the humanistic movements of the Renaissance, in many respects it was the salt in the humanistic contribution to the rise of the modern world."[29]

To state this point in the strongest possible way, Baron wants to maintain that without civic humanism, which grew on Florentine soil—and could only have grown in a republican atmosphere—the western world would not now have as part of its heritage political pluralism in both thought and form, an orientation toward the future rather than toward the past, or vernacular literatures. It is in these senses, rather than in "the discovery of the world and of man," as Burckhardt would have it, that the Italian Renaissance represents the birth of the modern world.

There have been a number of critical responses to the idea of civic humanism in the form in which Baron states it. One kind of critique raises questions about the adequacy of his methodology. Others, focusing on his conclusions, arrive at various judgments. One critic denies the existence of civic humanism altogether. Others believe that Baron has effectively demonstrated the existence of a civic humanism but that many of the larger conclusions he wishes to draw from his demonstration are not warranted. Still others, accepting the establishment of a Florentine civic humanism, raise the question—as Florentine historians—whether alternative explanations do not clarify or augment the theory in important respects. I shall discuss each of these types of response in turn.

*   *   *

An Italian critic, Gennaro Sasso, in a review essay of the first edition of the *Crisis*,[30] suggests that Baron is guilty of exalting Florence's struggle with Milan into an eternal moment of the human spirit. He cites the passage in which Baron asserts that Florence's relation to Milan in 1402 was analogous to that of Britain to Germany at Dunkirk in 1940: in both cases a historic moment came and went, and unforeseen developments upset the apparently inevitable course of fate. Baron believes that only from this perspective can we grasp adequately the psychological significance of the crisis of 1402 for the history of Florence.[31] Unfortunately, Sasso maintains, this methodological flaw—seeing the Florentine–Milanese struggle as an eternal moment—permeates Baron's study. For instead of investigating concretely the question of the internal nature and vitality of the Florentine and Milanese governments with a view to establishing the concrete ways in which they embodied political ideals, he has made them "ideal types."[32] For although Baron has clearly demonstrated that the political sentiment of liberty is embodied in the writings of the humanists, he has not demonstrated that these sentiments find expression in the real political life of Florence. Rather he has assumed that the government of Florence must have embodied the sentiments expressed by the humanists (thus taking the humanists' assessment at face value) and was therefore "good." Milan, as a tyrannical government, was "bad." The ideal types are not themselves established by concrete analysis but set up as the basis for the analysis that takes them for granted. This flaw raises the question: Why is Florence judged good in this schema? The answer is the cultural results it achieved. Cultural results that have contributed to the democratic development of the West have grown out of the Florentine Renaissance, and these results justify Florentine politics. But in making such an assumption, Baron has left the plane of political-historical analysis entirely.

Sasso has raised an important question. The methodological issue is a critical one. It is important to recall that Baron's thesis began to emerge in the 1920s, when he first used the phrase "civic humanism," and that he documented its presence during the 1930s while he was fleeing Hitler's Germany first for Italy and subsequently for the United States. It is not surprising that the way in which he finally formulated his thesis has an intrinsic relation to the rise of tyranny before his eyes and its opposition by the political democracies. Doubtless the attempt to demonstrate that political democracy and cultural pluralism were the hallmarks of the humanism that marks the real birth of the Renaissance and that this humanism was not, as earlier interpreters had believed, indifferent to politics or more intimately related to tyrannical than to republican politics, was an important motivation. The most problematic aspects of Baron's thesis rest on it.

It is difficult to believe that the growth of political democracy, the rise of vernacular literatures, and an attitude that looks toward future achievement rather than toward an ideal past would never have developed if they had not been bequeathed to the western world by republican Florence in the transition from the medieval to the modern worlds. It is one thing to say that humanism may have had a connection with all these things, another to say that humanism is responsible for them in the sense that without it they would not have come into being. In Baron, this thesis is asserted without being demonstrated. Nor could it very well be demonstrated, even on a superstructure much greater than the one Baron constructs. The rise of nation-states and their various political forms, the development of vernacular literatures, and the emergence of modern science with its explosive view of knowledge are much too complex to rest solely on the foundation of Renaissance Florence. But if these larger claims are problematic, what of the notion of civic humanism itself?

※ ※ ※

Jerrold Seigel denies that civic humanism ever existed.[33] In his view the older interpretations of humanism are much to be preferred, especially as most recently described by Paul O. Kristeller.[34] According to this older view humanists were professional rhetoricians and their interests were determined by that fact. They were never inspired by political considerations.

Since Baron's thesis rests principally on his interpretation of Leonardo Bruni and his new dating of Bruni's *Dialogues* and his *Panegyric to the City of Florence,* Seigel focuses his attention on these aspects of Baron's thesis. He argues that Bruni's *Dialogues* were not, as Baron believes, conceived and written at different times (the second after Giangaleazzo's death) but at the same time (both prior to his death). His "most powerful argument" in this connection is that Bruni follows very closely, in both the form and substance of his arguments, book 2 of Cicero's *De oratore.* There Cicero was addressing himself to the relation between knowledge and the ability to speak well. Bruni shows himself—and in the same way as Cicero—concerned with this question. Cicero's book is obviously of a piece; since Bruni imitates Cicero his two dialogues must also be of a piece. And since, further, it is acknowledged that dialogue 1 was written in 1401, that is, prior to the climax of the crisis with Giangaleazzo, the same must also be true for dialogue 2. Neither dialogue, in fact, had anything to do with the birth of a new civic spirit but both had to do with rhetoric, of which Bruni was a professional practitioner.

Seigel likewise finds the dating of the *Panegyric* in 1403 rather than 1400 unconvincing. The *Panegyric* refers to Giangaleazzo's capture of a number of cities. F. P. Luiso demonstrated years ago that this passage refers to the years 1397 to 1400 and not to 1402. But what of the fact that Bologna is included in this list, when it did not fall until 1402? The reference, Seigel maintains, is not to the historical event of 1402 but to rumors that were rife in Florence in 1400 when the city was on edge, rumors to which Bruni himself later referred in his history of Florence. Even more decisive is the fact that if the *Panegyric* had been written in 1403 it would surely have mentioned the death of Giangaleazzo, which it does not do.[35]

Baron responded one year later in the same journal to Seigel's critique.[36] Regarding Bruni's use of Cicero's *De oratore,* he maintains that even if everything Seigel says about his use of it is true (though there is much about it that could be disputed), the question would still remain to what extent he made use of it and, more importantly, when. Bruni could have used *De oratore* for dialogue 1 and then returned to it years later. However, Baron concludes, neither Seigel's contention nor this rejoinder is testable by reference to the texts, and the debate should turn on what the texts themselves tell us. What do they tell us?

Regarding the *Panegyric,* the critical passage contested by Seigel in his reference to Luiso reads as follows: "In Tuscany, he [Giangaleazzo] held Pisa, Siena, Perugia, and Assisi in his grip, and eventually he had even occupied Bologna." This list, Baron points out, proceeds chronologically. Pisa fell in 1399, Siena later that year, Perugia at the beginning of 1400, Assisi in May. Since Bologna is placed at the end of this list the time referred to must be subsequent to the fall of Assisi. The text itself thus supports the later dating. And if one accepts the post-1402 date of the *Panegyric,* the later date of dialogue 2 is also confirmed, since the latter cites the former.

What does the life of Bruni subsequent to the writing of these treatises indicate about his allegiances? Seigel attempts to show that throughout the remainder of his life Bruni's preoccupations were rhetorical and not political;[37] Baron, to the contrary, that Bruni's biography reveals a Florentine patriot whose principal intellectual occupation was the writing of a history of Florence that embodied a new political outlook in relation to past histories of the city.

Baron's analysis appears to have more textual support than Seigel's effort to dislodge it. But at this level the debate does not illuminate the broader issues involved.

*   *   *

Other intellectual historians have accepted some aspects of Baron's thesis, offering various qualifications. Kristeller, for example, whose interpretation of humanism Seigel would prefer to that of Baron, has written:

> Hans Baron in a series of studies has forcefully described this civic humanism which flourished in Florence during the first half of the fifteenth century, and it certainly deserves attention as one of the most impressive phases of Renaissance humanism, even though it would be quite mistaken to identify Renaissance humanism as a whole with this Florentine civic humanism. There was a good deal of "despotic humanism" even in fifteenth-century Italy, and it would be quite impossible to compare under the heading of "civic humanism" the entire political literature of the Renaissance period,

let alone the large body of humanist literature that was not concerned with political problems at all.[38]

Charles Trinkaus suggests that to state the issue in terms of civic versus despotic humanism is to miss the central point, namely, that the real influence of humanism lies in a different area altogether—that referred to by Kristeller as not concerned with political problems at all. He writes:

> a weakness in the concept of a 'civic humanism,' as both Hans Baron and Eugenio Garin have conceived it, is that it stresses the political and even the republican aspects of the idea too exclusively. The well-known fact that humanists with similar moral philosophies have served at both despotic and republican centres with equal praise for the ruling power has given rise to the facetious suggestion that there was also a 'despotic humanism.' May I suggest that the entire question has been too narrowly conceived, and that it is in the humanists' affirmation of an activist, constructivist, industrious view of man's nature, within a societal rather than a political nexus, that their significance may be discovered. The true significance of the Renaissance and of the humanist movement as a central part of it lies more in what Burckhardt and Michelet called "The Discovery of the World and of Man" than in a poorly founded, premature vision of political democracy.[39]

Eugene Rice sums up what is accepted and what questionable in the view of many intellectual historians while relating it to his study of changes in the idea of wisdom:

> The civic enthusiasm of Bruni, Palmieri, Manetti, and Alberti is only one facet of Italian humanism in the fifteenth century; and it would be misleading to suppose that ideas of wisdom which got their special flavor from this civic emphasis on active life were necessarily typical either of Italy or of the century as a whole. They appear, indeed, to have been limited both in time and place: to Florence, with the occasional exception of the Venetian Republic and to the first three-quarters of the century. Outside of Florence, the ideals of humanism and the burgher class were less closely allied, and speculation on the meaning of wisdom tended to reflect, not the novel interests of the *bourgeoisie*, but the traditional attitudes of princely or ecclesiastical governments or the more personal, often pessimistic sentiments of individual humanists. The

important consequence was a tendency to renew—or simply per-
petuate—the traditional emphasis on contemplative and religious
elements in the idea of wisdom, an attitude as typical of the period
as the more original position of Bruni.[40]

Wallace K. Ferguson raises another issue: the priority of Petrarch as
a founder of humanism, put into question by Baron's thesis. He finds
compelling the older and almost universal judgment that Petrarch inaugurated a new age and sees Dante as the transitional figure rather than
Petrarch, Petrarch as the seminal figure rather than Salutati or Bruni.[41]
Baron, in a friendly debate with Ferguson, replied that he considers Petrarch neither medieval nor Renaissance but rather like Moses, who was
allowed to see the promised land but not to enter it.[42] For intellectual
historians, the question of Petrarch's place remains fundamental in assessing the new consciousness of the Renaissance.

*   *   *

The presence of a new form of humanism in Florence raises the question:
What is its source and meaning? A number of Florentine social historians
have focused on this question during the generation after the first appearance of Baron's thesis and have thrown a different light on his interpretation.

Marvin Becker accepts the connection between culture and politics
that Baron wishes to establish but finds the connection in economic and
political developments internal to the Florentine state rather than in the
impact of external events on Florence.[43] Moreover, the critical events that
congealed a "civic humanism" he attributes to the years after 1343,
when a good many indexes point to profound changes within Florence
itself. The key to all change was the increased need for money to finance
wars of expansion in which Florence was engaged throughout Tuscany.
Until the 1320s the public treasury was more or less in balance. Communal debts could still be met by noble families who regarded the city
more or less as their fief. But from that time forward the debt progressively increased until, by the 1340s, it had reached sizable proportions.
The establishment of the *Monte,* or floating communal debt, in 1345
symbolized a turning point. "The *Monte* came to be so imbedded in civic
life that it was to assume the role of determinant in the formulation of
public policy."[44] Although contemporaries believed that the conditions
creating it would pass away, the debt never thereafter decreased but instead grew rapidly with each passing decade. As a result, government
spending and borrowing played an increasingly decisive role in Florentine politics. Guilds, the *Parte Guelfa,* wealthy families, and other cor-

porate bodies within the commune to which people had previously given as great or greater allegiance as to the commune itself, were now replaced by the commune as the object of allegiance, for every Florentine family with any wealth invested its money in the communal debt. When the debt was established in 1345 less than one hundred families had large-scale *Monte* holdings; by 1427 the number had increased twentyfold, and in most instances the amounts involved were thirty and forty times greater than earlier. The management of such great sums of money required a large, professional bureaucracy. The Florentine bureaucracy increased fivefold between 1343 and 1393; and crucial positions within it having to do with the management of money came to be filled by appointment (that is, by professionals) rather than by lot or popular election.

The wars against the Visconti near the end of the Trecento further intensified the tendencies that had emerged in the 1340s. In 1390 Florence resorted to forced loans (*prestanze*) which might be exacted several times a year, thus increasing the public debt even further. In 1427 the *catasto* or direct tax on the value of individual goods was introduced. It is hardly surprising that Leonardo Bruni, chancellor of Florence at this time (1427–44), asserted that wealth is to the city as blood is to the individual.

So also with other expressions of Florentine civic humanism: when Bruni extolled equality before the law, he was praising a much tighter state control over the lives of every citizen. The *vita civile* was an expression of the stake each citizen had in the survival of the Florentine state. Civic humanism, therefore, did not arise out of the wars with the Visconti, but out of the economic conditions brought on by Florentine expansion much earlier in the Trecento, which in turn caused a tightening of state control over and intervention in the life of each citizen. The ideas of the civic humanists followed and reinforced an economic reality.

Becker's analysis raises the question of whether external political factors can be given the weight that Baron gives them in his interpretation of civic humanism.

*   *   *

Lauro Martines has examined the problem from yet another perspective.[45] He studied the family backgrounds and the political and literary activities of eleven Florentine humanists: Salutati, Niccoli, Bruni, Poggio, Manetti, Marsuppini, Palmieri, Rinuccini, Alberti, and Pieruzzi. He found that all these men were born to wealth or acquired it, that is, that they belonged to the ruling class. This ruling class had increased its power in Florence after the revolt of the woollen workers—the so-called

Ciompi Revolution—in 1382. Again in 1387 and in 1393 they took more and more power away from the minor guilds until the lower middle class was left with only one-fourth of the seats in the legislative councils.

In view of the relation of the humanists to the ruling class, it was natural that they should have established an alliance between service to the state and humanistic studies. It is true, as Baron says, that during most of the Trecento the humanists lacked a definite connection with the public sphere. This connection was established by a group of *literati* who found themselves in the 1380s and especially in the 1390s belonging to the ruling oligarchy. This fact is not to deny that something decisive happened that affected the outlook of at least one group of these humanists in the crisis of 1400 to 1402, but it is to say that the social and political environment had already formed them to some extent, even if the crisis re-formed their intellectual vision. Moreover, Baron leaves very much in the background the oligarchic nature of the Florentine republican spirit and does not emphasize nearly as much as a modern historian should that when these men wrote extolling Florence's republican virtues, they were writing ideologically, that is, out of their own class interest. These virtues were what supported them in power. It is only natural that they should have been drawn to them.

The Florentine oligarchical republic ended in 1434 when the city came under the rule of one family, the Medicis. Martines asks what brought about this transformation in the conduct of the political class. He suggests two reasons, one political and the other economic.

Politically, one family had been prevented from gaining too much power through the fostering of equality among the ruling families. But after 1434 suspicion within this group grew so great that this equality was upset and the balance gravitated to one family, the Medicis. By the time Piero di Cosimo died in 1469 the Medicis could dispense with any one family or group of families if they chose, while they themselves became indispensable. The expulsion of Piero di Lorenzo in 1494 (after which Florence returned for a time to republican government) shows that these families could have done as much even in the 1460s. But their mutual suspicion prevented them from acting.

Economically, Florence had begun to decline by the 1450s. Many skilled workers were fleeing the city. The reason was that the wealthy class did not invest in business but instead turned Florence itself into a kind of business, loaning the city money (especially for war) and seeing this money returned with high interest. The Medicis, instead of developing policies to stimulate trade, "raised taxes on goods and increased interest rates on war loans so as to benefit the ruling clique."[46] These practices meant that the lower orders of citizens were continually drained, while the higher ranks rapidly accumulated money. The money accumulated by the wealthy, not being spent on business, was spent on lavish display: new family palaces, furnishings, works of art, clothing, jewelry, and dowries. Until around 1400 Florence had received an influx of new business families (who, until that time, often made their way into the political arena as well); but the failures after 1450 were not balanced by the rise of new businesses or by the penetration of businessmen into the ruling classes, where their presence might have acted as a force for more enlightened economic policy. The direction of economic change was toward agriculture. Martines concludes:

> An end to the large-scale rise of new men, commercial and industrial hard times, the concomitant pursuit of safer investment outlets, the pressure to spend lavishly as a mark of social rank—these trends made for a ruling class that had lost or was losing its political nerve. The upper classes became more exclusive and class conscious, and the oligarchy turned ever more sectarian, restricted and servile.[47]

This world provided the context for the decay of civic humanism. As politics became the privilege of an ever-diminishing number of families, less and less was left to action in real life. Thought became otherworldly; contemplation became once again an ideal, and much that had previously been ascribed to the actions of men now once again came under the goddess Fortuna. This otherworldliness can be seen in the paintings of Botticelli and Filippino Lippi, in the contrast between the early and late writings of Alberti, and in the *Disputationes camaldulenses* of Cristoforo Landino (1475). The contemplative ideal of Neoplatonism is a hallmark here, as it is in Giovanni Pico della Mirandola's *Oration* (1486). It is no accident, therefore, that civic humanism was replaced in Florence by the Platonic Academy of Marsilio Ficino. This intellectual transformation had its counterpart in the political arena and in the economic activities of the oligarchs that aggravated the political situation.

In 1494 the Medicis were overthrown and Florence returned once again for a few years to republican government, showing that that spirit had not died in the city. The question arises: Why did civic ardor in Florentine humanism fade between 1434 and 1494 if the republican spirit was still alive? The conclusion must be that more is required for civic humanism than desire; the reality itself is needed, that is, a political situation in which men can see a close relation between the civic life that actually exists and the sort of life they want, between what is and what they hope to attain. As Martines argues:

> The result was that men like Salutati and Bruni, Poggio and Ma-netti were as much at home with philological and literary questions as with political and historical ones. But in the second half of the century, when interest in political and historical reflection could no longer draw on the resources of a vigorous civic life, a convenient change ensued: subject matter of this sort was gradually purged from the program of humanism, and the *studia humanitatis* be-came more thoroughly literary, or much more purely concerned with idealistic and abstract questions.[48]

With the expulsion of the Medici, things that had been forbidden were suddenly possible again, and the republican spirit surged back. For a generation new intellectual energies were released in the social and polit-ical spheres. This generation produced Machiavelli, Guicciardini, and Giannotti. Moreover, "if something noteworthy was to be accomplished, it must be the work of specialists, of men who would bend all their ener-gies and passion to the political and social problems of the hour and whose study of history, ancient and modern, would bear the stamp of that ardor."[49] Such ardor existed in these historians and political writers of the first decades of the sixteenth century. They were, Martines con-cludes, as different from Salutati and Bruni as were Weber and Mann-heim from Burckhardt.

*   *   *

Gene Brucker, in a recent study of the history of Florence between 1378 and 1430,[50] maintains that the civic thesis of Baron, the statist thesis of Becker, and the class thesis of Martines do not fit well together or explain other facets of Florentine life. He believes, however, that a close study of Florentine government during these years, and especially of the *Consulte e pratiche* (record of political deliberations) provides a frame of reference that unites many otherwise loose strands.[51]

In an earlier study Brucker had argued (contrary to Becker) that between 1343 and 1378 Florence was still controlled by its corporate bodies, until the Ciompi Revolution revealed their weakness.[52] In his se-quel he recognizes the fact that constitutionally Florence did not change after 1382, but nonetheless profound changes took place both in the nature of the leadership and in the leadership's conception of politics.

The first change was the emergence during the 1380s of a group of upper-class merchant families into a position of political power. These families constituted "the most cohesive force in Florentine society through the Renaissance and beyond."[53] Through their rise to power Florence was transformed from a "corporate" to an "elitist" state. But the elite served as a new corporation, so to speak. The families that gained power came to a consensus among themselves regarding most issues of domestic and foreign policy. They could not control the political deliberations of the larger state assemblies, but as long as their inner cohesion remained unbroken there was continuity and stability in Florentine politics. Brucker thus disagrees with Becker's thesis that the elitist state appeared in the 1340s, arguing that even as Florence was developing its new polity in the 1380s, corporate loyalties of all kinds continued to express themselves, including above all the loyalty of the ruling families to one another.

The new regime reached the height of its power in the defeat of Giangaleazzo Visconti in 1402 and the conquest of Pisa in 1406. There is no indication, however, that the struggle with Giangaleazzo had the importance that Baron attributes to it. There was no panic, even after Bologna fell in June. Merchants continued to complain about heavy taxes and the stagnation of trade, but no more than usual. Florence did not attempt to attract new allies by some bold new policy. Diplomats were in Rome and Venice discussing terms of an alliance, and these overtures were supported by citizens who spoke in the *pratiche*, but with no sense of urgency or overwhelming need for an alliance. No agreement had been concluded when a report reached Florence on 12 September of Giangaleazzo's death. "The reaction to this news was muted, with no discernible sign of jubilation. . . . Neither the struggle nor the sacrifices ended with Giangaleazzo's death."[54] Public records for the year 1402 "reveal uncertainty and vacillation, doubt and disagreement, and abrupt shifts in attitude and policy that do not relate logically to events or circumstances."[55] If the Florentines "sensed that they were living through an historic 'moment of decision,' their demeanor did not indicate this awareness."[56]

Before the end of the decade, however, there is strong evidence in the public debates of a significant change in Florentine outlook, as seen in the style and content of the debates themselves.

> In seeking to persuade each other as well as the rank and file, the leaders systematically employed the skills of the logician and the rhetorician. Speeches became longer and more analytical; they were studded with allusions to historical precedents and references to classical authors. These innovations were not simply rhetorical gambits, but signs of a basic shift in historical outlook. Florentines

were being taught, in these debates, to view their past as a unique experience, filled with challenges and ordeals, but also with triumphs. If they did not yet link their origins directly with republican Rome, as the humanists were beginning to do, they did see the relevance of Roman history to their own problems. Though they still referred to divine grace as essential for Florence's prosperity, they placed increasing emphasis upon themselves as the makers of their destiny. They were proud of their demonstrated ability to maintain their freedom and their republican regime, and they looked with scorn and pity upon their neighbors, the Pisans and Pistoiese, who had contributed to their own downfall by failing to achieve civic unity.[57]

Brucker rejects the explanation that cultural lag accounts for the introduction into public debate of humanist ideas that had appeared some years earlier, for he finds "that internal developments were as important as threats from abroad in changing Florentine perceptions and points of view."[58] Moreover, even in foreign affairs, one cannot look exclusively at the struggle against Giangaleazzo but must consider, as the Florentines themselves did, the whole spectrum of their struggles with the church and with King Ladislas as well. Nonetheless, the evidence of these debates "does lend support to Baron's major thesis about the emergence in Florence of a new view of history and politics in the first decade of the Quattrocento."[59] The public debates were an ideal forum for introducing humanist attitudes. He suggests that "Bruni may have received some stimuli for the development of his ideology by listening to the debates in the palace."[60] However that may be, "ideas that had been nurtured in private by Salutati and his circle were being spread, through the medium of the *pratiche*, to a large group of citizens, whose minds must have been influenced by their exposure to humanist propaganda."[61]

Was this humanist propaganda simply the ideological standpoint of a ruling class, as Martines maintains? Brucker does not believe so. For he finds in the public debates, perhaps as another dimension of the new humanist ideas, greater concern for the general public good and a growing sophistication about the nature and functions of government. There is an ever stronger effort to consult, to persuade one's opponents, to exercise patience and seek moderate solutions. The records reveal an increasing capacity for analytical thinking and preoccupation with budgetary projections to determine whether and to what extent Florence could carry on its foreign wars. At the same time the government revised its policy in relation to the *contado* or rural districts around the city: whereas these had been exploited in the preceding century, efforts were now made to treat them more equitably. The same policy was instituted in Florence itself with the introduction of the *catasto* or direct tax in 1427.

Nonetheless, despite its growing professionalism and increasing tendency to think of the good of the state as a whole, the regime gave way to Medici rule in 1434. Its failure was due to the costly wars with Ladislas and Genoa between 1409 and 1414—the crises that had caused the larger-minded responses just mentioned—and, even more, the confrontation with Milan between 1423 and 1430. These conflicts led to an increase in the tax burden beyond what could be borne and to a scramble for public office as a means of offsetting losses incurred through taxation. These tensions produced rifts within a ruling elite that had until then managed to present a united front.

Even though the regime collapsed and was replaced by Medici rule, there were no constitutional changes. Moreover, rule by an elite group of families continued to be the norm, even though the families themselves changed and Cosimo himself exercised more direction on policy than anyone had done previously. The professionalism and sophistication of the bureaucracy also were not lost but continued in a direction that led to Machiavelli and Guicciardini. Thus it can be said that in some respect the civic humanist contribution to Florentine polity ran through the Quattrocento and into the Cinquecento.

＊　　＊　　＊

The most recent contribution to this debate, Quentin Skinner's history of political thought in the Renaissance, has placed Florentine civic humanism—whatever its impetus—within the larger framework, both spatial and temporal, of writings about polity.[62]

Skinner's analysis goes back to the century between 1200 and 1300, when many Italian communes developed republican institutions as the *popolani* in commune after commune rose against the nobility and set up rival administrations in the cities. A great deal of civil violence resulted, leading, after 1300, to the emergence of *signori,* strong political leaders who could enforce order. In order to protect against abuses of power, there began to appear many different kinds of defenses of republican liberty. There were two sources of these defenses: one was the rhetorical tradition of the *ars dictaminis,* whose practitioners were the direct forebears of the humanists; the other the tradition of scholastic philosophy.

In the manuals of letter writing (*ars dictaminis*) composed by a number of prehumanists after 1200, model speeches on political matters are included, which, in turn, led a number of *dictatores* to write about politics in the form of civic chronicles, advice books to guide city magistrates, even a play, Albertino Mussato's *Ecerinis* (1314) lamenting tyranny. Whatever the form, the writers all ask why *signori* are advancing in so many cities, and they all agree that the free cities are weakened by internal factions. They also attribute loss of civic liberty to the increase of private wealth (which some believe causes political factiousness). Baron contends that this bias is due to Franciscan influence on thirteenth-century writers. But the prehumanists were expressing Stoic rather than Franciscan beliefs, to wit, that those who covet wealth destroy the virtues.

How do these writers believe that republican values can be preserved? Through the abolition of personal and sectional interests and the equation of private good with the good of the city as a whole. But how is unity between individual and civil interests to be achieved? They give an answer that was to be developed by the humanists of the Quattrocento: if men are corrupt the best institutions will not work, and if they are virtuous the health of institutions is of secondary importance (a position later defended by Machiavelli and Montesquieu). They therefore ask how to promote men of virtue to serve as leaders, and respond that the traditional nobility must be bypassed and men from all classes be made eligible.

Scholastic writers base their ideas on Aristotle's *Ethics* and *Politics*, which were translated fully into Latin between 1240 and 1250. The scholastic theorists no less than the rhetorical writers were committed to an ideal of political independence and republican self-government. In so doing they hark back to Rome's republican period rather than to the empire as the age of Rome's greatest excellence, and they adopt a new attitude toward Cato and Cicero, leading figures in the republic. Formerly they were viewed as Stoic sages aloof from political life; now they are praised as great patriots and paragons of civic virtue. Baron is thus wrong, Skinner maintains, in arguing that this attitude appeared only in the early Quattrocento. Rather, "the main elements in this humanist historical consciousness were in fact formed with the arrival of scholastic political theory in Italy nearly a century before."[63] But scholastic writers are aware of the fragility of republican institutions and ask why they are so vulnerable. They do not believe, as the prehumanists do, that private wealth corrupts politics, but they do agree on the evil of factiousness. The relation between faction and tyranny they take from Aristotle, and the conclusion they draw is that civil discord is the principal danger to the liberty of city republics.

How can faction be avoided and peace secured? With the rhetorical theorists they agree that sectional interests must be set aside and the good of each individual equated with the good of the city as a whole. But how is this unity to be achieved? Here the scholastic writers diverge sharply from the prehumanists, emphasizing not a "true nobility," in other words virtuous individuals, but efficient institutions. To avoid factions or rival parties the ruler should be the whole body of the people, so that no such internecine fighting can in principle arise.[64] In defending this view the scholastics (particularly Marsilio of Padua in his *Defender of Peace*) argue that in delegating their authority to a ruler the people do not alienate it but remain the sovereign legislators at all times. Ultimate authority always remains in the hands of the people, though a ruler may exercise it for a particular time. But how is sovereignty that is delegated retained by the people? Through the imposition of three restraints: election, forcing rulers to govern according to law rather than their own discretion, and a system of checks.

By reviewing both the prehumanist and the scholastic traditions of political thought Skinner has shown that what Baron believed to be new in the early Quattrocento was in fact inherited from the city republics of medieval Italy. This view also does greater justice to the continuity between Petrarch and his successors than Baron is able to do.

Skinner then turns his attention to the relation between the humanists of the Quattrocento and this earlier thought of the *dictatores* and scholastics. Because Florence was politically stable (internally) by the beginning of the Quattrocento, the humanists no longer saw faction as the great problem but rather the use of mercenary troops. Their solution was the revival of an armed and independent citizenry (as in Aristotle's *Politics*, 3). Like the *dictatores* the humanists prefer republican Rome to the empire, but Bruni adds an original element: the connection between freedom and the greatness of commonwealths. Florence is great, he says, because its citizens are all engaged in the cultivation of the virtues. But this idea is fully in accord with the earlier notions of the *dictatores* that the health of a republic depends on developing the spirit of its citizens (not on perfecting the machinery of government) and that a citizen's worth is measured by his talent rather than by his lineage or wealth. Moreover, the latter idea requires a positive view of human nature or dignity and a rejection of Augustine's repudiation of the cardinal virtues.[65] By reconstructing the classical image of human nature that Augustine had tried to obliterate, they argue that although the human capacity for action is limited, the controlling factor is not providence but the caprices of fortune.[66] This led some (such as Poggio) to be pessimistic but others (notably Alberti in his preface to *On the Family*) to be strongly assertive of the power of human will.

At the same time, however, Quattrocento civic humanism was discontinuous with the Middle Ages. Humanists attacked scholastic method, especially its interpretation of Roman law. Moreover, they exalted activity (*negotium*) above leisure (*otium*). Baron has rightly stressed that this argument was first wholeheartedly embraced by the Florentine humanists of the early Quattrocento (Dante still thought of wisdom as purely intellectual rather than as a moral virtue).[67] Finally, as a result of their attack on scholasticism, the humanists developed a new view of history, inventing the notion of the Middle Ages and regarding it as having come to an end in their own time through their own innovations.

*   *   *

If Skinner has shown the richness of political thought relevant to Baron's thesis prior to the crisis of 1400–1402, J. G. A. Pocock, looking at the problem from the end point of Florentine republicanism (1494–1512 and 1527–30), especially with a view to illuminating the originality and genius of Machiavelli, proposes to reveal the consequences of that republicanism in the larger western (English and American) political tradition in the seventeenth and eighteenth centuries. He thus supports—though in his own way—Baron's most controversial contention, that Florentine republicanism was essential to the development of western democratic polity.[68]

What is of interest here is not the later permutations of the Machiavellian moment but only what was involved in its emergence. In order to grasp the innovations of the civic humanists it is necessary to understand the patterns of thought they inherited from the past, which provided the matrix of their ideas. One of the most compelling features of Pocock's complex treatment is the way in which he builds the context, so that the reader can see the sets of ideas with which the Florentine civic humanists were working and how their minds grappled with—in some cases transforming—these sets of ideas in relation to the political reality of the Florentine republic during its last years. There were four: first, the Augustinian Christian frame of reference; second, the Roman civic humanist modification of it by Boethius; third, the medieval view of the relation between the universal and the particular; and fourth, the Aristotelian political tradition, including Roman history as well.

Augustine rejected the idea that any fulfillment of human life was possible in political terms (the earthly city) and enjoined Christians to set their sights on the heavenly city, the city of God, in which alone justice (the preeminent political virtue) could be realized. History itself has no meaning; its meaning is given to it by the purposes of God, which lie outside history itself.

Yet Christians continued to be concerned with political history, and this concern expressed itself through the Greek notion of *arete* (civic excellence) and the Latin notion of *virtus* (virtue). Boethius, in his influential *Consolation of Philosophy*, written while he was in prison and as a reflection on his own downfall, inquires of God how He, who is perfect virtue, could allow virtue to become subject to fortune (as in his own case). Augustine would simply have responded that anyone who participates in the fallen city must expect injustice. But Boethius wants to understand how the heavenly city permits the earthly city to stand. Philosophy leads him to the view of the eternal now (*nunc-stans*), the view that to God all things are visible as a unity, so that the problem of historical succession does not exist. All Boethius can know is that the *nunc-stans* exists; he cannot share its vision. Redemption comes only through the grace of God, and although philosophy, faith, and virtuous practice might solicit it, they can never command it. History thus has only a private meaning. Its public meaning was restored through the papal church, which institutionalized the *nunc-stans*.[69] The only means of giving significance to time in this context was apocalyptic prophecy, through which it was claimed that redemption was to be found in the fulfillment of prophecy rather than in a timeless institution. Not surprisingly, most medieval heretics were apocalyptic.[70]

To the medieval mind the true is the universal, which is not time-bound; the particular cannot be true precisely because it is circumstantial, accidental, and time-bound. The problem this concept raises for political thought is illustrated in Sir John Fortescue's *In Praise of the Laws of England* (1468–71), in which he sets out to discover the universal principles on which English law is based, only to run up against his own presupposition that since "England" is a particular, there can be no body of universals concerning it. Thus English laws cannot be shown to be universal by any rational criterion, but only by virtue of their longevity, that is, by custom. This notion makes legislation difficult, for it takes a long time to establish a consensus. We find ourselves, in fact, in the paradoxical situation that when usage is well established a ruler does not really need to govern, he only needs to apply the law as built up through consensus (*jurisdictio*); but when an unprecedented event occurs, he actually does govern, inasmuch as there is no collective wisdom to tell him what to do; but in this case he does not govern by law but in the absence of it (*gubernaculum*).[71]

These patterns of political thought were the ones inherited by Renaissance humanists, and the problem they all present has to do with time; it is to find universal significance in the particular. It was this problem that led the humanists away from reading Aristotle's *Politics* in relation to the theme of natural law (through which people perceive the values inherent in nature and pursue them in society). Their orientation was rather the relation of the citizen to the city-state. Different groups of citizens in the Italian republics pursued many different ends. The problem was how to distribute power in such a way that the pursuit of individual ends (the particular) could also be related to the good of the republic as a whole (the universal). Aristotle's delineation of governments into monarchies (the one), aristocracies (the few), and democracies (the many) was crucial for their resolution of this problem. The one, the few, and the many were each to be entrusted with particular functions of government; thus each would rule and be ruled and no one group would predominate. Based on this analysis, it became usual to visualize society as a blend of the one, the few, and the many.

Polybius, who was translated from Greek into Latin between 1510 and 1520, set himself the task in book 6 of his *Histories* to explain Rome's military success. He did so by relating that success to its internal stability, achieved through balancing the one, the few, and the many. All cities, he asserted, must pass through Aristotle's sixfold classification (monarchy/tyranny, aristocracy/oligarchy, polity/democracy) if they were to escape instability. To his later readers (but not to Polybius) it seemed that if such a balance could be effected, then a regime that could last forever might be created.[72] Guicciardini held out such a hope; Machiavelli radically departed from it.

The myth of Venice came to be identified with the account of Polybius: Venice was a stable regime because it was a perfect blend of the one, the few, and the many—a myth as much of Florentine as of Venetian making.[73] Though at variance with the idea that Venice was an aristocracy of well-balanced elements (a view the Venetians apparently had of themselves), it came to predominate in Florence after the overthrow of the aristocratic Medici regime and the institutionalization, under Savonarola, of a constitution that included a consiglio grande, a signoria, and a gonfaloniere—which contemporaries identified with the many, the few, and the one of classical theory.

Machiavelli transforms all these inherited paradigms: he gives priority to time over eternity, to change over stasis, and to Rome (a republic based on change) over Venice. He accepts Boethius's notion of virtue and his contrast between virtue and fortune, and builds his new political paradigm upon it.

In *The Prince* Machiavelli is concerned with innovators and the ways in which (through their virtue) they have imposed their will upon their *fortuna*. In the spectrum between *institutio* and *gubernaculum,* he is interested in the extreme form of *gubernaculum,* the moment that the

ruler must rule without norms from the past to guide him, without legitimacy, as an innovator.

What Machiavelli does for the ruler in *The Prince* he does for the
republic in *The Discourses*. There are two daring and arresting hypotheses at the foundation of the latter (both of which Guicciardini was to
reject). The first is "that the disunion and strife among nobles and people
was the cause of Rome's attaining liberty, stability, and power—a statement shocking and incredible to minds which identified union with stability and virtue, conflict with innovation and decay."[74] The second is
that the ideal of stability is not the only value to be pursued. Stability
was pursued by Sparta and Venice, both of which lasted longer than
Rome, but its pursuit assumes that the sole purpose of the state is to
maintain itself. Rome, by contrast, created an empire, a choice that involved a preference for a more popular, as opposed to aristocratic, form
of government. Thus Rome is "the 'new prince' among republics, and
Machiavelli would rather study Rome than Venice as he would rather
study the new prince than the hereditary ruler: the short view is more
interesting than the long, and life in it more glorious."[75] "The Roman
path does not guarantee against ultimate degeneration, but in the present
and foreseeable future—in the world of accidental time, in short—it is
both wiser and more glorious."[76]

This conclusion leads Machiavelli, in *The Art of War*, to link warrior
and citizen in an inextricable bond. The citizen dedicates his life, the
warrior his death to the state; both thus perfect human nature by sacri-
ficing the particular to the universal. The enemy of the republic is corruption, for it creates inequality among citizens. Indeed, "the concept of
corruption is tending to replace that of the mere randomness of *fortuna*."[77] In the citizen as warrior, will replaces intelligence, action replaces prudence. Although Machiavelli's contributions to republican
theory were extraordinarily original, they were based on and limited to
his decision that "military dynamism was to be preferred before the
search for stability."[78]

In all his arguments Machiavelli carried out a drastic secularization
of political consciousness: he established that civic virtue and the *vivere
civile* may develop in the dimension of contingency. Citizens move
toward the goal of stability through their own time-bound wills. But if
they do not need the superhuman in order to become citizens, instead
achieving citizenship in the world of time and fortune, the earthly and
heavenly cities have once again split apart, and civic ends are divorced
from the ends of redemption. This suggestion is Machiavelli's most subver-
sive one.[79]

In grappling with politics in terms of the vicissitudes (particularities) of time—and in putting to rest the orientation of human life toward the eternal, the universal, and the wholly rational—the civic humanists introduced a historical consciousness that has ever since characterized western thinking. They were the first historicists in the western tradition (and perhaps in this sense the first "modern men"). When they began to write, words like stability, immobility, monarchy, authority, eternity, hierarchy, and universality dominated political writing; in their own works and subsequently (as a result, in important respects, of their influence) these had been replaced by republicanism, secularism, progress, patriotism, equality, liberty, and utopia. Only the terms reason, virtue, and experience survived from the earlier tradition of political thought.[80] Insofar as this is the case, civic humanism must be regarded as one of the most enduring contributions of Italian humanists generally to modern western culture.

*   *   *

Baron's hypothesis has proved to be a rich one indeed; it has led to a battery of new inquiries regarding the origin, nature, development, and influence of Italian humanism. All aspects of the thesis have been attacked, defended, and expanded in various ways. Although nothing like a synthesis can be said to have emerged, the result is certainly a more richly detailed picture of humanism than we have earlier possessed. As in the case of most other historical paradigms of equal power, this one is not likely to lead to a unanimous conclusion. But it has profoundly altered and enriched the study of humanism, and whatever the outcomes of continuing study prove to be, the terrain will forever look quite different as a result of the identification of civic humanism.

NOTES

1. J. Burckhardt, *The Civilization of the Renaissance in Italy*, trans. S. G. C. Middlemore (New York, 1954; orig 1860), 100.
2. Ibid., 158.
3. E. Garin, *Italian Humanism: Philosophy and Civic Life in the Renaissance*, trans. P. Munz (New York, 1965), 78. See the introduction and chaps. 1–2, especially chap. 2.
4. E. Garin, *Science and Civic Life in the Italian Renaissance*, trans. P. Munz (Garden City, NY, 1969), x, 19; and see, generally, 1–48.
5. E. Garin, "The Humanist Chancellors of the Florentine Republic from Coluccio Salutati to Bartolomeo Scala," in *Portraits from the Quattrocento*, trans. V. A. Velen and E. Velen (New York, 1972), 1–29. His orientation is heavily weighted in this direction in *La letteratura degli umanisti*, in the

series *Storia della letteratura italiana* 3, *Il Quattrocento e l'Ariosto* (Milan, 1965), 7–353.

6. Leon Battista Alberti, *The Family in Renaissance Florence,* trans. R. N. Watkins (Columbia, SC, 1969), 28. See the entire prologue, 25–32.

7. Quoted in Garin, *Italian Humanism,* 67.

8. Ibid., 75–76.

9. For a complete bibliography of the writings of Hans Baron, see *Renaissance Studies in Honor of Hans Baron,* ed. A. Molho and J. A. Tedeschi (Dekalb, IL, 1971), lxxi–lxxxvii. See also the two appreciations of his work, which open that volume, by Denys Hay (xi–xxix) and August Buck (xxxi–lviii). Relevant works by Baron along with critical appraisals will be cited as they are discussed in the analysis that follows.

10. See Garin's essay "Le prime ricerche di Hans Baron sul Quattrocento e la loro influenza fra le due guerre," in *Renaissance Studies in Honor of Hans Baron,* lix–lxx.

11. H. Baron, "Moot Problems of Renaissance Interpretation: An Answer to Wallace K. Ferguson," *Journal of the History of Ideas* 19 (1958): 28. Ferguson's "The Interpretation of Italian Humanism: The Contribution of Hans Baron," appears in the same journal on pp. 14–25. The issues are clearly articulated in both essays.

12. H. Baron, "Franciscan Poverty and Civic Wealth as Factors in the Rise of Humanistic Thought," *Speculum* 13 (1938): 1–37, esp. 2.

13. *Leonardo Bruni Aretino. Humanistisch-philosophische Schriften mit einer Chronologie seiner Werke und Briefe,* ed. H. Baron (Leipzig and Berlin, 1928; reprint, Wiesbaden, 1969), xi–xl.

14. See note 12.

15. "Franciscan Poverty and Civic Wealth," 18. For an introduction to Barbaro's treatise in which the relevant literature is cited and the introduction and book 2 are translated, see *The Earthly Republic: Italian Humanists on Government and Society,* ed. B. G. Kohl and R. G. Witt with E. B. Welles (Philadelphia, 1978), 179–228.

16. *Bulletin of the John Rylands Library* 22 (1938): 72–97.

17. *The Crisis of the Early Italian Renaissance,* 2 vols. (Princeton, 1955). At the same time he published *Humanistic and Political Literature in Florence and Venice at the Beginning of the Quattrocento* (Cambridge, MA, 1955). A revised one-volume edition of the *Crisis* with an epilogue appeared in 1966, also from Princeton University Press. *Humanistic and Political Literature* was reissued in 1968, and during the same year a companion to it appeared, *From Petrarch to Leonardo Bruni* (Chicago, 1968).

18. *Crisis,* 41 (all citations are from the 1966 reprint).

19. Ibid., 45.

20. Quoted, ibid., 188.

21. For the text of the *Laudatio florentinae urbis,* see Baron, *From Petrarch to Leonardo Bruni,* 232–63 (another edition by V. Zaccaria in *Studi medievali* 3d ser. 8 [1967]: 529–54); English translation in *Earthly Republic,* 135–75. For the text of the *Dialogi ad Petrum Paulum Istrum,* see *Prosatori latini*

del Quattrocento, ed. E. Garin (Milan, 1952), 39–99; English translation in *The Three Crowns of Florence*, ed. and trans. D. Thompson and A. F. Nagel (New York, 1972), 19–52.

22. Quoted, *Crisis*, 58.
23. See Machiavelli, *Discourses*, 2.2, 4, 5, in *The Prince and the Discourses*, intro. M. Lerner (New York, 1950).
24. *Crisis*, 332–53. For a translation of Boccaccio's and Bruni's lives of Dante, see *The Earliest Lives of Dante*, ed. F. Basetti-Sani, trans. J. R. Smith (New York, 1963) and for Bruni's life, in addition, *Three Crowns of Florence*, 57–73.
25. *Crisis*, 295–314.
26. Ibid., 323, 326ff. On Boccaccio's *Life* of Dante, see above, n. 24.
27. Ibid., 393–94. William J. Bouwsma has extended this influence into the sixteenth century. He sees the ideal of republican liberty expressed in civic humanism as a principal factor in Venetian politics. See *Venice and the Defense of Republican Liberty* (Berkeley, 1968); and his essay "Venice and the Political Education of Europe," in *Renaissance Venice*, ed. J. R. Hale (London, 1973), 445–66.
28. *Crisis*, 460–61.
29. Ibid., 461.
30. G. Sasso, "'Florentina libertas' e rinascimento italiano nell'opera di Hans Baron," *Rivista storica italiana* 69 (1957): 250–76.
31. Ibid., 261; see *Crisis*, 40.
32. It could be argued that something similar has taken place in William Bouwsma's attempt to use Baron's thesis as a basis for interpreting the later history of Venice; see note 27.
33. J. E. Seigel, "'Civic Humanism' or Ciceronian Rhetoric?" *Past and Present* 34 (1966): 3–48.
34. See P. O. Kristeller, "The Medieval Antecedents of Renaissance Humanism," in *Eight Philosophers of the Italian Renaissance* (Stanford, 1964), 147–65; idem, *Renaissance Thought: The Classic, Scholastic, and Humanist Strains* (New York, 1961); idem, *Renaissance Thought II: Papers on Humanism and the Arts* (New York, 1965); essays by Kristeller from a number of sources have been gathered in *Renaissance Thought and Its Sources*, ed. M. Mooney (New York, 1979).
35. Seigel, "'Civic Humanism,'" esp. 14–25.
36. H. Baron, "Leonardo Bruni: 'Professional Rhetorician' or 'Civic Humanist'?" *Past and Present* 36 (1967): 21–37.
37. Seigel's thesis that the principal preoccupations of the humanists were and always remained rhetorical rather than political is worked out in his *Rhetoric and Philosophy in Renaissance Humanism* (Princeton, 1968).
38. Kristeller, *Renaissance Thought II*, 46–47.
39. C. Trinkaus, *In Our Image and Likeness: Humanity and Divinity in Italian Humanist Thought*, 2 vols. (Chicago, 1970), 1:283. Trinkaus had made these same points earlier in a review of the first edition of *Crisis* in *Journal of the History of Ideas* 17 (1956): 426–32.

40. E. F. Rice, Jr., *The Renaissance Idea of Wisdom* (Cambridge, MA, 1958), 49.

41. Ferguson, "Interpretation of Italian Humanism," 25.

42. Baron, "Moot Problems," 28.

43. See his *Florence in Transition*, 2 vols. (Baltimore, 1967–68), esp. vol. 2, *Studies in the Rise of the Territorial State*. His thesis is succinctly stated in "The Florentine Territorial State and Civic Humanism in the Early Renaissance," in *Florentine Studies*, ed. N. Rubinstein (Evanston, IL, 1968), 109–39.

44. Becker, "Florentine Territorial State," 121.

45. L. Martines, *The Social World of the Florentine Humanists, 1390–1460* (Princeton, 1963).

46. Ibid., 289.

47. Ibid., 292.

48. Ibid., 302.

49. Ibid.

50. G. Brucker, *The Civic World of Early Renaissance Florence* (Princeton, 1977).

51. He writes: "Though known and exploited by scholars for more than a century, these debates have not been systematically studied nor their historical value fully appreciated. They constitute the most complete record of the political thought of any European community—urban, regional, national—prior to the English Civil War. For the years between 1382 and 1434, that record is comprehensive, with only a few lacunae" (ibid., 13).

52. G. Brucker, *Florentine Politics and Society, 1343–1378* (Princeton, 1962).

53. Brucker, *Civic World*, 18.

54. Ibid., 184.

55. Ibid., 185.

56. Ibid., 186.

57. Ibid., 299–300.

58. Ibid., 300.

59. Ibid., 301.

60. Ibid.

61. Ibid., 301–2.

62. Q. Skinner, *The Foundations of Modern Political Thought*, vol. 1, *The Renaissance* (Cambridge, 1978). Chapters 1–4 are most relevant to the present discussion.

63. Ibid., 54–55.

64. Ibid., 61.

65. Ibid., 91–92.

66. Ibid., 96.

67. Ibid., 107–8.

68. J. G. A. Pocock, *The Machiavellian Moment: Florentine Political Thought and the Atlantic Republican Tradition* (Princeton, 1975); idem, "*The Machiavellian Moment* Revisited: A Study in History and Ideology," *Journal of Modern History* 53 (1981): 49–72, which focuses on the debate

surrounding the transition between the Florentine republican tradition and the Atlantic tradition of the seventeenth and eighteenth centuries (not addressed in my discussion). See also the excellent review essay of the book by J. H. Hexter in *History and Theory* 16 (1977): 306–37, esp. 318–23, for a description of the central Machiavellian moment.

69. Pocock, *Machiavellian Moment*, 45.

70. Ibid., 46.

71. Ibid., 9–26.

72. Ibid., 76–80.

73. Ibid., 99–100.

74. Ibid., 194.

75. Ibid., 198.

76. Ibid., 199.

77. Ibid., 211.

78. Ibid., 218.

79. Ibid., 194.

80. See Hexter, review essay of *Machiavellian Moment*, 318.

8 ❧ HUMANISM IN FLORENCE
Charles L. Stinger

AMONG ITALIAN CENTERS OF THE *STUDIA HUMANITATIS*, FLORENCE holds primacy of place. There, in the late Trecento, Petrarch's legacy earliest took root. There for the next century first appeared the key achievements in classical scholarship, the revival of patristic studies, the main themes in humanist moral philosophy, and the development of a humanist historiography. Florentines during the fifteenth century stood at the vanguard, too, in areas influenced by the classical revival, notably painting, sculpture, and architecture. In vernacular poetry, Florentines held their own, and they made Tuscan *volgare* the standard literary language for prose fiction and for treatises on a whole range of intellectual issues, many of them paralleling works produced in Latin. Florentine humanists even made significant contributions to the fields of mathematics and science. Unrivaled as the intellectual capital of Italian humanism in the first half of the Quattrocento, this new Athens attracted, like a magnet, inquiring minds and creative talent from the whole of Italy.[1]

After 1450, other Italian cities—notably Rome and Naples, but also the smaller princely courts of Urbino, Ferrara, and Mantua—increasingly competed with Florence. Many Florentine humanists, or those whose careers had started there, found opportunities more attractive elsewhere. No longer preeminent in all humanist fields, the Florence of Ficino and Poliziano nonetheless remained at the cutting edge of philosophy and classical philology. Only with the turmoil of the early sixteenth century did Florentine humanism noticeably deteriorate. At the same time the imperial classicism of Julian and Leonine Rome and the editorial achievements of Aldo Manuzio's Venice threatened to put Florence in the shade. Yet in the mid-Cinquecento Florentines again assumed leadership roles. In the cultural world of the ducal court and in the Tuscan academies a revival of fifteenth-century humanist ideas took place. In this setting there emerged, at the end of the sixteenth century, the musical theories that eventually led to opera, and in the opening years of the seventeenth century Galileo found the most ardent supporters of the new science.

Before examining more closely the phases of Florentine humanism over this 250-year period and analyzing the various trends and accomplishments in scholarship and thought, one must consider briefly why

Florence proved so congenial a setting for the emergence of the humanist movement. Certain basic features of Florentine social, economic, and political life as they had developed by the later fourteenth century provide part of the explanation. Florentine wealth derived in large part from a widespread network of banking, commercial, and industrial activities—notably those involved in the production of luxury woolen cloth—that brought contact with the whole of Europe and the Mediterranean world. Risks were great, and achievement depended on a shrewd assessment of market opportunities and resourceful business organization. Intelligence, a cosmopolitan grasp of the world, persistence, and a keen eye for quality—virtues reflected in the bourgeois heroes of Boccaccio's *Decameron*—were the ingredients for success, and they encouraged an openness to the world and to the possibilities it offered.[2]

Moreover, within Florence's relatively open social and political structure, where feudal patterns no longer guided personal or public behavior, mercantile accomplishment provided the avenue to power and influence, especially in the later fourteenth and early fifteenth centuries. In this same period the various magistracies of the Florentine Republic and the proliferation of governmental posts overseeing such matters as the grain supply, the funded public debt, port facilities, and the subject communes of Tuscany presented most Florentine patricians with major public responsibilities. Urban planning, and undertaking such prominent public projects as the completion of the cathedral, the construction of the Ospedale degli Innocenti (the foundling hospital), and the sculptural embellishment of the baptistery and of Or San Michele also enlisted citizen involvement. The beauty, rational order, and healthfulness of early Quattrocento Florence could be celebrated as the creation of human planning and design. In short, Florentines found themselves in a secularized public world—the product of human deliberation—that closely resembled what they discovered in the Rome Cicero described and the Athens where Pericles had spoken and Socrates taught.[3]

Yet, especially in the late fourteenth and early fifteenth centuries, the quest for individual material gain and the competitive pursuit of worldly honors presented troubling conflicts with older assumptions of Christian morality. Florentines were anxious to reconcile the way they lived with what they should live for, and in this respect the rediscovered worlds of classical and Christian antiquity provided a fertile ground for developing new perceptions of selfhood and society. Humanism in Florence, then, did not remain an isolated phenomenon, a merely literary movement at the periphery of private and public life. Rather, it contributed answers to moral issues Florentines confronted in the conduct of their daily lives, and it inspired the exercise of creative intelligence in the pursuit of human virtue and fulfillment.[4]

This receptivity to humanist thought was also encouraged by the organization of intellectual life within the Arno city. In the first place, Florence lacked a major university. Indeed, the Florentine *studium* limped along on meager funding, often closing altogether during the frequent wars of the later fourteenth and early fifteenth centuries. This meant that during the years that the humanist movement took hold in Florence the established disciplines of medieval education, with their emphasis on Aristotelian logic, the deductive systems of scholastic philosophy, and a traditional set of problems in legal studies and theology, did not inhibit innovation. Unlike Venice, where the Aristotelianism of the University of Padua dominated higher education for the Venetian aristocracy in the fifteenth century, and in that way delayed the reception of humanism, Florentines confronted no such entrenched obstacle. Florence's intellectual life developed in more informal groupings than the institutional setting of the university—in the libraries of the urban monasteries, in bookshops, in the confraternities, and in suburban villas. The ties of friendship, the affinity of intellectual interests, the open give and take of earnest discussion, and the opportunity to meet directly with visiting humanist scholars to examine some newly acquired text or artifact brought Florentine humanists together in these "salons" or academies. The flexibility of these arrangements, similar to the settings of Plato's dialogues or Cicero's, encouraged wide-ranging rather than specialized intellectual pursuits. With no set curriculum, no lectures, no distinction of faculty and students, these intellectual circles promoted in Florentine minds the cultivation of human wisdom (*sapientia*) as against the acquisition of merely formal knowledge (*scientia*).[5]

At the same time, Florentine public life, in the office of chancellor, offered a tenured post for professional humanists to exercise their talents in Latin epistolography, oratory, and historiography. Much in the public eye and esteemed by the Florentine populace, the succession of humanist chancellors from Coluccio Salutati to Bartolomeo Scala served as spokesmen for the Florentine polity, defending its policies and articulating the city's character and achievements. In this way, a humanist stronghold emerged in the public heart of the city, the Palazzo della Signoria. Thence humanist insights into politics and history could inform a broad spectrum of Florence's citizenry.[6]

Neither did the church in Florence prove a stumbling block to the development of humanist thought. A number of Florentines in clerical orders were, in fact, humanists themselves, as will be seen. More importantly, humanism did not impinge upon many aspects of religious experience in Florence. The celebration of the cult, much of it in the form of processions and festivities that reinforced civic patriotism; the dissemination of the sacraments; the ritual oversight of the rites of passage from birth to marriage to death; the proceedings of ecclesiastical tribunals; and the management of charity, poor relief, and the care for the ill—all, for the most part, fell outside the intellectual and moral concerns of the humanists. This corporate and public religiosity formed an unquestioned assumption of Florentine life.[7]

Where Christianity did concern the humanists—as in fact it did—it was in making Christian teaching applicable to the circumstances and moral decisions of lay life. To this end Florentine humanists delivered sermons to confraternities, wrote dialogues and treatises, provided translations and editions of patristic texts, and even, as in the case of Giannozzo Manetti, engaged in Christian apologetics and scriptural exegesis. The humanists eschewed technical discussions of doctrine and authority: that was the province of scholastic theologians and canon lawyers. Rather they dwelt on the personal, subjective, and psychological aspects of religious belief, such as urging the responsible exercise of human free will, the pursuit of moral virtue, and the quest for salvation attainable through fulfilling the potential latent in mankind's creation in divine likeness. These concerns, in turn, reflected the humanists' persistent anthropocentric focus.[8]

If early Florentine humanism avoided controversy with religious authorities, this fact is in part explained, too, by the circumstances of the church as a whole in the conciliar era. Not until the later fifteenth century was the restored papacy able to intervene effectively in Florentine affairs, and only with the Counter-Reformation did the church in Rome, in the name of dogmatic orthodoxy, repress humanist inquiry. During the early Quattrocento, Popes John XXIII (the antipope elected following the Council of Pisa), Martin V, and Eugenius IV depended heavily on Florentine banking expertise and resources in their efforts to recover fiscal viability. All three pontiffs, moreover, found it necessary at various points in their pontificates to reside in Florence. In fact Eugenius, driven from Rome by a revolt of the populace, resided in the Arno city for a total of six years in the 1430s and early 1440s. While there, he officiated at the consecration of Florence's cathedral (1436), the dome of which Brunelleschi had just completed, and he presided over the Council of Union with the Greek Orthodox church (1439). During these decades, Florence could see itself as much the capital of Christendom as Rome, and the papacy, far from controlling the religious affairs of Florence, was cast in the role of humble suppliant to Florentine financial and political interests.

Moreover, in these same years, Florentine humanists made successful inroads into the papal secretariate, making these lucrative and intellectually influential positions within the inner circles of papal affairs outposts of Florentine cultural developments.[9]

The economic, social, political, and ecclesiastical life of Florence provided, then, favorable circumstances for the emergence of humanist ideas. Stimulus also came from another direction—previous achievements in literature and the arts. In Dante, Florence had produced Italy's greatest medieval poet, and one whose encyclopedic interests, empathy for the central mysteries of human life, poetic inventiveness, and moral grandeur placed him on a par with Homer and Vergil for his humanist readers. Dante's *Divine Comedy* continued to be read and commented upon throughout the Renaissance period, often in public recitations including those delivered from the pulpit of the cathedral. Laudatory sketches of his life appeared, too, frequently combined with those of Boccaccio and Petrarch, the other two "crowns" of Trecento Florentine letters. The *Comedy* proved inspiring to artists as well, notably Botticelli's extraordinary set of miniatures.[10]

But the arts possessed in Giotto, Dante's contemporary, their own font of inspiration. Giotto for subsequent Renaissance artists had, like Dante, pioneered the return to classical antiquity, and thereby restored to painting its expressive human power.[11] In Dante and Giotto Florentine humanists and artists had a heritage to live up to and a continuing inspiration for their own creations.

Various circumstances and trends in Florentine society and culture thus proved favorable to the city's gaining primacy as a humanist center. Yet this achievement was very much the result as well of individual inquiry, labor, and leadership.

＊　　＊　　＊

Humanism in Florence traces its beginnings to Giovanni Boccaccio (1313–1375)—not to the youthful Boccaccio whose early vernacular romances with their themes of love and gallantry reflect the refined gaiety and aristocratic charms of the Angevin court of Naples where he spent his adolescence, or even the Boccaccio of the *Decameron* (1348–51), but rather to the older Boccaccio, who after 1350 increasingly turned to classical scholarship.[12] An encounter with Petrarch in Florence in 1350, as the Father of Humanism was en route to Rome for the Jubilee, seems to have been instrumental in this shift. This first meeting initiated a friendship, maintained through correspondence, periodic visits, and the exchanges of mutual friends, that persisted for a quarter-century, until Petrarch's death in 1374.[13]

Despite numerous efforts, Boccaccio never managed to persuade Petrarch to take up residence in the city this much-traveled scholar always claimed as his *patria*. But from him Boccaccio drew the stimulus to enlarge the range and scope of his own interests in antiquity. These embraced a variety of endeavors. First, he seized advantage of opportunities to expand his knowledge of classical texts. Trips to Naples in 1355 and again in 1362–63 permitted investigations of the classical holdings in the famed library of the Benedictine abbey at Monte Cassino. From there he acquired various rare texts, including Varro's *De lingua latina,* Tacitus's *Annales,* and Martial's epigrams.[14] From such visits, from exchanges with Petrarch and loans from other friends, patrons, and admirers, and through purchases, Boccaccio over time amassed an impressive personal library of the Latin classics, probably the largest and finest private collection in Europe. Many manuscripts, written in his own hand and marked by the marginal notations of his attentive reading, still survive.[15] At the end of his life Boccaccio bequeathed this important collection of classical texts to the Augustinian monastery of Santo Spirito in Florence. There various Augustinian fathers and lay Florentines had joined Boccaccio in informal discussions of classical and humanistic topics, and there, after his decease, his manuscripts were preserved as a separate *parva libraria*—his spiritual testament to the next generation of Florentine humanists.[16]

The Latin literature of Roman antiquity absorbed most of Boccaccio's attention, but he pioneered as well a study of the Greek classics. Encouraged by Petrarch, Boccaccio arranged for Leontius Pilatus, a Calabrian Greek and representative of Byzantine learning, to come to Florence to teach Greek. Through Boccaccio's intercession, Leontius received appointment as professor of Greek studies at the Florentine *studium*—the first Greek chair in non-Byzantine Europe. While in Florence in the years 1360–62, he taught Boccaccio a smattering of Greek, discussed with him the works of various Greek poets, including Euripides, and in response to the Florentine's interests produced a Latin translation of Homer's *Iliad* and *Odyssey.*[17] Greek studies lapsed in Florence upon Leontius's departure and did not resume until Manuel Chrysoloras's much more decisive stay at the very end of the Trecento. But Boccaccio had at least identified the revival of classical Greek learning as a goal of humanistic studies.

The classical erudition Boccaccio slowly acquired is best reflected in his *Genealogia deorum gentilium,* begun shortly before 1350 and continually revised over the remainder of his life. This great compendium, the Greek learning of which Boccaccio owed largely to Leontius Pilatus, is a compilation, organized in fifteen books, of classical mythology, legends about the pagan gods, stories of heroes, and the lore of antiquity in general—all submitted to allegorical interpretation. As a reference work, the *Genealogia* kept Boccaccio's name before poets and artists throughout the Renaissance period.[18]

The *Genealogia* is basically literary in nature, and as such reveals the essential character of Boccaccio's classicism. His humanism was that of a poet and a grammarian, rather than, for example, that of an orator, a historian, a moralist, or a philosopher. In fact, Boccaccio devoted the last two books of the *Genealogia* to a defense of poetry. The issue was not an abstract one for Boccaccio. In 1362, in a period of personal anxiety, when he felt increasing tension between his cultural aspirations and the demands of a Christian life, he received what seemed an ominous warning from a saintly popular preacher of Siena, then on his deathbed. The preacher, Boccaccio was told, warned him to renounce, before it was too late, his worldly and decadent devotion to poetry and to literary studies. Distressed, Boccaccio wrote to Petrarch of his decision to abandon his writing and offered to turn over his library to his friend In reply Petrarch calmly reassured Boccaccio of the legitimacy, and indeed the religious value, of poetry and literature, citing the authority of Augustine and Jerome. Thus counseled, Boccaccio overcame his qualms, and in the *Genealogia* developed the Petrarchan theme of the *theologia poetica*. Poetry, Boccaccio argued, had from its origins close associations with theology, since the ancient poets, like the prophets, had dealt with the mysteries of the cosmos and of human nature. True, the pagan poets did not receive inspiration directly from the Holy Spirit, as the Hebrew prophets had; nonetheless their works reveal vestiges of the divine truth, hidden beneath the polytheistic myths. Poetry, far from being a worldly seduction, useless, vain, and lascivious, is the loftiest of gifts imparted to mankind, inspiring delight in understanding and conviction in the exercise of virtue. In this way Boccaccio both justified a sympathetic reading of the classical poets and defended his own scholarly and literary pursuits.[19]

In the years following Boccaccio's death, the Augustinian circle of Santo Spirito, in possession of his library and led by Luigi Marsili (1342–1394), a young Augustinian monk whom both Boccaccio and Petrarch had befriended, emerged as the focal point for continuing the two masters' humanistic studies. Within this group the central figure became Coluccio Salutati (1331–1406). Indeed, he soon dwarfed his contemporaries, dominating the direction of Florentine humanism in the late Trecento and by his efforts making the city by 1400 the capital of humanist studies in the peninsula.[20]

Born in the small commune of Buggiano, near Lucca but within the frontiers of Florentine Tuscany, Salutati grew up in the great university city of Bologna, where he received training as a notary, a vocation he practiced in various communes of the Florentine *contado*. In the mid-1360s he received a succession of appointments—as chancellor of Todi, to the papal chancery in Rome, then in Lucca. In 1375 he gained the prestigious position of chancellor of the Florentine Republic, a post he held to the end of his life.

Like Boccaccio, Salutati assembled a first-rate library of ancient texts. The largest collection in Europe at the end of the fourteenth century, it surpassed Boccaccio's in the number of volumes and included important new manuscript finds.[21] His massive personal correspondence also far exceeded Boccaccio's. Letters formed an important part of Salutati's literary production and served as the means by which he forged a network of humanist contacts throughout Italy.[22] Less remote than Petrarch, Salutati was more open in personal relations, promoting a spirit of fellowship in a common movement. A generous and inspiring teacher, he exerted a profound effect upon the many young disciples he attracted to Florence from other parts of the peninsula. These included figures like Pier Paolo Vergerio of Capodistria and Antonio Loschi of Vicenza, whose careers developed outside of Florence, as well as the Tuscans Leonardo Bruni and Poggio Bracciolini, who became the intellectual leaders of the next generation of Florentine humanism.[23]

Influential as these personal relations were, the real key to Salutati's humanist career in Florence was the chancellorship. At various points Boccaccio had served on embassies for the Florentine government, but he held no regular public appointment. Indeed, in the later 1350s he took clerical orders, which apparently enabled him, like Petrarch, to enjoy some income from ecclesiastical benefices. Salutati, who married in 1366, was thus the first prominent humanist to pursue a strictly lay career. Among other duties, being chancellor required Salutati to compose frequent public letters defending Florentine policy in conflicts with its peninsular rivals, notably the papacy and the Duchy of Milan. In so doing he first advanced several key political notions, which the subsequent generation of civic humanists developed much more fully. These included the centrality of liberty to fully developed civic life, the fundamental importance of mercantile and artisan elements in creating the conditions of equality conducive to self-government, and the assertion of historical claims for the republican foundations of the city of Florence itself. In many respects Salutati's political ideas remained medieval. Liberty, for instance, was ambiguously associated with republicanism, such that both monarchy and republics, legitimately constituted under the rule of law, drew his approbation as polities according the benefits of freedom to citizens and subjects alike.[24]

Where Salutati did eventually break from medieval assumptions was in his defense of the superiority of the active over the contemplative life. Medieval tradition had both asserted the primacy of the monastic life and associated intellectual activity with contemplative withdrawal. At various moments of depression and personal anxiety Salutati found such attitudes compelling, but the general thrust of his thought was to affirm the moral and spiritual value of the roles of husband, father, and citizen-scholar. In this Salutati drew inspiration from Cicero's career, particularly as more fully revealed to him in Cicero's letters *Ad familiares,* which the Florentine chancellor was largely responsible for unearthing in 1392. Whereas Petrarch in discovering Cicero's *Letters to Atticus* was dismayed at the portrait these revealed, prompting his famous letter to the shade of Cicero in Hades in which he reproached his literary hero for becoming involved in vain and useless quarrels, Salutati instead admired Cicero's participation in the political struggles of the late Roman republic as exemplary of the true citizen's civic duty.[25]

So effective was Salutati himself as a propagandist of Florentine interests against Milanese expansion in the 1390s that even the duke of Milan, so it was reported, regarded a Salutati letter as worth a thousand horses.[26]

The authority and esteem Salutati acquired as chancellor permitted him to influence Florentine public policy in other ways. For instance, he was primarily responsible for the decision of the Florentine signoria to appoint Manuel Chrysoloras to a chair of Greek studies at the Florentine *studium.* Chrysoloras, a leading representative of the Hellenic revival in fourteenth-century Byzantine culture, was far more knowledgeable in the Greek classics than Leontius Pilatus, and his sojourn in Florence from 1397 to 1399 proved decisive for the development of Greek studies there. Salutati never became proficient in the language himself, but he stimulated his younger protégés, most notably Leonardo Bruni, to master classical Greek, and even before Salutati's death significant scholarly advances had been achieved. The rich sources of Greek wisdom Cicero had admired, but which until then had remained largely unknown to the Latin West, in this way became available to the humanist curriculum.[27]

Salutati served, however, not merely as a forerunner to the developments of the Quattrocento. He was a significant humanist thinker in his own right. Certain humanist issues Salutati took up show his connection to earlier discussions. Thus, for instance, his *De laboribus Herculis,* a lengthy account of the classical myths surrounding the Greek demigod, pursues the idea of Boccaccio's *Genealogia* that the *theologia poetica* of the ancients includes moral and natural philosophy and theology. In seeing Hercules as a mirror of life, Salutati not only defended classical studies as permissible for Christians, but also tended to universalize the nature and meaning of human experience, thereby permitting an enlarged view of human potentiality within the world.[28]

In a similar way, Petrarch's moral philosophy set the agenda for much of Salutati's own thinking on the tasks of Christian life. In his most systematic work, *De fato et fortuna,* Salutati sought, in Charles Trinkaus's words, "to reconcile his active concept of human existence and his deep trust and faith in the Christian revelation."[29] How to reconcile divine providence with human free will was, in fact, a major concern of fourteenth-century theology as a whole. Salutati's answer, drawn in large part from an attentive study of two of St. Augustine's major works, *De Genesi ad litteram* and *De Trinitate,* was to affirm the dignity of man created in divine likeness. Human dignity, Salutati argues, consists in the freedom to will and act. The world human beings inhabit is neither preordained nor logically determined. Neither, however, is it subject to the blind caprices of fortune. Rather, human affairs, both individual and communal, are the responsibility of humans themselves. This point was central to Salutati's thought: the fundamental importance of humans assuming moral responsibility for the world in which they live. No clearer exemplar of true moral responsibility can be found, Salutati asserted, than Socrates. Though unjustly condemned, he refused to flee his native Athens, since to do so would be to fail to fulfill his duty to uphold the laws of the state.

Salutati was a transitional figure. Not a monolithic thinker, his works betray reservations, hesitancies, and vacillations. He never worked out a consistent political philosophy, and his enthusiasm for pagan culture, despite strenuous efforts, was never fully integrated into his Christian perspective. Salutati's Christian humanism thus remained, as Ronald Witt observes, an unstable mixture.[30] Yet as a scholar and a thinker Salutati opened the doors that led to the more enduring accomplishments of the fifteenth century.

*   *   *

During the first half of the fifteenth century, the humanist movement that had gradually taken root over the previous fifty years reached full flower in Florence. Restricted until this point to a coterie of enthusiasts, humanism now became pervasive as the culture of patrician Florence.[31] Earlier humanist notions now emerged in mature form, and significant areas of humanist studies, such as historiography, rhetoric, patristics, and aesthetic theory attained their first embodiments.

Underlying these developments was the extraordinary enlargement of humanist understanding of the ancient world made possible by the dramatic discoveries of classical texts. Numerous Latin authors, known only by reputation, now became available as texts to Renaissance readers, and important additions were made to the *opera omnia* of others. About half of what now survives as Cicero's works, for instance, resulted from humanist discoveries.[32] At the same time, the humanists' Greek studies illuminated the hitherto inaccessible world of Hellenic antiquity.

The most indefatigable, and successful, of the humanist bookhunters was Poggio Bracciolini (1380–1459).[33] Like so many other leaders of Florentine humanism, Poggio came from provincial Tuscany, in his case from Terranuova, a small town under Florentine jurisdiction located near Arezzo. In his late teens he came to Florence to prepare for the career of notary, and there fell under Salutati's influence. Through him he acquired a passion for humanist studies, and established lifelong friendships with other Florentine humanists of his generation. In 1403 he entered the papal secretariate, where he was employed for fifty years, except for a brief hiatus from 1418 to 1423, when he lived in England in the service of an English bishop. Though long connected to the papal court, Poggio's intellectual formation was Florentine, as were his most important intellectual ties. Indeed, late in life, in 1453, he returned to Florence to assume the position of chancellor, a post he held until his death. One should be reminded, too, that for much of the early fifteenth century the papal court fell within the Florentine political and cultural orbit. Hence, though for many years Poggio did not reside in Florence, he can rightly be claimed by the city on the Arno.

Poggio's greatest manuscript discoveries came during the period of the Council of Constance, 1414–18. As a member of the papal curia, Poggio accompanied John XXIII to Switzerland, but when the council deposed the pontiff in 1415, Poggio suddenly found time on his hands. Over the next two and a half years he made four lengthy journeys, exploring the manuscript holdings in the ancient abbey libraries of Switzerland, eastern France, and the Rhineland of Germany. Among the manuscript finds Poggio unearthed, many in decayed and neglected condition, were Lucretius's *De rerum natura*, Vitruvius's *De architectura*, and Statius's *Silvae*. What most excited Poggio's Florentine humanist friends, particularly Niccolò Niccoli and Leonardo Bruni, to whom he sent reports of his findings and transcriptions of the texts, were thirteen orations of Cicero (located at Cluny, Langres, and Cologne) and the first complete manuscript of Quintilian's *De oratoria institutione* (from St. Gall). These, when joined by Gerardus Landriani's discovery at Lodi in 1421 of Cicero's *Orator, Brutus,* and the complete *De oratore,* suddenly made available the most important classical Latin texts on the theory and practice of rhetoric. Rhetoric had constituted the key to Roman ideas of education, and, along with philosophy, represented the central intellectual discipline of antiquity.[34]

Discovery of the works of ancient authors formed for the humanists just the first step in "restoring" them to contemporary understanding. Over the centuries scribal errors had intruded into the texts, in part, the humanists believed, because of degenerate forms of handwriting and orthography. To overcome these deficiencies, Poggio, in transcribing texts and preparing copies for the libraries of his Florentine friends, developed a new style of script, sharply different from contemporary Gothic hand, which he called *littera antiqua* (though it was actually based on Carolingian minuscule). At the same time Niccoli, whose only scholarly treatise was devoted to Latin orthography, developed a second form of humanistic script, "italic."[35]

Niccolò Niccoli (1364–1437) stood for, in fact, the most ardent form of classicism in early Quattrocento Florence. The arbiter of style and taste for his generation, he possessed an almost fanatical devotion to everything antique, expending the wool textile fortune he inherited on collecting ancient sculpture, bronzes, and other artifacts. Above all, he acquired books, and he built up the largest and finest collection of ancient texts in Florence. His library included codices once in Salutati's possession but dispersed after the chancellor's death, as well as many of the finds Poggio and other humanists secured in transalpine monastic libraries. In fact, Niccoli continually pestered humanist travelers to make searches, sending them lists of *desiderata*. Niccoli's library included rare patristic as well as classical works. The church fathers indeed now became as much a subject for revival as the pagan classics. Admired for their Latin eloquence, Jerome, Augustine, Lactantius, and the other Latin fathers had, in fact, received classical rhetorical educations and shared many of the literary and cultural values of classical antiquity. To many early Quattrocento Florentines, most notably Ambrogio Traversari (1386–1439), the Camaldolese monk who was Niccoli's closest friend and collaborator, these Christian "classics" possessed a more authentic (because older) teaching, couched in a more persuasive and convincing form than scholastic works. Indeed, for Traversari the *studia humanitatis* and the *studia pietatis* are necessarily yoked.[36]

Niccoli and Traversari, along with Bruni, were also the leading proponents of Greek studies. Again, the first task after acquiring the rudiments of the language was the acquisition of Greek texts. Unlike the ancient Latin authors, Greek manuscripts were not accessible in the medieval collections of Europe. Rather, they had to come from Byzantium, and during the 1420s there arrived in Florence the two most successful procurers of manuscripts from the Greek East. The first, Giovanni Aurispa, a Sicilian humanist, had spent some time in the imperial chancery in Constantinople. From there he brought back over two hundred books, including all of Plato and most of the Neoplatonists, as well as many works in history and poetry. Niccoli apparently took advantage of Aurispa's stay in Florence during the years 1425–27 to acquire some of this Greek treasure, including an exceptionally beautiful codex of Aeschylus's and Sophocles's plays.[37] Two years after Aurispa's departure, Francesco Filelfo arrived in Florence, following a seven-year stay in the Greek capital. One of the leading humanists of the century, Filelfo lectured on Greek studies at the Florentine *studium* from 1429 to 1434. Although his personal relations with many of the Florentine humanists were often stormy, he did make accessible his important collection of Greek texts.[38]

A number of Florentine patricians assembled Greek libraries during the 1420s, including Antonio Corbinelli, Palla Strozzi, and Cosimo de' Medici.[39] Niccoli's, however, was the most important, and Cosimo, who had loaned Niccoli funds for book purchases, eventually in the 1440s provided for the housing of the deceased Niccoli's collection as the core of the splendid humanist library he had Michelozzo design for the rebuilt monastery of San Marco. This, the most beautiful and extensive humanist library of Quattrocento Florence, continued to provide public access for scholars of succeeding generations, until it was eventually consolidated into the Biblioteca Laurenziana, with its even finer architecture by Michelangelo.[40]

Possessed of the richest collection of Greek classical and patristic manuscripts in the Latin West prior to the Byzantine Bessarion's arrival for the Council of Florence in 1439 (Bessarion eventually bequeathed his library to Venice, where it formed the core of the famed Biblioteca Marciana), Florentine humanists had the textual resources from which to acquire an understanding of Greek literature and thought. An initial task of appropriation involved translation, and a large number of Greek works received Latin versions. Leonardo Bruni (ca. 1370–1444), the leading Greek classicist, made translations of Plutarch, Plato, and Aristotle, produced adaptations of Xenophon's *Greek History* and Procopius's *Gothic Wars,* and used Polybius along with other Greek and Latin sources to compile a narrative account of the Punic Wars.[41] The leading patristic translator was Traversari. He provided Latin versions of some two dozen works of the Greek fathers, including Basil, Gregory Nazianzus, Athanasius, and especially John Chrysostom.[42] Cicero himself engaged in the practice of translating from Greek into Latin (these have not survived), thus providing an important precedent for the humanists' endeavors. Moreover, translation was no mere passive activity, for it challenged both the scholar's grasp of the two languages and his sense of literary style. Indeed, the humanists discussed at length the approach and methods appropriate for various texts. In general they opposed as inadequate and inelegant the word-for-word practice of medieval translations, arguing for a more rhetorically polished Latin. They did so even for Aristotle's philosophical works, which in medieval Latin translation had provided the intellectual underpinnings for scholasticism. In fact, when Bruni provided a humanistic Latin rendering of Aristotle's *Nicomachean Ethics* (1416–17), it occasioned a controversy. The scholastic Alonso de Cartagena, while admitting he knew no Greek, rejected Bruni's translation as wholly inadequate, since it lacked the precision and rigor in terminology essential for philosophic inquiry. Bruni responded that it was ridiculous for one ignorant of Greek to criticize his translation, and, moreover, that the meaning of words should be established only through etymological analysis or through the usage of trustworthy authors, namely Cicero and the other ancients.[43]

The implications of this scholastic-humanist controversy extend beyond the narrower issue of proper translation to the meaning and purpose of language itself. For the scholastics language comprised the metaphysico-logical terminology by which a timeless system of rational certainty could be established. The *Nicomachean Ethics* thus provided the basis, when connected to Aristotle's *Physics* and *Metaphysics*, for structuring morality as an eternal pattern of cosmic order. Bruni, like the other humanists, instead regarded language in rhetorical, not logical terms. Language should be meaningful as an educative force, conducive to the *vita activa civilis*. Affective by nature, language is the creation of historical communities. In this way the Aristotle who mattered was the great thinker on issues of human community and citizen responsibility, and the *Nicomachean Ethics*, along with Aristotle's *Politics* (which Bruni translated in 1435), summed up Greek wisdom on man's existence as a *polis*-dwelling creature, that is, of philosophy conceived in anthropocentric, not cosmic terms. To reveal Aristotle's true meaning thus required rendering him in such a way that his ideas could serve as an active force for contemporary citizens of republics, with the power to persuade, convince, and exhort.[44]

Beyond translation, Florentine humanists also adopted the forms and content of Greek authors for creative works of their own. Bruni's youthful *Panegyric to the City of Florence*, for instance, drew upon Aelius Aristides's second-century panegyric on Athens, and his later *Funeral Oration for Nanni Strozzi* was inspired by Pericles's famous "Funeral Oration," in Thucydides's *History of the Peloponnesian War.*[45] Plutarch's lives similarly provided models for the writing of biographies. The dialogue form as created by Plato and adopted by Cicero for his philosophical works also proved a congenial vehicle for the humanists' treatment of a variety of issues in moral philosophy, religion, education, and politics. Two influential works in this genre were Bruni's *Dialogues to Pier Paolo Vergerio*, modeled on Cicero's *De oratore*, and Poggio's *On Avarice.*[46] Cultivating these classical literary forms permitted the humanists of the early Quattrocento to depart both from the systematic, formal treatises of the scholastics and from the discursive commentaries composed by Boccaccio and Salutati. By introducing humanist contemporaries as the interlocutors of their dialogues, they made their works seem engagingly immediate and humanly relevant to their audiences rather than theoretical, remote, and abstract.

Perhaps the most distinctive humanist achievement of the first half of the Quattrocento belongs to historiography. Here the seminal work was Bruni's *History of the Florentine People*. Begun upon his return from Rome to Florence in 1415, this project occupied him for the remainder of his life. Inspired by Livy's *History of Rome* and to some extent, too, by Thucydides's *History*, which he was among the first westerners to read since antiquity, Bruni treated the history of Florence from its origins to the death of Giangaleazzo Visconti, the tyrant of Milan, in 1402. His death freed Florence from jeopardy, and Bruni regarded it as opening the way for the extraordinary cultural creativity of Florentines in his own times. History for Bruni revealed neither a fortuitous succession of chance events nor the hand of divine providence. The record of human wisdom or folly, history was essentially the creation of human communities, particularly those of the Etruscans, the Romans, and the Florentines. Indeed, those communities that had had the most decisive impact on the development of human civilization had all been republics. Only republics, by providing for broad inclusion of citizens in the decision-making process and by extending the protection of just and equitable laws to the whole populace, generated the conditions for individuals to develop their creative talents. Just as the Roman Republic of the second and early first centuries B.C. represented one apex of human history, so Florence in the early fifteenth century constituted a second great age. In this way Bruni went beyond Salutati to embrace a full-fledged political philosophy of republicanism, and his history became a central work in the creation of an ideology of "civic humanism."[47]

Other Florentine humanists, stimulated by Bruni's achievement and by the high regard the ancients held for history, composed their own historical works. Thus Matteo Palmieri (1406–1475), whose *Della vita civile* (ca. 1433) espoused the same ethical and political values Bruni had earlier articulated, composed, shortly after Bruni's death, an account of the Florentine conquest of Pisa (1406). Like Bruni, Palmieri turned to a classical model, this time to Sallust.[48] Other historical writings include Giannozzo Manetti's *History of Pistoia*, Benedetto Accolti's history of the crusades, and Poggio's history of the Florentine people, written late in life when he served as Florentine chancellor. Indeed, the writing of a Florentine history became something of an expectation for the city's chancellors, and Bartolomeo Scala, the last of the Quattrocento chancellors, followed in the tradition.[49]

The public world, then, dominated the concerns of Florentine humanist activity in the opening decades of the fifteenth century. Poetry, so much a preoccupation of Petrarch and Boccaccio, receded into the background, with Carlo Marsuppini (1398–1453) the only notable practitioner, though he, too, was deeply involved in public life, succeeding Bruni as chancellor of Florence in 1444.[50] Nevertheless, humanism extended beyond merely literary pursuits to include science, mathematics, and the fine arts. Again acquisitions of classical sources and translation of Greek texts constituted important first steps. Early in the century Chrysoloras and Jacopo da Scarperia collaborated on a Latin version of Ptolemy's important *Geography*, a key work for ancient ideas of cartography.[51] Later, in the 1420s, Paolo Toscanelli's interest in mathematics, optics, and astronomy led him to investigate the work of Archimedes and other achievements of Hellenistic science and engineering.[52]

But the central figure in humanistic science and mathematics in the first half of the Quattrocento was Leon Battista Alberti (1404–1472).[53] The son of an exiled Florentine merchant-banker, Alberti's development and long career occurred primarily in Bologna, Rome, Mantua, and elsewhere. Yet while not, strictly speaking, a "Florentine" humanist, he nevertheless was decisively influenced by his sojourn in the Arno city during the mid-1430s, and his works had important influences there. Employed in the papal chancery, Alberti came to Florence in 1434 along with other members of the papal court. Florence, Eugenius IV's haven during his exile from the Eternal City, thus provided residence for nearly all the leading humanists of the day, and Alberti, like other humanists, benefited from this stimulus. Alberti was struck, too, by Florence itself, notably by the extraordinary advances in realism in Florentine painting achieved through the use of linear perspective. Inspired by what he saw and instructed by Brunelleschi and other members of the Florentine artistic community, Alberti composed his treatise *On Painting*. This work provided both a practical handbook to and a theoretical treatment of the new Florentine style. In this way aesthetic theory became a subject of humanist discourse, and artists joined scholars as practitioners of a humanistic discipline.[54]

A polymath, Alberti embodied the humanistic ideal of the universal man. For him, knowledge of the natural world, acquired through mathematical inquiry, was to be applied, through the virtue of hard work, to enhancing the human community. Activity, not contemplation, remained central to Alberti's ethical beliefs, and in building the world mankind realizes its inherent human dignity.[55]

Alberti thus shared the civic emphasis of Bruni's thought, but he extended this notion beyond Bruni's historico-political ideas to considerations of the natural world. Alberti's contemporary, Giannozzo Manetti (1396–1459), enlarged the theme of human dignity in another direction, to synthesize the new Renaissance idea of man as doer and creator (*homo faber*) with the Christian view of mankind created in the image and likeness of God. Manetti's *The Dignity of Man* is one of the most important humanist statements on the human condition and belongs to a series of reflections on human dignity and misery written in the mid and late Quattrocento. Drawing on patristic ideas, both Latin and Greek, Manetti praised humanity's inventive intelligence, those Promethean powers with which God has endowed him, and with which he has created human civilization.[56]

The optimism and assurance of Manetti's work reflects the general outlook of Florentine humanism in the early Quattrocento. Inspired by a much fuller knowledge of the ancient world, both classical and Christian and including Greek as well as Latin literature, and reinforced in their views through controversy with scholastic opponents and through the spread of the humanist movement itself, Florentine humanists of the early fifteenth century overcame the ambivalences and hesitations in Salutati's thought. By grasping the classical ideal of the orator, and by fully subscribing to the rhetorical values encompassed therein—in particular that humanity's essential characteristic is power of speech—they embraced the public world, seeing that arena of earthly government as the setting for human achievement and fulfillment. The *vita activa civilis* they regarded as fundamental to human happiness, and it also promoted the exercise of those virtues that lead to eternal beatitude.

*   *   *

Humanism in later fifteenth-century Florence shifted ground. The affirmation of the active life of the citizen gave way to the cultivation of the contemplative life. At the same time such humanist themes as human dignity became anchored in the more systematic philosophical and religious framework of Neoplatonism. If this return to metaphysics undermined the rhetorical culture of early Quattrocento humanism from one direction, this culture was eroded from the other through the return to poetry and to an emphasis on philological erudition in the work of Poliziano. In both respects, the public world of the orator gave way to the more esoteric inquiries of the scholar secluded in his study.

This dissipation of the civic impulse can be traced in several figures. There was Donato Acciaiuoli (1429–1478), friend of Manetti, translator of Bruni's *History* into Italian, and expositor of the moral and political Aristotle, but whose emphasis on the intersection of history and politics in asserting an image of citizen virtue attracted a diminishing audience.[57] In a similar way, Bartolomeo Scala, chancellor of Florence for the last third of the century, made his mark not as an intellectual leader but rather as the reformer of the chancery into a modern state bureaucracy. In rationalizing the chancery's structure and making more efficient its procedures, this humanist bureaucrat both enlarged the scope of its undertakings and made it more pliable to Medicean interests. While he, too, wrote a *History of Florence*, it lacked the thematic clarity of his predecessors' and stopped in midsentence at the year 1268. Telling, too, are the inclusion of an admiring portrait of the medieval Charlemagne and Scala's uncritical acceptance of the legends crediting the Carolingian emperor with rebuilding Florence.[58] Earlier Acciaiuoli, in his *Life of Charlemagne*, portrayed this medieval emperor as the ideal prince of wisdom and learning, responsible for the renewal of classical culture.[59] A renewed emphasis on princely leadership thus diluted the republican ideology of Bruni's civic humanism.

In fact, the growing dominance of the Medici and their increasing identification of family interests as those of Florentine policy altered the civic world that Bruni had celebrated. The change did not happen overnight. Under Cosimo de' Medici (in power 1434–64) republican appearances remained. But under his grandson Lorenzo (1469–92) the real locus of political authority in Florence had clearly gravitated from the Palazzo della Signoria to the lavish Palazzo Medici on the Via Larga. Alamanno Rinuccini (1426–1504), who maintained his republican convictions into this new Laurentian age, excoriated Lorenzo as a tyrant in his dialogue *On Liberty*, charging that his usurpations would lead to cultural and intellectual degeneration. Rinuccini, however, wrote from the embittered exile of his country villa, excluded from that participation in Florentine public life he viewed as so central to humanity's spiritual and moral well-being.[60]

Most other humanists of Laurentian Florence welcomed this shift from public space to the leisured retreat of suburban and country villa. Lorenzo himself, in fact, favored country life, the inspiration for much of the mythologizing nature poetry he wrote, and he created at Poggio a Caiano a classical villa, decorated with painted bucolic scenes. Typical of this change of intellectual setting and corresponding shift of mood are the *Disputationes camaldulenses* of Cristoforo Landino (1424–1504). Set in the monastic hermitage of Camaldoli, high up in the forested Apennines east of Florence, these dialogues composed in 1475 explore the relative advantages of the active versus the contemplative life. Lorenzo serves as spokesman for the former, Leon Battista Alberti—somewhat out of character—for the latter. Landino comes down decisively in favor of the primacy of the contemplative life, "for deeds die with men, but thoughts vanquish time." Landino returned to the ideal of the sage, arguing again with Petrarch that the Cicero who achieved the most was the philosopher who had abandoned politics. The real inspiration for Landino's thinking, however, was Plato, in particular the Plato of the *Republic* with its ideal of the philosopher-king, who longs for the lofty heights of pure thought and suffers in the cave where governing must take place.[61]

Platonism, indeed, runs all through Landino's thought, including his allegorizing commentaries on Vergil's *Aeneid* and on Dante's *Divine Comedy*. He was an important figure, too, in the Florentine Platonic Academy, the most influential intellectual community of Laurentian Florence. Established in 1462 when Cosimo assigned to Marsilio Ficino the Medici villa at Careggi, situated on the slopes near Fiesole overlooking Florence, the academy embodied the revival of the philosophical tradition Plato had inaugurated in the grove outside the walls of Athens.[62]

Plato had not been neglected by the Florentine humanists of the early fifteenth century. Salutati regarded acquisition of the complete Platonic *corpus* as a desideratum, and Bruni translated a number of Plato's early and middle dialogues, including the *Phaedo, Apology, Crito, Gorgias,* and *Phaedrus,* as well as the *Letters*. These revealed both the historical Socrates, citizen and educator of Athens, and the "political" Plato, analyst of rhetoric and committed to the reform of the *polis*.[63] For Bruni, Plato thus represented the *vita activa civilis* he admired in Cicero and in the moral and political works of Aristotle.

Interest in the more philosophical and religious Plato of the later dialogues stemmed from a group of Byzantine émigrés active in Italy in the middle decades of the Quattrocento. These Greek scholars first came in force to attend the Council of Ferrara–Florence in 1438–39. This ecumenical council was convened in hopes of resolving the long-standing schism separating Roman Catholicism and Greek Orthodoxy. After many delays, sessions began in Ferrara in 1438, then shifted to Florence, where Cosimo de' Medici agreed to underwrite expenses. The participants at length resolved the outstanding theological issues, though in the long term this resolution was inconsequential, since the demise of Byzantium following the Ottoman conquest of Constantinople forestalled any incentive to religious unification. The intellectual repercussions of the council were, however, significant.[64]

Among those attending the council was the enigmatic George Gemistus Pletho, mystic, religious cult leader, and creator of an esoteric religious system fusing Platonic and Neoplatonic views of the soul, immortality, and the metaphysical realm of the Ideas with elements of Christianity. Pletho engaged in discussions with a number of leading Italian humanists in Florence, and, according to Ficino, inspired Cosimo de' Medici with the idea of resurrecting the Platonic Academy in Florence.[65]

Pletho's impact on Florentine humanist thought was largely indirect, however. Ongoing interest in Plato in the years after the council consisted primarily of the fusillades exchanged, in Greek, among Byzantine émigrés, notably George of Trebizond and Bessarion, as to the relative merits of Aristotle and Plato as philosophers. These controversies centered on Rome, not Florence; and Rome, too, was where Nicholas of Cusa pursued his interests in Platonic theology. They established, however, the focus on the metaphysical and religious Plato, the Plato, for instance, of the *Laws* and the *Parmenides,* dialogues that had themselves been central to the Neoplatonists of antiquity.[66]

In Florence, a renewed attention to Platonic philosophy came with the appointment in 1456 of John Argyropoulos to a chair of Greek studies at the *studium*. This Byzantine émigré remained in Florence for fifteen years, lecturing on Aristotle's *Nicomachean Ethics* and *De anima,* but in so doing giving a sympathetic account of Platonic metaphysics and epistemology, and in private lessons further acquainting his Florentine students with the more speculative aspects of Platonic thought.[67]

These developments thus formed the background to the career of Marsilio Ficino (1433–1499), the foremost Neoplatonist of the Italian Renaissance. Ficino, the son of Cosimo de' Medici's personal physician, enjoyed the full patronage of the Florentine leader in his cultivation of Platonic studies. In youthful commentaries on Lucretius, Ficino already reveals a preoccupation with religious matters, but the real turning point in his intellectual development seems to have been work on the *Corpus Hermeticum,* that esoteric and mystical body of ancient religious lore which Ficino translated from Greek into Latin and presented to Cosimo in 1463. Ficino went on to translate all the works of Plato and the works of the ancient Neoplatonists, including Plotinus, Proclus, and Iamblichus. Since only a portion of Plato's own works had ever been rendered into Latin, this represented an extraordinary enlargement in humanist understanding of one of the most influential philosophical traditions of antiquity. Ficino also composed important philosophical works, chief among them *On Platonic Theology*, consisting largely of arguments for the immortality of the soul, which he dedicated to Lorenzo de' Medici.[68]

As the founder of Renaissance Neoplatonism, Ficino exerted a tremendous influence on European thought, which falls beyond the scope of this essay. Moreover, as a philosopher, much of his work stands outside the humanist's province. If not strictly speaking a humanist, Ficino nonetheless had important relations to the Florentine humanist tradition, both in the themes of his own thought and in the impact his Neoplatonism had on the direction of Florentine humanism in the later fifteenth century.

The theme of the dignity of man is central to Ficino's thought, and like Manetti and other Quattrocento humanists he celebrated humanity's capacity to create a civilized world. Yet, for Ficino, these achievements are to be transcended by the soul's quest for immortality and divinity, in which lies man's essential dignity. This emphasis on the soul meant that Ficino saw the human situation less in a social and ethical context than in a cosmic and metaphysical one. His vision was essentially religious. In this way, again, the earlier humanist interests in civic life, republicanism, and liberty receded.[69]

Another fundamental difference divides Ficino from early Quattrocento humanism. Inspired by the ideals of Ciceronian rhetoric, the humanists sought by articulating issues of public policy and citizens' responsibility to reach and inspire a broad spectrum of society. For Ficino, the intellectual must penetrate the veils that shroud the divine mysteries, must break through the bonds of the perceptible world to the realm of pure ideas and ultimately to God. The intellectual thus becomes the sage, the mystagogue. He initiates his disciples into the ultimate mysteries. The result is that much of Ficino's writing is esoteric and abstruse, consisting of symbols, images, and signs that must be deciphered, penetrated, and absorbed. Of necessity, his philosophy remained elitist, fully accessible only to those few chosen souls who joined him in the seclusion of the Florentine Platonic Academy at Careggi.[70]

Yet Neoplatonism had a greater impact on Florentine intellectual and cultural life than its recondite theosophy might suggest. In developing Neoplatonic ideas of love and beauty, Ficino inspired a generation of poets and artists. Here the key work was Ficino's *Commentary on Plato's 'Symposium' on the Subject of Love* (1469), composed as a series of speeches supposedly delivered by members of the Platonic Academy following a banquet held at Careggi on 7 November to commemorate the traditional date of Plato's birth and death. The dishes cleared, one of the banqueters read the *Symposium* and the other guests explained the meaning of the various speeches in the text. The *Symposium* represents Plato's fullest treatment of his idea of love as the impetus to knowledge of Truth and Beauty. For Ficino, love is exalted as the perpetual knot and link of the universe. Love is the cosmogonic principle, and the human soul in ascending in love draws nearer to God, ultimate love. At the same time this ascent involves higher realms of beauty, for love is the desire for beauty. Beauty itself is a kind of light or force shining from God through everything. In this way Ficino connected light, sight, love, and beauty as key elements of the Neoplatonic pursuit, an aesthetic vision that proved congenial to the artists and poets of Lorenzo's circle, among them Botticelli, whose *Birth of Venus* and *Primavera* seem to reflect these notions.[71]

Ficino's most famous disciple was Giovanni Pico della Mirandola (1463–1494), the precociously brilliant young prince of Concordia, who spent much of the last decade of his short life in Florence. A student of philosophy at the Universities of Ferrara, Padua, and later Paris, Pico regarded himself as a philosopher, preferring what he called a "Parisian" (in other words, scholastic) mode of disputation to the classical Latin of the humanists. In fact, in a famous letter to the Venetian humanist Ermolao Barbaro the Younger (1485), Pico defended the use of scholastic language for philosophical inquiry, denying that humanistic Latin provided a suitable means of discourse in this area. Such views made Pico equally unacceptable to the rigorous Ciceronians of Rome. Yet Pico, in a broad sense, can be regarded as humanistic, particularly in his development of the idea of human dignity, the subject of his famous *Oration* written to inaugurate his defense of his Nine Hundred Theses, and in his emphasis on the essential concord of all theological and metaphysical traditions. In pursuing this unity of truth, Pico drew particularly on the kabbalah, the medieval mystical tradition of Judaism. In this search for a secret wisdom transmitted down the centuries, Pico, like Ficino, emphasized a mystical-allegorical approach. Pico's vision, in fact, was more a poetic and religious than a philosophical one, as reflected in the title of a work he intended to write, but never did: *Poetic Theology.*[72]

If in their concern for a metaphysics Ficino and Pico remain somewhat outside the intellectual tradition of humanism in the narrower sense, no such disclaimers must be made for the other key intellectual of Laurentian Florence, Angelo Poliziano (1454–1494), who was one of the leading humanists of the century. Like Ficino, Poliziano depended on

Medicean patronage. He was an intimate companion of Lorenzo himself and served as a tutor in Lorenzo's household. Poliziano's achievements as a humanist lie in the fields of poetry and philology. His youthful, unfinished *Stanze per la Giostra* capture the carefree gaiety, the springtime ebullience of Florentine aristocratic society prior to the shock of the Pazzi Conspiracy, in which Lorenzo's younger brother, Giuliano, the hero of Poliziano's poem and the victor in the tournament that occasioned its composition, was assassinated. In this Italian poem, Poliziano evokes the image of the beautiful Simonetta Cattaneo, whose youthful charms before her premature death of consumption attracted the admiration of all Florence, and celebrates human love as the educative power that leads to fulfillment of *humanitas*. The poem's delicate mood of an innocent Golden Age is all the more poignant for the youthful demise of the poem's protagonists.[73]

For the most part, however, Poliziano wrote poetry in Latin, not Italian. Deeply read in the poetry of both Greek and Latin antiquity— early in his career he translated part of the *Iliad*—he composed odes, elegies, and epigrams of great refinement and elegance, particularly in his descriptions of the natural beauty of the Tuscan landscape. Besides Latin poetry, Poliziano composed a Sallustian account of the Pazzi Conspiracy, the *De Pactiana coniuratione commentarium*, though this was his only venture into history.[74]

As a scholar Poliziano's fame derives instead from his meticulous philological researches into classical texts, the fruit of his work as professor of Greek and rhetoric at the Florentine *studium*. In 1489 he published his *Miscellanea,* a collection of one hundred expanded textual notes, which reveal the depth of his classical erudition and important advances in such areas as the collation of manuscripts and textual criticism.

Though an admirer and friend of Ficino and Pico, Poliziano never shared their metaphysical flights and religious longings. Rather, as a grammarian and philologist, he focused on language as the conveyor of cultural tradition, of civilization, ultimately of *humanitas*. The arts of speech, not the mystic silence of the *theologia Platonica,* occupied Poliziano's mind. Language, too, for Poliziano was not an unchanging metahistorical reality. This view was the gist of his opposition to the Ciceronianism of the Roman humanist Paolo Cortesi, who asserted that imitation of Ciceronian style was the perfect vehicle for the expression of all topics. Poliziano instead argued for a more eclectic approach to classical antiquity, one that would allow for more individual expression.[75]

A bittersweet note runs through much of Poliziano's poetry, and the haunting specter of death. Poliziano, in fact, died young, in 1494, shortly before Pico did, and just as King Charles VIII of France was poised to enter a defeated Florence. Poliziano's funeral ode on the death of Lorenzo de' Medici, who died at age forty-three in 1492, provides an epitaph for the Laurentian age. The text for the remarkable musical composition of Heinrich Isaac, Lorenzo's favorite composer, the ode evokes the image of the laurel tree (a play on Lorenzo's name), so dear to all the Muses, under whose spreading boughs Apollo himself had sung. Now lightning has struck down this Laurel (under whose shelter happy Florence once rested in peace: *Stanze per la Giostra*, stanza 4), leaving all mute and none to hear.[76]

War and civic convulsions marked the closing years of the Quattrocento and opening decades of the Cinquecento in Florence. After the expulsion of Piero de' Medici, Lorenzo's son, in 1494, the central public figure in Florence was Savonarola, the firebrand Dominican preacher and prophet of the Eschaton. Many former *litterati* of Lorenzo's circle became ardent Savonarolans. Poliziano, and even more Pico, were drawn in their last years to the more somber Christianity of Savonarola, the religion of repentance and conversion, and both were buried in the cowl of a Dominican friar. Even Ficino initially believed in Savonarola's prophetic powers, before becoming disillusioned. The younger Laurentians, such as Giovanni Nesi and Girolamo Benivieni, all became converts to building the Savonarolan New Jerusalem in Florence, and Botticelli's late paintings reveal Savonarolan themes and imagery. With Ficino withdrawn in scholarly isolation to Careggi, the Neoplatonic court culture of Laurentian Florence came to an end.[77]

*   *   *

During the first third of the sixteenth century, humanism in Florence encountered serious difficulties. Nearly constant civic turmoil, provoked by the shifting fortune of the Italian Wars that convulsed the peninsula, disordered the city's intellectual life. High Renaissance Rome absorbed much of Tuscany's intellectual and artistic talent, while Venice outstripped it as a publishing center and as the leader in Greek studies. The Padua of Pietro Pomponazzi stood at the cutting edge of Renaissance Aristotelianism, perhaps the most important philosophical trend of the early Cinquecento.

At the same time, Florence's leading thinkers, Niccolò Machiavelli (1469–1527) and Francesco Guicciardini (1483–1540) owed relatively little to humanism in their highly original treatments of politics and history. True, both knew the Latin, if not the Greek, classics, and Machiavelli, in particular, pondered at length the meaning of Roman history;

but both drew more from their own experiences in public life, and both found the considerations of history and politics in Quattrocento humanism inadequate to the harsh, stern realities of their own times. For Machiavelli, the inexorable laws governing the acquisition and exercise of political power drove a wedge between the union of ethics and politics, between civic liberty and the personal fulfillment the civic humanists had sought. For Guicciardini, man seemed impotent before the overweening power of fortune. For both, humanist insights and aspirations seemed irrelevant to a world in which personal moral virtue mattered so little and impersonal force so much.[78]

Machiavelli and Guicciardini are Renaissance intellectuals of European significance. Their originality is such that sometimes they have been regarded in isolation from the Florentine milieu. It would be a mistake to do so. Machiavelli was a leading participant in the aristocratic discussion group that met in the Rucellai Gardens. This, the most vital intellectual community of early Cinquecento Florence, turned attention away from philosophy and literature to considerations of contemporary history and politics, and thus formed an attentive and sympathetic audience for Machiavelli's *Discourses on Livy.*[79] Similarly, Guicciardini's *History of Italy,* while written in retirement during the last years of his life, was avidly read and immediately recognized as a historical masterpiece, equal to or greater than the histories of classical antiquity.[80] Yet Machiavelli and Guicciardini were isolated in that neither inspired followers, and intellectual trends of early ducal Florence turned in a different direction.

In 1537, when Cosimo I came to power in Florence, the city's intellectual life was in serious disarray. The return to political stability aided efforts at cultural renewal, but much was owed as well to Cosimo's policies and patronage. He encouraged exiled scholars to return to Florence, promoted the revival of printing, and endorsed the creation of the Accademia Fiorentina, sanctioning its program of public lectures and its dissemination of learning in Italian. Through the work of people like Cosimo Bartoli (1503–1572), the heritage of Quattrocento Florentine humanism reappeared in new editions and translations.[81]

In sheer volume of literary production, the work of these mid-Cinquecento humanists is impressive, and by creating a readily digested Italian prose style they succeeded in popularizing learning beyond the circles of the Latin-writing elite. Yet these achievements must be set against clear negative tendencies. As elsewhere in the Italian peninsula, humanists drew back from exploring issues in politics, moral philosophy, and religion, and history writing became increasingly sterile. Both the absolutism of the ducal court and the increasingly repressive atmosphere of the Counter-Reformation discouraged creative thinking in these areas.

Yet intellectual timidity and unoriginality marked the humanists themselves. Too much attention was given to learning as merely the basis for civility and conversation. Increasingly, in the new academies that proliferated in later sixteenth-century Florence, like the Accademia degli Alterati, intellectual activity became a form of refined amusement. Intellectuals abdicated any responsibility for the society in which they lived. Concomitantly, humanist learning in these inward-looking academies of the late Cinquecento became increasingly detached from reality. The more authoritarian tendencies of Italian culture as a whole produced a concern for laws, definitions, and classifications in the study of texts. By applying abstract rules and principles to textual exegesis, humanists detached words from experience, knowledge from living. In so doing they emptied the *studia humanitatis* of its moral commitments to the formation of human character.[82]

If humanist history, political thought, and moral philosophy degenerated to the level of banality in the late Cinquecento academies, humanism did make creative contributions to two other intellectual endeavors: music and science. In fact, these two developments are interconnected, for Vincenzo Galilei (1520–1591), a professional musician and father of the famous physicist and cosmologist, published in Florence in 1581 his *Dialogo della musica antica e della musica moderna*, in which he called for sweeping changes in music. A protégé of Count Giovanni de' Bardi, patron of the Florentine Camerata, which had given attention to music in its discussions, and a friend of Girolamo Mei, a Florentine philologist resident in Rome, who had pioneered researches into ancient Greek music, Galilei contended that modern polyphony was wholly incapable of reproducing the psychological power so celebrated by the ancients in their accounts of Greek music. Greek music was originally monodic, Galilei argued, and so must modern music become if it were to express the intensity of words and feelings. Herein, indeed, lay music's special value as an art: it was capable of conveying passions and moods more directly to the mind of the hearer than any other form of human communication. The humanists of the Quattrocento, seeking to make spoken discourse serve the more subjective and affective experiences of human existence, found inspiration in rediscovered classical rhetoric, thus detaching language from its ties to logic and metaphysics. In effect, Galilei argued that music, too, should be divorced from theology and metaphysics and linked to rhetoric, thereby becoming a profoundly human art. Galilei's polemic helped inspire both the development of monody and the creation of the *stile recitativo*. This last was the key musical innovation in the musical dramas Jacopo Peri composed for the Medici court in

Florence, which culminated in his *Euridice* of 1600. In this way opera was born.[83]

Humanism facilitated, too, the birth of Galilean science. The humanists' recovery of Hellenistic texts in science and mathematics—including those of Archimedes, whom Galileo Galilei (1564–1642) took as his model for applying mathematics as a tool for physical investigation—their receptiveness to technological innovation, and their hostility to received authorities as such if these proved inconsistent with experience, contributed to Galileo's openness to the Copernican theory and to his eagerness to exploit the telescope as an instrument of astronomical observation. At the same time, Galileo published his important cosmological works in the form of personal letters and dialogues, that is, in the rhetorical forms of humanism. And he wrote them not in the technical Latin of the universities, but rather in Italian, in the clear, forceful prose the Accademia Fiorentina had cultivated in aiming to reach a nonspecialist, generally educated audience.[84]

Galileo's condemnation in 1633 forced his own late scientific work and those of his followers into more restricted, specialized directions. His science thus failed to become the basis of a general intellectual culture. In becoming isolated from other intellectual endeavors, science thus lost any connections to humanist impulses.[85] Yet, while Galileo's science drew from humanist roots, it also presented humanism with serious challenges (though no one in the debilitated state of humanistic studies in the dawning Age of the Baroque seems really to have confronted them). In the first place, Galileo's cosmos existed as a system of mathematical relations, as a universe of quantity not quality, devoid of color, soul, beauty, and moral goodness, and thus indifferent to precisely those aesthetic, religious, and ethical concerns that had been the focus of humanist thought. In the second place, the tremendously enlarged scale of the seemingly infinite universe, with its vast voids and myriad stars, seemed to dwarf the human scale. How were the creative acts of the human will and spirit relevant to the titanic forces of the universe?

In those fields in which Florentine humanists from the late Trecento on had made the most distinctive contributions—political thought, historiography, moral philosophy, and classical philology—Renaissance impulses had spent their force by the 1580s. The restless curiosity, the art of introspection, the concern for the moral formation of the individual, and an exalting of humanity's godlike powers to shape the course of history and civilization had all dissipated. Isolated from the political and religious world of the seventeenth century and inadequate to the new challenges in philosophy and science, Florentine humanism could not survive in the Age of the Baroque; and in the end neither Baroque opera nor the new science preserved the humanist elements that had been instrumental in their emergence.[86]

NOTES

1. No single scholarly work takes as its subject the entire history of Florentine humanism; but the importance of Florentines to Italian humanism as a whole gives them prominence in various general works. Of these, the most illuminating is E. Garin, *Italian Humanism: Philosophy and Civic Life in the Renaissance,* trans. P. Munz (New York, 1965). Key texts of the Florentine humanists can be found in E. Garin, ed., *Prosatori latini del Quattrocento* (Milan, 1952) and G. Ponte, ed., *Il Quattrocento* (Bologna, 1966). For the most part, students of Florentine humanism must refer to the more specialized studies indicated in the notes below.

2. Historians of Renaissance Florence have tended recently to concentrate more on economic, social, and political developments than on cultural matters. Note the review essays of R. Starn, "Florentine Renaissance Studies," *Bibliothèque d'humanisme et Renaissance* 32 (1970): 677–84, and G. Brucker, "Tales of Two Cities: Florence and Venice in the Renaissance," *American Historical Review* 88 (1983): 599–616. The best overview of Quattrocento Florence is G. Brucker, *Renaissance Florence* (Berkeley, rev. ed. 1983), of which chap. 6 is devoted to "Culture." For the *Decameron* as a "mercantile epic," see V. Branca, *Boccaccio: The Man and his Works,* trans. R. Monges (New York, 1976), 276–307.

3. The growth of government is a major theme of M. B. Becker, *Florence in Transition,* 2 vols. (Baltimore, 1967–68). For urban development, see R. A. Goldthwaite, *The Building of Renaissance Florence* (Baltimore, 1980).

4. Note esp. Becker, *Florence in Transition,* 2:245–50.

5. For the *studium,* see G. Brucker, "Florence and Its University, 1348–1434," in *Action and Conviction in Early Modern Europe: Essays in Memory of E. H. Harbison,* ed. T. K. Rabb and J. E. Seigel (Princeton, 1969), 220–36, and idem, "A Civic Debate on Higher Education (1460)," *Renaissance Quarterly* 34 (1981): 517–33. For the meetings of Florentine intellectuals, see A. della Torre, *Storia dell'Accademia Platonica di Firenze* (Florence, 1902).

6. E. Garin, "The Humanist Chancellors of the Florentine Republic from Coluccio Salutati to Bartolomeo Scala," in *Portraits from the Quattrocento,* trans. V. A. Velen and E. Velen (New York, 1972), 1–29.

7. R. C. Trexler has written extensively on church and religion in Florence. His most recent book is *Public Life in Renaissance Florence* (New York, 1980).

8. C. Trinkaus, *In Our Image and Likeness: Humanity and Divinity in Italian Humanist Thought,* 2 vols. (Chicago, 1970), esp. 615–50.

9. The weakness of the papacy vis-à-vis Florence is for G. Holmes a crucial factor in the emergence of the humanist movement: see *The Florentine Enlightenment, 1400–1450* (New York, 1969).

10. A useful anthology with introduction and notes is provided by *The Three Crowns of Florence: Humanist Assessments of Dante, Petrarca, and Boccaccio,* ed. and trans. D. Thompson and A. F. Nagel (New York, 1972). For Botticelli, see K. Clark, *The Drawings by Sandro Botticelli for Dante's Divine Comedy* (New York, 1976).

11. Note, for instance, Poliziano's poem in praise of Giotto, in *Renaissance Latin Verse: An Anthology,* ed. A. Perosa and J. Sparrow (Chapel Hill, 1979), 140.

12. Besides Branca, the best general introduction to Boccaccio is T. G. Bergin, *Boccaccio* (New York, 1981). For the shift in Boccaccio's career, note also J. Larner, *Culture and Society in Italy, 1290–1420* (London, 1971), 213–21.

13. E. H. Wilkins, *Life of Petrarch* (Chicago, 1961), 99–102.

14. R. Pfeiffer, *History of Classical Scholarship from 1300 to 1850* (Oxford, 1976), 20–24. The most extensive treatment of the humanists' manuscript discoveries remains R. Sabbadini, *Le scoperte dei codici latini e greci ne' secoli XIV e XV,* 2 vols. (Florence, 1905–14; reprint ed. by E. Garin, Florence, 1967).

15. See the catalog prepared for the *VI Centenario della morte di Giovanni Boccaccio: Mostra di manoscritti, documenti e edizioni. Firenze—Biblioteca Medicea Laurenziana, 22 maggio–31 agosto 1975,* 2 vols. (Certaldo, 1975).

16. A. Mazza, "L'inventario della 'parva libraria' di Santo Spirito e la biblioteca del Boccaccio," *Italia medioevale e umanistica* 9 (1966): 1–74.

17. Branca, *Boccaccio,* 115–19.

18. Ibid., 109; Bergin, *Boccaccio,* 230–45.

19. Branca, *Boccaccio,* 129–31; Trinkaus, *In Our Image and Likeness,* 693–97.

20. The leading contemporary authority on Salutati is R. G. Witt. Besides numerous articles he has published two books: *Coluccio Salutati and His Public Letters* (Geneva, 1976), and *Hercules at the Crossroads: The Life, Works, and Thought of Coluccio Salutati* (Durham, NC, 1983). Still significant is B. L. Ullman, *The Humanism of Coluccio Salutati* (Padua, 1963). Important discussions of Salutati's thought appear also in Garin, *Italian Humanism,* 27–36; Trinkaus, *In Our Image and Likeness,* 51–102, 555–62, 568–71, 662–74, 697–704; and H. Baron, *The Crisis of the Early Italian Renaissance,* 2 vols in 1 (Princeton, rev. ed. 1966), 104–26, 146–66, 295–314. Witt provides a sketch of Salutati's career, a bibliography, and an English translation of two of his letters in the anthology edited by him and B. G. Kohl with E. B. Welles, *The Earthly Republic: Italian Humanists on Government and Society* (Philadelphia, 1978), 81–118.

21. Ullman, *Humanism of Salutati,* 129–209.

22. The exemplary modern edition of his correspondence is: *Epistolario di Coluccio Salutati,* ed. F. Novati, 5 vols. (Rome, 1891–1911).

23. Witt, *Hercules at the Crossroads,* 287–310, 392–415.

24. Ibid., 368–91; Witt, *Salutati and His Public Letters,* esp. 51–57, 79–88.

25. Baron, *Crisis,* 104–26; Witt, *Hercules at the Crossroads,* 299–300, 350.

26. Witt, *Hercules at the Crossroads,* 158–59.

27. Ibid., 303–10.

28. Trinkaus, *In Our Image and Likeness,* 697–704; Witt, *Hercules at the Crossroads,* 212–26.

29. *In Our Image and Likeness,* 76. On pages 76–102, Trinkaus provides an extensive exegesis of this work; note also Witt, *Hercules at the Crossroads,* 315–30, 402.

30. *Hercules at the Crossroads,* 427.

31. L. Martines, *The Social World of the Florentine Humanists, 1390–1460* (Princeton, 1963) has shown how humanists, largely drawn from patrician ranks, created a cultural program that served the political and social interests of the urban elite. His book includes useful biographical sketches of most of the humanists active in Florence in the first half of the Quattrocento. G. Brucker, *The Civic World of Early Renaissance Florence* (Princeton, 1977), 300–18, demonstrates that after 1410 humanist attitudes and themes became increasingly prominent in the *pratiche,* where Florentine leaders debated issues of public policy.

32. Pfeiffer, *History of Classical Scholarship,* 33.

33. *Two Renaissance Book Hunters: The Letters of Poggius Bracciolini to Nicolaus de Niccolis,* ed. and trans. P. W. G. Gordan (New York, 1974); Pfeiffer, *History of Classical Scholarship,* 31–34. For a sketch of Poggio's career and bibliography, see *Earthly Republic,* 231–39. The most comprehensive treatment of Florentine humanism in the early Quattrocento is Holmes, *Florentine Enlightenment.*

34. For the fundamental importance of rhetoric, see H. H. Gray, "Renaissance Humanism: The Pursuit of Eloquence," *Journal of the History of Ideas* 24 (1963): 497–514, and J. E. Seigel, *Rhetoric and Philosophy in Renaissance Humanism* (Princeton, 1968).

35. B. L. Ullman, *The Origin and Development of Humanistic Script* (Rome, 1960); M. Meiss, "Toward a More Comprehensive Renaissance Palaeography," in *The Painter's Choice: Problems in the Interpretation of Renaissance Art* (New York, 1976), 151–75.

36. B. L. Ullman and P. A. Stadter, *The Public Library of the Renaissance: Niccolò Niccoli, Cosimo de' Medici and the Library of San Marco* (Padua, 1972); C. L. Stinger, *Humanism and the Church Fathers: Ambrogio Traversari (1386–1439) and Christian Antiquity in the Italian Renaissance* (Albany, NY, 1976).

37. Stinger, *Humanism and the Church Fathers,* 36–38.

38. Ibid., 38–39; D. Robin, "A Reassessment of the Character of Francesco Filelfo (1398–1481)," *Renaissance Quarterly* 36 (1983): 202–24.

39. R. Blum, *La biblioteca della Badia Fiorentina e i codici di Antonio Corbinelli* (Vatican City, 1951); A. Diller, "Greek Codices of Palla Strozzi and Guarino Veronese," *Journal of the Warburg and Courtauld Institutes* 24 (1961): 313–21.

40. For the creation of the San Marco library, see Ullman and Stadter, *The Public Library*.

41. For Bruni's Greek scholarship, see Pfeiffer, *History of Classical Scholarship*, 27–30; Baron, *Crisis*, index under "Bruni"; and E. Garin, "La 'retorica' di Leonardo Bruni," in *Dal Rinascimento all'Illuminismo: Studi e ricerche* (Pisa, 1970), 21–42. Baron has published the prefatory letters to Bruni's translations in *Leonardo Bruni Aretino. Humanistisch-philosophische Schriften mit einer Chronologie seiner Werke und Briefe* (Leipzig and Berlin, 1928; reprint, Wiesbaden, 1969). For Bruni's work on the ancient historians, see E. Cochrane, *Historians and Historiography in the Italian Renaissance* (Chicago, 1981), 18–19. Bruni is the central intellectual figure in Baron's *Crisis*. For a sketch of his life and bibliography, see *Earthly Republic*, 121–33.

42. Stinger, *Humanism and the Church Fathers*, 124–66.

43. Ibid., 100–13; Seigel, *Rhetoric and Philosophy*, 109–33. See also Chapter 19, in Volume 2 of this collection.

44. For a penetrating discussion of the meaning of language for the humanists, see N. S. Struever, *The Language of History in the Renaissance* (Princeton, 1970), esp. 63–82.

45. An English translation of Bruni's *Panegyric* appears in *Earthly Republic*, 135–75. Baron, *Crisis*, 191–224, 412–39, analyzes the genesis, sources, and themes of these two orations.

46. A partial English translation of Bruni's *Dialogues* appears in *Three Crowns of Florence*, 19–52; the most recent discussion of this work is D. Quint, "Humanism and Modernity: A Reconsideration of Bruni's *Dialogues*," *Renaissance Quarterly* 38 (1985): 423–45. A complete English translation of Poggio's *On Avarice* appears in *Earthly Republic*, 241–89.

47. Cochrane, *Historians and Historiography*, 3–20, underscores the originality of Bruni in creating a humanist historiography; for the ideological themes of Bruni's *History*, see Baron, *Crisis*, index under "Bruni," and Chapter 7, above.

48. Cochrane, *Historians and Historiography*, 26.

49. Ibid., 26–30.

50. Holmes, *Florentine Enlightenment*, 97–99, 106–8, 251, 253.

51. J. Gadol, *Leon Battista Alberti: Universal Man of the Early Renaissance* (Chicago, 1969), 70–81, 156–57, 197–99, has emphasized the importance of Ptolemy's scientific ideas of cartographic projection for Renaissance ideas of perspective and space. Note also, in general, S. Y. Edgerton, Jr., *The Renaissance Rediscovery of Linear Perspective* (New York, 1975).

52. The best short sketch of Toscanelli is E. Garin, "Paolo Toscanelli," in *Portraits from the Quattrocento*, 118–41. For the Florentine interest in Archimedes, note also C. Stinger, "Ambrogio Traversari and the 'Tempio degli Scolari' at S. Maria degli Angeli in Florence," in *Essays Presented to Myron P. Gilmore*, ed. S. Bertelli and G. Ramakus, 2 vols. (Florence, 1978), 1:280–82. Fundamental for Florentine interest in Hellenistic science and

mathematics is P. L. Rose, "Humanist Culture and Renaissance Mathematics: The Italian Libraries of the *Quattrocento,*" *Studies in the Renaissance* 20 (1973): 46–73.

53. The best general work on Alberti is Gadol, *Leon Battista Alberti.*
54. Gadol discusses Alberti's ideas on painting at length. There is an English translation: *On Painting,* ed. and trans. J. R. Spencer (New Haven, 1956). See also Chapter 38, in Volume 3.
55. Gadol, *Leon Battista Alberti,* 213–43.
56. Trinkaus, *In Our Image and Likeness,* 230–58; for other aspects of Manetti's scholarship and thought, see ibid., 573–78, 582–601, 726–34.
57. E. Garin, "Donato Acciaiuoli, Citizen of Florence," in *Portraits from the Quattrocento,* 55–117.
58. A. Brown, *Bartolomeo Scala (1430–1497), Chancellor of Florence: The Humanist as Bureaucrat* (Princeton, 1979); Accolti, too, emphasized medieval subjects: R. Black, *Benedetto Accolti and the Florentine Renaissance* (Cambridge, 1985).
59. Garin, "Donato Acciaiuoli," 88–89.
60. Rinuccini's treatise has been translated in *Humanism and Liberty: Writings on Freedom from Fifteenth-Century Florence,* ed. and trans. R. N. Watkins (Columbia, SC, 1978), 193–224. On Rinuccini see Garin, *Italian Humanism,* 78–81. A helpful overview of the Medicean regime under Lorenzo is J. R. Hale, *Florence and the Medici: The Pattern of Control* (London, 1977), 43–75.
61. Garin, *Italian Humanism,* 84–88. Note, most recently, A. Field, "A Manuscript of Cristoforo Landino's First Lectures on Virgil, 1462–63 (Codex 1368, Biblioteca Casanatense, Rome)," *Renaissance Quarterly* 31 (1978): 17–20.
62. For the establishment of the Florentine Platonic Academy and a general history of Platonism and Neoplatonism in the Italian Renaissance, see N. A. Robb, *Neoplatonism of the Italian Renaissance* (London, 1935).
63. E. Garin, "Ricerche sulle traduzioni di Platone nella prima metà del sec. XV," in *Medioevo e Rinascimento: Studi in onore di Bruno Nardi,* 2 vols. (Florence, 1955), 1:339–74.
64. J. Gill, S.J., *The Council of Florence* (Cambridge, 1959).
65. F. Masai, *Pléthon et le platonisme de Mistra* (Paris, 1956).
66. Garin, *Italian Humanism,* 81–84. The major monograph on George of Trebizond is J. Monfasani, *George of Trebizond: A Biography and a Study of His Rhetoric and Logic* (Leiden, 1976); Monfasani examines the Plato–Aristotle controversy in detail.
67. Garin, "Donato Acciaiuoli," 69–81 has emphasized the critical role of Argyropoulos in introducing Neoplatonism to Florence.
68. The major Ficino scholar is P. O. Kristeller. His work includes *The Philosophy of Marsilio Ficino* (New York, 1943) and his edition of Ficinian texts, *Supplementum Ficinianum,* 2 vols. (Florence, 1937). A good introduction is Kristeller's chapter on Ficino in his *Eight Philosophers of the Italian Ren-*

aissance (Stanford, 1964), 37–53. Among Kristeller's many articles dealing with Ficino and with Florentine Neoplatonism, there is most recently "Marsilio Ficino as a Man of Letters and the Glosses Attributed to Him in the Caetani Codex of Dante," *Renaissance Quarterly* 36 (1983): 1–47.

69. Note esp. Trinkaus, *In Our Image and Likeness,* chap. 9, "Humanist Themes in Marsilio Ficino's Philosophy of Human Immortality," 461–504.

70. E. Garin emphasizes these aspects of Ficino's thought: "Images and Symbols in Marsilio Ficino," in *Portraits from the Quattrocento,* 142–60.

71. For the text, English translation, introduction, and notes, see *Marsilio Ficino's Commentary on Plato's "Symposium,"* ed. and trans. S. R. Jayne, *University of Missouri Studies* 19 (1944): 1–235. For the impact on art, see E. H. Gombrich, "Botticelli's Mythologies: A Study in the Neoplatonic Symbolism of His Circle," in *Symbolic Images: Studies in the Art of the Renaissance II* (London, 1972), 31–81; E. Wind, *Pagan Mysteries in the Renaissance* (New York, rev. ed., 1968); and A. Chastel, *Art et l'humanisme à Florence au temps de Laurent le Magnifique: Études sur la Renaissance et l'humanisme platonicien* (Paris, 1959).

72. As with Ficino, the scholarship on Pico is enormous. For a critical assessment, see W. G. Craven, *Giovanni Pico della Mirandola, Symbol of his Age* (Geneva, 1981). For Pico's thought, note esp. Trinkaus, *In Our Image and Likeness,* 507–24, 753–60. An English translation of Pico's *Oration on the Dignity of Man* appears in *The Renaissance Philosophy of Man,* ed. E. Cassirer, P. O. Kristeller, and J. H. Randall (Chicago, 1948), 223–54. There is another English translation: Pico della Mirandola, *On the Dignity of Man, On Being and the One, Heptaplus,* ed. P. J. W. Miller (Indianapolis, 1965). For the text of the Nine Hundred Theses, see Giovanni Pico della Mirandola, *Conclusiones sive Theses DCCCC,* ed. B. Kieszkowski (Geneva, 1973). For Pico's controversy with Barbaro, see Q. Breen, "Giovanni Pico della Mirandola on the Conflict of Philosophy and Rhetoric," *Journal of the History of Ideas* 13 (1952): 384–412, and Gray, "Renaissance Humanism." For the Roman rejoinder to Pico's position, see J. F. D'Amico, "Paolo Cortesi's Rehabilitation of Giovanni Pico della Mirandola," *Bibliothèque d'humanisme et Renaissance* 44 (1982): 37–51.

73. For the text, English translation, introduction, and notes, see *The "Stanze" of Angelo Poliziano,* trans. D. Quint (Amherst, MA, 1979). For an introduction to Poliziano, see E. Garin, "The Cultural Background of Politian," in *Portraits from the Quattrocento,* 160–89.

74. An English translation of *The Pazzi Conspiracy,* along with a sketch of Poliziano's career and bibliography, appears in *Earthly Republic,* 293–322.

75. For Poliziano's philology and ideas of language, see Pfeiffer, *History of Classical Scholarship,* 42–46; A. D. Scaglione, "The Humanist as Scholar and Politian's Conception of the *Grammaticus,*" *Studies in the Renaissance* 8 (1961): 49–70; and A. L. Rubinstein, "Imitation and Style in Angelo Poliziano's *Iliad* Translation," *Renaissance Quarterly* 36 (1983): 48–70. See also Chapter 28, in Volume 3.

76. For the text of Poliziano's poem, see *Renaissance Latin Verse*, 140–41.

77. D. Weinstein, *Savonarola and Florence: Prophecy and Patriotism in the Renaissance* (Princeton, 1970), 185–226.

78. For the Florentine context of Machiavelli's and Guicciardini's thought, see F. Gilbert, *Machiavelli and Guicciardini: Politics and History in Sixteenth-Century Florence* (Princeton, 1965). For the political and social history of Florence in this period, see now J. N. Stephens, *The Fall of the Florentine Republic, 1512–1530* (New York, 1983).

79. F. Gilbert, "Bernardo Rucellai and the Orti Oricellari: A Study on the Origins of Modern Political Thought," *Journal of the Warburg and Courtauld Institutes* 12 (1949): 101–31.

80. Cochrane, *Historians and Historiography*, 295–305.

81. Fundamental is E. Cochrane, *Florence in the Forgotten Centuries, 1527–1800: A History of Florence and the Florentines in the Age of the Grand Dukes* (Chicago, 1973), 67–87. For Bartoli, see J. Bryce, *Cosimo Bartoli (1503–1572): The Career of a Florentine Polymath* (Geneva, 1983).

82. Cochrane, *Florence in the Forgotten Centuries*, 116–48; see also E. Cochrane, "A Case in Point: The End of the Renaissance in Florence," in idem, ed., *The Late Italian Renaissance, 1525–1630* (New York, 1970), 43–73. For similar tendencies in Italy as a whole, see P. F. Grendler, *Critics of the Italian World, 1530–1560: Anton Francesco Doni, Nicolò Franco, and Ortensio Lando* (Madison, WI, 1969), esp. chap. 5, "The Rejection of Learning for the Vita Civile," 136–61.

83. H. M. Brown, "Music—How Opera Began: An Introduction to Jacopo Peri's *Euridice* (1600)," in Cochrane, ed., *Late Italian Renaissance*, 401–43. See also Cochrane, *Florence in the Forgotten Centuries*, 156–58. S. Drake argues the connection between music and mechanics in the theories of the Galilei, father and son, in *Galileo Studies: Personality, Tradition, and Revolution* (Ann Arbor, MI, 1970), 43–62. See Chapter 39, in these volumes.

84. For persuasive arguments on the humanist context of Galileo's thought, see E. Cochrane, "Science and Humanism in the Italian Renaissance," *American Historical Review* 81 (1976): 1039–57.

85. The best treatment of the Florentine context of Galileo's campaign for Copernican cosmology and the repercussions of his papal condemnation is Cochrane, *Florence in the Forgotten Centuries*, 165–228. See Chapter 40, in these volumes.

86. For an incisive discussion of the shift in one humanist discipline, see E. Cochrane, "The Transition from Renaissance to Baroque: The Case of Italian Historiography," *History and Theory* 19 (1980): 21–38.

9 🙢 HUMANISM IN VENICE
Margaret L. King

VOKING LITTLE COMMENT IN GENERAL STUDIES, THE HUMANISM
of early Renaissance Venice (the fifteenth to early sixteenth centuries) has not, until recently, received scholarly attention in a full-
scale work.[1] The names of few Venetian humanists are household words.
Leonardo Giustiniani, perhaps, is remembered for his poetry; Francesco
Barbaro is studied for his views on marriage and the balance of power;
the profile of Ermolao Barbaro the Younger (Francesco's grandson) has
been emerging in recent decades as a philologist of undoubted first rank.[2]
Yet their faces are unfamiliar beyond a small circle of specialists. Curi-
ously, the city that dominated Mediterranean trade in the late Middle
Ages, that threatened to control the Italian peninsula in the Quattrocento, that generated sheer beauty in stone and color for several centuries
on end, is not noted for a humanist culture such as that which adorned
drabber and more volatile Florence.

At one level, at least, Venetian humanism may be judged a failure.
Modern scholars have said so. J. K. Hyde found it puzzling that Florence
was able to annihilate the early lead in the development of a classical
culture that Venice had in the fourteenth century because of her greater
proximity to ancient monuments and contacts with the East. Venice
failed to develop, Lino Lazzarini remarked, a humanist culture comparable to her political greatness. Aldo Oberdorfer judged the output of
Venetian humanism to be insignificant. There was in Venice, Berthold
Fenigstein observed, no class of humanists who sought wisdom for its
own sake. Georg Voigt had already noted, in his analysis comparing
"Spartan" Venice to "Athenian" Florence, the absence of a class of *letterati*, the varied quality of the participation of patricians in humanism,
and the paralyzing effect of insecurity on non-Venetian participants. Phi-
lippe Monnier, also noting the major presence of patricians, characterized humanism in Venice as "luxury," an amusement for a leisured elite.
According to Pier Giorgio Ricci, the citizen humanists of Venice, distracted, like the patricians, by other occupations, were not fully devoted
to studies and produced a culture focused on practical matters.[3]

Antonio Carile saw the solidity of political life, Venice's "politica
culturale," as an impediment to the development of subtlety in historical
writing. Guido Piovene observed, similarly, that the responsibilities to the

state felt by patrician humanists discouraged free expression, inhibiting exploration of the "revolutionary potential" of the word. Manlio Pastore Stocchi, deploring the repressive effects of aristocratic interest upon the development of pedagogy in Venice and the Veneto, pronounced that Venetian humanism was in fact excluded from the most brilliant achievements of contemporary Italian humanism. David Chambers remarked on the lack of a self-critical perspective in Venetian humanism. William Bouwsma linked the insufficiency of Quattrocento humanism to political life, but saw it as merely anachronistic, not fateful; in the next century, inspired by an experience of crisis to a renewed appreciation of her own liberty, Venice would produce a full-blown Renaissance humanism. Carlo Dionisotti, viewing the lush terrain of sixteenth-century Venetian literature, dismissed the preceding Latin culture of humanism as uncreative. Hubert Jedin diagnosed the lack of some vital quality, a "spiritual abstinence," as lying at the root of Venice's ceding leadership in humanist culture to Florence and Rome.[4]

It is perplexing, indeed, that so many sound judges find Venetian humanism hollow at the core: for humanism undoubtedly flourished in that city, scholars flocked there, and some men of vision or sensitivity or commitment to learning wrote there. How can her "failure" be explained?

At the beginning of the fifteenth century, when even in Florence Renaissance humanism was still young, the movement appealed to a group of young men of Venice's ruling class (a well-defined hereditary nobility).[5] They quickly dominated humanist culture, able to do so because of their elevated social position and their manifest abilities. The pattern they set endured for most of the century: most humanists in Venice were noblemen, and those who were not either were clearly assigned to subordinate positions or were gently, through neglect and suspended opportunity, urged to leave. Commoner humanists who remained adjusted their voices to conform to the tone set by patrician leaders in the realm of culture. The humanism of fifteenth-century Venice was thus a special animal: it was patrician humanism. It was open to novelty but closed to change, it welcomed new texts but abhorred new meanings, it praised eloquence but stifled criticism. Thus it fails, in a certain sense, as an intellectual movement: it fails to interest us because it did not produce great ideas that prefigure enlightened modernity and remind us pleasurably of ourselves. But in a certain sense it was profoundly successful: it reinforced in the intellectual realm the hegemony of a ruling class that did not wish to be disturbed by new ideas any more than it permitted challenge from rebellious subjects.

The patrician appropriation of humanism at the turn of the century constituted a cultural choice; the patrician relinquishment of humanism at the end of the century constituted another. These choices were made by no single act of will, but by a complex of individual decisions and events acting together with sufficient force to compel a shift in cultural patterns. These shifting patterns in the development of Venetian humanism will now be traced from fourteenth-century origins through three generations of Quattrocento humanism to the aftermath of that movement in the late fifteenth and sixteenth centuries.

*   *   *

In the Trecento, Venice was already rich, powerful, and old.[6] She had long enjoyed a major share of Mediterranean trade and had developed advanced shipping and commercial techniques. She possessed an empire of maritime colonies and protectorates—vast holdings for an island city, if not, perhaps, the *quartum et dimidium* of ancient Rome boasted by her doges. During this century, by a process beginning with the *Serrata* (closing) of the great council, she acquired a legally defined nobility, which alone had access to political power. By the last years of the century, as the role of the nobility coalesced and clarified, its consciousness matured as well. A commitment to common purpose developed as a small inner circle of noblemen imposed a collective discipline upon the whole class.

Intellectual culture in some ways reflected the ascendancy and cohesiveness of this social group.[7] Her chroniclers wrote works that consistently aimed at apology. Venice was described as having unfailingly followed the standard of justice and piety, led by faceless rulers followed by content and enthusiastic subjects. Authors and readers alike came from the upper strata of Venetian society. Their self-congratulatory public vision of Venice was to be perpetuated in the humanism of the next century. Poetry—in the vernacular but sparked with tuscanisms—constitutes another and distinct tradition of intellectual life. Their (again mostly patrician) authors' openness to mainland trends in style points to the following century, when Venetian humanists discoursed with humanists throughout Italy. That openness to innovation is seen also in the reception given in Venice to the Aristotelian tradition in philosophy, only recently imported from France and lodged in Italian universities (including neighboring Padua's). A newcomer, the scholastic tradition threw down deep roots in Trecento Venetian culture as members of Venice's citizen and noble classes, with or without professional goals, pursued advanced studies. It was to flourish even more vigorously, paired with humanism, in the Quattrocento.

While these intellectual traditions soon merged with humanism, a young proto-humanism had already come into existence by the last half of the Trecento. It was located in the circle of notaries and scribes employed by the government—conforming to a pattern seen elsewhere in Italy. A few figures of this chancery humanism stand out: Benintendi de' Ravagnani (chancellor to the brilliant mid-century doge and author Andrea Dandolo), Paolo de Bernardo (Ravagnani's notary), Raffaino de' Caresini (his successor as chancellor and historian), and Lorenzo de' Monaci (another historian, more famous than his fellows). Yet beyond these names, though the influence of humanism was diffuse in their circle, most are faceless. The mastery of technical skills with a practical object in view, it seems, was so stressed in Venice that the spur to broader cultural exploration was blunted. The chancery humanists appear to withdraw in the last years of the century from the public arena and talk mainly, in Latin letters, to their friends.

The lead they failed to take fell to a new group: the generation of young patricians who received their education from humanist teachers in the late Trecento. They grafted humanism to the inherited values of their class, which they identified with the interests of their city, and launched the next era's most characteristic intellectual movement: patrician humanism.

* * *

The decisive triumph at Chioggia in 1381 ended Venice's long struggle against her maritime rival, Genoa. In the years to come, she was to turn her eyes westward, to the Italian mainland vulnerable in its disorder. Over the two-year period 1404–6, she absorbed Padua, Vicenza, and Verona. These cities (along with Treviso, acquired in 1339) formed the basis of Venice's terra firma empire. It continued to grow throughout this period, changing life in Venice fundamentally. Captured lands provided rich revenues and an opportunity for land investment. The need to administer conquered cities resulted in employment opportunities for Venetian governors (patrician) and secretaries (commoner). Mainland matters occupied the government councils, which reapportioned their responsibilities and created new offices to meet the challenge presented. Venice had become a mainland power, and it came to participate in the struggles that marked the years leading to Italy's downfall in the sixteenth century.

The terra firma conquests inevitably affected cultural life. Now in contact with mainland social and intellectual elites, Venice absorbed Italian currents of thought and expression. At the same time that she learned from the advanced intellectual culture of mainland centers, she exported to them rulers equipped with a humanist education, prompt to convey with suitable eloquence the values implicit in Venetian laws and government practice, and eager to defend her policies. The conquest of the terra firma was cultural as well as military: these activities caused Venetian culture to be reshaped, encouraging the patrician appropriation of humanism as an instrument to refine self-consciousness and to define a public role. The story of the unfailing excellence of Venice, so often told by the medieval chroniclers to listeners of like mind, was now spread abroad in the lingua franca of educated Italians, humanist Latin.

*   *   *

A first generation of humanists born in the last three decades of the Trecento knew as young men the triumph of mainland conquest. They were mostly patrician and drawn from the inner circle of that ruling class. The few commoner humanists of these years were closely related to aristocratic circles. Very simply, patricians of high authority directed the formation of humanist culture during critical years in which its essential character was determined. They were aided in this task by foreign humanists, commoners of high literary reputation who served as companions of noblemen and as teachers of noblemen's sons. Transients, never residents, they were the catalysts of Venetian humanism. Much loved by their patrician friends and patrons, they left Venice for cities where the reverence for the new learning was greater and where men of their ilk could advance. In Venice, they could not.[8]

When they left, they left implanted in the young men they had taught and the mature men with whom they had conversed a love for the *studia humanitatis*. Patrician humanists collected books, circulated texts, imitated in written words ancient wisdom. Mutual enthusiasms fueled enduring friendships among patricians and between them and the small group of native commoners who shared their passion for learning. Their public lives obligated them to hours in the councils and to the strict observance of social conventions; in the alien languages and forms of the *studia humanitatis* they found relief. At the same time, though, they guided humanist culture in directions appropriate to the interests of their class. Humanist works (whether written by patricians themselves or by commoners who were their friends or servants) now defended aristocracy, representing as identical its aims and the welfare of Venice, portraying its activity as virtuous and benign. Not every humanist work written in this period undertakes this task, but enough do—and they are the most important products of the era—to make this tendency representative of the whole.[9]

The patrician Zaccaria Trevisan the Elder, a prime architect of Venetian humanism, spoke in several orations of Venice's special destiny, of the unique creativity and responsibility of a city's rulers, of the narrow universal hierarchy that embraces human society as a mirror of a more perfect order. These themes were to become familiar in later products of Venetian culture, which link Italian humanism and the particular ideology of the Venetian patriciate, committed to their city, jealous of their prerogatives, loyal to a metaphysics that dwarfs individual existence but provides order. Trevisan greatly influenced his young friend Francesco Barbaro, certainly the intellectual giant of this generation. His *De re uxoria* (*On Marriage*) gives the patrician humanism of Venice its legitimation. Not by mere coincidence does this first major work of Venetian humanism consist of a defense of nobility and a program for its perpetuation. The same confidence pervades his letters, written later in life, discussing statecraft and war.[10]

At the same time that Barbaro and Trevisan and their contemporaries introduced to Venetian humanism a persistent ideological mission, the allegiance to Aristotelian philosophy and Christian piety traditional in Venetian culture can be seen to persist in the newer humanist movement. Indeed, the Venetian conquest of Padua early in the century led to the Paduan "conquest" of Venice, an enthusiastic Aristotelianism that penetrated every outpost of the culture. The launching of patrician humanism coincided with the intensification of a tradition of Aristotelian philosophy. Thus the interests of the ruling elite were served in two ways in this first Quattrocento generation: its values and ideas were actively celebrated in a new language and style; and its existing metaphysical and theological assumptions were incorporated—an odd match though they sometimes made—with the new learning.

*   *   *

As adults, the humanists of the century's second generation were to experience unrelenting war on the mainland as Venice defended her recent conquests, and later, following Constantinople's fall, impending war at sea. They heard the complaints of other cities about her aggressive terra firma policies and her lack of Christian zeal in the pursuit of the Ottoman enemy, now her commercial partner. Humanists as well as statesmen responded to these charges, securing by words the status in the world Venice had won through arms and policy. Fewer patricians, relatively speaking, participated in humanist culture in this generation than in the first. Yet the presence among them of many men of major political and military importance makes their participation particularly striking. In the middle years of the century, a large fraction of Venice's political elite were humanists.[11]

Meanwhile, the participation of commoners increased, though not enough to challenge the patrician leadership of Renaissance culture.

Most were salaried and dependent, if resident in Venice, or they spent much of their careers abroad. While in Venice, they shared—by preference or compulsion—patrician perceptions of Venetian society and the world order. Foreign professionals—less mighty than before as intellectual figures—continued to flow through the city. But their influence was less than in the first generation, since natives and resident foreigners could be found (now that humanism was well rooted in Venice) to converse with learned patricians and to teach their sons and the sons of citizens bound to fill the ranks of the secretaries.[12]

In 1446—as a sign of the maturity of Venetian humanism—the senate created a public school for the training of that government secretariat. It mirrors the quality of the republic's commitment to the *studia humanitatis*: certain but limited. The utility of the humanities, rather than their ability to inform and illuminate human existence, was the main concern of the school's creators. Thus the public and institutional role of humanist culture was constrained at the same time that it was allowed an unprecedented place in the city's life. Yet the impact of the school on intellectual life was great. The teachers were long-term Venetian residents and shared the perceptions and values of their hosts. They taught not only secretarial candidates, but sons of patrician families. The school's existence lent prestige to humanism, and it coincides with the time that humanism became the culture of the ruling class.[13]

Even more aggressively in this generation than in the first, that class argued Venice's cause and elaborated the ideal of the aristocrat. They did so in orations delivered at home and abroad, in letters, in translations from the Greek of works picturing ideal rulers—implicit analogues of their contemporaries—and in their treatises and small works, which were more often apologies for Venice and her nobility than anything else. Such were the major works of Lauro Quirini, Giovanni Caldiera, and Domenico and Paolo Morosini, four of the principal authors of this generation.[14] In this period, moreover, history took its due place in Venice's humanist movement. Patricians urged commoners, transient and resident, to write histories of the city that would be eloquent and suitably laudatory. Meanwhile, some patricians themselves wrote history in a humanist genre: Francesco Contarini, Antonio Donato, and—masterfully—Bernardo Giustiniani. Their histories were celebrations of the city, conforming with Venice's medieval tradition.[15]

This humanism that militantly defended Venetian institutions and values is the perhaps predictable expression of a group of authors whose links to power were secure. At this moment, Venice had to explain herself to the Italian world, pointing to her benevolence, her piety, her reverence for peace, precisely when her aggressive terra firma policies and sluggish response to the Turks seemed most to accuse her. These authors wrote to persuade their fellow rulers that all was well; justice reigned. Venetian humanism became increasingly ideological.

While performing its apologetic task, meanwhile, the potential of humanism as a stimulus to spiritual liberation was in Venice carefully limited. The zeal for classical studies dimmed; taste leaned toward more sober historical, philosophical, and scientific texts. Ermolao Barbaro the Elder condemned the ancient poets. After renouncing some of his youthful compositions, Gregorio Correr's interests became sternly moralistic. Giovanni Caldiera, in order to save the ancient myths, reinterpreted them as allegories of Christian or philosophical doctrine, so that they could not tempt the imagination; they were Venetianized. Attention to religious and philosophical genres increased. Caldiera and the two patricians Candiano Bollani and Domenico Morosini wrote austere religious works. The two commoner humanists Domenico de' Domenichi and Pietro del Monte wrote systematic works on papal authority and matters of doctrine, while a third, Pietro Bruto, rampaged against the Jews. Anti-Semitism, indeed, formed a conspicuous strain of Venetian piety. It is harsh in Bruto's works and in the letters of Ludovico Foscarini, cool in the famous treatise by Paolo Morosini, the author also of an important work on providence and free will. He maintained that free will existed, but that it operated only in accord with the direction indicated by providence. His solution is Venetian, indeed, at the same time affirming orthodoxy and constraining the individual.[16]

The classical literature on which humanism depends implicitly argues for the freedom of the individual and the worthiness and diversity of his affects. These assumptions are absent from the Venetian humanism of this generation, which does, however, defend religious and philosophical orthodoxy and the authority of the church. This conservative component of Venetian humanism coexists with its other main purpose: the celebration of Venice. Its conservatism, indeed, is auxiliary to that task. Following in the steps of the first generation of humanists who had at the same time that they embraced the new learning domesticated it, the second generation crafted a mature humanist culture which performed an ideological mission well while it supported established intellectual traditions and moral values. A third generation of humanists will permit greater diversity while renewing the achievements of their predecessors.

*   *   *

Those humanists born after 1430 inherited a world with firmly established boundaries. In their generation, the nobility was to expand, dominated as before by an inner elite. Mainland possessions already secured were extended a little toward the end of this period as a consequence of the unfortunate war with Ferrara. That war (and other maneuvers) called forth biting anti-Venetian criticism, a continuing spur to the rhetorical defenses of the city. A battle against the Turks led to territorial loss but the continuation of trade privileges. Morale was high, revenues sound, building boomed. Humanists were fewer than before, and the political activities of the patricians among them somewhat less important. Perhaps in these years the challenges on the mainland and at sea did not inspire young intellectuals as greatly as before. Moreover, the task of shaping the humanist movement in Venice was already accomplished.

Still, the patricians remain the dominant group within humanist society. The participation of commoners was weak because of long absence or because of direct reliance on the government for employment. From this quarter there were unlikely to be heard voices raised against the prevailing patrician culture. Transient foreigners were numerous during this third stage of the evolution of fifteenth-century humanism in Venice; later they became even more so. As before, they came to provide companionship to learned nobles and to teach noblemen's sons.[17] But now they came with a new motive as well: to staff the printing presses that burgeoned in the last three decades of the century. While developing ties with resident humanists, common and noble, they achieved a certain independence—unprecedented in earlier generations of transients—since they drew their sustenance not directly from the patricians but from printer-entrepreneurs.[18]

Even before the advent of the press, humanism in Venice had broadened to permit a greater emphasis on the word. In earlier stages of the development of humanism in Venice, rhetoric had been considered a tool for other ends: a preparation for secretarial service or a means for the celebration of Venice and aristocratic values. In 1460, with the institution of a third public school, the study of rhetoric as an intrinsically worthy discipline gained prominence. But when Giorgio Merula took the chair of eloquence in 1468 after a long vacancy, he led the attention of Venetian humanists toward a narrow concentration on philology. The philological focus he advocated flourished, coinciding with the explosion of the printing industry. The science of textual criticism embodied in Merula and his successor, Giorgio Valla, became the ideal companion to the business of printing. Both these teachers, with their colleagues in the first San Marco school—Benedetto Brognoli and Marcantonio Sabellico—participated in the editorial activity of the presses, alongside the transient foreigners drawn to the new enterprise. Patricians were involved in editorial activity as well, but many henceforth became satisfied with a relatively passive patronage role. Others remained active and, like

Ermolao Barbaro the Younger and Girolamo Donato, engaged at the highest level in the study and criticism of texts. Philological interests and the business of printing thus converged in these years, spurring interest in neglected areas of classical literature while attending diligently to those aspects of the classical and Christian tradition which appealed to Venice's sober audience: science and mathematics, architecture and agriculture, history and law, philosophy and theology.[19]

The philological and editorial activities of this period constitute an independent tradition within Venetian humanism complementary to its main tendencies—its allegiance to Aristotelian philosophy and traditional Christianity and its preference for apologetic themes. The patricians Ermolao Barbaro the Younger and Girolamo Donato applied their philological skills to works by Aristotle or authors in the Aristotelian tradition, witnessing again in this generation the links between patrician humanism and traditional philosophy. That link is seen also in Niccolò Leonico Tomeo, a native commoner, who became the first expositor at Padua of Aristotle's works in the original Greek. The foreigner Giorgio Valla broadened the Venetian blend of humanism and philosophy to include science and mathematics in a vast encyclopedia, which envisioned the universe as an immense machine circumscribing the life of the individual human being. Patrician humanists of this generation, both clerical and lay, continued to write religious hymns and meditations, saints' lives, moral laments, and works on problems of church history or systematic theology, affirming the tradition of Christian orthodoxy. And humanists of this third generation wrote Venice's history, as did the commoner Marcantonio Sabellico, to the great delight of the senate. Both Ermolao Barbaro the Younger and Pietro Barozzi wrote treatises defining central patrician values. Girolamo Donato, finally, in many regards the most perfect exponent in its third generation of the phenomenon of patrician humanism, wrote a forceful defense of Venice.[20]

Patrician humanism, not yet old, was beginning to fade. Its sturdy tradition continued into the next generation and through the next century. But harbingers of a new era appeared. The unruly monk Francesco Colonna wrote the *Hypnerotomachia Poliphili*—that disorganized, fanciful, sensuous *pasticcio* of a romance, a shattered mirror of Venetian taboos and verities. The arrogant bronze condottiere on his swaggering horse exploded on a gray Dominican square. A printer beset with visions of grandeur took the road to Venice. The young aristocrat Ermolao Barbaro, rebellious in his soul, soon contemplated an act of disloyalty to his country and his ancestors, and was soon to act. The stern discipline that had characterized intellectual life through most of the fifteenth century was to dissolve as the patricians who had imposed it put down their reins.[21]

* * *

Italy was ravaged in 1494 by an invader from the north whose swift conquest warned of trials to come. At first aloof and secure in her lagoon, Venice did not long escape the battles that ripped Italy apart. By the League of Cambrai of 1508, France, Spain, and the empire joined the pope against Venice, and bloodied her troops at Agnadello in 1509. She rallied; by 1516, she was out of danger. But in a Europe of increasingly powerful nations, her role receded. Meanwhile, the aristocracy of Venice had expanded. Competition for power had become intense, leading perhaps to a new malaise at the turn of the sixteenth century. Although demoralization gave way after Cambrai to a new unity, the slow decline of the Venetian nobility as a ruling class had already begun. In coming years, wealthy noblemen tended increasingly to mainland investments, leaving the risks of commerce to citizen merchants. Yet Venice remained prosperous, sustained by her maritime commerce and by newly vigorous industries.[22]

Among them was the printing industry, which was to have in the next generations an immeasurable impact on intellectual life, not only in Venice but throughout Italy and Europe. It entered a distinctive phase under the leadership of Aldo Manuzio, who published pure texts unencumbered by commentary—first mainly Greek, then mainly Latin—in affordable editions. From his arrival in 1491 until his death in 1516, humanism in Venice centered on Aldo. In his shop worked a team of correctors and editors; around him flocked the humanists of Venice, pedagogues and secretaries, university professors and physicians, young or leisured noblemen. Despite the presence of some patricians in the Aldine circle, most of Aldo's associates were commoners. They continued the philological tendency within Venetian humanism, and they were the most active humanists in the decades following 1490, competing for position, thronging the printing houses, contending with one another in oral disputation and angry print, seeking patrons. But their humanist culture had become narrow and technical, concerned with the bare mechanism of language at the very time that Aldo nurtured hopes of the liberating power of the pure word.[23]

Meanwhile, patrician humanists tended to spectator roles. They gathered in their palaces and villas for intellectual conversation, speaking about philosophy and mathematics, science, medicine, and law, as well as the classics. They were an audience for the flourishing Venetian press.

They collected manuscripts and printed books and antiquities—works of art, coins, and medals surviving from a distant past. At the same time, they patronized the writers and artists of their generation. But these activities, too broad and unfocused to be genuinely productive, became an adornment of the leisured life, not a vehicle, as in the Quattrocento, for the expression of a powerful self-consciousness. That strong sense of self in commitment to a ruling class had weakened by the late fifteenth century. The figure of the nobleman seeking refuge from public responsibility became increasingly common. Some of the disenchanted noblemen of the early sixteenth century sought freedom in the inner life: in the monastery, in contemplation, in communion with God sealed by the assurance of salvation.[24]

Still the patrician humanism that had been born in the Quattrocento, though it foundered, survived. The reassertion of patrician discipline and renewed self-consciousness that followed Cambrai fostered it and yielded such famous sixteenth-century spokesmen as Gasparo Contarini, Daniele Barbaro, Agostino Valier, Paolo Paruta, and Niccolò Contarini. Among these and other patricians who participated actively in humanist culture, the philosophical and religious concerns typical of Venetian humanism in the fifteenth century remained central. Aristotelian philosophy still provided a metaphysical framework for these thinkers, and the contemplative ideal was still cherished, even by those who were themselves to lead active lives. Commitment to the church remained strong; personal religious experience found expression in prose and verse. This profound allegiance to inherited Christian and academic traditions accompanied a concern with the life and history of the city. History became the special province of the patricians as commoner humanists tended more intently to philological tasks. The position of official historian, created early in the sixteenth century, was held in these years by a series of patrician writers whose outlook on the past became increasingly rational and critical. Despite this tendency, however, the task of celebration was not abandoned.

For this era was, indeed, the great age of the Venetian myth. Sketched in some of the most interesting works of the century were the notions that had roots in the Middle Ages and which had been first wedded to humanism by Quattrocento authors: the eternity of Venice, the perfect balance of her governmental system, her historic commitment to liberty, the harmonious cooperation of her social classes encouraged by a just distribution of duties and rewards, her benevolent doges subject to law, her nobility's selfless devotion to the common welfare. These notions traveled far in the sixteenth century, no longer addressed by Venetians primarily to each other in reinforcement of common values, but more to the outside world, which was eager to hear of them.[25]

Thus patrician humanism survived into the sixteenth century. Yet it constituted but one tendency of sixteenth-century humanism, which included as well the culture of the philologists and encyclopedists, the classicism of teachers and secretaries, the book talk and trading generated by the presses. And it constituted but one strand of Venice's intellectual culture in this century: for the center of Venice's culture in the sixteenth century was not in humanism at all, but in vernacular literature and the arts. Under the leadership of the patrician Pietro Bembo, Venetian authors, mostly commoners, many foreign by origin, shed the Latin that had dominated expression, along with other restraints of Quattrocento humanism. There appeared a diversity of themes and sentiments, a previously prohibited sensuality, a critical voice. In a parallel development, the visual arts at about this time abandoned their fifteenth-century conservatism and adopted the language of color. An expressive range of softness, sensuality, and drama became newly available. In literature and the arts emerged a new stage of Venetian culture decidedly in contrast to the Quattrocento culture integrated by patrician humanists: the first sensual, the second sternly moralistic; the first emotive, the second rational; the first adrift from the political arena, aiming mainly to please and intrigue, the second focused on the political arena, aiming mainly to instruct and to command. Although much of the fifteenth-century tradition was inherited by the culture of the sixteenth, the balance had shifted. A cultural choice had once again been made.

*   *   *

These pages have traced the process by which patricians placed their seal upon humanist culture and subsequently receded, along with humanism itself, from center stage. Patrician humanism derived from a confluence, in the late Trecento and early Quattrocento of three major developments. One was the maturation of the patriciate as a class. A second was the embarkation on a program of terra firma expansion. A third, simultaneous with these social and political processes, was the availability to an elite within the ruling class, through the agency of resident teachers and publicly employed scribes, of the knowledge and perspectives basic to humanism. A ruling class that wished to defend its policies, affirm its benevolence, and command obedience found in humanism a means to do so.

Patricians assumed leadership of humanist culture about the turn of the fifteenth century. A first generation of humanists, patrician and commoner, absorbed the classical tradition thirstily, shaping the new learning to accord with the values and traditions of their city and its ruling class. A second generation, equipped with a humanist education, actively defended Venetian policies and principles. A third generation continued that mission, while a new fascination developed with the philological dimension of humanism. In the last years of the fifteenth century and early years of the sixteenth, while this humanism of earlier generations survived, patricians became relatively less important within humanism, and humanism itself played a smaller role in Venetian culture. The effects of this shift of equilibrium were already evident in the years following 1490 in the activities of Aldo's shop, in vernacular literature, and in the visual arts. By the turn of the sixteenth century, the circumstances that had encouraged the development of patrician humanism no longer existed or interacted as they had at the turn of the fifteenth. The task of defending patrician policy and shaping civic consciousness was left to those humanists who wished to assume it. And it was performed, and perhaps more effectively, by other media: by the ritual processions that frequently filled the piazza, and in the broad canvases that displayed in form and color the myth of Venice, and compelled belief.[26]

The patrician humanism of the Quattrocento had performed its mission: Venice had absorbed the new learning without disturbing the social balance that had been before, as it would be in the future, echoed in the realm of ideas.

NOTES

1. My *Venetian Humanism in an Age of Patrician Dominance* (Princeton, 1986) provides the full-scale work required. Otherwise, the literature on Venetian culture in the Renaissance is scattered but vast. The eighteenth-century general works by Giovanni degli Agostini and Marco Foscarini are venerable, still useful, and for some purposes excellent. The present generation of scholars has undertaken some synthetic studies of Venetian culture during the Renaissance period, as have W. Bouwsma and O. Logan in works dealing mainly with the sixteenth and later centuries. F. Gilbert gives an excellent sketch of the phenomenon of Venetian humanism in "Humanism in Venice." Studies of certain aspects of Venetian cultural history have appeared in several collections of essays, such as those by V. Branca, F. Gaeta, A. Pertusi, and M. Pastore Stocchi in vol. 3, pt. 1 (*Il Quattrocento* [Vicenza, 1980]) of the *Storia della cultura veneta*; by P. O. Kristeller in *La civiltà veneziana del Trecento* (Florence, 1956); by B. Nardi and G. Piovene in *La civiltà veneziana del Quattrocento* (Florence, 1957); by T. W. Elwert in *La civiltà veneziana del Rinascimento* (Florence, 1958); by Branca, E. Garin, L. Lazzarini, Nardi and P. G. Ricci in *Umanesimo europeo ed umanesimo veneziano* (Florence, 1963); by Branca and G. Cozzi in *Renaissance Venice,*

ed. J. R. Hale (London, 1973). The collection of essays on Venetian historiography edited by Pertusi is also invaluable for humanism: *La storiografia veneziana fino al secolo XVI: Aspetti e problemi* (Florence, 1970). Prior to this generation but extending into the 1980s, the tendency has been to very particular studies or monographs. This scholarly tradition, established in the earliest years of the investigation of Venetian culture, flourished in the late nineteenth and early twentieth centuries with the work of such scholars as R. Sabbadini and A. Segarizzi, among others. Later generations have offered more studies in the same genre, such as those of D. de' Bellis, L. Bertalot, V. Branca, N. Gianetto, P. Gothein, M. King, P. Labalme, P. Rigo, G. Tournoy, R. Weiss, or the many students of Gasparo Contarini, reviewed in the excellent historiographical guide of J. B. Ross. The volumes of microstudies offered by students and friends to V. Branca should also be noted: *Miscellanea di studi in onore di Vittore Branca*, 4 vols. in 6 (Florence, 1983). Similarly focused are modern text editions of key works providing prefatory material of great importance, for example, that of Lauro Quirini's treatises on nobility by K. Krautter and H. Roob, introduced by P. O. Kristeller; that of Pietro Barozzi's *De factionibus extinguendis* by F. Gaeta; that of Jacopo Zeno's *Vita Caroli Zeni* by G. Zonta. Some scholars have deviated from this tradition by attending to more general problems of Venetian cultural history—among them G. Cozzi, F. Gilbert, P. Grendler, M. Lowry, and P. Rose.

Full citations of the works mentioned in this brief review are given in the bibliography appended to this essay. Where authors are noted who have written several studies in the stated categories, only one representative work is listed in the bibliography. Henceforth, works cited in that bibliography will not be cited in full in the notes. The essays noted in the *Storia della cultura veneta,* the most recent and most comprehensive of their genre, are usefully consulted for further bibliography.

2. The following titles provide guidance to the many sources of further information about figures named. For Francesco Barbaro, see now the article by G. Gualdo in *Dizionario biografico degli italiani* (Rome, 1964), 6:101–3. For Ermolao the Younger, see Branca's "L'umanesimo veneziano," in *Storia della cultura veneta* 3.1:123–75. For Leonardo Giustiniani, see M. Dazzi, *Leonardo Giustiniani, poeta populare d'amore* (Bari, 1934), and the relevant sections of Labalme, *Bernardo Giustiniani.*

3. Hyde, review of L. Gargan, *Cultura e arte nel Veneto al tempo del Petrarca* (Padua, 1978), in *Renaissance Quarterly* 33 (1980): 95–96, p. 96; L. Lazzarini, "Un libro su Francesco Barbaro," *Archivio storico italiano* 7th ser. 20 (1933): 97–104, p. 97; A. Oberdorfer, "Di Leonardo Giustiniani umanista," *Giornale storico della letteratura italiana* 56 (1910): 107–20, p. 109; B. Fenigstein, *Leonardo Giustiniani (1383?–1446), venetianischer Staatsmann, Humanist und Vulgärdichter* (Halle am S., 1909), 29; G. Voigt, *Il risorgimento dell'antichità classica,* trans. D. Valbusa, ed. G. Zippel, 3 vols. (Florence, 1888–97; reprint ed. E. Garin, Florence, 1968), 1:410–11; P. Monnier, *Le Quattrocento,* 2 vols. (Paris, 2d ed., 1912), 1:168; P. G. Ricci,

"Umanesimo filologico," in *Umanesimo europeo ed umanesimo veneziano*, 160.

4. A Carile, "Aspetti della cronachista veneziana nei secoli XIII e XIV," in A. Pertusi, ed., *La storiografia veneziana*, 75–126 at 118; G. Piovene, "L'anacronismo," in *La civiltà veneziana del Quattrocento*, 9–10; M. Pastore Stocchi, "Scuola e cultura," in *Storia della cultura veneta*, 93–121 at 121; D. S. Chambers, *The Imperial Age of Venice, 1380–1580* (London and New York, 1970), 154; Bouwsma, *Venice*, especially chap. 2; C. Dionisotti, "Niccolò Liburnio e la letteratura cortigiana," in *Rinascimento europeo e Rinascimento veneziano*, ed. V. Branca (Florence, 1967), 26–37 at 30–36; H. Jedin, "Gasparo Contarini e il contributo veneziano alla riforma cattolica," in *La civiltà veneziana del Rinascimento*, 103–24 at 105. Gilbert reports similar comments of Burckhardt and the Trecento notary Paolo de Bernardo in his "Humanism in Venice," 13.

5. The interpretation of Venetian humanism outlined here is that presented in my *Venetian Humanism*.

6. For Venice's situation on the brink of and during the fourteenth century see especially F. C. Lane, *Venice: A Maritime Republic* (Baltimore, 1973); also R. Cessi, *Storia della Repubblica di Venezia*, 2 vols. (Milan, 1944); S. Chojnacki, "In Search of the Venetian Patriciate: Families and Factions in the Fourteenth Century," in *Renaissance Venice*, 47–90; G. Cracco, *Società e stato nel medioevo veneziano, secoli XII–XIV* (Florence, 1967); F. C. Lane, "The Enlargement of the Great Council of Venice," in *Florilegium Historiale: Essays Presented to Wallace K. Ferguson*, ed. J. G. Rowe and W. H. Stockdale (Toronto, 1971), 236–74; G. Luzzatto, *Storia economica di Venezia dall'XI al XVI secolo* (Venice, 1961); idem, *Studi di storia economica veneziana* (Padua, 1954); G. Ruggiero, *Violence in Early Renaissance Venice* (New Brunswick, NJ, 1980). Also useful are these older general works on Venice's history: W. C. Hazlitt, *The Venetian Republic, Its Rise, Its Growth, and Its Fall, A.D. 409–1797*, 2 vols. (London, 4th ed., 1915); H. Kretschmayr, *Geschichte von Venedig*, 3 vols. (Gotha, 1920; reprint Darmstadt, 1964); S. Romanin, *Storia documentata di Venezia*, 10 vols. (Venice, 1853–61).

7. For the fourteenth-century historiographical tradition, see the relevant studies in *La storiografia veneziana*, ed. Pertusi: G. Arnaldi, "Andrea Dandolo Doge-cronista," 127–268; A Carile, "Aspetti della cronachista veneziana"; G. Cracco, "Il pensiero storico di fronte ai problemi del comune veneziano," 45–74; Pertusi, "Gli inizi della storiografia umanistica del Quattrocento," 269–332; G. Fasoli, "I fondamenti della storiografia veneziana," 1–44. Elsewhere is S. Collodo's "Temi e caratteri della cronachista veneziana in volgare del Tre-Quattrocento (Enrico Dandolo)," *Studi veneziani* 9 (1967): 127–51. For Trecento literature, see A. Viscardi, "Lingua e letteratura," in *La civiltà veneziana del Trecento*, 179–205; also V. Lazzarini, *Rimatori veneziani del secolo XIV* (Padua, 1877), and R. Meneghel, "La 'Leandride' di Giovanni Girolamo Nadal," *Italia medioevale e umanistica* 16 (1973): 163–78. For the influence on Venice of Aristotelian philosophy

in this period, see especially P. O. Kristeller, "Il Petrarca," in *La civiltà veneziana del Trecento,* and idem, "Petrarch's 'Averroists': A Note on the History of Aristotelianism in Venice, Padua, and Bologna," *Bibliothèque d'Humanisme et Renaissance* 14 (1952): 59–65. For Venetian proto-humanism, see L. Gargan, "Il preumanesimo a Vicenza, Treviso e Venezia," in *Storia della cultura veneta,* vol. 2, *Il Trecento* (Vicenza, 1976), 142–70, and several studies of L. Lazzarini, especially his *Paolo de Bernardo e i primordi dell'umanesimo in Venezia* (Geneva, 1930); "Francesco Petrarca," in *Umanesimo veneziano,* 63–92; " 'Dux ille Danduleus,' Andrea Dandolo e la cultura veneziana a metà del Trecento," in *Petrarca, Venezia, e il Veneto,* ed. G. Padoan (Florence, 1976), 123–56; "Un libro su Francesco Barbaro." For Petrarch's influence specifically, see in addition to the works by Lazzarini already cited his "Amici del Petrarca a Venezia e Treviso," *Archivio veneto* 5th ser. 14 (1933): 1–14, and two studies by N. Mann: "Benintendi Ravagnani, il Petrarca, l'umanesimo veneziano," in *Petrarca, Venezia e il Veneto,* 109–22, and "Petrarca e la cancelleria veneziana," in *Storia della cultura veneta,* vol. 2, *Il Trecento,* 517–35. For Ravagnani, see also G. degli Agostini, *Notizie,* 2:322–31. For de' Monaci, see A. Pertusi, "Le fonti greche del 'De gestis, moribus et nobilitate civitatis venetiarum' di Lorenzo de Monacis, cancelliere di Creta (1388–1428)," *Italia medioevale e umanistica* 8 (1965): 162–211; M. Poppi, "Un'orazione del cronista Lorenzo de Monacis per il millenario di Venezia (1421)," *Atti dell'Istituto Veneto di scienze, lettere ed arti* 131 (1972–73): 463–97; idem, "Ricerche sulla vita e cultura del notaio e cronista veneziano Lorenzo de Monacis, cancelliere cretese (ca. 1351–1428)," *Studi veneziani* 9 (1967): 153–86; also degli Agostini, *Notizie,* 2:363–71. De' Monaci, who survived well into the fifteenth century, had a particularly strong impact on humanists of the first generation of that period.

8. The transient humanists of this first generation include, most notably, Guarino of Verona, active in Venice from 1414 to 1419; also Vittorino da Feltre (1415?, 1422–23), Cristoforo de Scarpis (intermittently 1416–25), George of Trebizond (intermittently, 1416–37), and Francesco Filelfo (1417–19, 1427–28). Gasparino Barzizza, teaching in nearby Padua, visited friends and pupils in Venice during 1407 and 1408. The literature describing these figures' Venetian careers and relations would too greatly strain this essay. Consult the main monographs on each figure, some of which are cited in King, *Venetian Humanism,* pt. 2, preface, note 13.

9. King, *Venetian Humanism,* pt. 2, preface, lists the following patrician humanists in the first generation: Francesco Barbaro, Giovanni Corner, Andrea Giuliani, Leonardo Giustiniani, Marco Lippomano, Jacopo Antonio Marcello, Zaccaria Trevisan the Elder, Daniele Vitturi (laymen); Fantino Dandolo, Pietro Donato, Pietro Marcello the Elder, Pietro Miani, Fantino Vallaresso (clerics); and the following commoners: the secretary Jacopo Languschi, and the physicians Niccolò Leonardi and Pietro Tommasi. Fantino Dandolo assumed his church career after a successful earlier career as Venetian politician and diplomat. Profiles of all these figures and those

named as Venetian humanists in the following notes appear in *Venetian Humanism*, pt. 2.

10. Trevisan's orations for his successor as captain of Padua, Pietro Rimondo (Petrus Arimundus; March 1407), and for the conferral of the doctorate on Pietro Marcello the Elder, bishop of Padua (16 October 1413) enunciate the themes given; they are published by P. Gothein in "Zaccaria Trevisan," *Archivio veneto* 5th ser. 21 (1937): 28–30 and 47–49. Barbaro's *De re uxoria liber* is edited by A. Gnesotto in *Atti e memorie della R. Accademia di Scienze, Lettere ed Arti in Padova* n.s. 32 (1916): 6–105; the preface and second part, translated by B. G. Kohl, is in *The Earthly Republic: Italian Humanists on Government and Society*, ed. Kohl and R. G. Witt with E. B. Welles (Philadelphia, 1978), 177–228. Barbaro's letters were edited by A. M. Quirini in his *Diatriba praeliminaris in duas partes divisa ad Francisci Barbari et aliorum ad ipsum epistolae ab anno Christi 1425 ad annum 1453*, 2 vols. (Brescia, 1741–43). Additional letters and a chronologically ordered catalog of those previously printed was published by R. Sabbadini: his *Centotrenta lettere inedite di Francesco Barbaro precedute dall'ordinamento critico cronologico dell'intero suo epistolario* (Salerno, 1884). A discussion of Barbaro's *De re uxoria* is found in King, *Venetian Humanism*, chap. 2.

11. King, *Venetian Humanism*, pt. 2, preface, lists the following patrician humanists in this second generation: the laymen Sebastiano Badoer, Girolamo Barbarigo, Zaccaria Barbaro, Niccolò Barbo, Paolo Barbo, Candiano Bollani, Niccolò Canal, Francesco Contarini, Federico Corner, Antonio Donato, Marco Donato, Jacopo Foscari, Ludovico Foscarini, Domenico Giorgi, Bernardo Giustiniani, Vitale Lando, Giovanni Marino, Barbone Morosini, Domenico Morosini, Lauro Quirini, Leonardo Sanuto, Zaccaria Trevisan the Younger, and the clerics Ermolao Barbaro the Elder, Marco Barbo, Pietro Barbo (later Pope Paul II), Gregorio Correr, Taddeo Quirini, Maffeo Vallaresso, Lorenzo Zane, Jacopo Zeno. Of the lay patricians named, all but three (Corner, Foscari, Lauro Quirini) held significant political office; twenty lay patrician humanists, therefore, held significant positions in a government in which perhaps one hundred individuals shared power. See the career analysis in the chapter cited.

12. Commoner humanists of the second generation include the teachers Benedetto Brognoli, Tito Livio Frulovisi, Filippo (da Rimini) Morandi, Pietro Perleone, the professor Giovanni Marcanova (resident of Padua), the secretaries Ulisse Aleotti, Febo Capella, Niccolò Sagundino, the physician Giovanni Caldiera, and the clerics Pietro Bruto, Andrea Contrario, Domenico de' Domenichi, Pietro del Monte, Michele Orsini (all resident abroad). The transient foreigners of this generation include the teacher Giovanni Pietro Vitali (da Lucca) d'Avenza (in Venice 1450–56), the private secretary (to Francesco Barbaro, among others) Flavio Biondo, the ambassador Gianozzo Manetti (1448), the bibliophile Ambrogio Traversari (1433), and the epigraphist Ciriaco d'Ancona (1443); for these, see the titles cited in King, *Venetian Humanism*, pt. 2, preface, notes 13–14.

13. Of a large literature on the San Marco school for the humanities, see especially B. Nardi, "Letteratura e cultura veneziana del Quattrocento," now reprinted in his *Saggi sulla cultura veneta del Quattrocento e Cinquecento* (Padua, 1971), 3–43; J. B. Ross, "Venetian Schools and Teachers, Fourteenth to Early Sixteenth Century: A Survey and a Study of Giovanni Battista Egnazio," *Renaissance Quarterly* 29 (1976): 521–66; A. Segarizzi, "Cenni sulle scuole pubbliche a Venezia nel secolo XV e sul primo maestro d'esse," *Atti del R. Istituto Veneto di Scienze, Lettere ed Arti* 75 (1915–16): pt. 2, 637–67; Pastore Stocchi, "Scuola e cultura." Previously founded was the Rialto school for philosophy, for which see the two studies by Nardi: "La scuola di Rialto e l'umanesimo veneziano," and "Letteratura e cultura"; now also F. Lepori, "La scuola di Rialto dalla fondazione alla metà del Quattrocento," in *Storia della cultura veneta,* 3.2 (Vicenza, 1980), 539–605.

14. Quirini's *Epistola ad Petrum Thomasium* (on nobility), with Niccolò Barbo and Francesco Contarini, *De nobilitate contra Poggium Florentinum,* and *De republica;* the first two ed. by K. Krautter, P. O. Kristeller, and H. Roob, in "Tre trattati di Lauro Quirini sulla nobiltà," in *Lauro Quirini umanista,* 67–73 and 74–98, respectively, and trans. by A. Rabil, in *Knowledge, Goodness and Power: The Debate over "Nobility" among Quattrocento Italian Humanists* (forthcoming); the last ed. C. Seno and G. Ravagnani also in *Lauro Quirini umanista,* 121–61. Caldiera's trilogy of moral philosophical works is in Oxford, Bodleian Library, cod. Laud. Misc. 717, esp. the third, *De praestantia venetae politiae, et artibus in eadem excultis tam mechanicis quam liberalibus [et] de virtutibus quae maxime reipublica[e] veneta[e] debentur, libri 5,* on fols. 101–48ᵛ. Domenico Morosini, *De bene instituta re publica,* ed. C. Finzi (Milan, 1969). Paolo Morosini's *Defensio venetorum ad Europae principes contra obtrectatores,* and *De rebus ac forma reipublicae venetae,* both in *Bibliotheca manuscripta ad S. Marci Venetiarum,* ed. G. Valentinelli, 6 vols. (Venice, 1868–73), 3:189–229 and 231–64, respectively. Analyses of these works may be found in King, *Venetian Humanism,* chap. 2.

15. Contarini, *De rebus in Hetruria a Senensibus gestis cum aduersus Florentinos, tum aduersus Ildibrandinum Petilianensem Comitem, libri tres,* ed. Giovanni Michele Bruto (Venice, 1623; reprint of Lyons, 1562). Donato's diminutive *Vitae ducum venetorum* is in Venice, Biblioteca Marciana, cod. Lat. X, 145 (3533), fols. 79–93. Giustiniani, *De origine urbis venetiarum rebusque gestis a Venetis libri quindecim,* in *Thesaurus antiquitatum et historiarum Italiae,* ed. J. G. Graevius, 5.1 (Leiden, 1722), cols. 1–172. For discussions of historiography in this period, see the essays in *La storiografia veneziana,* ed. A. Pertusi, particularly the editor's "Gli inizi della storiografia umanistica del Quattrocento." For Giustiniani's work in particular, see Labalme, *Bernardo Giustiniani,* chap. 10; and F. Gaeta, "Storiografia," in *Storia della cultura veneta,* 45–65.

16. The elder Barbaro's *Orationes contra poetas* (with *Epistolae*), ed. G. Ronconi (Florence, 1972) and Caldiera's *De concordantia poetarum philo-*

sophorum et theologorum (Biblioteca Apostolica Vaticana, cod. Urb. Lat.
1178, one of several manuscript versions, all preferred to the 1547 edition
of Venice, apud Cominum de Tridino Montisferati) deal with the perceived
threat of classical literature. For Correr's struggle with his love of secular
literature and eventual repudiation of it, see his own statements in the *Epistola ad Caeciliam Virginem*, in G. B. Contarini, *Anecdota veneta* (Venice,
1757), 213ff., and in the *Soliloquium ad Deum de vita sua et de vita et
obitu beatae memoriae Antonii Episcopi Ostiensis et Cardinalis patrui sui*,
ibid., 15ff. (The letter to Cecilia is available in a trans. by M. L. King and
A. Rabil in *Her Immaculate Hand: Selected Works by and About the
Women Humanists of Quattrocento Italy* [Binghamton, NY, 1983], 91–
105.) Caldiera expounded the Psalms (Modena, Bibl. Estense, cod. Est. Lat.
1000 [Alpha K, 3, 6]), Bollani expounded Genesis (*Libri XVIII in tria
priora capita Genesis*, Venice, Bibl. Marciana, cod. Lat. I, 44 [2038]); Domenico Morosini wrote religious works now lost, for which see pp. 7–8 of
C. Finzi's introduction to Morosini's *De bene instituta republica*, cited
above. De' Domenichi wrote many treatises on theological questions and
matters of ecclesiastical administration; see for example his *De reforma-
tionibus romanae curiae* (Brescia, 1495). Del Monte wrote the substantial
*Monarchia in qua generalium conciliorum materia de potestate prestantia
et excellentia Romani pontificis et imperatoris plenissime discutitur* (Rome,
1537). Bruto's *Epistola contra Judeos* (Vicenza, [1477]; GW 5658) and *Vic-
toria contra Judaeos* (Vicenza, 3 October 1489; H-C *4027; GW 5659) are
the notorious relics of an anti-Semitic upsurge in Vicenza. Foscarini's letters
can be scanned for anti-Semitic allusions: *Epistolae* (Vienna, Öster-
reichische Nationalbibliothek, cod. Lat. 441). Paolo Morosini's *De
aeterna temporalique Christi generatione in judaice improbationem perfi-
diae* (Padua, 28 April 1473; H 10924) was the first book published in
Padua. He discusses free will in his *De fato seu praescientia divina et liberi
humani arbitrii libertate* (Biblioteca Apostolica Vaticana, cod. Vat. Lat.
13157).

17. The patrician humanists of the third generation include: the laymen Ermo-
lao Barbaro the Younger, Bernardo Bembo, Antonio Bernardo, Domenico
Bollani, Antonio Calbo, Pietro Contarini, Marco Dandolo, Francesco
Diedo, Girolamo Donato, Pietro Marcello the Younger, Pietro Molin, Mar-
cantonio Morosini, Paolo Pisani, Daniele Renier, Marco Sanuto; the clerics
Francesco and Pietro Barozzi, Pietro Dolfin, Ludovico Donato, and Pietro
Foscari. The commoners include the teachers Giorgio Merula, Marcantonio
Sabellico, Giorgio Valla, the professor Niccolò Leonico Tomeo, the secre-
taries Marco Aurelio, Jacopo Ragazzoni, Paolo Ramusio, Antonio Vinci-
guerra, and the clerics Pietro Cirneo, Giovanni Lorenzi, and Francesco
Negri. The transients are multitudinous, including many foreigners who
stopped in Venice only briefly. Most notable are the public-school teachers
Giovanni Mario Filelfo (in Venice in 1460) and Gregorio (da Città di Castello) Tifernate (ca. 1463–66), the secretary-companions Girolamo Bologni
(ca. 1470), Paolo Marsi (intermittently, 1468–73), and Girolamo Aurelio

Augurello (1485), the poet and printer's aide Raffaele Zovenzoni (1470–73, 1474–ca. 1475), the students Luca Pacioli (1480s) and Urbano Bolzanio (ca. 1473), the soldier Coriolano Cippico (1470–74, with the Venetian fleet), the ambassador Filippo (Callimaco) Buonaccorsi (1476–77, 1486), Cardinal Bessarion (1463), the philologist and poet Poliziano (1480 and 1491). For the Venetian careers of these figures, see the titles cited in *Venetian Humanism*, pt. 2, preface, notes 13–14.

18. Of the extensive literature on the early history of printing in Venice, see especially these recent works and studies there cited: L. V. Gerulaitis, *Printing and Publishing in Fifteenth-Century Venice* (Chicago and London, 1976); P. F. Grendler, *The Roman Inquisition and the Venetian Press, 1540–1605* (Princeton, 1977); M. J. C. Lowry, *The World of Aldus Manutius: Business and Scholarship in Renaissance Venice* (Ithaca, NY, 1979), esp. chap. 1; E. Pastorello, *Bibliografia storico-analitica dell'arte della stampa a Venezia*, 1 (Venice, 1933); N. Pozza, "L'editoria veneziana da Giovanni da Spira ad Aldo Manuzio," in *Storia della cultura veneta* 3.2:215–44.

19. For the school of rhetoric, see the sources cited above, n. 13; also Gilbert, "Biondo, Sabellico." Merula's key role in the new philological trend of Venetian humanist culture was highlighted by V. Branca in several places; see especially "Ermolao Barbaro and Late Quattrocento Venetian Humanism," in *Renaissance Venice*, ed. Hale, 219ff., "Ermolao Barbaro e l'umanesimo veneziano," in *Umanesimo europeo ed umanesimo veneziano*, 196ff., and "L'umanesimo veneziano," 157ff. P. G. Ricci develops the same argument in "Umanesimo filologico," in *Umanesimo europeo ed umanesimo veneziano*, 169ff. For the notion of a shift in the focus of Venetian humanism from a rhetorical to a philological orientation, see also Gilbert, "Biondo, Sabellico." Gilbert locates that shift, however, in the early sixteenth century. Branca, in the studies named above, sees Barbaro's role as preeminent in forging the "new philology" of the late fifteenth century; see also his "L'umanesimo veneziano" for assessments of the contributions of Donato (166ff.) and Valla (161ff.). Gerulaitis, *Printing and Publishing*, sees a late-century tendency away from publication in the classics to a concentration on those subjects named (science and mathematics, etc.) more appropriate to professionals than amateurs. Philological skills were applied to the latter (especially to scientific and philosophical texts) as well as to the former.

20. For guidance to the scientific and philosophical work of Barbaro, see the studies named in the preceding note; for that of Donato, see especially P. Rigo's "Catalogo e tradizione"; for that of Tomeo, see, among several specialized studies by D. de' Bellis, especially her "La vita e l'ambiente." For Valla's work in humanism and mathematics, see especially P. L. Rose, "Humanist Culture and Renaissance Mathematics: The Italian Libraries of the Quattrocento," *Studies in the Renaissance* 20 (1973): 46–105. Notable among the religious works of this generation is Marco Dandolo's *Catena seu expositio graecorum patrum in psalmos: In Psalterium expositionum*

collectio e graeco in latinum versa M. D. interpreta (Venice, Bibl. Marciana, cod. Lat. I, 33 [2133]). Sabellico's successful history is his *Rerum venetarum ab urbe condita libri XXXIII*, in *Degl'istorici delle cose veneziane, i quali hanno scritto per pubblico decreto*, 10 vols. in 11, ed. A. Zeno (Venice, 1718–22), vol. 1. The younger Barbaro's (unfinished) *De officio legati* (ed. V. Branca with *De coelibatu* [Florence, 1969]) describes the duties of the Venetian ambassador, and Barozzi's *De factionibus extinguendis* (ed. F. Gaeta in *Il vescovo Pietro Barozzi e il trattato*) discusses the duties of the wise (Venetian) governor. Donato's *Contra Caroli Regis Francorum in Senatum Venetum calumnias apologia* (in D. Malipiero, *Annali veneti dall'anno 1457 al 1500*, ed. A. Sagredo, *Archivio storico italiano* 7.1–2 [1843–44]: 443–63) is the culmination in brief of the Venetian apologetic tradition, repeating many of the main arguments of Paolo Morosini's more extensive works (cited above, n. 14).

21. For Colonna and his work, see especially M. T. Casella and G. Pozzi, *Francesco Colonna, biografia e opere*, 2 vols. (Padua, 1959). The equestrian Colleoni of Verrocchio is known to travelers to Venice. For the printer Manuzio, see below. For Barbaro's disloyalty, see *Venetian Humanism*, chap. 2.

22. For a succinct account of the French invasion and consequent political disarray see L. Martines, *Power and Imagination: City-States in Renaissance Italy* (New York, 1979), 277ff. For the Cambrai crisis and sixteenth-century trends, in addition to general sources already cited, see especially F. Braudel, "La vita economica di Venezia nel secolo XVI," in *La civiltà veneziana del Rinascimento*, 81–102; F. Chabod, "Venezia nella politica italiana ed europea del Cinquecento," ibid., 27–55; G. Cozzi, "Authority and Law," in *Renaissance Venice*, ed. Hale, 293–345; J. C. Davis, *The Decline of the Venetian Nobility as a Ruling Class* (Baltimore, 1962); R. Finlay, "Venice, the Po Expedition, and the End of the League of Cambrai, 1509–1510," in *Studies in Modern European History and Culture* 2 (1976): 37–72; F. Gilbert, "Venice in the Crisis of the League of Cambrai," in *Renaissance Venice*, ed. Hale, 274–92 (also in Gilbert, *History: Choice and Commitment* [Cambridge, MA and London, 1977], 269–91); P. S. Leicht, "Ideali di vita dei veneziani del Cinquecento," *Archivio veneto* 5th ser. 14 (1933): 217–31; F. Seneca, *Venezia e Papa Giulio II* (Padua, 1962); U. Tucci, "The Psychology of the Venetian Merchant in the Sixteenth Century," in *Renaissance Venice*, ed. Hale, 346–78. Both Gilbert and Cozzi (in the studies cited) indicate a significant change in patrician culture, both psychological and institutional, from the late fifteenth to early sixteenth centuries linked to the experience of Cambrai. It should be noted, however, that neither the tendency to reinforce the monopoly of an inner oligarchy nor that toward the consolidation of patrician consciousness was new; both were evident in the fourteenth century with consequences extending through the fifteenth, as has been seen. These early sixteenth-century developments should be viewed as a renewal and intensification, provoked by a particular set of experiences, of tendencies already well rooted in Venetian culture. W.

Bouwsma in his massive *Venice and the Defense of Republican Liberty* (Berkeley, 1968) attributes to the Cambrai crisis an even more dramatic importance, seeing it as the catalyst of a modern secular political consciousness in Venice. L. J. Libby presents a similar argument in his "Venetian History and Political Thought After 1509," *Studies in the Renaissance* 20 (1973): 7–45. Both Bouwsma and Libby liken Cambrai to the crisis which, according to H. Baron, triggered civic humanism in Florence; see especially his *The Crisis of the Early Italian Renaissance,* 2 vols. in 1 (Princeton, 2d ed., 1966), a culmination of earlier studies.

23. For Aldo, see especially C. Dionisotti, "Aldo Manuzio umanista," in *Umanesimo europeo e umanesimo veneziano,* 213–43; Lowry, *Aldus Manutius,* and his two earlier studies: "The 'New Academy' of Aldus Manutius: A Renaissance Dream," *Bulletin of the John Rylands University Library of Manchester* 58 (1976): 378–420; "Two Great Venetian Libraries in the Age of Aldus Manutius," ibid., 57 (1974): 128–66. Aldo's Greek focus was intentional and his own, but was certainly facilitated by the abundance of Greek texts in Venice and the city's tradition of Greek scholarship. Branca demonstrates a relation between Ermolao Barbaro the Younger's Greek scholarship and Aldo's: "L'umanesimo veneziano," 156–57. For Greek learning in Venice, see A. Pertusi, "L'umanesimo greco," in *Storia della cultura veneta,* which updates and corrects D. J. Geanakoplos, *Greek Scholars in Venice* (Cambridge, MA, 1962). Typical of the commoner humanists around Aldo were such figures as Giovanni Battista Egnazio, Vettore Fausto, Marco Musurus, Giovanni Battista Ramusio, and Raffaele Regio; for guidance to literature on these figures, see *Venetian Humanism,* pt. 2, preface, note 16. Particularly vivid images of their struggle to gain and keep positions are offered by A. Medin, "Raffaele Regio a Venezia, epigrammi per la sua morte," *Archivio veneto tridentino* 4th ser. 1 (1922): 237–44, and Ross (dealing with Egnazio), "Venetian Schools," 536–56.

24. For patrician humanist culture in this era, see especially Logan, *Culture and Society,* chaps. 5 and 8. For the *convegni* and academies, see Rose, "The Accademia Venetiana." For the scientific orientation of patrician culture, see additionally idem, "Bartolomeo Zamberti's Funeral Oration for the Humanist Encyclopaedist Giorgio Valla," in C. Clough, ed., *Cultural Aspects of the Italian Renaissance: Essays in Honor of Paul Oskar Kristeller* (Manchester and New York, 1976), 299–310; Rose, "Humanistic Culture and Renaissance Mathematics"; and R. Massalongo, "Alessandro Benedetti e la medicina veneta del Quattrocento," *Atti del R. Istituto Veneto di scienze, lettere ed arti* 76 (1916–17): pt. 2, 197–259. Cozzi gives a particularly fine image of one member of this late patrician humanist culture in "Federico Contarini, un antiquario veneziano tra Rinascimento e Controriforma," *Bollettino dell'Istituto storico per la storia e cultura veneziana* 3 (1961): 190–221. The seekers of religious solitude were mainly in the circle of Gasparo Contarini; for the extensive literature on him see the bibliographical study of Ross, "The Emergence of Gasparo Contarini." For this tendency in the culture of Venetian aristocrats, see also S. Tramontin, "La cultura

monastica del Quattrocento dal primo patriarca Lorenzo Giustiniani ai Camaldolesi Paolo Giustiniani e Pietro Quirini," in *Storia della cultura veneta*, 3.1:431–57, esp. 453ff.

25. The myth of Venice is surely the concept most strenuously discussed by scholars of the period. See the review of essential literature in *Venetian Humanism*, chap. 2, note 231; also discussions of the myth by S. Chojnacki, "Crime, Punishment, and the Trecento Venetian State," in L. Martines, ed., *Violence and Civil Disorder in Italian Cities, 1200–1500* (Berkeley, 1972), 184–228 at 184ff.; R. Finlay, *Politics in Renaissance Venice* (New Brunswick, NJ, 1980), 27ff.; Logan, *Culture and Society*, chap. 1.

26. For this alternative means of securing cultural cohesion, see E. Muir's *Civic Ritual in Renaissance Venice* (Princeton, 1981) and earlier "Images of Power: Art and Pageantry in Renaissance Venice," *American Historical Review* 84 (1979): 16–52, and the literature there cited.

BIBLIOGRAPHY

Agostini, G. degli, *Notizie istorico-critiche intorno la vita e le opere degli scrittori viniziani*, 2 vols. (Venice, 1752–54).

Bellis, D. de', "La vita e l'ambiente di Niccolò Leonico Tomeo," *Quaderni per la storia dell'Università di Padova* 13 (1980): 37–75.

Bertalot, L. "Jacobi Zeni descriptio coniurationis patavine (das Ende des letzten Carraresen 1435)," *Quellen und Forschungen aus italienischen Archiven und Bibliotheken* 20 (1928–29): 333–58; reprinted in Bertalot, *Studien zum italienischen und deutschen Humanismus*, ed. P. O. Kristeller, 2 vols. (Rome, 1975), 2:103–30.

Bouwsma, W. J., *Venice and the Defense of Republican Liberty: Renaissance Values in the Age of the Counter-Reformation* (Berkeley, 1968).

Branca, V., "Ermolao Barbaro 'poeta' e la sua 'presentazione' alla corte degli Aragonesi," in *Classical, Medieval and Renaissance Studies in Honor of Berthold Louis Ullman*, ed. C. Henderson, 2 vols. (Rome, 1964), 2:385–411.

La civiltà veneziana del Quattrocento (Florence, 1957).

   Nardi, B., "Letteratura e cultura veneziana del Quattrocento," 99–145.

   Piovene, G., "L'anacronismo della Venezia quattrocentesca," 1–21.

La civiltà veneziana del Rinascimento (Florence, 1958).

   Elwert, T. S., "Pietro Bembo e la vita letteraria del suo tempo," 125–76.

La civiltà veneziana del Trecento (Florence, 1956).

   Kristeller, P. O., "Il Petrarca, l'umanesimo e la scolastica a Venezia," 149–78.

Cozzi, G., "Cultura politica e religione nella 'pubblica storiografia' veneziana del '500." *Bollettino dell'Istituto storico per la storia e cultura veneziana* 5–6 (1963–64): 215–94.

Foscarini, M., *Della letteratura veneziana ed altri scritti intorno essa*, ed. F. Berlan (Venice, 2d ed. 1854 [1752]).

Gaeta, F., ed., *Il vescovo Pietro Barozzi e il trattato "De factionibus extinguendis"* (Venice, 1958).

Giannetto, N., "Un'orazione inedita di Bernardo Bembo per Cristoforo Moro,"

Atti dell'Istituto Veneto di scienze, lettere ed arti 140 (1981–82): Classe di scienze morali, lettere ed arti, 257–88.

Gilbert, F., "Biondo, Sabellico, and the Beginnings of Venetian Official Historiography," in *Florilegium Historiale: Essays Presented to Wallace K. Ferguson*, ed. J. G. Rowe and W. H. Stockdale (Toronto, 1971), 275–93.

———, "Humanism in Venice," in *Florence and Venice: Comparisons and Relations*, Acts of Two Conferences at Villa I Tatti in 1976–77, 2 vols. (Florence, 1979–80), 1:13–26.

Gothein, P., *Francesco Barbaro (1390–1454): Frühhumanismus und Staatskunst in Venedig* (Berlin, 1932).

Grendler, P. F., *Critics of the Italian World, 1530–1560: Anton Francesco Doni, Nicolò Franco, and Ortensio Lando* (Madison, WI, 1969).

Hale, J. R., ed., *Renaissance Venice* (London and Totowa, NJ, 1973).

    Branca, V., "Ermolao Barbaro and Late Quattrocento Venetian Humanism," 218–43.

    Cozzi, G., "Authority and Law in Renaissance Venice," 293–345.

King, M. L., "A Study in Venetian Humanism at Mid-Quattrocento: Filippo da Rimini and his *Symposium de paupertate* (Study and Text)," *Studi veneziani* n.s. 2 (1978): 75–96; 3 (1979): 141–86; 4 (1980): 27–44.

Labalme, P. H., *Bernardo Guistiniani: A Venetian of the Quattrocento* (Rome, 1969).

Lauro Quirini umanista: Studi e testi, ed. V. Branca (Florence, 1977).

    Krautter, K., P. O. Kristeller, and H. Roob, eds., "Tre trattati di Lauro Quirini sulla nobiltà," 19–102.

    Seno, C. and G. Ravagnani, "*De republica,*" 121–61.

Logan, O., *Culture and Society in Venice, 1470–1790: The Renaissance and Its Heritage* (London and New York, 1972).

Lowry, M. J. C., *The World of Aldus Manutius: Business and Scholarship in Renaissance Venice* (Ithaca, NY, 1979).

Miscellanea di studi in onore di Vittore Branca, 4 vols. in 6 (Florence, 1983).

Pertusi, A., ed., *La storiografia veneziana fino al secolo XVI: Aspetti e problemi* (Florence, 1970).

Rigo, P., "Catalogo e tradizione degli scritti di Girolamo Donato," *Rendiconti dell'Accademia Nazionale dei Lincei* 8th ser. 31 (1976): 49–80.

Rose, P. L., "The Academia Venetiana, Science and Culture in Renaissance Venice," *Studi veneziani* 11 (1969): 191–242.

Ross, J. B., "The Emergence of Gasparo Contarini: A Bibliographical Essay," *Church History* 41 (1972): 22–45.

Sabbadini, R., "Antonio da Romagno e Pietro Marcello," *Nuovo archivio veneto* n.s. 30 (1915): 207–46.

Segarizzi, A., "Francesco Contarini, politico e letterato veneziano del secolo XV," *Nuovo archivio veneto* n.s. 12 (1906): pt. 2, 272–306.

Storia della cultura veneta, vol. 3, *Dal primo Quattrocento al Concilio di Trento,* part 1, *Il Quattrocento* (Vicenza, 1980).

    Branca, V., "L'umanesimo veneziano alla fine del Quattrocento, Ermolao Barbaro e il suo circolo," 123–75.

Gaeta, F., "Storiografia, coscienza nazionale e politica culturale nella Venezia del Rinascimento," 1–91.

Pastore Stocchi, M., "Scuola e cultura umanistica fra due secoli," 93–121.

Pertusi, A., "L'umanesimo greco dalla fine del secolo XIV agli inizi del secolo XVI," 177–264.

Tournoy, G., "Francesco Diedo, Venetian Humanist and Politician of the Quattrocento," *Humanistica lovaniensia* 19 (1970): 201–34.

Umanesimo europeo ed umanesimo veneziano, ed. V. Branca (Florence, 1963).

Branca, V., "Ermolao Barbaro e l'umanesimo veneziano," 193–212.

Garin, E., "Cultura filosofica toscana e veneta nel Quattrocento," 11–30.

Lazzarini, L., "Francesco Petrarca e il primo umanesimo a Venezia," 63–92.

Nardi, B., "La scuola di Rialto e l'umanesimo veneziano," 93–139.

Ricci, P. G., "Umanesimo filologico in Toscana e nel Veneto," 159–72.

Weiss, R., *Un umanista veneziano: Papa Paolo II* (Venice, 1958).

Zeno, Jacopo, *Vita Caroli Zeni*, ed. G. Zonta, in L. A. Muratori, *Rerum italicarum scriptores*, 19.6.1–2 (Bologna, 2d ed., 1940).

10 ❧ HUMANISM IN MILAN
Albert Rabil, Jr.

HUMANISM IN MILAN AND ITS SURROUNDING TERRITORIES (IN-cluding, preeminently, Pavia) first became visible during the reign of Giangaleazzo Visconti (1351–1402), who became the ruler of Pavia in 1378 upon the death of his father. His uncle Bernabò, who governed Milan, tied him to his own rule by marrying Giangaleazzo to his daughter Caterina. Since Bernabò had a number of sons of his own, Giangaleazzo's chances of ruling Milan were slim. But he improved upon them in the spirit of Italian Renaissance politics. In 1385 he went to Milan with a large entourage, ostensibly on a pilgrimage. When Bernabò and all his sons came out to meet him, Giangaleazzo took them all prisoner and afterward had them dispatched. He was greeted as a liberator and proceeded to insure his popularity by distributing much of Bernabò's property to the local nobility. No sooner was Milanese territory united under his suzerainty than his ambition led him to attempt to unite all of northern Italy into one state under his rule—a project in which he almost succeeded. He gained control of all the mountain passes to Switzerland, and thus of the trade routes, to the discomfiture of Venice; he not only conquered all of Lombardy but extended his reach also into Tuscany and by 1402 had captured Bologna, Siena, Pisa, and Perugia. Florence lay unprotected before him, when he became ill and died in September of that year. These latter events of his rule have become well known to students of the Italian Renaissance through the work of Hans Baron, in which Giangaleazzo's designs on Florence play an important role in the emergence of what Baron calls Florentine civic humanism.[1] When Giangaleazzo died, however, the extraterritorial pretensions of Milan evaporated, and the city turned back upon itself in a struggle for power among its many noble factions. Not until the emergence in 1412 of Filippo Maria Visconti (1392–1447), the last Visconti ruler of Milan, was Visconti hegemony restored. By then, however, Venice had decided to become a power in Lombardy in order to prevent Milanese control of trading passes; and Tuscany lay beyond the reach of Visconti power.

Milan was a beautiful example of what Burckhardt, Symonds, and others have described as the despotic Italian city-state, one ruled by a *signore* whose power is much more personal than dynastic.[2] The fundamental problem in Milan was that the merchant nobility was never integrated with the landed aristocracy, as happened in both Venice and Florence, so that when a ruler like Giangaleazzo died, his success evaporated in the struggle not only among his own heirs but also among the other noble families of Lombardy. This state of affairs continued throughout the Quattrocento, in fact until Milan lost its autonomy to Emperor Charles V in 1535.

*   *   *

The center of Milanese humanism at the turn of the fifteenth century was the chancery. The aristocracy, whether landed or merchant, seems to have produced no learned men, nor did it patronize the learned—there are no instances of works by Milanese humanists dedicated to any of them. Humanism, therefore, received its impetus from the duke, first directly through court service, then indirectly through ducal appointments to the University of Pavia and to some chairs in Milan.

It is not surprising that Milanese humanists praised Giangaleazzo and his successors. They defended the imposition of order on a recalcitrant state as a great good. This exaltation of order was escalated by the idea of Milan as an ideal state ruling over all of northern Italy—a humanist defense of Giangaleazzo's dynastic ambitions.

But although the emergence of humanism in Milan owes many of its thematic interests as well as its physical support to the Visconti, its cultural springs were the works of Petrarch and Florentine humanism, especially of Salutati. During the latter years of his life Petrarch was connected with the courts of Milan[3] and Padua;[4] his eight years in Milan were his longest continuous residence anywhere, and he remained a great favorite of the Visconti, whom he also served in several capacities. Petrarch may be said to have set the pattern for humanist support of the princely courts of Lombardy. Even more significantly, Petrarch left most of his books to Padua, and when Padua was conquered by the Visconti in 1388 and 1392 most of these works were transferred to Pavia, where they were studied, copied, and annotated by Lombard humanists. Pasquino Cappelli possessed Petrarch's *Epistolae familiares,* and Giovanni Manzini annotated them. Astolfino Marinoni copied the Petrarchan Vergil, and Gasparino Barzizza read *De viris illustribus.* Petrarch's work was the inspiration for the humanist circle around Salutati in Florence, with whom the Milanese humanists were in contact. Salutati corresponded with Cappelli, Manzini, and Antonio Loschi, who had studied under Salutati and worked in the Florentine chancery in the 1380s.[5] Relations between Salutati and Loschi led to further contacts with Florentine humanists, notably Bruni.[6] The classical interests of the Milanese humanists were encouraged by the large collection of classical manuscripts in the Visconti library, one of the largest in Italy at that time.

All of these influences may be seen at work in the careers of several of these early humanists. Pasquino Cappelli (ca. 1340–ca. 1398),[7] was the powerful secretary—functionally a chancellor in a bureaucracy not so highly differentiated as it was to become later in the century—of Giangaleazzo, who may have known Petrarch and who also owned an impressive collection of books. Salutati wrote to Cappelli in 1392 about his dream of a republic of men of letters who could love one another despite political struggle,[8] a view shared by many humanists. A few years later, in 1398, Salutati had occasion to lament the fortune of Cappelli, who, having been accused of treason in connection with Giangaleazzo's military defeat in 1397 by Mantua, was languishing in prison; he cited Cappelli's fate as an example of the turning of the wheel of fortune, comparing Cappelli to Callisthenes, the philosopher treated so cruelly by Alexander the Great.[9]

Giovanni Manzini wrote a neo-Senecan tragedy dealing with the defeat of Antonio della Scala by the Visconti (which occurred in 1387), probably modeled on the *Ecerinis* of Albertino Mussato.[10] Manzini was a man of arms as well as a man of letters. He participated in the battle between the Visconti and della Scala that he later dramatized. Manzini characterized Giangaleazzo as, like himself, a man of both arms and letters. He was a disciple of Petrarch and probably a court tutor, for we know he taught the son of Cappelli.

But the best known of the early Milanese humanists was Antonio Loschi (1368–1441), Cappelli's successor from 1398 to 1404.[11] Loschi's association with Salutati was an intimate and decisive one. He was a student of Salutati's in Florence, and, as noted, also worked in the chancery. When he subsequently assumed a position in the Milanese chancery he was instrumental in introducing to Milan the literary currents already present in Florence. When Manuel Chrysoloras left Florence in 1400 he went to Pavia for a time, where Loschi studied Greek under him. Loschi's *Inquisitio artis in orationibus Ciceronis*, a commentary on eleven Ciceronian orations, intended in reality to be a tract on rhetoric, was conceived in the daily colloquies with humanists in Pavia, particularly with Astolfino Marinoni; the work was highly regarded by humanists, as reflected in its widespread distribution both in manuscript and later in printed editions during the fifteenth century. Gasparino Barzizza's later commentaries on Cicero's speeches were heavily indebted to the method Loschi developed: a sixfold scheme beginning with a summary and background, then moving on to descriptions of the branch of rhetoric, type of argument, order and number of parts of the speech, analysis of each part with particular attention to the commonplaces and argumentation of the "confirmatio" and "confutatio," and concluding with the style or list of figures of speech and thought.[12] The themes that appear in Loschi's commentary reflect clearly the emphases of Florentine humanism from Brunetto Latini to Salutati, Vergerio, and Bruni, as well as the school of Chrysoloras and the new connection established there between Cicero and Plato: the connection between the art of speaking and the art of governing, between the laws of nature and a state based on reason.

In his tragedy *Achilles*, dealing with the Trojan War but having in mind the struggle within the communes of Italy, he stressed—as had Manzini—the inexorable turning of the wheel of fortune, and he emphasized the restoration of order by the Visconti.[13] This ideal of order, having even cosmic dimensions, was opposed to the Florentine ideal of an unpredictable freedom of movement and expression. In exalting republican liberty Florence proclaimed itself the true heir of the Roman republic and in this respect opposed to Milan.

The polemical exchange between Salutati and Loschi on the occasion of Giangaleazzo's attempt to subdue all of northern Italy (1397–1402) was a striking instance of letters serving arms. Loschi, in his invective against Florence, opposed liberty to peace. Through arms the Visconti were attempting to bring peace to Italy. Liberty means strife, instability, constant danger. Worthy of Cicero, Loschi's invective is a political manifesto. Florence is made responsible for all the unrest of Italy. The argument is clearly put forward that it is necessary to restore tyranny in order to restore peace and tranquility.

Salutati's response is likewise a manifesto. Not only does he represent Florence as the direct heir of Roman freedom, but he paints Milan as the most advanced point of barbarism in the Latin world. He describes Milanese tyranny as an attempt to snuff out freedom in which alone culture can flower and civilization prosper. To the immobile peace invoked by Loschi, he opposes the life of commerce, a population vibrant and active, a productive countryside, and, finally, knowledge.[14]

Despite their political differences, Salutati's dream of a republic of men of letters transcending politics prevailed, and their personal links remained unbroken. When Salutati died in 1406 Loschi, who by then had left Milan, as well as other leaders of Milanese culture, genuinely lamented his passing.[15] Uberto Decembrio, for example, while predicting that the walls of Florence would fall into ruin, said that Salutati's name would live as do the names of Scipio and Cato. I came to Florence myself, said Decembrio, not so much to see the city as to meet its chancellor.[16]

*   *   *

Loschi's view that the Visconti were trying to bring peace to Italy through arms was echoed by Uberto Decembrio (1370–1427), a friend of Loschi's. From 1391 until 1407 Decembrio worked for Bishop Pietro Filargo, who became the godfather of his son Pier Candido (1392–1477) and, ten years later, Pope Alexander V. Uberto was sent on a number of missions on behalf of the bishop, one to Florence, where he met Salutati, and another to Prague where Wenceslas ruled, a period he regarded as the high point of his life. In 1402 he wrote a paean to the Milanese conqueror of Bologna, exhorting him to march immediately against Florence. When he left the service of Filargo he entered directly into the service of the Visconti. He regarded himself as a mediator between the duke and the populace. But between Giangaleazzo's death in 1402 and Filippo Maria's ascension to power in 1412, Milanese territory was under the control of various condottieri. One of these, Facino Cane, a cruel and tyrannical man,[17] had him thrown into prison (1411–12), sick and far from his children who took refuge in Genoa. When Filippo Maria Visconti took power, Uberto was released, entered his service, and remained with him until his death in 1427.

If the ambassadorship to Prague was the major event of his public career, his meeting with Manuel Chrysoloras in Pavia was the most important event in his intellectual life. Chrysoloras was in Lombardy for three years (1400–1403) and spent some of that time in Pavia. He had been sent primarily on a political mission by Emperor Manuel Palaeologus to solicit help against Turkish pressure. Although he was unsuccessful in this respect, he did succeed in establishing a small group of Greek enthusiasts in Milan: Uberto and his sons Angelo and Pier Candido, and Antonio Loschi. The fact that it was the first incursion of Greek studies into Lombardy indicates that the study of Greek was not at that time connected with the university.

While Chrysoloras was in Lombardy, he and Decembrio collaborated in translating Plato's *Republic,* an effort that was not entirely successful—Bruni passed a harsh judgment upon it. Pier Candido later wrote that Chrysoloras did not possess any grace in the Latin language, and that Uberto, though he attempted to revise the translation stylistically, was distracted by the adversities of the time, not the least of which was his own imprisonment. Despite the harsh judgment of the more refined Florentines, the translation of Plato's political work was an important event in Milanese humanism. The idea of a state ruled by reason and guided by philosophers or in which the king himself was a philosopher, made its way rapidly in Italian and wider European circles. The Chrysoloras–Decembrio translation circulated widely and even penetrated beyond the Alps. As a direct heir, Pier Candido took up the revision of this translation for Humphrey, Duke of Gloucester.[18]

After his unfortunate period of imprisonment, Decembrio turned to the study of moral philosophy, composing *De modestia* for his first-born Modesto and then *De candore* for Pier Candido. He also wrote a dialogue in two books, *Moralis philosophiae dyalogus*. But his most important work was his *De republica* in four books, dedicated to Filippo Maria Visconti, each book preceded by a prologue. The interlocutors are, in addition to Decembrio himself, Leon and Simone Moriggia, Manfredo della Croce, abbot of S. Ambrogio and a close friend of Giovanni Maria Visconti, an orator at the Council of Constance. The dialogues are rich in historical allusions and personal reminiscences. They recall the splendor of Milan in classical times when the arts flourished and rhetoricians, philosophers, and poets crowded the city—he mentions Vergil of Mantua, Catullus of Verona, Ovid, and in later times Ambrose and Augustine. Then followed the crash, silence, and exile of the liberal arts and the triumph of material activity, until, finally, the Visconti restored letters as protectors of the *studium* and the library of Pavia. (Later, in his preface to his revised translation of the *Republic*, Pier Candido also recalls the flourishing of letters and virtue during the reign of Giangaleazzo.) The work seems to view the history of Milan as an oscillation between order and anarchy. The prose of the moralist is permeated with a sense of the fragility of human fortune.

Although inferior to Salutati and to his friend Loschi in his learning, Uberto perhaps gave a more solid gift to the culture of his time in his rough but important attempt to make Plato's politics known. His heritage lived in his sons, Pier Candido—who worked in Milan under the Visconti and later also under the Sforza—and Angelo—who taught in Guarino's school in Ferrara. But his influence was important also in his "colloquies," in which he proclaimed with sincere passion the triumph of the new culture.

✳   ✳   ✳

Paul O. Kristeller regards Pier Candido Decembrio as "probably the most important representative of humanism in Milan during the first half of the fifteenth century."[19] Pier Candido's long career as a literary figure intertwined with his political activities. He knew the principal men of culture of his time—his letters reveal that Valla and Poggio were his friends, Panormita and especially Filelfo his enemies, and his relations with Guarino and Bruni uneven.[20] He was also well acquainted with most of the regions of Italy and Europe, inasmuch as he was sent on many missions by Filippo Maria Visconti. His most original work is related to his political activity, his *Biography of Filippo Maria*, acclaimed by Burckhardt, interesting because it draws on the experience and observations accumulated over a quarter-century. Less significant, but also related to politics, is his eulogy of Milan in response to Bruni's praise of Florence.[21] His other works do not generally reveal such a connection but they do reveal versatility: Latin poems, one oration, a number of historical works, a grammatical treatise, several works of interest to historians of science, and several theoretical treatises—an early work *De septem liberalium artium inventoribus*, and later moral, religious, or philosophical treatises: *De origine fidei, De vitae ignorantia,* and *De immortalitate*.[22] Decembrio also composed a number of works in the Lombard vernacular, including a life of Petrarch.[23]

Of equal significance to his own literary activity was his work as a translator. He translated a number of works from Latin into Italian, the most important of which were the historical works of Caesar and of Curtius (in conformity, perhaps, with the tastes of the Viscontean court). He also translated parts of a number of Greek writers into Latin (Appian, Diodorus Siculus, Homer's *Iliad*, Plutarch, Plato), of which his translation of Plato's *Republic* was the most important. This work, together with his biography of Filippo Maria, constitutes his most important contribution as a humanist to his culture.

His letters reveal that he desired to take on again the work his father had undertaken in order to succeed where his father had fallen short. It was not perfect, however, and it was almost immediately rendered in another version by the Sicilian Cassarino (whether at the instigation of Panormita is not known, though Decembrio thought so). Its importance consists in the fact that he resumed the work after reading Aristotle; he wanted to confront Plato's conception of justice with Aristotle's. Completed in 1441, the translation received mixed reviews. Archbishop Francesco Pizolpasso wrote that in dedicating the work to the duke of Gloucester (to whom Pizolpasso had introduced him) Decembrio had fulfilled a promise Bruni had failed to fulfill, a comment that annoyed Bruni. Others said that Decembrio did not translate directly from the Greek but rather sought to clean up the version completed by Chrysoloras and his father Uberto. Pier Candido himself said that he had labored not for the moment but for humanity in every age; he had attempted to render not only what Plato said but what he felt. And Gloucester was pleased with the work, declaring that he was happy to live in a time in which, through the learned Italians, a wisdom worthy of men was being restored at last to the world.

When Filippo Maria died, Pier Candido worked for the Ambrosian Republic (1447–50), even adding to the end of his biography of Filippo

Maria an exaltation of liberty recovered. With the advent of Francesco Sforza, however, he left the city for the papal court, where Nicholas V (1447–55) summoned him to the post of *magister brevium* and to the task of translating Greek works into Latin. The next six years were perhaps the happiest of his life. When Nicholas died in 1455, Decembrio went to Naples, where he served Alfonso until the latter's death in 1458; thence to Ferrara and finally, in 1460, back to Milan, to which he had returned at least twice in the interim on diplomatic assignments. The next six years in Milan were among his most miserable, though it was during this period that he wrote his life of Francesco Sforza and other biographies in order to make a living. In 1466 he returned to Ferrara, where he remained until 1474, summoned home during the latter year by Galeazzo Maria Sforza who accused him of speaking ill of the Sforzas. He returned to defend himelf and died in Milan in 1477.

*   *   *

Cappelli, Loschi, and the two Decembrios were tied to the Milanese chancery. The other center of humanist studies was the university, though this developed only slowly after the turn of the century. The first significant teacher of rhetoric at Pavia was Giovanni Travesi.[24] Loschi probably attended his school. So also, at the same time, did Gasparino Barzizza of Bergamo (1360–1430), the future champion of Ciceronianism, who studied closely with Travesi between 1387 and 1392 and on 13 July of the latter year received his arts degree in grammar and rhetoric with Travesi as his sponsor. (In 1413 at Padua he received his doctor of arts degree.)[25] From Travesi Barzizza inherited the intense attention to specific texts. Though not deaf to the Petrarchan heritage, Travesi was tied to the scholastic tradition, as his commentary on Boethius illustrates. In addition to Travesi, Barzizza was thoroughly familiar with the humanist circles of the Visconti court. He knew Loschi and the other humanists well and read the works of Petrarch. His particular contribution to humanism was to unite textual analysis to the newer humanist interest in the classics and their application to the problems of contemporary life.

He was not, however, immediately able to develop his talents in Milan and Pavia. Although he probably worked at the Visconti court between 1384 and 1392 and again between 1400 and 1403, and taught for two years at Pavia, 1404–6, the recall of Travesi to the post Barzizza held during the latter year forced him to seek employment elsewhere.[26] From March until September 1407 he lived in the Barbaro home in Venice, initiating the Latin studies of Francesco Barbaro. Then he was called to a teaching post in Padua, where he spent fourteen uninterrupted years,

1407 to 1421. He wrote nothing that survives prior to 1407; everything he subsequently produced was the outcome of his teaching program at Padua. His was one of the earliest humanist schools, and his activity as educator influenced the more famous schools of his friends Guarino of Verona and Vittorino da Feltre. Among his students were Leon Battista Alberti and Francesco Filelfo.[27]

In 1421 he was called to Milan by Filippo Maria Visconti, by which time he was a renowned educator. The specific occasion of Barzizza's recall to Milan was the discovery by Gerardo Landriani, bishop of Lodi, of an important manuscript collection of Cicero's rhetorical works. Among these were some that until then were unknown, such as the *Brutus,* and others known only in part, such as *On the Orator* and *Orator.*[28] Landriani was unable to decipher the codex and asked Barzizza to do so and to have a fair copy made for him. Cosimo Raimondi of Cremona, a student of Barzizza's, made copies under his supervision.[29] Guarino sent one of his pupils to obtain copies of these texts in 1422, at the same time writing to Barzizza that he would take first place in promoting Ciceronian studies in Italy as a result of this discovery. Flavio Biondo came to Milan during the same year and transcribed the *Brutus* to send to Guarino and to Leonardo Giustiniani in Venice.[30]

The find at Lodi was one of the most exciting discoveries of the humanists, and it led to a manuscript mania in Milan.[31] Between 1420 and 1430 there was great fervor in seeking out and studying ancient writers. Landriani discovered another codex in 1422, and when Flavio Biondo came to transcribe the *Brutus* he discovered the *Caesares* of Aurelius Victor. Additional texts were discovered by Pier Candido Decembrio and Giovanni Lamola[32] in 1426 and 1427. The duke, though he preferred reading stories and poetry in the vernacular (or French romances), looked favorably upon this more advanced culture, which also brought fame to his city.

From his many epistles and orations, one sees that Barzizza was an outstanding representative of this new classical culture. He studied Quintilian as well as Cicero and Seneca, placing the moral thought of the latter two on a par with that of Aristotle. He recognized the value of Aristotle's *Rhetoric,* part of his argument being that every discipline should be given equal weight in the curriculum (an implicit criticism of the priority heretofore given to logic). He annotated Dante and gave his annotated copy to Guiniforte. But his principal writings are related to his activities as teacher. Three in fact were written explicitly for his students. *The Vocabularium breve* (1417–18) contains an etymology of many Latin words divided into categories according to meaning. It was later often printed, first in Venice in 1509. *Orthographia* was written in two redactions, the first in Padua about 1417, the second after the discovery of the Lodi manuscript in 1421. It is divided into four parts, the first two dealing with the general order of sentences and with the spelling of Greek words (making use of Chrysoloras's *Erotemata* in Guarino's Latin translation), and containing an inventory of Latin words. These two parts are best represented in the manuscript tradition and were the only ones later printed. The other two parts dealt with Latin pronunciation and punctuation. For his son Guiniforte he wrote *De compositione*[33] about 1420, illustrating principles of rhetoric and style and drawing especially on Cicero and Quintilian. His work moves in the same direction as the later *Rhetoric* of George of Trebizond and the *Elegances* of Lorenzo Valla.

When Gasparino died in 1431 his son Guiniforte (1406–1463)[34] petitioned for his chair, unsuccessfully for the moment, since the position went to Antonio da Rho, who held it only briefly. Guiniforte had a very promising beginning. Perhaps by 1416, certainly by 1419, he had been introduced to Greek studies by Guarino. He received his arts degree in Pavia in 1422, studied law there, and in 1425—when still only nineteen—received a professorship in moral philosophy at the University of Pavia. After his father's death he taught briefly in Novara (lecturing on Terence and on Cicero's *On Duties*), worked for a year in the service of Alfonso of Aragon, then returned to Milan, where he succeeded his father from 1435 to 1441. His inaugural lectures were on the letters of Seneca and the rhetoric of Cicero. During this period he wrote a commentary in the vernacular on Dante's *Inferno* (1440), perhaps making use of the notes his father had given him. After 1441 Guiniforte served as secretary to Filippo Maria Visconti until the latter's death in 1447. In this capacity he was sent on several missions—to Alfonso, and to popes Eugenius IV and Nicholas V. After the death of Filippo Maria he went to Ferrara, where he lived until he was recalled to Milan by Francesco Sforza in 1455 to tutor his son Gian Francesco. Early in 1457 we find him actually serving in this capacity. He composed his *De liberis educandis* for his young pupils, actually a summary of pseudo-Plutarch's essay on education.

Despite his precocious beginning and the high hopes his father and others placed in him, his accomplishments as a humanist were not great. In part this was due to the double duty he did as teacher and courtier. In addition to the works mentioned, he wrote a number of orations and letters (many unpublished) and a defense of marriage (to which Giovanni Pontano responded with a defense of free love). Guiniforte's career illustrates the intimate connection of the life of the humanist with the politics of the Milanese court and, specifically, the disruption suffered by many during the period of transition from the Visconti to the Sforza regimes.

✼ ✼ ✼

The high moment in Lombard humanist culture occurred during the brief period in which Antonio Beccadelli, called Panormita (1394–1471)[35] and Lorenzo Valla (1407–1457)[36] lived and worked between Milan and Pavia, surrounded by a host of lesser figures, both friends and enemies.

Panormita became immediately well known in humanist circles throughout Italy when he published his *Hermaphroditus* (1425), a collection of Latin epigrams inspired by the *Priapea* and Martial, by Horace, Plautus (whom he subsequently studied in close detail), and Catullus; the title plays on the multiplicity of amorous situations, and the poems are questionable in their morals and sexually explicit. The humanists reacted to it immediately. Loschi wrote that he found it "most delightful." Poggio stated that although he found the book enjoyable and full of pleasure, nevertheless, Christians should not forget that things are permitted to pagans that are not permitted to poets who know God, and suggests that Panormita turn to more serious things. If Vergil wrote some *Priapea* in his youth, Panormita should not forget that in his older age he was more serious, as also was Terence.[37] In defense of his work, Panormita said that he did not judge the lives of the poets by their writings, that poets often play with words that do not correspond to their way of life. In fact, however, Panormita's style of life mirrored his poetry very closely! He was a lover of youth, both male and female. He was a lover also of learning, but of its rebellious rather than formal side—he praised and respected his teacher Gasparino Barzizza, but he spent his time with the young Valla. And while in personal life he was given to love, in professional life he was given to polemics. It was perhaps for all these reasons that Panormita was called to Milan in 1429 as both court poet and professor at the Pavian *studium*. Until he departed for southern Italy in 1434 he remained the favorite of Filippo Maria, a poet who gave luster to the court simply by his presence there (he was crowned poet by Emperor Sigismund in 1432); and in this capacity he lived in luxury in Pavia, at least until his last year at the university.

He was, indeed, much like the duke, whom he characterized (in his *Gallicae*, a rich picture of the cultural ambience in the Milanese court) as one who did not love knowledge but supported it because it was fashionable and allowed it to influence him. Panormita also allowed learning to influence him, but he experienced no inner conflict between the pleasant life he preferred and the life of learning. When he was accused of wasting his youth and his talents, he responded to his critic (in this case

Francesco Barbavara, 1432) in a way that underlined the criticism, point-ing out that he had begun a commentary on Plautus which he had not completed, as well as two political discourses and other letters, commen-taries, and orations. The text of Plautus he had received from Guarino, and he took it with him, together with Guarino's nephew, Ludovico Fer-rari, when he left Pavia for Genoa and Naples in 1434. On both counts Guarino was much distressed! He did, however, compose his *Poematum et prosarum liber* while teaching at Pavia; it is the first and perhaps only humanist anthology of different kinds of prose and verse. Prose letters in it deal with universal themes—love, sadness, friendship, melancholy, the sweetness of solitude. The anthology includes examples of elegy, polemic, apology, and oratory.

Panormita did not carry all with him in Milan and Pavia. Maffeo Vegio (1407–1458)[38] also frequented the Pavian *studium*. His flight from the plague to the Villa Pompeiana in 1423 inspired his *Pompeiana*. His *Supplementum* to the *Aeneid* drew the praise of Catone Sacco (and an accusation of plagiarism from Decembrio). He was a friend to all the learned and the great who lived and studied in the city, among whom he represented the mild, chaste voice of an Augustinian humanism. For him there was a harmonious bond between the Latin poets and the Christian fathers. His treatise *On the Education of Children,* so full of autobio-graphical references, expresses faith in the capacity of children to be ex-cited by learning when their teachers do not humiliate them and views education as a social enterprise forging the bonds of society and inspiring us to love our neighbors.[39] Although Vegio knew Panormita, he always remained aloof from him.

Others, however, were deeply hurt by Panormita. Francesco Barba-vara and Antonio Cremona, both secretaries in the Viscontean chancery, are good examples. From 1425 Barbavara enjoyed great prestige with the duke, who entrusted him with many important assignments. In 1429 he was created a notary, and though not himself a humanist writer or scholar, belonged to the circle of humanists and was one of their chief supporters at the court. Many of them called him a "Maecenas," and Panormita seemed especially indebted to him, describing him variously as "a divine man," "an immortal man," "a most holy man." In 1432 he suddenly lost favor with the duke, perhaps in connection with the polem-ics involving Panormita and Antonio da Rho. He was sent for a time as consul to Savona but shortly thereafter returned to the good graces of the duke, who sent him on subsequent missions, most notably to the Council of Basel.[40]

Antonio Cremona belonged to the humanist circle encouraged by Barbavara and even followed him into exile, describing him in a letter to

Francesco Pizolpasso as maintaining a stoic serenity in his disgrace and remaining unchanged in his fidelity to his ruler.[41] Antonio corresponded with a number of well-known humanists: Poggio, Valla, Decembrio, and Bruni.[42] He was a man of arms as well as of letters, a lover of women and of good company. He was naturally drawn to Panormita, with whom he also exchanged many letters. After he left Milan, however, the contact between them virtually ceased; Panormita lamented that several of his letters had had no response. In 1437 Cremona, now a monk, wrote to Antonio Pessina, also a friend of Panormita's who had belonged to the same circle, that he had found peace at last in the purity of nature and in poverty.

In other cases Panormita entered into polemical relations with former associates. Antonio da Rho (1398–1450/1453), a Franciscan who achieved the title "master of theology" in 1425, was also trained in and devoted to humanist studies.[43] He was appointed by the duke in 1431 to succeed Gasparino Barzizza and in his capacity as teacher produced his *De imitatione* (1430–34) as a reference book on eloquence. He listed synonyms and dealt with literary matters and with history of every kind, offering in each case many examples as illustrations. His orientation was Ciceronian, including the avoidance of rare terms. Valla, later in his *Adnotationes in errores Antonii Raudensis* (1442), accused him of plagiarizing materials written by himself in Milan and later used in his *Elegances of the Latin Language*. The polemic with Valla arose subsequent to his stay in Milan, but he carried on a continuous polemic with Panormita while there. Like Panormita he was a poet, and despite the fact that he was also a priest, he wrote lascivious verses rivaling the *Hermaphroditus*. An *Apology* written in 1430 against his detractors reveals a knowledge of many of the same Latin poets who inspired Panormita— Plautus, Catullus, Tibullus, Propertius, and Martial. Not only did he defend his own poetry, but he attacked Panormita, allying himself with Panormita's humanist rival, Pier Candido Decembrio. The attacks were anonymous, which doubly annoyed Panormita, who threatened to make Antonio feel the force of "Sicily the mother of poets."

In the midst of the tumult that began to increase around him, Panormita for a time in 1433 replaced Valla in the Pavian chair of rhetoric (though his stipend was much reduced). By then he had decided to leave, and in the winter of 1434 he departed for the milder climate of the court of Alfonso of Aragon.

*   *   *

Lorenzo Valla was the actual successor of Barzizza in the chair of rhetoric. He came to Pavia at the end of 1431 and began his course there, continuing through the following year. Panormita himself attended Valla's classes, even though fifteen years his elder, and, according to Valla, not only learned much from him but was also grateful to him, at least until the break between the two, brought on, Valla says, by the success of his book on the true good.[44] In his first redaction of *De voluptate* Valla included Panormita among the interlocutors, but after their break he replaced him in subsequent redactions with Vegio, and included as well a number of others from the Milanese-Pavian circle of humanists: Antonio da Rho (who became the Christian interlocutor), Pier Candido Decembrio, and Catone Sacco.[45]

There are pages in the *De voluptate,* even in its subsequent redactions, that mirror the pleasurable life characteristic of this circle of learned men. For example, in his defense of Epicurus, he maintains the superiority of prostitutes over virgins and of the laws of Plato over the laws of Augustus regarding adultery. (One must keep in mind in this connection that Plato's *Republic* circulated freely in the Pavia-Milan circle in Decembrio's translation.) In his attempt to restore the natural world, he emphasizes the sensual life, carnal love, beautiful women— wives, lovers, prostitutes—as well as the need for a city less tormented, more reasonable, more natural, without war; in sum, more human. As Decembrio writes to Cremona, it is not the pleasure of Panormita, but the natural and human pleasure of Lorenzo. Perhaps there is also in this dialogue, albeit unconsciously, a dream of a world in which the wise and learned govern the state, an ideal characteristic of so many of the humanists.[46]

But pleasure was not Valla's only concern in Pavia. He also prepared lectures that constituted the earliest formulations of the materials later to be organized in the *Elegances of the Latin Language.* More related to his immediate future, however, was an attack on Bartolo's *De insigniis et armis,* a work, Valla said, that the jurists regarded as more eloquent than Cicero, though it was filled with nothing but empty words. Valla wrote to his friend, the jurist Catone Sacco, demonstrating the inferiority of Bartolo to the jurists of antiquity. This attack, despite the generous support given him by Catone, caused such a violent reaction within the law faculty that—as Bartolomeo Facio, then in Milan, wrote about the matter—Valla was saved by Panormita, who allowed him to take refuge in his home. In March 1433 Valla left Pavia for Milan and was officially replaced by Panormita and another of his former students, Antonio da Asti.

Valla taught in Milan for a time; there he met Facio, had some contact with Raudensis, but above all met Ciriaco d'Ancona, with whom he discussed biblical codices and even borrowed some from him.[47] Thus Valla's later *Collationes* were also born in Lombardy.

But Panormita and Antonio da Asti were poor substitutes for Valla; and students in Pavia were grieved to lose so learned a teacher. With Valla's departure, the heroic age of Pavian humanism was over. In 1436 Vegio also left, decrying the bacchanalian behavior of the students and their impiety even in church. The real successor of Valla and Panormita in Milan was Francesco Filelfo, though he did not arrive until 1439.

* * *

Francesco Filelfo (1398–1481) was the center of the cultural life of Milan for many years. Born in Tolentino, he studied law, philosophy, and rhetoric (the latter under Gasparino Barzizza) at Pavia from 1416. In 1421 he traveled to Constantinople where he studied Greek for six years, learning it well enough to compose verse in the language. He married while there Theodora Chrysoloras, daughter of his teacher John Chrysoloras and a blood relation of the emperor. Upon his return, he taught briefly in Bologna, then in 1429 was invited to the Florentine *studium*. There he remained for five years expounding among the Latins Livy, Cicero, and Terence, and among the Greeks Homer, Thucydides, and Xenophon. He also lectured on Dante. But enmity developed between Filelfo and two Florentines who attended his lectures, Niccolò Niccoli and Carlo Marsuppini. When the latter was temporarily chosen to succeed Filelfo in 1431 the enmity became irreconcilable. In 1433 he sided with the Albizzi faction against the Medici (with whom his humanist rivals were friendly), and in 1434 when Cosimo de' Medici returned Filelfo left for Siena, where he remained for four years and wrote his *Commentationes Florentinae de exilio* against the Medici.[48] Finally in 1439 he was called to Milan. Until the end of the Visconti regime and subsequently during the reign of Francesco Sforza, Filelfo was the leading intellectual in the city.

Apart from his own letters, judgments about Filelfo's character have depended on the letters of Ambrogio Traversari and the invectives of Poggio Bracciolini, two Florentine contemporaries, both friends of Niccolò Niccoli who defended the latter against Filelfo. Modern scholars have by and large followed the characterization of Filelfo as a groveling courtier, avaricious, lacking in moderation, and capable of vilifying or befriending the same person (e.g., Cosimo de' Medici) as the occasion demanded. Eugenio Garin, for example, labors all the negative personal qualities of Filelfo's character, perhaps reflecting the Florentine judgment of Filelfo's contemporaries.[49] Recently an attempt has been made for the first time to redress the balance, to investigate the specific charges and their accompanying circumstances, in relation to Filelfo's Florentine years (1429–34). The charges against him have been shown to be largely fabricated. Presumably the same writer will continue her work and complete a full-length study of Filelfo's life and character, which has not been done since Carlo de' Rosmini published his study in 1808.[50] Whatever the ultimate judgment about Filelfo's character, his dominant position in the cultural life of Milan over a period of almost forty years through his teaching, writings, and the collection of a treasured library is uncontested.

Filelfo not only knew in Milan, and was respected by, all the learned and powerful, but his relations extended beyond the city to all the famous in Italy and beyond Italy to Hungary and Turkey. He brought learned Greeks to Milan, developed a school around himself, collected codices, and created a library. He taught many who became editors of texts, including most of the leading scholars of his day. His curiosity and industry led to many editions of classical writers, which grew out of his teaching. Thus his importance to his culture was very great.

*   *   *

When Filippo Maria died suddenly in 1447, Filelfo, like many other humanists in Milan, was for a time disoriented. He enclosed himself with his books, not knowing which way to turn. Filippo Maria had only one child, an illegitimate daughter, Bianca Maria, whom he married to the condottiere Francesco Sforza in 1443. But he never made provision for his successor—some said because he hoped that chaos would prevail after he died. The citizens of Milan proclaimed the Ambrosian Republic, a political experiment that lasted for three years. Filelfo wanted to leave the city during this period, but the republican government denied him permission. Struggles among the local nobility, usual in Milanese politics, failed to establish order but instead increased political chaos, to the point where people were ready to welcome Francesco Sforza as the new duke in 1450.[51] Filelfo was there to give the welcoming oration.

Francesco Sforza (1450–66) was a warrior—the most successful condottiere in Quattrocento Italy—who learned to become a statesman. He ruled wisely and carefully. His successors were more devious and extravagant. He was succeeded by his son Giangaleazzo Sforza (1466–76), who lived in great luxury and created sufficient offense to be assassinated through a conspiracy of three men, one of them the poet Girolamo Olgiati, in December 1476. Upon his death he left a young son, who was proclaimed duke and for whom Cicco Simonetta, the powerful secretary of both Francesco and Giangaleazzo, ruled. Simonetta, as a foreigner distrusted by the local nobility (he was from Sicily), depended on the support of Giangaleazzo's widow, Bona, who controlled Milan through her young son. Lodovico Il Moro Sforza, another of Francesco's sons (and the first born after Francesco became duke), who was in France at the time of Giangaleazzo's murder, returned determined to take power. He succeeded in 1479 when, on 7 September, he was reconciled with Bona, sealing Simonetta's fate. Lodovico assumed the reins of power with his young nephew and had Simonetta sent to prison and later beheaded. Cicco's brother, Giovanni, was also sent to prison but was subsequently spared because he had written *Commentaries* honoring Francesco Sforza; in fact Lodovico had these published between 1481 and 1483, probably in order to help legitimate his own reign as a direct descendant of Francesco.[52] Lodovico effectively held the reins of power in his own hands after 1480, and when the young duke died in 1494 he received also the title of duke of Milan from Emperor Maximilian—the first Sforza duke legitimated by imperial decree.[53] His rule ended in 1500 when he was taken prisoner by the French; he languished in a French prison for eight years until he died in 1508.

Francesco and Lodovico were the best of the Sforza rulers; both were men of great talent. It was under Francesco that many artistic and humanistic projects were initiated and under Lodovico that they developed in important ways during the waning years of the century.

*   *   *

As soon as Francesco Sforza assumed power Filelfo began his *Sforziade*—conceived as a new *Iliad*—exalting Sforza rule; he worked on the poem for the remainder of his stay in Milan, over twenty years. It was perhaps the greatest sale of poetry in recorded history; in actuality it was, as he said, history told in verse rather than a true poem.

He was not, however, satisfied with his new lord and patron. He turned to Alfonso of Naples (1443–58) and to Pope Nicholas V, receiving the patronage of both, as well as of Nicholas's successors. For Paul II (1464–71) he translated Xenophon's *Cyropaedia*, a work translated earlier by Poggio, which Filelfo intended to correct; he was rewarded well for it. Between 1458 and 1465 he wrote *De iocis et seriis*, ten books of verse. In 1471 he began a course of lectures on Aristotle's *Politics*. When Paul II was succeeded by Sixtus IV (1471–84) Filelfo turned to him, and in 1475 was appointed to a chair in Rome; he began lectures on Cicero attended by all the high ecclesiastics of the city. In 1476 he decided to transfer his family to Rome, but his third wife died before the move could be made. Finally in 1481 he was reconciled to the Medici and returned to Florence, where he died on 31 July.

✻   ✻   ✻

Even before Filelfo left Milan for the last time in 1475 his pupils had begun to carry forward the classical revival he had put into high gear. Three of them did more to enrich the library of Milan than any other figures.

The first, Gabriel Pavero Fontana (b. 1420) from Piacenza, taught rhetoric and wrote poetry and prose, the latter including grammatical works, commentaries, and editions of classical texts. Like his teacher he knew both Greek and Latin and was not averse to polemics, taking up Filelfo's cause against Giorgio Merula and quarreling with other humanists as well.[54]

The second, Bonaccorso Pisano,[55] established an early friendship with Filelfo, who wrote for him a letter of recommendation to Pavia where he studied Greek in 1456, and then—with another recommendation from Filelfo to Piero de' Medici—he opened a private school at Pisa in 1461. In 1470 Filelfo invited him to Milan; he actually came in 1474–75, at the same time as he published two commentaries, one on Julius Caesar with an index—which became famous—of the places in Caesar's *Gallic War* and the other on Plautian words worthy of being remembered. In Milan he opened a school of rhetoric and untiringly devoted himself to defending classical culture through publications of Latin and Greek texts. In 1475 he prepared for publication a compendium of Valla's *Elegances,* the *De variis loquendi regulis* of Agostino Dati (another student of Filelfo), Ovid's *Metamorphoses* with the commentary by Lactantius Placidus, the *Scriptores historiae Augustae,* and Valerius Maximus (dedicated to Cicco Simonetta, Bonaccorso's sponsor until his fall in 1480). After this great activity in relation to Latin texts he turned his attention primarily to Greek. Before 1478 he published the *Lexicon Graeco-Latinum* of Giovanni Monaco (translated by Crastoni), followed by *Aesop's Fables* in Latin and Greek with a life of Aesop by Maximus Planudes, a Greek–Latin Psalter (dated 1481—the only one of his Greek texts for which the date of publication is actually given), the idylls of Theocritus, Hesiod's *Works and Days,* Greek accents and diphthongs by Sassolo of Prato, and the *Erotemata* of Chalcondylas and Moschopoulos. The only Latin text he edited during these latter years was Cicero's *Epistolae familiares.*

The third, Cola Montano, exercised not a little influence in Milan as both teacher and editor.[56] Between 1469 and 1472 he taught oratory and for his students published a compendium of Priscian's divisions of oratory. But although as a teacher he was popular with his students, he did not receive the protection of Galeazzo Maria Sforza or the support of his colleagues. He was imprisoned and then condemned to exile for some epigrams attributed to him written against Gabriel Pavero, from 1473 teacher of the duke's brother. His republican spirit inspired the rancor of Girolamo Olgiati and his companions, which, despite his condemnation, he did not abandon. His perhaps seditious passions were not shared by his Milanese colleagues, preoccupied as they were with points of grammar; they would not be distracted from their learned work by political intrigues.

⁎   ⁎   ⁎

The publication of Greek texts points to the study of Greek by Lombard humanists. The best of the Greek teachers in Italy from the time of Chrysoloras, John Argyropoulos (1415–1487), was in constant contact with Milan.[57] In 1456 Donato Acciaiuoli wrote about him to Filelfo, who welcomed him most warmly. Filelfo ever afterward spoke of him with great respect, and Galeazzo Maria Sforza continued to receive letters from him. But Argyropoulos soon left the city without teaching there and without exercising any direct influence. Connections were maintained with the Greeks, however. Filelfo sent his son to study in Constantinople and corresponded with learned Greeks continually. Bessarion, Gaza, and others wrote to him, sent him their works, and asked for manuscripts, news, and advice. In January 1458 Demetrius Castrenus came to Milan and after teaching privately for a few months received an official position in October.

A few years later, in 1462, Pier Candido Decembrio put forward the candidacy of Constantinus Lascaris for the chair of Greek. When this happened Castrenus left the city, and Lascaris was appointed in July 1463. He in turn left at the end of 1464 to follow his pupil Ippolita Sforza to Naples when she married Alfonso II. Lodovico Il Moro tried in vain some time later (1488) to bring Lascaris back to Milan. Lascaris wrote his *Epitome* for Ippolita; it was published in Milan in 1476, the first Greek book printed there. In 1480 Bonaccorso Pisano offered, as a pledge of his friendship to Pomponio Leto, a bilingual edition of this compendium, together with other Greek texts and the Latin interpretation of it by the monk Giovanni Crastoni. In 1496 Lascaris wrote that Milan had been a place of disembarkation in his peregrinations and the diffusion of Greek his joy—not surprisingly, for he had seen the downfall of Constantinople and the ruin of its civilization; thus there is an almost missionary zeal in his teaching of Greek. In the introduction to his grammatical writings he provided a brief history of the development of

Greek studies in Italy. He felt that the impulse coming from Florence (Traversari, Guarino, Bruni, Marsuppini, and others) through the teaching of Chrysoloras created a new spring of Hellenic studies in Italy. He praised Argyropoulos, his teacher, Gaza, the author of a grammar in four books, Castrenus, Callistus, and Chalcondylas. The last two were destined to succeed him in teaching Greek in Lombardy. He decided, he said, to compose a more organic grammar, being dissatisfied with current texts. His book had a great success among the Latins.

Andronicus Callistus made a brief visit to Milan between 1475 and 1476. He was a friend of both Filelfo and Pisano, together with whom he purchased for two hundred ducats six manuscripts of Greek and Latin works written by the most learned men. After Andronicus's departure, there was no Greek teacher in Milan for almost fifteen years, though Greek was taught in Pavia by Giorgio Valla (who possessed 151 Greek manuscripts)[58] until he moved to Venice, where he continued to teach it until his death in 1500. Finally, in 1491 Lodovico Il Moro, after having failed to lure Lascaris, obtained the services of Demetrius Chalcondylas from Florence. On 6 November 1491 Chalcondylas opened his course in Milan with an oration in praise of elegant letters. Among his students were Baldassare Castiglione and Gian Giorgio Trissino; among his works were his edition of Isocrates in 1493 and of Suidas's *Lexicon* in 1499.

✳   ✳   ✳

Lodovico Il Moro's rise to power after 1479 coincided with the passing of the old guard of humanist studies. Filelfo left the city in 1475 never to return, and Pier Candido died in 1477. The central figure at the court related to the humanist disciplines was now Giorgio Merula (1430–1497) who, despite poor health, was made professor in Pavia and then at Milan in 1482.[59] A student of Filelfo's, he continued the tradition of Filelfo's circle, emphasizing philological studies; he was editor and student especially of Plautus, Martial, Juvenal, and the *Scriptores rei rusticae*.

Merula remained on the friendliest terms with Ermolao Barbaro the Younger (1453–1493) from the days of his own teaching in Venice. When Barbaro came to Milan as an ambassador in 1488 and 1489 he lived in Merula's home and was in touch with all the learned Lombards. At this time he was interested in astrology and hermeticism on the one side and logic on the other.[60] He professed to be delighted with the subtlety of logic, which he studied in Pavia. In Milan Galeazzo Pontico Facino filled his head with exorcisms and incantations and his house with books on magic.[61] It seemed that these two kinds of interests dominated the Lombard landscape intellectually, notwithstanding the critical philological and editorial work of Merula and his students.

Merula was employed by the duke not primarily to do philological work but rather to write a history of the rulers of Milan, both the Visconti and the Sforza. Decembrio and Simonetta had produced two excellent biographies of Francesco Sforza. But Lodovico wanted a comprehensive history written, doubtless to legitimate the Sforza claim to power. Merula was entrusted with this larger task. He did much work in verifying older sources, finding documentation, and refuting legends. But when he died in 1494 he had only arrived at the year 1339. While Merula was still working on his history, Tristano Calco (before 1455–1515) was entrusted with the same task.[62] Instead of continuing where Merula ended, he went over the same ground again, even finding sources (especially legal) that Merula had overlooked. Both produced recognizably humanist works; as Eric Cochrane elaborates:

> The history of Milan was traced back no further than the date of the foundation of the city established on the authority of Livy. The achievements of the Visconti were dissociated from their ancestry, which in turn was made much more recent. The fabulous size attributed by their sources to the Gothic armies was hidden behind such phrases as 'quidam tradunt.' Epigraphical evidence was used to check the accounts of the chronicles, and bulls and charters were quoted at length to bridge the gaps that the chronicles had left.[63]

In Merula's work the historical periodization is sharply delineated, and the thesis that Matteo Visconti was a pious prince excommunicated by power-hungry popes forcefully sustained. Calco's narrative is precise in detail, quoting documents at great length, and it places the history of Milan in the context of the history of northern Italy. The incompleteness of their accounts, however, left the task of completing the history of Lombardy to a less capable younger man, Bernardino Corio (1459–1513).[64] He was hardly a humanist historian and found himself incapable of dealing with the barbarism that disturbed the tranquility of Milan beginning with the French invasion of 1494. But retreating from history into chronicle in the second half of his work, he was able to bring his account down to the present; it was his work's comprehensiveness that caused it to be recognized and consulted.[65]

The best work in Milan at the end of the century was not in historical but in philological studies. Emblematic of the new emphasis was the discovery on 5 September 1496 of a manuscript at Bobbio that recalled the more heroic earlier age of humanism in Lombardy. It contained, among others, works of Rutilius, Terence, Frontinus, and the hymns of Prudentius. Philological studies were led in the city by Demetrius Chalcondyles and Giorgio Merula. The praise of Poliziano is testimony that their work was of high quality.

Merula combined a sincere love of the classics with a litigious spirit. After a conflict with his old teacher Filelfo, he engaged in one with his old friend Poliziano, which led finally to the intervention of Lodovico himself and Jacopo Antiquario, who told Merula to keep silent. In his *Miscellanea*[66] Poliziano had praised Merula's work on Juvenal and had made use of his philology. He had also criticized it, but with discretion. Merula, however, was extremely irritated by the criticism. Not content with the praise, he accused Poliziano of plagiarism. Poliziano complained to Lodovico about this attack. Merula wrote directly to Poliziano asking him for a copy of his comments. Poliziano responded that he had always respected and praised Merula and that he had never knowingly offended him. But Merula would not be reconciled. One can perhaps understand his polemic against Filelfo, who was himself just as litigious, but this polemic at the close of his life was an unfortunate one, involving as it did not only Poliziano but also Filippo Beroaldo the Elder,[67] the two best philologists of their generation. Merula's polemics were not published at the time of the debate; but if they had been his work would have done greater honor to his adversary than to himself. Merula's critical work has been forgotten, while Poliziano's exercised a great influence on subsequent philologists.[68]

٭ ٭ ٭

Although humanist culture continued under Lodovico, the moving forces of cultural life in his court were popular poetry, feasts and plays, music and songs, machines of various kinds, and works of art. Many celebrated the cultural primacy of Milan, reminiscent of the humanist panegyrics during the earlier decades of the century. The tradition is reflected in the *Treatise on Architecture* (ca. 1460–64) by Antonio Averlino (Filarete), in the first twenty-one books of which he conceived Sforzinda and Zogalia, ideal cities filled with every type of building and organized according to principles of symmetry laid down by Leon Battista Alberti, which became characteristic of Renaissance architecture. He was connected in minor ways with work on the cathedral and the castle (from 1454) and actually began for Francesco Sforza the construction of the Ospedale Maggiore (1456–65), the first hospital with symmetrical cross-shaped wards, though he was replaced in 1465 by Guiniforte Solari after disputes with Francesco Sforza—at which time he also withdrew the dedication to Francesco of his *Treatise* and offered it to Piero de' Medici, simultaneously leaving Milan for Florence.[69]

The poet who celebrated Milan as the Athens of Italy was a transplanted Florentine, Bernardo Bellincioni (1452–1492).[70] Born into a poor Florentine family, his talent was brought to the attention of Lorenzo de' Medici, who became his patron and with whom he exchanged poems. In 1482 he left Florence with Cardinal Francesco Gonzaga and early in 1483 sought, without success, to establish himself in Milan. But by 1485 he was settled in the city, where he spent the remainder of his life. He was an intimate of Lodovico, whom he praised in many poems. In 1488 he was sent on the mission to bring Isabella of Aragon to Milan to marry Giangaleazzo. In 1490 he wrote *La festa del paradiso* on the occasion of her marriage to Duke Giangaleazzo, and established a relationship with her that endured—though this did not prevent him from also writing eulogies to Beatrice d'Este, who married Lodovico in 1491, even though there was intense rivalry at court between the legitimate duke's wife and the wife of the actual ruler of Milan.

The poets who filled Lodovico's court were in effect courtiers whose poetry oscillated between buffoonery designed to make people laugh and verse composed especially for banquets and plays. Of the many court poems the *Libellus de carcere* is expressive of the most sincere feelings. The court found its center of gravity in its banquets and luxury and in the farces associated with them. Luxury and pomp characterize the *Danae* of 1496 by Taccone, author also of *La favola d'Atteone*.[71] *La festa del paradiso* by Bellincione, already mentioned, was performed with mechanical machinery constructed by Leonardo da Vinci.

*   *   *

Milanese humanism produced very little that was memorable in humanist literature, even though important texts like Valla's *On Pleasure* and his *Elegances* had their inception in Milan. But Milan was very important for the propagation and dissemination of humanist culture, through the school of Barzizza and his successors and through the discovery and editing of classical texts, beginning with the famous discovery at Lodi in 1421. Indeed, it was in the editing and publication of classical texts in both Latin and Greek that, later in the century, Milanese humanists made their greatest contributions to humanist culture. Here the position and work of Filelfo was seminal. Less significant but also important was the philological work of Merula and his coworkers and the historical studies of Merula, Calco, and Corio. Milanese humanism suffered from the divided loyalties of the humanists: the requirements of their service at court and their humanist studies. Uberto and Pier Candido Decembrio and Guiniforte Barzizza, especially the latter, are examples of humanists whose accomplishments were less than their promise, in part because of the double duty they did as courtiers and humanist scholars and writers. In both its accomplishments and its limitations, the humanist culture of Milan reveals the universal elements of humanist culture and local variations that bear comparison with the contrasting cultures of the other major city-states of Italy during the Quattrocento.

NOTES

This essay is based primarily on the essays of Eugenio Garin in *Storia di Milano* (Milan, 1955–56), 6.4, "La cultura milanese nella prima metà del XV secolo," 546–608; and 7.4, "L'età Sforzesca dal 1450 al 1500," 540–97; and his more recent "La cultura a Milano alla fine del Quattrocento," in *Milano nell'età di Ludovico Il Moro* (Milan, 1983), 1:21–28. I would like to thank Professor Paul O. Kristeller for a critical reading of both the earlier and the later drafts of this essay.

1. See H. Baron, *The Crisis of the Early Italian Renaissance,* 2 vols. in 1 (Princeton, 2d ed., 1966). See also Chapter 7 above, an examination of the Garin–Baron thesis.

2. See J. Burckhardt, *The Civilization of the Renaissance in Italy,* trans. S. G. C. Middlemore (New York, 1954), pt. 1; and J. A. Symonds, *The Renaissance in Italy,* vol. 1, *The Age of the Despots* (New York, repr. 1960), esp. chap. 3.

3. On Petrarch and the Visconti, see F. Novati, in *F. Petrarca e la Lombardia* (Milan, 1904), 9–84; and V. Rossi, *Scritti di critica letteraria* (Florence, 1930), 2:3–91. See also E. H. Wilkins, *Life of Petrarch* (Chicago, 1961), chaps. 20–24; idem, *Petrarch's Eight Years in Milan* (Cambridge, MA, 1958).

4. See Petrarch's *Testament,* ed. and trans. T. E. Mommsen (Ithaca, NY, 1957), 21–25, text 78–81; and idem, "How a Ruler Ought to Govern His State," trans. B. G. Kohl in *The Earthly Republic: Italian Humanists on Government and Society,* ed. B. G. Kohl and R. G. Witt with E. B. Welles (Philadelphia, 1978), 25–78.

5. Coluccio Salutati, *Epistolario,* ed. F. Novati, 5 vols. (Rome, 1891–1911), 2:166–68, 335–42, 375–80, 386–93 (to Cappelli); 3:327–30 (to Manzini); 2:354–58, 394–99, 3:634–40 (to Loschi).

6. See J. E. Seigel, *Rhetoric and Philosophy in Renaissance Humanism* (Princeton, 1968), 41.

7. See D. M. Bueno De Mesquita, "Cappelli, Pasquino de'," *Dizionario biografico degli italiani* (Rome, 1975), 18:727–30.

8. Salutati, *Epistolario,* 2:337.

9. Ibid., 3:327–30.

10. The tragedy is not extant. See Garin, "La cultura milanese," 6:549, n. 3.

11. See M. L. King, "Goddess and Captive: Antonio Loschi's Poetic Tribute to Maddalena Scrovegni (1389), Study and Text," *Medievalia et humanistica* n.s. 10 (1980): 103–27, bibliography on Loschi, 108, n. 2.

12. G. W. Pigman III, "Barzizza's Studies of Cicero," *Rinascimento* n.s. 21 (1981): 123–63 at 130–31.

13. The work was published together with the *Ecerinis* of Mussato, ed. Felice Osio and Niccolò Villani (Venice, 1636), with the statement that the two tragedies were found together in a manuscript of the works of Mussato.

14. The central part of Salutati's response has been published with an Italian translation by E. Garin in *Prosatori latini del Quattrocento* (Milan, 1952), 8–37.

15. See Salutati, *Epistolario*, 4:474–78, esp. 476–78 for Loschi's response to Salutati's death.

16. F. Novati, "Aneddoti viscontei," *Archivio storico lombardo* 4th ser. 10 (1908): 193–216 at 195. For other sources on Uberto, see Rossi, *Il Quattrocento* (Milan, 1933), 67, n. 23.

17. On him, see D. M. Bueno De Mesquita, "Cane, Facino," *Dizionario biografico degli italiani* (Rome, 1974), 17:791–801.

18. See M. Borsa, "Correspondence of Humphrey Duke of Gloucester and Pier Candido Decembrio," *English Historical Review* 19 (1904): 509–26. See especially the last letter, an oration (525–26) in which Pier Candido comments on the earlier work of his father and Chrysoloras.

19. P. O. Kristeller, "Pier Candido Decembrio and His Unpublished Treatise on the Immortality of the Soul," in his *Studies in Renaissance Thought and Letters*, 2 vols. (Rome, 1956–85), 2:281–300 at 282. For the literature on Decembrio, see the article by R. Sabbadini in *Enciclopedia italiana* 12 (1931): 457. And see especially, M. Borsa, "Pier Candido Decembrio e l'umanesimo in Lombardia," *Archivio storico lombardo* 20 (1893): 5–75, 338–441; F. Gabotto, "L'attività politica di Pier Candido Decembrio," *Giornale ligustico* 20 (1893): 161–99, 241–80; and E. Ditt, "Pier Candido Decembrio, Contributo alla storia dell'umanesimo italiano," *Memorie del Reale Istituto Lombardo di scienze e lettere, Classe di lettere, scienze morali e storiche* 24 (1930): 21–108.

20. Kristeller, *Studies*, 2:283. On his various missions for the Visconti, see Borsa, "Pier Candido Decembrio," 11ff.

21. Decembrio's biography of Filippo Maria, in addition to his life of Francesco Sforza, his life of Ercole d'Este, his eulogy of Niccolò Piccinino, and his eulogy of Milan, have been published in a critical edition: *Opuscula historica*, ed. A. Butti, F. Fossati, and G. Petraglione, in *Rerum italicarum scriptores* 20.1 (Bologna, 1925–58).

22. Kristeller has published a critical edition of *De immortalitate* in his *Studies*, 2:567–84 (appendix 4).

23. The most complete listing of Decembrio's works is V. Zaccaria, "Sulle opere di Pier Candido Decembrio," *Rinascimento* 7 (1956): 13–74; additions and corrections to this list in Kristeller, *Studies*, 2:561–65.

24. On him, see V. Rossi, "Un grammatico cremonese a Pavia nella prima età del Rinascimento," *Bollettino della Società Pavese di storia patria* 1 (1901): 16–46; reprinted in *Scritti di critica letteraria*, 3:19–30.

25. G. Martellotti, "Barzizza, Gasperino," *Dizionario biografico degli italiani* (Rome, 1965), 7:34–39 at 34–35.

26. G. Mainardi, "Il Travesio, Il Barzizza e l'umanesimo pavese," *Bollettino della Società Pavese di storia patria* 52 (1953): 13–25, has shown that Rossi, "Un grammatico cremonese," erred in treating Barzizza's departure as a result of rivalry between him and Travesi; the evidence reveals that the low level of remuneration forced Barzizza to seek support for his family elsewhere.

27. On Barzizza, see now G. Martellotti, "Barzizza, Gasperino"; and R. G. G. Mercer, *The Teaching of Gasparino Barzizza with Special Reference to His Place in Paduan Humanism* (London, 1979), which focuses on his courses during the Paduan years, chaps. 3–8. There is an extensive bibliography of printed sources cited, both primary (156–57) and secondary (157–62) as well as of manuscripts utilized (152–56). See also Pigman, "Barzizza's Studies of Cicero," who is in some respects critical of Mercer; his study includes a critical text of Barzizza's life of Cicero.

28. See Sabbadini, *Storia e critica*, 77–78, 84. The whole text of all three works goes back to the Lodi manuscript.

29. For sources on Raimondi, see Rossi, *Il Quattrocento*, 71, n. 66. Raimondi was also a defender of Epicurus. His *Defensio Epicuri* has been published with an Italian translation by E. Garin in *Filosofi italiani del Quattrocento* (Florence, 1942), 133–49.

30. See R. Fubini, "Biondo, Flavio," *Dizionario biografico degli italiani* (Rome, 1968), 10:536–57, bibliography, 557–59; A. Mazzocco, "Biondo Flavio and the Antiquarian Tradition" (Ph.D. diss., University of California, Berkeley, 1973); and idem, "Decline and Rebirth in Bruni and Biondo," in *Umanesimo a Roma nel Quattrocento*, ed. P. Brezzi and M. Lorch (Rome and New York, 1984), 249–66.

31. See R. Sabbadini, *Le scoperte dei codici latini e greci ne' secoli XIV e XV*, 2 vols. (Florence, 1905–14; rev. ed. by E. Garin, Florence, 1967), 121–50.

32. See R. Sabbadini, "Cronologia documentata della vita di Giovanni Lamola," *Propugnatore* n.s. 3 (1890): 417–36; and idem, "Nuove notizie di Giovanni Lamola," *Giornale storico della letteratura italiana* 31 (1898): 244–45.

33. Critically edited by R. Sonkowsky (Chapel Hill, NC, 1959). His *Epilogus ac summa praeceptorum*, which treats succinctly some of the points developed in *De compositione*, has also been edited by Sonkowsky in *Classical, Medieval and Renaissance Studies in Honor of B. L. Ullman*, ed. C. Henderson, 2 vols. (Rome, 1964), 2:268–76.

34. See G. Martellotti, "Barzizza, Guiniforte," *Dizionario biografico degli italiani* (Rome, 1965), 7:39–40, bibliography, 40–41.

35. See now, G. Resta, "Beccadelli, Antonio," *Dizionario biografico degli italiani* (Rome, 1965), 7:400–405, bibliography, 405–6. His *Liber rerum ges-*

tarum Ferdinandi regis has more recently been edited by Resta (Palermo, 1968).

36. See Chapter 13 below, and the sources cited there.

37. Poggio, *Epistolae*, 2:40, in *Opera omnia*, ed. R. Fubini, 4 vols. (Turin, 1964–69), 1:177–78.

38. See Rossi, *Il Quattrocento*, 283–84, bibliography, 307, notes 2–6.

39. Maffeo Vegio, *De educatione liberorum et eorum claris moribus, libri sex*, bks. 1–3 ed. M. W. Fanning (Washington, DC, 1933); bks. 4–6 ed. A. S. Sullivan (Washington, DC, 1936).

40. N. Raponi, "Barbavara, Francesco," *Dizionario biografico degli italiani* (Rome, 1964), 6:141–42.

41. *Ottanta lettere inedite del Panormita tratte dei codici milanesi*, ed. R. Sabbadini (Catania, 1910), 51ff.

42. Ibid., 46–53.

43. See R. Fubini, "Antonio da Rho," *Dizionario biografico degli italiani* (Rome, 1961), 3:574–77.

44. G. Mancini, *Vita di Lorenzo Valla* (Florence, 1891), 23ff.

45. On the redactions of Valla's *De voluptate*, see M. Lorch, "Introduction," *De vero falsoque bono* (Bari, 1970), xxx–lvii; and idem, *On Pleasure*, trans. A. K. Hieatt and M. Lorch (New York, 1979), 7–46.

46. For a discussion of *De voluptate*, see Chapter 13, below. On the Milanese ambience that produced it, see Lorch's introduction to the English translation of *On Pleasure*, 16–26, esp. 22.

47. Mancini, *Vita di Lorenzo Valla*, 83–84.

48. A selection from his *Commentationes Florentinae de exilio* has been published with an Italian translation by E. Garin, *Prosatori latini del Quattrocento*, 494–517, with a bibliographical note, 491, and additional bibliography, 492.

49. Garin, "L'età Sforzesca," 7:541–61, esp. 545–48.

50. C. de' Rosmini, *Vita di Francesco Filelfo da Tolentino*, 3 vols. (Milan, 1808), containing also many texts and documents in the appendix to vol. 3. But see now D. Robin, "A Reassessment of the Character of Francesco Filelfo (1398–1481)," *Renaissance Quarterly* 36 (1983): 202–24. See also idem, "Unknown Greek Poems of Francesco Filelfo," *Renaissance Quarterly* 37 (1984): 173–206.

51. Still useful on the Sforza is C. M. Ady, *A History of Milan Under the Sforza*, ed. E. Armstrong (London, 1907); see, more recently, C. Santoro, *Gli Sforza* (Milan, 1968); F. Malaguzzi-Valeri, *La corte di Lodovico Il Moro*, 4 vols. (Milan, 1913–23); and *Storia di Milano*, vols. 6 and 7.

52. On the fate of Giovanni Simonetta after Lodovico's reconciliation with his sister-in-law, see Bernardino Corio, *Storia di Milano*, ed. A. M. Guerra (Turin, 1978), 1410–29. On the relation of his *Commentaries* to these events, see G. Ianziti, "The First Edition of Giovanni Simonetta's 'De rebus gestis Francisci Sfortiae commentarii': Questions of Chronology and Interpretation," *Bibliothèque d'humanisme et Renaissance* 44 (1982): 137–47.

53. The imperial diploma was given on 5 September 1494, just prior to the

death of the legal duke, Giangaleazzo, on 27 October. Maximilian gave the diploma to Lodovico because, as he said in the preamble, Lodovico was the first-born son of Francesco Sforza after the latter became duke, and because Maximilian (who possessed the power to bestow the title on whomever he wished, since Milan had reverted to the empire after the death of Filippo Maria Visconti) judged Lodovico "the only person worthy of being raised to this rank." But Maximilian said it was to be kept secret for the present. See Ady, *History of Milan*, 149, 154.

54. See Garin, "L'età Sforzesca," 7:564–65, bibliography, n. 1. The standard biography is F. Gabotto and A. Badini-Confalonieri, *Vita di Giorgio Merula* (Alessandria, 1893).

55. See G. Ballistreri, "Bonaccorso da Pisa," *Dizionario biografico degli italiani* (Rome, 1969), 11:464–65.

56. See Garin, "L'età Sforzesca," 7:566–68, bibliography, 567, n. 1.

57. See G. Cammelli, *I dotti bizantini e le origini dell'umanesimo*, vol. 1, *Manuele Crisolora;* vol. 2, *Giovanni Argiropulo;* vol. 3, *Demetrio Calcondila* (Florence, 1941–54); and D. J. Geanakoplos, *Interaction of the 'Sibling' Byzantine and Western Cultures in the Middle Ages and Italian Renaissance (330–1600)* (New Haven, 1976).

58. D. J. Geanakoplos, *Greek Scholars in Venice* (Cambridge, MA, 1962), 236, 295.

59. See Gabotto and Badini-Confalonieri, *Vita di Giorgio Merula.*

60. See Garin, "L'età Sforzesca," 7:590 and n. 1.

61. Ermolao Barbaro the Younger, *Epistolae, orationes, carmina*, ed. V. Branca (Florence, 1943), 2:14–50.

62. See F. Petrucci, "Calco, Tristano," *Dizionario biografico degli italiani* (Rome, 1973), 16:537–41; and the following note.

63. E. Cochrane, *Historians and Historiography in the Italian Renaissance* (Chicago, 1981), 114–17 at 115.

64. F. Petrucci, "Corio, Bernardino," *Dizionario biografico degli italiani* (Rome, 1983), 29:75–78; and Cochrane, *Historians and Historiography*, 117–18.

65. Cochrane, *Historians and Historiography*, 118.

66. See the discussion of this work in Chapter 28, in these volumes.

67. On him, see M. P. Gilmore, "Beroaldo, Filippo, senior," *Dizionario biografico degli italiani* (Rome, 1967), 9:382–84; and K. Krautter, *Philologische Methode und humanistische Existenz: Filippo Beroaldo und sein Kommentar zum Goldenen Esel des Apuleius* (Munich, 1971).

68. See Garin, "L'età Sforzesca," 7:593–95, and 594, n. 1, for manuscripts and early printed sources of the debate. On the debate, see M. Santoro, "La polemica Poliziano-Merula," *Giornale italiano di filologia* 5 (1952): 212–33. See also Gabotto and Badini-Confalonieri, *Vita di Giorgio Merula*, 318ff.; and A. Perosa, "Documenti di polemiche umanistiche," *Rinascimento* 1 (1950): 178ff.

69. See A. M. Romanini, "Averlino (Averulino), Antonio, detto Filarete," *Dizionario biografico degli italiani* (Rome, 1962), 4:662–67.

70. See R. Scrivano, "Bellincioni, Bernardo," *Dizionario biografico degli italiani* (Rome, 1965), 7:687–89.

71. The latter has been published: *L'Atteone e le rime di Baldassare Taccone,* ed. F. Bariola (Florence, 1888).

11 & HUMANISM IN ROME
John F. D'Amico

ROME HAD A NATURAL ATTRACTION FOR HUMANISTS SEEKING TO recover classical civilization, yet Rome did not become a center for humanism until the middle of the Quattrocento.[1] The relatively slow establishment of humanism in the Eternal City resulted from the political and religious problems that plagued her as the home of the western church's central government. The long absence of the papacy and its bureaucracy—the Curia Romana—in Avignon and the divided loyalties caused by the great western schism prevented the development of a settled atmosphere in which humanists could prosper. This institutional situation was important, since to a great extent the history of humanism in Rome was bound to the fortunes of the papacy and the curia. Nevertheless, throughout the Quattrocento humanists did come to Rome and, once the limits imposed by the city's ecclesiastical rulers had been accepted, they often stayed for long periods and adopted intellectual attitudes and interests that betrayed a distinctively Roman stance. As humanists began to feel increasingly secure in Rome after the papacy's permanent return in the 1440s, they learned how to adapt their interests and talents to the needs of the papacy and the curia. They invented the means by which to integrate their humanist secular concerns—especially their desire to recover the purity of the Latin language—with the ideological presuppositions of a theocratically organized state.

Rome made special demands on any group wishing to find a comfortable home there. It had a special socio-political constitution and old traditions that did not change easily. Accommodation was essential if humanists were to receive the benefits of residence in the city. Roman society centered on a series of courts—the papal court, the curia, as well as other prelatial and secular courts—and the humanism that developed in response to these institutions can be termed "curial humanism," thereby identifying the element of dependence that characterized such a courtly state. In many ways the integration of humanism into Rome's uniquely constituted society and religious ambience, with its official celibacy and theocratic claims, makes it the most spectacular success story in the history of Italian humanism. Until the Sack of Rome in 1527 crippled its supporting society, Roman humanism was a constantly growing and assertive movement.

*   *   *

Major humanists such as Poggio Bracciolini and Leonardo Bruni, as well as less well-known writers and scholars such as Giovanni Aurispa, Bartolomeo della Capra, Antonio Loschi, Cenci dei Rustici, and Jacopo Angeli da Scarperio found a part-time home in Rome and employment in the Curia Romana under a variety of popes during the trying years of the schism. While employment prospects were precarious during the schism, Rome's potential as an employment center for humanists was well understood. No less a figure than Coluccio Salutati advised Leonardo Bruni to seek his fortune in Rome, where his ability to write good Latin won him an attractive post in the curia. The appeal of the curia was so great, in fact, that Salutati feared Rome might displace Florence as the great center for humanist studies.[2] Salutati need not have worried; Rome's attraction in the early Quattrocento to humanists was not lasting. Bruni, like other humanists—especially his fellow Tuscans such as Poggio—never accepted Rome as a permanent home; it was a place to visit for inspiration and to work for financial security but not a place to spend one's life or to house one's family. While this ambivalence became modified over time and with humanist success on a large scale, it remained a factor in humanist life in the Eternal City throughout the Renaissance. Poggio, despite decades of service in Rome and in the curia, never considered Rome his primary home and left it in old age to become the Chancellor of the Republic of Florence, while still holding his curial office.[3]

Romans found nothing extraordinary in the peripatetic characteristics of the humanists. In many ways Rome was a city lacking in a prominent or large native population. Estimates of Rome's population in the early Quattrocento place it as low as fifteen thousand. Even if this number is greatly underestimated, Rome had suffered extensively from the political dislocations of the late Trecento and early Quattrocento, and she had to depend on immigration to provide the personnel needed to staff the curia if she were to recover her former prestige. Immigration had always been a factor in Rome's life and contributed to its cosmopolitan atmosphere.[4] The immigrants who found themselves in Rome were mostly Italians, with the Neapolitans seemingly the largest group. Non-Italians were also numerous, especially Germans and Frenchmen. While the humanists were disproportionately Tuscans, such prominent humanist patrons as Cardinal Bessarion and Johann Goritz were non-Italian.

This diversity required the formation of some unity through a community based on common humanist interests.

The Tuscans were central to the spread and composition of humanism in Rome. They translated to Rome the new concerns for classical civilization as a model for a renewed modern society. But Florence and Rome were very different places. The Florentine Republic was a government of bankers, merchants, and other nonaristocratic professionals struggling to control the city's fortune.[5] The humanists had been successful in convincing the new politically powerful bourgeoisie that an education in classical languages and culture was the proper attribute for a servant of a modern state and of a modern self-made man. Through this new humanist education, the Florentines could equal the feudal aristocracy of northern Europe and southern Italy.

Rome was in many ways the exact opposite of Florence. She was dominated by an ecclesiastical-theocratic court that did not believe that it had to justify its actions to men. (The local nobility, while still strong, was being weakened by the popes throughout the Renaissance and seems not to have had a major influence in directing the city's intellectual life.) Moreover, this courtly society had long-established medieval traditions, which, if not hostile to humanism, certainly did not feel that it required the new educational and cultural movement for fulfillment. Rome's clerical ambience was potentially at odds with the essentially secular concerns of the humanists, but the possibility of conflict was avoided partly because many humanists willingly accepted the clerical state as proper for advancement and security. Such men were in better positions to deal with the religious and ideological demands of the papacy and to emphasize those elements in humanism which most nearly combined their secular values with the religious presuppositions of the papacy.

In attempting to describe the manner in which humanism successfully reconciled possible disagreements and antipathies, integrated itself into Rome's society, and provided a new development in humanism, it is best to begin with the reign of Pope Martin V (1417–31), under whom the papacy returned to Rome and began to rebuild its fallen political power. From Martin's reign till the Sack of Rome humanism steadily grew. It was not, however, a straight line of growth; there were high points and some periods of uncertainty. After Martin there were two basic subdivisions: the reign of Nicholas V (1447–55), which initiated the period of humanist growth with papal support, and the reign of Sixtus IV (1471–84), which marked the maturation of Roman humanism. Overall, the Quattrocento was a period of advancement and consolidation for humanism in Rome.

*   *   *

The attitude of the Renaissance papacy toward humanism was pragmatic. The popes viewed humanism as an aid in reestablishing the papacy's central position in contemporary culture, which had been lost as a result of the schism and the growth of secular government and bourgeois society. For most of the popes patronage of humanism provided a means of displaying their cultural sensitivity, but they expected that the humanists would in turn prove to be loyal servants, performing the required tasks for the clerical hierarchy and curial bureaucracy.[6] With the exception of Paul II's suppression of the Roman academy, the individual popes either supported humanism or remained indifferent to it and allowed their subordinates to act for them. Although papal patronage of artistic programs is generally better known and more appreciated, the patronage extended to humanism both tied the humanists closely to the ecclesiastical hierarchy and gave incentives to humanists to intensify the process of accommodation.

Martin V and Eugenius IV (1431–47) were both too preoccupied with political problems to give their full attention to any other activity.[7] What money they had was used to improve the physical state of the city. Utility was primary in their minds. Still, during their pontificates humanism continued to thrive in the curia and individual humanists, such as the historian of ancient Rome and medieval Italy Flavio Biondo (1392–1463), made productive use of their time in the curia. The period of Eugenius's residence in Florence in the 1430s, after his expulsion from the city by republican forces, and the success of the Council of Ferrara–Florence in "uniting" the Orthodox and western Christian churches both helped to make the papacy more cognizant of humanism's mastery of Latin and Greek and its possible uses to the church. Indicative of this recognition was the entrance of the most famous of all native-born Roman humanists, Lorenzo Valla (1407–1457), into the curia under Eugenius.[8]

The election of Nicholas V marked the major advance of humanism in the curia.[9] Before his election Nicholas had been a respected intellectual with close ties to Florence and the Medici. More of a book collector than a creative scholar, he appreciated humanism as a vital element in his projected renewal of the clergy. The humanists' knowledge of Greek appealed to him as the means of making available to western Christians a vast body of Greek material that had been largely inaccessible during the Middle Ages. He employed a variety of humanists as translators of Greek classical and patristic texts, consisting of both new translations and retranslations. These books and other classical and Christian works formed the basis of Nicholas's library, which was placed under the direction of the Tuscan humanist Giovanni Tortelli (ca. 1400–1466).[10]

Nicholas's patronage of humanism made the papacy seem to be an enthusiastic advocate of the new culture in the service of the church and set a model that could be followed by other clerics in justifying their support for humanism. Nicholas's example was not forgotten, even if it was not universally followed.

This active patronage was not continued by Calixtus III (1455–58).[11] A Spaniard by birth and a jurist by training, Calixtus had advanced through faithful service to the Aragonese king of Naples. His Spanish background made him sensitive to the new advances of the Turks after their capture of Constantinople (1453), and he devoted much of his energy to an unrealized crusade against the Turks. Nepotism was another of his activities, and he made his nephew, Rodrigo Borgia, a cardinal. Calixtus neither helped nor hindered humanism.

More was expected of his successor, Pius II (1458–64), Aeneas Silvius Piccolomini.[12] Pius had enjoyed an international reputation as a humanist before his decision to take orders seriously. As pope, however, he did not actively advance humanism. Like his predecessors, he was concerned with a crusade against the Turks. Intent on memorializing his name, Pius spent large sums in building a Renaissance city at Pienza, instead of caring for Rome's physical and intellectual needs. His humanist patronage to a great degree coincided with his nepotism and advancement of fellow Sienese.

Paul II (1464–71)[13] was a product of the nepotistic system of the Renaissance papacy. He owed his position in the church hierarchy to his uncle Eugenius IV. Paul's relationship to humanism presents a major problem because of his suppression of the Roman academy (which will be discussed in detail below). Paul was by temperament ill-disposed toward humanist literary and historical interests. Though an avid collector of ancient gems and interested in ancient art (he died unexpectedly while discussing the relocation of an obelisk near the Vatican), he was less appreciative of ancient literature, which he judged in many cases immoral. But this indifference or even antipathy would not have mattered had not bureaucratic and political issues moved Paul to active hostility. His famous suppression remains critically important to any evaluation of humanism in Rome. Here it is necessary to realize that Paul's actions against the Roman academy resulted from his personality and from those of the other actors in the drama, and that humanism suffered no serious reversal as a result of the pope's actions.

In Sixtus IV[14] humanism found a new patron who had an old-fashioned scholastic theological education. While untouched by humanist educational ideals, Sixtus proved to be especially open to humanism as an element in the life of his court. This receptivity did not require either his active seeking out of humanists or his appreciation of what they did, but rather his realization that papal patronage of humanism was an aspect of modern government and proof of a ruler's cultural sensitivity. Sixtus understood that he could capitalize on literary and scholarly patronage to advance the prestige of the papacy in its dealings with secular courts and to attract nonclerical attention and respect. Like Nicholas V, Sixtus made a major contribution to scholarship by reorganizing the Vatican Library and opening it to broader use. Equally important for the history of Roman humanism, Sixtus offered a model for artistic and literary support that inspired his nephew, Julius II.

The next three popes may be treated summarily. Innocent VIII (1484–92)[15] was a weak individual who left little imprint on events. Intellectually the most famous event of his reign was the aborted debate announced by Giovanni Pico della Mirandola to discuss nine hundred theses with any scholar, and the pope's condemnation of thirteen of these propositions; by and large the Roman humanists sympathized with Pico but did not approve of his hubris.[16] Alexander VI (1492–1503),[17] like his uncle Calixtus, was more interested in nepotism than humanism, although he and his family did employ some humanists in sensitive posts;[18] essentially Alexander did not involve himself in cultivating intellectual pursuits. Pius III (1503),[19] the nephew of Pius II, might have been a great humanist pope had he reigned more than a month. He had been a major advocate of humanism while a cardinal and had done much to integrate humanist culture into the curial and ecclesiastical establishment.

Julius II (1503–12)[20] was probably the strongest personality to sit on the papal throne during the Renaissance and one of the dominant characters of the Renaissance period. His policies increased the political power and prestige of the papacy and permitted Roman society to become the most dynamic of its day. Eminently egotistical, he wished to memorialize his name and fame through artistic and literary patronage. While his artistic support has received the bulk of scholarly attention, Julius understood that a government required a large body of literary men and scholars if it were to be perceived as a central element in contemporary life. Indeed, it well may be said that Roman humanism reached its apex under Julius, when humanists easily moved into and within the bureaucracy and the ecclesiastical structure and when their presence was accepted as natural and desirable.

Leo X (1513–21),[21] the son of Lorenzo "il Magnifico" de' Medici, seemed to many to represent humanism itself ascending the papal throne. This view was a misperception. Although he was humanistically educated by such men as Angelo Poliziano and was a true devotee of humanist culture, he expended most of his energy in advancing his family's fortunes. He patronized a large number of humanists, but often his support fell to men of mediocre talent. The large amount of money spent on useless wars and the increasingly aggressive posture of Martin Luther and his supporters in Germany marked Leo's pontificate as a turning point; humanism in Rome had reached its highest level and now began its descent. Leo was unable and unwilling to fulfill the high expectations generated at the time of his election.

Adrian VI (1522–23)[22] seemed to justify the worst fears of the Roman humanists and bureaucrats and to confirm the sense of decline. Adrian was foreign to Rome's Renaissance culture. Having been educated in scholastic philosophy and theology and having served as regent for Charles I in Spain, he naturally directed his attention away from Rome to the problems facing the church in northern Europe. His careful management of money and his poor choice of some subordinates alienated him from a society that required and expected papal largess. The hostility directed against Adrian really was in no way warranted by his actions. The succession of Clement VII (1523–34),[23] Leo X's cousin, to the papal throne was met with great expectations by all curialists, but Clement followed his relative's disastrous foreign policy, which led to the Sack of Rome.[24] He failed to initiate any major revitalization of Roman society and merely watched helplessly as Rome's intellectual dominance passed away. With the Sack the society that had supported Rome's culture ceased to exist and its humanism became vestigial.

*   *   *

The popes provided the essential background to humanism in Rome, but they did not affect the fortunes of every man directly. There existed individuals and institutions that could act as patrons to humanism even when a pope was indifferent to it. Certainly the most important of these institutions was the Curia Romana, the largest and most advanced bureaucracy of its day.[25] This bureaucracy required a large number of literate men to staff its various offices. Since all its work was done in Latin until the end of the Quattrocento, the expertise in that language the humanists could provide made them the ideal applicants to staff many offices. The curia was anxious to present its linguistic experts as proof of its modern qualities. In employing the humanists, it did not give them a free hand but bound them closely to its traditions; yet the humanists were willing to accept these working conditions because they realized that much money and security could be received from service in the curia.

Naturally not all the offices in the curia were equally attractive to the humanists. Those requiring legal qualifications normally fell outside the humanists' abilities and interests. Within the bureaucracy the division that employed the largest number of humanists was the chancery.[26] It produced many of the official bulls by which the curia expressed its decisions. The office that included the largest number of humanists was the scriptorship; these officials were charged with the task of composing, correcting, and analyzing the bulls. A large percentage of humanists held a scriptorship at one time or another in their careers. However, the office that most clearly demonstrates humanist advancement in acceptance by the curia was the apostolic secretariate. Originally the secretaries were scriptors specifically assigned to the pope to do his most pressing work. Their number varied, and they were divided into two categories, the regular secretaries and the domestic or private secretaries. Under Leo X the duties received greater specificity when secretaries assumed particular areas of concern; Leo's rationalization laid the foundation for the modern secretariate. The secretaries prepared the new government documents, the papal briefs, which were shorter and less elaborate than the papal bulls; the popes used the briefs to express their opinions on a number of topics rather than to respond to special requests as they did in the bulls. The secretaries worked closely with the popes, frequently becoming their confidants, and they were often rewarded with benefices or other tangible signs of appreciation. Throughout the Renaissance the secretariate was increasingly staffed by men with humanist credentials, including some well-known and respected individuals. Moreover, the humanists came to consider the secretariate especially theirs because of the literary qualities required to compose papal briefs, and they willingly defended the office's dignity against the claims of other curialists to precedence.[27] The high point of humanist presence in the secretariate came under Leo X, when he appointed the two Ciceronian stylists Pietro Bembo (1470–1547) and Jacopo Sadoleto (1477–1547) to the office.[28]

As part of the curial bureaucracy, the humanists increasingly identified their own needs with those of their employer. Since the curia was a hierarchical and conservative institution, the humanists respected its ingrained rights and defended them with great tenacity. This adaptation can be seen in their willingness to embrace one of the curia's newer traditions, the venality of offices, which became the standard procedure for staffing nonspiritual offices by the end of the Quattrocento. The humanists, like other curialists, saw their offices as investments that they had to protect; hence they would allow no substantive change without major opposition. A further example was the ease with which the humanists embraced the clerical state when it became a requirement for curial advancement.[29] While the humanists were aware of the limits the curia could place on their time for scholarship and literary composition and of the need to reform the institution in order to make it more responsive to the religious needs of the people, they never worked to alter the institution as constituted.[30]

Although entrance into the curial bureaucracy was to an extent dependent on one's literary qualifications, no such ability sufficed for advancement in the ecclesiastical hierarchy. Despite the growing number of clerics among them, few humanists were promoted to the episcopate, and even fewer to the cardinalate. Generally promotion to an episcopal see was a function of a man's success as a curialist or as a servant of some powerful secular or religious power.[31] Nevertheless, a few humanists did reach the episcopate as a result of their literary talents being recognized and deemed worthy of support. Often these men were able to continue their work as creative scholars or as editors and commentators. The Neolatin poet Giannantonio Campano (1429–1477), the editor Andrea Bussi (1417–1475), and the Latin lexicographer and grammarian Niccolò Perotti (1429–1480) were some of the most outstanding examples of humanist bishops.[32] Like their fellow bishops these men tended to be nonresidents, content to leave the running of their dioceses to others while they continued their scholarly lives in Rome and served the pope in other functions.

Even more restrictive in its membership was the College of Cardinals.[33] In general the college contained men of princely or administrative backgrounds whose appointments fulfilled political needs. While distinguished theologians were elected, humanists seldom were. In the Quattrocento Cardinal Bessarion, Cardinal Francesco Todeschini-Piccolomini, and his uncle Pius II show that humanists could rise to the cardinalate; but none of these men owed their position to their literary or scholarly abilities alone or primarily. The humanist and Hebrew scholar Adriano Castellesi da Corneto (1458–1522?) received his cardinal's hat because of his close association with Alexander VI as his secretary.[34] In the Cinquecento both Pietro Bembo and Jacopo Sadoleto were made cardinals in recognition of both their service to the curia and their literary reputations. Essentially, however, the cardinalate was a position a humanist could not realistically aspire to obtain.

*   *   *

While few humanists could expect to receive a bishopric and even fewer dream of a cardinalate, the humanists had many other employment opportunities in Rome outside the curia. Especially important in providing employment and some social dimension to their lives in Rome were the various *familiae* or households in the city.[35] The Roman *familia* was an important institution in the city's social fabric and performed valuable service in integrating humanists into Rome's special ambience. It consisted of those men—women were never explicitly mentioned as participants in this celibate society—who helped the popes, cardinals, or secular lords to perform their duties. The papal *familia* grew greatly in number throughout the Renaissance and reached two thousand members under Leo X; it was the largest of the *familiae,* and humanists were to be found scattered through its various subdivisions, especially as secretaries, chaplains, chamberlains, and domestic prelates. They held similar positions in cardinalatial *familiae.* Just prior to the Sack of Rome the *familia* of Cardinal Alessandro Farnese, later Paul III, numbered 700 souls, but usually cardinals employed an average household of approximately 120 members. With as many as twenty cardinals resident in Rome, and granting that several of these cardinals were too impoverished to maintain even average-sized staffs, the cardinals' *familiae* were an obviously important employment source for humanists. Membership in a cardinal's *familia* could also gain that prelate's assistance when a humanist wished to secure a curial post or even a bishopric. Secular *familiae,* as well as some clerical ones, also employed humanists as tutors to children. Some humanists made their careers passing from the employ of one *familia* to another. Domizio Calderini, who served as an apostolic secretary under Sixtus IV, held posts in the *familiae* of Cardinals Bessarion, Pietro Riario, and Giuliano della Rovere until his death in 1478. A generation later Scipione Forteguerra, called Cateromachus (1466–1515), served four cardinals—Domenico Grimani, Alessandro Farnese, Franciotti della Rovere, and Giulio de' Medici.[36]

In addition to providing support through employment, these *familiae,* especially those of the cardinals, could provide humanists with meeting places. A large, rich *familia* could bring together men of a variety of occupations and interests who could form a small intellectual community to discuss literary or artistic questions. Certainly the most famous of these gatherings were those at the palace of Cardinal Bessarion, which brought together familiars and outside intellectuals attracted by the cardinal's learning and generosity. Bessarion's group was especially devoted to Greek studies and Neoplatonic philosophy.[37] Cardinal Todeschini-Piccolomini used his *familia* in a similar manner. Not only did these cardinals offer the humanists a forum for discussion and official recognition, but they also could control the development of discussions and direct the humanists along those lines which would be most acceptable to the curia. Thus in part these *familiae* determined the way humanism would develop in Rome, provided some supervision for its growth, and regulated the rewards available to individual humanists.

These gatherings at cardinals' palaces had one major disadvantage for the humanists. They were more or less official groups under the patronage and control of men who were representatives of the curia. Such official surroundings limited freedom of discussion and expression. Not surprisingly, the humanists wished to have their own centers where they could meet and discuss what they wished without fear of overstepping their welcome or broaching topics unappreciated by the establishment. The humanists wanted some form of self-governing and self-defining organization aimed at disseminating and encouraging common ideas. The answer to this search was the creation of the so-called Roman academies, institutions created by and for humanists.

*   *   *

The Roman academies were informal gatherings lacking set membership, meeting places, or agendas.[38] They depended on the generosity of one man who opened his house to other humanists and allowed them to use it as a center. Often this individual gave a sense of direction to the others, who followed his lead in intellectual matters. Despite their informal character, these academies, which continued to meet until the Sack of Rome, were important in giving organization and form to humanist thought in Rome. The humanists could discuss the type of literary or historical questions that most particularly aroused their interests. They also served as a means of integrating newcomers into the Roman humanist traditions and providing to younger members an opportunity to learn from more experienced individuals the best procedures for advancement in the curia and the ecclesiastical hierarchy.

The first and most influential of these academies was that led by Giulio Pomponio Leto (1427–1494).[39] Leto was the illegitimate offspring of a southern Italian noble family; his fascination with Roman antiquity led him to Rome to study Latin and the physical remains of Roman life. Leto's devotion to the Roman past bordered on the eccentric. He was consumed with the desire to understand Roman antiquity and use it as a standard for his own life. He was not alone in this pursuit, and he attracted to his side many other humanists who wished to make the recovery of ancient civilization and its imitation the central element in their intellectual lives. This allegiance to the ancients led members of the academy to change their names to more fully classicized forms. Unlike most Roman humanists Leto did not enter the service of either the church or the curia. Rather, he earned his money teaching at the University of Rome, the Sapienza.[40] While many humanists were employed at the university throughout the Renaissance, the Roman university was never a major force in shaping Roman humanist thought. It was generally too professional in orientation and too mediocre to offset the curia as an employment center.

Little information exists on the activities of Leto's academy. Leto's close collaborator in the academy, Bartolomeo dei Sacchi, called Platina (1421–1481),[41] indicated that the members held discussions of literary and historical topics, read their original compositions, and enjoyed general conviviality, often over dinner. In addition to the study of the major ancient writers and historians, Leto devoted special attention to the study of ancient Roman archaeology and encouraged his students and fellow academicians to do the same.[42] Leto searched the Roman ruins in an attempt to discover the ancient locations mentioned in literary sources; in time this search was even extended to Christian monuments. Although many of Leto's identifications were ultimately rejected, his attitude toward archaeology inspired some of his students to follow in his footsteps. His work inaugurated an important and fruitful field of investigation.

The crucial event in the history of Leto's academy was its suppression by Paul II.[43] The story of the suppression has been told often, and by now the general outline of events is clear and can be summarized quickly. The key figure in the drama was Platina. In addition to his membership in Leto's academy, Platina was a curialist who had purchased a post in the College of Abbreviators, which Pius II had recently established. Paul II dissolved the college as part of a reform of the curia. Platina indignantly complained of his deprivation and threatened to appeal to a general council against the pope's actions, a remedy specifically forbidden by Pius II. This angered Paul, and he was moved to action when he learned, seemingly from some cardinals, that several members of the Roman academy planned to overthrow the papal government and reinstate a republic. Paul acted quickly in 1468 and ordered the arrest of Platina and several other academicians. The suppression coincided with other problems within the Roman humanist community, since Leto was himself at that time in Venice, preparing for a trip to the East in order to study Greek. The pope had him extradited and imprisoned, together with Platina and other academicians. At least some of the prisoners were subjected to torture.

The charges levied by the pope against the humanists have been historically important since they have been interpreted as proof that the humanists of the academy as a group were irreligious and anticlerical and that humanism was essentially hostile to its clerical ambience and was perceived as such. Paul labeled the humanists as heretics, sodomites, neopagans, and republicans. Our knowledge of the academy and the lives of its various members gives some circumstantial support to these accusations but little direct evidence to demonstrate that there was a revolutionary-pagan-homosexual conspiracy brewing in the Roman academy.

Certainly Leto's academy showed no marked interest in religion or theological questions.[44] Leto personally seems to have been indifferent to religion in general and contemptuous of some aspects of it. This indifference seems to have been shared by other humanists in the academy. The tradition of changing names from Christian to classical forms also contributed to this irreligious aspect. But indifference is not active opposition to Christianity, as the pope charged. Some academicians did express anticlerical sentiments, but these remarks may have been more the result of a too close proximity with clerical superiors and a resentment of the limited advancement prospects for those who remained outside orders. When everything is considered, there is little evidence to support Paul's belief that the academy was a center for antireligious propaganda and paganism.

Doubtless there were some practicing homosexuals in the Roman academy. Leto himself was suspected of more than pedagogical interest in the students he was teaching while in Venice; he was, in fact, in prison for homosexuality when Paul had him extradited to Rome. But there is no proof that the academy as a whole was homosexually oriented or that there were sinister sexual practices going on at its meetings. Further, clerics or men deporting themselves as clerics are especially open to such an accusation.

The charge of republicanism on the surface had greater support. Under torture Platina confessed that Filippo Buonaccorsi (d. 1496), who went by his academic name "Callimachus Experiens," had expressed anticlerical opinions and called for the overthrow of the priests and the establishment of a republic after the model of ancient Rome. But apart from such rhetorical expressions, there was no action to produce a change in the government. Nevertheless, the papacy was alive to such threats, and after Cola di Rienzo and the republican plots against Eugenius IV (successful) and Nicholas V (unsuccessful), the touchiness of the popes on this issue is understandable. Still, there was no real republican uprising planned, and even if the humanists had so acted, they would have found no followers. In truth, the humanists in Rome showed no practical interest in political questions and tended to confine their study of antiquity to literary, historical, and archaeological arenas. The ecclesiastical dominance in the city and the non-Roman background of most humanists caused them to shun politics.

In short, Paul's suppression expressed his own dissatisfaction with the classical leanings of the humanists and his touchiness over the complaints voiced by Platina as well as a sensitivity to any hint of political irregularity. While there were, no doubt, some clerics in Rome who shared Paul's attitudes, his action against the academy cannot be read as a programmatic response on the part of the papacy or the religious establishment toward humanism. Indeed, the institutions Paul wished to defend and protect from the humanists did not share his concerns. The curia rehired the humanists Paul persecuted. Platina, the central figure in initiating the events, had an illustrious career after Paul's death, serving as the first official librarian of the Vatican under Sixtus IV. He composed a famous history of the popes in which he took the opportunity to blacken the name of his persecutor. Leto was allowed to return to his teaching post at the university.

Neither did Paul destroy the Roman academy. After Paul's death the academy was able to reorganize under Leto's direction for the special purpose of celebrating the birthday of the city of Rome. Certainly the new academy had no intention of making the same mistakes as its predecessor; it organized itself as a religious confraternity and received the patronage of a cardinal. Its activities did change insofar as the members took greater cognizance of the religious character of their specific urban environment. More and more of the humanists in the academy devoted their time not only to classical commentaries, Neolatin poetry, archaeology, and classical history but also to composing works with a decidedly religious tone, poems praising the saints and the popes, short theological treatises, and, like Platina, religious history. These new activities did not replace the traditional ones but supplemented them, and gave to Leto's second academy a breadth that the first had lacked, helping to ensure that it would continue undisturbed.

After Leto's, the next academy was that of Paolo Cortesi (1465–1510).[45] Cortesi belonged to a family with close associations with the curia, and he himself served as an apostolic secretary. Educated partly in Rome, he also had long-standing connections with the humanist circle around Poliziano in Florence. Cortesi was an avid student of classical and Neolatin writings and produced the first critical assessment of Renaissance writers, *De hominibus doctis dialogus* (ca. 1491). He is most famous for a youthful epistolary polemic with Poliziano (ca. 1489) on the imitation of Cicero, which Cortesi vehemently defended. Like other humanists, including his brother Alessandro (d. ca. 1489), a poet and respected orator in Rome, Cortesi took orders and directed his career toward ecclesiastical advancement. He was very sensitive to the need for integrating humanist education and culture into Rome's clerical and ecclesiastical establishment. He wrote a theological handbook, the *Liber sententiarum* (1504), in classical Latin in order to demonstrate that humanist Latin could express Christian doctrine; and his last composition, *De cardinalatu* (1510), one of the few humanist texts to discuss a clerical theme, argued for the integration of humanist and Christian ideas as a model for the life of a cardinal or any man with important political responsibilities.

Cortesi's academy functioned both as a means of tutoring younger humanists in the ideas and topics dominant in Roman humanism and of developing set themes that could be accepted as standard by the humanist community. Latin composition was the central interest of his academy, and Cortesi's Ciceronian Latin, which was also the favored Latin style in Rome, was its chief literary concern. But Cortesi and his academicians had broader interests, and the study of Petrarch's verse and its imitation also appealed to them. Essentially Cortesi's academy acted as a conduit for the movement and training of humanists into the various courts in Rome, and it seems to have ended when he left Rome in 1503 to devote himself fully to original composition as a means of career advancement.

There were several academies after Cortesi's; some had specific aims, such as the study of antiquities, but generally they were even more informal than Leto's and Cortesi's. However, two groups do stand out and merit special consideration. One was patronized by the curialist Johann Goritz (d. 1527), whose members were especially devoted to Neolatin poetry.[46] Goritz supplied the members of his group with the opportunity to express their poetic talents when he had constructed in the church of Sant'Agostino in Rome an altar dedicated to Saint Anne and adorned with a statue of the Virgin, the Christ Child, and Saint Anne by Andrea Sansovino.[47] Each year humanists would meet there and place on the statue their poems celebrating the statue, its figures, Goritz, and other members of the academy. These poems were collected as the *Coryciana*, based on the Latin form of Goritz's name, and printed by Blasio Palladio (d. 1547), a respected orator and subsequently an apostolic secretary. Included in the *Coryciana* was Francesco Arsilli's *De poetis urbanis*, which glorified the Rome of Leo X by comparing it to that of Augustus. The *Coryciana* stands as one of the monuments of Roman humanism.[48]

The other academy that had more or less definite characteristics was that of Angelo Colocci (1484–1549).[49] Colocci was a curialist who, after his wife's death, took orders and eventually became bishop of Nocero. He opened his *horti* or gardens to other humanists as a literary meeting-place. Colocci's interests were especially broad, including not only Latin and Italian literature but also Spanish and Portuguese. He was also devoted to Greek studies and assisted in the publication of Greek texts in Rome. His academy, however, was primarily concerned with Latin eloquence, and it was in some sense a continuation of Cortesi's group.

A negative result, which attests to the effectiveness of these academies in binding together Roman humanist thought, was the extent to which the members of the academies eventually became sterile intellectuals. Too often the academies amounted to the same men meeting in the same place, discussing the same topics, with the same conclusions. Intellectual vitality weakened as the city and the curia experienced difficulties in the second decade of the sixteenth century. The best example of this decline is the famous case of the prosecution of the Belgian humanist Christophe Longueil (1488–1522).[50] Longueil had come to Rome to master Ciceronian style and had been supported by both Bembo and Sadoleto. His friends thought so highly of him that they moved to have conferred on him honorary Roman citizenship. However, this plan was blocked by some humanists, who argued that the Belgian was not worthy of such an honor because he had once delivered an oration praising the ancient Franks at the expense of the Romans. A charge of treason against Rome was laid and a public debate between Longueil and a member of the Roman academy, the orator Celso Mellini (d. 1519), was planned. The debate never occurred because Longueil fled the city in fear for his life.

The event demonstrates not only that Longueil was less than mentally stable, but also that Roman humanism had become parochial and intolerant. It was in its last stages and had begun a decline that was to end with the Sack of Rome, when the humanist community largely dispersed. Despite this melancholy end, Roman humanism had developed a set attitude toward classical and Christian topics that allows us to discuss it as a unity—to sketch its major elements, the extent to which it succeeded in its goals, and its differences from other humanist centers.

*   *   *

Whatever the sterility that ultimately overtook Roman humanism, it did produce a large variety of original writings and editorial work that marked it off as a distinctive element in Italian Renaissance humanism. When looking to Roman humanism to identify its distinctive elements we should not expect to find altogether new activities or interests, but rather a particular emphasis on topics common to humanism in general. Roman humanists stressed those matters which reflected their special concerns as well as those which fitted most naturally with their social, political, and religious ambience. Where Roman humanism did become unique was in those areas in which it stressed the relationship between its culture and the papal ideology.

A clear example of the way the Roman humanists pursued a traditional humanist activity but treated it in a manner to meet their particular needs is the Latin language. All humanists began their work with reverence for the Latin language; it was the revival of the Roman tongue and its cultural ingredients that had inspired the humanists from the beginning. But in Rome the Latin language was given a centrality that, if not unique, was very one-sided. Latin not only supplied the centralizing element of humanist thought but also responded to the secretarial needs of the curia, which encouraged their concentration on Latin style. Latin was thus the medium that could bind the humanists and their culture to the papacy and the curia on several levels.[51]

Like all humanists, Romans were not ignorant of the importance of Greek and Greek scholarship to a proper appreciation of Latin antiquity. Nevertheless, the cultivation of Greek was very much a secondary element to them. Not that there were lacking those who wished to advance Hellenic scholarship, nor were these men without their followers: Cardinal Bessarion's patronage of Greeks seeking refuge in Italy from the Turks and his encouragement of Italians in their study of Greek provided Rome with an important advocate for Hellenism. Similarly, Nicholas V had given important support to Greek scholarship by his translation program. As noted above, Angelo Colocci supported the printing of Greek texts in Rome, and Leo X did the same with the establishment of a Greek college.[52] There were some important teachers of Greek in Rome, most notably George of Trebizond.[53] But all these activities in no way should diminish the realization that Greek scholarship was not central to Roman humanism. Nor should the presence of Hebrew scholars in the curia and the religious orders in Rome be read as a major interest in that language, with its special religious significance among Roman humanists.[54] Rome had to await the Counter-Reformation for Hebrew scholarship to receive its due. Finally, vernacular literature was also a minor humanist concern in Rome, except for the cultivation of Petrarchan verse, which was interpreted as a form becoming to court life.[55]

In seeking the pure Latinity of the ancients as well as favoring an idiom that appealed to their employers, Roman humanists naturally moved to the study and imitation of Cicero. Ciceronianism was a Europewide phenomenon and in no way peculiar to Rome.[56] Nevertheless, Roman humanists did develop the Ciceronian movement more fully than other humanists and gave it an ideological interpretation that bound it closely to the papacy and the curia. Ciceronianism is a much maligned literary movement, and it has been seen as essentially a sterile activity. Yet Ciceronianism did fascinate Roman humanists; it is necessary to appreciate this fact and to treat it as a fundamental characteristic of their thought.

Ciceronianism was an attempt on several levels by many humanists to locate in time the perfect expression of the Latin language, and in so doing to recapture and recreate the cultural ideals that undergirded ancient civilization. The humanists asserted a direct relationship between the Latin language and the culture of the ancients, which could be restored only through the study and imitation of ancient writers. While all humanists accepted the imitation of the ancients as necessary in some form, they disagreed over who should be imitated and how exclusively. Some preferred an eclectic approach, others the use of unusual words and syntax, and some the imitation of the best, in other words, Cicero. Hence Ciceronian imitation was interpreted by its advocates as the best means of reestablishing contact with the lost traditions of the ancients and of making moderns write, and no doubt think, like the ancients. This preference for Cicero was strongest among those who were actively engaged in secretarial and teaching positions. Ciceronianism offered a standard that could be accepted and copied by all; it gave uniformity in style. These qualities made it attractive to the humanists in the curia, and it is not surprising that Rome produced the major defenders of Ciceronian imitation in the Renaissance.[57]

Poggio Bracciolini was the first Roman humanist specifically to proclaim the imitation of Cicero as central to humanism. His opponent was Lorenzo Valla, who based himself on Quintilian and advocated an eclectic approach. This dispute rapidly became personal and never dealt fully with the question of imitation. Sometime around 1489 Angelo Poliziano and Paolo Cortesi revived the debate on the propriety of Ciceronian imitation in a more valuable manner. Poliziano, representing the eclectic, Greek, and vernacular orientation of Florentine humanism, rejected Cortesi's Ciceronianism by emphasizing the necessity of self-expression. Cortesi responded by noting that the best was what should always be cultivated, and the best was Cicero. Like a true son, Cortesi continued, a Ciceronian remains himself but still follows in the footsteps of his father. The next chapter in the dispute came in 1512 when Gianfrancesco Pico della Mirandola (1496–1533), the nephew of the famous philosopher and critic of humanist Latin, Giovanni Pico, debated Pietro Bembo, the soon-to-be Ciceronian secretary to Leo X. Pico rejected Ciceronian imitation for basically philosophical reasons. He argued that there exists a perfect exemplar of the best style, which no man nor any time could claim as his own; to Pico the ancients had no monopoly on the best. Bembo counterargued that only the best should be imitated and that true imitation in no way destroys a man's talents but rather allows him to advance beyond his limits. The final assault on Ciceronianism as practiced in Rome came from Desiderius Erasmus in his *Ciceronianus* (1528). Erasmus rejected Ciceronian imitation in general as sterile and specifically labeled the Roman variety as a form of neopaganism. This last charge, reminiscent of Pope Paul's attacks on the Roman academicians, has had some historical consequences by presenting the Roman humanists' literary and religious interests as in some manner trivial and antireligious. But instead of representing an antireligious buffoonery, in the hands of the Romans Ciceronianism was very much part of a well-defined attitude toward the ancient heritage and Christianity.[58]

We may posit a parallelism between the orthodoxy that pervaded the religious climate of Rome and the orthodoxy represented by the Ciceronian movement. Ciceronian language was cultivated for its sonority, its clear but elegant presentation, and its ability to present a topic in a compelling manner. As used by the Roman humanists it had the advantage of providing a means of praising and exalting the established authority in a language that made historical comparisons to the ancient Roman world and culture obvious. Modern Christian Rome could be praised in the language of the Roman Empire and a direct equation posited through vocabulary and syntax between the Roman Empire and its civilization and the Roman church as the new defender of that culture. Lorenzo Valla, despite his earlier opposition to Ciceronianism, had proclaimed the nexus between the language of the Roman Empire and its culture and the church as the new propagator of that language and culture.[59] The Roman Ciceronians, in a sense, took this equation one step further by singling out Ciceronian Latin as the unique means of expressing this identification. The Roman humanists understood language and culture as a unity; the Ciceronians felt this unity as strongly as others and maintained that they had found the perfect vehicle to proclaim it. Erasmus was correct in realizing that there was an essential bond between the religious beliefs of the Ciceronians and the language they used, but he erred in the identification of the content of that thought.

Ciceronianism also was a valuable instrument for men who had to function in a court and to please those in power with their literary ability. Rome had numerous occasions for oratorical displays, and Ciceronian Latin was the preferred form for them. As John O'Malley has demonstrated in his study of preaching in Rome before the Sack,[60] this oratory could be more than mere praise of the patron and his noble deeds; but in general the Ciceronians preferred to do precisely that. To praise a patron in the words of the great Roman orator doubtless encouraged him to identify himself with the lost Roman culture and its revival through the medium of the humanists, and thereby implied the need to support this reviving medium. It also demonstrated the talent of a particular orator in a literary form that was well known to his audience and had a set body of rules for judging his product. In the eyes of the Romans, the more perfectly one mastered Ciceronian form, the more deserving one was of patronage.

A good example of an individual who embodied this literary ideal and used it in a manner pleasing to the Roman establishment was Tommaso Fedra Inghirami of Volterra (1470–1516).[61] He was a member of the Roman academy, a cleric, a papal scriptor, a professor of rhetoric at the University of Rome under Leo X, and a very popular orator. He was especially prominent in assisting in the revival of Roman theater that had been begun by Leto. Inghirami used his mastery of Ciceronian Latin to ingratiate himself to cardinals and other important prelates and spoke on several important occasions. His oratory embodied those themes of glorifying the church and its adherents by comparison to ancient Rome which the Roman humanists and their superiors found most acceptable. For Inghirami Cicero's eloquence was a language that befitted empire. But the empire was no longer that of the ancient Romans, but rather that of the church with the pope at its head. Just as Cicero had made the Latin language an imperial tongue, fit to rule, so this revived ancient idiom could serve the same purpose for the popes. Ancient Roman culture and ideas were thus fully renewed in modern Roman dress.

This dependence on Ciceronianism had a parallel in the concentration on the verse of Vergil, like Cicero a prime representative of the Golden Age of Latin, as the preferred poetic form. Again the court environment encouraged poetry, and Vergil was the most renowned of Latin court poets. His verse was created to praise the great deeds and men of the Roman world, and the humanists adapted its meter to their needs. Certainly the most famous exponent of this form was Marco Girolamo Vida (1485–1566).[62] For Julius II Vida composed a *Juliad,* now lost, that seemingly exalted the pope in terms befitting a Roman hero. His greatest poem was the *Christiad,* which took the story of Christ as its theme and made an equation between the founder of Christianity and the founder of ancient Rome. It enjoyed great popularity throughout Europe in the Renaissance.

A valuable example of the uses of poetry and oratory to praise the special political and ecclesiastical establishment of Rome is the celebration planned by the city council of Rome for the unveiling of a statue of Leo X that had been commissioned from the Bolognese sculptor Domenico Amio.[63] The intention of the council was to hold the festivities on 21 April 1521, the occasion of the *Palilia,* the birthday of Rome. There were to be theatrical displays as well as a special oration and poem in honor of the pope and the statue. Delays, however, prevented the event as planned from taking place, and Leo died before it could be rescheduled. Despite this setback, the oration and the poem were duly composed and still exist. The oration is usually attributed to Blosio Palladio, the editor of the *Coryciana;* while there are some doubts about this attribution,

Blosio seems to be the best candidate. The poem was written by C. Silvanus Germanicus, a professor at the University of Rome. Germanicus was, clearly, a German, but little is known about his activities. Like Blosio he belonged to the Goritz academy, and some of his work was published in the *Coryciana*. His selection for this event indicates that he was appreciated by the humanists. Both Blosio and Silvanus took the occasion to present an imperial reading of papal history. They compared the papal church to the Roman Empire and presented the popes as the successors to the Roman emperors. Like their predecessors, the popes rule the world; indeed they actually have authority over greater areas than had the emperors at their zenith. Since the festivities were to be held on the Capitol, the ancient center of imperial Rome, the identification between the ancient empire and the new Christian one was made even more explicit. All the Roman humanists acknowledged the new "imperial" character of the papacy.

Oratory and poetry were two forms of classically inspired activity in Rome. Humanists, further, under the influence of Leto devoted much of their effort to the editions of commentaries on classical writers, and to the study of artistic and archaeological remains of the ancient world. While the classical commentaries were not unique to Rome, their cultivation in the humanist circles did mark a particular element in Roman humanism's study of the ancient past, while archaeology was of obvious appeal to men living in Rome. Archaeology takes on added significance since it was closely allied to the artistic revival of the high Renaissance. Also popular with some of Leto's pupils was the revival of ancient theater, which appealed to the cardinals and other rich patrons as a proper court entertainment. As noted, Tommaso Fedra Inghirami was a prominent follower of Leto in reviving theater.

Printing came to Rome in 1468 when two Germans, Arnold Pannartz and Konrad Sweynheym, brought a press to the city. While they published a variety of types of literature, it was the *editiones principes* of the classical authors that have earned them the gratitude of subsequent generations.[64] They used local humanist talent as editors for their enterprises. Appropriately enough, the first text they issued was Cicero's *Familiar Letters*. New texts encouraged the production of commentaries, and they were written on both ancient poets and prose writers. In these commentaries their authors tried to provide historical and literary information that would make the works more accessible and understandable; it was a form of literary archaeology. Leto led the way, producing a commentary on Vergil, and he inspired his students to follow his example. One of those who did was Paolo Marsi (d. 1484), who contributed commentaries on several poets, especially Ovid. Another was Aurelio Brandolini (1454–1497), a popular poet and orator who, like his master, gave his attention to Vergil.[65] Niccolò Perotti wrote a commentary on Martial that became an enormous catalog of Latin words. This form did not appeal to all and was to an extent identified by those opposed to it with Rome. Aldo Manuzio, the famous Venetian printer, was a Roman and studied with Leto. Aldo, however, did not approve of the type of commentary his teacher wrote, and he devoted his energies to producing the texts themselves rather than extended reflections on them.

Interest in ancient art and archaeology had an especially important effect on the art of the high Renaissance. Leto had led the way, and others advanced his methods. Most famous of Leto's archaeological students was Andrea Fulvio (ca. 1470–1527).[66] Like his mentor, Fulvio supported himself as a teacher and ignored Greek studies, devoting all his time to Latin literature and archaeology. He collected a large number of inscriptions and details of ancient monuments. In 1514 he produced a major study of Roman antiquities, the *Antiquaria urbis*. Raphael, the perfect courtly painter, was also fascinated by the ancient remains of the city and advocated their preservation. His interest led him also to investigate the great ancient theorist of architecture, Vitruvius, who, like Cicero and Vergil, provided an ancient model the Romans felt was normative. The humanist Marco Fabio Calvo translated Vitruvius into Italian for Raphael and helped him interpret the text. After Raphael's death Calvo produced an important plan of ancient Rome.[67]

*   *   *

Architecture, oratory, poetry, archaeology, classical commentaries and editions, all these enterprises absorbed to a greater or lesser extent the scholarly attention of the humanists. But they were not blind to the necessity of providing a clear justification for their intellectual interests to the clerical world that controlled Rome and the curia. Above all, they had to demonstrate how humanist education and culture should be proper attributes to the clergy, since an increasing number of them became clerics and wished to advance in the hierarchy. This goal was best met through the presentation of works with theological or religious themes that appealed to the pope, cardinals, and other prelates.

The most obvious of these humanist endeavors that combined the humanist concern for language and history with the special Christian or ecclesiastical theme was the creation of a genre of humanist biographies of the popes.[68] From the middle of the Quattrocento, humanists employed their knowledge of ancient historical models as the means by which to praise the deeds of their clerical patrons. Nicholas V, Pius II, Paul II, Julius II, Leo X, Adrian VI, and Clement VII all enjoyed humanist histories. The first of the genre, and the most important, was Giannozzo Manetti's *Life of Nicholas V.* Manetti presented humanist learning as an element in the reform of the clergy and Christian culture that Nicholas had envisioned. Platina took as his topic all the popes as a means of expressing his gratitude to Sixtus IV for his support of humanism and of Platina in particular. Through these histories Roman humanists found the means of presenting their interpretation of what clerical patronage should be.

When humanists dealt with theological topics they seldom strayed very far from accepted norms, since they did not wish to establish new doctrines. Rather, they followed trends that had official approbation, thereby demonstrating their loyalty and willingness to support the dominant clerical will. The humanists searched for a safe, congenial orthodoxy. One aspect of theological thought, or better the history of Christian thought, which especially attracted the humanists and satisfied the requirement of congenial orthodoxy was the study of the church fathers. Indeed, the humanists had almost a monopoly in this area.[69] Roman humanists, like other humanists, found the fathers of the church, both Latin and Greek, especially attractive because of their mastery of ancient rhetoric and literature. The Christian fathers were seen as extensions of classical antiquity. Rome became a center for the translation of Greek patristic texts into Latin, the study of the Latin fathers, and the production of editions of their works. In a famous oration given on the feast of St. Thomas Aquinas in the Church of Santa Maria sopra Minerva, Lorenzo Valla compared scholastic theologians unfavorably to the church fathers and located the latter's superiority in their training in ancient rhetoric.[70] For Valla and other Roman humanists, rhetoric was a more fitting adjunct to Christian thought than Aristotelian scholasticism. This rhetorical ability made Christian teachings more compelling and attractive, and therefore more effective. The fathers were the models for the humanists' *theologia rhetorica*, which Charles Trinkaus has identified as a major characteristic of humanist religious thought.[71]

Valla's criticism of Aquinas in his oration, however, was not the normal humanist attitude toward the Dominican theologian. Rome in general was a center for the propagation of Thomistic theology, which was interpreted as most conducive to papal power.[72] Part of the Roman Thomist revival included special liturgical ceremonies on the saint's feast day, 7 March at Santa Maria sopra Minerva, which included an oration in honor of the saint. Valla's oration was one of them. Humanists were often chosen for the delivery of these orations, and they were much more positive toward Aquinas's contribution than Valla was. The humanists found in Aquinas a scholastic thinker much more congenial to their needs than the other professional theologians, since he offered a clarity and directness in exposition that the humanists appreciated.

One humanist who found a valuable model in Aquinas was Paolo Cortesi. Cortesi, who has already been discussed as a leader of the Roman academy and as a defender of Ciceronianism, also produced a theological treatise.[73] His *Liber sententiarum* was a humanist refashioning of basic Christian doctrines. Written in Ciceronian Latin, the text covered every major Christian doctrine, usually summarily, with discussions of patristic and scholastic opinion but without using traditional theological vocabulary. In expounding these basic doctrines, Cortesi surveyed scholastic authorities, but he generally showed a preference for Aquinas and his followers, although he often used a Thomist-Scotist axis from which to develop a topic. In general when citing Aquinas, he praised him for his clarity and orthodox thought. Cortesi wrote the treatise in order to demonstrate that humanist Latin could successfully deal with any subject matter. He wished to show that humanist education and culture properly belonged to the clerical state and that humanists must be cognizant of theological questions. In short, he believed that theologians must be more humanistic and humanists more theologically aware. This view represented the need of humanists, who had devoted their lives to the curia and the church and wished to defend their intellectual interests and convince their superiors that they should be rewarded for their actions.

Cortesi expanded his view of the relationship between humanist and cleric in his final work, *De cardinalatu*.[74] *De cardinalatu* was written in a highly artificial classical Latin, often using archaic forms. The aim of the treatise was to show that humanist learning could be combined with traditional scholastic and Christian themes in providing the moral and intellectual basis to make proper choices in a world that was markedly lacking in morality. It established the cardinal, a particularly important Roman humanist patron, as a new ideal humanist type. The cardinal had the duty to be educated in the *studia humanitatis* and to undertake the responsibility of advancing humanism. He could no longer be content with the limited world of scholastic theology, canon law, or medieval administration, but must also embrace the values of humanist culture. No matter what actions he might engage in—advising the pope, governing his diocese, or judging another man's action—humanistic learning provided the basis for the proper evaluation of any situation and a guide for making the proper choices. Humanism, in Cortesi's rendition, was a vital and natural attribute to a cardinal, and by extension to the church. Not surprisingly, *De cardinalatu* has been compared to Machiavelli's *The Prince* and Castiglione's *The Book of the Courtier*. Like these two other writers, Cortesi wished to explain to his audience the special lessons necessary to survive and prosper in an Italy suffering from social and political upheaval. But unlike his two near contemporaries Cortesi still believed that the Quattrocento Latin humanist tradition maintained its value as a moral guide. Hence, he wrote his treatise in a highly erudite Latin, while Machiavelli and Castiglione turned to the vernacular. Unlike Machiavelli, Cortesi believed that morality retained its value in an unstable world, and unlike Castiglione he directed his attention to a group that still commanded some discretionary power and decision-making authority. Cortesi's was a message fitted to the clerical-humanist ambience of Rome.

The belief that underlay Cortesi's *De cardinalatu*—that humanism could be accommodated to the needs of the church and be made more secure as a result—could be maintained only as long as the society in which humanism had to function was receptive to it and felt no great economic or political pressures to regroup and modify itself. From the mid-Quattrocento till 1527 such pressures were lacking, and humanism easily found a comfortable home for itself in Rome, once certain ground rules had been accepted. Humanism thus formed a relatively cohesive intellectual movement, which advanced in prestige and centrality. Like humanism in other centers, the Roman variety conditioned generations of men to form and accept specific cultural models that could bind them to Rome's special socio-political establishment. Roman humanism's unique success lay in convincing the rulers of the medieval church that this procedure fitted them also.

NOTES

1. Two works of late nineteenth-century German scholarship are valuable for the general history of Rome in the Renaissance. F. Gregorovius, *History of the City of Rome in the Middle Ages*, trans. A. Hamilton (London, 1900), vols. 5–8, contains much information on the various aspects of Roman life. L. von Pastor, *History of the Popes from the Close of the Middle Ages*, trans. F. I. Antrobus et al. (London and St. Louis, 1891–1910), vols. 1–11, remains basic. Pastor, however, was especially weak on intellectual history, and he lacked sympathy for humanism. He posited an artificial distinction between a "Christian" and a "pagan" humanism, which has had regrettable overtones in subsequent historiography. More recent one-volume surveys of Renaissance Rome are B. Mitchell, *Rome in the High Renaissance: The Age of Leo X* (Norman, OK, 1973), and P. Partner, *Renaissance Rome, 1550–1559: A Portrait of a Society* (Berkeley, 1977). From an art-historical perspective, see P. Portoghesi, *Rome in the Renaissance*, trans. P. Sanders (London, 1977). For papal policy, which had an influence on humanism, see in addition to Pastor, J. A. F. Thomson, *Popes and Princes, 1417–1517: Politics and Popes in the Late Medieval Church* (London, 1980). For the finan-

cial state of the papacy, see P. Partner, "Papal Financial Policy in the Renaissance and Counter-Reformation," *Past and Present* 88 (1980): 17–62. Recent scholarship in English has given increased attention to Rome's intellectual and religious conditions. The influence of humanism on Rome's character is the subject of J. W. O'Malley, S. J., *Praise and Blame in Renaissance Rome: Rhetoric, Doctrine, and Reform in the Sacred Orators of the Papal Court, ca. 1450–1521* (Durham, NC, 1979). O'Malley has also published an important monograph on an influential figure in Rome's intellectual life, *Giles of Viterbo on Church and Reform: A Study in Renaissance Thought* (Leiden, 1968). Also valuable are O'Malley's collected essays, *Rome and the Renaissance: Studies in Culture and Religion* (London, 1981). From a broader perspective is J. F. D'Amico, *Renaissance Humanism in Papal Rome* (Baltimore, 1983), which tries to relate humanism to Roman society in general and has as its thesis that humanism formed a cohesive and distinctive identity in Rome up to the Sack of Rome in 1527. Also arguing for a close relationship between religion and humanism is C. L. Stinger, *The Renaissance in Rome: Ideology and Culture in the City of the Popes, 1443–1527* (Bloomington, IN, 1985). On an individual pope and the humanists, see E. Lee, *Sixtus IV and Men of Letters* (Rome, 1978). J. Monfasani, *George of Trebizond: A Biography and a Study of His Rhetoric and Logic* (Leiden, 1976), has much information on humanists in Rome. Two recent collections of essays provide studies on particular aspects of Renaissance Rome, especially humanism: *Rome in the Renaissance: The City and the Myth,* ed. P. A. Ramsey (Binghamton, NY, 1982), and *Umanesimo a Roma nel Quattrocento* (Rome and New York, 1984).

2. See R. Weiss, "Jacopo Angeli da Scarperia (c. 1360–1410/11)," in *Medioevo e Rinascimento: Studi in onore di Bruno Nardi,* 2 vols. (Florence, 1955), 2:801–27. For Bruni, see also G. Griffiths, "Leonardo Bruni and the Restoration of the University of Rome (1406)," *Renaissance Quarterly* 26 (1973): 1–10.

3. See J. D. Folts, "In Search of the 'Civic Life': An Intellectual Biography of Poggio Bracciolini (1380–1459)," (Ph.D. diss., University of Rochester, 1976), and P. G. Gordan, "Poggio at the Curia," in *Umanesimo a Roma nel Quattrocento,* 113–26.

4. See J. Delumeau, *Vie économique et sociale de Rome dans le seconde moitié du XVIe siècle,* 2 vols. (Paris, 1957), 1:135–220, and C. W. Maas, *The German Community in Rome, 1378–1525* (Rome, 1981), for a study of one immigrant group.

5. See Chapter 8, above. For Florentines in Rome, see A. Esch, "Dal medioevo al rinascimento: uomini a Roma dal 1340–1450," *Archivio della Società romana di storia patria* 94 (1971): 3–10; idem, "Florentiner in Rom 1400: Namenverzeichnis der ersten Quattrocento-Generation," *Quellen und Forschungen aus italienischen Archiven und Bibliotheken* 51 (1972): 476–525; and R. Lefevre, "Fiorentini a Roma del'400: I Dati," *Studi romani* 20.1 (1972): 186–97.

6. See on the clericalization of humanism, C. Dionisotti, "Chierici e laici," in

his *Geografia e storia della letteratura italiana* (Turin, 1967), 47–73, and A. Prosperi, "Intellettuali e chiesa all'inizio dell'età moderna," in *Storia dell'Italia, Annali 4, Intellettuali e potere,* ed. C. Vivanti (Turin, 1981), 161–252.

7. See in general, L. G. Gabel, "The First Revival of Rome, 1420–1484," in *Renaissance Reconsidered: A Symposium* (Northhampton, MA, 1964), 13–25. For Martin V, see Pastor, *History of the Popes,* vol. 1; also P. Partner, *The Papal States under Martin V* (London, 1958). For Eugenius IV, see J. Gill, S. J., *Eugenius IV: Pope of Christian Reunion* (Westminster, MD, 1961), and J. W. Stieber, *Pope Eugenius IV, the Council of Basel and the Secular and Ecclesiastical Authorities in the Empire: The Conflict over Supreme Authority in the Church* (Leiden, 1978).

8. See R. Weiss, *The Renaissance Discovery of Classical Antiquity* (Oxford, 1969), chap. 2; A. Mazzocco, "Biondo Flavio and the Antiquarian Tradition" (Ph.D. diss., University of California, Berkeley, 1973), idem, "Decline and Rebirth in Bruni and Biondo," in *Umanesimo a Roma nel Quattrocento,* 249–66, and J. A. White, "Towards a Critical Edition of Biondo Flavio's 'Italia illustrata': A Survey and an Evaluation of the Manuscripts," ibid., 267–94. For Valla see Chapter 13, below.

9. See Pastor, *History of the Popes,* vol. 2; J. B. Toews, "Formative Forces in the Pontificate of Nicholas V," *Catholic Historical Review* 54 (1968–69): 261–84; and C. W. Westfall, *In This Most Perfect Paradise* (University Park, PA, 1974).

10. For the Vatican Library, see M. Bertola, *I due primi registri di prestito della Biblioteca Apostolica Vaticana* (Vatican City, 1942); J. Bignami-Odier, *La bibliothèque vaticane de Sixte IV à Pie IX* (Vatican City, 1973), D. Mycue, "Founder of the Vatican Library: Nicholas V or Sixtus IV?" in *Libraries and Culture: Proceedings of the Library History Association* 4th ser. (Austin, TX, 1981), 121–33. For Tortelli, see G. Mancini, "Giovanni Tortelli: Cooperatore di Niccolò V nel fondare la Biblioteca vaticana," *Archivio storico italiano* 78.2 (1920): 161–82. For other libraries in Rome, see the essays in *Scrittura, biblioteche e stampa,* ed. P. Farenga et al. (Vatican City, 1980).

11. See Pastor, *History of the Popes,* vol. 2; M. Mallet, *The Borgias* (London, 1969), chap. 4.

12. See Pastor, *History of the Popes,* vol. 3; R. J. Mitchell, *The Laurels and the Tiara: Pope Pius II, 1405–1464* (Garden City, NY, 1962); and R. B. Hilary, "The Appointments of Pope Pius II," *Catholic Historical Review* 64 (1978): 33–35.

13. See Pastor, *History of the Popes,* vol. 4; R. Weiss, *Un umanista veneziano: Papa Paolo II* (Venice, 1958); and A. Andrews, "The 'Lost' Fifth Book of the Life of Pope Paul II by Gaspare of Verona," *Studies in the Renaissance* 17 (1970): 7–45.

14. See Pastor, *History of the Popes,* vol. 4; D. Cortese, "Sisto quatro: Papa antoniano," *Il Santo* 7 (1972): 211–81, and E. Lee, *Sixtus IV and Men of Letters.*

15. See Pastor, *History of the Popes,* and R. Weiss, "In Obitv Vrsini Lanfredini: A Footnote to the Literary History of Rome under Pope Innocent VIII," *Italia medioevale e umanistica* 2 (1959): 353–66.

16. See J. F. D'Amico, "Paolo Cortesi's Rehabilitation of Giovanni Pico della Mirandola," *Bibliothèque d'humanisme et Renaissance* 44 (1982): 37–51.

17. See Pastor, *History of the Popes,* vols. 5 and 6, and Mallet, *The Borgias,* chaps. 5–11.

18. See R. Garnett, "A Laureate of Caesar Borgia," *English Historical Review* 17 (1902): 15–19.

19. See Pastor, *History of the Popes,* vol. 6, and A. A. Strnad, "Francesco Todeschini-Piccolomini: Politik und Mäzenatentum im Quattrocento," *Römische Historische Mitteilungen* 8–9 (1964–65): 101–425.

20. A modern biography of Julius is greatly needed. See Pastor, *History of the Popes,* vol. 6; J. F. D'Amico, "Papal History and Curial Reform in the Renaissance: Raffaele Maffei's *Breuis Historia* of Julius II and Leo X," *Archivum historiae pontificiae* 18 (1980): 157–210; L. Patridge and R. Starn, *A Renaissance Likeness: Art and Culture in Raphael's "Julius II"* (Berkeley, 1980); and F. Gilbert, *The Pope, His Banker and Venice* (Cambridge, MA, 1980). For a recent treatment of the humanist ambience in Rome under Julius, see E. Kai-Kee, "Social Order and Rhetoric in the Rome of Julius II (1503–1513)" (Ph.D. diss., University of California, Berkeley, 1983). See also E. Rodocanachi, *Le Pontificat de Jules II, 1503–1513* (Paris, 1928).

21. See Pastor, *History of the Popes,* vols. 7 and 8; Mitchell, *Rome in the High Renaissance;* D'Amico, "Papal History and Curial Reform." Old but still valuable is W. Roscoe, *The Life and Pontificate of Leo the Tenth,* 2 vols. (London, 1910), especially in the Italian translation with much illustrative material by Conte Luigi Bossi (Milan, 1816). Covering the period also is E. Rodocanachi, *La première Renaissance de Rome au temps de Jules II et Léon X* (Paris, 1912). For a critical treatment of the culture of Leo's Rome, see D. Gnoli, "Il secolo di Leone X" in his *La Roma di Leone X* (Milan, 1938), 341–84. For the humanistic ambience of Leonine Rome, see also V. de Caprio, "Intellettuali e mercato del lavoro nella Roma medicea," *Studi romani* 29 (1981): 29–46, and idem, "L'area umanistica romana (1513–1527)," ibid. 29 (1981): 321–35.

22. See Pastor, *History of the Popes,* vol. 9.

23. Ibid.

24. See J. Hook, *The Sack of Rome, 1527* (London, 1972), and A. Chastel, *The Sack of Rome, 1527,* trans. B. Archer (Princeton, 1983).

25. For the curia, see the general discussion in N. del Re, *La Curia Romana* (Rome, 1972). The best discussion of the curia in the Renaissance remains W. von Hofmann, *Forschungen zur Geschichte der kurialen Behörden vom Schisma bis zur Reformation,* 2 vols. (Rome, 1914); for further bibliography, see D'Amico, *Renaissance Humanism in Papal Rome,* 19–28 and notes. For a specific aspect of curial life, see B. M. Hallman, *Italian Cardinals, Reform, and the Church as Property, 1492–1563* (Berkeley, 1985).

26. In addition to the citations in the previous note, see also H. Bresslau,

Handbuch der Urkundenlehre für Deutschland und Italien (Leipzig, 1912), 1:287–352; P. Rabikauskas, S. J., *Diplomatica pontificia (Praelectionum lineamenta)* (Rome, 1972), 75–140, and "Chancellerie apostolique," in *Dictionnaire de droit canonique*, 7 vols. (Paris, 1924–65), 3:465–71. A general discussion in English can be found in Thomson, *Popes and Princes*, chap. 5.

27. See J. F. D'Amico, "De Dignitate et Excellentia Curiae Romanae: Humanism and the Papal Court," in *Umanesimo a Roma nel Quattrocento*, 83–112.

28. For Sadoleto, see R. Douglas, *Jacopo Sadoleto 1477–1547: Humanist and Reformer* (Cambridge, MA, 1959).

29. See Dionisotti, "Chierici e laici," for discussion.

30. See D'Amico, *Renaissance Humanism in Papal Rome*, chap. 9.

31. See D. Girgensohn, "Wie wird man Kardinal? Kuriale und ausserkuriale Karrieren an der Wende des 14. zum 15. Jahrhundert," *Quellen und Forschungen aus italienischen Archiven und Bibliotheken* 57 (1977): 138–62, and Thomson, *Popes and Princes*, chap. 3.

32. See F. di Bernardo, *Un vescovo umanista alla corte pontificia: Ginnantonio Campano (1429–1477)* (Rome, 1975); M. D. Feld, "Sweynheym and Pannartz, Cardinal Bessarion and Neoplatonism: Renaissance Humanism and Two Early Printers' Choice of Texts," *Harvard Library Bulletin* 30.3 (1982): 282–335; and the collected essays on Perotti in *Res publica litteraria* 4 (1981) and 5 (1982).

33. For the Renaissance cardinalate, see D. Hay, "Renaissance Cardinals," *Synthesis* (Bucharest) 3 (1976): 35–46, and D'Amico, *Renaissance Humanism in Papal Rome*, index and above, note 31. For the cardinals' economic problems, see D. S. Chambers, "The Economic Predicament of Renaissance Cardinals," *Studies in Medieval and Renaissance History* 3 (1966): 289–313.

34. See D'Amico, *Renaissance Humanism in Papal Rome*, 16–18.

35. Ibid., chap. 2, for discussion and bibliography.

36. Ibid., 46.

37. See Feld, "Sweynheym and Pannartz."

38. See A. della Torre, *Paolo Marsi da Peschina: Contributo alla storia dell'-Accademia Pomponiana* (Rocca S. Casciano, 1903), and D'Amico, *Renaissance Humanism in Papal Rome*, chap. 4.

39. See V. Zabughin, *Giulio Pomponio Leto: Saggio critico*, 3 vols. (Rome, 1909–12); for more recent bibliography, see D'Amico, *Renaissance Humanism in Papal Rome*, index.

40. See A. J. Dunston, "A Student's Notes on Lectures by Giulio Pomponio Leto," *Antichthon* 1 (1967): 86–94; see also D. S. Chambers, "*Studium Urbis* and *gabella studii*: The University of Rome in the Fifteenth Century," in *Cultural Aspects of the Italian Renaissance: Essays in Honor of Paul Oskar Kristeller*, ed. C. Clough (Manchester and New York, 1976), 68–110.

41. For Platina, see C. Trinkaus, *In Our Image and Likeness: Humanity and Divinity in Italian Humanist Thought*, 2 vols. (Chicago, 1970), 1:294–97;

and R. J. Palermino, "Platina's History of the Popes" (M.Litt. thesis, University of Edinburgh, 1973). The edition of Platina's *History of the Popes*, ed. G. Gaida, contains a valuable introduction, *Liber de Vita Christi ac Omnium Pontificum* (Città di Castello, 1913–32).

42. See Weiss, *Renaissance Discovery of Classical Antiquity*, index.

43. See A. J. Dunston, "Pope Paul II and the Humanists," *Journal of Religious History* 7.4 (1973): 287–306; R. J. Palermino, "The Roman Academy, the Catacombs and the Conspiracy of 1468," *Archivum historiae pontificiae* 18 (1980): 117–55, and D'Amico, *Renaissance Humanism in Papal Rome*, 92–97.

44. For a different view, see Feld, "Sweynheym and Pannartz."

45. For Cortesi, see J. F. D'Amico and K. Weil-Garris, *The Renaissance Cardinal's Ideal Palace: A Chapter from Cortesi's "De Cardinalatu"* (Rome, 1980); D'Amico, "Paolo Cortesi's Rehabilitation"; idem, *Renaissance Humanism in Papal Rome*, index; and idem, "Contra divinationem: Paolo Cortesi's Attack on Astrology," in *Renaissance Studies in Honor of Craig Hugh Smyth* (Florence, 1985), 1:281–91.

46. See T. Simar, *Christophe de Longueil, humaniste (1488–1522)* (Louvain, 1911), 194–203, and P. P. Bober, "The 'Coryciana' and the Nymph Coryciana," *Journal of the Warburg and Courtauld Institutes* 40 (1977): 223–39.

47. See L. Geiger, "Der alteste römische Musenalmanach," *Vierteljahrschrift für Kultur und Literatur der Renaissance* 1 (1886): 145–61, and V. A. Bonita, "The Saint Anne Altar in Sant'Agostino: Restoration and Interpretation," *Burlington Magazine* 124 (1982): 268–80.

48. See J. Ruysschaert, "Les péripéties inconnues de l'édition des 'Coryciana' de 1524," in *Atti del convegno di studi su Angelo Colocci* (Jesi, 1972), 45–60.

49. See *Atti del convegno di studi su Angelo Colocci*; F. Ubaldini, *Vita di Mons. Angelo Colocci*, ed. V. Fanelli (Vatican City, 1964); and V. Fanelli, *Ricerche su Angelo Colocci e sulla Roma cinquecentesca* (Vatican City, 1979).

50. See Simar, *Christophe de Longueil*, and D. Gnoli, *Un giudizio de lesa romanità sotto Leone X* (Rome, 1891).

51. For Renaissance Latin, see J. IJsewijn, *Companion to Neo-Latin Studies* (Amsterdam, 1977), and J. F. D'Amico, "The Progress of Renaissance Latin Prose: The Case of Apuleianism," *Renaissance Quarterly* 37 (1984): 351–92.

52. See A. Hobson, "The Printer of the Greek Editions 'In Gymnasio Mediceo ad Caballinum Montem,' " in *Studi di biblioteconomia e storia del libro in onore di Francesco Barberi* (Rome, 1976), 331–35.

53. See Monfasani, *George of Trebizond*.

54. For examples of Hebrew scholars in Rome, see A. Kleinhans, "De vita et operibus Petri Galatini, O.F.M., scientiarum biblicarum cultoris (c. 1460–1540)," *Antonianum* 1 (1926): 145–78, and H. Galliver, "Agathius Guidacerius, 1477–1540: An Early Hebrew Grammarian in Rome and Paris," *Historia Judaica* 2.2 (1940): 85–101.

55. See Mitchell, *Rome in the High Renaissance*, for the vernacular.

56. See I. Scott, *Controversies over the Imitation of Cicero* (New York, 1910), for discussion and translations of important texts.

57. See D'Amico, "Progress of Renaissance Latin Prose," and idem, *Renaissance Humanism in Papal Rome*, chap. 5.

58. These texts are available in Scott, *Controversies*.

59. See D'Amico, *Renaissance Humanism in Papal Rome*, 119–20.

60. See O'Malley, *Praise and Blame in Renaissance Rome*.

61. See ibid., index; D'Amico, *Renaissance Humanism in Papal Rome*, index; J. M. McManamon, "The Ideal Renaissance Pope: Funeral Oratory from the Papal Court," *Archivum historiae pontificiae* 14 (1976): 5–70, and F. Cruciani, "Il teatro dei Ciceroniani," *Forum italicum* 14 (1980): 356–77.

62. See M. Di Cesare, *Vida's Christiad and Vergilian Epic* (New York, 1964). For the text, see Marco Girolamo Vida, *The Christiad: A Latin–English Edition*, ed. and trans. G. C. Drake and C. A. Forbes (Carbondale, IL, 1978).

63. See H. H. Brummer and T. Janson, "Art, Literature and Politics: An Episode in the Roman Renaissance," *Konsthistorisk Tidskrift* 45 (1976): 79–93, and D'Amico, *Renaissance Humanism in Papal Rome*, 134–37.

64. See Feld, "Sweynheym and Pannartz," and Lee, *Sixtus IV and Men of Letters*, chap 3.

65. For Brandolini, see Trinkaus, *In Our Image and Likeness*, index; O'Malley, *Praise and Blame in Renaissance Rome*, index; and J. M. McManamon, "Renaissance Preaching, Theory and Practice: A Holy Thursday Sermon of Aurelio Brandolini," *Viator* 10 (1979): 354–73.

66. See R. Weiss, "Andrea Fulvio, antiquario romano (ca. 1470–1527)," *Annali della Scuola Normale Superiore di Pisa* 2d ser. 28 (1959): 1–44.

67. See F. Castagnoli, "Raphael and Ancient Rome," in *The Complete Works of Raphael* (New York, 1969), 569–84, and P. N. Pagliara, "La Roma antica di Fabio Calvo: Note sulla cultura antiquaria e architettonica," *Psicon* 8–9 (1977): 65–87.

68. See M. Miglio, *Storiografia pontificia del Quattrocento* (Bologna, 1975), and D'Amico, "Papal History and Curial Reform." For a specific history, that of Nicholas V, see L. Onofri, "Sacralità, immaginazione e proposte politiche: La *Vita* di Niccolò V di Giannozzo Manetti," *Humanistica Lovaniensia* 28 (1979): 27–77.

69. See C. L. Stinger, "Greek Patristics and Christian Antiquity in Renaissance Rome," in *Rome in the Renaissance*, 153–69.

70. See J. W. O'Malley, "Some Renaissance Panegyrics of Aquinas," *Renaissance Quarterly* 27 (1974): 174–92, and H. H. Gray, "Valla's *Encomium of St. Thomas Aquinas* and the Humanist Conception of Christian Antiquity," in *Essays in History and Literature Presented by Fellows of the Newberry Library to Stanley Pargellis*, ed. H. Bluhm (Chicago, 1965), 37–51. An English translation of the oration can be found in *Renaissance Philosophy: New Translations*, ed. L. A. Kennedy (The Hague, 1973), 17–26.

71. See Trinkaus, *In Our Image and Likeness*, index.

72. See J. W. O'Malley, "The Feast of Thomas Aquinas in Renaissance Rome: A Neglected Document and Its Impact," *Rivista di storia della chiesa in Italia* 35 (1981): 1–27.

73. See the translation of the introduction to the *Liber sententiarum* in *Renaissance Philosophy: New Translations*, 29–37; and G. Farris, *Eloquenza e teologia nel "Prooemium in librum primum sententiarum" di Paolo Cortesi* (Savona, 1972), and D'Amico, *Renaissance Humanism in Papal Rome*, chap. 6.

74. See Weil-Garris and D'Amico, *Renaissance Cardinal's Ideal Palace*, and D'Amico, *Renaissance Humanism in Papal Rome*, index.

12 &~ HUMANISM IN NAPLES
Mario Santoro

I N TRACING THE ESSENTIAL CHARACTERISTICS AND DEVELOPMENT OF
humanism at Naples, I shall limit this discussion to the culture of the
Aragonese period (1442–1501). Contrary to the beliefs of older historians, humanism in Naples was not something "imported."[1] Indeed,
when one reads the celebration by writers in that age of the cultural
renewal brought about by the Aragonese monarchy, one cannot escape
the conviction that in the eyes of contemporaries the new dynasty marked
a decisive turning point in Neapolitan cultural life. The rebirth seemed
to contemporaries more conspicuous by comparison with the depressed
condition of Neapolitan culture in the last years of the Angevin regime.[2]
But even allowing for exaggeration, humanism asserted itself decisively
in Naples under the rule of Alfonso I (1442–58).

The humanistic renewal was initiated through the presence of outstanding scholars from other parts of Italy—Valla, Manetti, Facio, Panormita, and others. Nevertheless, Neapolitan humanism soon assumed
novel characteristics of its own and made Naples one of the greatest
intellectual centers of Italy and Europe. The "Neapolitanization" of humanism did not spell provincialism, but rather the recasting of humanist
ideas in relation to the historical and cultural experiences of Naples. It is
no accident that this process paralleled the institution of collaborative
ties between the monarchy and the Neapolitan nobility. The parallel development was made possible by the fact that humanistic studies were
not actually new in the fifteenth century but dated back to the early fourteenth century and the court of King Robert (1309–43), and that they
had remained alive in alternating phases through the Angevin era until
the time of King Ladislas (1386–1414).[3] It was not by chance that the
jurist Paride del Pozzo, in dedicating to Diomede Carafa his *Libellus syndacatus officialium* celebrating the cultural policies of Ferrante (1458–
94), compared that sovereign to Frederick II and King Robert, under
whom the grand tradition of studies restored by Ferrante had reached its
highest levels.[4]

Even so, Neapolitan humanism cannot be simply identified with the
humanism of southern Italy. Although the capital played a strong centralizing role, there were forms of humanistic culture that reflected local
conditions. Examples that come easily to mind are the "Greek human-

ism"[5] in Calabria, Puglia, and Sicily where the classical heritage was strong; and the spontaneous cultural life that developed around famous princely families such as the Acquaviva of Atri and the Caracciolo of Melfi.

Even in limiting ourselves to Naples we must recognize that humanism was only one among a number of other cultures in the capital and that it was in competition with many of them.[6] There was, for example, a fundamental antipathy between the science of nature and the science of man (the *studia humanitatis*). When Pontano, in his dialogue *Aegidius*, attempted a reconciliation between "physics," theology, and eloquence, he did so with an eye to the enemies of the humanists, the "new philosophers," the "barbarians," the logicians, the grammarians, and the "Hellenizers." All of the latter constituted a lively presence in the convents, the university, and even the royal court at Naples, and one must take account of them in order to understand the cultural debate that took place under the guidance of Pontano's teachings.[7]

Finally, it must be noted that even within the humanistic circle attitudes and points of view depended on the geographic and social origins, the cultural interests, the moral convictions, and even the personalities of its most important representatives. Thus, even though humanists belonged to the same cultural climate, men like Panormita, Pontano, Tristano Caracciolo, Antonio de Ferrariis Il Galateo, and Jacopo Sannazaro gave to their humanist works their own peculiar stamp; each had a profound effect on Neapolitan culture and within the larger arena of Italian and European culture.

*   *   *

Essential, then, for the inception[8] of the grand era of Neapolitan humanism was the fervid and intense cultural activity carried on in the court of Alfonso the Magnanimous, "the grand lamp of literature."[9] Independently of the limits and quality of his culture, Alfonso, through his impassioned love of literature, his fanatic, even ingenuous, cult of the "ancients," his unqualified generosity to scholars, men of letters, and artists, embodied in exemplary fashion that model of the patron-prince whom contemporaries celebrated and who represented a strong pole of attraction for intellectuals from every part of the peninsula. The cultural operation he enlivened and encouraged had already been shaped by the dominant themes of the humanist ideology: the cult of the "book," faith in the exemplary value of the ancients, the duty to recover the patrimony of the past and draw from it lessons for the present. "[Alfonso] used to say that the best advisers he had were the dead, meaning books, since those showed him what he had to do without fear, dishonor, mercy, or even respect."[10]

An important instance of the sovereign's direct and diligent participation in the intellectual life of the court was the literary gathering that took place every day after dinner in his library, called "the hour of the book." Not less significant was the care with which Alfonso oversaw the formation and growth of the library, which was destined to become one of the richest and most valuable collections on the peninsula.[11] And it was not by chance that among the books acquired for the library the classics—Livy, Plutarch, Quintilian, and the Latin poets—occupied a privileged position.

The circle formed around the sovereign—that circle which Minieri Ricci called the "Alfonsine Academy," the first nucleus of the future Pontanian Academy—engaged in the common work of research through "colloquies" and the philological analysis of texts. Their presence made the court a place of lively discussion, and in the process they contributed to its growing prestige.[12]

In their years at Alfonso's court, Lorenzo Valla (1407–1457) and Bartolomeo Facio (1400–1457) contributed significantly to making Neapolitan culture visible to humanist culture elsewhere in Italy and Europe. Valla composed some of his major works, including the *Dialecticae disputationes*, the *Elegantiae*, the *Annotationes* on Livy; only the *Historia Ferdinandi regis* remained unfinished. Valla's high philological achievement, with its task of restoring the language of ancient wisdom and recovering the patrimony of Roman civilization, pointed to the ideals of a culture addressed to the formation and enrichment of moral and civil conscience, and against the disputes of medieval dialecticians, against the metaphysical abstractions of the theologians, against an empty formalism.[13] Facio's works ranged from lexicography, as in *De verborum priscorum significatione*, to history and biography, as in *De rebus gestis ab Alphonso primo* and *De viris illustribus*, to his discussion in moral treatises of some of the central themes of humanistic culture, such as happiness and the dignity of man, as in *De humanae vitae felicitate* and *De excellentia ac praestantia hominis*.[14]

The theme debated in the latter treatise was also addressed in one of the most famous and symbolic works of humanistic culture, *De dignitate et excellentia hominis*, composed at Alfonso's invitation by Giannozzo Manetti between 1451 and 1457 in polemic against the opinions expressed by Facio. Against the thesis of Facio, who identified the excellence of the human condition with the supranatural life, Manetti celebrated the earthly conditions of man, his superiority over all other animals, his exceptional gifts of body and spirit. Without dwelling on this well-known work, it is essential to emphasize its fundamental motif, which was destined to have a great development in Neapolitan humanistic culture: the optimistic concept of the strivings of the human being who, far from being discouraged by the evil and dangers of life, shows his most authentic and innate moral endowments precisely in the struggle in which he is constantly engaged.

The presence of Greek scholars, or experts in the Greek language, represented another important interest in Alfonso's circle. Among those brought by the monarch to improve knowledge of the Greek language and, most of all, to increase by means of Latin translations knowledge of the texts from the cultural patrimony of ancient Greece, were Giorgio da Tiferno, Pier Candido Decembrio, Theodore Gaza, and George of Trebizond. Theodore Gaza, during his brief and troubled residence in Naples, made an unforgettable impression on the Neapolitan humanists. George of Trebizond was the author of the *Rhetoricorum libri,* which became an important text for the study of rhetoric and poetics.[15]

In a different order of ideological and literary concerns can be placed another outstanding scholar who also participated for some time in Alfonso's circle: Flavio Biondo (1392–1463). An ardent advocate of the interests and vitality of Catholic Rome, Flavio Biondo made a vigorous appeal for a crusade against the Turks, especially in his discourse, *De expeditione in Turchos.*[16] In this work, dedicated to Alfonso, he asserted with lucid argumentation, based on a full reconnaissance of the regions under Turkish domination, that if the Christian princes had been harmoniously united against the invading Turkish imperialism, the outcome of the crusade would have been favorable. Certainly Flavio Biondo brought to the attention of the intellectuals in Alfonso's circle a theme of burning significance, destined to remain for a long time in Italian and European culture one of the greatest themes of western civilization. But what is of particular interest here is the method, of which Biondo offered a significant example, of analyzing a political problem based on both geographical reconnaissance and use of the lessons of history.

Antonio Beccadelli, called Panormita (1394–1471), the principal moving force and protagonist in the cultural activities of the circle, assumed the primary responsibility of coordinator and director. Panormita was also one of the most prominent personalities of intellectual society in Quattrocento Italy and especially in Aragonese Naples.[17] His youthful work, the *Hermaphroditus,* secured his fame as a poet with its striking success, while his *Epistolae gallicae* bespoke a sense of his rare artistic abilities—abilities confirmed later in the collection of his *Epistolae campanae.* In his last years, with *De dictis et factis Alphonsi regis,* he took up with novel results a celebrated genre of the classical tradition and wrote one of the most lively and incisive examples in the literature of persuasion. With the *Liber rerum gestarum Ferdinandi regis* he left a major work of Neapolitan historiography, but he was, above all, a principal organizer of culture.[18]

Panormita's long intellectual career began at Naples in 1435 with the meeting with Alfonso of Aragon in Sicily that fixed his destiny. In those difficult years Alfonso was engaged in the conquest of the Neapolitan kingdom, and Panormita carried out a number of important and delicate tasks, giving proof of his political and administrative abilities, securing the sovereign's trust, and sealing with him a close cultural friendship. Therefore, when the king finally entered Naples, he already counted Panormita among his most trusted and closest collaborators. From that moment until his death, Panormita took on the role of protagonist in the political and cultural life of the dynasty, first under Alfonso and then under his successor, Ferrante. It is impossible to estimate the extent of his role in encouraging and directing Alfonso's passion for literature and shaping his literary tastes. But certainly Panormita played a momentous role, if one considers his diligent and constant work for the growth of the library collection, his skillful work as a mediator between the court and scholars of other countries, and above all his direction of the literary gatherings in the sovereign's circle. His activities reached their apex after the death of Alfonso and the accession of Ferrante.[19] The literary circle ceased to meet at the court and met instead at Panormita's home, a move that signaled the transition of an elite, courtly culture to a culture more open to the city and to everyday life—a cultural change of decisive importance. The *Porticus antoniana* was soon to become the Accademia Pontaniana, which set in motion that process of Neapolitanization of culture that was destined to give Neapolitan humanism its unmistakably original character.

✻　　✻　　✻

A significant testimony to the arrival of humanistic culture in the official culture of Aragonese Naples is the renewal of the university's academic structure. Reformed during the reign of Alfonso mainly for goals of professional education, the university experienced a decisive change under the cultural policies of Ferrante with the establishment in 1465 of four chairs of humanities, of which one was for Greek literature. In this way the *studia humanitatis* made their official entry into the structures of university culture.[20]

But even though the opening of the university to the *studia humanitatis* was brought about by the will of the sovereign and by the king's principal collaborators in cultural policy, Panormita and Ferrante's royal secretary, Antonello de Petruciis[21]—so that the change was not the result of a struggle of the new culture against the methods and curriculum of traditional culture (as happened at other universities in the peninsula, for example, at Padua)—still, the struggle was not completely lacking at Naples, nor was the confrontation any less ardent between the *studia humanitatis* and the methods and tendencies of the traditional university culture represented, in various ways, by the older disciplines. For example, instruction in Greek, first by Constantinus Lascaris—though for only a year—was a major factor in the growth of the program (common to more advanced humanistic culture throughout the peninsula) of recovering the original reading of ancient texts against the distortions and alterations of medieval translations. Also significant is the particular attention paid at Naples to Aristotle and the Aristotelians within the framework of general cultural renewal.[22] A good example of this emphasis was the praise given by Pontano to Giovanni Attaldi, a teacher of philosophy at the university. According to Pontano, this man related philosophy to the dignity of the grand classical tradition as opposed to old-fashioned teachers burdened by the sophisms of the logicians of northern Europe:

> For a long time I have been bewailing the condition of philosophy, because after having been cultivated by the Greeks, then honored by the ancient Romans, it subsequently lost so much of its old refinement and dignity among the French and British, and among some men in our own country. John Actaldus, a noble teacher, a man of great intellect, the best teaching, and a quality of judgment that placed him among the most select, finally consoled me. For not content with the many interpreters whom he saw and studied with as a young man, he investigated all of the writings of Aristotle by a different method, seeking not so much those sophistical subtleties as the things themselves. He introduced the hope that it would presently come about that a more lucid philosophy would appear, not one that would be dragged into such different and opposed meanings and offer students an occasion for quarreling rather than for thinking rightly. For he hears and understands the philosophers speaking in his own Greek language, he handles our ancient authors, he compares the ancient Latins with the ancient Greeks.[23]

Thus Aristotelianism was renewed under the influence of humanistic philology and restored from a state of abstract sophisms to its fundamental function of a great guide to living. It assumed, not only in the university but also in that most active intellectual center, the Pontanian Academy, a dominant function, without disparaging the study of Plato and the Platonists.

The long and profitable instruction carried on in the university by one of the first holders of a chair of humanity, the Neapolitan Giuniano Maio, is related to some of his works, conceived in the classroom and written for class use, but soon in circulation. One of them, *De priscorum proprietate verborum*, was printed by Moravo in 1475 and in fifteen years went through at least six editions, not counting reprintings. Others were an edition of Pliny's letters (also printed by Moravo, in 1476) and an edition of selected orations of Cicero, published by the same printer in 1480. A disciple of Valla, Maio profited from his master's teachings but emphasized instead his own propensity for a very broad concept of Latinity; he drew from the literary traditions of all the ancients without exclusions or limitations. Thus he sought to contribute to the restoration of Latin studies against the "barbarians." In preparing his editions of Pliny and Cicero, Maio shows that he was conscious of the moral and intellectual value of studying these works, beyond simple formal concerns. Thus, for example, with regard to Cicero, it was not by chance that Maio's selection favored the political orations, for he placed emphasis on the exemplary character of the moral and civil values that Cicero preached. For Maio, to study Cicero meant not only to recover lessons in oratory but even more to provide great lessons for living.[24]

Maio dedicated the major share of his activity to teaching, for besides university instruction he carried on private tutoring and was the preceptor of princely children, such as Pietro, Alfonso, Carlo, and Isabella of Aragon. Not only did he participate actively in the life of the Pontanian Academy, but the king appointed him to several important offices. A testimony of his devotion to the sovereign and of his disposition to compete with the most important Aragonese writers in elaborating the dynasty's ideology was the treatise *De majestate*, composed in the vernacular around 1492. This work took its place in the genre of ethical-political treatises, one of the most important and significant genres of Aragonese humanist literature.

Besides such scholars as Bartolomeo Filalite (Bartolomeus Philaletes), Antonio Carcillo, Giovanni Siculo, and Baldassare Officiano, two authoritative and renowned neo-Neapolitan professors contributed decisively to the affirmation and development of humanistic culture in the University of Naples: the Milanese Aurelio Bienato and the Florentine Francesco Pucci, who began teaching at the university in 1470 and 1484, respectively.[25] Both remind us of the fertile relations between Naples and Milan and between Naples and Florence. The appointment to the

University of Naples of Aurelio Bienato was very probably prompted by Ippolita Sforza, the learned princess, daughter of Francesco Sforza and pupil of Constantius Lascaris. She came to Naples in 1465 as the wife of Alfonso, duke of Calabria, the future King Alfonso II. Even for Naples royal marriages obviously constituted an important channel of cultural, as well as political, relations with the other states of the peninsula. Ippolita—one among a number of women from the upper class who became important in the cultural life of Italy, especially during the second half of the Quattrocento—in her new surroundings became an ambassador and mediator of the culture of her country of origin, exercising this function so effectively because she was endowed with a natural grace and a refined literary education. She not only saw to appointment to the university of her teacher, Constantius Lascaris and, later, of Bienato, but also, in the course of more than two decades spent at Naples before her premature death in 1488, she encouraged literary studies and was the generous patron of writers and men of letters. In their turn, other Aragonese princesses exercised an important role of cultural mediation in the courts they entered as wives. Eleanora, a daughter of Ferrante, entered the court of Ferrara in 1471 as the wife of Ercole d'Este; Beatrice, another daughter of Ferrante, was married in 1476 to Matthias Corvinus, king of Hungary; and Isabella, daughter of Alfonso II, was married at Milan to Giangaleazzo Sforza.

Bienato was closely tied to the views of Valla, his teacher; however, he emphasized the grammatical aspects of Valla's work more than his thought—it is worth mentioning the success and popularity of Bienato's compendium of Valla's *Elegantiae* as well as his careful and precise commentary on Quintilian's *Institutiones oratoriae*. Francesco Pucci, by contrast, reminds us of the political and cultural relations between Naples and Florence, which were very significant in the years before his appointment but became closer and even more cordial in the 1480s until the death of Lorenzo de' Medici in 1492, who, together with Ferrante, was one of two grand advocates of the policy of equilibrium. A pupil of Poliziano, Pucci made himself both within and outside the University of Naples an advocate of his teacher's philological methods. But Pucci was also independent and original, for while he continued his master's teaching in a methodological sense, he also directed and carried out his studies on writers and questions that reflected specific new interests.

The sovereign gave both Bienato and Pucci important posts, such as the office of *librero major* that Pucci held for about a decade after 1491. The close and open participation of these two professors (and especially Pucci) in Neapolitan cultural life is attested above all by their inclusion among the fellows of the Pontanian Academy. Also very significant is the portrait of the Florentine that emerges from one of Pontano's dialogues, *Aegidius*, in which Pucci figures as one of the principal interlocutors. He appears as the energetic interpreter of a fundamental aspect of Pontano's thought—the reconciliation of eloquence with natural science and theology. But independently of Poliziano, Pucci stands out for his marked and fervent predilection for Vergil and his original studies of the poet, as well as for his archaeological interests—studying Greco-Roman monuments in the Phlegraean fields near Naples. The affirmation in the *Aegidius* of the originality of Pucci's studies in comparison with those of his Tuscan master—just as in the same dialogue Pontano praises the originality of the Roman scholar Pietro Tamira, disciple of Giulio Pomponio Leto—perhaps does not simply attest to the new cultural destiny of the two scholars at Naples, but rather is proof of a more general opposition between the methodology represented by Poliziano and Leto and the philologico-literary methodology adopted by Pontano's circle.

✳   ✳   ✳

Although humanism acquired a prominent place in the university, humanist culture in Naples had its most congenial seat in the Pontanian Academy. Taking hold of the city and promoting the union of the most active components of the capital's cultural life, the academy became in a short time one of the grandest and most active intellectual centers of Italy, first under the guidance of Panormita and, after his death in 1471, under Giovanni Pontano (1422–1503)—whence it took its name—the greatest protagonist of culture in Aragonese Naples and one of the greatest protagonists of Renaissance civilization.

All the evidence we have from Pontano's works—especially his dialogues *Antonius, Actius,* and *Aegidius*—provides us with an extremely lively and varied picture of the gatherings of the academy's fellows.[26] These gatherings were characterized by a great variety of themes, from history, poetics, politics, archaeology, and morals; by a common disposition to confront and reexamine commonly shared intellectual commitments; and by a desire to ground the topics and questions of their discussions in concrete reality in light of the teachings of the ancients. Through its growing prestige and great success in representing the entire Neapolitan intellectual community, the academy constituted a magnetic pole for all scholars who came to the capital either from other parts of the kingdom or from other states of the peninsula. Therefore, in addition to the usual court relations, it was most of all through the group around Pontano that deep and intense relations were established between Naples and other Italian intellectual centers, such as Venice, Florence, Ferrara,

Milan, and Rome. Through a great openness to the ideas and opinions of others (and by a consistent aversion to "logicians," "Hellenizers," and grammarians in the narrowest sense), the fellows of the academy brought to the discussions a sincere spirit of tolerance. But this disposition for tolerance did not imply indifference and complicity with regard to the vices of society or the corruption of morals, which the humanists strongly and ruthlessly denounced, often using irony and even sarcasm, as, for example, in Pontano's *Charon* and Galateo's *Heremita*.

*   *   *

The academy's openness to intellectuals of diverse social backgrounds, coming from different regions, and motivated by various political, moral, and cultural interests, helps to explain the great variety of topics and questions addressed in the discussions and, at the same time, the broad range of opinions and viewpoints. Around Panormita and Pontano were gathered members of the citizen nobility, such as Tristano Caracciolo; the barons, including Belisario and Andrea Matteo Acquaviva; representatives of the new nobility, such as Antonello de Petruciis and Diomede Carafa himself;[27] representatives of the minor nobility and bourgeoisie, such as the Neapolitans Enrico Poderico or Pietro Golino, called Compatre (Godfather), or Jacopo Sannazaro; natives of the kingdom operating between the capital and their original province, such as Antonio de Ferrariis, Il Galateo;[28] foreigners who were Neapolitanized, such as Francesco Pucci; and finally foreigners who, for various reasons, stayed in the capital for different lengths of time. The participation of this last group, coming from different centers of the peninsula, enhanced the multiplicity of themes and opposing ideas and backgrounds. Because of this great diversity the academy has been characterized as seemingly rambling, disorganized, and eclectic. In reality it reflects the disposition, so typical of Pontano, to base dialogue on a diversity of experience and to oppose every kind of academicism and dogmatism. But in addition to this diversity and openness there was a common faith in the humane function of culture, in the civilizing function of literature, in the inalienable value of reason, and in the essential humanity of the divine power of poetry.

The conclusion of one of Pontano's last works, *De immanitate*, symbolizes this faith: it is an exaltation of the civilizing function of literature that can be seen as the humanist's spiritual testament.[29] It is a peremptory reaffirmation of a belief that seemed threatened or endangered by the growing dominance of the irrational and contingent marked by the political, social, and moral crisis brought on by the French invasion:

Humanity and the study of civic life must be more zealously cultivated. The liberal arts [are] the ornaments and bonds of a cultivated human society. A mind must not only be perfected in civic
customs but also raised to heavenly things, and it must be considered what would be especially pleasing to that highest and best
parent and guide of the whole universe, and by which arts above
all we can be similar to the gods themselves. But we shall be most
similar to them if we withdraw as much as possible from the nature of beasts and by taming the affections common to beasts, join
ourselves to reason. Following reason we shall rule even over the
other living creatures with excellence and we shall approach the
gods themselves as nearly as possible.[30]

*   *   *

The fidelity of Pontano and his circle to an ideal of culture interpreted as
the knowledge and study of the art of living is reflected in the deliberate-
ness with which they based their literary activity explicitly on the Ciceronian principle of the indissoluble union of *eloquentia* and *sapientia*.
And it is very significant that one of the protagonists of Pontano's circle,
Il Galateo, was directly involved in the so-called "crusade against the
barbarians" announced by Ermolao Barbaro the Younger. With his dic-
tum, "What matters to me are not words but meanings, erudition not
elocution," Galateo placed the emphasis on his interest in "things" and,
at the risk of overstepping the boundaries of humanistic orthodoxy,
transformed the pair *sapientia–eloquentia* into *sapientia–facta*. "Barbarism is to be avoided more in acts than in words." In this way we can
understand the predominant interest (already noted) of Pontano's circle
in Aristotle, the philosopher of the earthly city and of the experience of
the moral and civil life. This concept also explains their interest in St.
Thomas. Equally significant was their interest in the church fathers, especially St. Augustine, as the Christian writers who were most congenial
to humanistic culture and who were, along with the ancients, the teachers of the most authentic human values.

Pontano's circle highlighted, with their cult of the ancients, the disposition typical of humanistic learning: a critical reading of texts. They
succeeded in situating the teaching and models of the ancients in relation
to their own experience by a constant comparison of these models to the
events, problems, and questions of contemporary reality. Thus the examination of any work will be fruitful only if account is taken of the
historical reality transformed by the author in the myths developed in
his own poetry.

A good example of such works by Pontano are treatises that were formerly considered to be lacking in originality, abstractly reechoing themes and precepts from Aristotle's ethical writings. But more recent scholars, beginning with Giuseppe Toffanin,[31] have seen in them a fundamental witness to Pontano's recognition of the problems confronting contemporary society, and thus of the political and moral teachings to be drawn from it.

*   *   *

Tristano Caracciolo asserts in his *Praecepta ad filium:* "When, through the kindness of the highest God, you have arrived at the age at which you begin to know how to make discriminations among things for yourself, let me bring to you this inevitable judgment sent from heaven to mortals: be sure that you know yourself."[32] And later, drawing on a statement from Cicero, he explained that the motto "Know thyself" is not fulfilled in the knowledge of one's own mind, but also entails knowledge of the real essence of man, of the parts of which he is composed, and of the actions proper to the human condition: "Therefore, first know yourself, but not only as Cicero wishes, that is, your mind; but I want you to know yourself as a man and what parts you consist of, and by what source you direct them and what you are likely to do according to your condition." In placing man at the center of his moral inquiry, Pontano explained that the man to whom he was referring was not the abstract and isolated man, but the "social" man, the real man called to live concretely in society with his passions, instincts, and public and private enthusiasms:

> I confess that I am a man living in the society and assemblies of men, occupied daily with many things, and judging not only actions but also by times, places, persons, business. I am not content with present concerns unless I also consider their relation to the future. I consider virtue herself gentle, mild, favorable at times, and patient. Sometimes, [it] turns us aside a little from the road and advances through bypaths, and an account is taken not only of itself but also of many things, both domestic and public.[33]

This passage attests to the broad realistic perspective from which Pontano—and with him, in different ways, the most diligent protagonists of Neapolitan humanism—formulated their approach to classical authors, their inquiry on the human condition in contemporary culture, and the circumstances and themes of their poetic compositions. From such a perspective, the inquiry was articulated in two different but complementary directions—an investigation of the interior state of man and the relation of man and society at both the private and public levels. Viewing man as a rational creature, they sought to measure the distance between this ideal and the growing irrationality of private and public life in a society becoming more and more out of control and unpredictable.

As I have emphasized elsewhere,[34] it was not by chance that contemporaries expressed great admiration for Pontano's exemplary capacity to combine with equal zeal responsible political action and fervid literary activity. Galateo wrote:

> This is what I admire most in Pontano. He was a man thoroughly occupied in great matters—in the affairs of kings—but he was not a stranger to the rustic life. He was so diligent in his study of letters that a man of leisure would not have been able to do more, but at the same time he was not at all ensnared in business, either public or domestic.[35]

In effect, the concomitance and interaction of the two activities—political and literary—constitute perhaps the most striking attribute of Pontano's personality, as they do to a certain extent of Panormita's, Carafa's, and Caracciolo's. Thus, Pontano's political experience enabled him to endow his literary production with a constant concern for specific and real situations, while his literary culture, his study of the great masters of the past, and his humane learning were certainly of great value in the conduct and events of his diplomatic and political life.

*　　*　　*

Important evidence—which can be used only in part and with caution—of the cultural interests and different types of readers in Neapolitan society, is provided by the works published in Naples in the first decades after the introduction of printing in the capital.[36] It has been observed that the data gained from summary, comprehensive examinations must be used with extreme caution above all because the introduction of printing did not result in the immediate substitution of the printed book for the manuscript codex. Without dwelling at this point on the various reasons for the survival of manuscript book production, suffice it to say that for several decades there coexisted two complementary levels of the circulation of books; the aristocratic level marked by the production and circulation of manuscripts, which were limited to the valuable libraries of princes and nobles or to specialized and selective scholarly collections; and the level of the printed book, which was of broader and more "popular" diffusion, responding to the desires, tastes, and different needs of the several layers of society, including, sometimes, manuscript users.

The types of books selected for printing were determined more by the process of the market than by objective scholarly criteria. Although this process can only partially suggest a hierarchy of values and indexes of interest, these selections do offer precious indications of the book market, of the diverse uses and destinations of books, of different means of diffusion, and, in part, of the tastes of the public or at least certain segments of the public. For example, the large number of legal texts printed for students of law and court practice at the university level was unexceptional. Likewise, the striking numbers of printed medical works (some of which were rather famous) and numerous printed works of religious edification are readily explicable.

As regards instead the printing of literary works, the data are at first glance surprising but finally rather indicative. The number of Latin classics printed, destined for school or for the average reader, was rather limited. For example, Cicero was more often the teacher of Latin style, *ars scribendi*, but sometimes the Cicero of the *De officiis*, teacher of an *ars vivendi;* there was the Ovid of the *ars amandi* and the *Heroides;* Seneca, Terence, and the lyric Horace, whom humanistic culture favored at the expense of the satirist. Also significant were the editions of Manilius's *Astronomicon*, which attests to the broad interest at Naples in astronomy, due to the presence of Buonincontri. Oddly, there were no early editions of Vergil printed at Naples. This poet, who in the circle of Pontano and Sannazaro played a dominant role in the canon of Latin authors, was issued for the first time at Naples only in 1510, with the publication of the *Bucolics* from the printing press of Giovanni Antonio Canneto. And a first edition of Vergil's *Aeneid* at Naples appeared only in 1535.[37] Probably the very rich collection of Vergil manuscripts in the court library, as well as of manuscripts possessed by nobles and scholars, helps to explain this lack of early editions of Vergil.[38]

Certainly not without significance are the editions of writings by the humanists themselves. These can attest the preferences and choices of university instruction, as in the intense editorial activity of Giuniano Maio with the printer Moravo; or interests and themes of great topicality, as Giorgio Fieschi's poem *Eubois* and Carlo Sorrentino's *Cohortatio ad Italos contra Turcas;* or witness the large reading public of the works of humanists such as Pontano.

Very important and significant was the great number of works in the vernacular, which not only attest to the large and growing fortune of the vernacular in Neapolitan culture but also offer an articulate panorama of the popularity of vernacular writers, from the great writers of the Trecento to translations of the Latin works of early humanists to the original writings of Neapolitan poets and authors, including Pietro

Jacopo de Jennaro, Perleoni, Marino Jonata, and Masuccio. There is not space to treat here the many and varied questions suggested by this imposing patrimony of printed works in the vernacular—they range from strictly linguistic subjects to diverse genres and forms of the pre-Aragonese and Aragonese vernacular literature, from the relation between learned and popular literature to the interaction between humanistic culture and vernacular literature. It is particularly important to record here—while bearing in mind a more defined picture of the major intellectual centers of Aragonese Naples—the monumental role that the circle of Frederick of Aragon played in the development, direction, and fate of vernacular literature at Naples—and, broadly speaking, for southern Italy.[39] Frederick, called the literary prince, had had among his teachers Elisio Calenzio, Latin poet and fellow of the Pontanian Academy, and had evidenced from childhood a striking interest in literary culture. In his circle he did not limit himself to merely bestowing favors and protection on poets and writers (though numerous books were dedicated to him), but participated directly and with a critical outlook in the literary events of Naples, especially in matters of publication in the vernacular and the problems connected with the use and patronage of vernacular literature. As has been noted, his meeting in 1476 with Lorenzo de' Medici was very indicative, followed by Lorenzo's sending of the collection made for the Aragonese library accompanied by a letter written by Poliziano.[40] This episode explicitly proved the disposition of the young prince to a critical approach to vernacular texts, especially to "those which had been written poetically in the Tuscan language."

But one must remember that those who participated in the life of the circle, at least for the decade of the 1470s, had already completed their literary education and developed their interests and tastes, and had already chosen certain directions and set their artistic experience. A good example is Masuccio who, in the 1450s, in an early group of *novelle*, had already given an indication of his qualities as a narrator.[41]

To be sure, vernacular literature in Aragonese Naples must not be reduced to only the activity of poets and writers working within or near Frederick's circle. In reality, it was very rich and varied, in large measure recalling the forms and structures of pre-Aragonese vernacular traditions as well as those of other important centers in the Neapolitan kingdom. There existed a wide range of writings, of genres and stylistic approaches in both verse and prose. Examples among prose works include Francesco del Tuppo's *Esopo,* Loise de Rosa's *Ricordi,* Diomede Carafa's *Memoriali,* Orso degli Orsini's *Governo et exercitio de la militia,* and Ceccarela Minutolo's *Lettere.* In my opinion, Frederick's circle exercised a fundamental function in relation to discussion and investigation of the developing "linguistic crisis."[42] And it was no coincidence that the major poet of the circle and the best personal friend of the prince, Jacopo Sannazaro, marked with his *Arcadia*—especially in the edition published by Summontio in 1504—the exemplary success of the adoption of the Tuscan model.

But it is also necessary to emphasize the close relations between Frederick's circle and the literary society gathered in the Pontanian Academy. Not only were several of the great, highly placed participants in the prince's literary circle at the same time fellows (and in the case of Sannazaro protagonists) of the academy, but beginning with Frederick many also valued Latin and joined the study of the classics with the reading of vernacular authors, applying classical models to works in Italian. Thus, the members of Pontano's circle did not disdain the use of the vernacular in literary works, using Italian beyond the obvious practical need of communication. Rather, several humanists who usually wrote in Latin had recourse to the vernacular as a function of the particular nature and audience of the work. Examples of these cases include Giuniano Maio's *De maiestate* and Antonio de Ferrariis Il Galateo's *Espositione del Pater*.

Not less striking seems to me the affinity between the poetic principles held by the vernacular poets of the circle and the model of poetics codified by Pontano's group. For example, there was the principle of originality defended by Perleoni that reflected the position of Panormita, whom Elisio Calenzio in Pontano's dialogue *Antonius* makes the explicit upholder of the imitation of the classics.[43] A good example is the case of Sannazaro, who wrote both in the vernacular (for example, his *Rime* and *Arcadia*), and in Latin (for example, *Eclogae piscatoriae* and *De partu Virginis*). To both languages Sannazaro brought the most refined sensibilities and artistic skill—that craftsmanship which his teacher's poetics, absorbed and adopted by him, had prescribed.

           *   *   *

"Lamp of the orators and mirror of the poets": thus did Masuccio call his friend Pontano in the *Esordio* to *Novelle III*. Here he placed the accent on the poetic teaching that represented the high achievement of the "humanities" in the humanistic myth of poetry. It is not by chance that in frequent eulogies Pontano was most often recalled by contemporaries as a poet.[44] To be sure, poetry, defined as individual composition, as philological research on the texts of the ancients, and as the study of questions of poetics, occupied a privileged position in the activity of Pontano and the Neapolitan humanists. But we must add at once that the other fields of literary activity, which were demonstrated in Pontano's versatile personality, were no less important and fruitful than those of the poetic experience.

In the specific spheres of poetic experience Pontano's doctrine was characteristic of Neapolitan humanism. Here humanism developed with constant diligence in two parallel and complementary directions: theoretical reflections on questions of poetics, suggested and verified by the approach to ancient authors, and creative originality.

It was not by chance that the model of the *Hermaphroditus,* Panormita's collection famous as a turning point and a bold new example in the tradition of humanistic poetry,[45] was, beginning with Pontano, a fundamental point of reference for humanists' training and literary education and, at the same time, the basis of any artistic apprenticeship. With the suggestion of the autonomy of art implicit in the distinction between *mens* and *charta procax,*[46] this work attempted the revitalization of the classical tradition in a modern key. With the identification of craftsmanship as the essence of poetic creation, the way was opened for the very controlled autonomous exercise of the art but led at the same time to reflection and discussion on the problems of poetics.

The discussion of the general and specific themes of poetics linked the study of the ancients, above all Aristotelian rhetoric (through the important contribution of George of Trebizond's *Rhetoric*) with the experiences of contemporary culture; study of the ancient poets and examination of their compositions constituted a constant in the conversations of the academy fellows. This focus is reflected in marked fashion in the course of Pontano's artful literary production from its important beginning, the *Charon,* down to the *Actius,* which symbolized his arrival at a mature and organic theory of art.[47]

Pontano's poetics were characterized by increasing recognition of formal structure—craftsmanship. But this emphasis did not lead him to eschew his own experienced reality. On the contrary, the poet is called upon, in his view, not just to reproduce according to the dictates of *mimesis* and *prepon,* but even to render more admirable (*admirabiliorem*). It was not by chance that Pontano himself, in developing and elaborating the principles of his doctrine, accentuated the cognition of a poetic reality different from the pure reality of nature and of events. "For this reason, because truth by itself would not be able to offer this, now they overlay the truth with imaginary and fabled inventions, now they contrive things that are altogether opposed to the truth and to the nature of things."[48] Nor was it by chance that in his last years he dedicated his more diligent and affectionate efforts to the composition and revision of that work from which he had above all gained his fame: *Urania*. He explicitly compared this poem to Vergil, having perfected and enriched Manilius's poem as Vergil had brought to perfection his Lucretian model:

> Empedocles by his poem uncovered the nature of things for the human race, Dorotheus Sidonius the discipline of astronomy. Lucretius and Manilius were their Latin imitators. Good Christ! What abundance, what ornament, how much glitter sparkles from the very bright lights of the first [Lucretius]. He snatches the reader anywhere he wishes, he makes good what he intends; he exhorts, deters, incites, withdraws with the greatest subtlety and artifice; everything [is said with] greatness and grace, where necessary, and with that admiration concerning which there has been a dispute. So that if those redder marks of age are cleansed away, by which Virgil later cast light on Roman poetic, nothing at all would appear missing. But as to the other [Manilius]—if some splendor of poetic ornament is missing—it was recently added and supplied by our old man. His *Uranus*, I believe, posterity will perhaps judge more freely, because I certainly think they feel less envious about it [the *Urania*].[49]

The most prestigious poets of the academy, or in any case tied to the intellectual life of the academy, from Calenzio to Gabriele Altilio, Girolamo Carbone, Michele Marullo Tarcaniota, and Jacopo Sannazaro, were in various ways collaborators in and contributors to Pontano's theory of poetics. Apart from the meaning, richness, and variety of the production, resulting from the concurrent activities of so many poets, it is necessary to emphasize the importance of the theoretical debate and of the conclusions that by the end of the century Pontano and some of his most congenial fellows, most of all, Sannazaro, were able to offer to the culture of the early Cinquecento. I am not referring only to the individual questions of the moment, such as imitation in regard to poetry and to history (the *oratio soluta*), which were important and were confronted and discussed with great balance. Above all, I am referring to that doctrine of *admiratio* on which more or less all Pontano's circle agreed and which was to have a decisive impact on the tradition of poetics in sixteenth-century Neapolitan culture, from Minturno to Tasso. Finally, I am referring to that decisive displacement of grammatical research in favor of the literary formalism that accompanied or prefigured the codification of Bembo's model.[50]

✳ ✳ ✳

Granted the diverse personalities, thematic and stylistic directions, cultural depth, and artistic sensibility, still all the individual poets can be characterized in varying degrees by the discipline with which they practiced their art, by their constant fidelity to the canon of stylistic and metrical devices corresponding to genres, by the desire to rival in imitation and emulation the models of the ancients, by the clever play of myth and metaphor to bring out explicit or hidden relations with autobiographical experience transfigured through memory, and by the evocation of fables or of rhetorical stylization.

A frequent and deeply felt moral obligation and an urgent insistence both on religious and philosophical motives stemmed from naturalism and Neoplatonism as well as from the new Lucretian awareness of the inescapably contingent quality of the human condition. But together with these qualities, the humanistic faith in the redeeming quality of poetry was worked into a suggestive mythology in the *Hymni naturales* of Michele Marullo Tarcaniota,[51] an original intellectual and poetic figure who was closely tied to the milieu and culture of Neapolitan humanism, particularly to Pontano. Since it is not possible in this essay to dwell on all these poets, I have decided to limit myself to some brief remarks on the two most important ones, Pontano and Sannazaro.[52]

Contemporaries described with admiration the plurality of themes and genres that Pontano had utilized during his long career as a poet. Summonte has observed that while many poets composed only elegiac poetry, others only heroic poetry, still others only verse of six syllables, Pontano treated every genre of poetry with equal skill: "But not even among the Greeks (as far as I have read up to now) do we have anyone who has written both in poetry and in another genre at the same time."[53] And such variety, far from indicating an eclectic, if skilled literary exercise—by implication lacking any profound inspiring motif—in fact demonstrated, on the one hand, an attitude of real delight in artistic experimentation expressed in several different modes, and on the other, the intrinsic disposition of the poet, probably as a reflection of his interest in the human condition in all of its aspects, to translate into poetic images his own experience and his treatment of the varied aspects and levels of existence. Therefore, as I have stated,[54] Pontano's entire poetic corpus in all its vast articulation of themes and forms can be seen as the transcription and mythicizing of the poet's human and intellectual experience in the various realms of existence. It ranges from the pleasant *relaxatio* of daily life to a tolerant and free eroticism, from the happy communion with the vivid beauty of nature to the emotions and memories of domestic intimacy, from the affectionate comradeship with friends and guests to an intense and heartfelt sympathy for the local people, customs, tra-

ditions, and voluptuous and splendid canvas of the city that he loved as
an adopted homeland. Finally the corpus includes an ambitious and enthusiastic inquiry into the mysteries of the starry heavens, a meditation
on death, and a consoling faith in the survival of personal glory assured
by the miracle of the word.

Thus, from first drafts of *Pruritus* done after the manner of Panormita to the whimsical intellectual play of the *Amores,* one experiences
the vivid evocations of scenes and figures of the carefree and tolerant life
at the baths of Baia—evocations in which the literary models become
rediscovered and revived in the reality of thoughtless gaiety that marked
a pause of *relaxatio* in the breathless rhythm of the tasks and duties of
daily life (*Hendecasyllabi seu Baiarum*). The clearest example of Pontano's poetry of domestic sentiment is found in his *De amore coniugali.*
There he treats the death of Lucius in the mournful tones of *Jambici* and
the fabulous scenes from the pastoral world in his *Eclogae,* composed in
emulation of the Vergilian model. There is a suggestive evocation in his
Eridanus of the story of his famous love affair experienced toward the
end of his life; the melancholy gallery of portraits of the dead framed in
the memory by virtue of the word in the *Tumuli;* the astrological poetry
of *Urania* and *Meteororum liber;* and finally the poetry of the hard-
working and tranquil country life in *De hortis Hesperidum.* It is evident
that in his poetic career, Pontano over the course of time developed an
ever greater predilection for Vergil—a Vergil whose quality as a model
and whose Neapolitan character were emphasized by Pontano and his
fellows. At the same time, it is also evident that Pontano was working at
the ambitious task of highlighting moral and doctrinal topics through
suggestive symbols and myths. In this task he brought together doctrine
and art, knowledge of the human condition and fate—seen in terms of
the grandiose and mysterious system of the universe—and consummate
craftsmanship.

Needless to say, there was in all of Pontano's poetry an extraordinary felicity of language that the poet reinvented and shaped in faithfully
following his literary traditions. Thus, he could express with incomparable modernity the most diverse sentiments and different human and
intellectual experiences, from the miracle of the *Neniae* to the marvelous
depiction of mythography in the *Urania.*

*   *   *

Pontano's poetics found in Jacopo Sannazaro (1457–1530) writing both
in the vernacular and in Latin, its greatest and most original collaborator
and heir. Students of Sannazaro frequently insisted on his refined sensibility and artistic skill as the most striking characteristic of his poetic

production. In fact, the poet's artistic, linguistic, and stylistic diligence, evident in the long, minute work of revision of his various compositions, both in Latin and Italian, from *Arcadia* to *De partu Virginis,* gave a precise measure of the extraordinary care with which Sannazaro strove to perfect his writings in accordance with his literary beliefs. Although it is true that craftsmanship constitutes the figure of the poet's workmanship, still one must avoid the temptation in a critical essay to reduce the dimensions of his poetry to mere literary accomplishments. One must not dismiss or belittle the real sentimental and ideal motivations that are reflected or contained in these compositions.

Sannazaro's entire thematic, even in its most diverse structural and stylistic articulations, had its roots in the poet's moral state, in his intense emotional life, and in the consciousness with which he confronted contemporary reality and his own historic and existential condition. For this reason, from the matrix of an enchanting and melancholy awareness of reality there originated two visions on which the poet generally based his work: he attempted through his autobiographical experiences to represent and evoke the real, and he idolized an Edenlike world remote from the conflicts and violence of everyday life and set apart by innocence and human solidarity.

Literary artifice and autobiographical themes were combined in the structure of the various compositions so that they were transformed into moments and tales exemplary of an existential condition that lacked specific historical references and allusions. For example, there is a change from the first redaction of the *Arcadia,* where initially prose was subordinated to the poetic texts, to a later redaction in which prose is primary, with a corresponding change in the work's prevailing lyrical character to one of narrative. The position favored in *Eclogues* reveals emulation of Sienese models, including the projection stamped in these models of a congenial idolization of a world of evasion. These changes marked the beginning of the pastoral romance, the novelty of which Maria Corti has emphasized.[55] They are evidence of a conceptual, not merely formal, transformation; for the "story" takes its shape as an exemplary projection in a literary structure of Dantesque resonance—the reference to the *Vita nuova* is obvious—of an amorous experience recovered in memory in its sweetness and melancholic tenderness. And it was not by chance that frequent allusions to persons and events of Aragonese Naples were inserted in these stories. Although other stories of other personages did have a specific function in the context of the work, they also recalled, more or less openly, the real world of the poet.

The farces, generally speaking, represent rather successful and surely important experimentation with those plays destined for the court.

And even they reveal topics and sentiments stemming from the poet's affective sensibility, as the sentiment of the transience of human fate in *La Giovane e la Vecchia*. Even the *Rime,* which were dedicated in their definitive redaction to Cassandra Marchese and published posthumously in 1530 shortly after the poet's death, represented the codification of the model of Bembo's Petrarchism.[56] The composition of both parts of the collection is characterized by the intrinsic literary transfiguration of autobiographical themes, in addition to its formal value. Therefore, in my opinion, the *Rime* represent not only a model example of the triumph of Bembo's school, but also the poetic mirror of an interior life of intense emotion.

Although one cannot divide Sannazaro's poetic history schematically between works written before and after his exile, certainly the experience of the years lived on French soil (1501–4) had a striking bearing not just on his intellectual and moral biography but also on the development and orientation of his poetry.[57] To be sure, in his last period of activity, he continued to write polished and correct compositions in Italian; thus, not by chance did he leave, in addition to the collection of the *Rime,* other compositions that are now contained in the *Rime sparse.* But Sannazaro decidedly favored Latin for the composition of his most ambitious works, destined in his opinion to secure his fame; these works ranged from the *Elegiae* to the *Eclogae piscatoriae* and *De partu Virginis.* The vast popularity of *Piscatoriae*—only consider, for example, its mention in the prologue to canto 46 of Ariosto's *Orlando Furioso*—was due not just to the novelty of its genre, which becomes a model for many imitators in the course of the century and beyond. Its success also lay in its refined formal elaborations and in the suggestive references to the landscape of the Neapolitan region, to the bay and the islands that came to form a magical backdrop on which the speakers interwove their love songs.

A clearer tie with reality is found in the *Elegiae,* with the poet's usual ability to arouse reevocation, regret, and nostalgia, memories of youth and of beloved places that recalled former states of mind, friends, and colleagues, most of all Pontano.

Very different is the case of *De partu Virginis,* a work elaborated at great length and the object of Sannazaro's most minute and tireless labors both on the formal level and in the area of religious and theological questions. The concurrence in the ample repertory of sources of classical authors, most of all Vergil, with Christian writers, such as Juvencus, Prudentius, and Paulinus of Nola, attests the further success of an important vein of Neapolitan humanism—the rereading of the ancients' message as the anticipation and prerevelation of the Savior's coming. In order to evoke the event of the Nativity and to present the Annunciation as the choral participation of God's creatures in the miraculous event, the poet drew from his memory's archive images, motifs, metaphors, and myths from both the classical and the Christian traditions, forging them into a new suggestive representation.

The beauty of book 3, which in the past some scholars have viewed as a useless appendix, has now been recognized. This book makes clear the humanistic and Christian consciousness with which the poet evoked the exceptional event. The song of the River Jordan metaphorically signified the homage of the ancient world to the Redeemer who opened to mankind the path to a metatemporal destiny. To be sure, at the base of the conception and composition of *De partu* there lies Sannazaro's profound religious sentiment, but perhaps the message that the poet wanted to express in this work should not be reduced to the poetic exaltation of the Christian event, but implies a more specific and committed moral and human obligation. Read against the background of the political, social, and moral reality of the early sixteenth century, *De partu* reveals a serious, though hidden, demand for society to recover the essential values of revelation, peace, concord, and love from a world marked by violence, conflict, hatred, and egoism. Sannazaro explicitly created the bridge between Vergil's prophecy and the fullness of the event (compare the *Eclogue*, 4.4–7):

> The last age of the Sibylline song has now come,
> Great ages are renewed through the completion of cycles.
> Certainly this is the sibyl, these are Saturnian ages,
> This new offspring descends from the high heaven.[58]

It is not surprising that the adoring shepherds before the manger greet the Christ child with the very words of the Vergilian *Eclogue* (4.15–17):

> Then you will take on the life of the gods and you will see the heroes mingled together with the gods; and will you yourself be seen by them and rule the pacified earth through the virtues of your father?[59]

Symbolic is the blissful amazement of the Jordan before the marvelous phenomena of the unexpected spring, of the unusually flowered river bank, of the happy songs that are raised to heaven to announce the coming of the Lord. The solemn praise of God's infinite power, based not on any earthly means of power and destruction but instead on the gifts of redemption and salvation, acquires a deeper significance if one notes the veiled opposition to the current sway of armed force, power, and wealth recalling the disasters, destruction, and disorder of contemporary society.

> He will not seek riches or honors—that glory and virtue of his father—after he has already taken on mortal members voluntarily and fragile limbs. He will not assault the rule of Cyrus or the Caspian rulers, he will not overthrow proud Babylon for its spoils or climb the Capitoline hill in a tall chariot with soldiers and with the senate joyfully accompanying him on all sides.[60]

*   *   *

While in the area of poetic experience the study of writers was polarized toward formal values, without of course disregarding the human and cultural motivations contained in their *Fabulosum commentum*, in their works of politics, morals, history, and customs, their attention was turned with constant and growing engagement toward the reality of the contemporary world. At several levels, the humanists were becoming the interpreters and consciences of that world. To be sure, there was no indication in the composition of these works of any growing lack of concern for the requirement of form. The institutional requirement to clothe the message of wisdom (*sapientia*) in the form of eloquence (*eloquentia*) ensured that the work possessed classical decorum. At the same time, a beguiling power of mediation and persuasion was present in that form of literary composition, based on the imitation of ancient models and on careful stylistic research, which could and often did seem to exhaust the dimensions and sense of these writings.

In fact, one can discern in the entire literary production of Neapolitan humanism (as indeed in all humanistic literature) the erudite use of the instruments of rhetoric borrowed from the teachings of the ancients and made the object of intensive study and theoretical reflection. Therefore, the choice of various genres was not by accident, and within each genre the choice of structures, divisions, stylistic levels, and even diction was carefully considered. In addition to relying on classical models for such choices, Neapolitan humanists also used important texts of fifteenth-century writers. Likewise in theoretical discussions they were not limited to reworking and reelaborating precepts and examples from the classical tradition, but tackled themes and proposals from very recent cultural debates. But even at this rhetorical level they were able to make substantial and occasionally innovative contributions in their writing, and sometimes even critical advances in their reflections. Thus, they accentuated and developed the code of the genre's model in new directions and with broader perspectives, while they revised or recodified traditional models. The liveliness and interest in the discussion of the writing of history found in Valla's preface to his *Gesta Ferdinandi regis* immediately comes to mind. Likewise, Pontano discussed in the *Actius* the theory of historiographical style, which his followers continued with some modifications in conversations mentioned by Bernardo Rucellai.[61] Another example is Pontano's refinement and enrichment of ethical-social treatises, following the Aristotelian and Ciceronian models and characterized by a systematic and demonstrative structure. Consider too the very widespread use of the epistle as a discursive, occasional treatise, as it was by and large employed in Galateo's writings. Another case in point is Pontano's dialogues, which profoundly revised the structure and character of the Platonic and Ciceronian models under the strong influence of Lucian and to some extent the humanistic tradition, mainly Alberti's dialogues. Finally, bear in mind biography, a genre that already had a long tradition, but which was transformed profoundly under the growing importance of Plutarch and received a new ethical and psychological dimension in the works of Tristano Caracciolo.

But after these striking, though strictly literary, changes, the most important aspect of this literature seems to be the widespread duty of the humanists to project in their writings their own understanding of reality and to express judgments, principles, and precepts that reflect specific situations and the demands of their own experience. It was above all in this regard that Neapolitan intellectuals, especially the major ones such as Pontano, Carafa, Tristano Caracciolo, and Galateo, achieved in their work great and fruitful results.

If one leaves aside the literary production of other cities of the kingdom, often linked to the political presence of the barons, who were frequently in conflict with the centralizing culture of the capital, this entire humanistic literature can be characterized by the close relation, based on consensus and collaboration, between intellectuals and power, at least until the fall of the dynasty. Therefore, the political choices of these men more or less openly friendly to the dynasty constituted the general perspective that was set forth in the different works in which the writers expressed the results of their studies and reflections.

Therefore, one can clearly notice over time the passage from an original disposition to codify and propose a model of the prince corresponding to the popularity and growing prestige of the Aragonese monarchy to a lengthy and complex period in which these writers both continued and developed theoretical statements of the essential qualities of the prince and also turned their attention to the internal structure of the institution of monarchy. This second concern became a severe and merciless inquiry, especially on the moral and social level, of the vices, moral bankruptcy, errors, and contradictions of society at the time of the crisis of 1494. The dramatic trauma—political, moral, and existential—provoked by the descent of Charles VIII, and the collapse of the dynasty and the values associated with it, brought on a new attempt at defining reality and, thus, inquiry into the possibility of rational human control of human destiny.

All these writers in various degrees participated with great diligence through their works in a grand intellectual adventure. It has been justly observed that the first apologetic writings in verse and prose born in the court milieu in Alfonso's time were far from becoming mere empty adulatory compositions. They already reflected a "political" direction—the more or less profound intention to contribute to the formulation and celebration of a dynastic ideology.[62]

Even if the recurrent thematic motifs of these writings idealized the sovereign's real attitudes and behavior, in fact they proposed to the monarch himself a model for him to adopt and strive to attain. Pontano's *De principe*, written between 1463 and 1464,[63] initiated the process of idealization and characterization of a model prince based on a careful reading of the canonical sources from Aristotle and Cicero to St. Thomas and on the experience of the reigns of Alfonso and Ferrante. At the same time, this treatise revitalized the tradition of the mirror of princes (*Speculum principis*) in Neapolitan culture, which was destined to be enriched in the course of time by works such as Pontano's *De fortitudine, De liberalitate, De beneficentia*, and *De magnificentia*, as well as Maio's *De maiestate* in the vernacular. In these treatises, seeking the union of *eloquentia* and *sapientia*, Pontano combined his ideological outlook with his literary obligation to exact stylistic control. But it is important to note that there was already in *De principe* a tendency to gauge the ideal prince against contemporary reality. And this tendency revealed even more clearly in the course of time a movement in the direction of that "realism" which had been, as already noted, the more striking and fertile characteristic of the political and moral investigations of Neapolitan humanism. And already in 1472 with *De oboedientia* (in tune with Ferrante's centralizing policy), Pontano had identified the condition of family and political order, and did not hesitate to admit the possibility of the prince being exempted from an absolute morality for the common good of the country: "There might be such a great power of utility and in so great a cause that one must sometimes turn aside from uprightness, but only a little and without serious dishonor."[64] This passage reflects the fundamental importance of "public utility," or the common good, and implies the recognition of political conduct that does not conform to ordinary morality.

In this school of "realism" is also found Diomede Carafa's *Memoriali*, written in Italian and placing a striking accent on using the lessons of experience. In this work the practical precepts of behavior suggested for princes help to frame realistic codes of social and political conduct. The various treatises of Tristano Caracciolo belong to a more specific social perspective, based not on any abstract morality but on the reality of events. A member of the citizen nobility and one of the greatest protagonists of Neapolitan humanism, Caracciolo approached reality from the viewpoint and interests of his class. But his discourses transcend the boundaries of class and city to investigate the questions and motives of the moral life and of existence itself. This period of over thirty years of rapid historical change was signaled by various triumphs and defeats for his class, including the transition from the practice of traditional occupations, mainly arms and court service, to other fields of activity. All these changes were subjected to his investigations chronologically in three works: *Nobilitatis neapolitanae defensio*, *Quid sit iuvenibus amplectendum* (a review of the skills proper to young noblemen), and *Disceptatio priscorum cum iunioribus de moribus suorum temporum* (a lively confrontation between two generations).

The social and political topic of nobility, recurrent in humanistic literature, assumed in Neapolitan culture a new meaning in the context of the monarchy's centralizing policy, which relied on the collaboration of the citizen nobility against the centrifugal power of the barons. Naturally, since the writer's outlook was reflected, the approach to the topic in each work—the various treatises that either directly or indirectly dealt with the topic of nobility—exhibited the dialectical vision of the question in concrete Neapolitan reality, seen and discussed from diverse and often opposing points of view. A good example is in two treatises by Galateo: *De distinctione humani generis et nobilitate* and *De nobilitate ad Gelasium*. As a provincial, a native of Galatone, and a physician who was not directly interested in the problems and fortunes of the nobility, Galateo viewed the question from a rigorously moral point of view. His was a harsh polemic against the degeneration of nobility that in the second treatise came to include the entire nobility defined as a class of holders of hereditary titles. Elio Marchese handled the question very differently in his discourse, *Liber de neapolitanis familiis*, which analyzed the phenomenon of the decadence of old families and the rise of new ones, attributing the cause for success to the *virtù* of individuals while admitting the frequent uncontrollable impact of *fortuna*.[65]

But even though in his treatises on nobility Galateo seems to indulge in an abstract model of nobility identified with the individual's *virtù*, in other writings he confirms and enlarges his ruthless and sharp polemic against the vices and injustices of contemporary society. A good example is the treatise *De educatione*, a violent polemic against the Spanish and the French and an exaltation of education framed in terms of opposing foreigners' "barbarism" with the tradition of the Italians' "humanity."

A very striking, though somewhat empirical, realism characterized another important style of humanistic treatise, which was destined to have a flowering in sixteenth-century literature: the literature of comportment. Examples include Carafa's *Memoriali* (his *Memoriale alla serenissima Regina d'Ungheria*), precepts for Beatrice of Aragon in her conduct in both public and private life, and his *Tractato dello optimo cortesano*, norms to his son on his comportment in court life, which anticipated Castiglione's *Courtier*. Also very significant are Tristano Caracciolo's *Praecepta ad filium* and *Opusculum ad marchionem Atellae*, written during the crisis of 1494, which show an awareness of treacherous and mutable reality and anticipate della Casa's doctrine of "discretion."[66]

Likewise, political interests and attention to pressing problems and themes of contemporary reality are revealed in historical writings based on the rhetorical tradition of Livy and Sallust, writings that Eduard Fueter has judged all too unfavorably.[67] These include Valla's *Gesta Ferdinandi regis*, Panormita's *Liber gestarum Ferdinandi regis*, and Pontano's *De bello neapolitano*, which signaled the coming of that model of political history[68] Bernardo Rucellai would adopt in his *De bello italico*,[69] opening the path to Machiavelli's historiography.[70]

Biography presents another perspective on realism, marked by an analysis of the individual's interior state: the tangle of the passions and the contrast between *virtù* and *fortuna*. This genre reached its highest achievements especially in the writings of Tristano Caracciolo: *Vita Serzannis Caraccioli, De Joanne Baptista Spinello Cariatis comite*, and in the author's masterpiece, *De varietate fortunae*, a central text of Neapolitan humanism.

*   *   *

The descent of Charles VIII (1494–95) and the crisis it precipitated signals a decisive turning point, not only in Italian political history but also in the history of society and of intellectual and moral life. I have already discussed at length in my writings the significance of this crisis and of its impact on the consciousness of Italian intellectuals and especially on the consciousness of Neapolitan humanists.[71] Here I shall say only that this event marked a transformation in Pontano's intellectual and moral itinerary, as reflected in his late writings, *De fortuna, De prudentia*, the dialogue *Aegidius*, and *De immanitate*.

Confronted with such an upsetting reality, marked by the fortuitous, the irrational, and the unpredictable, Pontano took up again the theme of fortune. *Fortuna* was an old topic that had been often handled with new meaning in humanistic culture and had as a correlative the power of *virtù*. But now *fortuna* presented widespread, unwonted gravity, affecting the very reality of the human condition and the possibility of man's controlling his own destiny. In *De fortuna* Pontano conducted a penetrating and precise inquiry into the phenomenology of the fortuitous. Dwelling in *De prudentia* on the effect of what is problematic, on insecurity, on risk, on the possibilities of reason, he entrusted to prudence (which fulfills the function of mediation between reason and reality) the task of controlling man's choices and conduct in public and private life. Pontano's thesis implied a dramatic and dynamic conception of existence. Prudence was no longer delegated the function of choosing the things to avoid and those to follow from within a closed, motionless system. Now prudence had to make this choice in an extremely fluid, variable, and unpredictable context, distinguishing favorable conditions and opportunities from unfavorable ones, adapting to change, altering methods and behavior with the times, alternating the use of force with the use of cunning according to the circumstances: "Be both lion and fox," as Machiavelli later put it.

Pontano's doctrine of prudence affected all moral life, but it had a special bearing on political life. To cite only one example: the rape of the Sabine women, which symbolized an event judged immoral within the context of a traditional or absolute morality, now became a positive and useful political act, justified by necessity, since it ensured the survival and great destiny of the Roman state.

This doctrine of prudence is reflected in the whole of Neapolitan culture after 1494, as the foundation for any understanding of reality and any moral or political model in all fields of human activity, aiming to reconcile faith in reason with consciousness of the contradictory and shifting rhythm of experience. Pontano's doctrine passed beyond the confines of the city and kingdom and spread throughout Italian and European culture. Perhaps a more thorough consideration of Pontano's teaching and of the Neapolitan writers who continued and elaborated his doctrines would give an indication of the heritage that Neapolitan humanistic culture offered to Renaissance civilization.

NOTES

This essay has been translated by Benjamin G. Kohl, a contributor to these volumes, who was aided on some knotty problems of translation by John Ahern,

Dante Antolini Professor of Italian at Vassar. Professor Santoro corrected and approved the translation. The editor subsequently recast parts of the literal translation into a more idiomatic English rendering.

1. See M. Santoro, "La cultura umanistica," in *Storia di Napoli* (Naples, 1974), 4.2:315–498 at 318.

2. See F. Sabatini, *Napoli angioine* (Naples, 1975), 152.

3. See G. Billanovich, *Petrarca letterato*, vol. 1, *Lo scrittoio del Petrarca* (Rome, 1947); idem, "Pietro Piccolo da Monteforte tra Petrarca e Boccaccio," in *Medioevo e Rinascimento: Studi in onore di Bruno Nardi*, 2 vols. (Florence, 1955), 1:3–76; idem, "La tradizione del 'Liber de dictis philosophorum antiquorum' e la cultura di Dante, del Petrarca e del Boccaccio," *Studi petrarcheschi* 1 (1948): 111–23; idem, "Tra Dante e il Petrarca," *Italia medioevale e umanistica* 8 (1965): 1–44; idem, "Il Petrarca, il Boccaccio, Zanobi da Strada e le tradizioni dei testi della cronaca di Ugo Falcando e di alcune vite dei Pontefici," *Rinascimento* 4 (1953): 17–24. See also G. di Stefano, "Per la fortuna di Valerio Massimo nel Trecento: Le glosse di Pietro da Monteforte e il commento di Dionigi da Borgo San Sepolcro," *Atti dell'Accademia di scienze di Torino, Classe di scienze morali* 96 pt. 2 (1961–62): 272–314; A. Altamura, *La letteratura dell'età angioina* (Naples, 1952); idem, *Studi e ricerche di letteratura umanistica* (Naples, 1956); and A. Pertusi, *Leonzio Pilato fra Petrarca e Boccaccio* (Venice, 1964).

4. Paride del Pozzo, *Libellus syndacatus officialium* (Naples, 1485); this work is dedicated to Diomede Carafa.

5. M. Gigante, "La civiltà letteraria," in *I Bizantini in Italia* (Milan, 1982), 615–51.

6. See M. Fuiano, *Maestri di medicina e filosofia a Napoli nel Quattrocento* (Naples, 1973); and C. de Frede, "Biblioteche e cultura di medici-filosofi napoletani del '400," *Gutenberg Jahrbuch* (1961): 89–96. On the School of Salerno, see P. O. Kristeller, "The School of Salerno: Its Development and Its Contribution to the History of Learning," *Bulletin of the History of Medicine* 17 (1945): 138–94, repr. in his *Studies in Renaissance Thought and Letters*, 2 vols. (Rome, 1956–85), 1:495–552.

7. A rather revealing episode in the humanist offensive against the "barbarians" even at Naples is represented in the exchange in 1480 between Ermolao Barbaro the Younger and Galateo: see M. Santoro, "Scienza e humanitas nell'opera del Galateo," *La Zagaglia* 2.5 (1960): 25–40, 50–63; and idem, "La cultura umanistica," 364ff.

8. E. Garin, "La letteratura degli umanisti," in *Storia della letteratura italiana* (Milan, 1966), 3:159.

9. Still fundamental is B. Croce, *La Spagna nella vita italiana durante la Rinascenza* (Bari, 5th ed., 1968). See also the recent essay of E. J. Rao, "Alfonso of Aragon and the Italian Humanists," *Esperienze letterarie* 4.1 (1979): 43–52.

10. P. Collenuccio, *Compendio de le istorie del regno di Napoli*, ed. A. Saviotto (Bari, 1928), 290ff.

11. Fundamental is T. de Marinis, *La biblioteca napoletana dei re d'Aragona*, 4 vols. (Milan, 1947–52), *Supplemento*, 2 vols. (Verona, 1969).

12. See Santoro, "La cultura umanistica," 339.

13. On Valla and his relations with the Aragonese court and culture, see G. Mancini, *Vita di Lorenzo Valla* (Florence, 1891), 90ff.; F. Gaeta, *Lorenzo Valla: Filologia e storia nell'umanesimo italiano* (Naples, 1955); G. Billanovich and M. Ferraris, "Le 'Emendationes in T. Livium' del Valla e il Codex Regius di Livio," *Italia medioevale e umanistica* 1 (1958): 245–64; M. Fois, *Il pensiero cristiano di Lorenzo Valla nel quadro storico-culturale del suo ambiente* (Rome, 1969). Still useful, if rather general, is A. Soria, *Los humanistas de la corte de Alfonso el Magnanimo (según los epistolarios)* (Granada, 1956).

14. See P. O. Kristeller, "The Humanist Bartolomeo Facio and His Unknown Correspondence," in *From Renaissance to Counter-Reformation: Essays in Honor of Garrett Mattingly*, ed. C. H. Carter (New York, 1965), 56–74.

15. During his stay at Naples from 1452 to 1455, George of Trebizond was the champion of Aristotelianism against the followers of Bessarion, such as Gaza. Of particular importance are his Latin version of the pseudo-Aristotelian *Problemata* and the work *In perversionem Aristotelis a quodam Theodoro Cage editam*, dedicated to Alfonso and kept in the Aragonese Library: see de Marinis, *La biblioteca*, 2:76. On George of Trebizond, see J. Monfasani, *George of Trebizond: A Biography and a Study of His Rhetoric and Logic* (Leiden, 1976); and Chapter 31, in Volume 3.

16. Flavio Biondo, *Scritti inediti e rari*, ed. B. Nogara (Rome, 1927), 31ff. See also F. Cerone, "La politica orientale di Alfonso d'Aragona," *Archivio storico per le provincie Napoletane* 27 (1902): 3–93, 384–456, 553–634, 794–852; 28 (1903): 154–212.

17. See G. Resta, *L'epistolario del Panormita, Studi per un'edizione critica* (Messina, 1954), and his "Introduzione" to A. Panhormita, *Liber rerum gestarum Ferdinandi regis* (Palermo, 1968).

18. See M. Santoro, "Panormita aragonese," *Esperienze letterarie* 9.4 (1984): 3–25.

19. Still fundamental is E. Pontieri, *Ferrante d'Aragona, re di Napoli* (Naples, 2d ed., 1969). General works include B. Croce, *Storia di Napoli* (Bari, 1953); and, above all, G. Galasso, *Mezzogiorno medievale e moderno* (Turin, 1965).

20. See C. de Frede, *I lettori di umanità nello Studio di Napoli durante il Rinascimento* (Naples, 1960); and M. Fuiano, *Insegnamento e cultura a Napoli nel Rinascimento* (Naples, 1971).

21. See M. Santoro, *Uno scolaro del Poliziano a Napoli: Francesco Pucci* (Naples, 1948), 27ff.

22. In his dialogue *Charon*, Pontano had already indicated the limits of Platonic doctrine, while emphasizing Aristotle's superior specificity: see Giovanni Pontano, *I Dialoghi*, ed. C. Previtera (Florence, 1943), 15.

23. *De oboedientia*, in *Opera omnia soluta oratione composita* (Venice, 1518), 1:19v.

24. On Maio, see F. Gaeta, "Introduzione" to Giuniano Maio, *De maiestate* (Bologna, 1956); de Frede, *I lettori*, 47–48; Fuiano, *Insegnamento e cultura*, 30–31; and Santoro, "La cultura umanistica," 348–51.

25. See A. Miola, "Su un umanista milanese lettore di retorica nello Studio di Napoli," *Atti della Società italiana per il progresso delle scienze* (Naples, 1910), 897–99; and Santoro, "La cultura umanistica," 353ff. On Pucci, in addition to the volume of Santoro, *Uno scolaro del Poliziano*, see M. Fuiano, "La Scuola del Pucci e Antonio Seripando," *Atti dell'Accademia Pontaniana* n.s. 19 (1970), 197–292.

26. For an important record of these gatherings, see Alessandro D'Alessandro, *Geniales dies* (Lyons, 1673), 1:1: "Accersebat plerunque nos in hortos amoenissimos, ubi aediculas habebat, Iovianus Pontanus in nostra Parthenope, vir memoria quidem nostra omnibus bonis artibus, atque omni doctrine praeditus. . . . Illoque conveniebamus complusculi, quibus bonarum artium studia, eaedemque disciplinae, atque non absimilis discendi facultas erat. Detinebat demulcebatque nos vir ille fandi dulcissimus, egregia quadam et illustri oratione, sermoneque perquam lepido et venusto, totos plerunque dies: tanta in eo comitas, tantusque lepos erat." On this author, see D. Maffei, *Alessandro D'Alessandro, giureconsulto e umanista* (Milan, 1956).

27. On Carafa (1461–1523), see the fundamental book of T. Persico, *Diomede Carafa, uomo di stato e scrittore del secolo XV* (Naples, 1899); and G. Paparelli's "Introduzione" to his recent edition of the *Tractato dello optimo cortesano* (Salerno, 1971). See also P. Pieri, "L'arte militare italiana della seconda metà del secolo XV negli scritti di Diomede Carafa," in *Ricordi e studi in memoria di Francesco Flamini* (Naples, 1931), 87–103; idem, "Il 'Governo et exercitio de la militia' di Orso degli Orsini e i 'Memoriali' di Diomede Carafa," *Archivio storico per le provincie napoletano* n.s. 19 (1933): 99–125; M. Santoro, "Machiavelli e l'umanesimo," *Cultura e società* 1 (1959): 21–43; G. Paparelli, "Umanesimo e paraumanesimo napoletano: D. Carafa," in *Da Dante al Seicento* (Salerno, 1971), 71–107; L. Miele, "Tradizione ed 'esperienza' nella precettistica politica di Diomede Carafa," *Atti dell'Accademia Pontaniana* n.s. 24 (1976), 1–11.

28. Scholarly interest in Il Galateo has grown in recent decades—see the following: E. Garin, *Italian Humanism: Philosophy and Civic Life in the Renaissance*, trans. P. Munz (New York, 1965), 72–74; Santoro, "Scienze e humanitas"; F. Tateo, "Il pensiero civile di A. de Ferrariis," in *Studi su Antonio de Ferrariis* (Galatone, 1970), 13–32; P. A. de Lisio, "L'umanesimo problematico di A. de F., Galateo," in his *Studi sull'umanesimo meridionale* (Naples, 1973), 19–59; S. Martelli, "La 'Vituperatio literarum' di A. de Ferrariis, Galateo," *Misure critiche* 2.3 (1972): 43ff., reprinted in *Dal progetto al rifiuto*, ed. P. A. de Lisio and S. Martelli (Salerno, 1979), 65–106; G. Paparelli, "La disputa delle arti," in *Feritas, humanitas, divinitas*

(Florence, 1960),52ff; G. Griggio, "Tradizione e rinnovavamento nella cultura del Galateo," *Lettere italiane* 26.4 (1974): 415–33; M. Santoro, "La cultura umanistica," 364ff.; L. Miele, "Moralismo e utopia nell'*Esposizione del pater*," in his *Saggi galateani* (Naples, 1982), 5–23; D. Moro, "Tre note per la biografia di Antonio Galateo," *Esperienze letterarie* 4.3 (1979): 81–102; E. Garin, "Antonio de Ferrariis," in his *Educazione umanistica in Italia* (Bari, 1971), 172ff.; M. Santoro, "Il Galateo," in his *Fortuna, ragione e prudenza nella civiltà letteraria del Cinquecento* (Naples, 1967), 67–96; V. Zacchino, "Il 'De educatione' di A. Galateo e i suoi sentimento antispagnuoli," in *Atti del congresso di studi sull'età aragonese* (Bari, 1969), 620–42; A. Jurilli, "Problemi lessicali nell'*Esposizione del Pater Noster* di Antonio Galateo," *Lingua e storia di Puglia* 9 (1980): 45–58; A. A. Memola, *Catalogo delle opere di Antonio de' Ferrariis (Galateo)* (Lecce, 1982); L. Miele, *Saggi galateani* (Naples, 1982); and idem, "Per una rilettura dell-'*Esposizione del Pater* di A. de Ferrariis Galateo," *Esperienze letterarie* 9.4 (1984): 39–55. On the erroneous attribution to Galateo of *De bello hydruntino* and on the writings of his contemporaries on the war of Otranto, see *Gli umanisti e la guerra otrantina: Testi dei secoli XV e XVI*, ed. F. Tateo (Bari, 1982); *Otranto 1480*, ed. A. Laporta (Lecce, 1980); D. Moro, "I Turchi ad Otranto (1480–81)," *Quaderni dell'Istituto Nazionale di Studi sul Rinascimento meridionale* 3 (1986): 99–121. In addition, see F. Tateo, "Diagnosi del potere nell'oratoria di un medico," in *Chierici e feudatari del mezzogiorno* (Bari, 1984), 1–20.

29. M Santoro, "Il 'De immanitate' testamento spirituale del Pontano," *Partenope* 1 (1960): 5–15. The treatise was recently edited by L. Monti Sabia (Naples, 1970).

30. Pontano, *De immanitate*, 46.

31. G. Toffanin, *Giovanni Pontano fra l'uomo e la natura* (Bologna, 1938).

32. "Postquam Dei summi benignitate ad id aetatis perveneris ut iam rerum discrimina per te noscere incipias, sententiam coelo missam mortalibus necessariam tibi suggeram: Nosce scilicet te ipsum." And: "Te igitur primum nosce, neque tantum ut Cicero vult, idest animum tuum, sed volo hominem te scias et quibus constes partibus, undene illas ducas et quae iuxta tuam conditionem acturus sis . . ." (Tristano Caracciolo, *Praecepta ad filium*, Biblioteca Nazionale di Napoli, MS, IX.C.25, fol. 121v).

33. Pontano, *De oboedientia*, in *Opera*, 38v.

34. Santoro, *Fortuna, ragione e prudenza*, 27ff.

35. Antonio de Ferrariis (Il Galateo), *Epistole*, ed. A. Altamura (Lecce, 1959), 119.

36. For a discussion of questions related to the beginning of printing, see *Il libro a stampa, I Primordi*, ed. Marco Santoro (Naples, 1970); see also his fundamental work, *La stampa a Napoli nel Quattrocento* (Naples, 1984).

37. See A. Jurilli, "La fortuna editoriale delle opere di Virgilio nell'Italia meridionale fino al XVIII secolo," in *Atti del convegno virgiliano di Brindisi* (Perugia, 1983), 66–69.

38. See G. C. Alessio, "Appunti sulla diffusione manoscritta di Virgilio nel Mezzogiorno d'Italia," in *Atti del convegno virgiliano di Brindisi* (Perugia, 1983): 361–81.

39. On Frederick, see L. Volpicella, *Federico d'Aragone e la fine del regno di Napoli nel 1501* (Naples, 1901); M. Corti, "Introduzione" to P. J. de Jennaro, *Rime e lettere* (Bologna, 1956), 159–60; M. Santoro, "Masuccio fra Salerno e Napoli," *Atti dell'Accademia Pontaniana* n.s. 11 (1962): 309–40.

40. For the attribution of the letter to Poliziano, see M. Santoro, "Poliziano o il Magnifico?" *Giornale italiano di filologia* 2 (1948), reprinted in his *Note umanistiche* (Naples, 1970), 79–99.

41. See Santoro, "Masuccio fra Salerno e Napoli," 320ff.

42. See G. Folena, *La crisi linguistica del Quattrocento e l'Arcadia del Sannazaro* (Florence, 1952); A. Altamura, "La letteratura volgare," in *Storia di Napoli* (Naples, 1974), 4:501–72; M. Santagata, *La lirica aragonese* (Padua, 1979).

43. Thus spoke Perleone in the preamble of his *Canzoniere* dedicated to Frederick of Aragon: "I cannot be silent about those who only were called learned and wise, nurtured on a foreign and unnatural gruel; these can be called similar to a horse, who is free by nature but tied to his stall by cunning, so that he can only feed on that which is given to him" (Giuliano Perleoni, *Compendio di Sonecti et altre Rime de varie texture, intitolato lo Perleone, recolte tra le opere antiche e moderne de l'humile discipulo et imitatore devotissimo de' vulgari poeti Giuliano Perleonio dicto Rustico Romano* [Naples, 1492]). See G. Ferraù, *Pontano critico* (Messina, 1983).

44. See E. Percopo, "Gli scritti di G. Pontano," *Archivio storico per le provincie napoletane* 62 (1937): 222–25.

45. See F. Arnaldi, "Introduzione" to *Poeti latini del Quattrocento*, ed. F. Arnaldi et al. (Milan, 1964).

46. M. Santoro, "La cultura umanistica," 448ff.

47. F. Tateo, "La poetica di G. Pontano," *Filologia romanza* 6.3 (1959): 277–303; 6.4:337–69. Rather important was the judgment of Paolo Cortesi on Pontano, in his *De hominibus doctis*, ed. G. Ferraù (Palermo, 1979), 45ff.

48. Pontano, *Actius*, in *I Dialoghi*, 235. For the evolution of Pontano's style and his first experiences—following the example of Panormita—in the adoption of the most renowned models, see G. Parenti, "Pontano o dell'allitterazione: Lettura di Parthenopoeus I.7," *Rinascimento* n.s. 15 (1975): 89–110. See also L. Monti Sabia, "Esegesi critica e storia del testo nei Carmina del Pontano (a proposito di Parth. I.13 e II.12)," *Annali della Facoltà di Lettere e Filosofia dell'Università di Napoli* 12 (1969–70): 219–35; idem, "L'estremo autografo di G. Pontano," *Italia medievale e umanistica* 22 (1980): 293–314. On the character of humanist "letters," especially with respect to formal structure, see G. Martellotti, "Critica metrica del Salutati e del Pontano," in *Critica e storia letteraria: Studi offerti a Mario Fubini* (Padua, 1970), 352–73, reprinted in his *Dante e Boccaccio e altri scrittori dall'umanesimo al romanticismo* (Florence, 1983), 273–302.

49. *Actius*, in *I Dialoghi*, 238. See also the penetrating observations of L. Monti Sabia, "Virgilio nella poesia del Pontano," in *Atti del convegno virgiliano di Brindisi*, 47–63.

50. Rather more important was the inquiry carried out by Pontano in *De sermone* of the diverse levels of language determined by the diverse destinations of the discourse: see S. Lupi, "Il 'De sermone' di G. Pontano," *Filologia romanza* 2 (1955): fasc. 8. See also F. Tateo, "Il linguaggio 'comico' nell'opera di G. Pontano," *Acta conventus neo-latini Lovaniensis*, ed. J. IJsewijn et al. (Louvain, 1973), 647–57; and G. Ferroni, "La teoria classicistica della facezia da Pontano a Castiglione," *Sigma* 13 (1980): 69–96.

51. Fundamental on Marullo remains the monograph of B. Croce, *M. Marullo Tarcaniota: Le elegie per la patria perdute e altri suoi carmi* (Bari, 1938), reprinted in his *Poeti e scrittori del pieno e tardo Rinascimento* (Bari, 1945), 1:269ff. Among more recent studies and important contributions are G. Luck, "Marullus und sein dichterisches Werk, Versuch einer Würdigung," *Arcadia* 1 (1966): 31–49; D. de Robertis, "M. Marullo Tarcaniota," in *Storia della letteratura italiana* (Milan, 1966), 3:556–66; F. Tateo, *Tradizione e realtà nell'umanesimo italiano* (Bari, 1967), 129ff.; and C. F. Goffis, "Il sincretismo lucreziano-platonico negli 'Hymni naturales' del Marullo," *Belfagor* 24 (1969): 386–417.

52. For an introduction to individual poets, consult the fine anthology, *Poeti latini del Quattrocento*. Still useful is A. Altamura, *L'umanesimo nel Mezzogiorno d'Italia* (Florence, 1941). On Calenzio, see L. Monti Sabia, "L'umanitas di Elisio Calenzio alla luce del suo epistolario," *Annali della Facoltà di Lettere e Filosofia dell'Università di Napoli* 11 (1964–68): 175–251; and for Carbone, P. de Montera, *L'humaniste Napolitain Giovanni Carbone et ses poésies inédites* (Naples, 1935).

53. See Summonte's letter to Sannazaro as preface to the edition of Pontano's poetry published at Naples in 1505, reprinted in the appendix to Giovanni Pontano, *Carmina*, ed. J. Oeschger (Bari, 1948), 460.

54. Santoro, "La cultura umanistica," 381.

55. M. Corti, "Il codice bucolico e l'*Arcadia* di Jacopo Sannazaro," *Strumenti critici* 2 (1968): 141–67. See also Corti's important contributions in "L'impasto linguistico dell'*Arcadia*," *Studi di filologia italiana* 22 (1964): 593–619, and "Rivoluzione e reazione stilistica nel Sannazaro," in *Metodi e fantasmi* (Milan, 1969), 305–23. See also the fine edition of Sannazaro's *Opere volgari* (Bari, 1961), edited by the late Alfredo Mauro, one of the most serious and able students of the Neapolitan vernacular in the fifteenth century.

56. See P. V. Mengaldo, "La lirica volgare del Sannazaro e lo sviluppo del linguaggio poetico rinascimentale," *Rassegna delle letteratura italiana* 66 (1962): 436–82.

57. On Sannazaro's last years there is a need for further careful and exact study, especially on the context and relations of Neapolitan and European culture in the first three decades of the sixteenth century.

58. Vergil, *Opera*, ed. R. A. B. Mynors (Oxford, 1972), *Eclogues* 4.4–7.

59. Ibid., 4.15–17.
60. Jacopo Sannazaro, *De partu virginis*, ed. A. Altamura (Naples, 1948), 1.3.422–28.
61. Santoro, *Fortuna, ragione e prudenza*, 135–40.
62. G. Resta, "Introduzione" to his edition of Panhormita, *Liber rerum gestarum*, 14ff.
63. S. Monti, "Ricerche sulla cronologia del 'Dialoghi' del Pontano," *Annali della Facoltà di Lettere e Filosofia dell'Università di Napoli* 10 (1962–63): 247–352. See also L. Miele, "Tradizione letteraria e realismo politico nel 'De principe' del Pontano," *Atti Accademia Pontaniana* n.s. 32 (1983): 301–21.
64. *De oboedientia*, 35v.
65. For an analysis and English translation of Caracciolo's treatise and Galateo's two letters on nobility, see *Knowledge, Goodness, and Power: The Debate over "Nobility" Among Quattrocento Italian Humanists*, ed. A. Rabil Jr., forthcoming.
66. M. Santoro, *Tristano Caracciolo e la cultura napoletana della Rinascenza* (Naples, 1957), 118–19.
67. See E. Fueter, *Geschichte der neuren Historiographie* (Berlin, 3d ed., 1963).
68. Cf. G. Toffanin, *Machiavelli e il tacitismo* (Naples, 1972); and M. P. Gilmore, "Individualism in Renaissance Historians," in his *Humanists and Jurists: Six Studies in the Renaissance* (Cambridge, MA, 1963), 38–60.
69. See M. Santoro, "Fortuna e prudenze nel 'De bello italico' del Rucellai," in *Fortuna, ragione e prudenza*, 135–78.
70. On the relation between Pontano and Machiavelli, see Santoro, "Machiavelli e l'umanesimo"; idem, "Machiavelli e il tema della fortuna," in *Fortuna, ragione e prudenza*, 179–231. See also B. Richardson, "Notes on Machiavelli's Sources and His Treatment of the Rhetorical Tradition," *Italian Studies* 26 (1971): 24–48; and R. Belladonna, "Pontanus, Machiavelli and a Case of Religious Dissimulation in Early Sixteenth-Century Siena (Carli's *Trattati nove della prudenza*)," *Bibliothèque d'Humanisme et Renaissance* 37 (1975): 377–85.
71. See M. Santoro, "Il Pontano e l'ideale rinascimentale del 'prudente,'" *Giornale italiano di filologia* 17 (1964): 29–54; and "Fortuna e 'prudenza' nella lezione del Pontano," in *Fortuna, ragione e prudenza*, 23–66. See also P. A. de Lisio, *Gli anni della svolta* (Salerno, 1976).

B ❧ ITALY'S LEADING HUMANIST

13 ❧ LORENZO VALLA
Maristella Lorch

ALTHOUGH LORENZO VALLA'S FAMILY ORIGINATED FROM NORTH-ern Italy, he was born in Rome in 1405 or 1407, where he also spent his youth.[1] His uncle, Nicola Scrivani, was a papal secretary. Valla seems to have had a tutor for learning Greek, but he was otherwise a self-taught man, a condition that led one of the most influential papal secretaries, Poggio Bracciolini, to accuse him of ignorance, largely because he had never studied "philosophy." Valla, however, declared himself to be primarily a grammarian, but also an orator and a rhetorician. In the footsteps of Quintilian's *Institutiones oratoriae*—with which he fell in love at a very early age and to which he dedicated his first work (now lost), a comparison between Cicero and Quintilian—he thought of rhetoric as the highest human art, encompassing all that man produces. At the same time, he also studied jurisprudence extensively and with great enthusiasm. Indeed, it can be said that Valla applied himself within the classical Roman tradition to every field of study directly concerned with man as an individual and as a member of society.

Valla wanted to remain in Rome and pursue a career as a papal secretary, but his desire was blocked. At the invitation of his friend, Antonio Beccadelli (Panormita), he went then to Pavia in 1431. There he published his first extant work, *De voluptate* (*On Pleasure*)—for many years now the principal object of my study[2]—which he had conceived even earlier in Rome. *On Pleasure* is a dialogue among a Stoic, an Epicurean, and a Christian on the true and false good (*voluptas* and *honestas*, pleasure and virtue, respectively). The thesis, categorically asserted by Valla in the preface, is that pleasure is the one and only good. The Epicurean understands it as "the encounter of the senses with the external object," the Christian as a substance or essence, an act of faith and hope, and in the final analysis the love of God, the original cohesive force of life itself. The essential ingredients of Valla's thought find a full articulation in *On Pleasure:* his polemical, aggressive approach to scholasticism and to humanistic Stoicism (from Cicero) in the name of an original concept of life inspired by faith, hope, and love and by a concept of language and rhetoric drawn from Quintilian.

The *studium* in Pavia where Valla taught for two years (1431–32) was, in contrast to the Rome of Pope Martin V, a cultural center thriving with philosophical and theological disputes, to which Valla contributed a polemic against the barbarous Latin of the well-known jurist Bartolus, the result of which was that he had to flee Pavia in fear of his life in 1433. He went to Milan where he diffused a revised version of his dialogue on pleasure, giving it the title *De vero falsoque bono* (*On the True and False Good*). The setting was changed to a convent in Pavia, and the interlocutors became Lombard scholars of irreproachable moral and religious reputations. Panormita, the Epicurean in *On Pleasure,* had not only become Valla's enemy but had also, because of his immoral behavior, apparently caused the misinterpretation of Valla's thesis. The change in interlocutors allowed Valla to clarify his point.

In 1435 Valla obtained a position at the court of Alfonso of Aragon with the title of secretary. He remained there over a decade. The king's controversy with the pope over the legitimacy of his kingdom was undoubtedly behind the work for which Valla was best known until recently, the *Declamatio* or *De falso credita et ementita Constantini donatione* (*Discourse on the Forgery of the Alleged Donation of Constantine,* 1440).[3] In this work Valla challenged the very document on which the papacy based its right to temporal power. Meanwhile, Alfonso had become reconciled with the pope, and although he probably dismissed the whole issue raised by the *Declamatio,* Valla suffered serious difficulties from it. He added to them when he refuted two bishops well known in Naples, one in a juridical debate, the other with respect to the authenticity of the false letter of Jesus to Abgar of Edessa. Moreover, a dispute with a popular preacher, Antonio da Bitonto, on the origin of the Apostle's Creed, induced him to refute its apostolic origin. He also addressed a letter to the College of Jurists in Naples asking them to correct a passage of Gratian's *Decretals.*

The result of all this controversy was that in 1444 Valla was summoned to trial by the tribunal of the Inquisition. The trial, of which a distorted account is given in Poggio's *Antidotum,* provoked a *Defensio* from Valla. He was freed through the intervention of Alfonso, ran the risk of being retried during a brief sojourn in Rome in 1446, escaped from Rome to Naples, and from there addressed to Pope Eugenius IV an *Apologia* in which he defended the ideas expressed in the works he had thus far composed.[4]

Prior to his trial, in 1438–39, Valla composed his *Dialecticae disputationes* (*Dialectical Disputations*),[5] in which he attacked Aristotelian-scholastic dialectic in the interest of clarity and simplicity. Specifically, he reduced Aristotle's logical categories from ten to three, based the three retained on their conformity to ordinary Latin usage, and, most important, attempted to subordinate this revised conception of logic to rhetoric. It is here that he made explicit his debt to Quintilian, whom he highly praised throughout and whose authority he exploited in maintaining the supreme importance of rhetoric.

His *De libero arbitrio* (1435–43) also made its appearance during these years.[6] In it he developed a critique of philosophy and a religious viewpoint analogous to that in *On Pleasure*. The question he raises in the treatise is whether God's foreknowledge is compatible with freedom of the human will. By using as examples the pagan gods Zeus and Apollo, Valla shows that Apollo, though he foreknows what will happen, does not cause events. Thus foreknowledge seems compatible with free will. But since in the Christian view God is one and causes all events, that is to say, he predestines events, philosophy cannot resolve the question. The issue is resolvable only in religious terms, through humility and faith.

Valla's work on free will became widely known as a result of the Protestant Reformation—the reformers praised it. But the work best known in his own lifetime and one for which he was justly famous was his *Elegantiae linguae latinae* (*Elegances of the Latin Language*), intended to restore the classical purity of Latin in grammar, phraseology, and style before its corruption by the barbarians. The *Elegances* was an important work in humanist philology and a major influence on subsequent humanists, beginning most notably with Erasmus.[7]

During his latter years in Naples (1446–48), subsequent to his trial, Valla was engaged in revisions of his earlier works: *On Pleasure*, the *Dialectical Disputations*, and the *Elegances*. He also revised his *Gesta Ferdinandi regis Aragonum* (*The Deeds of Ferdinand, King of Aragon*), which he had written during a brief absence from Naples in 1446;[8] and he composed his defense of these historical writings against Bartolomeo Facio, *Antidotum in Facium* (1447).[9]

In the autumn of 1446 King Alfonso led an expedition against Francesco Sforza and his allies, the Florentines and the Venetians. In moving north, he stopped at Tivoli, and there Valla joined his patron, met the newly elected Pope Nicholas V in Rome, and submitted to Poggio his emendation of Livy. In 1448 he finally saw his dream realized: he obtained a position in the papal curia. The departure from Naples must have been made easier by the increasing enmity of his former friends, Panormita and Facio.

Nicholas had promised Valla that he would make him *scriptorem et secretarium*. Valla was appointed composer of the pope's letters (*scriptor literarum apostolicarum*) but Nicholas never appointed him *secretarius,* a position of higher prestige and responsibility. In 1450, however, the pope reconfirmed his position of *scriptor* in a personal note delivered to Cardinal Nicholas of Cusa, a fellow humanist and friend of Valla. Valla conserved the note jealously, as he tells us in his *Antidotum II* against Poggio.[10] The following pope, Calixtus III, finally appointed him *secretarius* in 1455, guided by the strong support of Giovanni Tortelli, the pope's librarian.

Meanwhile, however, jealousy and personal resentment on the part of Poggio, the old-time, powerful papal secretary who had forced young Valla to leave Rome for Pavia in 1431, had flared up. The bomb exploded at the end of 1451 with an exchange of reciprocal violent invectives. Although Poggio left Rome to become chancellor of Florence in 1453, he never ceased to oppose Valla who, he wrote, "spent his energy and his life in talking against and ruining the reputations of the most learned and holy scholars, both those dead and those still living." Poggio succeeded for a time in stopping Valla's nomination as a secretary.

In 1450, after a period of private tutoring, Valla obtained a chair at the Roman *studium* in competition with the famous Greek scholar George of Trebizond. For a semester the two exchanged unfriendly remarks, apparently one defending and the other attacking Valla's lifelong "friend," Quintilian. Even though George soon gave up his chair in Rome, the hostility between the two persisted. They argued over such issues as the relative merits of Greek and Roman generals, Aristotelian and scholastic philosophy, and the interpretation of the Vulgate. It is perhaps ironic that among Valla's students might have been Poggio's children!

In Rome Valla worked actively at reediting his *Elegances,* which had become a true best seller. In 1450, induced by Cardinals Bessarion and Nicholas of Cusa, he took up once again his work on the New Testament. The *Adnotationes in Novum Testamentum* were dedicated to Pope Nicholas V in 1453. (They were first printed through the instigation of Erasmus in 1504.) In addition, Valla participated in Pope Nicholas's project of translating all the major Greek works into Latin, working on Herodotus and Thucydides. Valla celebrates this project in his prologue to the Latin version of Thucydides's *History* (summer, 1452), which is actually a dedicatory letter to the pope and a treatise on the role and function of translation.[11]

Between 1455 and 1457 Valla delivered three addresses that epitomize his lifelong intellectual activity and thus are important clues to the interpretation of his thought. One is the "Oratio in principio sui studii" ("Oration on the Beginning of His Own Studies"), the prolusion to his lectures, consisting of a praise of the liberal arts and an exhortation to the young to pursue them. In it he reflects on what makes the arts survive all human crises. The second address is "Sermo de mysterio Eucharistiae" ("Sermon on the Mystery of the Eucharist"), delivered on Maundy Thursday 1456 or 1457, dealing with the mystery of transubstantiation. The last was on 7 March 1457, when he was invited by the Dominicans of Santa Maria sopra Minerva in Rome to deliver a praise in honor of St. Thomas Aquinas. His "Encomium Sanctae Thomae" can be truly read as a synthesis of his ideas.[12] Shortly afterward he died.

Recently there has been a proliferation of editions of Valla's works and of historical, philosophical, and theological studies based on them or meant to encourage the further publication of reliable modern editions. Valla emerges from this recent attention as the most powerful figure among fifteenth-century Italian humanists, among whom he is also, in many respects, the most controversial. The enthusiastic reaction Erasmus had to Valla's works, the positive judgments of Luther and Ulrich von Hutten among other northern European scholars and religious figures, and the publication and diffusion of some of his controversial writings in central and northern Europe while they were disappearing from circulation in Italy, make him from a philosophical-theological point of view the most important link between Italian and transalpine humanism.[13]

*   *   *

In 1936 the Italian historian Delio Cantimori observed that "living theological thought in Italy had been laicized by Ficino, Pomponazzi, and their followers after the first attempts had been carried out by Valla. The problems of theology had become for the humanists . . . cultural intellectual problems."[14] In his view Valla is actively fighting against ecclesiastical institutions. More recent interpreters like Fois and Di Napoli[15] have attempted to defend Valla's orthodoxy in light of the theological renewal instituted by Vatican II. Other recent interpreters, for example, Vasoli and Gaeta,[16] have begun to move in another direction. Gaeta in particular states that the problem of Valla's orthodoxy is a false one, for the obvious reason that humanism developed within the framework of a Christian conception of life. The problem that should concern us is "the relation of the new humanistic culture to the expression that theology assumes within the Aristotelian-scholastic system." The issue is not Valla's personal religious convictions but the more general one of "a theology freed from a metaphysical-scholastic structure."[17] What we should look for in Valla is a theology different from that of the Counter-Reformation. Certainly Valla, with his repeated claims of orthodoxy and his militant attitude in defense of the church of Christ (with which he opens his earliest work—*On Pleasure*—and closes his last—"Encomium to St. Thomas") aims at reforming the contemporary Christian vision of life. What one must avoid, however, is the attempt to justify Valla's powerfully aggressive philological linguistic theory within the limits of Catholic piety, to make him an instrument in support of one's particular Catholic tradition.

Vasoli observes that it is equally dangerous and in fact impossible to try to elaborate from Valla's individual works a Vallian philosophical or theological system. The problem should therefore be phrased in different terms: What are the specific historical results that Valla's works have contributed to theological methodology? This line of thinking may be followed to discover the reasons for the influence Valla exercised on northern European scholars and religious thinkers. Gaeta points out, in support of this contention, that those who defend Valla's orthodoxy and so contest the connection Valla–Luther, are oblivious of the connection Valla–Erasmus. He contends that *On Pleasure* has a direct relation to Erasmus's colloquy, *Epicureus* (and, I would add, an even stronger connection to the *Praise of Folly*), and that Valla's *De professione* is closely related to Erasmus's *Enchiridion*. Moreover, Erasmus published Valla's *Annotations on the New Testament* in 1504, a project that put him on the road to publishing his own *Annotations* in 1516 and later. In line with Valla, Erasmus conceives the possibility of the "cohabitation of holy religion and true literature." In sum, then, if one wants to define Valla's orthodoxy, it should be in pre-Tridentine terms, recognizing that Valla's philological-critical method is in strong opposition to the structure and tradition of the church of the Counter-Reformation.

But what forms did this opposition assume? What were Valla's aims? His tools? Both Gaeta and Vasoli point to the interpretations of a Dominican, Salvatore Camporeale,[18] as the one who sets the problem in the right terms by focusing on Valla's method instead of on his orthodoxy, primarily on his concept of rhetoric derived from Quintilian. Reading Valla's works in the context of contemporary theological debates, Camporeale discovered that Valla lived in the midst of a deep theological crisis in relation to which he called for radical cultural renewal. Accordingly, the fact that he points to Paul as the ideal authority should be interpreted not only as a call to evangelical purity but also as the rehabilitation of the theology of the apostles and church fathers, that is, of a theology in which rhetoric had not yet been displaced by Aristotle's metaphysics and dialectics. It is significant that in his rhetorical work Valla should attack contemporary theologians as "an army of ants admirable perhaps for their activity but incapable of the originality of the ancient theologians."

Camporeale's most original contribution is to be found in his analysis of the *Dialectical Disputations* and the *Annotations on the New Testament*. With regard to the *Dialectical Disputations* Camporeale discovered that it had been completed by 1439 and was already diffused by 1440–42. The trinitarian problem discussed in book 1, chapter 13 is directly connected with the debates at the Council of Ferrara–Florence, and Valla shows his inclination for the position of the Greek theologians. Facio, Poggio, and Lauro Quirini, among others, attack him and arouse the attention of the Inquisition. After his trial in 1444 Valla revised the work, giving greater attention to theological problems. He revised it once again (1453–57) as a result of his polemic with Poggio in 1452, emphasizing his revulsion for the old "Ciceronian" point of view that Poggio represented. With regard to the *Annotations*, Camporeale discovered that the first version was completed in 1435–36 and revised in 1443, prior to his trial. This version circulated in Naples and Rome in an unofficial way. Poggio's polemic induced Valla to revise it and dedicate it to Pope Nicholas V in 1453. Thus Camporeale demonstrated that the works of Valla should be read in relation to his enemies' attacks.

In their final elaboration the *Dialectical Disputations* introduce a Vallian concept of rhetoric "that goes much beyond that of Aristotelian rhetoric, which was purely the science of discourse and was counterposed to logic as the technique of argumentation through rational processes. . . . Rhetoric for Valla is a science that comprehends all forms of the study of human language. It comprehends all other disciplines and cultural expressions."[19] The Aristotelians stressed the dichotomy between dialectic and rhetoric, between reason and popular speech. The consequence of Valla's position is that philosophy ceases to be metaphysical speculation, logic ceases to be the autonomous analysis of a rational structure, and rhetoric goes much beyond the art of persuasion. Valla's great novelty is the application of his linguistic-rhetorical method to philosophical and especially to theological questions.

*   *   *

Let us look more closely at Valla's rhetorical method. Rhetoric is the field in which the humanists emerge as original thinkers. For Valla in particular the *ars rhetorica* ceases to be a discipline concerned simply with speaking and writing, an art that, so regarded, can be learned in school. It is rather a philosophy in the original sense of the word, conceiving language as man's point of contact with his environment. As such it embraces all arts and disciplines. Rhetoric thus provides a new method of approach to intellectual problems.

Valla found this new point of departure in Quintilian, which accounts for his early and continued enthusiasm for that writer. Quintilian, in the first century after Christ, wrote what looks on the surface like a manual of rhetorical precepts. In reality, however, he vigorously opposes the rhetorical schools of his time. Much more self-consciously than Cicero, whom he outdistances in this sense, Quintilian establishes language as the expression of the relation between an individual and his world, a relationship that both reveals and creates that world. Valla accepted this implicit philosophical position and used it polemically in relation, on the one hand, to Aristotelian metaphysics and the dialectic of contemporary scholasticism and, on the other hand, to the so-called humanist *schola antiqua.*

In opposition to Aristotelian-scholastic philosophy, which was deductive in its method, deriving particular conclusions from universal, axiomatic truths, Valla offered a rhetorical method based on induction. The inductive method works by means of the individual concrete example, inducing truth from it, that is, allowing the truth that the example contains to come to the surface. Valla elaborates on this issue in detail in his *Dialectical Disputations.* Valla was equally opposed by Bruni, Guarino, Poggio, and Facio. According to this group, the texts of the ancients are regarded as perfect expressions of eloquence and wisdom. In ethics or moral philosophy, they admired and encouraged the imitation of Cicero, especially of his concept of *virtus* or *honestas* as the highest aspiration of man's *humanitas.* Cicero in his philosophical works, principally in *De officiis,* defends *honestum* as good for its own sake, in strict agreement with Stoic ethics: only by overcoming all forms of selfish personal interest in the name of a universal principle of reason can *homo* function as a *civis,* placing himself wholeheartedly at the service of a public good. He thus contributes to a form of government that affords peace and harmony, achieving a kind of divine self-sufficiency on earth. What Hans Baron and Eugenio Garin define as civic humanism feeds on this ideal.

Against both Aristotelians and fellow humanists Valla regarded a literary text—be it Plato's, Aristotle's, or Cicero's—as the expression of man's interactions with his environment. The Aristotelian scholastics with their deductive method and the humanists who look to the past as a norm both sacrifice the particular and the individual in each human situation. Valla admires Quintilian precisely because he establishes language as the expression of the relation between an individual and his world. It is, in fact, precisely this relation—one that changes according to time, place, and circumstances—that for both Quintilian and Valla is the subject of investigation.

Thus for Valla a text is a laboratory for investigation. It must be studied as an example of what is unique and unrepeatable in a particular moment of human history. The complex, multifaceted reaction of man to the object (*res*) produces a variety of linguistic expressions. Of these, common everyday language is the most immediate. To use and to interpret poetic language is most difficult because of its intense metaphorical potentialities. Though aware of the function of such forms of language, Valla's critical philology takes into account first common everyday language, the *verba usitata et propria*. In the *Elegances* he addresses repeatedly the students of Latin (*cultores latinae linguae*) and those who are intensely interested in the beauty of language (*bene loquendi studiosissimi*), stating that he offers them with his book an analytical methodological instrument for reaching what Quintilian calls the admirable elegance of the Latin language (*mira sermonis latini elegantia*). What he means by elegance is a new concept of grammar, syntax, and style. The *Elegances* present us first with a morphological study of grammar and syntax, the *partes orationis*. Then they investigate the *verborum significatio*, in other words, the semantic structure of the language. *Grammatica* thus acquires for Valla an epistemological significance and function as "the doctrine of the basic principles of language." It is on this basis that Valla develops his idea of rhetoric as philological criticism.

Philology, as the comprehensive study of a text, implies also a knowledge of history, jurisprudence, the natural sciences, philosophy, and theology. For this reason Valla thought of himself as a universal man, learned in every branch of knowledge, and he declared himself to be first of all a grammarian and a rhetorician, but at the same time a philosopher and a theologian. In his invectives against Bartolomeo Facio, he also claims to be an expert in music, astronomy, civil law, Greek, and "infinite other disciplines," a statement he repeats in his *Apologia* to Pope Eugenius IV. Making due allowance for the polemical tone of many of these assertions, one can nevertheless conclude that he applied himself to all the disciplines concerned with man, the *studia humanitatis* or humanities, and that he did so in his function as a philologist.

Thus philology became for Valla a true philosophy in the sense that it is an attitude and a critical habit, which contributes to place activity in a perspective that results not so much in the discovery and rediscovery of texts and authors as in a change in the sense of culture arising from these texts. This philology truly leads to the discovery of a world, because it restores historical concreteness through which a world emerges.

The kind of knowledge that philology conveys does not share the objectivity of mathematical knowledge, simply because its *res* or subject partakes of the multiplicity of contacts between man and nature. Nevertheless, a form of objectivity is certainly imposed by the respect that the philologist, in his search for man's historical identity, must constantly profess for the infinite variety of the natural world outside of man and for nature and human nature meeting constantly in ever-changing ways. Undaunted by the obvious limitations that such knowledge implies, the philologist-philosopher Valla plows ahead enthusiastically, from the beginning of his authorship to its end. Judging from the way Valla applied his method to different texts as expressions of different fields of "man's interaction with his environment," his way of looking at reality can certainly be regarded as a new science concerning man.

*   *   *

Perhaps the best way to illustrate both Valla's intellectual development and his philological method, and a fitting way to conclude this essay, is to analyze a particular passage in which both are revealed. When I wrote the introduction to my critical edition of Valla's *On Pleasure* over twenty years ago, I instinctively chose book 3, chapters 12–14 as an example of what I then defined as Valla at his best in the use of his philological method. In the intervening years critical attention devoted to Valla and my own continuing preoccupation with his thought allows me to return to these passages in order to show what I could only intuit earlier. I shall first state briefly the argument of *On Pleasure,* book 3; second, discuss Valla's attack on Boethius in book 3, chapter 12; third, trace the evolution of chapter 12 in Valla's revisions; fourth, relate chapter 12 to chapters 13 and 14; and finally, suggest the implications of the development and substance of these passages for Valla's other works.

In book 3 of *On Pleasure,* usually described as the "Christian" book, Valla reaches a solution to the problem of the true good. He approaches it first through a refutation of Aristotle's theory of virtue as a mean between two extremes, a refutation he calls the *demonstratio falsi boni.* He then turns to the *demonstratio veri boni,* of which chapters 12 through 14 are the crowning statement. The Christian interlocutor begins his demonstration of the true good by relating the concept of *honestas* or virtue—the moral principle of the philosophers that has just been disposed of in the refutation of Aristotle's conception of virtue—to a concept of virtue that serves pleasure. This moral principle will in the end be discovered to be Christian virtue or *christiana honestas.* The argument begins with a myth similar to one with which Cicero opens the *De inventione.* Serving man and god was initially expressed by two words, *utilitas* and *honestas.* The former points to self-interested behavior, to an expediency that limits humans to physical life; the latter reveals a vague longing for contact with the mystery that is divinity, a contact that has been irremediably lost. Valla's Christian interlocutor rejects the emptiness of this conception of *honestas,* though he praises the aspiration to go beyond the sensual, an aspiration that suggests a tension in the desire to regain an original sense of mystery. Christ, whose appearance in the unfolding of Valla's theory of pleasure is sudden, almost miraculous, makes the true virtues tangible for us through his words. The *honestas* of the Christian consists in faith, hope, and love: faith in human strength through faith in its creator, hope in a temporal sense through the hope of transcending the limits of the sensual and the laws of expediency; love not as patience (resignation) but as joy. Thus the solution of the problem of *honestas* lies in uniting it with *voluptas*. In a Christian context, *honestas* suggests the sacrifice that *christiana honestas* implies: the joyful, hopeful attitude by which human beings face evil in nature and life, inspired by an instinctive faith in the final reward, a faith that makes that reward superior to any humanly conceivable prize.

The *voluptas/caritas* or pleasure/love for God that is the final reward is revealed to Valla's Christian interlocutor by the words of Scripture, particularly Psalm 36:8 (the translation of which Valla subjects to a sharp analysis): "Thou shalt inebriate them with the plenty of thy house; and thou shalt make them drink of the torrent of pleasure." Thus it is that the incitement to the renunciation of earthly pleasures cannot come from an outside *honestas*, a virtue that pursues good for the sake of good, but comes instead from a deep faith in and hope for a full self-realization.

This demonstration of the true good leaves no doubt that Valla's intention is to prove that *honestas* is not a form of self-perfection for the pursuit of good for its own sake, a pursuit nourished more by the intellect than by the heart, thus stressing human self-sufficiency. *Honestas* does not stand any chance of survival when faced by a pleasure/love that directs and inspires human life in all its significant actions (*in magnis*) such as building, buying, and marrying, as well as in the satisfaction of primary needs (*in minimis*) such as eating and sleeping.

At the same time, earthly pleasure, an essential aspect of pleasure as love, can be justified only if it is conceived as a reflection of an active human experience in its totality. Pleasure/*caritas* is this active experience par excellence. The degree of its intensity depends ultimately on the intensity of the desire that urges us on from experience to experience until we reach into the origin and motivation of all experiences, an all-encompassing love. Since this all-encompassing love is found in Christ, supreme *voluptas* is identification with him in his incarnation. In Valla's theory of pleasure these are the existential prerequisites for the achievement of the goal, the true virtue that leads us to pleasure as the true good. Inspired and motivated by pure joy, *honestas* itself becomes pure joy.

Since, from this Christian point of view, "the actions of men were empty and worthy of punishment before they were illuminated by the light of truth and kindled by the heat of charity, which is Christ," the pagan world, apart from the Jews, is condemned. The condemnation is based on the fact that they were recompensed for what they desired; they are of course not recompensed for what they did not desire.

All this discussion sets the stage for Valla's attack on Boethius in chapter 12. Boethius is chosen as the object of attack because he is the first in a long series of thinkers who employed classical philosophy in the service of Christian theology. In Valla's view Boethius is responsible for the most serious "philosophical sin," namely, having introduced into Christian discourse the terminology of pagan philosophy (*sermo gentilis*). Valla's opposition to Boethius thus takes the form of an attack on his "philosophical method," to which Valla opposes his own method inspired by Quintilian's concept of rhetoric. Thus the refutation of Boethius is intrinsic to Valla's argument in favor of his rhetorical method.

Boethius concludes from the premises "whoever is good possesses a good" and "beatitude (happiness) is a good" that "every good (or virtuous) person is happy." His error in reasoning thus is, in Valla's view, due to his ignorance of the word *bonum,* a good. In the major premise the good in question is virtue, which is an action; but in the minor premise happiness is a quality. The syllogism mixes action and quality. It is the error of a philosopher. Because Boethius took philosophy as his mistress, paying her more honor than he paid his religion, he could not solve the problem of the true good or show that the good are always happy and the evil always miserable. An orator, instead, who knows the meaning and function of a word in a sentence, uses them, not abstractly as a philosopher does, but in the context of human life, as tools in the service of life. How much more advantageous it would have been for Boethius to speak as an orator rather than as a dialectician! Among the philosophers, if one word goes wrong the whole argument falls, as in the case of Boethius. But in the rhetorical method, the object of which is to illuminate real objects or ideas, the richer the *res* to be illuminated the clearer will be the vision and the stronger the conviction of the orator; the language will in turn reflect this clarity and strength of conviction. Thus he concludes: "Farewell, then, farewell to Philosophy, and let her, as though she were a loose woman of the stage, remove her foot from the sacred temple, and cease to sing, or to prate, like a sweet siren drawing men to their deaths; since she herself is afflicted with foul diseases and many wounds, let her leave it to another physician to cure and care for the sick."

In the earliest version of chapter 12 (1431), Boethius was only mentioned incidentally: "What then? Don't the good and the evil aim at the same point, as Boethius declared, while the former longs for the future, the latter for the present goods?" The second version of the passage in 1433 expands the development of the example of Boethius, pointing out that as a philosopher he could not resolve the problem of the relation between virtue and happiness, since on earth the wicked sometimes prosper and the good do not. It is only in the third revision, however (after 1444), that Valla makes explicit the use of his rhetorical method to undermine dialectic. It is then that he makes the distinction between action and quality (12.3) and spells out the way Boethius has gone wrong through the misapprehension of a word. In the period between these two revisions Valla had completed his *Dialectical Disputations,* in which he had developed his rhetorical method as opposed to the philosophers.

This clear appeal to his contribution toward a new method is reflected in the alternative endings of the second and third versions. In the second version he writes:

> Thus should Boethius have proceeded. He should have dedicated to the reading of Quintilian the time and energy he spent in writing his dialectical work. In this way he would have avoided erring in his interpretation of rhetoric and he would have appeared to us as a more serious and religious philosopher.

The third version reads:

> Boethius ought to have worked in this way; he, like many others, was deceived by excessive love of dialectics. But how much error has been in dialectics and how no one has ever before written carefully about it, and how it is really a part of rhetoric—about all these things our Lorenzo here has begun to write, very much in accordance with the truth in my opinion.

The development of the text between 1431 and 1444 shows clearly that Valla was looking for a convincing formulation of his rhetorical method as the only method capable of responding adequately to philosophical-theological problems.

In chapters 13 and 14 Valla applies his rhetorical method to an important theological issue: our love for God. Should God be loved for himself (in scholastic terms, as the *causa finalis*) or as the source of all the goods we enjoy (as the *causa efficiens*)?

Chapter 13 opens with the declaration that all things are loved for two reasons, either because they bring joy or because they receive joy. Both elements concur in God. In the 1431 and 1433 versions Valla limits himself to commenting: "He created us from nothing ready to enjoy good things, so that we ought to love him more than ourselves." Although God and the things are the same, "he distinguishes himself from them by *a particular property*" (emphasis added). Hence "our happiness is not God himself but descends from God, as the joy we get from a beautiful thing is not the thing itself." What is added after 1444 is a detailed study of that *particular quality* which distinguishes God from his creatures. The aim of Valla's study is to discover what generates beatitude or happiness in man.

Pleasure had already been found by the Epicurean in book 1 to be "a union of what receives and is received." This statement is now supported by the fact that God—who creates pleasure—is in the unique condition of also being loved as "what is received," while man who experiences pleasure loves him. Valla's originality, however, is revealed in his style, rude and abrupt, in the nervous impatience with which he deals with words. Boethius's argument had been ridiculed because it depended, *philosophico more,* on one word as the key to his solution of the issue at stake (human happiness). Valla, *rhetorico more,* does not care about the word itself that defines this happiness. "Loving itself is delight [*delectatio*] or pleasure [*voluptas*] or beatitude [*beatitudo*] or charity [*caritas*], which is the final end or goal for which all other things are" (13.2). What matters is the end, the reward that keeps the tension alive which is life.

Valla's originality is evidenced equally by his approach to the next issue, the much debated question whether God should be loved as final cause—as an end in himself—or as efficient cause—as the cause of the goods that man enjoys. He comes down on the side of saying that God should not be loved for himself, as if love and delight existed for the sake of an end and were not themselves an end. In keeping with the thesis that pleasure is the highest good, God should be loved as efficient cause, the giver of pleasure.

It is a third issue, however, that arouses Valla to make full use of his dialectics. The issue centers on the point that "everything was created by God with the greatest possible wisdom and prudence." Everything God has created is a good. But only those goods that fall in our world of perception exist for us. Hence what is deprived of sensual perception (for example, a diamond) has been created for the sake of those who perceive. This statement implies that between to be (*esse* or *substantia*) and to be happy (*bene esse* or *qualitas*) what concerns us directly is the *bene esse* that involves the feeling of joy. Consequently, the just are happy not simply because they exist, but because they are open to the perception of what is good for them, the *bene esse*. God has created the world neutral, for the good of the just and the evil of the unjust. In this sense one should understand the statements that "God created evil" and that demons and the damned "have no good." It would have been better for them not to exist at all, because they lack the opening that would allow them to interpret or use existence, *esse* or *substantia*, for their own good, *bene esse*. Thus pleasure is received (by those who love God) from creatures, but much more from the Creator. Since he is the source of good and since the good is manifold, God is the source of goods. In his love must be included all forms of virtue. In this context, the antithesis between *voluptas* and *honestas* vanishes. Rather, we discover *voluptas* in its divine essence by experiencing, though with different intensity, the attraction we have for what is contingent and perishable. *Honestas* in this context is the gate to *voluptas,* an open attitude toward or acceptance of life on earth but with due awareness of the mystery of existence.

The various transformations through which passed the passage I have analyzed from *On Pleasure* provide a benchmark for observing these transformations in his other works as well.

Valla wrote his now lost treatise, *Comparison of Cicero and Quintilian,* at the same time as the earliest version of *On Pleasure.* From his praise of Quintilian in other sources we know that he had already arrived at his conception of the opposition between philosophy and rhetoric, an opposition already evident in the condemnation of Boethius in the earliest version of *On Pleasure.* In the second version (1433) this condemnation is elaborated in his rejection of Boethius's contention that the good are always rewarded and the evil punished in this life. The conclusion Valla had reached is that only a different conception of philosophical theology could deal with problems of human existence. Consequently, he rejected rationalistic philosophy as an abstraction from life and argued that rhetoric, a science more strictly tied to human life, must help theology in solving the problems of human existence. This point of view is reflected in a number of works Valla composed in the late 1430s and early 1440s. In the preface to book 4 of the *Elegances* (from 1441), for example, Valla defends himself against those who accuse him for exhorting Christians to read pagan literature. He makes the argument Erasmus will adopt from him later, that if we condemn pagan literature we must condemn at the same time all cultural expressions of ancient civilization. Such a wholesale rejection would make life as we know it impossible. The alternative is the acceptance of all the human sciences which, as Quintilian proved, are included in the *eloquentia rhetorica,* and the subjection of all these human arts to the Christian religion. In the *Collatio Novi Testamenti* (1443) Valla makes clear that the specific task of the superior art of rhetoric is the reconstruction of a text. In this capacity rhetoric serves as "the rebuilder of the Temple of Jerusalem." The "individual words of the Holy Scriptures are like individual gems and precious stones out of which the celestial Jerusalem is built." No other art—canon law, medicine, astronomy—can claim the same priority in rebuilding the temple of God. In his dialogue *On Free Will* Valla suggests that the Christian religion and rationalistic philosophy propose two antithetical conceptions of life and that the Christian tradition has always condemned such philosophy as the mother of heresies. Commensurate with this view is his contention, also in the preface to book 4 of the *Elegances,* that "the only eloquent people are those whom I have listed as columns of the church, beginning with the apostles, among whom Paul seems to be prominent because of his eloquence." The union of theology and rhetoric lies at the beginning of the Christian tradition.

This point of view finds expression as a new methodology in the *Dialectical Disputations,* published in their original version in 1438–39. For the next twenty years Valla continued to develop and deepen his commitment to rhetoric. He was particularly affected by his trial at the hands of the Inquisition in 1444. Thereafter, he revised all his earlier productions in order to make clear not only his critique of rationalistic philosophy but the application of the new methodology he proposed as its replacement, as he did in the passage analyzed from *On Pleasure.* But in these subsequent revisions his philosophical opponents now include not only ancients like Boethius and medieval theologians like Thomas Aquinas, but contemporary humanists like Poggio and Facio who championed Stoicism. Valla's polemics with these two humanists, among others, reveals his opposition to what he regarded as their conservative tendencies. His dismantling of scholastic theology and his opposition to Stoicism were in the interests of a living *rhetorica eloquentia,* an eloquence that, setting aside all abstractions and reifications, would address itself to the problems of human life in the service of the Christian religion. Valla, like his northern disciple, Erasmus, sought in eloquence— the art of persuasion—and in a return to the sources of both pagan and Christian traditions, a renewal of thought and religion in his own time.

NOTES

1. The standard edition of Valla's works is *Opera omnia,* ed. E. Garin, 2 vols. (Turin, 1962), which includes, in vol. 1 (pp. 1–235), the standard sixteenth-century edition of Valla's works, *Laurentii Vallae Opera* (Basel, 1540). Separate editions of Valla's major works will be cited as mentioned in the text. On Valla's life, see G. Mancini, *Vita di Lorenzo Valla* (Florence, 1891) and R. Sabbadini in L. Barozzi and R. Sabbadini, *Studi sul Panormita e sul Valla* (Florence, 1891), 48–148. Among recent studies, see M. Fois, *Il pensiero cristiano di Lorenzo Valla nel quadro storico-culturale del suo ambiente* (Rome, 1969); Fois deals extensively with Valla's life and works in

relation to the historical and literary environment in which he worked; see his bibliography of Valla's life, 649–51 and works, 651–56 (preceded by a bibliography of works by humanists contemporary with Valla). See also G. di Napoli, *Lorenzo Valla: Filosofia e religione nell'umanesimo italiano* (Rome, 1971).

2. For the critical edition, see *De vero falsoque bono,* ed. M. Lorch (Bari, 1970). For an English translation that also includes the Latin text, see *On Pleasure,* trans. A. K. Heiatt and M. Lorch (New York, 1979). For a study of the work, see M. Lorch, *Valla's Defense of Life: A Theory of Pleasure* (Munich, 1985).

3. *De falso credita et ementita Constantini donatione Declamatio* (usually called simply *Declamatio*), ed. W. Schwahn (Leipzig, 1928); and, with an English translation, *The Treatise of Lorenzo Valla on the Donation of Constantine,* trans. C. B. Coleman (New Haven, 1922). For a study of the *Donation,* see V. de Caprio, "Retorica e ideologia nella Declamatio di L. Valla sulla Donazione di Constantino," *Paragone* 338 (April 1978): 35–56.

4. *Antidotum primum,* ed. A. Wesseling (Amsterdam, 1978); *Apologus,* ed. S. Camporeale, in *L. Valla, umanesimo e teologia* (Florence, 1972), 503–34.

5. *Repastinatio dialectice et philosophie,* ed. G. Zippel (Padua, 1982), vols. 1–2. In addition to the studies mentioned below in note 13, see Chapter 29 in these volumes, note 16.

6. *De libero arbitrio,* ed. M. Anfossi (Florence, 1934); critical edition with French translation, ed. J. Chomarat (Paris, 1983); text with Italian translation, *Prosatori latini del Quattrocento,* ed. E. Garin (Milan, 1952), 524–65; translated into English by C. Trinkaus, in *The Renaissance Philosophy of Man,* ed. E. Cassirer, P. O. Kristeller, and J. H. Randall (Chicago, 1948), 155–82; and in *Renaissance Philosophy,* vol. 1, *The Italian Philosophers,* trans. A. B. Fallico and H. Shapiro (New York, 1967), 40–65.

7. The prefaces have been published with an Italian translation in *Prosatori latini del Quattrocento,* 594–631. For studies of the *Elegances,* see Chapter 29, Volume 3, note 16.

8. *Gesta Ferdinandi regis Aragonum,* ed. O. Besomi (Padua, 1974).

9. *In Bartholomeum Facium ligurem recriminationes libri IV,* ed. M. P. Regoliosi (Padua, 1982).

10. *Antidotum primum,* intro., 23–24.

11. The proem is amply discussed by Camporeale, *L. Valla, umanesimo e teologia,* 125–31.

12. See, on this work, S. Camporeale, "L. Valla, tra Medioevo e Rinascimento, Encomium Sanctae Thomae—1457," *Memorie Domenicane* n.s. 7 (1976): 3–190; and published separately (Pistoia, 1977).

13. The literature on Valla's thought is vast. Following are some general discussions of his thought as well as special studies useful for the present essay: S. Camporeale, *L. Valla, umanesimo e teologia;* idem, "Da Lorenzo Valla a Tommaso Moro: Lo statuto umanistico della teologia," *Memorie Domenicane* n.s. 4 (1973): 9–101; R. Fubini, "Intendimenti umanistici e riferimenti patristici dal Petrarca al Valla," *Giornale storico della letteratura italiana*

95 (1974): 521–78; F. Gaeta, *Lorenzo Valla: Filologia e storia nell'umane-simo italiano* (Naples, 1955); E. Garin, *La cultura filosofica del Rinascimento italiano* (Florence, 1979), 60–92; P. O. Kristeller, *Eight Philosophers of the Italian Renaissance* (Stanford, 1964), 19–36; G. Radetti, introduction to his *Scritti filosofici e religiosi* (Florence, 1953), a translation into Italian of some of Valla's works; idem, commentary and bibliography in "L'epicureismo nel pensiero umanistico del Quattrocento," *Grande antologia filosofica* (Milan, 1964), 6:839–961; idem, "La religione di L. Valla," in *Medioevo e Rinascimento: Studi in onore di Bruno Nardi,* 2 vols. (Florence, 1955), 2:595–620; J. E. Seigel, *Rhetoric and Philosophy in Renaissance Humanism* (Princeton, 1968), 137–69; C. Trinkaus, *In Our Image and Likeness: Humanity and Divinity in Italian Humanist Thought,* 2 vols. (Chicago, 1970), vol. 1, chap. 3 (the term *theologia rhetorica* was first used by Trinkaus); R. Waswe, "The 'Ordinary Language Philosophy' of Lorenzo Valla," *Bibliothèque d'humanisme et Renaissance* 41 (1979): 255–71; idem, "The Reaction of Juan Vives to Valla's Philosophy of Language," *Bibliothèque d'humanisme et Renaissance* 42 (1980): 595–609.

The following are also discussed in the present essay: G. Farris, "Teologia e paolinismo in L. Valla," *Studium* 68 (1973): 671–83; F. Gaeta, "Recenti studi su L. Valla," *Rivista della storia della chiesa in Italia* 29 (1975): 560–77; H.-B. Gerl, *Rhetorik als Philosophie: Lorenzo Valla* (Munich, 1974); E. Grassi, *Rhetoric as Philosophy* (University Park, PA, 1980); E. Marino, "Umanesimo e teologia (a proposito della recente storiografia su L. Valla)," *Memorie Domenicane* n.s. 3 (1972): 198–218; C. Vasoli, "Nuove prospettive su L. Valla," *Nuova rivista storica* 57 (1973): 448–58.

14. D. Cantimori, *Umanesimo e religione del Rinascimento* (Turin, 1975), 4–7. The book is a series of essays; the quotation is taken from an essay written in 1936.

15. Fois, *Il pensiero cristiano;* Di Napoli, *Lorenzo Valla.*

16. Vasoli, "Nuove prospettive"; Gaeta, *Lorenzo Valla,* "Recenti studi."

17. Gaeta, *Lorenzo Valla,* 571.

18. Camporeale, *L. Valla, umanesimo e teologia.*

19. Ibid., 79–80.

C&HUMANIST CULTURE AND THE MARGINS OF SOCIETY

14&ITALIAN HUMANISM AND THE BYZANTINE ÉMIGRÉ SCHOLARS

Deno J. Geanakoplos

NY REASSESSMENT OF THE ROLE OF THE ÉMIGRÉ BYZANTINE
scholars in the development of Italian Renaissance thought and
learning must take cognizance of the fact that at the time that the
Italian Renaissance developed there was a parallel "Renaissance" taking
place also in the Byzantine East.[1] The latter, more accurately termed the
Palaeologan "revival of learning," had begun earlier in the thirteenth century. This revival of culture under the Palaeologan dynasty was expressed
in the emergence of certain realistic qualities in painting, a further development in mystical beliefs, and, what will be the exclusive focus here, a
greater intensification than ever before of the study of ancient Greek literature, philosophy, and science. Byzantinists disagree as to the precise
causes of the Palaeologan intellectual revival, which took firm hold, notably, after the Greek recovery of Constantinople from the Latins in
1261.[2] But there is no doubt that it was characterized by somewhat different and more intensive methods of study than earlier Byzantine revivals of classical Greek learning.[3] An understanding of the characteristics
of this Palaeologan intellectual revival is vital, as I shall try to show,
because the recovery of Greek learning in the Italian Renaissance was
influenced not only by the contents of Palaeologan learning but by such
considerations as its methods of teaching, curricula of study, and attitudes toward the corpus of disciplines in the Byzantine cultural tradition.

It is the principal thesis of this essay—in my view it is an important
reason to reevaluate the role of the Byzantine scholars—that the development of Greek learning in the Italian Renaissance was the result primarily of the fusion, however imperfect in certain respects, of various

The author wishes to thank the *Rivista di studi bizantini e slavi* 3 (1983): 129–57,
for permission to reprint this essay. The bibliographical note 1 has been added, other notes
have been updated, and minor editorial changes have been made to the text.

elements of the Palaeologan Renaissance with those of the Italian. This consideration is one of which most western Renaissance historians are unaware, often lacking a knowledge of Greek, and, no less important, of late Byzantine cultural developments.

This thesis, however, must be qualified to take into account such considerations as Italian receptivity or lack thereof toward certain kinds of Greek learning on account of intellectual differences, ethnic prejudices, or even divergent methods of academic organization. My method in reassessing the significance of the Greek émigrés in Italy will be first to point out the Italian historical milieu for the reception of Greek learning and its agents of transmission—the émigrés—then to outline the main characteristics of this little-known Palaeologan revival of Greek literature, philosophy, and science, along with Byzantine attitudes toward such learning. Then, in the main body of the essay, I shall deal with the activities of the more important émigrés in the three principal centers of the Italian Renaissance: Florence, Rome, and Venice-Padua, each of which experienced a period of primacy in Greek studies. Finally, I shall draw a few general conclusions about the significance of the Byzantine émigrés' contribution to Italian Renaissance thought and learning.

✻   ✻   ✻

What was the state of Greek learning in Italy at the outset of the Italian Renaissance, roughly 1350? Scholasticism then held sway with its primary focus on Aristotelian logic and philosophy, and attempts were being made to reconcile Aristotle with Christian theology. But unless we understand the method, word-for-word (*verbum ad verbum*) translation, and intent of scholastic translators from the Greek such as William of Moerbeke,[4] we shall fail to comprehend the need felt later by Italian humanists and virtually all Byzantine émigré scholars to retranslate most of these ancient Greek texts. The scholastic versions had served to whet western appetites for Greek logical, metaphysical, and scientific works, but virtually all the literary, rhetorical, and historical works, along with several important writings of Aristotle[5] and most of Plato, were either unknown in the West or left untranslated by the scholastics.

With the dawn of the early Italian Renaissance and humanist emphasis on classical Latin literature, the receptivity of Italian men of letters to ancient Greek literature was accordingly intensified. In Florence in particular, the birthplace of so-called "civic" humanism with its focus on Roman republicanism, Greek works pertaining to the activities of civic life, the *vita activa*, were now welcomed, especially those concerning ancient Athens, the rhetorical qualities of whose statesmen were looked upon as models to emulate. In this social ambience of the Italian urban areas, we see, then, a general readiness for appreciation of certain Greek works, especially rhetorical. But the degree of receptivity varied. Leonardo Bruni, for example, may well have considered making a Latin translation of Plato's *Republic*. Quite possibly, however, he was not sophisticated enough to appreciate the subtleties of the work, or he may have disliked its "communistic" concepts and praise of despotism, however benevolent.[6]

As for the Byzantine émigrés, they found the Italian intellectual terrain well prepared for them, because the Italian humanist focus on the *studia humanitatis* was very similar to the rhetorical training so fundamental to the Palaeologan Renaissance. Paul O. Kristeller has astutely remarked that the learning and interests of the Italian humanists had more links to the Byzantine didactic tradition than to the humanists' western predecessors, the scholastics.[7]

It is important now to turn to a vital but inadequately explored area: Palaeologan methods of teaching and exegesis, curricula, and attitudes toward various ancient Greek writers. The young Byzantine student, after learning grammar and composition, a process requiring a great deal of memorization, advanced to the study of the Greek orators.[8] Rhetorical studies were important in Byzantium if simply for the government's need of a well-trained, articulate bureaucracy (not to speak of the inordinate Byzantine love for rhetorical expression), a situation comparable to the Italian cities' need for "professional" humanists. (Isocrates was more esteemed in Byzantium than Demosthenes, apparently because of his more "didactic" qualities.)[9] The most esteemed manuals on rhetoric used by the Byzantines were those of Hermogenes of Tarsus and his follower Aphthonius. Hermogenes's value lay in his pragmatic and highly effective analysis of the various kinds of rhetoric, and his concrete information on precisely how the rhetorician can create desired effects on his audience through observing specified rhetorical "forms" (*ideas*).[10]

The Byzantine curriculum, then, strongly emphasized rhetoric, but unlike the parallel *studia humanitatis* of Italy, particularly in the earlier Florentine stage of humanism, it also included metaphysical philosophy, mathematics, and pure science. It was the Byzantine aim to impart an all-encompassing education (based on the traditional *enkyklios paideia*), the culmination of which lay, theoretically, in theology.[11] Attesting to the organic unity of late Byzantine education is the fact that, as far as I can ascertain, every scholar who dealt with literature in the Palaeologan Renaissance also concerned himself with science.[12] Maximus Planudes, the great *literatus*, wrote a little-known work on mathematics and was even interested in Arabic numerals.[13] I stress this point because the huge scope of learning and interests manifested by such Byzantine émigrés in Italy as George of Trebizond, John Argyropoulos, and Bessarion will contrast strongly with the narrower Italian interests of the *studia humanitatis*, which, for some time at least, excluded metaphysical philosophy and science.[14]

During the Palaeologan Renaissance there was a far more intensive and systematic study than ever before of the entire range of classical pagan Greek works: literary, philosophical, and scientific. And the Byzantine church seemed for the first time not to object to the reading of such texts.[15] The works of the leading ancient commentators on Aristotle and Plato were now carefully analyzed.[16] In addition, Palaeologan scholars studied more closely the ancient historians, Thucydides in particular, possibly because of the very difficulty of his text.[17] But the chief intellectual emphasis seems to have been on poetry, particularly the classical dramas and lyric poetry, perhaps owing to the greater challenge offered by the more refined style of these texts. Thus *systematic* study of the great tragedians and Aristophanes, along with attempts to correct and establish accurate texts, were now for the first time undertaken.[18]

In their teaching at Padua and Florence the Greek émigré scholars, and the Latins who followed them, taught the Greek dramas in the order they seem to have been read in Palaeologan Byzantium, in the case of Euripides first the easiest, *Hecuba,* and with Aristophanes, first the *Plutos.*[19] In philosophy, Plato and Aristotle were both read in the Byzantine schools from at least the eleventh century on. There was no such polarization between them as was to some degree the case in the West during the scholastic period and especially after the Byzantine Pletho's discourse on their differences in Florence.[20]

Finally, there is a unique Palaeologan scholarly technique, used in poetry and prose, which is never considered in discussing Byzantine influences on the Italian Renaissance of Greek learning, that termed *schedographia*. Following this technique Byzantine scholars, after dividing the entire text before them into passages of several lines each, would write a comment or an elaborate paraphrase explaining each passage. This comment would include a careful analysis of terms employed, homonyms, antonyms, syntax, and so forth. Each passage of the original text would alternate with a schedographic passage.[21] It seems safe to affirm that the fruits of this practice of *schedographia* were applied by many of the Byzantine scholars (such as Musurus) to their teaching in Italy.[22]

✻   ✻   ✻

With that background in mind, it is possible to consider the Byzantine émigrés' activities in Florence, the first center of Greek studies in Italy. The initial holder of the Greek chair in the Florentine *studium* was the southern Italian-Greek Leontius Pilatus, appointed in 1361 through the mediation of Boccaccio.[23] Agostino Pertusi has recently shown that Pilatus's translation of Homer into Latin, the first since antiquity, despite almost unanimous Renaissance and modern condemnation, was as accurate as could be expected for his time. It was not in the flowing humanist style of Bruni, but rather word-for-word as was then the fashion in Byzantine southern Italy.[24] Pertusi also demonstrates that Pilatus resided for years in Crete, whence probably came much of his remarkable knowledge of Greek mythology, imparted to Boccaccio for composition of the latter's *Genealogia deorum*.[25] As for Petrarch's Greek teacher, Barlaam of Calabria, perhaps only Byzantinists realize that his command of Greek was so good that he taught a course in Constantinople on the teachings of the difficult early Byzantine (or late ancient) mystical theologian, pseudo-Dionysius the Areopagite.[26]

With Manuel Chrysoloras's arrival in Florence in 1397 to teach Greek at the invitation of the signoria, the enthusiasm generated by his efforts became so contagious that a wave of interest in Greek studies spread over much of northern Italy.[27] Since Chrysoloras lacked adequate texts to teach properly, he had first to compose a Greco-Latin grammar. This, notably, was modeled on the typical Palaeologan type of grammar called *Erotemata*.[28] It is tantalizing to speculate on how Chrysoloras taught Greek. After rudimentary instruction in grammar using the *Erotemata*, Chrysoloras, I believe, probably continued with the method of teaching literature followed in Byzantium. After reading aloud in Greek a passage of an ancient author, first alone and then with the class, he would then carefully analyze it, probably incorporating information drawn from Byzantine scholia (marginal comments on manuscripts) or from *schedographia*.[29]

To Chrysoloras, it seems, goes the credit for first establishing the subsequently standard humanist method of Greek translation into Latin, so expertly applied by his student Leonardo Bruni. Instead of word-for-word translation, he prescribed rendering a passage in the spirit of the text (*ad sententiam transferre*), while at the same time avoiding an overly free translation.[30] It is of interest also that Chrysoloras himself, probably for the use of his students, began to translate into Latin Plato's *Republic*. Perhaps too busy, he did not finish the task. Translation of the *Republic* was later taken up by one of Chrysoloras's pupils in Milan, Uberto Decembrio, who was then in the service of the despot Giangaleazzo Visconti of Milan. But Uberto's translation was rather unsatisfactory, and the work was later corrected and refined by Uberto's son, the leading Milanese humanist Pier Candido Decembrio.[31] A letter of Salutati's mentions that Chrysoloras in Florence began, in addition, to translate Ptolemy's

Geographia (further evidence of Palaeologan scientific interests transplanted to Italy). His translation was completed, not too accurately, however, by his pupil Jacopo Angeli da Scarperia, who dedicated the work to his patron, the later Cretan pope of Pisa, Alexander V. (There is another—perhaps earlier—dedication of the work by Scarperia, to Pope Gregory XII.)[32]

Inspired by Chrysoloras, almost all his Italian pupils—Pier Paolo Vergerio, Guarino of Verona, Bruni, Roberto Rossi, Scarperia, Cenci dei Rustici, and others—became humanists noted for their knowledge and promotion of Greek studies. Bruni in particular translated a number of Aristotle's works, notably the *Politics,* in humanist fashion to replace the literal version of William of Moerbeke.[33] At the end of his introduction to the *Politics,* Bruni stressed, in evident contrast to the scholastics, the *flumen aureum* (golden stream) of Aristotle's style as well as thought.[34] It may have been from Chrysoloras that Bruni derived additional knowledge of the enormous range of Aristotle's works. Thus he translated (or in some cases retranslated) Aristotle's *Rhetoric, Ethics, pseudo-Economics,* and logical writings. These versions were not always completely accurate (as the Greek John Argyropoulos later put it, they were too freely rendered),[35] but in general they preserved the textual nuances and style more faithfully than did the scholastic renderings. Bruni in addition translated several of Plato's less difficult works as well as Plutarch's *Lives,* probably again at the inspiration of Chrysoloras.[36] According to Chrysoloras Plutarch was the best author with whom to start Greek study, as he most successfully bridged the gap between Greeks and Romans.[37] Indeed, owing primarily to the individual and civic virtues extolled in Plutarch (a very popular author in Byzantium), almost every Latin humanist who knew Greek tried his hand at translation of this author.[38]

In line with early Florentine humanist interest in what has been called "civic" humanism, Bruni sought out Greek rhetorical texts that might offer material to glorify the republicanism of his city. Thus in his *Laudatio* he drew heavily on the *Panathenaicus* of the Greek orator Aelius Aristides.[39] The main reason for his use of Aristides apparently was to draw the analogy between the democracy of Athens, which had saved Greek culture from the Persians, and the republicanism of Florence, then locked in struggle with the despotic Visconti of Milan. Moreover, Aristides provided new and more effective Greek rhetorical material for his purposes.[40] Baron believes that Bruni was the first Italian humanist not merely to imitate Greek political ideals but to apply them creatively to the contemporary events of his own epoch.[41]

A catalytic event for Greek studies in Italy was the Council of

Ferrara–Florence, assembled in 1438–39 to reunite the two churches. At this council, to quote a modern critic, the Greek scholars in attendance conducted a kind of continuing "seminar" in Hellenic studies for the Latins.[42] An official interpreter for the Latins was the Camaldolese monk Ambrogio Traversari,[43] the first Latin since Burgundio of Pisa in the twelfth century to translate Byzantine church fathers into Latin.[44] The number of Latin scholars present at the council is remarkable, including many celebrated humanists, for example Bruni, Traversari, Vergerio, Poggio Bracciolini, Lorenzo Valla, Leon Battista Alberti, and the philosopher Nicholas of Cusa. Opportunities for intellectual exchange were frequent. We know for instance that Mark of Ephesus, the most intransigent antiunionist Greek bishop, permitted Traversari to examine the manuscripts he had brought with him from Constantinople.[45]

It is now more widely realized that the early Florentine humanists such as Niccolò Niccoli were as interested in the ancient church fathers (including the Greek) as in classical learning. When Leonardo Bruni, for instance, heard of the rediscovery in Rome of the text of St. Basil's *Discourse to Christian Youth on Study of the Pagan Classics,* he pounced upon it, translating it into Latin. His version, which was subsequently widely disseminated, was one of the very first Greek patristic works in translation to be printed (ca. 1470–71).[46] No wonder, for discovery of a work by the highly esteemed Basil supporting, though with qualification, the reading of pagan Greek literary works for their moral value and aid in interpreting the Greek Scripture was powerful justification for combating the accusation of paganism levied against the early Italian humanists.[47]

The most remarkable development at the Council of Ferrara–Florence was the appearance of the Byzantine Platonist George Gemistus Pletho of Mistra. At banquets hosted by Cosimo de' Medici, Pletho held forth on the pagan philosophic doctrines not only of Plato but of his Neoplatonic followers such as Iamblichus and Proclus, no few of whom the West now learned of for the first time. In addition, he introduced the occult, arcane works of the Pythagoreans, Hermes Trismegistus, and the Chaldaic oracles.[48] Many scholars maintain that Pletho's lectures and writing had a considerable immediate impact on his Florentine audience. That they were impressed, even enraptured, seems clear, but that they really understood the nuances of this highly sophisticated Byzantine philosophic exegete is, I believe, extremely doubtful.[49] It was during the council that Pletho wrote his famous treatise, *On the Differences Between Plato and Aristotle.* It was, according to certain scholars, because of the apparently excessive emphasis placed by the Italian scholars on

Aristotle that Pletho denigrated Aristotle and exalted Plato, which tended to create a greater polarization between the two philosophers than existed in the Byzantine tradition, in which they were not viewed as genuinely antagonistic.[50] Pletho's treatise thus seemed to sharpen for the West the differences between the two and provided the impetus for an accurate translation of all of Plato as well as Aristotle. It is notable that Marsilio Ficino's later translation and interpretation of Plato were drawn from and based in considerable part on the Byzantine tradition, on Michael Psellus, Pletho, Bessarion, and other Byzantine Platonists. Ficino even knew Pletho's tract, *De fato*.[51] More concrete evidence of Pletho's direct contact with the Florentine humanists is offered by the corrections that still survive in his hand on a manuscript containing Bruni's work in Greek on the constitution of Florence.[52]

The figure whose appearance in Florence helped most to reorient Florentine humanism away from its primarily rhetorical emphasis was not Pletho but rather the Byzantine professor John Argyropoulos, who later occupied a chair in Greek philosophy at the Florentine *studium* (1456–71).[53] It was during his teaching tenure that the Florentines began, for the first time I believe, fully to understand what Pletho had spoken about and especially, as Garin maintains, to view Greek learning in the total context of ancient Greek philosophy and civilization.[54] Ironically, Argyropoulos, who had taught in Constantinople at the higher school called the Catholicon Mouseion,[55] had been subsequently brought to Florence by several young Florentine Aristotelians in order to expound not Plato but Aristotle. In the morning Argyropoulos publicly taught and interpreted Aristotle's writings on natural science, notably physics, and on his metaphysics, ethics, and other subjects. In the afternoon, however, in his own home, to a select group of students, he expounded on the philosophical and "theological" doctrines of Plato, on the Pythagoreans, the Chaldaic oracles, and on the various Neoplatonic successor schools.[56] So deep an impression did his Platonic teaching make that, according to Eugenio Garin, Jerrold Seigel, George Holmes, and Deno Geanakoplos, Argyropoulos deserves primary credit for the shift in the focus of Florentine humanism from rhetoric—that is, eloquence—to metaphysical philosophy, particularly Platonism.[57] Argyropoulos's emphasis on understanding Plato as well as Aristotle was undoubtedly an expression of Palaeologan interest in both philosophers. Reflecting also his Byzantine sense of the wholeness of culture (the traditional *enkyklios paideia*), Argyropoulos taught Greek philosophy as a developing organic unity, beginning with the pre-Socratics, the Pythagoreans, and Orpheus, and proceeding systematically to Socrates, Plato, Aristotle, and their

successors.[58] Moreover, he did not feel, as many Italian humanists might
well have, that he was humbling himself intellectually in writing a small
tract on logic modeled on Aristotle's *Organon*. His profound knowledge
of both Latin and Greek (he had received a doctorate from Padua University)[59] made him the ideal interpreter to explicate the teachings of
Plato and Aristotle to the Latins. It remained for the Florentine Ficino,
who apparently did not study formally with Argyropoulos but, I believe,
was at least indirectly influenced by his teaching,[60] to produce the Renaissance synthesis of Catholic Christianity and Neoplatonic thought.

The importance of Florence under Ficino as a center for the radia-
tion of Platonic thought is too well known to need repetition. I should
mention, however, still another Byzantine, the Athenian Demetrius Chalcondyles, a student of Pletho at Mistra, who in 1476 succeeded Andronicus Callistus's successor Argyropoulos, in the Florentine *studium*.
According to the German scribe, Hartmann Schedel, who earlier in 1463
had copied down Chalcondyles's inaugural address on the establishment
of the first Greek chair at Padua, Chalcondyles when in Florence had
explained to Ficino (difficult) passages in Plato's *Dialogues*.[61]

Angelo Poliziano, who very probably studied with Argyropoulos, is
an outstanding example of a Florentine humanist who was able to take
what the Byzantines offered and, fusing it with his deep knowledge of
Latin literature, to apply it to benefit his own works in Latin and even
Italian, for example, in his important essay *Miscellanea;* in other pieces
of criticism on Greek epic, lyric poetry, and rhetoric; and in his translations of Plutarch, Homer, and other Greek authors. What Poliziano
gained particularly from Byzantine interpretations of ancient Greek literary and rhetorical works was a new awareness of the subtlety and
nuances of classical style as well as content, both in poetry and in prose.[62]
Poliziano was one of the first Italian humanists to give lectures on Aristotle on the basis of the Greek text, to which his attention was directed
by the Venetian Ermolao Barbaro the Younger as well as by Argyropoulos.[63]

The Florentine humanist mastery of Greek style, together with an
increasing knowledge of Greek vocabulary, syntax, and structure,[64] probably carried over into Florentine historical writing, especially after translation into Latin of works by the major Greek historians.[65] Bruni, in
writing his *History of Florence*, was very likely influenced by the work
of Plutarch and Polybius as well as such Romans as Livy and the Florentine Villani.[66] And Machiavelli, as has been shown by Gennaro Sasso,
drew upon the work of Polybius, and far more, of course, on the Latin
and vernacular Italian historical traditions.[67]

※   ※   ※

While Florence's primacy in Greek letters extended to the end of the Quattrocento, Rome's rise to prominence in Greek studies began in the mid-fifteenth century, during the pontificate especially of Nicholas V, and continued for about fifteen years, from about 1440 to 1455.[68] The principal "institution" in Rome for Greek scholarship was the so-called academy founded by Pope Nicholas and Bessarion, the Byzantine cardinal of the Roman church. Its prime purpose was the translation into Latin of Greek classical and patristic writings.[69] Bessarion's academy included, besides Greeks, learned Latins of the curia who knew Greek, such as Giovanni Tortelli, who journeyed to Byzantium to study there even before Constantinople's fall,[70] as did a number of other Latins in this period.

The major translators in the papal court were two Byzantines, the polemical Cretan George of Trebizond, and the more irenic Theodore Gaza from Thessalonica, intense rivals but each highly competent. A biography of George has recently been written by John Monfasani, which elucidates many obscure points in this period of Roman primacy, while revealing new aspects of the career of a truly major humanist.[71] From Crete in 1415, George of Trebizond, at the age of twenty, came to Venice, invited by his patron, the Venetian patrician Francesco Barbaro, for whom he probably translated manuscripts and to whom he probably taught Greek in exchange for Latin lessons. It was George's primary aim to learn and then to teach *Latin* rhetoric in Italy, enriched by his background of Palaeologan Greek studies. George studied Latin with the greatest Latinist of the day, Vittorino da Feltre. With his wide background of interests, derived at least in part from the influence of the broad scope of Palaeologan education, he engaged in a very wide range of intellectual activities, including rhetoric, logic, Greek and Latin apocalyptic literature, philosophy, and theology.[72] Most important, through his Latin treatise *Rhetoricorum libri V,* he brought to the awareness of western humanists the writer whom Bessarion called "the greatest glory of Greek rhetoric,"[73] Hermogenes. (None other than Lorenzo Valla wrote that George was then on the way to becoming the greatest rhetorician of Italy in the Latin language.)[74] In the *Rhetoricorum libri V,* George set forth the contents of Hermogenes's masterful analysis of ways to move an audience. In this work George was able to fuse the Byzantine Hermogenean rhetorical tradition with the Latin tradition of Cicero, which he greatly esteemed.[75] Some Byzantine scholars, however, tended to denigrate Ciceronian rhetoric, notably John Argyropoulos,[76] perhaps because Cicero was the only authority for most Latins who did not know the Greek sources of rhetoric.

George's treatise on rhetoric, after its gradual assimilation by the

Italian humanists, became the leading Italian and, later, northern Renaissance rhetorical text, supplementing or even supplanting the rhetorical writings of Cicero and Quintilian. George also was the first humanist in Italy, even before Valla, to write a treatise (in Latin) on logic, a field generally considered the domain of the scholastics.[77]

At the request of Pope Nicholas V and Bessarion, George translated into Latin no less than eleven major Greek texts, some never before translated, others rendered for the first time in the humanist manner. His versions were often criticized, but George's translations were as a whole well executed, the flaws in most cases being attributable rather to factors over which he had little or no control. For example, George's papal patron insisted that in his translation of Eusebius's *De praeparatione evangelica*, he delete any statements reflecting Eusebius's Arian beliefs.[78] George's method of translation was sensible, to adhere closely to the original in the case of scientific texts (Aristotle and Ptolemy especially) but to provide a more flexible rendering in the case of the Greek historians and the fathers of the Byzantine church.[79]

His translation of Ptolemy's capital work on astronomy and mathematics, the *Almagest,* which was already available in the faulty twelfth-century Latin version of Gerard of Cremona, was of extraordinary importance for the future development of mathematics and astronomy.[80] Believing that Ptolemy's text had been corrupted by his Arab translator, George, at the personal suggestion of Bessarion, appended a lengthy commentary to his translation, explicating Ptolemy's astronomic theories on the basis of, or rather often in disagreement with, the ancient Greek commentary of Theon of Alexandria, hitherto unknown in the West.[81] George's commentary, but not his translation, was then evaluated but sharply condemned by the Italian curial scholar, Jacopo da Cremona, who had previously translated Archimedes.[82] George's version of Ptolemy's *Almagest*, nevertheless, subsequently became standard, although, surprisingly, the Greek text was not printed until much later, in 1538.[83] George, in addition, rendered into Latin for the first time pseudo-Ptolemy's work, the *Centiloquium,* containing one hundred aphorisms dealing primarily with astrology,[84] a subject that contributed much to the development of Renaissance astronomy. For Nicholas of Cusa, George translated into Latin Plato's *Parmenides.*[85] Nicholas, though very interested in Platonism and the Dionysian writings, probably never learned Greek well. He himself relates that when, before the Council of Ferrara–Florence, he represented the Basel conciliarist party in Constantinople, he there sought out Greek manuscripts[86] (probably of Plato), and that it was during his boat trip back home from Constantinople that he conceived the main philosophical ideas for his chief work, *De docta ignorantia.*[87]

In addition to scientific and literary translations, George rendered into Latin more of the Greek church fathers than is generally realized, including works of Gregory of Nazianzus, Basil, Gregory of Nyssa, Athanasius, and more strikingly of Cyril of Alexandria and Eusebius's *De praeparatione evangelica,* the last of which soon became very popular in Italy. He also produced a Latin version of the extremely valuable homilies of John Chrysostom on Matthew, then hardly known in the West except for a small portion of an ancient Latin version and the little-used rendering of the twelfth-century Burgundio of Pisa. George's many translations had a far wider dissemination than has hitherto been recognized.[88] He therefore played a major role in promoting a greater knowledge of both ancient Greek classical and Byzantine ecclesiastical learning in Italy.

Striking advances have recently been made in the study of New Testament textual criticism in the Renaissance. These advances are concerned primarily with the Greek scholarship of Lorenzo Valla, secretary in the papal curia during the mid-fifteenth century. In 1444, in Naples, even before he went to Rome, Valla had undertaken a comparison (*Collatio,* he entitled his work) of Jerome's Vulgate text and the Greek New Testament, a work, we are told, that the Byzantine Cardinal Bessarion, an intimate of Valla, read through.[89] Valla himself notes that he had heard from "quidam Graeci" (certain Greeks)—probably Gaza and Bessarion—of errors existing in a passage, or rather passages, of Jerome's Latin Vulgate version.[90] Salvatore Camporeale admits Bessarion's influence on Valla in at least one important textual reading, that of John 21:22.[91] It seems almost certain, then, that the Byzantine émigrés—"some learned scholars," as Mario Fois puts it—exercised no slight influence on the development and possibly even the genesis of Valla's thought with regard to a Latin New Testament text corresponding more closely to the Greek original than the several existing Latin Vulgate versions—a process of thought that later resulted in Valla's epoch-making *Annotationes.*

Valla is also credited with suspecting the authenticity of the apostolic authority of the "Dionysian" corpus of mystical writings.[92] They were already suspect in the eyes of certain early Byzantine theologians such as the sixth-century Hypatius of Ephesus.[93] Valla himself, in his *Annotationes,* refers to the suspicions of "certain very learned Greeks of our time" who (in accord with one Byzantine view) associated the Dionysian writings with the fourth-century Apollinaris of Laodicea.[94] It is therefore again plausible to believe, without gainsaying any of Valla's remarkable historical acumen, that he was probably influenced in his suspicions by Greek scholars in the papal curia such as the erudite Theodore Gaza, though evidently in this case not by Bessarion, who held to the traditional view of authorship of the Dionysian writings.[95]

The increasing availability of Byzantine texts and commentaries on the New Testament may well have contributed also to the western interest in St. Paul, as evidenced by the almost simultaneous studies of the Pauline writings produced by Ficino, John Colet, Lefèvre d'Etaples, Johann Reuchlin, and, later, of Erasmus.[96] One cannot help but wonder whether certain Greek commentaries on Paul, the very important ones of Origen in particular, now made known to Italian humanists in the original Greek version, did not foster questions about the accuracy of the Latin text and western interpretations thereof.[97]

The manuscripts used by George of Trebizond, Gaza, Niccolò Perotti (Bessarion's secretary), perhaps Valla, and others, for making translations from ancient Greek authors or Greek fathers very often came from Bessarion's Greek manuscript collection, the greatest in the Renaissance.[98] Of course Bessarion was not alone in collecting Greek codices; Antonio Corbinelli, Cenci dei Rustici (who secured Chrysoloras's library), Giovanni Aurispa, and Giorgio Valla, among other Latins, assembled an impressive number.[99] Yet through his many codices on Greek mathematics in particular, Bessarion was able considerably to promote mathematical study.[100] Euclid and Archimedes had already been translated by the indefatigable scholastic William of Moerbeke.[101] But, as Paul Rose has shown, Bessarion was instrumental in inculcating in Regiomontanus, a German humanist who later became the Renaissance's leading mathematician, an intense interest in Archimedes and in the pseudo-Aristotle's *Mechanica,* both works of first importance for dealing, among other things, with stresses and balances,[102] and in the treatise of the fourth-century Byzantine Pappus, who also wrote on mechanics. Partly as a result of Bessarion's patronage, mathematics in time became, among the humanists, a veritable appendage to the *studia humanitatis.*[103] Rome's less important period of efflorescence in Greek studies in the late fifteenth and early sixteenth centuries I shall have to pass over here.[104]

*　　*　　*

Venice and its satellite city Padua, with its great university, constituted in many ways a single nucleus of culture. I shall therefore deal with them together. In Venice there existed the largest of the Greek émigré communities in Italy, one reason why Bessarion called Venice *alterum Byzan-*

tium. But despite Venice's centuries-long connections with the Greek East, Venetian humanism did not clearly emerge until intellectual influences flowed to Venice from nearby Padua and Florence. Nevertheless, with the coming of the Greek exiles before and especially after 1453, there was a genuine intensification of Venetian humanist interests.[105] At Padua (as in other Italian universities) the medical school and the school of letters constituted a single faculty: hence Paduan interest in employing professors who could teach not only literary but also scientific subjects. At Padua, from the time at least of the Averroist Pietro d'Abano (early Trecento), the scientific and other writings of Aristotle were above all studied but, notably, for a long time not from the original Greek text but in the Arab Averroist translations and interpretations.[106]

The long supremacy at Padua of the so-called "Averroist" tradition—I personally prefer Kristeller's less ambiguous and more accurate term, "Italian secular Aristotelianism"[107]—which flourished especially during the mid and later fifteenth century, began seriously to be challenged on the arrival of the Byzantine émigrés with what they considered to be their more authentic texts of Aristotle and other scientific authors. Yet the Greek versions of Aristotle did not make any really effective impact in Padua—they were in fact resisted—until espousal of their cause by the leading Venetian humanists Ermolao Barbaro the Younger and Girolamo Donato, both of whom had studied with Greek teachers. Partly under the influence of the Byzantines, especially Theodore Gaza with whom he had studied in Rome, Barbaro—who had contempt for scholastic philosophy but was enamored of Greek literature, philosophy, and science—began to insist at Padua on recognition of the greater authority of the ancient Greek and early Byzantine commentators for explicating Aristotle.[108] As recently shown by Kristeller, in his translation of the Byzantine commentator Themistius, Ermolao, despite his antipathy for the scholastics, still utilized the old scholastic translation but into it, interlinearly, he interpolated material drawn from other Greek commentators.[109]

Earlier in 1463, as noted above, the Venetian senate, at the urging primarily of Bessarion and perhaps Filelfo, had established the first chair for the teaching of Greek at Padua University, to which it appointed the Byzantine Demetrius Chalcondyles. In his inaugural orations Chalcondyles, like virtually all the Byzantines, lamented the corrupt manuscripts and translations of Aristotle and other Greek authors in use in Italy.[110] (The Byzantine émigrés, Pletho for example, also criticized Averroës's versions of Aristotle, and some liked to point out that Averroës knew no Greek.)[111] With medicine and letters so closely associated at Padua, it seems very probable that at Padua Chalcondyles taught not only Greek grammar and literature but also scientific treatises, especially those of Aristotle.[112]

In 1470 the Venetian senate received from George of Trebizond, then in Rome, the dedication of his Latin translation, the very first, of Plato's important treatise, the *Laws*. In his dedicatory letter, George hyperbolically affirmed that the founding fathers of the Venetian state must have known Plato's *Laws* when they drew up their mixed constitution![113]

The rivalry between the entrenched Averroist tradition at Padua and the increasing support for the Greek versions of Aristotle grew more intense in the last decade of the fifteenth century. At this time, not long after Barbaro began teaching there, the leading Averroists were Nicoletto Vernia and his pupil and successor Agostino Nifo. Edward Mahoney has shown that seven years before his death in 1499, Vernia sharply attacked Averroës's interpretation of Aristotle's views on the immortality of the soul, going as far as to condemn Averroës's view as "perversam opinionem Averrois."[114] In his reversal of opinion Vernia had evidently been gradually influenced by the activities of Barbaro, the Byzantine exiles, and particularly by the manifest superiority of the Greek texts of the ancient commentators now available. Already in 1472 Bessarion had bequeathed to Venice his entire library of Greek manuscripts, which contained many scientific treatises of Aristotle.[115] In any case, as a result of Vernia's semidefection, the changing view of his successor Nifo, certainly Barbaro's efforts, and, not least, the impact of the new Greek manuscripts put forward by the Byzantines, the Venetian senate in 1497 appointed a Greek, Niccolò Leonico Tomeo, born in Venice, to a chair to read Aristotle "in the Greek [text]."[116]

This event was a veritable triumph for the Greek text, meaning the traditional Byzantine interpretation, of the Aristotelian corpus. For what Tomeo began above all to emphasize in his lectures was the Aristotelian texts as explicated by the ancient Greek and early Byzantine commentators.[117] These included Simplicius, Philoponus of sixth-century Alexandria (who anticipated the fourteenth-century impetus theory of projectile motion),[118] Themistius, and, finally, the philosopher Alexander of Aphrodisias, who is noted particularly for his commentary on Aristotle's *De anima*.[119] The questions of the unity of the intellect and the immortality of the soul had for some time been burning issues at Padua among the so-called Averroists, not least because Aristotle himself was not always clear on certain points.[120] Averroës's hitherto prevailing commentary on *De anima* thus began to be challenged by the interpretation provided by Alexander of Aphrodisias. The Greek commentators (who had been increasingly studied during the Palaeologan Renaissance)[121] left a wide range of materials on Aristotle's works, and in this period of the Italian Renaissance certain pseudo-Aristotelian writings were being studied— the *pseudo-Economica, pseudo-Mechanica,* and *pseudo-Problemata.*[122] The idea had finally taken firm hold at Padua not only that the Greek manuscripts provided surer texts than those coming secondhand via Arab translations, but also that ancient Greek commentators could provide more authentic interpretations of Aristotle's works.

The significant role of the Byzantines in the Greek academy and publishing house of Aldo Manuzio I have discussed in detail elsewhere.[123] I shall restrict myself here to only a few observations. The Cretan Marcus Musurus, Aldo's leading collaborator and also professor of Greek at the University of Padua, edited a very large number of first editions of Greek authors, including the complete works of Aristophanes and the writings of Plato. Less well known but hardly less impressive was Aldo's edition in 1495–98 of the works of Aristotle in Greek,[124] possibly as a response to the earlier publication in Latin, in 1472, of Aristotle's works with all of Averroës's commentaries. This Greek edition was of the highest importance because it provided for the first time reasonably accurate Greek texts of Aristotle. During the following years Aldo edited for the first time (probably with the aid of Musurus) Greek texts of the commentators Themistius and Alexander of Aphrodisias, while Musurus, evidently alone, edited the Greek authors Pausanias and Hesychius,[125] though, perhaps surprisingly, not the historian Polybius.[126] Polybius was popular in Venetian and Florentine humanist circles, especially with Machiavelli and Francesco Guicciardini, not only because of his analytical power, style, and stress on the theory of the mixed constitution, but also because he was, as Vergerio had earlier put it, "that Greek who alone tells us so much about an early period of Roman history."[127]

The teachings of Musurus and Tomeo at Padua, though overlapping in time, evidently differed somewhat in scope. As successor to Chalcondyles's Greek chair, Musurus's primary emphasis was apparently on Greek literature, especially the poets and dramatists, including Planudes's noted collection of poetry, the *Greek Anthology.* As inheritor of the Palaeologan methods of textual criticism established by Demetrius Triclinius, Thomas Magister, and Manuel Moschopoulos,[128] Musurus doubtless analyzed for his students the complex meters of ancient drama following the views of Triclinius, who in the fourteenth century had rediscovered a manuscript of Hephaestion explaining this technique.[129] This recently recovered knowledge of metrics, so vital for understanding ancient Greek poetry, Musurus applied to his own "Hymn to Plato," which prefixed his famous *editio princeps* of Plato in 1513.[130]

Tomeo, whose name is probably unfamiliar to many Renaissance historians, must have stressed Aristotle's philosophy in his teaching at Padua but, to judge from his published editions of Greek texts and his translations into Latin,[131] in the broad sense of philosophy to include Aristotle's metaphysics, moral and natural philosophy (physics), as well as biology and logic. Special mention should be made of Tomeo's translation (which became standard) of pseudo-Aristotle's *Mechanica*.[132] This work, with Archimedes's *Mechanica*, occupies a place in leading to the development of early modern science with its emphasis on the new "quantitative" physics (based on mathematics) rather than the older "qualitative" Aristotelian physics.[133] Philology also interested Tomeo, as can be seen by his contribution to the textual tradition of Plutarch's *Moralia*.[134] Tomeo was named by the Venetian government preceptor to the many high-ranking English students studying at Padua, including the later famous Cardinal Pole. In a letter to the latter, Tomeo requested a copy of More's *Utopia* in exchange for one of his own writings.[135]

Yves Renouard believes the most valuable of all Aldine editions was the *Rhetores Graeci*, which included Aristotle's *Rhetoric* and *Poetics* (both omitted from Aldo's Greek edition of Aristotle). The *Rhetores Graeci* was edited in 1508 primarily by the Cretan Demetrius Ducas.[136] Hermogenes's works occupy at least half of the edition, in contrast to the *Rhetoric* of Aristotle, which has a distinctly minor place. This difference reflects the diverse attitudes of Byzantium and the West toward Aristotle's *Rhetoric*. In Byzantium it could not compete with Hermogenes's much more impressive treatises. In the medieval West, however, where Aristotle's *Rhetoric* was relatively little known (through William of Moerbeke's scholastic translation), it was, because of its extensive discussion of the emotions, read by scholastic philosophers in connection with Aristotle's *Ethics* and *Politics*.[137] The *Rhetoric* was later retranslated in humanist fashion and thereafter rather widely read by Renaissance rhetoricians, although it was subsequently displaced in popularity by Hermogenes.

As for Aristotle's *Poetics*, which also had been translated by William, its contents were misinterpreted by western medieval and early Renaissance scholars, who read the work in conjunction with Aristotle's *Organon* (logical writings).[138] Not apparently until the impact of the Byzantine émigrés and the work of the Renaissance humanists Ermolao Barbaro and Giorgio Valla was it interpreted as a treatise on aesthetics, as Aristotle had evidently intended.

To return to the little-known Tomeo: As a youth he had studied with his compatriot Chalcondyles in Florence.[139] Thus he too was to some extent in the Palaeologan tradition, as well as constituting a link between Florentine and Paduan humanism. Tomeo was very open-minded; in explicating Aristotle he several times admitted that Aristotle was wrong on certain points. Once he even affirmed his preference for Averroës's interpretation on a particular question over Aristotle's position. Tomeo's views on the debated questions of the unity of the intellect and immortality of the soul led in part to those of Pietro Pomponazzi, who in 1516 declared his belief in the concept of the immortality of the individual soul while affirming he could not prove it.[140] Like the Palaeologan scholars, Tomeo was interested in both Plato and Aristotle and tried (rather like Bessarion, who really favored Plato) to conciliate them.[141] Tomeo's career then marks the final end of the conflict among the Greeks (though certainly not among the Latins) over the relative merits of Plato and Aristotle begun at Florence almost a century before. His career, finally, may be taken as a kind of capstone to the contribution of the Byzantine scholars in Italy. For at his death in 1531,[142] virtually all the literary, philosophic, and scientific Greek works had been transmitted to Italy, and by the end of the century they were either published in the original Greek text or translated into Latin or, in some cases, even into Italian.

✻   ✻   ✻

It was not until the Italian Renaissance that the complete range of the ancient Greek writings, including many of the more profound and complex works of the ancients, and, in part, of the Byzantine period, came to the West. In particular there were brought for the first time all the philosophical writings of Platonism, the remainder—much more than we realize—of Aristotle and Aristotelian-inspired writings, and the Greek sources of Stoicism and of Epicureanism. Even more striking and numerous were the works of literature transmitted by the Byzantines: the tragedians and Aristophanes, all the lyric poetry of Pindar, Theocritus, and others, and the epic poems of Hesiod and especially Homer, as well as the great Greek historians and orators, especially Lysias, Isocrates, and Demosthenes. In rhetoric the entire Byzantine corpus was brought, notably Hermogenes and Aphthonius, the importance of whose new translations, along with the commentary on Ptolemy, have been discussed above. All these writings constitute a remarkably broad range of literary, scientific, and philosophic masterpieces without which modern western culture would be quite different from what it is today.

In the transmission of almost all these works it was, as we have seen, the Byzantine émigrés who were the main protagonists, though of course Latins too made a very considerable contribution. But were the Byzantines simply transmitters of the ancient Greek legacy for which, as one modern scholar puts it, Constantinople was merely the "custodian" and its scholars simply the "world's librarians"?[143] We have seen that the transmission of Greek learning was not a simple process but one that should be viewed in its many ramifications, including the problems of its reception, assimilation, and diffusion throughout Italy. In this entire process the émigrés were not merely transmitters but also interpreters in matters of textual meaning and nuances of style. Indeed, in the case of the more complex works, the Byzantine tradition alone could unlock and authentically interpret the treasures brought to the West.

But the most fundamental criterion, I believe, for evaluating the Byzantine scholars' contribution to the learning of the Italian Renaissance is to ascertain whether their work of teaching, editing, and publishing texts resulted in any way in altering the patterns of thought current in Italy at the time of each of the three periods discussed. At the beginning of Florence's period of primacy, the desire to learn the long-neglected Greek language and literature was, through Chrysoloras's inspired teaching, transformed into a veritable mania that spread rapidly from Florence through much of Italy. And during the latter half of the Florentine period, the shift in the orientation of Florentine humanism from rhetoric to emphasis on metaphysical philosophy was not so much the work of the Italian humanists or of Pletho's banquet speeches in Florence as, primarily, the result of the teaching of the bilingual Argyropoulos, a true representative of the Palaeologan Renaissance. It was his teaching that proved decisive for shifting the axis of Florentine humanism, thus paving the way, as Garin puts it, "for the triumphant entry into Florence of the Platonic 'theology.' "[144] This fact does not, of course, mean that Argyropoulos alone was responsible for this change of direction. The change in the Florentine government from republicanism to Medici "despotism" certainly lessened the opportunities for "civic" humanism, and of course in the educational backgrounds of Ficino and especially Pico della Mirandola, Aristotelian scholasticism had a very firm place.

During the period of Roman primacy it was Bessarion's leadership that not only produced the first translations of many important Greek works, but also substantiated the view that, in the search for the most authentic interpretation, whether in ancient science, philosophy, or biblical studies, the preferred interpreters were generally the ancient Greek or early Byzantine commentators, those closer in time to the original. Bessarion, a pupil of Pletho at Palaeologan Mistra, was probably the most able of the Greek émigrés, especially in terms of vision and of combining Byzantine and Latin patterns of thought and methods.[145] Indeed, his widespread patronage and influence can be detected in almost every endeavor notable for the advancement of Greek learning in the Quattrocento. Through the force of his personality and his patronage of both Byzantine and Italian scholars; the size and variety of his manuscript collection;[146] his treatise demonstrating the easier assimilability to Christianity of Plato over Aristotle;[147] his probable inspiration of Valla in biblical scholarship and certainly of Regiomontanus in mathematics; also his role in founding the chair of Greek at Padua; and, not least, his feeling for the organic unity of the entire Christian church of both East and West as in patristic times,[148] Bessarion played a greater and more wideranging role than any other Byzantine émigré in the development of Italian Renaissance learning.

Finally, in the period of Venetian-Paduan preeminence, we have seen that the émigrés edited for the Aldine press virtually all the major Greek authors in the original text. Moreover, the Byzantine scholars, with the aid of Barbaro, as evidenced in Tomeo's subsequent appointment at Padua, were able to promote recognition of the greater authority of the Greek text of Aristotle and the interpretations of his Greek commentators over, and finally even in place of, the medieval Greco-Latin and Arabo-Latin versions of Aristotle.

Can we say that the Byzantine émigré scholars were very original? Probably not, I think, except for Bessarion, Argyropoulos, and perhaps George of Trebizond and Theodore Gaza.[149] They were generally uncreative, as was typical of Byzantine scholars of the Palaeologan period, upon whose shoulders the ancient Hellenic tradition weighed all too heavily. But how many Quattrocento Latin humanists and philosophers were truly original in thought? Aside from Nicholas of Cusa (himself inspired, among others, by Plato and the pseudo-Dionysius) and perhaps Valla, Pico, and Poliziano, very few were truly original thinkers until Leonardo da Vinci and Galileo.

In this reevaluation we should not forget that the Byzantine accomplishments would have been impossible without certain basic considerations or qualities present in Renaissance Italian life: the growing desire, initially at least, of Italian humanists within the increasingly sophisticated context of urban Florence and other city-states to find perfected models for imitation and justification of their intensified secular values. Later, the generous patronage of the papacy, and then the economic strength of Venice, provided the opportunity for Aldo and the Greeks to exercise their talents. Let us not forget, too, the Italian scholars who even before 1453 went to Constantinople to learn Greek, such as Guarino, Scarperia, Filelfo, and Tortelli. Nor should we neglect the fundamental contribution of Italian humanists with knowledge of Greek, such as Bruni, Poliziano, Ficino, and Barbaro, who—along with the relatively few Byzantines with an acute knowledge of Latin—were in the main responsible for adapting the new Greek learning and concepts to their own native Latin and Italian traditions. I must mention also the invention of printing itself, which, fortunately for the fate of Greek learning, occurred at almost the very moment that the Byzantine state was being extinguished by the Turks.

Finally, it should be stressed, despite the basic significance of Greek, that in the last analysis it was a foreign language to the Italian humanists and that only a relatively small minority of them actually mastered the language.[150] Yet this minority, it would appear, included virtually all or most of the major formative Italian thinkers in the Renaissance. And these men, on the basis of the assimilation of the Greek cultural inheritance, with its body of rich concepts and ideas, into their Latin and native vernacular traditions, were—at least in part—able to inspire and lead to the more genuinely creative efforts that followed from the early sixteenth century onward in the works of Leonardo, Machiavelli, Galileo, and others.

Bearing in mind the various achievements of the Byzantine émigré scholars and the qualifications I have pointed out, it seems to me that the revival of Greek learning in Italy, which was carried out primarily by the Byzantine émigrés and cannot easily be separated from them, probably did more than any other single factor not to begin but—once it had begun on the basis of Latin literature—to *widen* the intellectual perspective of the Italian Renaissance.[151] And this widening was accomplished by the émigrés essentially through their making possible the fusion, sometimes imperfect, of many elements of learning of the Palaeologan Renaissance with those of the emerging Italian Renaissance.

NOTES

1. The question of the Byzantine émigré scholars' influence on Italian Renaissance humanism, especially those representing the late Byzantine Palaeologan "Renaissance," has not hitherto been systematically studied. Yet several centuries ago it was believed, erroneously, that the emigration of Byzantine refugee scholars from Constantinople and the Byzantine East after 1453 actually began the Italian Renaissance. With the present essay, the most recent study of the Byzantine Palaeologan contribution to Italian Renaissance humanism is D. J. Geanakoplos, "A Reevaluation of the Influences of Byzantine Scholars on the Development of the *Studia Humanitatis*, Metaphysics, Patristics, and Science in the Italian Renaissance (1361–c. 1531)," in *Proceedings of the Patristic, Medieval, and Renaissance Conference* (Villanova, 1978), 3:1–25; idem, *Interaction of the "Sibling" Byzantine and Western Cultures in the Middle Ages and Italian Renaissance (330–1600)* (New Haven, 1976). See further, S. Runciman, *The Last Byzantine Renaissance* (Cambridge, 1970), which focuses on learning within Byzantium; and K. Setton, "The Byzantine Background to the Italian Renaissance," *Proceedings of the American Philosophical Society* 100 (1956): 1–76.

A valuable tool for study is still E. Legrand, *Bibliographie hellénique ou description raisonnée des ouvrages publiés en grec par des grecs au XVe and XVIe siècles,* 4 vols. (Paris, 1885–1906; reprinted Paris, 1962), which includes sketches of the more important Greek refugee scholars and an analytical catalogue of their publications. But Legrand omits treatment of some leading Byzantine émigrés, including Demetrius Ducas. For his biography (and others, especially in Venice and Padua), see D. J. Geanakoplos, *Greek Scholars in Venice* (Cambridge, MA, 1962), republished as *Byzantium and the Renaissance* (New Haven, 1978). On late Byzantine learning, see B. Tatakis, *La philosophie byzantine* (Paris, 1949); R. R. Bolgar, *The Classical Heritage and Its Beneficiaries* (Cambridge, 1958); L. D. Reynolds and N. G. Wilson, *Scribes and Scholars* (Oxford, 2d ed., 1974). On Byzantine and Italian humanists up to 1600, see D. J. Geanakoplos, *Byzantine East and Latin West* (Oxford, 1966). For the Greek dramatists, see A. Turyn, *The MS Tradition of the Tragedies of Aeschylus* (New York, 1943); idem, *The MS Tradition of the Tragedies of Sophocles* (Urbana, IL, 1952); idem, *The MS Tradition of the Tragedies of Euripides* (Urbana, IL, 1957). See, more recently, H. Hunger, *Die hochsprächliche profane Literatur der Byzantiner* (Munich, 1978).

On individual Byzantine humanists in Italy, see A. Pertusi, *Leonzio Pilato fra Petrarca e Boccaccio* (Venice, 1964); the pioneering G. Cammelli, *I dotti bizantini e le origini dell'umanesimo,* 3 vols. (Florence, 1951–54), vol. 1, *Manuele Crisolora;* vol. 2, *Giovanni Argiropulo;* vol. 3, *Demetrio Calcondila;* F. Masai, *Pléthon et le platonisme de Mistra* (Paris, 1956); P. O. Kristeller, "Byzantine and Western Platonism in the 15th Century," in *Renaissance Thought and Its Sources,* ed. M. Mooney (New York, 1979), 150–63; idem, "The Renaissance and Byzantine Learning," in *Renaissance Concepts of Man* (New York, 1972), 64–100; L. Mohler, *Kardinal Bessarion als Theologe, Humanist, und Staatsmann,* 3 vols. (Paderborn, 1923–42); H. Vast, *Le Cardinal Bessarion* (Paris, 1878); J. Monfasani, *George of Trebizond: A Biography and a Study of His Rhetoric and Logic* (Leiden, 1976); C. Stinger, *Humanism and the Church Fathers: Ambrogio Traversari (1386–1439) and Christian Antiquity in the Italian Renaissance* (Albany, NY, 1976). Finally, see the following by D. J. Geanakoplos: "The Discourse of Demetrius Chalcondyles on the Inauguration of Greek Studies at the University of Padua in 1463," *Studies in the Renaissance* 21 (1974): 18–44; "The Italian Renaissance and Byzantium: The Career of the Greek Humanist-Professor John Argyropoulos in Florence and Rome (1415–87)," in *Conspectus of History* (Muncie, IN, 1974), 1:12–28; "Theodore Gaza, a Byzantine Scholar from the Palaeologan 'Renaissance' in the Italian Renaissance," *Medievalia et humanistica* n.s. 12 (1984): 61–81; and, most recently, "The Career of the Little-Known Renaissance Greek Scholar Nicholas Leonicus Tomaeus and the Ascendancy of Greco-Byzantine Aristotelianism at Padua University (1497)," *Δώρημα στὸν I. Καραγιαννόπουλο, Byzantina* 13 (1985): 357–72. I am writing a monograph on the Greek scholar Peter of Candia (Pope Alexander V) and his influence in the Italian Renaissance.

2. On causes of the Palaeologan revival, see Geanakoplos, *Interaction*, 17–21, 85–91, 285–86; idem, "The Byzantine Recovery of Constantinople from the Latins in 1261: A Chrysobull of Emperor Michael Palaeologus in Favor of Hagia Sophia," in *Continuity and Discontinuity in Church History: Essays to G. Williams*, ed. F. Church and T. George (Leiden, 1979), 104–17. See also A. Vacalopoulos, *Origins of the Greek Nation: The Byzantine Period* (New Brunswick, NJ, 1970), 1:46–57; 2:157–61; cf. Runciman, *Last Byzantine Renaissance*, 55f. and 14f.

3. See especially H. G. Beck, "Intellectual Life in the Late Byzantine Church," *Handbook of Church History* 4 (1968): 505–12, who points out the greater intensity of study in the Palaeologan than in earlier Byzantine renaissances and the apparently less constricting attitude of the Greek church. Cf. N. G. Wilson, "The Church and Classical Studies in Byzantium," *Antike und Abendland* 16 (1970): 68–77.

4. On Moerbeke's method of translation, see Geanakoplos, *Interaction*, 266; Kristeller, *Renaissance Concepts*, 69; and G. Holmes, *The Florentine Enlightenment, 1400–1450* (New York, 1969), 115–17, who discusses the dispute with the scholastic bishop of Burgos, a critic of Bruni's humanist translations and supporter of the "accuracy" of Moerbeke's word-for-word rendering. Some modern scholars now prefer many of the scholastic translations as being more faithful to the original. The humanist ones were often virtually copies of the scholastic, but rendered only superficially more "rhetorical."

5. The principal Aristotelian texts translated after 1350 were the *Eudemian Ethics* and the pseudo-Aristotelian *Mechanica*. See E. Garin, "Le traduzioni umanistiche di Aristotele nel secolo XV," in *Atti e memorie dell'Accademia Fiorentina di scienze morali. La Columbaria* 16 (1949–50): 55–103.

6. On Bruni, see now C. Vasoli, in *Dizionario biografico degli italiani* (Rome, 1972), 14:618–33; and Holmes, *Florentine Enlightenment*, 30–31. Chrysoloras first in Florence and Uberto Decembrio later in Milan continued translation of Plato's *Republic*. It was completed by Pier Candido Decembrio: see E. Garin, "Ricerche sulle traduzioni di Platone nella prima metà del secolo XV," *Medioevo e Rinascimento: Studi in onore di Bruno Nardi*, 2 vols. (Florence, 1955), 1:361–63. For Bruni's abhorrence of certain ideas in the *Republic*, see Bruni, *Epistolarum libri viii*, 2 vols. ed. L. Mehus (Florence, 1741), no. 9, 4.

7. Kristeller, "Italian Humanism and Byzantium," in *Renaissance Concepts*, 75.

8. R. Browning, "Byzantine Scholarship," *Past and Present* 28 (1964): 3–30; and Runciman, *Last Byzantine Renaissance*, 15–16.

9. See Geanakoplos, "Reevaluation."

10. On Hermogenes in Byzantium, see especially G. Kustas, "The Function and Evolution of Byzantine Rhetoric," *Viator* 1 (1970): 55–73; and idem,

"Studies in Byzantine Rhetoric," *Theologia* 45 (1975): 413ff. See also Monfasani, *George of Trebizond*, 248–55.

11. F. Fuchs, *Die höheren Schulen von Konstantinopel im Mittelalter* (reprinted Amsterdam, 1964), 41–45; Reynolds and Wilson, *Scribes and Scholars*, chap. 2 and 121–33; Browning, "Byzantine Scholarship," 3–20; and Runciman, *Last Byzantine Renaissance*, 53–54, 31–33. In the later Byzantine period *enkyklios paideia* came to refer to the *general rudiments* of Byzantine education.

12. My friend, the eminent scholar A. Turyn, has expressed this view to me.

13. On Planudes's writings, see especially A. Turyn, "Demetrius Triklinios and the Planudean Anthology," *Festschrift N. Tomadakes* (Athens, 1973), 403–50. See also Geanakoplos, *Interaction*, 101 and bibliography 326, n. 17, including his interest in mathematics. See also I. Ševčenko, "Théodore Métochites, Chora et les courants intellectuels de l'époque," *Art et société à Byzance sous les Paléologues* (Venice, 1971), 29f.; Runciman, *Last Byzantine Renaissance*, 59–60; and now Hunger, *Die hochsprächliche profane Literatur.*

14. On the *studia humanitatis*, see P. O. Kristeller, *Renaissance Thought: The Classic, Scholastic, and Humanist Strains* (New York, 1961), 9f. and 19f.

15. See Beck, "Intellectual Life," 505–12; Wilson, "Church and Classical Studies," 68–77; and Runciman, *Last Byzantine Renaissance*, 33–34 and cf. 29f.

16. Runciman, *Last Byzantine Renaissance*, 83, 17; Tatakis, *La philosophie byzantine*, 233, 251, 287, 299.

17. This view was also expressed to me by Professor Turyn.

18. On Palaeologan study and edition of the tragedians and Aristophanes, see especially the works of Turyn, cited above in note 1. See also Hunger, *Die hochsprächliche profane Literatur*, 1:37–41; 2:67–77.

19. Kristeller, *Renaissance Concepts of Man*, 74–75.

20. On their nonpolarization in Byzantium, see Tatakis, *La philosophie byzantine*, 250–58; also Geanakoplos, "Theodore Gaza," text for notes, 47–49. On the enormous diffusion of Aristotle in Byzantium, see A. Wartelle, *Inventaire des manuscrits grecs d'Aristotle et de ses commentateurs* (Paris, 1963). The extent of the diffusion of Plato in Byzantium is less clear.

21. On *schedographia*, see Hunger, *Die hochsprächliche profane Literatur*, 29ff.

22. Ibid., 29f., cites the example of Moschopoulos's use in Byzantium of *schedographia* in manuscripts known later to the Italian Renaissance.

23. G. Brucker, "Florence and Its University, 1348–1434," in *Action and Conviction in Early Modern Europe: Essays in Memory of E. H. Harbison*, ed. T. K. Rabb and J. E. Seigel (Princeton, 1969), 231–33; Geanakoplos, *Interaction*, 66.

24. Pertusi, *Leonzio Pilato*, 433–37.

25. A. Pertusi, "Leonzio Pilato a Creta prima del 1358–59: Scuole e cultura a Creta durante il secolo XIV," *Kretika Chronika* 15–16 (1961–72): 363ff.

26. See Barlaam's writings in *Patrologia Graeca*, ed J.-P. Migne (Paris, 1865),

vol. 151, cols. 1243–1364. On his career, see J. Meyendorff, *A Study of Gregory Palamas* (London, 1964), 42–62; and Tatakis, *La philosophie byzantine*, 263–66.

27. Cammelli, *Manuele Crisolora*, 34ff.; Geanakoplos, *Greek Scholars in Venice*, 24f.; and Setton, "Byzantine Background to the Italian Renaissance," 57.

28. On the *Erotemata*, see A. Pertusi, "*Erotemata*: Per la storia e le fonti delle prime grammatiche greche a stampa," *Italia medioevale e umanistica* 5 (1962): 329–51. Cf. Geanakoplos, *Greek Scholars in Venice*, 219–20, 286.

29. On Chrysoloras's teaching method in Florence, see Cammelli, *Manuele Crisolora*, 81–85. The evidence comes mainly from his students Cenci dei Rustici and Guarino of Verona, whose Greek teaching (doubtless modeled on that of Chrysoloras) is described in his son's treatise, trans. in W. H. Woodward, *Vittorino da Feltre and Other Humanist Educators* (Cambridge, 1897, reprinted with intro. by E. F. Rice, New York, 1963), 159–78. On *schedographia*, see above, text for notes 21–22.

30. Cammelli, *Manuele Crisolora*, 88–92, esp. 91. See preface of Chrysoloras's pupil, Cenci dei Rustici, to the *Bacchus* of Aristides, where Cenci explicitly cites the translating principle of Chrysoloras: L. Bertalot, *Studien zum italienischen und deutschen Humanismus*, ed. P. O. Kristeller, 2 vols. (Rome, 1975), 2:132–33.

31. Cammelli, *Manuele Crisolora*, 89; on Uberto see M. Borsa, "Un umanista vigevanasco del secolo XIV," *Giornale ligustico* 20 (1893): 81–111; and on Pier Candido, see idem, "Pier Candido Decembrio e l'umanesimo in Lombardia," *Archivio storico lombardo* 20 (1893): 5–75, 338–441.

32. See R. Weiss, "Jacopo Angeli da Scarperia," in *Medioevo e Rinascimento: Studi in Onore di Bruno Nardi*, 27, 58 n. 16.

33. Vasoli's article on Bruni in *Dizionario biografico degli italiani* (Rome, 1972), 14:618–33; Holmes, *Florentine Enlightenment*, 95.

34. See *Filosofi italiani del Quattrocento*, ed. E. Garin (Florence, 1942), 118, passage from the end of Bruni's preface to his Latin translation of Aristotle's *Politics*. But Bruni, basing his views on Cicero, in praising Aristotle's style was thinking of the popular writings of Aristotle now lost. Aristotle's preserved works are only the lecture notes of his students and not really eloquent.

35. Cammelli, *Giovanni Argiropulo*, 180; but cf. 93, where earlier Argyropoulos praises Bruni's person. Cf. Holmes, *Florentine Enlightenment*, 263.

36. Cammelli, *Manuele Crisolora*, 88–89.

37. Ibid., 88. See also Chrysoloras's letter (in Greek) to Salutati: *Epistolario di Coluccio Salutati*, ed. F. Novati, 5 vols. (Rome, 1891–1911), 4:333 (quoted in Holmes, *Florentine Enlightenment*, 18).

38. Cammelli, *Manuele Crisolora*, 89, on Chrysoloras's reading of Plutarch with his students.

39. H. Baron, "Imitation, Rhetoric, and Quattrocento Thought in Bruni's *Laudatio*," in his *From Petrarch to Leonardo Bruni* (Chicago, 1968), 115–71.

40. Ibid., 155–56.

41. Ibid., 151–53.

42. See Setton, "Byzantine Background," 71.

43. On Traversari, see Stinger, *Humanism and the Church Fathers,* who stresses Traversari's indebtedness in learning Greek to the Greek monk Scaranus.

44. On Burgundio, see M. Anastos, "Some Aspects of Byzantine Influence in Latin Thought," *Twelfth Century Europe and the Foundations of Modern Society* (Madison, WI, 1961), 138–49; and especially P. Classen, "Burgundio von Pisa," in *Sitzungsberichte der Heidelberger Akademie der Wissenschaften, Philosophisch-historische Klasse* (Heidelberg, 1974): 128f.

45. See *Ambrosii Traversarii . . . latinae epistolae,* ed. L. Mehus, 2 vols. (Florence, 1759); and D. Traversari, *Ambrogio Traversari e i suoi tempi* (Florence, 1912).

46. See, on Bruni's version of Basil, L. Schucan, *Das Nachleben von Basilius Magnus "Ad adolescentes"* (Geneva, 1973), 62–76. See also Geanakoplos, *Interaction,* 270 and notes 15, 18. Basil's work is listed in *Gesamtkatalog der Wiegen Drücke* (Leipzig, 1928), vol. 3, no. 3700. See D. J. Geanakoplos, "St. Basil, Christian Humanist of the Three Hierarchs and Patron Saint of Greek Letters," *Greek Orthodox Theological Review* 25 (1980): 94–102.

47. Geanakoplos, *Interaction,* 270–72 and references.

48. On Pletho, see F. Masai, *Pléthon;* A. della Torre, *Storia dell'Accademia Platonica di Firenze* (Florence, 1902), 438ff.; Kristeller, *Renaissance Thought and Its Sources,* 156–58.

49. This is the opinion of Kristeller, *Renaissance Thought and Its Sources,* and G. Monfasani, *George of Trebizond,* 203, based on della Torre, *Storia dell'Accademia Platonica,* 438ff.

50. See Tatakis, *La philosophie byzantine,* 250–58; Kristeller, *Renaissance Thought and Its Sources,* 157; E. Garin, *Portraits from the Quattrocento,* trans. V. A. Velen and E. Velen (New York, 1972), 50, showing that Argyropoulos "did not set Pletho against Aristotle." See also Holmes, *Florentine Enlightenment,* 257–59.

51. Pletho's *De Fato* constituted part of his *Laws.* See *Traité des lois,* ed. C. Alexandre and A. Pelissier (reprinted Amsterdam, 1966), 64–78; Kristeller, *Renaissance Thought and Its Sources,* 156, 304 n. 42. Of course, Ficino's approach to Plato was heavily indebted to Augustine and other western authors, and he used whatever earlier Latin translations were available.

52. Masai, *Pléthon,* 68.

53. On Argyropoulos, see Cammelli, *Giovanni Argiropulo;* Garin, *Portraits from the Quattrocento,* chap. 3; J. E. Seigel, "The Teaching of Argyropoulos and the Rhetoric of the First Humanists," in *Action and Conviction,* 237ff.; and Geanakoplos, "Italian Renaissance and Byzantium," 12–28.

54. Garin, *Portraits from the Quattrocento,* 71, 75, and esp. 82.

55. At the so-called Xenon. Fuchs, *Die höheren Schulen,* 71.

56. See esp. Garin, *Portraits from the Quattrocento,* 68–83.

57. Ibid., 70, 80; Seigel, "Teaching of Argyropoulos," 237ff.; Holmes, *Florentine Enlightenment,* 262–65; Geanakoplos, "Career of John Argyropoulos," 28.

58. Garin, *Portraits from the Quattrocento*, 75–79.

59. Cammelli, *Giovanni Argiropulo*, 23–26.

60. On the influence of the Byzantine tradition on Ficino, see Kristeller, *Renaissance Thought and Its Sources*, 161–62. Nothing concrete seems to be known about links between Ficino and Argyropoulos.

61. Geanakoplos, *Interaction*, 254, 296. Ficino himself says he consulted Chalcondyles before publishing his Plato translation: see *Supplementum Ficinianum*, ed. P. O. Kristeller, 2 vols. (Florence, 1937), 2:105.

62. On Poliziano, see Garin, *Portraits from the Quattrocento*, chap. 6, esp. 171–73 for his relations with Argyropoulos and other Greeks.

63. On Poliziano's lectures (and manuscripts, especially on Aristotle), see I. Maïer, *Les manuscrits d'Ange Politien* (Geneva, 1965), 189, 227–28, 323–24, 336–38, 432–34; I. del Lungo, *Florentia: Uomini e cose del Quattrocento* (Florence, 1897), 133f. and 175f. See Geanakoplos, "Career of . . . Nicholas Leonicus Tomaeus," and J. Facciolatus, *De Gymnasio patavini* (Padua, 1752), on Tomaeus and his work on Aristotle in Padua. Mention should be made of Francesco Filelfo, one of the Quattrocento's best Hellenists (he even wrote Greek verse) who, however, was in Florence only briefly, spending most of his life in Milan. On him, see Chapter 10 in this volume and sources cited there.

64. Kristeller, *Renaissance Thought and Its Sources*, 142–43.

65. Thucydides and Herodotus were translated by Lorenzo Valla, and Polybius by Niccolò Perotti (earlier paraphrased by Bruni), while Xenophon's *Cyropaedia* was translated by Filelfo and paraphrased by Poggio, and his *Hellenica* paraphrased by Bruni.

66. Bruni was influenced by Polybius, as shown by B. L. Ullman, "Leonardo Bruni and Humanist Historiography," in his *Studies in the Italian Renaissance* (Rome, 2d ed., 1973), 324–25. Also on Polybius's influence on Bruni, see Baron, *Crisis of the Early Italian Renaissance*, 410, 508 n. 14.

67. See G. Sasso, "Polibio e Machiavelli: Costituzione, potenza, conquista," *Giornale critico della filosofia italiana* 40 (1961): 50–86.

68. In 1380–81 the Byzantine Simon Atumano seems briefly to have taught Greek in Rome to Raoul de Rivo, evidently for ecclesiastical purposes. See G. Fedalto, *Simone Atumano monaco di studio* (Brescia, 1968), 105; Setton, "Byzantine Background to the Italian Renaissance," 49–50.

69. On Bessarion, see Mohler, *Kardinal Bessarion*, esp. pt. 3; Vast, *Cardinal Bessarion;* and now the entry on him by L. Labowsky in *Dizionario biografico degli italiani* (Rome, 1967), 9.686–96.

70. On Tortelli, see Holmes, *Florentine Enlightenment*, 251; Monfasani, *George of Trebizond*, 38, 80–81; and esp. G. Mancini, "Giovanni Tortelli: Cooperatore di Niccolò V nel fondare la Biblioteca vaticana," *Archivio storico italiano* 78.2 (1920): 161–268.

71. Monfasani, *George of Trebizond*, 69–179.

72. Ibid., passim.

73. *Cent-dix lettres grecques de François Filelfe*, ed. E. Legrand (Paris, 1892); Monfasani, *George of Trebizond*, 25.

74. Monfasani, *George of Trebizond*, 177.
75. Ibid., 265, 272, 290ff.
76. Garin, *Portraits from the Quattrocento*, 82; Cammelli, *Giovanni Argiropulo*, 176–78.
77. Monfasani, *George of Trebizond*, 313. On p. 306 Monfasani says that Valla completed his work one year before George finished his manual. Even before 1400 the humanist Vergerio had taught logic in Padua, though apparently writing no work on it.
78. Geanakoplos, *Interaction*, 272 and n. 22; Monfasani, *George of Trebizond*, 78.
79. Monfasani, *George of Trebizond*, 76, notes.
80. Ibid., 232–33, 104–5.
81. On Bessarion's suggestion, see ibid., 108 and n. 165.
82. Ibid., 105.
83. See J. E. Sandys, *A History of Classical Scholarship*, 3 vols. (Cambridge, 3d ed., 1921), 2:490: edited by Grynaeus at Basel.
84. Discussed in *Collectanea Trapezuntiana: Texts, Bibliographies, and Documents of George of Trebizond*, ed. J. Monfasani (Binghamton, NY, 1985). The *Centiloquium* is now believed to be an Arabic work.
85. See, on Plato's *Parmenides*, R. Klibansky, *The Continuity of the Platonic Tradition . . . with Plato's Parmenides* (Millwood, NY, 1982). P. O. Kristeller, "A Latin translation of Gemistos Pletho's *De fato* by Johannes Sophianos dedicated to Nicholas of Cusa," in *Nicolò Cusano agli inizi del mondo moderno: Atti del congresso internazionale in occasione del V centenario della morte di Nicolò Cusano Bressanone, 1964* (Florence, 1970), 175–93.
86. See M. Honecker, "Nikolaus von Cues und die griechischen Sprache," *Sitzungsberichte der Heidelberger Akademie der Wissenschaften, Philosophisch-historische Klasse* 28 (Heidelberg, 1938): fasc. 2, 13. Also, on reports of the conciliar and papal envoys in Constantinople, see E. Cecconi, *Studi sul concilio di Firenze* (Florence, 1869), dix ff. and dixxvi ff. Finally, on the *Docta ignorantia*, see E. Van Steenburghe, *Le Cardinal Nicolas de Cues* (Paris, 1920), 27–28.
87. Monfasani, *George of Trebizond*, 341–44. Greeks with whom Nicholas of Cusa had conversations on the boat while returning to the council may possibly have helped inspire or develop some of his ideas.
88. See Monfasani, *Collectanea Trapezuntiana*. It is also shown in his *George of Trebizond*, passim.
89. *Collatio Novi Testamenti*, ed. A. Perosa (Florence, 1970). For Bessarion's help on special passages in the *Collatio*, see xxiv, xlix. See also S. Camporeale, *L. Valla, umanesimo e teologia* (Florence, 1972), 366, 389; and M. Fois, *Il pensiero cristiano di Lorenzo Valla nel quadro storico-culturale del suo ambiente* (Rome, 1969), 416–19.
90. On "quidam Graeci," see Fois, *Il pensiero cristiano*, 417.
91. *Collatio novi testamenti*, xxxiv.
92. In his *Opera omnia*, ed. E. Garin, 2 vols. (Turin, 1962), 1:852b, Valla

wrote: "de libris Dionysii nemo veterum habuit mentionem neque Latinorum neque Graecorum." See Camporeale, *L. Valla*, 429–30.

93. See *Oxford Dictionary of the Christian Church* (Oxford, 1963), 402; Runciman, *Last Byzantine Renaissance*, 44.

94. Camporeale, *L. Valla*, 429–30.

95. Ibid., 428, 429. See also Geanakoplos, "Theodore Gaza," 71.

96. N. A. Robb, *Neoplatonism of the Italian Renaissance* (London, 1935).

97. On Origen's commentaries on St. Paul, see E. Wind, "The Revival of Origen," in *Studies in Art and Literature for Bella Costa Greene*, ed. D. Miner (Princeton, 1954), 412–24. For other Italians (such as Traversari), see Stinger, *Humanism and the Church Fathers*, 33, 152.

98. On Bessarion's collection, see L. Labowsky, "Bessarion Studies," *Medieval and Renaissance Studies* 5 (1961): 108–62; idem, "Il Cardinale Bessarione e gli inizi della biblioteca Marciana," *Venezia e l'oriente fra tardo Medio Evo e Rinascimento*, ed. A. Pertusi (Venice, 1966), 159–82.

99. On most of these collections, see Stinger, *Humanism and the Church Fathers;* R. Blum, *La biblioteca della Badia Fiorentina e i codici di Antonio Corbinelli* (Vatican City, 1951); R. Sabbadini, *Carteggio di G. Aurispa* (Rome, 1931); J. B. Heiberg, "Beiträge zur Geschichte Georg Vallas und seiner Bibliothek," *Centralblatt für Bibliothekswesen* 16 (1896): 1–129.

100. See P. L. Rose, *The Italian Renaissance of Mathematics* (Geneva, 1975), esp. 44–46, noting his influence on Regiomontanus.

101. See Geanakoplos, *Byzantine East and Latin West*, 23, 26.

102. See Rose, *Italian Renaissance of Mathematics*. See also P. L. Rose and S. Drake, "The Pseudo-Aristotelian Question of *Mechanics* in Renaissance Culture," *Studies in the Renaissance* 18 (1971): 75–76.

103. Rose, *Italian Renaissance of Mathematics*, 44–46, 49, 56. Cf. E. Cochrane, "Science and Humanism in the Italian Renaissance," *American Historical Review* 81 (1976): 1039–57 on science and the *studia humanitatis*.

104. On this period, see Geanakoplos, *Greek Scholars in Venice*, 215–17, 248–49.

105. Ibid., 70, 33–40.

106. Nevertheless, Pietro d'Abano, who spent most of his life in Paris, being only briefly in Padua at the end of his life, had sought Greek manuscripts of Aristotle in Constantinople and had translated his *pseudo-Problemata*. On d'Abano, see L. Norpoth, "Zur Biobibliographie und Wissenschaftslehre des Pietro d'Abano," *Kyklos: Jahrbuch für Geschichte und Philosophie der Medizin* 3 (1930): 293–353. L. Thorndike, *A History of Magic and Experimental Science*, 8 vols. (New York, 1923–58), vol. 2, chap. 70, 874–947; idem, "Peter of Abano and Another Commentary on the *Problems* of Aristotle," *Bulletin of the History of Medicine* 29 (1955): 517–23.

107. P. O. Kristeller, *Renaissance Thought II: Papers on Humanism and the Arts* (New York, 1965), 111–18; idem, "Renaissance Aristotelianism," *Greek, Roman and Byzantine Studies* 6 (1965): 163. But Averroism continued to be taught at Padua even through the sixteenth century.

108. For Ermolao's study with Gaza while Barbaro's father was Venetian ambassador to Rome, see V. Branca, "Barbaro, Ermolao," *Dizionario biografico degli italiani* (Rome, 1964), 6:96–99. For Donato, see V. Branca, "Ermolao Barbaro and Late Quattrocento Humanism," in *Renaissance Venice*, ed. J. R. Hale (London, 1973), 227f.

109. P. O. Kristeller, *Studies in Renaissance Thought and Letters*, 2 vols. (Rome, 1956–85), 1:352–53. See also Branca, "Ermolao Barbaro," 225–27.

110. Geanakoplos, "Discourse of Demetrius Chalcondyles," 135; expanded upon in *Interaction*, chap. 13, esp. 246.

111. Kristeller, *Renaissance Thought and Its Sources*, 161.

112. Geanakoplos, *Interaction*, 246.

113. Monfasani, *George of Trebizond*, 102–3.

114. E. P. Mahoney, "Nicoletto Vernia on the Soul and Immortality," in *Philosophy and Humanism: Festschrift for Paul Oskar Kristeller*, ed. E. P. Mahoney (New York, 1976), 144, 149ff.

115. Geanakoplos, *Interaction*, 177–78; and Labowsky, "Il Cardinale Bessarione," 159–82.

116. For document of appointment, see Facciolatus, *De Gymnasio patavini*, under a.1497; see pp. 56–57.

117. See Geanakoplos, "Career of . . . Nicholas Leonicus Tomaeus."

118. See trans. in D. J. Geanakoplos, *Byzantium: Church, Society and Civilization Seen Through Contemporary Eyes* (Chicago, 1984), no. 384.

119. On Aristotle's *De anima*, see E. Cranz on Alexander of Aphrodisias, in *Catalogus Translationum et Commentariorum*, ed. P. O. Kristeller, F. E. Cranz, and V. Brown, 6 vols. to date (Washington, DC, 1960–), 1:77–135.

120. See Kristeller, "Renaissance Aristotelianism," 131.

121. See the example of George Scholarios, cited in Runciman, *Last Byzantine Renaissance*, 83.

122. "Pseudo" usually means that a work was probably not by Aristotle but by one of his students. For Aristotelian commentaries, see *Commentaria in Aristotelem Graeca*, ed. Berlin Academy (1882–1909).

123. Especially in my *Greek Scholars in Venice*, 116–66, 226ff., and passim.

124. See A. Renouard, *Annales de l'imprimerie des Alde* (Paris, 3d ed., 1834), 1:7–16.

125. On these authors, see Geanakoplos, *Greek Scholars in Venice*, 154, 149, 154–55. Simplicius was first edited by the Greek Calliergis (208).

126. The Greek text of Polybius was not published until 1530, ed. by Obsopoeus: see Sandys, *History of Classical Scholarship*, 2:105.

127. Woodward, *Vittorino da Feltre*, 106.

128. See Reynolds and Wilson, *Scribes and Scholars*, 65–66, 39–40. See also Turyn on the manuscript tradition of Aeschylus, Sophocles, and Euripides (cited above, note 1).

129. Reynolds and Wilson, *Scribes and Scholars*, 65–66.

130. For a translation of part of this poem, considered by E. Legrand the best poem in Greek since antiquity, see Geanakoplos, *Greek Scholars in Venice*,

152–53. On a pupil of Musurus, see now M. Sicherl, *Johannes Cuno* (Heidelberg, 1978).

131. For these works, see Legrand, *Bibiographie hellénique*, 3:281–84, 336–39, 438–44, etc. His most important manuscript (there are not many) is his letter book in the Vatican, published in great part by Cardinal Gasquet in *Cardinal Pole and His Early Friends* (London, 1927).

132. See Rose and Drake, "Pseudo-Aristotelian Question," 79–80, 68.

133. Kristeller, "Renaissance Aristotelianism," 173–74.

134. See A. Turyn, *Dated Greek Manuscripts of the 13th and 14th Centuries in the Libraries of Italy* (Chicago, 1972), 1:xx, 85–87.

135. On Thomas More (and other English students), see Gasquet, *Cardinal Pole*, 11ff., 66ff.

136. Renouard, *Annales de l'imprimerie*, 54; Geanakoplos, *Greek Scholars in Venice*, 227.

137. Monfasani, *George of Trebizond*, 165. On Aristotle, the emotions, and rhetoric, ibid., 246.

138. E. Tigerstedt, "Observations on the Reception of the Aristotelian 'Poetics' in the Latin West," *Studies in the Renaissance* 15 (1968): 12–14, 21.

139. Cammelli, *Demetrio Calcondila*, 36; Paolo Giovio, *Elogia doctorum virorum*, trans. F. A. Gragg (Boston, 1935), 129.

140. On Pomponazzi, see Kristeller, *Renaissance Concepts of Man*, 18–19, 38–41. On Tomeo's connection with Pomponazzi, see P. Sherrard, *Greek East and Latin West* (London, 1959), 173–75. For the first attempt at a biography of Tomeo see Geanakoplos, "Career of . . . Nicholas Leonicus Tomaeus," 357–72.

141. See Legrand, *Bibliographie hellénique*, 3:283, quoting a contemporary Paduan professor referring to Tomeo as "doctus disciplinae Platonicae et Aristotelicae." Geanakoplos, "Career of . . . Nicholas Leonicus Tomaeus," 366–67.

142. Janus Lascaris, another important Byzantine scholar, died in 1534, but his last years were far less important than his earlier. See Geanakoplos, "Career of . . . Nicholas Leonicus Tomaeus," 367–71.

143. Setton, "Byzantine Background to the Italian Renaissance," 76, himself quoting Neumann.

144. Garin, *Portraits from the Quattrocento*, 80.

145. On Bessarion's achievements, see L. Mohler, *Aus Bessarions Gelehrtenkreis*, 3 vols. (Paderborn, 1942); and Vast, *Cardinal Bessarion*.

146. Tomeo was a protégé of Bessarion and used his manuscripts: see Rose and Drake, "Pseudo-Aristotelian Question," 97f.; and esp. Geanakoplos, "Career of . . . Nicholas Leonicus Tomaeus," 364ff.

147. See the Latin text with Italian translation in *Filosofi italiani del Quattrocento*, ed. Garin, 276–83.

148. Geanakoplos, *Interaction*, 14, 293.

149. Argyropoulos, besides his work of synthesizing Greek philosophy and culture into an organic whole in his teaching in Florence, wrote a treatise on

tyranny: see Garin, *Portraits from the Quattrocento,* 69–80. On Gaza, see now Geanakoplos, "Theodore Gaza."

150. Kristeller, *Renaissance Thought,* 16.

151. Geanakoplos, *Greek Scholars in Venice,* 1.

15 ❧ THE ITALIAN RENAISSANCE
AND JEWISH THOUGHT
David B. Ruderman

reprinted where?

O NE NOTABLE EXAMPLE OF THE ASYMMETRY BETWEEN GENERAL European and Jewish historiography is their respective treatments of the Renaissance period. At least since the appearance of Jacob Burckhardt's classic study, *The Civilization of the Renaissance in Italy,* historians have thoroughly discussed the significance of this cultural epoch, often with great intensity and acrimony. Despite their diverging and often contradictory perspectives, few would now argue with Burckhardt's initial assessment that the Renaissance marks a momentous transformation in European civilization in general and in Italian culture in particular.[1]

In striking contrast, the meaning of the Renaissance, especially in Italy, is far less clear for the history of Jewish civilization. The flourishing of a small, enlightened Jewish society during the late fourteenth and fifteenth centuries in Italy has long been recognized, but the precise ways in which the majority culture symbiotically affected the Jewish community and its intellectual life have not been thoroughly elucidated.[2] To what extent were Jews earnestly preoccupied with the concerns of Renaissance culture? Was there a Jewish humanist movement comparable to that of Italian culture of the period? Can one legitimately speak of a Jewish Renaissance in Italy coterminous with the Italian Renaissance? Was there something unique about the development of Jewish thought in the Italian Renaissance to distinguish it from that of other enlightened Jewish civilizations in Spain, Provence, or Turkey? Did Italian Renaissance culture actually exert a decisive influence on Jewish thought or did its impact constitute no more than a passing fad or superficial encounter? When weighed against other factors affecting Jewish culture throughout the European continent—such as the expulsion from Spain, the creation of new Jewish settlements in the Ottoman Empire and eastern Europe, dramatic developments in Jewish political organization, in religious law and ethics, and in mystical speculation—was the Renaissance relatively less important to Jews, even those living in Italy, than to Christians living in the same era?[3]

Such questions have not been fully answered; only in recent years have researchers of Jewish civilization begun to address them seriously. In many respects, the cultural and intellectual history of Italian Jewry is still in its infancy. Extant sources still remain unpublished and even unstudied. The manuscript and printed writings of many of the major cultural luminaries have yet to be investigated carefully and systematically.[4] Moreover, because general historians have often disagreed as to the specific character of the Renaissance or of humanism, "Renaissance" influences on Jewish culture have not always been easily understood nor properly assessed by Jewish historians. Because of the obvious gaps of knowledge that currently exist, it is still premature to establish a clear and comprehensive conceptual framework in which to place Italian Jewish thought in this period, and in later years as well. In thus treating the subject of the impact of the Renaissance environment on some major Jewish thinkers, this essay can offer something less than a synthesis of this period—instead a tentative statement of general and fluid impressions, a preliminary report of recent research, as well as a sense of what yet needs to be explored before a complete picture emerges.[5]

*　　*　　*

Any serious consideration of Jewish thought in the era of the Renaissance should first assess the particular social and economic circumstances determining Italian Jewish life. At least three factors are of primary importance in this regard. First of all, Italian Jewish communities, especially the majority situated in the northern and central regions of the peninsula, were relatively small and recent, consisting of only a few families with limited political power and institutional resources. Second, these fledgling communities were composed of Jews who were primarily immigrants with diverse cultural and religious backgrounds—either migrants from other regions in Italy, or French, German, or Spanish Jews. Under such circumstances, the process of political and social self-definition and differentiation that these communities underwent from the late fourteenth century to well into the sixteenth was naturally accompanied by considerable stress, internal conflict, and often bitter struggles over religious and political authority. Third, the economic power of these communities was concentrated in the hands of a small number of relatively affluent banking families who exerted considerable influence over the political and cultural life of their own communities. Not surprisingly, the major Jewish thinkers of this period were aligned to this group; their intellectual activities were supported by these privileged patrons of higher culture in a manner not unlike that of their counterparts in the Christian world of letters.[6]

In addition to these three factors, one should also stress the relatively benign relations that existed between certain Jews and Christians in Italy, which facilitated the intense interaction between the two communities, at least until the mid-sixteenth century. That certain Christian intellectuals were more positively disposed to Jewish culture should not imply that traditional animosities between Jews and Christians did not persist in this era. One need only recall that in the same period in which some Christian humanists studied Hebrew texts with Jews, pogroms, blood libels, and forced religious debates were still as prevalent as they had been in previous centuries. Nevertheless, some Jews had more access to Christian society than before, and, accordingly, their impact on certain sectors of that community was more profound. Since Jews were not only recipients of external culture but also served directly in their own right to shape particular aspects of Christian culture in this era and in subsequent ones, this essay must consider the extent to which the Jewish presence was a factor in the Italian Renaissance. How did the role of Jews and Judaism in Renaissance civilization affect, in turn, the self-perception of Jews and their own sense of cultural dignity?

All three of the major intellectual traditions of Renaissance culture affected Jews living in the fifteenth century and at the beginning of the sixteenth and will constitute the foci of this inquiry. They are Aristotelianism, humanism, and Neoplatonism, the latter reflected especially in the writings of Giovanni Pico della Mirandola and his circle. A separate consideration of the impact of each of these traditions on Jewish thought should not obscure, however, the obvious interrelatedness of all three. Ideas and cultural concerns found within each tradition affected simultaneously Jewish intellectuals, who, like their Christian counterparts, often drew indiscriminately and eclectically from variegated sources of knowledge. Yet in responding to the new concerns raised by Renaissance culture, they generally favored one tradition over another in adopting their own particular solutions. Despite the overlapping categories in their thought, a consideration of the distinct influence of each of these traditions on the major Jewish intellectual figures of the period thus appears warranted.

On the basis of such an examination, some observations about the character of the interaction between the Italian Renaissance and Jewish thought will be proposed. A fresh look at this relationship should also lead to an appraisal of the way this period has previously been viewed by earlier Jewish historians. It also elicits some reflection on the correlation between Renaissance Jewish thought and later Jewish intellectual responses to modern European civilization in the period of the Enlightenment and after.

*   *   *

Due to the recent work of Charles Schmitt and others, the dominant role of Aristotelian philosophy and the scholastic tradition in Renaissance culture has now been fully recognized.[7] The Peripatetic tradition not only survived during the Renaissance but even flourished in all the major Italian universities, utilizing newly discovered materials and fresh translations of Aristotle and his commentators, and absorbing some of the new linguistic-humanistic methodology for the study of ancient texts. Despite strong opposition to specific Aristotelian views expressed throughout the period, all the diverging medieval schools of the Peripatetic tradition—the Averroists, Thomists, Scotists, Albertists, and Ockhamists—markedly persisted, even coexisting with other systems of thought, often found in the thinking of the same person.[8]

For fifteenth-century Italian Jews, the scholastic tradition remained a dominant aspect of their intellectual life, the rich legacy of Judeo-Arabic philosophy, as exemplified by Moses Maimonides, amplified and refined by Christian scholastic influences of the later Middle Ages. The Latin scholastic traditions especially inspired the writings of Italian Jewish philosophers in the thirteenth and fourteenth centuries—figures such as Hillel of Verona, Judah Romano, and Emanuel of Rome.[9] Christian scholastic influences were also widespread among Spanish and Provençal Jews throughout the fourteenth and fifteenth centuries.[10]

The most prominent Jewish scholastic living in fifteenth-century Italy was Elijah Delmedigo (1460–1493). Born and raised in Crete, where he also died, Delmedigo spent considerable time among scholastic academic circles in Venice and Padua, where he acquired his fame as an authority on the writings of Averroës. His most important legacy consisted of a large corpus of translations and original treatises, explicating the doctrines of Averroës to a learned and distinguished audience of Christians including Domenico Grimani and Pico della Mirandola.[11] Having access to Hebrew translations of the famous Arabic philosopher that were unavailable to his Christian contemporaries, Delmedigo, as other Jews before him, elected as his life work the translation and publicizing of Averroës's doctrines predominantly to non-Jews.[12] Of special significance was the publication during his lifetime of five of his works under the patronage of Domenico Grimani in Venice in 1488.[13] Taking full advantage of the new authority and wider diffusion of the printed word, Delmedigo's publications clearly crowned his previous literary achievements, adding considerable luster to an already distinguished career in the company of elite intellectual circles.[14] Besides his translations, Delmedigo wrote two major treatises on Averroës, explicating in the first Averroës's doctrine of the unity of the intellect, and in the second his theory of conjunction.[15]

For Delmedigo, the goal of philosophy was limited to the clarification of previous philosophic doctrines, in his case, those of Averroës. Thus as he explained to Pico: "Just as Averroës explained Aristotle's words fully, I have to explain the words of Averroës, since such wisdom has almost been lost in our day."[16] Delmedigo's perception of the restricted role of philosophy is especially evident in his *Behinat ha-Dat* (*Examination of the Faith*), his major work of Jewish philosophy, written in Hebrew at the request of his student, Saul Cohen Ashkenazi, in Crete in 1490.[17] In clarifying the traditional problem of the relation between faith and reason, Delmedigo relied heavily on his Arabic mentor Averroës, especially *The Decisive Treatise,* but went further than Averroës in limiting the application of philosophic reasoning to matters of faith. Averroës had maintained in *The Decisive Treatise* that Scripture was to be interpreted esoterically to conform with reason. While there was for him only one truth, Scripture could be interpreted on three different levels of understanding: rhetorically for the masses, dialectically for the theologians, and demonstratively for the philosophers. But all three groups were obliged to assent to three major principles of faith—belief in God, prophecy, and reward and punishment. When each group accepted the principles of religion according to their proper mode of understanding, no conflict between philosophy and revelation existed for Averroës.[18]

Delmedigo generally followed Averroës's basic assumptions about restricting philosophy to philosophers. He likewise maintained that philosophers must accept certain principles of Judaism but, unlike Averroës, he disallowed the philosopher from rationally interpreting the principles of Judaism. The Jewish people were identified by a specific set of beliefs, which for the sake of social harmony were resistant to philosophical investigation. While recommending the study of philosophy, Delmedigo departed from his teacher in holding that philosophy and religion each maintained their separate methodologies. The goal of Judaism was to implant in every Jew an understanding of divine truth; philosophy was circumscribed to clarifying earlier philosophical doctrines. In the case of disagreement between the two, the truths of Judaism clearly had the upper hand. Maintaining a position that paralleled the Paduan school of secular Aristotelians, especially the followers of the views of Siger of Brabant (ca. 1240–ca. 1284) and John of Jandun (ca. 1275–1328), Delmedigo's inquiry into the relation of faith and reason fits squarely into an intellectual context of contemporary philosophical discussion in Italy as well as a long tradition of speculation among earlier medieval Jewish philosophers.[19]

Delmedigo's collaboration with the illustrious Florentine Neoplatonist, Giovanni Pico della Mirandola, was clearly the most distinguished feature of this Jew's career, superseding in importance his philosophic writings and even his translations.[20] In 1480, Pico met Delmedigo in Padua, initiating a relationship of some five years out of which Pico acquired a more solid grounding in Averroistic philosophy. He asked Elijah to translate Averroës's paraphrase of Plato's *Republic*.[21] Elijah later translated other works of Averroës for Pico, wrote a commentary on *De substantia orbis* and a treatise on essence, being, and unity that clearly influenced Pico's own writing on the subject.[22] Of particular interest was Delmedigo's elucidation for Pico of certain kabbalistic concepts on the doctrine of the *Sefirot* and the *Ein Sof*, his acquisition for Pico of a translation of Menahem Recanati's (late thirteenth to early fourteenth century) mystical commentary on the Pentateuch, and his compilation of a list of essential works of kabbalah, which he presented to Pico, works with which he was apparently familiar. The knowledge Pico acquired from Delmedigo regarding Averroës, and to a lesser extent the material prepared for him on the kabbalah, had a formative impact on Pico's syncretistic theology and are reflected in the outlines of Pico's thinking published in his famous theses presented in Rome in 1486.[23] While Delmedigo, in his *Beḥinat ha-Dat*, was extremely critical of both the kabbalah and the traditional Christian exegesis of Jewish sacred texts,[24] he did not hesitate to expound for Pico kabbalist doctrines to which he did not subscribe. Apparently, Delmedigo's clarification of kabbalah paralleled the role he had earlier assumed in explicating philosophical texts. A philosopher is essentially an expositor of earlier philosophic views; he may elucidate concepts, even kabbalistic ones, without affirming their veracity with respect to his own religious faith. By placing kabbalistic concepts in the framework of philosophical analysis, Delmedigo also associated himself with an approach to Jewish mystical sources particularly characteristic of other Italian Jews—the fusion of kabbalah and philosophy. This approach is especially important in understanding Pico's attitude to Jewish mysticism and will be considered later in this essay.

Italian scholasticism molded the intellectual interests of other eminent Italian Jews besides Elijah Delmedigo. Judah Messer Leon, who lived in Italy at the end of the fifteenth century in Ancona, Bologna, Padua, Venice, Mantua, and Naples, earned a doctorate in philosophy and medicine and was even granted the unique privilege of conferring medical degrees on his own students.[25] Messer Leon's intellectual commitment to the study of Aristotle and Averroës closely parallels that of

Delmedigo's. Though clearly differing in personality and to a great extent in academic interests,[26] Messer Leon shared with his Jewish contemporary a view of philosophy as primarily the elucidation of earlier philosophical texts, while maintaining a subordinate position for rational thought in relation to fundamental Jewish beliefs.[27] Although two of his original works on Jewish thought are no longer extant, it is possible to reconstruct partially the direction of his scholastic interests from those works that are preserved. The latter include scholastic commentaries on grammar, logic, and rhetoric.[28] With respect to the first two subjects Messer Leon's philosophical method, like Delmedigo's, is essentially limited to expounding Averroës's commentary on Aristotle's fundamental works. Utilizing the Hebrew translation of Averroës's middle commentary on the *Organon,* for example, Messer Leon composed a paragraph-by-paragraph commentary on Averroës, carefully harmonizing it with a Latin text of Aristotle, noting any difficulties in the text, and attempting to explain them. In his commentary on the *Isagoge,* he slavishly copied from Walter Burley's (ca. 1275–1345) commentary on Aristotle's logic and apparently relied heavily on Paul of Venice (ca. 1370–1429) in writing his commentary on the *Posterior Analytics* and on the *Categories.*[29] When Messer Leon came to compose a treatise on rhetoric, some years after completing his earlier commentaries, the same scholastic methodology of textual explication, unswerving reliance on earlier authorities, and the reconciliation of all textual "dubia" still dominated the style and structure of his work.[30]

David, the son of Judah Messer Leon (ca. 1460–1530s), shared with both his father and Elijah Delmedigo a scholastic orientation that influenced the form and content of his extant writings.[31] His philosophical works, especially his *Magen David* and his *Tehilah le-David,* constitute original expositions of his thought in contrast to the linear commentaries of his father and those of Delmedigo. However, David too understood his primary role as a philosopher to be one of explicating earlier philosophical positions; he chose to elucidate the philosophy of Moses Maimonides in a work he called *Ein ha-Koreh.*[32] As an expositor of a Jewish philosophical authority, David felt obliged to present a reliable explication of the philosopher's views, severely maligned in the earlier commentary of Moses Narboni (d. 1362), even when David himself could not uphold a particular Maimonidean position.[33] In his other writings, he offers a systematic presentation of Jewish beliefs by clarifying earlier philosophical positions of Jewish and Arabic thinkers—especially those of Averroës and Ibn Sina.[34] And like Delmedigo before him, he considers the elucidation of earlier philosophical views to include those found in kabbalistic works. In *Magen David* he argues against Menahem Recanati's view of the *Sefirot* by quoting verbatim an earlier contemporary, Isaac Mar Hayyim (late fifteenth century).[35] But in so doing, he clearly treats his material as a philosopher and not as a kabbalist. Kabbalah for David is equivalent to other speculative fields of knowledge and accordingly can be reduced to rational analysis.[36] Precisely like Delmedigo, he is naturally inclined to expound any earlier intellectual idea, even that voiced by a kabbalist. And like his father, he clearly understands the kabbalah to be a philosophic system conceptually related to Neoplatonic thought.[37]

David ben Judah's views closely parallel those of Delmedigo and Averroës on the relation between Judaism and philosophy. Like Delmedigo, David acknowledges the superiority of Torah over philosophy. Like Averroës, he sees philosophy as a necessary tool for the study of Scripture, sharpening human reason and bringing the human mind from potentiality to actuality. But while philosophy is necessary, it is not sufficient to transform the mind to a higher level, one of communion with God. In the first part of *Tehilah le-David*, David, like Delmedigo, elucidates the fundamental principles of Judaism, which cannot be proved by rational analysis.[38]

David ben Judah differed from Delmedigo, however, in deviating from Averroistic positions by adopting, even copying, the views of Thomas Aquinas. His theology of Judaism consists of a merging of Averroist and Thomist sources with a particular emphasis on dogmatic theology.[39] Whether he was influenced in this direction by his father's views is virtually impossible to surmise, in view of the absence of Judah's theological writings.[40] What is clear, however, is his indebtedness to the views of Thomas, Judah ha-Levi, and the Spanish Jewish philosopher Abraham Bivago, particularly in his extended analysis of faith and miracles. In his special emphasis on the significance of faith in attaining truth, in his concept of divine grace, and in his delineation of the relation between religious love and the divine commandments, David Messer Leon introduced into Italian Jewish thought religious themes that were to become more prominent throughout the sixteenth century.[41] Nevertheless, as an expositor of earlier philosophical authorities, as a systematizer of religious beliefs heavily reliant on Thomas and Averroës, Messer Leon reveals a striking affinity to the scholastic interests of his father and of Delmedigo. Clearly different in many respects from both in the direction his theology took, he nonetheless was clearly wedded, like them, to the scholastic world of his contemporaries.[42] For all three Jewish thinkers, it was necessary to formulate their Jewish faith by reference to Aristotelian texts or through scholastic modes of study and investigation.

* * *

Judah Messer Leon, and to a lesser extent David his son, parted company, however, with Elijah Delmedigo in widening their intellectual horizons beyond scholasticism. Messer Leon's intellectual interests were broader than his contemporary's in absorbing profoundly the influence of the humanistic studies of his day. In composing his Hebrew work *Sefer Nofet Zufim*, Messer Leon introduced for the first time to his Italian Jewish readers a new genre of rhetorical writing that placed him squarely in the center of a new and dominant expression of Renaissance cultural life of the fifteenth century, that of Italian humanism.[43]

With Poggio Bracciolini's famous discovery of Quintilian's rhetorical handbook in 1416, rhetoric began to assume a broader and more important place in the culture and educational program of Renaissance Italy.[44] In Greek antiquity, rhetoric as an independent subject of inquiry either had been rejected out of hand or had been treated as a subordinate part of philosophy. Only with the Latinists Cicero and Quintilian was rhetoric integrated with philosophy into a broader scheme of education and learning. With Cicero, the ideal of true eloquence, a harmonious union of wisdom and style, was elevated to a societal ideal. Rhetoric had a beneficial end—the development of high moral character—when combined with the knowledge of philosophy. In the Middle Ages, by contrast, Judeo-Arabic philosophy generally maintained the attitude of Greek philosophy regarding rhetoric. Like theology, it was considered inferior to scientific or demonstrative reasoning; its only useful function was to persuade the uneducated masses, those incapable of understanding demonstrative proofs. In the Latin West, however, rhetoric assumed a more important place, although it was confined to practical purposes—the composition of letter-writing manuals, thematic sermons, or grammar textbooks.[45]

By the fourteenth century with the revival and imitation of classical antiquity, the humanists reclaimed rhetoric as a significant and independent part of the new *studia humanitatis*, which also included grammar, poetry, history, and moral philosophy. As a reaction to the more technical philosophical interests of the scholastics, the humanists revived the Ciceronian ideal, the combination of wisdom with eloquence. Throughout the Renaissance, scholastics and humanists debated the question of the legitimacy of philosophy over rhetoric, drawing from either the Greek or the Roman traditions to substantiate their positions.[46]

It is in this context, in the centrality of the debate over philosophy and rhetoric between the humanists and scholastics, that Messer Leon's *Sefer Nofet Zufim* can best be understood.[47] The novelty of Messer Leon's rhetorical compendium lies not only in his use of most of the major classical sources available in his day for the mastery of the rhetorical art; more significant is the bold hypothesis suggested by the work and its general implications for Italian Jewry—the projection of a "good and righteous man," gifted in the oratorical art and so combining his knowledge and noble character as to produce a new and effective leadership for the Jewish community.[48]

The image of the orator construed by Judah Messer Leon corresponds directly to that of Cicero and Quintilian, revived by the Italian humanists to uplift the place of rhetoric in relation to the study of philosophy, to strive for that blend of wisdom and eloquence exemplified in the new humanist leader who by his speech and personal example would directly affect the moral fiber of society. This image was in direct opposition to that of medieval Jewish thought, exemplified by the posture of Messer Leon's contemporary, Elijah Delmedigo, and earlier by that of Moses Maimonides. For Averroës and for the entire tradition of medieval Jewish philosophy, rhetoric's status was decidedly inferior to that of demonstrative argumentation. Its function was merely to persuade the multitude, and if used to disclose the esoteric philosophic insights of the elite, it was potentially dangerous, for the masses would then be exposed to ideas corrosive to their simple faith.[49] Despite their common scholastic backgrounds, Delmedigo apparently objected to Messer Leon's ennoblement of the rhetorical art; he may also have taken exception to similar ideas voiced by Messer Leon's student, Yohanan Alemanno (1433–ca. 1504), for precisely the same reason.[50]

What is most interesting about Messer Leon's grafting of the Ciceronian ideal onto Judaism is his attempt to portray his new image of leadership as an intrinsic part of Jewish tradition in the first place. The orator is equated with a good and righteous man, one who is "perfect in his character and philosophic notions." The Latin ideal of *vir bonus* is equated with the traditional Jewish ideal of the Zaddik[51] and also appears to be related to another designation of a leader, one that most probably encapsulates the image Messer Leon conceived of himself. This image was that of the *homo universalis*, the ḥakham kolel, the leader who was obliged to lead his community by right of a unique combination of broad and substantive learning together with good character. The prerogative to lead, even to impose his authority on those unwilling to listen to him, articulated so well by his son David,[52] clearly helps to explain Judah's own career in the Jewish community, his self-righteous and aggressive behavior, and his sense of superiority in dealing with other Jewish leaders.[53] Projecting the image of the complete Jewish leader in *Sefer Nofet Zufim*, he was also, in a real sense, describing himself.[54]

As he Judaized the civic orator, so too did he treat the entire field of rhetoric as conceived by the classical theoreticians. The model of classical oratory was initially conceived not in Greece or Rome but in Israel itself, so he claimed. The novelty of the rhetorical art had been anticipated by the divine Torah:

> For when I had studied the Torah in the habitual way, I had not been able to fathom that it embraced that science (of rhetoric) or part of it. Only after I had learned, searched and mastered it [rhetoric] in all its depth from the writings of the Gentiles, could I visualize, when returning to the Holy Scriptures, what they were like. Now the eyes of my understanding were opened and I saw that there was, in fact, a great difference between the pleasantness and elegance of speeches . . . and all this found, in this [genre], among the rest of the nations, the difference resembling that between the "hyssop out of the wall" and "the cedar that is in Lebanon" (1 Kings 5:13).[55]

If indeed the entire Hebrew Bible, especially its prophetic orations, were the font and exemplar of the rhetorical art, it followed not only that rhetoric was a worthy subject for Jews but also that it was incumbent upon them to appreciate and to master a discipline that had been theirs in the first place. Moreover, the idea that rhetoric had first been perfected by the Hebrews offered to Jews a satisfying reassurance regarding the intrinsic worth of their own cultural legacy. Judaism was not out of fashion with the times; on the contrary, it was avant-garde; it had long ago anticipated every seeming novelty appearing in the cultural world of the non-Jews. The humanist revival of the art of rhetoric thus served to highlight from a previously ignored perspective the unique contribution of Judaism to western civilization.[56]

The compendium that Messer Leon compiled represented an eclectic selection of the traditional and more recently available classical texts on rhetoric. It was based heavily on Averroës's middle commentary of Aristotle's *Rhetorica*, as well as on the pseudo-Aristotelian *Rhetorica ad Alexandrum*, but it also included Cicero's *De inventione*, the most popular *Rhetorica ad Herrenium*, Fabius Laurentius Victorinus's *Explanationes in rhetoricam M. Tullii*, and Quintilian's *Institutio oratoria*.[57] Notwithstanding the originality of his use of sources, Messer Leon's mode of presentation characteristically follows that of his other works written in a scholastic mold: a linear commentary establishing one source as the basis of his presentation and an excursus of the basic source working out any difficulties by reference to other sources. He then supplements his theoretical remarks with illustrative material from the Bible to demonstrate his theory of the biblical origin of rhetoric.[58] By following tenaciously the scholastic method of inquiry and by relying heavily on Averroës on the one hand while invoking the authority of Cicero and Quintilian on the other, *Sefer Nofet Zufim* uniquely embodies the cultural tension between scholastic and humanistic elements in Messer Leon's thought.

Notwithstanding its scholastic format, the sheer novelty of the subject and approach of *Sefer Nofet Zufim* was not lost on its author. Incorporating newly published rhetorical works to substantiate a daring hypothesis of Jewish cultural superiority and consciously deciding to disseminate his work in printed form, Messer Leon creatively and expeditiously responded to an intellectual challenge of his day. Like Delmedigo, Messer Leon, some years later, was fully attuned to the dramatic changes wrought in his cultural world by the invention of the printing press and by the potent authority it was to claim in fashioning intellectual change.[59]

The influence of *Sefer Nofet Zufim* on Messer Leon's contemporaries has never been systematically investigated, but it is apparent nevertheless that Judah's effort served to inspire Jewish humanist interests well into the sixteenth century. Most apparent is the influence Judah had in this discipline on his son, David. David's humanistic proclivities cannot be fully documented since a number of his writings in this area are lost, but there is no doubt that he was not unlike his father. In his *Shevah Nashim*, he displays a substantial awareness of the classical sources of rhetoric and poetic theory. He mentions five of Cicero's works, quotes Quintilian among other classical writers, and even refers to Petrarch's remarks on love.[60] He mentions that he wrote sermons, ostensibly based on classical theory; but these are no longer extant.[61] Most importantly, he strongly articulates his father's ideal image of the *homo universalis,* an image that understandably included mastery of the art of persuasion. And like his father, he absorbed humanistic values without surrendering his scholastic orientation to learning.[62]

Another clear example of Judah Messer Leon's humanist influence is the case of Abraham ben Mordecai Farissol (1452–ca. 1528), his younger contemporary who apparently made his acquaintance when both of them were living in Mantua in the early 1470s. Judging by the evidence of materials probably used in Farissol's classroom in the neighboring community of Ferrara, this young Jewish pedagogue introduced to his Jewish students the rudiments of rhetorical theory, which he may have mastered through his contact with Judah Messer Leon and his works. Farissol's students learned about the qualities of a good speaker and the four Aristotelian causes of an address, while practicing the proper form of humble apology that opened the exordium of a sermon. Their rhetorical skills were also enhanced by studying a model epistolary collection in Hebrew, at least one of whose letters was penned from the hand of Messer Leon himself. Most likely, under Messer Leon's influence, Farissol's young students studied elementary grammar and logic, humanistic subjects preferred and upgraded in Messer Leon's other writings, all intimately known to Farissol as well.[63]

Whether under Judah Messer Leon's direct influence, the significance of rhetorical skills was well appreciated by his Florentine contemporary, Moses ben Yoab, who apparently addressed his congregation in Italian while composing polished Hebrew sermons that displayed a knowledge of classical theory.[64] The importance of elegant style in writing letters is particularly evident in the outstanding collection of model Hebrew epistles assembled by Solomon of Poggibonsi and by numerous other collections assiduously gathered and even printed by Italian Jews well into the next century.[65]

The most outstanding example, however, of Judah Messer Leon's humanistic influence on a contemporary Jew is that of Yohanan Alemanno. Alemanno, who was awarded a doctoral degree after completing his medical studies under Judah Messer Leon's tutelage, apparently was also affected by his mentor in his humanist interests.[66] Alemanno lived in a number of Italian cities throughout the fifteenth century but spent most of the time in the stimulating intellectual environment of Florence and in direct contact with one of its major intellectual figures, Giovanni Pico della Mirandola.[67] Alemanno's appreciation of the importance of *Sefer Nofet Zufim* for a Jew well rounded in Jewish and classical sources is attested by the prominent place he assigns the book in his ideal curriculum of Jewish study.[68] More generally, Alemanno shared with his teacher the image of a new Jewish leader, both wise and eloquent, committed to inculcating a large audience of followers through his persuasive rhetoric. In the introduction to his *Commentary on the Song of Songs* commissioned by Pico himself and entitled *Shir ha-Ma'alot le-Shlomo*, Alemanno skillfully presents an encomium of virtues in praise of King Solomon, the perfect embodiment of the ideal Jewish leader as perceived to suit the needs of Italian Jewish culture in his day.[69] While the specific dimensions of King Solomon's learning as delineated by Alemanno, particularly in the arcane fields of magic, alchemy, and the like, might have been distasteful to Messer Leon, the general portrait of Solomon as an imposing scholar and orator certainly would have appealed to him. Equally engaging to him would have been the form of Alemanno's composition. Based on rhetorical epideictic discourse, Alemanno created a new genre in Hebrew literature, appropriating the humanist norms of style, moral exemplification, and communal patriotism in constructing his biography of Solomon.[70] For Alemanno, it was entirely appropriate for a Hebrew writer to produce, in the style of Petrarch's *De viris illustribus,* a literary work on the exemplary life of an author and king.[71] Moreover, it was not surprising to him that the most worthy exemplar of such a hero should be located in a biblical setting and not in a classical one. Sharing a common perception with his teacher, Judah Messer Leon, Alemanno had no doubt that the classical ideal of sagacity and virtue revived by Italian humanism was more fully personified by the figure of an ancient Hebrew sage than by either a Cicero or a Plato.

*   *   *

Even more decisive than the impact of scholasticism or humanism on Italian Jewish thought in this period was that of Neoplatonism, associated primarily with Giovanni Pico della Mirandola. Out of a mutually stimulating interaction and prolonged study of Jewish texts between Pico and his associates and a number of contemporary Jews, one of the most unusual and obscure currents in the intellectual history of the Renaissance, the Christian kabbalah, emerged. While in the case of both scholasticism and humanism, the interaction between Renaissance and Jewish culture was generally one-sided, whereby Jews were primarily recipients of cultural forms and ideas which they absorbed and appropriated into their own cultural experience,[72] the encounter with Pico and the Neoplatonists was substantially different. The interaction was indeed a mutual one. Jews were certainly affected by the rich and variegated intellectual currents emanating from the Florentine school, but they also had the opportunity in a very real and concrete way to exercise influence on an area of western thought.[73] In a relatively unprecedented manner, Christians actively desired to understand the Jewish religion, its culture, and its texts in order to penetrate more deeply their own spiritual roots. For the first time in the history of western thought, postbiblical Judaism as conceived by Christians was neither negative, irrelevant, nor peripheral to their culture; on the contrary, to a select but influential group of Christian scholars, Judaism had intrinsic worth and represented a significant dimension of the human experience. As one scholar has recently written: "Through Pico's introduction of Christian Cabbala, a contemporary and modern Jewish movement affected the development of the European mind and soul."[74] Such a major reevaluation of contemporary Jewish culture by Christians was also to leave a noticeable mark on Jewish thinking and Jewish self-consciousness in the period.

While the beginning of the Christian kabbalistic study in the Renaissance generally has been attributed to Pico, the count of Mirandola was hardly the first Christian to pursue the study of rabbinic and kabbalistic texts. As Gershom Scholem has pointed out, by the time Pico decided to master Jewish sources, especially kabbalistic ones, he consciously or unconsciously conjoined himself to a long tradition of Christian interpretation of Jewish texts and of the kabbalah originating in Spain in the early fourteenth century.[75] Essentially through the activity of Jewish converts to Christianity, rabbinic homilies and kabbalistic texts had been exhaustively combed for hints of Christian truths that could be used by Christian missionaries and polemicists to demonstrate the veracity of their newfound faith and the perversity of Judaism. As earlier Christian disputants had assiduously collected Christian "testimonia" from the Old Testament to legitimate the new Christian faith in opposition to the "stubborn" errors of the Jews, these Spanish apostates extended the approach to include the postbiblical writings of the Jews. The narrative and imaginary character of rabbinic homilies and kabbalistic discourses were particularly susceptible to the new Christian exegesis. Converts like Raymund Martini (1220–1285), Abner of Burgos (ca. 1270–1340), and Pedro de la Cavalleria (fifteenth century) were especially skillful in locating particularly obscure and ambiguous passages in Jewish literature that could be implanted with christological meaning. By the fifteenth century, these Christian readers of Jewish writings boldly expanded their activity to include the fabrication of newly created homiletic and kabbalistic collections, written in Hebrew and Aramaic, cleverly designed to preserve the same style and outward appearance of authentic Jewish writings.[76] The most notorious of these authors was Paul de Heredia, whose writings reached Italy and were probably known to Pico himself during the time preceding the Spanish Inquisition.[77] But Paul was not the only creator of such materials. Abraham Farissol testified that he had examined in his home in Ferrara a collection of Christian forgeries originating in Spain, similar but not identical to those invented by de Heredia.[78] Such materials were widely used and circulated throughout the sixteenth century in Italy and elsewhere by such well-known converts as Paulus Ricius and Petrus Galantinus and may even have been used by certain church circles as a deliberate tactic in encouraging Jews to approach the baptismal font.[79]

That Pico and his colleagues in Florence shared with these earlier converts a sincere devotion to missionary activity among the Jews need not be doubted, but this fact would not explain in itself their newly discovered passion for unraveling the mysteries of arcane Jewish texts. Pico's attraction to the kabbalah can best be understood by placing it in the broader context of his intellectual background and philosophical development. While nurtured in the cultural world of Italian humanism,

Pico was more than a humanist; above all he was a metaphysician and a theologian.[80] His philosophy was fashioned through intense encounters with a number of contemporary intellectual movements, which he syncretized in his own unique manner of thinking and which facilitated his entrance into the world of Jewish mysticism. Of decisive importance was his prolonged study of scholastic philosophy in Padua and later in Paris. While in Padua between 1480 and 1482, he attended courses with the leading Averroist of the day, Nicoletto Vernia, and also gained the acquaintance of Elijah Delmedigo, among others, as discussed above.[81] His Paduan studies may eventually have furthered his kabbalistic studies in at least two ways. From the study of Averroës, Pico may already have come to appreciate the existence of a universal core of knowledge available only to a philosophical elite who could decipher a hidden concordance of truth that effectively transcended the seeming differences separating Platonists from Peripatetics, Christians from Jews.[82] More tangibly, Pico's relationship with Delmedigo clearly opened for him a direct avenue to Jewish learning, beginning with a rich philosophical tradition but leading eventually to an equally fertile mystical legacy.

From an intense exposure to the thought of Marsilio Ficino, the leading Neoplatonist of Florence, Pico gained an even broader perspective in which to place his kabbalistic studies. From Ficino, he derived the vital concept of *prisca theologia,* or ancient theology.[83] This idea, first articulated by Ficino, maintained that a single truth pervades all historical periods. Ficino argued that a direct line of thinking can be traced back to Plato through such pagan writers as Zoroaster, Hermes Trismegistus, Orpheus, Aglaophemus, and Pythagoras. By discovering, translating, and misdating the primary writings of these authors, Ficino came to argue that all of them believed in God, that underlying the external differences between each of them and between their work and the sacred writings of Christians was to be found a unity and harmony of religious insight, a basic core of universal truth. The history of culture was nothing more than the accretions and predilections of particular cultures and traditions, which had surrounded the common nucleus with a tapestry of disparate customs, ideas, and artistic expressions. In this new statement of the universal history of mankind, every philosophy and every religion thus possessed some good. Moreover, there was no longer any clear demarcation between philosophy and religion. The traditional reason–faith problem that had engaged a philosopher like Delmedigo had little relevance to thinkers like Ficino or Pico.[84] For them, the end of philosophy was piety and the contemplation of God, and thus the subject of philosophy could be located simultaneously in an Aristotelian demonstration, an Orphic chant, or a Hebrew commentary. Moreover, their search for truth constituted a search for the earliest, the most ancient expressions of wisdom from ages supposedly more profound and more spiritually inclined than their own. Their genealogy of knowledge through pagan sources to Plato could eventually lead to an era prior to the Greek master, to the birthplace of all wisdom, that is, to the Hebrew Bible and the Mosaic tradition itself. By universalizing all religious knowledge, Ficino and Pico fashioned an open and more tolerant theology of Christianity; in searching for the source of universal truth in ancient cultural and religious settings distant and alien from their own, they came to appreciate the centrality and priority of Hebrew culture in western civilization.[85]

While ancient theology led Pico back to the beginnings of Jewish civilization, the concept of poetic theology employed by the Florentine Neoplatonists facilitated his concentration on the kabbalah.[86] For Pico, the ancient pagan religions had concealed their secret truths through a kind of "hieroglyphic" imagery of myths and fables designed to attract the attention of their following while safeguarding their esoteric character by not fully divulging their divine secrets.[87] Thus, in studying the Orphic hymns, Pico wrote: "In this manner, Orpheus interwove the mysteries of his doctrines with the texture of fables and covered them with a poetic veil, in order that anyone reading his hymns would think them to contain nothing but the sheerest tales and trifles."[88] But so too Moses had addressed the Hebrews with his face veiled and had revealed to the many only what they were capable of understanding. The spiritual understanding of the Mosaic law was available only to an elite within the Jewish people, the kabbalists. The wisdom of their literature had not been conceived in the Middle Ages—so thought Pico—but reflected instead the real intentions of Moses himself as conveyed to him by divine revelation. The kabbalah therefore constituted that part of the Jewish tradition in which the essential divine truths could be located. The kabbalah corresponded to both the divine secrets extrapolated from the Orphic hymns by the Neoplatonists and the divine secrets of Christ revealed to St. Paul as understood through the mystical writings of pseudo-Dionysius the Areopagite (early sixth century). In outward appearance, pagan, Jewish, and Christian theologies appeared to have little in common; but by unraveling their inner cores, an unsuspected affinity could be discerned.[89] For Pico the kabbalah was the key to lay bare the secrets of Judaism, to reconcile them with the mysteries of other religions and cultures, and thus to universalize them. Through kabbalah, the essential differences between Judaism and Christianity could be eradicated: "Taken together, there is absolutely no controversy between ourselves and the Hebrews on any matter, with regard to which they cannot be refuted and gainsaid out of the cabalistic books, so that there will not even be a corner left in which they may hide themselves."[90] By extracting from Jewish culture its vibrant and indispensable sparks of divine consciousness as manifest in the kabbalah, Pico made Judaism lifeless and ghostly; it had no rationale to exist in and of itself. It only had meaning in its merger with the esoteric, ageless, and catholic divine truths that were the common possession of all humanity.

The kabbalah for Pico was not merely an individual tile in the universal mosaic of divine mysteries about to be unearthed by the Florentine and his associates; it was in fact for him the central piece around which the other tiles might cluster. The humanist tradition had sensitized Pico to the importance of language and communication in understanding and appreciating the inherent character of any culture, and this feature was precisely what Pico found attractive in the study of kabbalah—its cultivated sense of the meaning of language as a vehicle for penetrating deeply the underlying significance of human experience. For the kabbalists, the words and letters of "the holy language," if correctly deciphered, could restore a means of direct communication with God himself.[91] The techniques of letter combination (ars combinandi) associated with the school of Abraham Abulafia were particularly fascinating to Pico.[92] Kabbalistic language thus provided him with a unifying principle, a powerful tool for fathoming the harmonious agreement of all cultures and tongues, all corruptions of the veritable divine words once spoken at Sinai.

Kabbalah also represented power for Pico, a means of enhancing man's ability to control his own destiny, to tap the higher spiritual powers of the cosmos for his benefit and delight. In fusing the kabbalah with the cultures of pagan antiquity, Pico also juxtaposed it with magic, with the traditions associated with the ancient Hermes Trismegistus, whose writings had been recently brought to prominence by Marsilio Ficino.[93] For Pico, kabbalah was more than a spiritual tradition of passive piety or meditation. It was, rather, a higher form of licit magic establishing a direct link between heaven and earth whereby man could capture the divine effluvia in order to transform himself into a divine being. Kabbalah in this active, theurgic sense, when fused with hermetic magic, could help to prove the divinity of Christ.[94] It could also enable man to assert his true nobility and dignity as a true "magus" with divine power.

Pico's fascination with the kabbalah, and subsequently that of a surprising number of other Christians in later centuries, thus had real meaning in the broader context of his religious quest and syncretistic thought. As for earlier Christians, it was also for him an effective strategy for converting Jews. But it was clearly more than that. It was a natural outgrowth of his scholastic, humanistic, and Neoplatonic studies. He was led to Hebraic culture by his preoccupation with ancient theology and to Jewish mysticism by his attraction to poetic theology. And in its refined sense of language, its ubiquitous grasp of human power, it provided Pico and later students of Christian kabbalah a dramatically potent instrument to make sense out of the highly complex and variegated intellectual world in which they lived.[95]

Pico's writings that deal with the kabbalah include his commentary on Girolamo Benivieni's *Canzone d'amore* and his commentary on the first twenty-seven lines of the Book of Genesis, the *Heptaplus*. But even more important is the outline of his views as presented in his famous nine hundred theses published in Rome in 1486, written as a manifesto of the perceived unity of all truth.[96] Of the nine hundred theses, two parts are specifically concerned with the kabbalah: forty-seven conclusions "according to the Hebrews" and seventy-two kabbalistic conclusions according to Pico's "own opinion." In addition, Pico uses the kabbalah in a number of his conclusions regarding other categories of human knowledge. Because of the research of the late Chaim Wirszubski, the precise manner in which kabbalistic thought was joined to Pico's thought is now more fully understandable.[97] Wirszubski, in a number of studies on the kabbalistic conclusions, demonstrated how Pico expanded the use of the kabbalah by Christians in ways never before imagined.

After mastering a kabbalistic idea, Pico could place it in an entirely different intellectual context either by Christianizing it or by relating it to an idea found in Hermetic writings, in a Chaldean oracle, a Zoroastrian statement, an Orphic poem, or a Neoplatonic insight on love.[98] An example of the latter is Pico's understanding of the Neoplatonic concept of the *mors osculi*, the kiss of death, discussed at length by Pico in his commentary on Benivieni's *Canzone d'amore* and later repeated by other Neoplatonists such as Leone Ebreo, Celio Calcagnini, Francesco Giorgio, Egidio of Viterbo, Baldassare Castiglione, and Bruno.[99] Ultimately Pico derived this remarkable idea of a spiritual kiss between the lover and the beloved, the union of the soul with its divine source at the moment of the death of the body, from Menachem Recanati's *Commentary on the Pentateuch*, translated from the Hebrew by Flavius Mithridates and from an interpolation by the latter in Gersonides's *Commentary on Job*. In so doing, Pico uprooted a kabbalistic idea from its source and applied it in an entirely novel fashion to illustrate a Neoplatonic concept.[100]

But Pico's innovation in using the kabbalah went even beyond placing a kabbalistic idea he found in Jewish sources into an entirely alien context. For Pico also appropriated the methods of kabbalistic thought, removed them from their original Jewish thought system and applied them to his own thought system, totally unrelated to the ways they had been employed by Jewish kabbalists. Thus, as Wirszubski so aptly explained, Pico's innovation was not merely to write a Christian commentary on the Jewish kabbalah but also to create a mystical commentary on Christianity based initially on Jewish thought but ultimately becoming a mystical distillation of its own accord.[101] As an example of this second usage of kabbalistic methodology in Pico's thought, Wirszubski offers, among others, Pico's commentary on the first word of the Hebrew Bible, "Bereshit." By demonstrating how the first letter of the word "Bet" (which signifies for the Jewish kabbalists the Sefirah—hokhmah [wisdom]) can be related to other Hebrew letters, Pico was able to derive the Christian trinity, relating it as well to the Neoplatonic concept of three basic processes found in the thought of Proclus.[102] By manipulating the number–letter symbolism of the kabbalists for his own purposes and by integrating his findings with a Neoplatonic idea, Pico successfully metamorphosed the Jewish concept into a Christian one. The kabbalist approaches employed by Jews were now estranged from their original cultural and spiritual source in Judaism and instead confronted a new mixture of radically different associations and meanings blended together from pagan and Christian modes of thinking. The Jewish kabbalah, in Pico's hands, was literally recast into a Christian kabbalah.

Understandably, Pico's creative thinking on the kabbalah depended to a great extent on his Jewish teachers. They served him by initially making accessible to him Latin translations of Hebrew works, by offering him personal instruction in Hebrew and Aramaic, by studying with him Jewish ideas as found in a wide array of Jewish exegetical, kabbalistic, and philosophical texts, and by integrating these ideas with concepts familiar to Pico and his associates from the ancient corpus of writings they had enthusiastically studied.

The critical role of Elijah Delmedigo in translating and conveying to Pico aspects of Averroistic thought as well as exposing to him some preliminary kabbalistic notions has already been mentioned. Even more important was the role of a Jewish convert to Christianity, Guglielmo Raimondo Moncada, better known as Flavius Mithridates.[103] This former Sicilian rabbi abandoned Judaism early in his career and was soon noticed by a number of Christian intellectuals, especially Pico himself. After preaching before the pope and his associates in Rome in 1481, he joined Pico and proceeded over the course of the following years to translate for him some forty kabbalistic and other works, still extant in some 3,500 folio pages. This massive undertaking included translations of almost all the major kabbalistic works available to Pico's contemporaries and those which most decisively influenced the course of Pico's thinking. They include Recanati's commentary, the writings of the thirteenth-century kabbalist Joseph Gikatilia, Abraham Abulafia's commentary on Maimonides's *Guide to the Perplexed*, a new translation of the Book of Job systematically employing Gersonides's commentary on the biblical book as well as Gersonides's *Commentary on the Song of Songs*, and Joseph Ibn Waker's *Sefer ha-Shorashim*, a glossary of kabbalist symbols, to mention only a few. Mithridates's efforts to make available to the Christian intellectual reading public such a large body of Jewish knowledge constitutes in itself a critical moment in the infiltration of Jewish thought into the Christian world. It clearly corresponds to the earlier efforts of Ficino to translate the large corpus of Hermetic writings previously unknown to the Latin world. Both Ficino's and Mithridates's translations constituted major events in the intellectual development of Renaissance Neoplatonism, the former shaping Ficino's theology, the latter Pico's.[104]

But Mithridates, as Chaim Wirszubski has clearly shown from his study of his Roman sermon, functioned in more than the capacity of translator. His *Sermo*, delivered some five years before Pico's conclusions, already establishes the new trend of utilizing esoteric Jewish ideas to prove the mysteries of the Christian faith. Although Mithridates never mentioned the kabbalah, he spoke instead of an ancient arcane Talmud, a "vetus talmud" containing implicit Christian secrets. Like Pico and unlike earlier Christians who quoted from Jewish sources, he employed ancient Jewish texts not to refute Judaism but rather to verify Christianity. Relying heavily on the earlier work of Raymund Martini, Mithridates consciously fabricated his sources, claiming to deduce dramatic revelations from made-up authorities. Pico probably read Mithridates's sermon and was apparently impressed by Mithridates's erudition and by his willingness to exploit his knowledge of Judaism to authenticate the Christian faith.[105]

Even more substantial were Mithridates's modifications of the translations he made for Pico. By interpolating passages to reveal a Christian or magical stance, his own way of thinking had a direct impact on Pico's initial impression of Jewish texts. Thus by a slight interpolation in Joseph Ibn Waker's kabbalistic glossary, Pico was led to believe that the kabbalah actually hinted at the trinity.[106] By relying on Mithridates's translation of the Book of Job, he came to appreciate the philosophical and astrological conception of the Jewish philosopher Gersonides in understanding the sacred text.[107] He learned what he thought was Maimonidean philosophy through Mithridates's translation of Abraham Abulafia's commentary on the *Guide to the Perplexed*.[108] As Wirszubski has persuasively demonstrated, "Pico formed his view of kabbalah not only because he read them with Christian eyes and preconceived ideas but also because he read them in translations weighted by interpolations to invite Christian interpretations."[109] Thus the whole character of Pico's kabbalistic thinking was shaped conclusively by a comprehensive exposure to Jewish sources skillfully patterned through the stamp of Flavius Mithridates.

Besides Delmedigo and Mithridates, Pico was directly influenced by another Jewish savant, Yohanan Alemanno, the student of Judah Messer Leon, a doctor and prolific writer who lived in Florence for an extended period of time at the end of the fifteenth and early sixteenth century.[110] Aside from Pico, he had personal contact with other Christian intellectuals including Pico's nephew Alberto Pio, Domenico Benivieni, and Paride da Ceresara, a distinguished Mantuan humanist and alchemist.[111] His relation to Pico is attested by his own account in the opening of his *Song of Solomon's Ascents:* "When I came to take shelter in the shadow of this cherub, crowned with divine lights, a prince perfect in knowledge, the Lord, who shields him and his intelligence day and night and is never separated from him, stirred his mouth and tongue to ask me if, in my vain life, I had seen any brilliant light among the commentators on the Song that is Solomon's . . . this is my lord, called Count Giovanni della Mirandola."[112] Pico asked Yohanan in 1488 to explain the allegorical sense of the *Song of Songs* after learning of Yohanan's own study of the biblical work. Yohanan's writing apparently influenced Pico's thoughts on the same subject and probably constituted only a part of an ongoing contact between the two. Alemanno betrays the profound influence of the Florentine ambience in his own writings considerably more than Pico's previous teachers in Judaism. His references to Neoplatonic and hermetic sources and their fusion with Jewish kabbalistic concepts clearly mirror similar efforts on the part of Pico. Because of the similarity of their intellectual systems, it is difficult to determine who stimulated the other. Alemanno's writings have yet to be studied exhaustively, but what is already clear is that he too, in ways more subtle than Mithridates, undoubtedly affected Pico's theological development, most obviously his study of the *Song of Songs,* during the later years of Pico's life. While there is little doubt how profoundly Pico's thought influenced Alemanno, the latter's impact on his illustrious Christian colleague has yet to be elucidated precisely.[113]

Thus Pico, through the influence of his Jewish teachers and through his own synthetic powers, became the pioneer figure in the gradual penetration of contemporary Jewish thought into fifteenth-century European culture. Pico's Christianization of kabbalistic techniques and his amalgamation of magic and Jewish mysticism, while officially condemned by the church, were enthusiastically received by a notable number of

Christian thinkers in Italy, France, Germany, and England well into the eighteenth century. Christian kabbalah through Pico left its mark on Renaissance culture through its integration with Neoplatonism; it also influenced both the Catholic and the Protestant Reformations through its impact on such thinkers as Egidio of Viterbo, Francesco Giorgio, Cornelius Agrippa, and Johann Reuchlin, to name only a few. Its remarkable persistence as a formative factor in post-Renaissance cultural developments in art, literature, and even scientific thought is only now fully coming to light.[114]

*   *   *

Beyond the impact of Pico's kabbalistic studies on Christian thought is the noticeable effect of such activity on contemporary Jewish culture. That Pico's syncretism affected deeply the thought of one of his close Jewish associates is fully attested by the writings of Yohanan Alemanno.

During Alemanno's long sojourn in Florence, he composed a number of significant works that reveal distinctly his involvement with the cultural concerns of Pico and his colleagues. In his two major Hebrew compositions, *Heshek Shlomo* and *Hai Olamin,* and in his informative notebook compiled over a number of years, Alemanno occupied himself with themes—the immortality of the soul, the unity of truth, the dignity of man—and with special fields of inquiry—magic and Neoplatonism—that paralleled precisely those of Pico's intellectual circle. Of particular importance is Alemanno's coadunation of magic and the kabbalah.[115] Alemanno was surely not the first Jewish thinker to introduce discussions of magic into his Hebrew writings; for this endeavor, Alemanno himself found ample precedents in the writings of such fourteenth-century Sephardic Jewish writers as Samuel Zarza, Samuel Ibn Motot, Judah Ibn Malkah, and Joseph Ibn Wakar.[116] Neither was the attempt to integrate the kabbalah with another system of thought completely alien to earlier kabbalists in Italy, individuals like Abraham Abulafia, Menahem Recanati, or the author of the *Ma'arakhet Ha-Elohut,* who had anticipated Alemanno's integration by already combining philosophical ideas with kabbalistic ones.[117] Yet the degree to which Alemanno recast the kabbalah from a magical and Neoplatonic perspective clearly separates him from his predecessors and displays unmistakably the powerful influence of Pico's thinking.

Like Pico, Alemanno imparted to the kabbalah a new understanding by equating it with a higher form of magic, a method superior to natural magic or to astrology. Kabbalah now constituted much more than speculation on the divine mysteries; it provided human beings with the capability to influence the heavens. Thus Moses was really a kabbalistic magician, the Torah was ultimately an instrument of magic, and both the tabernacle and the holy temple were in fact instruments for performing magical functions to those who understood their true purpose.

Alemanno's total commitment to magic and to its legitimation as a distinctly Jewish discipline is made especially evident in an ideal curriculum of Jewish study he drafted, which is found in his notebooks. Alemanno not only supplements a list of traditional philosophical works of his Judeo-Arabic predecessors to include classic kabbalistic and magical sources; he also boldly suggests that magic is the pinnacle of all human knowledge. It marks for him the total spiritual development of the complete man and the height of Jewish spiritual development. Magic is validated as a Jewish discipline because it constitutes the ancient wisdom of Israel as conceived by Solomon. Rather than an artificial grafting of a foreign limb alien to Jewish tradition, the discovery of magic for Alemanno was indeed the restoration of Israel's rightful inheritance.[118]

Equally innovative was Alemanno's use of Neoplatonic sources and integration of them with the kabbalah. As with magic, Alemanno was able to find ample precedents in Jewish tradition for his amalgamation of Judaism with Neoplatonism, beginning with such thinkers as Isaac Israeli and including especially the Spanish Neoplatonists, Solomon Ibn Gabirol and Abraham Ibn Ezra as well as the later Isaac Ibn Latif (thirteenth century). But Alemanno exceeded all of them in his absorption of Neoplatonism and particularly in his attempt to force the kabbalah into a Neoplatonic mold.[119] Thus Alemanno could demonstrate that Plato's theory of ten ideal numbers as discussed in Aristotle and a similar determination found in the *Liber de causis* corresponded precisely to the ten *Sefirot*.[120]

Alemanno's magical and Neoplatonic interpretation of Judaism and in particular the kabbalah reveals the way Renaissance culture could profoundly affect the thinking of one Jewish intellectual in close liaison with Pico and his associates. Yet Alemanno was not an isolated case of such obvious stimulation. Ideas similar to those of Alemanno are found in a number of sixteenth-century Italian Jewish thinkers who were even more conversant than Alemanno in magical and Neoplatonic sources. While their influence was eclipsed by the new system of Lurianic kabbalah emanating from Safed by the end of the sixteenth century, their hybrid systems of thought suggest the substantial impression Pico made on at least one group of contemporary Jewish writers.[121]

These thinkers were not the only Jews affected by the Florentine philosopher. While Pico's interest in Jewish sources, especially the kabbalah, differed radically from earlier Christians in the multiple ways he used these sources, he still shared with them a traditional Christian willingness to attract Jews to the baptismal font. This point is certainly suggested by a letter written by Marsilio Ficino to Domenico Benivieni describing a series of disputations at Pico's home between two Jews, Elijah Delmedigo and another named Abraham, against Flavius Mithridates.[122] The prolonged discussions centered not on issues of philosophical import but rather on subjects relating to the traditional polemics debated between Jews and Christians for centuries and still disputed even in the relatively tolerant surroundings of Renaissance Italy by the late fifteenth century.[123] Ficino testifies: "They [the Jews] insist that the divine words of the prophets do not refer at all to Jesus but were intended in another sense. They turn them all in a different direction, so far as they are able, wresting them from our hands; nor does it seem that they will be easy to refute unless the divine Plato enters the debate, the invincible defender of the holy religion." The fact that one of the clear by-products of the close relationships Pico and others in his group had fostered with contemporary Jews was often the conversion of the latter to Christianity can hardly go unnoticed. For Flavius Mithridates was only the most conspicuous of the converts associated with Pico; he was later joined by other Jews who were apparently so attracted to the social and intellectual climate surrounding the Florentine that they too converted: Jews such as Dattilo, one named Clemente, another named Fortuna. Other luminaries of Pico's circle like Sabastiano Salvini and Santi Pagnini revealed openly their passion to convert Jews. And by the sixteenth century, such converts clearly associated with Christian kabbalist circles were even more noticeable—men like Petrus Galatinus, Emmanuel Tremellius, Sixtus of Siena, and Paulus Ricius. Statements by Abraham Farissol and perhaps Elijah Delmedigo in their fifteenth-century Hebrew writings already may have expressed the later fears of the sixteenth-century Jewish community toward a growing number of proselytes, initially attracted by the warm respect extended to Jews and their rich cultural heritage by enlightened Christians, but who ultimately abandoned Judaism and who, like Mithridates, even defiantly turned against their former religion by attacking the foundations of the Jewish faith.[124]

By the latter half of the sixteenth century, Jews came to recognize and fear the Christian use of the kabbalah as an effective missionary tactic avidly pursued by a growing number of Christian missionaries, most of them former members of the Jewish community.[125] Thus one clear effect of Pico's theological syncretism on Jewish culture was the successful conversion of a small but conspicuous number of Jews and their eventual involvement in proselytizing activities among their former coreligionists. In this sense, Renaissance culture represented a continuum of the medieval Jewish–Christian relationship in its undiluted concern with the conversion and "salvation" of its Jewish minority.

A consideration of the impression Pico and Florentine Neoplatonism made on Italian Jewry would be incomplete without mention of the most illustrious Jew of the Italian Renaissance, Judah ben Isaac Abravanel, better known as Leone Ebreo (ca. 1460–ca. 1523).[126] Unlike the case of Alemanno, however, there is no firm evidence that Leone ever visited Florence or that he ever met Pico before the latter's death in 1494.[127] Yet without assuming that Leone knew intimately the cultural ambience of Pico's circle, it becomes most difficult to comprehend the genesis of his well-known work, the *Dialoghi d'amore*.[128] More than any other Jewish work written during the Renaissance, Leone's composition has been linked to the same literary and intellectual currents associated with the Florentine school of Ficino and Pico. Exhaustively studied by numerous scholars and passionately hailed as the most truly representative Jewish work of Renaissance culture,[129] Leone and his treatise on love still remain somewhat of a mystery to contemporary scholarship regarding the peculiar background of the author and the extraordinary literary and intellectual sophistication of his final printed work. In view of the seminal importance of Leone Ebreo to Renaissance culture, how might he be understood in relation to the other expressions of contemporary Jewish culture discussed above?

Most studies of the *Dialoghi* have focused on its relationship with the Neoplatonic discussions of love initiated in Florence by Ficino and with the literary genre of the *trattati d'amore,* of which the *Dialoghi* has been considered to be the most distinguished masterpiece.[130] Inspired by Plato's *Symposium* and by his *Phaedrus*, Ficino first formulated a theory of Platonic love that was widely imitated and expanded upon by other Italian writers well into the sixteenth century. Ficino spoke of love as a force common to all existing things, which universally connected the entire world. Driven by a basic restlessness, the lover rises in successive stages of loving until at last he reaches the boundless love of wisdom, perceiving the idea of beauty itself by contemplating God.[131]

In the direct tradition launched by Ficino, a large number of love treatises and prose commentaries on love verses subsequently appeared in Florence, including Pico's own commentary on Giovanni Benivieni's *Canzone d'amore* and elaborate discussions of love by Pietro Bembo, Francesco Cattani da Diacceto, Mario Equicola, and Castiglione. Though not identical with any of these works, Leone's work has generally been placed together with them, and considered as the most widely received work of this genre, the primary source of which was Ficino.[132]

The *Dialoghi d'amore* represents a loosely structured series of three discourses (a fourth is apparently missing), dealing with an encyclopedic variety of questions generally unified by the idea of love. The love between the two participants of the dialogue, Philone and Sophia, provides the ornamental frame for the three sections, dealing roughly with each of the following subjects: the definition of the essence of love and desire, the broad community of love, and the origins of love in the universe. Because of the complexity of the work, it would be impossible here to summarize Leone's major ideas as articulated by his two characters.[133] Yet at least three basic threads of the work need to be mentioned briefly before discussing its significance for Jewish thought of the period.

One of these major motifs is the kinship between love and intelligence, constantly reiterated throughout the dialogues.[134] Like Maimonides, Leone maintains that intellectual preparation is necessary to reach man's highest beatitude. The most authentic love is one whose object is the intellect. At the moment of illumination by the agent intellect, man enjoys his most intense felicity, the intellectual vision of God, where a union of love and knowledge is wonderfully realized. This highest act of union Leone characteristically expresses by the sexual term of *coppulazione,* the copulation of the human and divine intellect.[135] Throughout his work, Leone thus deliberately affirms the identity of rational and religious illumination.

Another of the major themes developed by Leone is the image of the love circle.[136] The image constitutes a natural development of the cumulative portrait of love that emerges especially in the last two dialogues. For love is the principle governing the whole universe, the force of interaction and unification between the material, intellectual, and divine worlds. Since love is the omnipresent law of the universe, even God loves his creatures which are inferior to him for the sake of his own self-perfection. When men sin, their sins adversely affect God, and thus, out of an act of pure paternal beneficence, God loves all his beings and is deeply involved in their righteous strivings. Men in turn love what is superior to them, desiring to ascend ultimately to God from whence they came. Through love men increase in perfection and consequently add to the world's perfection by striving to attain their fit position in a harmonious order depicted as a revolving love circle—a circular line from God descending to the first matter and then up again to the conjunction of the human intellect and the divine beauty. In this circular revolution, all beings love not only what is superior to them but also what is inferior to them.[137] Thus Leone dramatically conceives of the world as a dynamic organism in which love represents the universal bond that vivifies the entire universe. Clearly not unnoticed by his Christian readers, God's beneficent love as portrayed by Leone strikingly conforms to the concept of divine grace and Christian charity.[138] Out of a genuine concern for his creation, God's love is beneficently offered, inspiring the uninterrupted revolution of the circle.

Of special attraction to the *Dialoghi's* Jewish readers was Leone's employment of Greek and pagan mythology, his depictions of the stories of the pagan deities as allegories that represented poetically to him various levels of truth. Like Pico, Leone's poetic theology allowed him the possibility of finding equivalence between two apparently disparate spiritual traditions. Thus Philone tells Sophia how Plato's view of creation may be harmonized with that of Moses.[139] The myth of the Androgynes was really what the Book of Genesis had depicted in the figure of Adam. When the first man was created, Adam and Eve were in reality housed in one body, one name "Adam" sufficing to describe their dual character. By creating Eve, God divided the two, thus conforming to the fable related by Plato. By deciphering the essence of the two accounts of creation, Leone was able to penetrate the unitary truth common to both.

Leone's successful effort to syncretize scholastic, Neoplatonic, Jewish, and pagan sources into his dramatic narrative obviously drew from a wide variety of materials available to him during his lifetime. Clearly indebted to Ficino and Pico, the *Symposium,* and some of the Platonic dialogues, he also relied on Islamic sources—Averroës, al-Farabi, Avicenna, al-Ghazzali, and Jewish sources—Maimonides, Ibn Gabirol, and Crescas.[140] While a precise determination of their influence is yet to be made, he undoubtedly was affected by the writings of his father, on the one hand, and by those of his older contemporary Johanan Alemanno.[141] But the work he finally achieved was clearly much more than the sum of its composite sources. Its unusual acceptance and popularity among a wide Christian literary audience in Italy, France, Spain, and elsewhere are remarkable in that the author never denied his Jewish ancestry or the superiority of the Mosaic tradition.[142] Its approval has to be attributed to the sheer quality of the work, its dramatic effect, its tasteful style, its rich speculative content, and apparently because of the deeply religious elements injected into its discussion of Neoplatonic love, which provided it with a broad universal appeal.[143] The astounding success of the *Dialoghi,* however, hardly helps to explain the unusual circumstances of the work's evolution. In fact, it seems to encumber even more a reasonable explanation of how a Spanish Jewish émigré reared in a scholastic tradition, living for only a short time in a number of southern Italian cities, was capable of producing such a sophisticated and learned work so different, indeed so alien, to his known background and experience. In short, the work and the author do not neatly fit together at all. How did Judah Abravanel actually become Leone Ebreo?

Already some fifty years ago, Isaiah Sonne, in a number of studies, raised this central problem in understanding Leone and his work.[144] Focusing on the question of the original language of the *Dialoghi,* Sonne astutely pointed out that Judah remained in the locale of his family throughout his entire life, that he was basically a product of Spanish Jewish culture proudly cultivated by his own family during their entire sojourn on Italian soil, and that his proper social and cultural milieu was never the Italian nor especially the Florentine literary and intellectual world but only a Jewish one circumscribed by the recent colony of Spanish Jews living in Naples, Genoa, Venice, or Ferrara. Sonne thus hypothesized that Leone Ebreo wrote his original work in Hebrew and was introduced in Rome at the end of his life to a Christian literary circle that assisted him in translating the work, albeit in unfinished form, into Italian.[145] Only in 1535, some years after his death, did this same circle first publish the Italian translation.

In the absence of more concrete evidence regarding the secret prehistory of the *Dialoghi,* Sonne's theory still failed to explain the puzzling dichotomy between the work and its author. More recently Carlo Dionisotti has offered some additional evidence, which at least supplies some small pieces of the puzzle surrounding his life and composition, if not resolving the entire mystery of Leone.[146] Dionisotti reported the discovery of a manuscript of the third book of the *Dialoghi,* clearly drafted before the first known printed edition, that contained minor variations with more Latinisms but still displayed the sophisticated literary taste of a disciplined oration written in Tuscan Italian. Even more remarkable is a document, first discovered by Roberto Weiss, of a collection of Latin commemorative poems written in Rome in 1522.[147] At the end of the collection a Hebrew poem appears, apparently written by Leone. If this poem can be attributed definitely to Leone, the document thus establishes his place, toward the end of his life, amid a Roman humanist circle of poets who wrote primarily in Latin on military themes. Despite the fascinating indication of Leone's acceptance within such a group, the enigma regarding Leone still remains. None of the members of this circle appears capable of assisting Leone, let alone composing, in their own right, such a sophisticated Italian work composed in a Tuscan linguistic ambience.[148] The mystery seems even more pronounced, as Dionisotti observed, for how could such a work, brilliantly crafted in the *volgare,* be written by a virtual stranger to the Italian literary tradition? How could a Jew like Leone become saturated in Tuscan literary tradition from a relatively brief sojourn, not in Tuscany, but in southern Italy? Where are the traces of linguistic and stylistic travail necessarily accompanying the literary development of a foreigner writing in an alien tongue? The audacious act of composing such a work defies complete understanding on the basis of the extant data regarding Leone's whereabouts. The secrets surrounding Leone might best be solved, concluded Dionisotti, by Hebrew rather than by Italian scholars.[149]

Indeed the most promising directions researchers might now follow in exploring the yet unanswered questions surrounding Leone involve a more careful investigation of the potential influence of Leone's Jewish contemporaries on his intellectual development, particularly his father Isaac Abravanel and the previously mentioned Yohanan Alemanno.[150] But barring the possibility of future dramatic discoveries regarding Leone, the most celebrated Jewish writer of Renaissance Italy ironically remains a most elusive figure.

One fact is certain, however, in assessing the significance of Leone Ebreo to Jewish thought in the Renaissance period. Whatever the original language of his composition, Leone's work was known to both a Christian and a Jewish intellectual world in Italian or Latin.[151] The ultimate language of the *Dialoghi* seems to signal a more substantial feature of the entire work. Even more than Alemanno, Leone seems to accept at face value the ideals and intellectual assumptions inherent in Pico's dual concepts of ancient theology and poetic theology. Leone, like Pico, believed in a universality of knowledge, upholding a vision of the commonality of all humanity that transcended the particularistic cultures and traditions of world civilizations. Undoubtedly, Leone never denied his Jewish background; he proudly affirms it throughout his work, but it in no way obviates the obvious novelty of his thinking. He wrote for all men, not only for Jews; his message of a universal bond of love was ultimately directed to the widest possible audience, and thus in its final form, the work had to appear in a language accessible to a large number of people. Leone had no cause to negate his Jewish origins in the light of the central role of Judaism in the *prisca theologia* of human civilization. But despite his Jewish affirmation, it was most appropriate for him to refer as well to pagan myths or even to quote St. John.[152] As for Spinoza after him, for Leone Jewish civilization was most relevant when it transcended its own exclusivity, when it became the province of all men and all nations.[153] Whether or not Leone personally remained a faithful Jew during his lifetime (and there is no reason to assume he converted), his work demonstrates beyond a doubt the degree to which his intellectual proclivities and his spiritual temperament extended far beyond the Jewish community.

*   *   *

Having examined how three major traditions of the Italian Renaissance—scholasticism, humanism, and Neoplatonism—affected Jewish thought by the beginning of the Cinquecento, we might now address again the questions posed at the beginning of this essay. Did the Renaissance exert a decisive influence on Jewish thought? Was there a Jewish Renaissance that paralleled the Italian Renaissance? Despite obvious lacunas of research, some answers to these questions have already been offered by previous historians. In the nineteenth century, the historian Heinrich Graetz found in the enlightened Jewish culture of the Renaissance period a model worthy of emulation for contemporary Jews still fettered, so he thought, in the bonds of obscurantism and medieval fanaticism.[154] Jewish culture and thought in the Renaissance period has been similarly regarded by twentieth-century Jewish historians as a positive change in the reception by traditional Jews of external secular forms of culture.[155] Sharing a perspective of traditional Judaism that was predominantly east European Ashkenazic, often narrow, and generally intolerant to cultural change or pluralism, these more secularly inclined historians were clearly enamored of the Italian Jewish environment that offered them a refreshingly different case study of a traditional Jewish society more open and more receptive to cultural change than that which they had intimately known. In holding up a single monolithic concept of Jewish traditional society and by generally approaching Renaissance culture from a superficial and overly romantic perspective mainly derived from Burckhardt, their idealized portrait of Jewish culture in the Renaissance was imprecise, unbalanced, and highly apologetic. By maintaining a fundamental opposition between a traditional Jewish culture, antirationalistic and unreceptive to external culture, and an open, rational, tolerant Renaissance culture, they tended to distort the nature of Jewish culture in its medieval setting as well as the heterogeneous character of Renaissance civilization.[156] The history of Jewish culture was often reduced to a treatment of the supposed tension between the core and the shell, the original essence and its external borrowings, the *Volksgeist* versus the *Zeitgeist*.[157]

More recently, a number of younger scholars have attempted to view this period from a different perspective than that of the scheme of rationalism versus antirationalism. Robert Bonfil has attempted to shift the emphasis from focusing on external influences in Jewish culture to what he calls an internal Jewish development. Instead of concentrating exclusively on the dramatic yet often superficial ways in which every contemporary fad or modish philosophy affected the life-style of Jews, this historian would prefer to examine Jewish culture from an inwardly directed perspective in which every change or development in Jewish culture need not be reduced facilely to external influences. While advocating this revision, he also offers his own definition of Jewish culture in the Renaissance. For him, Jews primarily responded to the cultural world of their contemporaries by reasserting their own national consciousness, their own sense of uniqueness and cultural superiority, a feeling reinforced by the newly awakened interest in Judaism on the part of their Christian contemporaries.[158]

Another approach, recently put forward by Arthur Lesley, has even taken exception to posing the general question of how Renaissance culture influenced the Jews. In its place, it substitutes what is considered to be a more manageable and realistic way of understanding the period, using primarily the tools of contemporary literary history. This emphasis shifts from the wider history of culture to Hebrew literary activity, to the norms shared by Italian-Latin and Hebrew literature of the period and to the question of whether a humanistic movement among Jews existed in this era.[159]

On the basis of the evidence explored in this chapter, it would appear to me that any broad characterization of Jewish culture or thought in the Renaissance period would still be premature.[160] Yet some initial impression of this cultural experience seems appropriate on the basis of the areas treated above and in response to the reconstructions of this epoch presented by others. It does appear legitimate to me to ask how Italian culture in all its multiple dimensions influenced Jewish intellectual activity, with the proviso that in asking the question one approaches it without a subjective or distorted view of the nature of either Jewish or Renaissance culture. To focus exclusively on internal Jewish development seems both ambiguous and misleading in placing undue emphasis on organic developments at the expense of external factors. It seems to deny arbitrarily the complex and subtle ways in which Jewish thought was shaped in any period by interaction with its majority culture.[161] The question of whether there existed a Jewish humanist movement is certainly a worthy one to ask. But it cannot be substituted for the broader question of how to understand the symbiotic relationship between the Jewish and Christian cultures in the Renaissance. The Renaissance was more than its humanist movement, and similarly Italian Jewish thought of the period was shaped by much more than humanistic concerns, as this essay has demonstrated.[162]

How then might one characterize the development of Jewish

thought at the end of the fifteenth century in the context of the Italian Renaissance? On the basis of the limited evidence discussed above, it appears misleading to speak of a Jewish Renaissance in the same way one might speak of the Renaissance in western civilization. Jewish thought was not radically transformed in the same way the thought of the majority culture seemed to be affected—there was no major cultural shift, no rebirth, and certainly no new vision of mankind. The Renaissance appears to carry less significance for the history of Jewish thought than it does for that of general culture.

Nevertheless, if one is not entitled to speak of a Jewish Renaissance, one might legitimately speak of a real impact of Renaissance culture on Jewish cultural processes and thought. The evidence considered in this essay underscores a cultural efflorescence among certain Jews stimulated and eagerly responsive to the external environment in which they lived. Whatever the ultimate impact of Renaissance culture on their own Jewish identities, some of them, at least, now talked about Judaism in entirely novel terms and expressed themselves in a new cultural idiom. The language of Renaissance Jewish culture was now enlarged and enriched to include references to Greek and pagan mythology; it revealed a preoccupation with the elegances of proper style in oral and written communication, as well as an increasing tendency to draw from a wide array of pagan and Christian, classical and contemporary sources when writing about Jewish matters for either a Christian or a Jewish audience. The most clearly discernible difference between Jewish writing at the end of the fifteenth century and that of previous centuries is the relative change in the universe of discourse—new terms of reference, new literary sources, new ideas, and new modes of self-expression.

Of all the major traditions of Renaissance culture that affected contemporary Jewish thought, Pico's syncretistic philosophy and Renaissance Neoplatonism may well have constituted the most intense and most significant interaction between the two cultures. Especially in this area, Jews made the greatest impression on contemporary Christians, while Christians in turn left a lasting mark on Jewish thought. The importance of Pico to Renaissance Jewish culture seems to lie primarily in the novel challenge he posed to the continuity of Jewish national existence. He introduced Jews for the first time to the image of a universal cultural experience transcending either Christianity in its present form or Judaism. He argued for a new cultural world in which all separatisms would be obliterated, and the best of every nation and culture, including Judaism, would be fused into a universal human spirit. With Pico and with Renaissance culture in general, Jews entered for the first time into a new dialogue with the western world. Jewish–Christian polemical and apologetic thinking in the Middle Ages had generally been restricted to demonstrations of the superiority of one faith over the other. By the end of the fifteenth century, however, the conditions of the Jewish–Christian dialogue seem to have been altered substantially. Pico no longer simply juxtaposes a superior Christian faith to an inferior Jewish one. He argues instead that a human cultural experience consisting of the best of all previous religious and national cultures was infinitely superior to Jewish culture. Though still clothed in Christian guise, Pico's cultural image uniquely adumbrated for Jews the chasm between their own national aspirations and their growing desire to participate in and belong to a larger family of humanity. How much richer and more meaningful would the Jewish heritage become, so Pico argued, if the walls of separation between Jew and Christian could now be broken down, whereby the essence of Jewish culture would then be shared by all mankind? What greater appeal could Pico offer to enlightened Jews than the promise of mutuality in place of separatism, of spiritual concord among all men instead of hatred and divisiveness? In a real sense, Pico's religious syncretism had ushered in a new dimension to Jewish–Christian relations, one that would become a dominant factor in challenging the viability and justification of Jewish particularity in the modern western world. And Pico's philosophy constituted only a part of the new cultural challenge that the Renaissance as a whole presented to Jews. Not only the Christian kabbalah, but certainly humanism in general, ultimately threatened Jewish culture in a similar way. For it too juxtaposed a cultural experience open to all mankind, transcending the seemingly irreconcilable differences between peoples and religious faiths.[163] One need not deny the deep Christian coloring of Renaissance culture by emphasizing this dominant image of a new universal human experience open to Jews and Christians. Christians still preoccupied themselves with converting Jews, as they had done for centuries before, but the specific character of their dialogue with Jews was different—more subtle, more intellectually stimulating, and ultimately more persuasive.

In this context of a new universal image of human experience, Jews were pressed to respond creatively to a dramatically new intellectual and spiritual challenge. Clearly, one major way to justify themselves and their own distinctiveness was to evoke a renewed image of the superiority of Jewish culture, to emphasize, as Judah Messer Leon had done, the original role and centrality of Judaism in western culture.[164] The bold image of Plato and Aristotle having learned from Jeremiah or Moses seemed as convincing a rationalization as any that Jewish culture still played a major role in the history of mankind. Whether such assertions signified an expression of vigor and self-confidence or of weakness and insecurity is not always easy to determine. Did Messer Leon actually believe that by labeling rhetoric an originally Jewish discipline it was indeed so, or were later sixteenth-century Jews who used similar apologetic clichés of Jewish superiority equally convinced of their claims? The contemporary historian in reading such statements cannot readily decipher the psychological attitude—whether confidence or insecurity—accompanying their writing.[165] What is clear, however, is that the constant need to evoke such myths of Jewish superiority might in fact signal a clear manifestation of spiritual crisis inherent in the recognition that everything of value need not be found only in Judaism and that a Jew might be enticed to look elsewhere to satisfy his own spiritual and cultural appetites.

Thus, ideological statements regarding Jewish superiority were only one way of coping with the new challenge posed by Renaissance culture. Clearly another response was conversion, as advocated by Flavius Mithridates and other former Jews intimately involved in the new Christianity of Pico and his associates. And between the two extremes, of reasserting Jewish specificity or of surrendering totally any Jewish affiliation, lay a wide array of other responses. One could affirm his Jewishness like Leone Ebreo, while speaking in the idiom and within the conceptual framework of the new universalism. Or one could remain solidly within Jewish culture by expanding the character of Judaism to include magic, Neoplatonism, and the prisca theologia, as Yohanan Alemanno had done. In this case, remaining a Jew at least implied the recognition of the relative value of other cultural experiences and the need to reexamine Judaism in their light. All of these approaches adopted by Italian Jews in the fifteenth and sixteenth centuries had been partially anticipated before their time.[166] The novelty of their cultural world did not necessarily lie in the responses they fashioned in understanding themselves in relation to their majority culture. It lay rather in the particular way in which the majority culture now addressed its Jewish minority. By defining the matrix of Jewish intellectual activity in a Renaissance environment as primarily a set of responses to the new universal image of mankind projected by the Renaissance, it may be easier to grasp the dynamic cultural setting of Jews living in Italy at the end of the fifteenth century and the beginning of the sixteenth. Moreover, it might also suggest the underlying significance of this age for Jewish history and thought in subsequent centuries. Earlier students of this period have seen in Renaissance Jewish culture the seeds of modern Jewish consciousness—an intellectual world increasingly secular, rational, and less traditional, and an age already prefiguring for Jews the world of the eighteenth-century Enlightenment and beyond. The limitations of their perspective have already been pointed out. Yet perhaps this understanding of Jewish Renaissance culture is correct in at least one respect: the Italian Renaissance did offer certain Jews a preview of the intellectual and cultural challenges their descendants would face with growing regularity and intensity in the modern world. In sensing a greater urgency to justify their own particularity before an intellectual community increasingly ecumenical and cosmopolitan in spirit if not in practice, Renaissance Jews had entered the modern age.

NOTES

The following is a list of books and articles for the reader seeking a broad introduction to the subject of this essay. General studies of Jewish civilization in Renaissance Italy include: C. Roth, *The Jews in the Renaissance* (New York, 1959); M. A. Shulvass, *The Jews in the World of the Renaissance* (Leiden, 1973); I. Zinberg, *A History of Jewish Literature,* ed. and trans. B. Martin (Cincinnati, OH, 1974), vol. 4; and R. Bonfil, *Ha-Rabbanut be-Italyah bi-Tekufat ha-Renesance (The Rabbinate in Italy in the Period of the Renaissance)* (Jerusalem, 1979). This book is to be published in English in the Littman Library of Jewish Civilization by Oxford University Press. The first three are limited by their particular biases toward the nature of Jewish traditional culture on the one hand, and their idealized vision of Renaissance culture on the other. Bonfil's work, which purports to be an institutional history of the rabbinate, is in fact a more expansive social and cultural history of Italian Jewry in the fifteenth and sixteenth centuries. For a portrait of one Jewish intellectual living in Renaissance Italy, see my *The World of a Renaissance Jew: The Life and Thought of Abraham ben Mordecai Farissol* (Cincinnati, OH, 1981). A recent book of essays dealing with sixteenth-century Jewish thought, including a number of studies related to the Renaissance, is *Jewish Thought in the Sixteenth Century,* ed. B. Cooperman (Cambridge, MA, 1983). S. W. Baron, in *A Social and Religious History of the Jews* (New York, 1969), devotes a large part of volume 13 to Jewish life in Renaissance Italy.

There is no good published introduction in English to Elijah Delmedigo and Jewish Aristotelianism in Renaissance Italy. See M. D. Geffen, "Faith and Reason in Elijah Delmedigo's *Behinat ha-Dat (Examination of the Faith)* and the Philosophic Backgrounds of His Work" (Ph.D. diss., Columbia University, New York, 1970). A new critical edition of Delmedigo's *Behinat ha-Dat* has recently been published by J. J. Ross (Tel Aviv, 1984). On Judah Messer Leon and Jewish humanism, see R. Bonfil's introduction to the reproduction of *Sefer Nofet Zufim,* Mantua, ca. 1475 (Jerusalem, 1980); ed. and trans. by I. Rabinowitz, *The Book of the Honeycomb's Flow by Judah Messer Leon* (Ithaca, NY, 1983); A. Altmann, "*Ars Rhetorica* as Reflected in Some Jewish Figures of the Italian Renaissance," in *Jewish Thought,* 1–22; and A. M. Lesley, "Hebrew Humanism in Italy: The Case of Biography," *Prooftexts* 2 (1982): 163–78.

The impact of Pico and Renaissance Neoplatonism on Jewish thought is treated by M. Idel, "The Magical and Neoplatonic Interpretations of the Kabbalah in the Renaissance," in *Jewish Thought,* 186–242. On Christian kabbalah, see the classic essay of G. Scholem, "Zur Geschichte der Anfänge der

Christlichen Kabbala," in *Essays Presented to Leo Baeck* (London, 1954), 158–
93. On Mithridates, Pico's teacher and Hebrew translator, and Pico's Hebraic
learning, see C. Wirszubski, *Sheloshah Perakim be-Toledot ha-Kabbalah ha-
Nozrit* (*Three Chapters in the History of the Kabbalah*) (Jerusalem, 1975); and
Mekkubal Nozri Koreh Ba-Torah (*A Christian Kabbalist Reads the Torah*)
(Jerusalem, 1977). On Leone Ebreo, see A. M. Lesley, "The Place of the *Dialoghi
d'amore* in Contemporaneous Jewish Thought," in *Volare alla divina bellezza:
Ficino and Renaissance Neoplatonism*, ed. O. Z. Pugliese and K. Eisenbichler,
forthcoming; and M. Idel, "Kabbalah and Ancient Theology in R. Isaac and
Judah Abravanel" (Hebrew), in *The Philosophy of Love of Leone Ebreo*, ed. M.
Dorman and Z. Levy (Haifa, 1985). An English translation of Leone Ebreo's
work is entitled *The Philosophy of Love*, trans. F. Friedeberg-Seeley and J. H.
Barnes (London, 1937).

For a recent consideration of Jewish historiography of the Renaissance
period, see R. Bonfil, "The Historian's Perception of the Jews in the Italian
Renaissance: Towards a Reappraisal," *Revue des études juives* 143 (1984): 59–
82.

1. J. Burckhardt, *The Civilization of the Renaissance in Italy*, trans. S. G. C.
   Middlemore (reprint, New York, 1954). For a sampling of the literature on
   interpreting "the Renaissance," see W. K. Ferguson, *The Renaissance in
   Historical Thought* (Cambridge, MA, 1948); E. Garin, "Interpretations of
   the Renaissance," in *Science and Civic Life in the Italian Renaissance*, trans.
   P. Munz (Garden City, NY, 1969); P. O. Kristeller, *Renaissance Thought
   and Its Sources*, ed. M. Mooney (New York, 1979); *The Renaissance: A
   Reconsideration of the Theories and Interpretations of the Age*, ed. T. Hel-
   ton (Madison, WI, 1961); F. Chabod, *Scritti sul Rinascimento*, 2 vols.
   (Turin, 1967), esp. 2:73–144; A. Chastel et al., *The Renaissance: Essays in
   Interpretation* (London and New York, 1982); W. J. Bouwsma, "The Renaissance and the Drama of Western History," *American Historical Review*
   84 (1979): 1–15.

2. Some of the earlier studies include Roth, *Jews in the Renaissance;* Shulvass,
   Jews in the World of the Renaissance; Baron, *Social and Religious History,*
   13:159–205; Zinberg, *History of Jewish Literature;* and, more recently,
   Bonfil, *Ha-Rabbanut,* esp. chap. 6, which focuses more on sixteenth-
   century developments.

3. Compare, for example, the recent volume, *Jewish Thought,* where the Renaissance is a part of but not the central focus of the volume.

4. See J. Sermoneta's comments in this regard on I. Barzilay's *Between Faith
   and Reason: Anti-Rationalism in Italian Jewish Thought, 1250–1650* (The
   Hague and Paris, 1967), which he reviews in *Kiryat Sefer* 45 (1970): 539–
   46 (Hebrew). It should be added, however, that in the past fifteen years
   since Sermoneta made these comments, a considerable amount of new work
   has appeared, primarily from scholars in Israel and the United States. Much
   of this work is mentioned in the notes that follow.

5. Since this essay focuses on certain aspects of Italian Jewish thought substantially influenced by the Italian Renaissance, it obviously ignores other di-

mensions of Jewish thought, such as that shaped by the uninterrupted study of rabbinic texts, still a primary expression of Jewish culture in this period. Rabbinic culture in this period is discussed by Bonfil in *Ha-Rabbanut*. On the evolution of Jewish thought and culture in earlier periods, particularly in Christian Spain and Provence, see the earlier volumes of S. W. Baron's *Social and Religious History*. See also *Jewish Society Through the Ages*, ed. H. H. Ben Sasson and S. Ettinger (New York, 1971), especially the essays by Twersky, Ben Sasson, and Beinart; Y. Baer, *A History of the Jews of Christian Spain*, 2 vols. (Philadelphia, 1961–66). A more comprehensive treatment of Jewish culture, including such areas as music, art, science, and literature, is beyond the scope of this essay. Also lacking is a consideration of more popular expressions of Jewish culture and of the extent to which the writings of a Jewish intellectual elite are representative of other segments of Jewish society. Understandably, all of these areas need to be fully integrated with the subject matter of this essay before a history of Jewish culture in this period can be written.

Some additional remarks should also be made about the parameters of this essay. It deals primarily with Italian Jewish thought in the second half of the fifteenth century. However, the impact of certain Renaissance trends on Italian Jewry extends well into the sixteenth and even into the early seventeenth century. It is anomalous that Leon Modena, the Venetian rabbi of the late sixteenth and early seventeenth centuries, is often referred to as a typical Renaissance rabbi! There exists no complete synthesis of Jewish thought in this later period, but the following recent works should be noted: Bonfil, *Ha-Rabbanut*, esp. the final chapter; idem, "Change in Cultural Patterns of Jewish Society in Crisis: The Case of Italian Jewry at the Close of the Sixteenth Century," in *The Transformation of Jewish Society in the Sixteenth and Seventeenth Centuries*, forthcoming; idem, "Cultura e mistica a Venezia nel '500," in *Gli ebrei e Venezia*, ed. G. Cozzi (Milan, 1987), 469–509, 543–48. M. Idel, "Major Currents in Italian Kabbalah Between 1560–1660," *Italia Judaica* 2 (1986); idem, "Particularism and Universalism in Kabbalah 1480–1650," in *The Transformation of Jewish Society in the 16th and 17th Centuries*, forthcoming; idem, "Differing Perceptions of the Kabbalah in the Early Seventeenth Century," in *Jewish Thought in the Seventeenth Century*, ed. I. Twersky and B. Septimus (Cambridge, MA, 1987), 137–200.

In addition to this temporal limitation, there is a spatial one. Italy, especially at the end of the fifteenth century, was a temporary haven for Spanish Jews and Conversos fleeing the Iberian peninsula in search of religious freedom. Some of these immigrants remained; many others moved on to Turkey, Israel, and elsewhere. In this sense, Italian Jewish culture should be viewed as a part of a larger Jewish civilization throughout the Mediterranean basin. For the purposes of this essay, however, the subject of immigrants and temporary residents is not treated, with the outstanding exception of Judah Abravanel and, to a lesser extent, his father, Don Isaac.

It should be obvious from the above that in writing this essay, I have selected themes and individual authors (some of whose literary output extends into the early sixteenth century) who most clearly exemplify the most interesting interactions between Renaissance and Jewish thought, and the consideration of whom allow some initial observations about the character of such interactions. Needless to say, such a choice is somewhat arbitrary, reflecting the personal interests and proclivities of the author.

6. For the social and economic background of Jewish life during the Italian Renaissance, see the works of Roth, *Jews in the Renaissance*, Shulvass, *Jews in the World of the Renaissance*, and Bonfil, *Ha-Rabbanut*. See also A. Milano, *Storia degli ebrei in Italia* (Turin, 1963). The social setting of one Jewish intellectual in this period is treated in Ruderman, *World of a Renaissance Jew*.

7. See especially P. O. Kristeller, "Renaissance Aristotelianism," *Greek, Roman and Byzantine Studies* 6 (1965): 157–74; N. W. Gilbert, "Renaissance Aristotelianism and Its Fate: Some Observations and Problems," in *Naturalism and Historical Understanding: Essays on the Philosophy of John Herman Randall, Jr.* (Buffalo, 1967), 42–52; C. B. Schmitt, "Towards a Reassessment of Renaissance Aristotelianism," *History of Science* 11 (1973): 159–93; idem, *Aristotle and the Renaissance* (Cambridge, MA, 1983). On the distinction between Aristotelianism and scholasticism, which I follow in this essay, see Schmitt, "Towards a Reassessment," 160–61.

8. See P. O. Kristeller, "Florentine Platonism and Its Relation with Humanism and Scholasticism," *Church History* 8 (1939): 201–11. On the coexistence of scholasticism and other systems of thought in Pico's thinking and in contemporary Jewish thought, see below.

9. See especially J. Sermoneta, "La dottrina dell'intelletto e la fede filosofica de Jehudah e Immanuel Romano," *Studi medievali* 3d ser. 6 (1965): 3–78; idem, "Hillel ben Shemu'el mi-Verona u-Mishnato ha-Pilosofit" (Ph.D. diss., Hebrew University, Jerusalem, 1965); Hillel ben Shemu'el of Verona, *Sefer Tagmule ha-Nefesh*, ed. J. Sermoneta (Jerusalem, 1981) [a second volume is forthcoming]; J. Sermoneta, "Jehudah Ben Moshe Daniel Romano, Traducteur de Saint Thomas," in *Homage à Georges Vajda*, ed. G. Nahon and C. Touati (Louvain, 1980).

10. See G. Vajda, *Isaac Abalag, Averroiste juif, traducteur et annotateur d'al-Ghazali* (Paris, 1960); S. Pines, "Scholasticism After Thomas Aquinas in the Teachings of Hasdai Crescas and His Predecessors," *Israel Academy of Sciences and Humanities Proceedings* 1 (1967): 101 pp.

11. M. D. Geffen, "Insights into the Life and Thought of Elijah Delmedigo Based on His Published and Unpublished Works," *Proceedings of the American Academy of Jewish Research* 41–42 (1973–74): 69–86; idem, "Faith and Reason," introductory chapter; B. Kieszkowski, "Les rapports entre Elie Delmedigo et Pic de la Mirandole (d'après le ms. lat. 6508 de la Bibliothèque Nationale)," *Rinascimento* 2d ser. 4 (1964): 41–91; *Sefer Beḥinat ha-Dat*, ed. Ross, introduction.

12. On earlier Jewish translators, see Roth, *Jews in the Renaissance*, 64–85; A. Ivry, "Remnants of Jewish Averroism in the Renaissance," in *Jewish*

Thought, 243–45. A complete list of Delmedigo's translations is found in Geffen, "Insights," 85–86.

13. Geffen, "Faith and Reason," 30.

14. On Delmedigo's relation with Ermolao Barbaro the Younger, see the latter's *Epistolae, orationes, carmina,* ed. V. Branca (Florence, 1943), 1:87–90. On his correspondence with Pico and his influence on the latter, see Kieszkowski, "Les Rapports"; U. Cassuto, *Gli ebrei a Firenze nell'età dell' Rinascimento* (Florence, 1918), Hebrew trans., *Ha-Yehudim be-Firenze bi-Tekufat ha-Renesans* (Jerusalem, 1967), Hebrew ed. cited, 221ff.; Geffen, "Faith and Reason," 29ff.

15. Geffen, "Faith and Reason," 12ff.

16. MS Paris heb. 968, fol. 3a, trans. in Geffen, "Faith and Reason," 256.

17. Printed three times: Basel, 1629; Vienna, 1833; and most recently Tel Aviv, 1984, ed. J. J. Ross.

18. This is summarized by Geffen, "Faith and Reason," chap. 1; and see M. Fakhry, "Philosophy and Scripture in the Theology of Averroes," *Medieval Studies* 30 (1968): 78–89. For a somewhat different view, see M. Mahdi, "Averroes on Divine Law and Human Wisdom," in *Ancients and Moderns: Essays on the Tradition of Political Philosophy in Honor of Leo Strauss,* ed. J. Cropsey (New York and London, 1964), 114–31.

19. Geffen, "Faith and Reason," chaps. 2–3; Ross, Introduction to *Beḥinat ha-Dat.* Earlier discussions of Delmedigo's philosophy include A. Hübsch, "Elia Delmedigo's Bechinath ha-dath und Ibn Roschd's Facl ul-maqâl," *Monatschrift für Geschichte und Wissenschaft des Judenthums* 31 (1882): 555–63, 32 (1883): 28–46; J. Guttmann, "Elia del Medigo's Verhältnis zu Averroës in seinem Bechinat Ha-Dat," in *Jewish Studies in Memory of Israel Abrahams* (New York, 1927), 192–208; J. Perles, *Beiträge zur Geschichte der hebräischen und aramäischen Studien* (Munich, 1884), 177–99; and see Ivry, "Remnants of Jewish Averroism," 16–35.

20. See the references cited in n. 13, above.

21. Geffen, "Faith and Reason," 17; P. O. Kristeller, "Giovanni Pico della Mirandola and His Sources," in *L'Opera e il pensiero di Giovanni Pico della Mirandola nella storia della umanismo* (Florence, 1965), 1:58, 118–19.

22. Geffen, "Insights," 85–86; Kieszkowski, "Les rapports."

23. Kieszkowski "Les rapports," 58ff.; Geffen, "Faith and Reason," 28–29.

24. *Beḥinat ha-Dat* (Vienna, 1833), 38, 43, 45, 47, 53, 58, and passim; M. Mortara, "Expurgated Passages in the Printed *Sefer Beḥinat ha-Dat*" (Hebrew), *Oẓar tov* (Hebrew supplement to *Magazin für die Wissenschaft des Judenthums*) 1 (1878): 082–084. These passages are discussed at length in Ruderman, *World of a Renaissance Jew,* chap. 4. See also Ross, Introduction to the *Beḥinat ha-Dat,* 25ff.

25. D. Carpi, "R. Judah Messer Leon and His Activity as a Doctor" (Hebrew), *Michael* 1 (1973): 277–301 (republished in *Korot,* 6 [1974]: 395–415 and in abbreviated form in English as "Notes on the Life of Rabbi Judah Messer Leon," in *Studi sull'ebraismo italiano in memoria di Cecil Roth* [Rome, 1974], 37–62); R. Bonfil, introduction to *Sefer Nofet Ẓufim.* V. Colorni,

"Note per la biographia di alcuni dotti ebrei vissuti a Mantova nel secolo XV," *Annuario di studi ebraici* 1 (1935): 172–75; C. Rosenberg, "Cenni biografici di alcuni rabbini et letterati della Communità Israelitica di Ancona," *Saggio degli scritti in lingua ebraica degli Eccelentissimi Rabbini Vivanti et Tedeschi* d.v.m. (Casale Monferato, 1932), V–XLVIII; S. Simonsohn, *History of the Jews in the Duchy of Mantua* (Tel Aviv, 1978), 717; *Book of the Honeycomb's Flow,* Rabinowitz's introduction.

26. On his exceptional arrogance, see his remark quoted by Carpi, "R. Judah Messer Leon," 293. On Messer Leon's disputes with his contemporaries, see M. A. Shulvass, "The Disputes of Messer Leon with His Contemporaries and His Attempts to Exert His Authority on the Jews of Italy" (Hebrew), *Zion* 12 (1947): 17–23; and Bonfil, introduction to *Sefer Nofet Ẓufim,* 1ff.

27. Bonfil, introduction to *Sefer Nofet Ẓufim,* 7ff.

28. See the almost complete list of Messer Leon's compositions written by David of Tivoli and published in S. Schechter, "Notes sur Messer David Leon," *Revue des études juives* 24 (1892): 120; in I. Husik, *Judah Messer Leon's Commentary on the "Vetus Logica"* (Leiden, 1906), 5; in Bonfil, in his introduction to *Sefer Nofet Ẓufim,* 6; and in Rabinowitz, *Book of the Honeycomb's Flow,* xlvi–l.

29. Husik, *Judah Messer Leon's Commentary,* 9, 17, passim; Bonfil, *Sefer Nofet Ẓufim,* introduction, 6–7; S. Rosenberg, "Logic and Ontology in Jewish Philosophy of the Fourteenth Century" (Hebrew with English summary; Ph.D. diss., Hebrew University, Jerusalem, 1974), 47–49.

30. See below, and Bonfil, *Sefer Nofet Ẓufim,* introduction, 11ff., who compares this scholastic approach with that pursued in the Ashkenazic academies of rabbinic learning of northern Italy.

31. On David, see T. T. Rothschild, "The Philosophy of R. David ben Judah Messer Leon" (Hebrew with English summary; Ph.D. diss., Hebrew University, Jerusalem, 1978); idem, "Sefirot as the Essence of God in the Writings of David Messer Leon," *Association for Jewish Studies Review* 7–8 (1982–83): 409–25; idem, "The Concept of the Torah in the Thought of R. David Messer Leon" (Hebrew), *Meḥkarei Yerushalayim be-Maḥshevet Yisra'el* 2 (1981–82): 94–117.

32. *Ein ha-Koreh,* MS Oxford-Bodleian 1263; Rothschild, "Philosophy of . . . Messer Leon," 35–39, 120ff.

33. Rothschild, "Philosophy of . . . Messer Leon," 35–39, 120ff.

34. Ibid., 119ff.

35. E. Gottleib, "Or Olam of R. Elhanan Sagi Nahor" (Hebrew), *Michael* 1 (1973): 144–68 also in *Meḥkarim be-Sifrut ha-Kabbalah* (*Researches in the Literature of the Kabbalah*), ed. J. Hacker (Tel Aviv, 1976), 404–12. On Isaac Mar Ḥayyim, see now M. Idel, "The Epistle of R. Isaac of Pisa (?) in Its Three Versions" (Hebrew), *Kovez al Yad* n.s. 10 (20) (1982): 163–214; idem, "Between the Concept of Sefirot as Essence and Instrument in Kabbalah in the Renaissance Period" (Hebrew), *Italia* 3 (1982): 89–111.

36. See David's comments quoted in Schechter, "Notes sur Messer David Leon," 120, 126; and Rothschild, "Philosophy of . . . Messer Leon," 60ff.

37. Compare David's statement on the affinity between Kabbalah and Plato in Schechter, "Notes sur Messer David Leon," 122, with that of his father, quoted in S. Asaf, "From the Hidden Treasures of the Library in Jerusalem" (Hebrew), *Minḥah le-David: Koveẓ Ma'amarim be-Ḥokhmat Yisra'el R. David Yellin* (*Present to David: A Collection of Essays in Jewish Thought in Honor of David Yellin*) (Jerusalem, 1935), 227. Compare Rothschild, "Philosophy of . . . Messer David Leon," 24.

38. Rothschild, "Philosophy of . . . Messer David Leon," chap. 7.

39. Ibid., esp. 300–305.

40. Yet note the parallel of their views regarding Kabbalah and Plato referred to in n. 37, above; and their antagonism to the philosophy of Gersonides: compare Judah's view in Husik, *Judah Messer Leon's Commentary*, 93 ff., and Asaf, "From the Hidden Treasures," 226–27, with David's view in *Ein ha-Koreh*, published by P. Perreau in *Hebraeische Bibliographie* 8 (1865): 64–65, and in *Tehilah le-David* (Constantinople, 1567), 79a, 80a, 80b, chaps. 19 and 22.

41. Rothschild, "Philosophy of . . . Messer David Leon," esp. chaps. 7–8.

42. Rothschild's view of David ben Judah as a transitional figure between the crisis and subsequent decline of scholastic philosophy and the rise of kabbalah ("Philosophy of . . . Messer David Leon," 301ff.) is clearly indebted to R. Bonfil's view of sixteenth-century Jewish thought (*Ha-Rabbanut*, chap. 6). Bonfil similarly describes Judah Messer Leon's thinking (introduction to *Sefer Nofet Ẓufim*, 5) in the context of a supposed beginning of a "crisis" in scholastic philosophy. I consider both characterizations somewhat misleading, for scholasticism in both Judah's and David's times had not yet experienced a major crisis or decline. Both figures fit well into the heterogeneous intellectual climate of fifteenth- and sixteenth-century Italian scholasticism. The hybrid character of their thought, instead of being indicative of declining scholastic influence, might also suggest the continued vitality and openness of Aristotelianism among Italian Jewish thinkers well into the sixteenth century.

43. See *Sefer Nofet Ẓufim* and the English trans. by Rabinowitz.

44. J. J. Murphy, *Rhetoric in the Middle Ages* (Berkeley, 1974), 359.

45. P. O. Kristeller, "Philosophy and Rhetoric from Antiquity to the Renaissance," in *Renaissance Thought and Its Sources*, 211–59; Murphy *Rhetoric in the Middle Ages*, pt. 2; Altmann, "Ars Rhetorica," 1–5.

46. Kristeller, *Renaissance Thought and Its Sources*, 243–54; H. Gray, "Renaissance Humanism: The Pursuit of Eloquence," *Journal of the History of Ideas* 24 (1963): 497–514, reprinted in *Renaissance Essays from the Journal of the History of Ideas*, ed. P. O. Kristeller and P. P. Weiner (New York, 1968), 199–216; J. E. Seigel, *Rhetoric and Philosophy in Renaissance Humanism* (Princeton, 1968); Q. Breen, "Giovanni Pico della Mirandola on the Conflict of Philosophy and Rhetoric," *Journal of the History of Ideas* 13 (1952): 384–426.

47. See A. Melamed, "Rhetoric and Philosophy in *Sefer Nofet Ẓufim* of R. Judah Messer Leon" (Hebrew), *Italia* 1 (1978): 7–38.

48. Altmann, "*Ars Rhetorica*," 8–11.

49. Ibid., 3–4.

50. Geffen, "Faith and Reason," 377. This view is shared by A. Lesley, first articulated in a paper entitled "Two Renaissance Jewish Thinkers on the Place of Philosophy in Jewish Education," presented at the annual meeting of the Association for Jewish Studies, 21 December 1975. See also M. Idel, "The Study Program of R. Yohanan Alemanno" (Hebrew), *Tarbiz* 48 (1979): 328–29.

51. Altmann, "*Ars Rhetorica*," 8–11.

52. See below, n. 62.

53. Bonfil, introduction to *Sefer Nofet Zufim*, 4.

54. See *Book of the Honeycomb's Flow*, 35: "the most effective speakers in all generations have been morally sound and good men: lands are called after their names (Ps. 49:12). . . . It is impossible for a speaker to succeed in persuading with even the most wholly persuasive of words unless both his mouth and his heart be whole."

55. Ibid., 145 (I have used Altmann's translation of the passage, 13).

56. See Altmann's perceptive comments in this regard ("*Ars Rhetorica*"), 8, 13, especially on the potential seeds of secularism in Messer Leon's approach to seeing Scripture as great literature. See also Bonfil, introduction to *Sefer Nofet Zufim*, 13–15, and his citation of similar approaches by other Italian Jews in his "Expressions of the Uniqueness of the Jewish People During the Period of the Renaissance" (Hebrew), *Sinai* 76 (1975): 36–46.

57. Messer Leon's sources are discussed by Bonfil, introduction to *Sefer Nofet Zufim*, 10–22; Altmann, "*Ars Rhetorica*," 6–7; *Book of the Honeycomb's Flow*, liv ff.; and much earlier by N. Brüll, L. Löw, and M. Steinschneider (full references in Bonfil, 23, n. 83).

58. Bonfil, introduction to *Sefer Nofet Zufim*, 10–12.

59. See Bonfil's remarks in this regard, ibid., 13. On the impact of the printing press on Renaissance culture, see E. Eisenstein, *The Printing Press as an Agent of Change*, 2 vols. (Cambridge, 1979). Her insights might be applied successfully to other aspects of the study of Jewish culture in the period.

60. Rothschild, "Philosophy of . . . Messer Leon," 29–32; M. Steinschneider, "Zur Frauen-literatur," *Israelitische Letterbode* 10 (1884): 88–105, 113–33, 139–47; 11 (1885): 52–92; 12 (1886): 63 ff. See also idem, *Letteratura delle donne* (Rome, 1880); and *Shevah Nashim*, MS Parma 1395.

61. Rothschild, "Philosophy of . . . Messer Leon," 32; and Cassuto, *Ha-Yehudim*, 258, on his Hebrew letters.

62. David Messer Leon, *Kevod Hakhamim* (Berlin, 1899; reprinted Jerusalem, 1970), 54, 65; and see Bonfil, introduction to *Sefer Nofet Zufim*, 4; and *Ha-Rabbanut*, 41–42.

63. D. Ruderman, "An Exemplary Sermon from the Classroom of a Jewish Teacher in Renaissance Italy," *Italia* 1 (1978): 7–38; idem, *World of a Renaissance Jew*, chap. 2.

64. U. Cassuto, *Un rabbino fiorentino del secolo XV* (Florence, 1908).

65. M. D. Cassuto, *Ha-Yehudim be-Firenze bi-Tekufat ha-Renaissance*, trans. from Italian [U. Cassuto the Italian name] by M. Hartum (Jerusalem, 1967), 256ff.; S. Simonsohn, "From the Letters of Solomon of Poggibonsi" (Hebrew), *Kovez Al Yad* 5, bk. 6, pt. 2 (1966): 381–417; I. Sonne, "Eight Letters from Ferrara from the 16th Century" (Hebrew), *Zion* 17 (1952): 148–56; W. Zeitlin, "Bibliotheca epistolographia," *Hebraeische Bibliographie* 22 (1919): 32–47; *Letters of the Carmi Family, Cremona, 1570–77* (Hebrew), ed. Y. Boksenboim (Tel Aviv, 1983).

66. See Carpi, "R. Judah Messer Leon."

67. On Alemanno's life, see A. M. Lesley, "The Song of Solomon's Ascents: Love and Human Perfection According to a Jewish Associate of Giovanni Pico della Mirandola" (Ph.D. diss., University of California, Berkeley, 1976); Cassuto, *Toledot*, 235ff.; B. C. Novak, "Giovanni Pico della Mirandola and Jochanan Alemanno," *Journal of the Warburg and Courtauld Institutes* 45 (1982): 125–47.

68. Idel, "Study Program."

69. Lesley, "Hebrew Humanism in Italy," 169–72; idem, "Jewish Adaptation of Humanist Concepts in Fifteenth-Century Italy," unpublished paper presented at the annual meeting of the Renaissance Society of America, 22 March 1985.

70. Lesley, "Hebrew Humanism in Italy," 71–72.

71. Ibid., 72.

72. Of course, a scholar like Delmedigo exerted some influence on the thinking of his Christian associates, including Pico, through his interpretations of Averroës, but his influence as a teacher of Jewish learning was relatively less significant than such figures as Mithridates and Alemanno, considered below.

73. See M. Idel, "Magical and Neoplatonic Interpretations," 186–88. See also, on the general subject, Cassuto, *Toledot*, 214–54; J. Perles, "Les savants juifs à Florence à l'époque de Laurent de Médicis," *Revue des études juives* 12 (1886): 245–57; J. L. Blau, *The Christian Interpretation of the Cabala in the Renaissance* (Port Washington, NY, 1944, reprinted 1965); F. Secret, *Les kabbalistes Chrétiens de la Renaissance* (Paris, 1964); idem, "Pico della Mirandola e gli inizi della cabala cristiana," *Convivium* n.s. 25 (1957): 31–47; Baron, *Social and Religious History*, 13:172ff.

74. F. A. Yates, *The Occult Philosophy in the Elizabethan Age* (London, 1979), 21.

75. G. Scholem, "Zur Geschichte der Anfänge." For earlier Christian use of Jewish texts, see A. Funkenstein, "Changes in the Patterns of Christian Anti-Jewish Polemics in the 12th Century" (Hebrew), *Zion* 33 (1968): 125–44; J. Cohen, *The Friars and the Jews* (Ithaca, NY, 1982).

76. Scholem, "Zur Geschichte der Anfänge." See also Y. Baer, *History of the Jews*, vol. 2, chap. 14; F. Castro, *El manuscrito apologetico de Alfonso de Zamora* (Madrid, 1950).

77. On Paul, see A. Freimann, "Paulus de Heredia als Verfasser der kabbalis-

tischen Schriften Igeret-ha-sodot und Galie Raze," in *Festschrift zum seib-zigsten Geburtstage Jacob Guttmanns* (Leipzig, 1915), 206–9; F. Secret, "L'Ensis Pauli de Paulus de Heredia," *Sefarad* 26 (1966): 79–102, 253–71.

78. Ruderman, *World of a Renaissance Jew*, 47–51.

79. See above, n. 72, and below, n. 125.

80. Kristeller, "Giovanni Pico della Mirandola," 56.

81. Ibid., 58–64.

82. This is the view of E. Garin, *Giovanni Pico della Mirandola, vita e dottrina* (Florence, 1936), 65–68; and B. Nardi, "'La mistica averroistica et Pico della Mirandola," in *Umanesimo e Machiavellismo*, ed. E. Castrelli (Padua, 1949), 55–74, which Kristeller rejects, "Giovanni Pico della Mirandola," 64.

83. Kristeller, "Giovanni Pico della Mirandola," 65ff.; C. B. Schmitt, "Perennial Philosophy from Agostino Steuco to Leibniz," *Journal of the History of Ideas* 27 (1966): 505–23; idem, "Prisca Theologia e Philosophia Perennis: Due temi del Rinascimento italiano e la loro fortuna," *Il pensiero italiano del Rinascimento e il tempo nostro* (Florence, 1970), 211–36; D. P. Walker, *The Ancient Theology: Studies in Christian Platonism from the Fifteenth to the Eighteenth Century* (Ithaca, NY, 1972); C. Trinkaus, *In Our Image and Likeness: Humanity and Divinity in Italian Humanist Thought*, 2 vols. (Chicago, 1970), 2:722ff.; F. Yates, *Giordano Bruno and the Hermetic Tradition* (London, 1964), chaps. 1–2.

Recently, W. Craven, *Giovanni Pico della Mirandola, Symbol of His Age* (Geneva, 1981), has questioned some conventional notions about Pico's philosophy, specifically his supposed universalism, his involvement in ancient theology, and his use of the kabbalah as a general hermeneutic. Craven instead claims that Pico only dabbled briefly in ancient theology and saw in kabbalah only a Christian apologetic resource for use against the Jews (see esp. 98, 107, 121, 125, 129). I cannot here refute Craven's challenging assessment of the overall picture of Pico presented by Kristeller, Garin, Wind, Yates, and others, one generally followed in this essay. Suffice it to say that Craven displays only a superficial awareness of Pico's knowledge and creative use of the kabbalah and has read little of the recent scholarship summarized in this essay. (He mentions only F. Secret as his major source on the subject, 4.) Because of this deficiency, it seems premature to conclude, as he does, that the study of Pico's kabbalistic sources has had little effect on the general interpretations of his philosophy (3–4).

84. Schmitt, "Perennial Philosophy," 519.

85. See esp., Trinkaus, *In Our Image and Likeness*, 2:741–42.

86. On poetic theology, see the references in n. 83, above, and especially E. Wind, *Pagan Mysteries in the Renaissance* (New York, rev. ed. 1968), chap. 1. For another view, see Craven, *Giovanni Pico della Mirandola*, 106ff.

87. Wind, *Pagan Mysteries*, 17.

88. Giovanni Pico della Mirandola, *De hominis dignitate*, ed. E. Garin (Florence, 1942), 162; quoted in Wind, *Pagan Mysteries*, 18.

89. Wind, *Pagan Mysteries*, 20.

90. Pico della Mirandola, *Oratio*, trans. E. Forbes in *The Renaissance Philosophy of Man*, ed. E. Cassirer, P. O. Kristeller, and J. H. Randall (Chicago, 1948), 282–83; also quoted by Trinkaus, *In Our Image and Likeness*, 2:758.

91. W. J. Bouwsma, "Postel and the Significance of Renaissance Cabalism," in *Renaissance Essays*, ed. P. O. Kristeller and P. P. Wiener (New York, 1968), 252–66, at 257–58 (originally published in *Journal of the History of Ideas* 15 [1954]: 218–32).

92. Yates, *Giordano Bruno*, 95–96; and see the studies of Wirszubski discussed below.

93. Ibid., chap. 5; idem, *Occult Philosophy*, chap. 2; D. P. Walker, *Spiritual and Demonic Magic from Ficino to Campanella* (London, 1958).

94. Giovanni Pico della Mirandola, *Opera omnia* (Basel, 1557), 105: "Nulla est scientia quae nos magis certificet de divinitate Christi quam magis et Cabala."

95. Bouwsma, "Postel," 266.

96. On the theses, see the works of Wirszubski cited in n. 97, below.

97. Wirszubski, *Sheloshah Perakim;* idem, *Mekkubal Noẓri*. The major points of these works, as well as those of Wirszubski's studies of Mithridates (see below), are succinctly described by M. Idel, "Two Books on Christian Kabbalah of Professor Chaim Wirszubski" (Hebrew), *Eshkolot* n.s. 4 (11) (n.d.): 98–103. Wirszubski's book-length manuscript on Pico, finished before his death, will soon be published by Harvard University Press.

98. Wirszubski, *Sheloshah Perakim*, 48.

99. See Wind, *Pagan Mysteries*, chap. 10, esp. 154–55.

100. Wirszubski, *Sheloshah Perakim*, 14ff.; Idel, "Two Books," 101–2.

101. Wirszubski, *Mekkubal Noẓri*, 22; Idel, "Two Books," 101–2.

102. Wirszubski, *Mekkubal Noẓri*, 27ff.; Idel, "Two Books," 101–2.

103. On Mithridates, see R. Starrabba, "Guglielmo Raimondo Moncada Ebreo convertito siciliano del secolo XV," *Archivio storico siciliano* n.s. 3 (1878): 15–91; F. Secret, "Qui était l'orientaliste Mithridate," *Revue des études juives* 16 [116] (1957): 96–102; idem, "Nouvelles precisions sur Flavius Mithridates, maître de Pico de la Mirandole et traducteur de commentaires de kabbale," in *L'Opera e il pensiero di Giovanni Pico*, 1:169–83; C. Wirszubski, *Flavius Mithridates, Sermo de passione domini* (Jerusalem, 1963); idem, "Flavius Mithridates" (Hebrew), *Israel National Academy for Sciences Proceedings* 1 (1966): 1–10; idem, "Flavius Mithridates' Christological Sermon" (Hebrew), in *Yiẓḥak Baer Jubilee Volume* (Jerusalem, 1960), 191–206; idem, "Liber redemptionis, An Early Version of the Kabbalistic Commentary on the Guide to the Perplexed of Abraham Abulafia in Its Latin Translation of Flavius Mithridates" (Hebrew), *Israel National Academy of Sciences Proceedings* 3 (1970): 135–49; idem, "Giovanni Pico's Book of Job," *Journal of the Warburg and Courtauld Institutes* 32 (1969): 171–99; idem, "Giovanni Pico's Companion to Kabbalistic Symbolism," in *Studies in Mysticism and Religion Presented to Gershom G. Scholem* (Jerusalem, 1967), 353–62.

104. Cf. Idel, "Two Books," 99.

105. Wirszubski, *Flavius Mithridates, Sermo*, esp. 20–28.

106. Wirszubski, "Giovanni Pico's Companion"; also Idel, "Two Books," 100.

107. Wirszubski, "Giovanni Pico's Book of Job."

108. Wirszubski, "Liber redemptionis."

109. Wirszubski, "Giovanni Pico's Companion," 361.

110. On Alemanno, see the works of Idel, Novak, and Lesley mentioned above in notes 50, 67, 69, and 73.

111. Lesley, "Song of Solomon's Ascents," 3; Novak, "Giovanni Pico della Mirandola," 127.

112. Translated in Lesley, "Song of Solomon's Ascents," 27–29.

113. See Idel, "Magical and Neoplatonic Interpretations"; idem, "Differing Conceptions"; Lesley, "Song of Solomon's Ascents," 49–50; Novak, "Giovanni Pico della Mirandola."

114. The subsequent development of the Christian kabbalah is treated comprehensively by F. A. Yates, especially in her studies mentioned above in notes 74 and 83. Her thesis on the relationship between hermeticism-kabbalah and science was first stated in *Giordano Bruno* and more forcefully in "The Hermetic Tradition in Renaissance Science," in *Art, Science and History in the Renaissance*, ed. C. S. Singleton (Baltimore, 1967), 255–74. Her views have elicited considerable discussion. See especially, R. S. Westman and J. E. McGuire, *Hermeticism and the Scientific Revolution* (Los Angeles, 1977); *Occult and Scientific Mentalities in the Renaissance*, ed. B. Vickers (Cambridge, 1984). The literature on Christian kabbalah is much too expansive to describe here, but see the recent volume of studies, *Kabbalistes chrétiens* (Paris, 1979). On Egidio, see J. W. O'Malley, S. J., *Giles of Viterbo on Church and Reform: A Study in Renaissance Thought* (Leiden, 1968). On Giorgi, see C. Wirszubski, "Francesco Giorgio's Commentary on Giovanni Pico's Kabbalistic Theses," *Journal of the Warburg and Courtauld Institutes* 37 (1974): 145–56. On Agrippa, see C. G. Nauert, Jr., *Agrippa and the Crisis of Renaissance Thought* (Urbana, IL, 1965) and the many studies of P. Zambelli, including "Agrippa von Nettesheim in den neueren kritischen Studien und in den Handschriften," *Archiv für Kulturgeschichte* 51 (1969): 264–96. On Reuchlin, see C. Zika, "Reuchlin's *De verbo mirifico* and the Magic Debate of the Late Fifteenth Century," *Journal of the Warburg and Courtauld Institutes* 39 (1976): 104–38; J. Freedman, *The Most Ancient Testimony* (Athens, OH, 1983), 71–98.

115. Besides Idel's studies, "Magical and Neoplatonic Interpretations" and "Study Program," see Novak, "Giovanni Pico della Mirandola"; F. J. E. Rosenthal, "Yohanan Alemanno and Occult Science," in *Prismata: Naturwissenschaft geschichtliche Studien: Festschrift für Willy Hartner* (Wiesbaden, 1977), 349–61; and G. Scholem, "An Unknown Composition from Yohanan Alemanno" (Hebrew), *Kiryat Sefer* 5 (1928–29): 273–77.

116. On these thinkers, see G. Vajda, *Recherches sur la philosophie et la kabbale dans la pensée juive du Moyen Âge* (Paris, 1962); idem, *Juda ben Nissim ibn Malka, philosophe juif marocain* (Paris, 1954); idem, "Recherches sur

la synthèse philosophico-kabbalistique de Samuel ibn Motot," *Archives d'histoire doctrinale et littéraire du Moyen Âge* 27 (1960): 29–63; and Idel, "Magical and Neoplatonic Interpretations."

117. Idel, "Magical and Neoplatonic Interpretations," 188–91; idem, "Major Currents in Italian Kabbalah"; and articles cited above, n. 35.

118. Idel, "Magical and Neoplatonic Interpretations," 198–215.

119. Ibid., 215–24.

120. Ibid., 221–24.

121. Ibid., 224–29; Idel, "Major Currents in Italian Kabbalah." See also my forthcoming book on Abraham ben Hananiyah Yagel (1553–ca. 1623), tentatively entitled *The Perfect Kinship: Kabbalah, Magic, and Science in the Cultural Universe of a Sixteenth-Century Jewish Physician* (Cambridge, MA, 1988).

122. Marsilio Ficino, *Opera omnia* (Basel, 1576), 1:873. The letter is discussed at length in Ruderman, *World of a Renaissance Jew,* chap. 4.

123. On earlier Jewish–Christian debates in fifteenth-century Italy, see Ruderman, *World of a Renaissance Jew,* chaps. 5–7, and the bibliography presented there.

124. This is my thesis in *World of a Renaissance Jew,* chap. 4. Craven, *Giovanni Pico della Mirandola,* 98, understands Pico's use of the kabbalah in a similar fashion as a "God-sent apologetical weapon for use against the Jews."

125. I. Sonne, "The Place of Kabbalah as a Means of Incitement of the Church in the Seventeenth Century" (Hebrew), *Bizaron* 36 (1957): 7–12, 57–66; K. Stow, *Catholic Thought and Papal Jewry Policy 1555–1593* (New York, 1977); Idel, "Differing Conceptions of Kabbalah."

126. Bibliography on Leone is quite extensive. Besides the works cited below, some of the earlier studies include B. Zimmels, *Leo Hebreaus, ein judischer Philosoph der Renaissance* (Breslau, 1886); idem, *Leone Hebreo: Neue Studien* (Vienna, 1892); H. Pflaum, *Die Idee der Liebe, Leone Ebreo* (Tübingen, 1926); C. Gebhardt's edition and massive study, *Leone Ebreo: Dialoghi d'amore* (Heidelberg, 1924); G. Saitta, "La filosofia di Leone Ebreo," in *Storici antichi e moderni* (Venice, 1928). See, more recently, S. Damiens, *Amour et intellect chez Léon l'Hébreu* (Toulouse, 1971); the new Hebrew edition of the *Dialoghi* translated and edited by M. Dorman, entitled *Yehudah Abravanel, Siḥot al ha-Ahavah* (Jerusalem, 1983), and the critical review by A. Lesley in *Renaissance Quarterly* 38 (1985): 145–48; the Hebrew collection of essays entitled *The Philosophy of Love of Leone Ebreo* (Hebrew), ed. M. Dorman and Z. Levy (Haifa, 1985); and Lesley, "Place of the *Dialoghi d'amore.*"

127. This point is persuasively argued by I. Sonne, *Intorno alla vita di Leone Ebreo* (Florence, 1934), who discounts the testimony of Amatus Lusitanus.

128. So argued in Roth, *Jews in the Renaissance,* 131.

129. For example, see Pflaum, *Idee der Liebe,* 145; J. Guttmann, *Philosophies of Judaism* (Garden City, NY, 1966), 294.

130. See especially, A. R. Milburn, "Leone Ebreo and the Renaissance," in *Isaac Abravanel: Six Lectures,* ed. J. B. Trend and H. Loewe (Cambridge, 1937), 131–57; Damiens, *Amour et intellect;* J. C. Nelson, *The Renaissance*

Theory of Love: The Context of Giordano Bruno's Eroici Furori (New York, 1958); E. Garin, *Italian Humanism: Philosophy and Civic Life in the Renaissance*, trans. P. Munz (New York, 1965), chap. 4; T. A. Perry, *Erotic Spirituality: The Integrative Tradition from Leone Ebreo to John Donne* (University, AL, 1980).

131. P. O. Kristeller, *The Philosophy of Marsilio Ficino* (New York, 1943), esp. 111–15, 263–87.

132. See Pflaum, *Idee der Liebe*, 70ff; Nelson, *Renaissance Theory of Love*, esp. chap. 2.

133. An excellent summary of the work is provided by Perry, *Erotic Spirituality*, chap. 1.

134. This topic is discussed thoroughly by Damiens, *Amour et intellect.*

135. See W. Melczer, "Platonisme et Aristotélisme dans la pensée de Léon L'Hébreu," in *Platon et Aristotle à la Renaissance* (Paris, 1976), 298.

136. Leone Ebreo, *Philosophy of Love*, 335ff., 449ff.; M. Idel, "Sources of the Image of the Circle in the *Dialoghi d'Amore*" (Hebrew), *Iyyun* 28 (1978): 156–66.

137. Milburn, "Leone Ebreo and the Renaissance," 150.

138. Ibid., 154; Damiens, *Amour et intellect*, 179.

139. Leone Ebreo, *Philosophy of Love*, 345ff.

140. On Leone's medieval sources, see S. Pines, "Medieval Doctrines in Renaissance Garb? Some Jewish and Arabic Sources of Leone Ebreo's Doctrines," in *Jewish Thought*, ed. Cooperman, 365–98.

141. Relatively little has been written on Don Isaac's intellectual influence on his son. See B. Netanyahu, *Don Isaac Abravanel: Statesman and Scholar* (Philadelphia, 1953), 80, 286 n. 7; Pines, "Medieval Doctrines," 374–75; Idel, "Sources of the Image," 159–60; and idem, "Kabbalah and Ancient Theology in R. Isaac and Judah Abravanel" (Hebrew), in *Philosophy of Love of Leone Ebreo*, ed. Dorman and Levy, 73–112. On Leone's relationship with Alemanno, see Pflaum, *Idee der Liebe*, 67–70; Idel, "Sources of the Image," 164–65; Lesley, "Place of the *Dialoghi d'Amore*"; Dorman, introduction to his Hebrew edition, 52–58.

142. This fact is emphasized by J. Klausner, "Don Judah Abravanel and His Philosophy of Love" (Hebrew), *Tarbiz* 3 (1931): 67–98. See Idel, "Kabbalah and Ancient Theology," and Lesley, "Place of the *Dialoghi d'amore.*"

143. Cf. Melczer, "Platonisme et Aristotélisme," 293ff.

144. I. Sonne, "On the Question of the Original Language of the *Dialoghi d'amore* of Judah Abravanel" (Hebrew), in *Ziyyunim. Kovez le-Zikhrono shel Y. N. Simḥoni (Notes: A Collection in Memory of Y. N. Simhoni)* (Berlin, 1928–29), 142–48; idem, "Traces of the *Dialoghi d'amore* in Hebrew Literature and the Printed Hebrew Translation" (Hebrew), *Tarbiz* 3 (1932): 287–313; idem, *Intorno alla vita.* Dorman, in his introduction, 86–95, summarizes Sonne's arguments.

145. Sonne, "On the Question," 147–48, where he refers to a letter of Tolomei Claudio (1543), which suggests that the work was translated into Italian from the original, "in langua sua." Lesley, in "Place of the *Dialoghi*

d'amore," also argues in favor of Hebrew as the original language of the work.

146. C. Dionisotti, "Appunti su Leone Ebreo," *Italia medioevale e umanistica* 2 (1959): 409–28.

147. Ibid., 425–28.

148. Ibid., 428.

149. Ibid., 419ff.

150. See n. 141, above.

151. On the knowledge of Leone's work among Christians, see Pflaum, *Idee der Liebe,* 149–54; Dorman, introduction, 96ff.; among Jews, see Sonne, "Traces of the *Dialoghi d'amore.*"

152. He quotes St. John in *Philosophy of Love,* 330. My emphasis here is somewhat different from that of Moshe Idel in his recent essay on Isaac and Judah Abravanel and their respective attitudes toward ancient theology. Idel maintains that both father and son polemicized with the Christian view of ancient theology. Unlike their Christian counterparts, who acknowledged two "independent" paths to universal truth, that of paganism and Christianity, they claimed that there was only one path to the truth, which came exclusively from Jewish revelation. They had little interest in ancient pagan writers, with the exception of Plato, who was made a student of Jeremiah and the Hebrew prophets and thus "Judaized" in their hands. By subordinating Plato to Jewish revelation, Judah and Isaac only allowed ancient theology to infiltrate Judaism to the extent that it served to promote their notion of Jewish superiority. Idel thus views the *Dialoghi* not as a work of universal truth but as a Jewish polemic against the claims of Pico and ancient theology as understood by contemporary Christians. See also a similar view in his "Kabbalah, Platonism, and *Prisca Theologia:* The Case of R. Menashe b. Israel," in a forthcoming volume devoted to the thought of Menasseh ben Israel; and Lesley, "Place of the *Dialoghe d'amore,*" which also emphasizes the Jewish "apologetic" tendency in the *Dialoghi.*

  To my mind, Idel somewhat distorts the view of ancient theology as understood by Ficino, Pico, and other contemporary Christians. Instead of allowing pagan philosophy a totally independent status, they also subordinated it to the truth of their own religious heritage in precisely the same manner as that of the Jews. (Lesley puts it this way in "Place of the *Dialoghe d'amore*": "If the Florentines could turn pagan myths into secret avowals of Christian truth, if they christened pagan myths, Abravanel would circumcise them.") They also utilized the myth that Plato had learned from Jeremiah, as Idel admits, and they claimed that the truths of pagan philosophy came from a single fountain, which was the Mosaic revelation and which led ultimately to their own Christian religion. (See the summaries by Schmitt and Walker of ancient theology, above, n. 83.) Furthermore, Idel exaggerates the polemical quality of Leone's work. No doubt, Judah affirmed the superiority of the Jewish faith as the font of all pagan and Christian truth, but he expressed this affirmation in a veiled and subtle manner. If his work had been conceived as a polemic with Christianity,

Christians would not have read it with such great interest and delight. Idel may be right in detecting a vindictive and victorious tone in the *Dialoghi*, but it was so faint that it went unnoticed and unappreciated by its large readership. More striking to the latter was its universal and human message.

153. On the potential influence of Leone on Spinoza, see E. Solmi, *Benedetto Spinoza e Leone Ebreo* (Modena, 1903); Damiens, *Amour et intellect*, 174ff. However, H. A. Wolfson, *The Philosophy of Spinoza*, 2 vols. (Cleveland and New York, 1958), 2:277, discounts any relationship between the two. He contends that any common passages are no more than "philosophic commonplaces."

154. H. Graetz, *Divrei Yemei Yisra'el*, ed. and trans. S. P. Rabinowitz (Warsaw, 1916), vol. 6, chap. 12.

155. Roth, *Jews in the Renaissance*; Shulvass, *Hayyei ha-Yehudim*; Zinberg, *History of Jewish Literature*, vol. 4.

156. See Bonfil, *Ha-Rabbanut*, 180ff., earlier discussed in his "Expressions of the Uniqueness," 36–46, and by Sermoneta in his review of Barzilay's *Between Faith and Reason*. See Bonfil's even clearer recent formulation, "Historian's Perception of the Jews." Bonfil there calls the approaches of Roth and Shulvass "Burckhardtian trends in Jewish-Italian Renaissance historiography."

157. My formulation here is indebted to an unpublished manuscript by Arthur Lesley.

158. In his recent essay, "Historian's Perception of the Jews," for example, Bonfil writes of "shifting our focus from stressing imitation or even adaptation to non-Jewish values and standards, whatever they may have been, to internal Jewish wrestling with the problem of maintaining the validity of Jewish cultural uniqueness while confronted with changing non-Jewish values and standards" (80). See his *Ha-Rabbanut* and "Expressions of the Uniqueness," as well as his two recent essays on Italian Jewish culture in the sixteenth and early seventeenth centuries, "Change in Cultural Patterns" and "Cultura e mistica," where he continues to refine his earlier position. See also my review of Bonfil's book in *Association for Jewish Studies Newsletter* 26 (1980): 9–11.

159. See Lesley's essays mentioned above, n. 69, esp. his "Jewish Adaptation of Humanist Concepts." See also his "Recovery of the Ancients in Sixteenth-Century Italy," paper delivered at the Association for Jewish Studies, 17 December 1985. He is preparing a forthcoming book entitled *All the Wisdom of Solomon: The Jewish Humanist Movement in Italy, 1450–1600*.

160. I should stress again that any full characterization of Jewish culture in the Renaissance period must take into account the more complex developments of the sixteenth century, where some "Renaissance" trends persisted in Jewish intellectual life, despite the increasing isolation and ghettoization of the Italian Jewish community. See above, n. 5, especially Bonfil's "Change in Cultural Patterns," where this "paradox" is discussed.

161. See my review of Bonfil's book, cited above, n. 158. I should add that Bonfil's latest formulation of his approach, "Historian's Perception of the Jews," appears more balanced and less ambiguous than his earlier ones. See also

6 &∿ BOOK-LINED CELLS: WOMEN AND HUMANISM IN THE EARLY ITALIAN RENAISSANCE
Margaret L. King

A LESSANDRA SCALA ASKED CASSANDRA FEDELE, "SHALL I MARRY, or devote my life to study?" Fedele responded, not very helpfully, "Do that for which your nature has suited you."[1] Both women understood that the pursuit of learning required deliberate choice, the repudiation of ordinary goals, and an extraordinary commitment of energies. Both married.

The condition of the learned woman in the early Renaissance will be described here. That description will help us to understand not only why Scala and Fedele chose as they did, but why they felt they had to choose at all. First, some common patterns in the careers of learned women will be outlined. The perceptions learned women had of themselves will then be explored, and the perceptions of them held by learned men. This study will conclude with an assessment of the significance of the phenomenon of the learned woman of the early Italian Renaissance for the later development of woman's role in the society of the learned. Her achievements and her failures are still with us.

* * *

By participating in the humanist movement as it emerged in fourteenth- and fifteenth-century Italy, women took part in a community of learning essential to the development of Renaissance civilization and consequential for the evolving intellectual life of modern Europe. Women constituted a small minority among humanists; yet their participation was significant. There were perhaps a dozen who could easily be named; perhaps another twenty, less visible, could be identified; others perhaps existed whose identities will elude us; perhaps three, in these centuries, were famous. But their significance is not in numbers.[2]

The women humanists typically came either from the court cities of

Reprinted by permission of New York University Press from *Beyond Their Sex: Learned Women of the European Past,* ed. P. H. Labalme, copyright 1980 by New York University. Modified and updated.

Lesley's gentle critique of Bonfil in "Hebrew Huma
"Recovery of the Ancients."

162. One additional question for Lesley concerns his us(
humanist movement." Is it legitimate to characterize th
ities of a small handful of Jewish writers—primarily M
manno—as a movement, the cultural or political progr(
claim a sizable following within the Jewish community?

163. Cf. Altmann, "*Ars Rhetorica*," 10–13.

164. See Bonfil, "Expressions of the Uniqueness"; Idel, "Kabbal,
Theology"; Lesley, "Recovery of the Ancients."

165. Thus Bonfil's assertion that Messer Leon's vigorous stateme
rhetorical supremacy in the fifteenth century expressed vig(
confidence, while Judah Moscato's sixteenth-century comments
supremacy in music reflected weakness and spiritual decline, ap
warranted to me. See R. Bonfil, "Some Reflections on the Place o1
de Rossi's *Me'or Enayim* in the Cultural Milieu of Italian Ren(
Jewry," in *Jewish Thought*, ed. Cooperman, 34.

166. It is instructive in this regard to compare the style and subsequent au(
of Solomon Ibn Gabirol's *Mekor Ḥayyim (Fons vitae)* with that of Le(
Dialoghi.

northern Italy, ruled by despots, or from the Veneto. They came from prominent families. Some (such as Battista Montefeltro, Cecilia Gonzaga, and Costanza Varano) were the daughters of ruling families. Some (such as Isotta Nogarola, Cassandra Fedele, and Laura Cereta) belonged to the urban aristocratic and professional elite. Often they were born into families that specialized in learning. Some even came from families that specialized in learned women. Battista Montefeltro, Costanza Varano, Cecilia Gonzaga, and the sixteenth-century poet Vittoria Colonna were all related, as were the three Nogarolas (Angela, Isotta, and Ginevra) and the later poet Veronica Gambara.[3] Learned women, therefore, came from a limited set of environments specifically favorable to their education and advancement.

They were educated, typically, by men. Some were educated by their fathers. Alessandra Scala was trained by her father Bartolomeo, one of Florence's great humanist chancellors in the fifteenth century.[4] Laura Cereta studied with her father Silvestro, a member of Brescia's solid government elite.[5] Caterina Caldiera studied assiduously with her father Giovanni, a physician, whose enthusiasm for his daughter's genius is revealed in the prefaces to two works he wrote for her.[6] His words may suggest the pride in their learned daughters felt by other fathers whose words have not survived. "[Our] little daughter," Giovanni wrote his brother, "exceeds all others in excellence of mind, in depth of character, and in knowledge of the liberal arts, not according to my judgment alone but to that of the wisest men who flourish in this [barbarous] age."[7]

Other women were educated by tutors. The Nogarola sisters were taught by Martino Rizzoni, himself a student of Guarino of Verona.[8] Cassandra Fedele was taught by Gasparino Borro, for whom she expresses deep respect in a letter written after her training had ended.[9] Olimpia Morata studied with two brothers, one expert in Greek, one in medicine and natural philosophy.[10] Cecilia Gonzaga's education is best known. She joined her brothers as pupils of Vittorino da Feltre in the Casa Giocosa (joyous house), a pioneering humanist school founded and protected by the marquis of Mantua, her father.[11]

Trained by wise fathers and excellent teachers in the languages, literature, history, poetry, and moral philosophy of the ancients, the learned women of this epoch often showed early and brilliant promise.[12] Costanza Varano was sixteen when she recited a Latin oration, universally acclaimed for its fineness, to Bianca Maria Visconti.[13] Cecilia Gonzaga had mastered Greek by age eight.[14] Isotta Nogarola and Cassandra Fedele were still young when their glory peaked.[15] Laura Cereta's literary career was well under way before her marriage at age fifteen, and it may have culminated at age eighteen, twelve years before her death.[16] Olimpia

Morata's career flowered soon after her appearance at the d'Este court at age fourteen.[17] The precocity of these women was remarkable even in an age that valued precocity. But their early achievements form an intriguing contrast with the difficulties several of these women experienced when advancing age necessitated hard decisions about adult roles.

A young woman was free to be studious. There were no other demands made of her, and the period of adolescence for those with literary interests was a period of freedom. But that freedom could not last into adulthood. A young woman eventually confronted a choice between two futures: marriage and full participation in social life on the one hand; or abstention from marriage and withdrawal from the world.[18] For learned women, the choice was agonizing. To marry implied the abandonment of beloved studies. Not to marry implied the abandonment of the world. It was this dilemma that faced Alessandra Scala, with whose question to Cassandra Fedele this essay began. Both understood the implications of a decision for marriage. Some learned women did in fact marry, and their studies virtually ended with their marriage: among these, in addition to Scala and Fedele, were Costanza Varano and Ginevra Nogarola. Others withdrew from the world, either to a convent, like Cecilia Gonzaga, or to a self-imposed solitude at home, like Isotta Nogarola. Others, having married, survived their husbands to devote years of solitary widowhood to renewed pursuits of knowledge: among these, Laura Cereta.[19] The community of marriage, it seems, inhibited the learned woman from pursuing studious interests, and it certainly prevented her from realizing ambitions she might have cherished for greatness. The freedom of solitude permitted, in some cases, the learned woman to develop intellectual capacities—but that freedom, perhaps more apparent than real, was purchased at the cost of solitude. I shall return to consider what feelings experienced by learned women might have persuaded them to seek freedom in the book-lined cells of the solitary life. First, some preliminary judgment should be made about the achievements of the learned women of the early Italian Renaissance.

Learned women achieved competence in the difficult material of humanist studies and composed works in most of the usual genres: letters, orations, dialogues, treatises, and poems. Much of their writing is mediocre; but then much that was written by male humanists is mediocre as well. The greatest number, perhaps, of their works constitute mere declarations of competence. Chief among these is Cassandra Fedele's oration on the liberal arts, recited at the University of Padua in 1487.[20] The oration is unoriginal—though it won Cassandra great fame. It is remarkable not in itself but because a woman had acquired the skills necessary to compose it without error and to deliver it with poise to an audience of some of Europe's most learned men. Other works by learned women were written to achieve political or social ends sought by male relatives. Costanza Varano's oration to Bianca Maria Visconti and letter to King Alfonso of Aragon were written to obtain for her brothers the lordship of Camerino, and Battista Montefeltro's oration to Emperor Sigismund was designed to enlist that monarch's aid in restoring to her husband and her son-in-law their ancestral lands.[21] Perhaps the finest works produced by learned women are those that directly or indirectly describe their authors' struggles to gain recognition and to pursue their studies. These works include Isotta Nogarola's dialogue on Adam and Eve and Laura Cereta's letters on her own life.[22] The achievement of learned women in this age was substantial: they participated more than adequately in the secular society of the learned.

Yet their achievement is flawed. Its deficiency is seen not in what learned women did in fact achieve, but in what they failed to achieve. Their accomplishments, on the whole, did not match their early promise. Their ambitions, too often, were not realized. Their success was disturbed by too many defeats.

Only a few learned women continued to write—and presumably to labor at their studies—after the brilliant years of youth. Among the learned women whose mature years yielded little or no intellectual activity are Maddalena Scrovegni, known for her learning in the Paduan years of her early widowhood; Cecilia Gonzaga, whose youthful retirement to a convent was encouraged by the Venetian cleric Gregorio Correr; Ginevra Nogarola, who had enjoyed in her adolescence the same acclaim as her sister; Cassandra Fedele, whose productive years ended with her marriage at age thirty-three but who lived in near silence for sixty thereafter, pursued perhaps by the memory of past glory. And Isotta Nogarola and Laura Cereta, two among those who continued their studies, perhaps until death, did not find the tranquility they sought in dedicating themselves to their pursuit of knowledge. The ambitions of the learned women of the Renaissance were thwarted: some never achieved goals they were capable and apparently desirous of achieving; others achieved partial goals at inordinate cost.

This pattern of failure in the careers of learned women was due, certainly, in part to the absence of opportunities for them to enter learned professions—but this issue will be left to another place. The concern here is with the attitudes held by women and men that also help to explain this pattern of failure. They were not less important than social obstacles to the realization of ambitions among learned women, and they are more elusive.

* * *

Remarkable people sometimes know they are remarkable. Laura Cereta did. She enjoyed her studies; she understood her talents; she delighted in describing to those who asked and to some who did not how she had progressed to her present stage of knowledge. Gradually her talents emerged, she reported; as her mind acquired small particles of knowledge, she learned to supply words to adorn them; her mind yearned for studies even more challenging; as her understanding expanded, so did her diligence; she loved philosophy above all; she burned with desire for mathematics; she delved deeply into theology, and she found there knowledge not "shadowy and vaporous" but "perpetually secure and perfect."[23] At birth she had been given the name of Laura, whom Petrarch had immortalized in his sonnets. Now she labored in imitation of Petrarch to lend that name still grander eternity.[24] Cereta was proud of her mind. She was unique.

Learned women more typically betray their fragile self-confidence. "Even the wisest and most famous men would fear to attempt to praise you adequately," Costanza Varano wrote in her oration to Bianca Maria Visconti; "What then can I, an ignorant, unlettered, and inexperienced girl hope to do?"[25] Cassandra Fedele began her oration to the learned doctors of Padua with a more elaborate but similar demurral: "I shall contain my timidity, although I know it might seem to many of you audacious that I, a virgin too young to be learned, ignoring my sex and exceeding my talent, should propose to speak before such a body of learned men, and especially in this city where today (as once in Athens) the study of the liberal arts flourishes."[26] Isotta Nogarola apologizes not only for being a woman with pretenses of learning but for being a woman at all, in a work that is, I believe, the most important written by a woman in the early Italian Renaissance: the *De pari aut impari Evae atque Adae peccato,* a dialogue on the relative responsibility of Adam and Eve for the fall of mankind from grace.[27] Nogarola condemned Adam in this dialogue, but based her defense of Eve, paradoxically, on the weakness of female nature. Eve, who had been created imperfect, could not be held responsible for universal sin: "For where there is less intellect and less constancy," Nogarola wrote, "there there is less sin; and Eve [lacked intellect and constancy] and therefore sinned less."[28] Eve's ignorance was natural and deliberately planted by God; but Adam had been created perfect and could be expected to behave perfectly: "When God created man, from the beginning he created him perfect, and the powers of his soul perfect, and gave him a greater understanding and knowledge of truth as well as a greater depth of wisdom."[29] Nogarola's uncertainties about her role as a woman—put into question by her confrontation with the world of male learning—culminate here in the clear conviction that woman was in fact created inferior to man and that all women had to bear the burden of this first act of creation.

Nogarola gives voice in this dialogue and in her other works to a concern shared certainly to some degree by several and perhaps by all. Her success in the society of the learned was inhibited by her membership in the female sex. The acuity of her mind could be undermined by the frailty of her nature. Not surprisingly, learned women on occasion regretted having been born female and attempted to distance themselves from other women. Not surprisingly, other women despised them.

Both Nogarola and Cereta were attacked by other women and fought to distinguish themselves from the unlettered members of their sex. Nogarola had addressed a letter to her compatriot, Guarino of Verona.[30] When Guarino did not reply after several months, the women of Verona ridiculed Nogarola, condemning her arrogance in approaching so great a man and rejoicing in her humiliation by his silence. Desperately, she wrote Guarino a second time, reproaching him for having exposed her to the mockery of her sex:

> There are already so many women in the world! Why then . . . was I born a woman, to be scorned by men in words and deeds? I ask myself this question in solitude. I do not dare to ask it of you, who have made me the butt of everyone's jokes. . . . For they jeer at me throughout the city, the women mock me. [I, a woman, in turning to you, a man, am like a donkey yoked to an ox; when I fall in the mud, as I must, when dragged by so strong a beast, neither my own kind, nor yours, will have anything to do with me.] I cannot find a quiet stable to hide in, and the donkeys tear me with their teeth, the oxen stab me with their horns.[31]

Nogarola's literary ambitions had exposed her to the envy and hostility of her sex. Laura Cereta, too, was the object of fierce criticism by women. She responded with spirit, understanding both the envy that may have motivated the attacks and the self-destructiveness implicit in any attack on women by women: these women search out others who have risen above them by their genius and destroy them with poisonous envy, she wrote. "I cannot bear the babbling and chattering women, glowing with drunkenness and wine, whose impudent words harm not only our sex but even more themselves." "Inflamed with hatred, they would noisily chew up others, [except that] mute, they are themselves chewed up within." Virtue and learning, she concludes, are not acquired through destiny but through effort; these women who are unable to ascend to knowledge fall into sloth and sink into the filth of pleasures.[32]

Less pained than Nogarola by the attacks of other women, Cereta more easily defends herself and more aggressively turns on her enemies.[33] She ruthlessly condemns empty women, who strive for no good but exist to adorn themselves and do not understand that their condition is one of servitude: these women of majestic pride, fantastic coiffures, outlandish ornament, and necks bound with gold or pearls bear the glittering symbols of their captivity to men who are proud enough to be free.[34] For Nogarola, women's inferiority derived from the order of things, from a divine decree asserted at the hour of creation; for Cereta it is derived from women themselves, who lack the will to be good, to be learned, to be free: "For knowledge is not given as a gift, but [is gained] with diligence. The free mind, not shirking effort, always soars zealously toward the good, and the desire to know grows ever more wide and deep."[35]

Nogarola and Cereta clearly reveal their attitudes toward themselves as women and as learned women; others speak less fully, but sufficiently to persuade us that the consciousness of womanhood in the quest for intellectual integrity was probably general.[36] Being women, they were burdened. To succeed wholly, they would have had to cast off that burden—but it was a burden that could not be cast off. Or they would have had to elevate the whole of their sex—but this they were powerless to do. The ambitions of the learned women of the Renaissance were thwarted in part because, being women, they were vanquished from within: by their own self-doubt, punctuated by moments of pride; and by their low evaluation of their sex, which undermined their confidence further and which was confirmed by the behavior of other women, for whom the intellectual strivings of a few threatened their condition of comfortable servitude.

The learned women, conquered from within, capitulated and withdrew from battle. They withdrew from study altogether, into marriage or into grief. They withdrew to convents and to good works and to silence. They withdrew from secular studies, where men excelled, and took up sacred studies, appropriate for women, and formed cloisters of their minds. They withdrew from friendships, from the life of their cities, from public view, to small corners of the world where they worked in solitude: to self-constructed prisons, lined with books—to book-lined cells— which may serve as a symbol for the condition of the learned women of this age.

There, they fascinated men. Matteo Bosso recalled years later his after-school visits to Isotta Nogarola in her "libraria cella"—literally, her book-lined cell.[37] Ludovico Foscarini was struck by the same image of that learned woman—by then committed to sacred study and religious exercises—in her solitude: "In my mind I see again your little cell [*cellulam tuam*] redolent of sanctity."[38] Years earlier, Antonio Loschi had been inspired by a similar image of Maddalena Scrovegni: "Your virtues, your manner of life . . . so moved me, and a vision of your little cell [*sacellum*], that one place in your father's house which you had chosen and set aside for silence, for study, and for prayer, was so fixed in my soul that it first gave birth to this meditation within me."[39] Women enclosed themselves in studious solitude, and men applauded. And women sought their approbation. When learned women withdrew from the public discourse of the learned, they may have been moved in part by the powerful spur of male opinion. They were defeated, it is suggested, from within—but the attitudes toward them held by male contemporaries were sharp probes that could penetrate deep within the hearts where that battle raged that ended in surrender.

✳   ✳   ✳

Male humanists praised learned women extravagantly.[40] Angelo Poliziano went to Venice, he said, specifically to meet Cassandra Fedele. His famous letter to her, which followed upon their meeting, praises her highly indeed; for he compared her favorably with Giovanni Pico della Mirandola, his friend and one of that century's monumental geniuses.[41] Costanza Varano's first public oration won Guiniforte Barzizza's warm commendation of Varano and of her grandmother, the learned Battista Montefeltro, who had had the wisdom to cultivate in her young relative a simulacrum of her own excellence.[42] In an age in which learning was prized, learning in women was prized as well—all the more because it was rare.

But such praise is treacherous. For the women who competed with learned men and who had the boldness to equal or exceed them were not in recognition of their excellence admitted to the company of men—yet they were excluded from the company of women.[43] Like divine miracles, they were both wondrous and terrible; as prodigies, they had exceeded— and violated—nature. Male by intellect, female in body and in soul, their sexual identity was rendered ambiguous: they were, to borrow Nogarola's imagery, rejected by donkeys and oxen alike, expelled from either stable, abandoned, restless, and sleepless. Not quite male, not quite female, learned women belonged to a third and amorphous sex.

The ambiguous sexual identity of learned women was assumed from the early age of humanism. In dedicating his book *De claris mulieribus* (*Concerning Famous Women*) to Andrea Acciaiuoli, Boccaccio declared that learned women to have so far exceeded the rest of womankind that her sexual being had in fact been transformed by a miraculous divine act: "And when I saw that what Nature has taken from the weaker sex

God in His liberality has granted to you, instilling marvelous virtues within your breast, and that He willed you to be known by the name you bear (since in Greek *andres* means "men"), I [judged] that you should be set equal to the worthiest men, even among the ancients."[44] Her very greatness, Boccaccio reasons, in which she equals male greatness, suggests that Andrea was not so much a talented female as a woman transformed by the Creator himself and made—not a man—but a being of compound and indefinite sexuality.

Other men in the next century would, like Boccaccio, in the rhetoric of praise question and transform the sexual identity of intelligent women. Lauro Quirini found that Isotta Nogarola had attained greatness by overcoming her biological nature: "Rightly, therefore, should you also, famous Isotta, receive the highest praises, since you have indeed . . . overcome your own nature. For that true virtue which is proper to men you have pursued with remarkable zeal . . . [such as] would befit a man of the most flawless and perfect wisdom."[45] Pietro Dabuson said of Cassandra Fedele that she was the "miracle" of the age; for a male soul had been born in one of female sex.[46] Angelo Poliziano understood that Fedele had, by attaining deep learning, detached herself from her sex, abandoning symbolic objects associated with women in favor of those associated with men: instead of wool, books; instead of a needle, a pen; instead of white dyes to blanch the skin, black ink to stain the page in the process of poetic creation.[47] She can be compared with the muses, the sibyls, the Delphic priestesses, any of the learned women of antiquity, Greek or Roman; "We know this, certainly, we know that [the female] sex was not by nature stupid or condemned to dullness."[48] Cassandra, too, had overcome her sex, had created a man within her womanliness and had become a creature of ambiguous identity, belonging to a third and unknown sex beyond the order of nature. The learned women of the Renaissance, in the eyes of their male contemporaries and friends, ceased, in becoming learned, to be women.

Whatever they were—and shortly there will be sketched the image that was applied to them—they aroused fear and anger in male contemporaries, who then joined to constrain these brilliant creatures perceived as threats to the natural and social order. Perhaps the most brutal attack was an anonymous one upon Isotta Nogarola: she was accused of incest. Having aroused her enemy's anger by repudiating through her intellectual activity a role proper for women, he responded, not surprisingly, with an assault on her sexual integrity. He wrote:

[She], who has won such praise for her eloquence, does things which little befit her erudition and reputation—although this saying of many wise men I hold to be true: that an eloquent woman is never chaste; and the behavior of many learned women also confirms its truth. . . . But lest you approve even slightly this excessively foul and obscene crime, let me explain that before she made her body generally available for promiscuous intercourse, she had first permitted, and indeed even earnestly desired that the seal of her virginity be broken by none other than her brother, so that by this tie she might be more tightly bound to him. Alas for God in whom men trust, "who does not mingle heaven with earth nor the sea with heaven," when she, who sets herself no limit to this filthy lust, dares to engage so deeply in the finest literary studies.[49]

Other women were the victims, not of overt hostility, but of kind persuasion: male friends urged them to retreat from full participation in intellectual life, offering advice perhaps as inimical to their progress as heated opposition. Leonardo Bruni, in outlining for the daughter of Battista Montefeltro a program of humane studies, cautioned against the study of rhetoric—the one discipline the knowledge of which would enable a woman to participate publicly in intellectual discourse: "To her [that is, the woman student] neither the intricacies of debate nor the oratorical artifices of action and delivery are of the least practical use, if indeed they are not positively unbecoming. Rhetoric in all its forms . . . lies absolutely outside the province of woman."[50]

Learned women, then, were sometimes attacked, and sometimes urged to achieve less than could be expected of their talents and their hopes. They were also urged to be chaste. Cassandra Fedele and Isotta Nogarola were praised for their chastity; the latter, clearly influenced by men who preferred that she, as a learned woman, maintain her chastity, voluntarily committed herself outside the boundaries of organized religious life to celibacy.[51] Now the social function of chastity in the Italian Renaissance is a complex problem that calls for serious exploration. It is perilous to generalize; but since the theme of chastity in relation to the learned women is so prominent, a tentative hypothesis is required. When learned women (or men, for that matter) themselves chose a celibate life, it is suggested, they did so at least in part because they sought psychic freedom.[52] When, by contrast, men urged chastity upon learned women, they did so at least in part to constrain them. These fearful creatures of a third sex threatened male dominance in both the intellectual and the social realm. Chaste, they were perhaps less awesome. And chastity suited the stony asexuality that they possessed, or that they were seen as possessing. Learning and chastity were indissolubly linked—for in undertaking the life of learning women repudiated a normal life of reproduction. *She* rejected a sexually active role for the sake of the intellectual life; *he* insisted on her asexuality because by means of intellect she had penetrated a male preserve. Chastity was at once expressive, I propose, of the learned woman's defiance of the established natural order and of the learned man's attempts to constrain her energies by making her mind the prison for her body. In the first case, chastity is a source of pride and independence; in the second, it is an instrument of repression.

The tension between these two facets of chastity in relation to the learned woman is evident in Antonio Loschi's poetic tribute to Maddalena Scrovegni.[53] Scrovegni, widowed while still young, had returned to her father's house in Padua and undertaken a life of study there in the small *sacellum* mentioned earlier. There Loschi, a young humanist, had conversed with her and, impressed by her learning and virtue, was inspired to write a poem, accompanied by a dedicatory letter and exposition, in her honor. Struck by the image of this learned woman in her book-lined cell, Loschi built for her, as he put it, "on poetic foundations," a grander edifice, in which she might sit and reign. He called this larger and worthier edifice the Temple of Chastity, and Scrovegni herself the personification of chastity. The temple was perched on a mountain; the mountain rose from a broad plain; the broad plain, an island, was bounded by sea; temple, mountain, plain, and sea were set in the frozen land of Scythia, the home of the Amazons. The temple was huge, white, immaculate, symbolic of virtue. Within the temple's deepest recess was a room—reminiscent of Scrovegni's cell—on the walls of which were carved images in relief of ancient and mythological figures noted for their chastity. Like the mind itself, one of whose principal functions is memory, this cave contained images of the past: for it was in fact the analogue, not only of Scrovegni's studious cell, but of her mind as well, by both of which she was enclosed. There in the center she sat imperious on crystal throne, surrounded by her handmaidens Modesty, Virginity, Frugality, and others. A powerful, monumental figure, she dominates the space around her—and yet she is dominated by it. She is queen within her own domain, but she is constrained: rigid on her throne, engulfed by the massive weight of temple walls, denied access to the realm of sensation and pleasure by the very guard who, defending her, repels the assaults of Venus and her son, isolated on an uncharted island in a remote and frigid land. Loschi's tribute to Scrovegni is ambivalent indeed: as it honors her for that virtue concomitant with knowledge, it confines her to a timeless and frozen desert.

The ambivalence discernible in Loschi's encomium of Scrovegni is characteristic, it seems, of male attitudes toward learned women. At the very moment that they praised learned women, learned men undermined them. They perceived such women as desexualized, or of distorted sexuality, as neither male nor female, but as members of a third sex; and these creatures of a third sex aroused in them fear and anger that provoked, sometimes hostile retaliation, and sometimes sweet persuasion to passive roles and to the ultimate passivity of chastity. For the phenomenon of the learned woman, whose learning destroyed the integrity of her sexual identity, they fashioned a fitting image: that of the armed maiden, a fusion of the icons of Athena, the chaste goddess of wisdom, and of the Amazons, fierce warriors ruthless to men. Male admirers repeatedly likened learned women to the Amazon queens and to other female warriors of myth and history. Angelo Poliziano's encomium of Cassandra Fedele opens with the words that Vergil wrote for Camilla, the warrior maiden of the *Aeneid:* "*O decus italiae virgo.*"[54] Boccaccio's catalog of famous women includes a great number of armed women, of warrior maidens, of female aggressors, several of whom combined with their martial energy a love of learning, and who suffer, interestingly, gross humiliation.[55] And behind these visions of female warriors lay the vision of Athena, martially armed, unnaturally born, coldly virginal, and though female, defined not by sex but by intellect. The chill refinement of the symbol of wisdom coalesced with the ferocity of the Amazons. These images from antiquity were invested with fresh meaning when they were jointly applied to the learned woman: they expressed the relation men perceived between wisdom in women and preternatural aggression. Learned women fascinated learned men, and men applauded, of course, their retreat to quiet studies apart from male society. There, in solitude, they were both magnificent and chained: fierce goddesses in book-lined cells. Thus confined, it is no wonder they won no battles.

*   *   *

Let us not leave her there, but reflect for a last few brief moments on the achievement of the learned woman of the Renaissance. She received no degrees. She wrote no truly great works. She exerted no great influence on emerging trends in the history of ideas. She was probably unhappy. But she was perhaps the earliest figure of the type of the learned woman who is still with us. She was educated and excelled in the highest tradition of learning available to male contemporaries—not in needlework, not in graceful conversation, not in tinkling accomplishments, but in the languages and literature that were the vehicles of the most profound thoughts the age produced. And she exercised her knowledge publicly, at least at some point in her career—not in the cloister, not in the hermitage, nor merely within the well-insulated walls of domesticity—but in the marketplace, for the learned to hear and to judge.

The achievement of the learned women of the Renaissance was enormous, and has not wholly been surpassed. Certainly, many more women are educated now than were educated then; many more seek careers in the public realm; and many are successful in attaining positions of authority—success that no Renaissance woman I know of enjoyed. But the inward experience of today's learned women is perhaps no more tranquil than that of the women who have been discussed. Many learned women still doubt themselves—more than men do. Many men still view learned women with hostility—and their hostility is still often blended with fascination. Many women still choose between marriage and learning; and many must adjust their expectations of love, of marriage, of motherhood in order to pursue an active intellectual life; or, in order to permit themselves the warmth of these relationships, they must adjust their intellectual goals. Few women have not had to face these choices; few men, perhaps, have had to. It is perhaps the last barrier to the achievement of female equality in the society of the learned—and it is obstinate. What the learned women of the Italian Renaissance attained, we have attained, in greater quantity; but what they suffered we have not escaped. We have confined their demons in a Pandoran box, from which they erupt to haunt us: book-lined cells; armed maidens; the thwarting of ambitions.

NOTES

1. Fedele's response to Scala, on the basis of which Scala's query can be assumed, is in *Clarissimae feminae Cassandrae Fidelis venetae epistolae et orationes posthumae,* ed. G. F. Tomasini (Padua, 1636), 167: "Mea itaque, Alexandra, utrum Musis an Viro te dedas ancipitem esse; id tibi de hac re eligendum censeo, ad quod te magis proclivem natura constituit."

2. I am concerned with the period 1350–1530. Laura Cereta, Cassandra Fedele, and Isotta Nogarola (all from the fifteenth century) achieved considerable fame. Nine others, to my knowledge, achieved some visibility: Cecilia Gonzaga, Battista Montefeltro (or Malatesta, her name by marriage), Olimpia Morata, Angela Nogarola, Ginevra Nogarola, Alessandra Scala, Maddalena Scrovegni, Ippolita Sforza, and Costanza Varano. For the learned women of the Italian Renaissance, see M. L. King, "Thwarted Ambitions: Six Learned Women of the Early Italian Renaissance," *Soundings* 59 (1976): 280–300, with bibliography at 301–4; the relevant essays in *Beyond Their Sex: Learned Women of the European Past,* ed. P. A. Labalme (New York, 1980), esp. P. O. Kristeller, "Learned Women of Early Modern Italy: Humanists and University Scholars," 91–116; M. L. King and A. Rabil, Jr., *Her Immaculate Hand: Selected Works by and About the Women Humanists of Quattrocento Italy* (Binghamton, NY, 1983), translation with biographical introductions and bibliography. These works should be consulted for guidance to primary and secondary bibliography for the figures considered here. In addition to the works already there cited, the following

studies may be noted: on Battista Montefeltro (Malatesta), G. Franceschini, "Battista Montefeltre Malatesta, signora di Pesaro," *Studia oliveriana* 6 (1958): 7–43, with a bibliography of editions of her poems on p. 9, n. 2; A. degli Abati Olivieri Giordani, *Notizie di Battista Montefeltro moglie di Galeazzo Malatesta signore di Pesaro* (Pesaro, 1782); on Olimpia Morata, G. Agnelli, *Olimpia Morata* (Ferrara, 1892); R. Bainton, *Women of the Reformation*, vol. 1, *Germany and Italy* (Minneapolis, 1971), 253–66; J. Bonnet, *Vie d'Olympia Morata: Épisode de la Renaissance et de la réforme en Italie* (Paris, 3d ed., 1856); C. A. B. Southey, *Olympia Morata, Her Times, Life, and Writings* (London, 1834); R. Turnbull, *Olympia Morata, Her Life and Times* (Boston, 1846); D. Vorlander, "Olympia Fulvia Morata—eine evangelische Humanistin in Schweinfurt," *Zeitschrift für Bayerische Kirchengeschichte* 39 (1970): 95–113; and editions of her works by C. S. Curione, *Olympiae Fulviae Moratae foeminae doctissimae ac plane divinae orationes, dialogi, epistolae, carmina, tam Latina quam Graeca* (Basel, 3d ed., 1570); and L. Caretti, *Opere*, Deputazione provinciale ferrarese di storia patria, *Atti e memorie* n.s. 2 (1954), pt. 1 (*Epistolae*) and pt. 2 (*Orationes, dialogi et carmina*); on Costanza Varano, P. M. Chiappetti, *Vita di Costanza Varano* (Jesi, 1871); B. Feliciangeli, "Notizie sulla vita e sugli scritti di Costanza Varano-Sforza (1426–1447)," *Giornale storico della letteratura italiana* 23 (1894): 1–75; D. Michiel, *Elogio di Costanza da Varano* (Venice, 1807); and editions of her works by T. Bettinelli, *C. Varaneae Sfortiae Pisauri Principis orationes et epistolae*, in *Miscellanea di varie operette* 7 (Venice, 1743), 295–330, by G. Lami, in *Catalogus codicum manuscriptorum qui in Bibliotheca Riccardiana Florentiae adservantur* . . . (Livorno, 1756), 145–50, and by Feliciangeli, "Notizie sulla vita," 50–75. For manuscript versions of works by these and other learned women, see also the indexes of P. O. Kristeller, *Iter Italicum, a Finding List of Uncatalogued or Incompletely Catalogued Humanistic Manuscripts of the Renaissance in Italian and Other Libraries*, 3 vols. to date (Leiden and London, 1963–83). An issue related to that of the production of learned women is feminist writing by women or men. For that issue, see esp. C. Fahy, "Three Early Renaissance Treatises on Women," *Italian Studies* 11 (1956): 30–55; W. Gundersheimer, "Bartolommeo Goggio: A Feminist in Renaissance Ferrara," *Renaissance Quarterly* 23 (1980): 175–200; P. H. Labalme, "Venetian Women on Women: Three Early Modern Feminists," *Archivio veneto* 5th ser. 197 (1981).

Since the major studies cited above went to press, several works have appeared on the problem of the learned woman of the Renaissance. For that problem in general, see J. R. Brink, *Female Scholars: A Tradition of Learned Women Before 1800* (Montreal, 1980); on a smaller scale, S. G. Bell, "Medieval Women Book Owners: Arbiters of Lay Piety and Ambassadors of Culture," *Signs* 7 (1982): 742–68. On Italian women, I know of only M. K. Blade's *Education of Italian Renaissance Women* (Mesquite, TX, 1983), which I have not been able to consult. For English women, see S. W. Hull, *Chaste, Silent and Obedient: English Books for Women*,

1475–1640 (San Marino, CA, 1982); *The Paradise of Women: Writings by Englishwomen of the Renaissance,* ed. B. Travitsky (Westport, CT, 1981); R. M. Warnicke, *Women of the English Renaissance and Reformation* (Westport, CT, 1983); L. Woodbridge, *Women and the English Renaissance: Literature and the Nature of Womankind, 1540–1620* (Urbana, IL, 1984); noteworthy here too is C. Jordan, "Feminism and the Humanists: The Case of Sir Thomas Elyot's *Defence of Good Women,*" *Renaissance Quarterly* 36 (1983): 181–201.

    I have focused here on women learned in the humanists' sense of the term and have excluded women patrons, religious writers, and poets. For a full understanding of the situation of the learned women, attention must be given to these as well, and to the wider problems of the role of women—learned or unlearned—in Renaissance culture and society. Scholars are currently engaged in exploring such problems as women and the printing industry, women and lay piety, women as viewed by the western learned tradition (philosophy, theology, and medicine), as well as studying specific monumental women figures (such as Christine de Pizan) or the discussion of women by major authors (such as Shakespeare).

3. Costanza Varano and Cecilia Gonzaga were granddaughters, and Vittoria Colonna a great-granddaughter, of Battista Montefeltro; Angela Nogarola was aunt of Isotta and Ginevra; Veronica Gambara was Ginevra's granddaughter.

4. Fedele's letter to Bartolomeo Scala, *Cassandrae Fidelis,* ed. Tomasini, no. 109, congratulates him for having undertaken his daughter's education. Alessandra may have studied at the university in Florence; but she could not, as a woman, be admitted, and she may have pursued instead higher studies with professors engaged to give her private instruction.

5. A. Rabil, Jr., *Laura Cereta: Quattrocento Humanist* (Binghamton, NY, 1981), 4ff.

6. His *Catonis expositio pro filia erudienda* and his *De concordantia poetarum, philosophorum at theologorum;* for manuscripts and editions, see M. L. King, "Personal, Domestic, and Republican Values in the Moral Philosophy of Giovanni Caldiera," *Renaissance Quarterly* 28 (1975): 535–74, nn. 7 and 9, respectively.

7. "Tam praeclaro ingenio, tanta optimorum morum experientia et liberalium disciplinarum eruditione filioli nostra excellere cunctos non meo juditio, sed etiam sapientissimorum omnium hominum qui nostra hac sevissima temporum tempestate floruerunt vissa est" (*Catonis expositio,* Modena, Biblioteca Estense, cod. Campori, app. 293, fol. 1).

8. E. Able, "Praefatio" to his edition of the works, *Isottae Nogarolae Veronensis opera quae supersunt omnia, accedunt Angelae et Zeneverae Nogar-epistolae et carmina,* 2 vols. (Budapest, 1886), 1:xvi–xvii.

9. *Cassandrae Fidelis,* ed. Tomasini, preface, 21–25 and no. 14.

10. Olimpia Morata, "La Vita," *Opere,* ed. Caretti, 1:37–38; see among several letters particularly no. 3 to Chilianus Sinapius, 59–60.

11. *Vittorino da Feltre and Other Humanist Educators: Essays and Versions,* ed. W. H. Woodward (Cambridge, 1897; reprint with intro. by E. F. Rice, New York, 1963), 29–92, for the Mantuan school.

12. For indications of the kinds of studies women pursued, see the letters of Leonardo Bruni to Battista Montefeltro (trans. in *Vittorino da Feltre,* 123–33), and of Lauro Quirini to Isotta Nogarola (trans. in *Her Immaculate Hand,* 111–16). Here and henceforth, where the works cited have been translated, the translated source is given; recourse must be made to that source for notice of the original edition.

13. The oration to Bianca Maria Visconti (trans. in *Her Immaculate Hand,* 39–41). For her age at this time, see Feliciangeli, "Notizie sulla vita," 24, n. 1.

14. Ambrogio Traversari reported her accomplishment in a letter to Niccolò Niccoli, in *Ambrosii Traversarii generalis Camaldulensium aliorumque ad ipsum et ad alios de eodem Ambrosio latinae epistolae,* ed. L. Mehus, 2 vols. (Florence, 1759), vol. 2, no. 50, and in *Veterum scriptorum ac monumentorum historicorum, dogmaticorum, moralium, amplissima collectio,* ed. E. Martène and U. Durand (Paris, 1724), vol. 3, no. 20.

15. Nogarola was already famous at age eighteen and participated most actively in the world of humanism in the five ensuing years (see M. L. King, "The Religious Retreat of Isotta Nogarola," *Signs* 3 [1978]: 807–22, at 807–11); Cassandra Fedele's most remarkable achievement is dated 1487, when at age twenty-two she spoke to an assembly at the University of Padua (her "Oration for Bertucio Lamberto," trans. in *Her Immaculate Hand,* 69–73).

16. Rabil dates her letters, the main evidence of her literary activity, between January 1485 and March 1488; at the latter date, she was eighteen years old. Cereta died at age thirty in 1499: *Laura Cereta,* 3ff.

17. Caretti, introduction to Morata's *Opere,* 37ff.

18. Giovanni Caldiera provides supporting evidence for this statement. He defined the following different conditions of women: virgins destined for marriage; married women; widows; nuns; servants (slaves); prostitutes. Since maidens and widows would pass through the condition of matrimony at some time or would already have done so, respectable women, neither servants nor prostitutes, were seen to have only two choices: marriage and the convent. See King, "Personal, Domestic, and Republican Values," 555–56.

19. For the choices made by Fedele, Gonzaga, and the Nogarolas, see King, "Thwarted Ambitions." For Scala's marriage, see G. Pesenti, "Alessandra Scala, una figurina della Rinascenza fiorentina," *Giornale storico della letteratura italiana* 85 (1925): 259ff.; for Varano's, who died less than three years after her marriage, see Feliciangeli, "Notizie sulla vita," 42–45; for Cereta's marriage and widowhood see Rabil, *Laura Cereta,* 9ff.

20. "Oration for Bertucio Lamberto," trans. in *Her Immaculate Hand,* 69–73.

21. For Varano's oration to Bianca Maria, *Her Immaculate Hand,* 39–41. Her letter to the King of Aragon may be found in her *Orationes et epistolae,* ed. Bettinelli, 310–14, and *Catalogus,* ed. Lami, 149–50. Battista Montefeltro's oration to Sigismund trans. in *Her Immaculate Hand,* 35–38.

22. Nogarola's dialogue trans. in *Her Immaculate Hand*, 57–69. Many of Cereta's letters were published in *Laurae Ceretae brixiensis feminae clarissimae epistolae jam primum e manuscriptis in lucem productae*, ed. G. F. Tomasini (Padua, 1640); among these, those most revelatory of her own life and feelings I judge to be the prefatory letter and numbers 32, 37, 45, 46, 50, 54, 56, 58, 59, 64, 65, 66, and 71. Rabil's *Laura Cereta* provides a complete study of the correspondence and publishes previously unedited works; *Her Immaculate Hand* publishes five key letters by and to Cereta, 77–86 and 122–25.

23. Cereta, *Epistolae*, ed. Tomasini, 3: "His igitur sat eram contenta litteris quae possint non umbram mihi, vel fumum, sed perpetuo securum aliquid, perfectumque largiri."

24. Ibid., 20: "Ego potius omnem hanc insumpsi operam mihi, ut Laurae nomen, miro Petrarcae preconio cantatum, novior altera in me custodiat aeternitas."

25. This passage condensed from *Her Immaculate Hand*, 39–40.

26. *Her Immaculate Hand*, 70.

27. See n. 22, above. This work also discussed in King, "Religious Retreat," 818–20, and idem, "Thwarted Ambitions," 288.

28. Nogarola, trans. in *Her Immaculate Hand*, 59.

29. Ibid., 63.

30. This exchange is also discussed with fuller documentation in King, "Religious Retreat," 809–10, and "Thwarted Ambitions," 284–85.

31. "Sepissime mihi cogitanti mulieres quanti sint, venit in mentem queri fortunam meam, quoniam femina nata sum, que a viris re atque verbis derise sunt. Hanc enim coniecturam domi de me facio, ne queram foris, qui me sic ludibrio habueris. Nam tanta erumna afficior ut nihil supra. . . . Gaudebam cum hanc ad te dedi; arbitrabar equidem id valde ad laudem meam pertinere, quoniam testimonio sententie tue nihil erat quod me assecutam esse non putarem. 'Nunc pol merores antevortunt gaudiis,' cum aliter evenire intelligam. 'Usa sum te nequiore meque magis haud respectus es quam si nunquam gnata essem. Per urbem enim irrideor, meus me ordo deridet, neutrobi habeo stabile stabulum, asini me mordicus scindunt, boves me incursant cornibus.' " My free translation is based on the text in *Epistolario di Guarino Veronese*, ed. R. Sabbadini, 3 vols. (Venice, 1915–19), 2:305–6; also published by Abel in Nogarola's *Opera*, 1:79–82. I have included the words in brackets, exercising due caution; they are implied by Nogarola's elaborate allusion to Plautus's *Aulularia*, 226–35. Her reference is to a scene in which a poor man refuses to marry his daughter to a rich man, comparing himself with a donkey, the prospective bridegroom with an ox. When a donkey presumes to consort with an ox, the poor man complains, and stumbles in the mud, he can expect sympathy from neither the poor (the donkeys) nor the rich (the oxen). In adapting these comments on the abyss between social classes, Isotta apparently had in mind not the divisions between the poor and the rich (she was vastly richer than Guarino), but a social division more pertinent to her own case, that between males and

females. Here, then, she sees herself as the female "donkey," dragged down by the male "ox" and consequently ostracized by both her kind and his. Nogarola has borrowed heavily from Plautus but omitted a section that would make her thought complete. The omitted sentence, which her reader—the learned Guarino—would have understood from context, I have supplied. Furthermore, I have translated *ordo* as "sex." It is those of Isotta's sex, the women of Verona, who mock her, as we know from Guarino's reply (*Epistolario*, ed. Sabbadini, 2:306–9). Interestingly, a man's *ordo* was the social group to which he belonged: the noble "order," the secretarial "order," the *ordo litteratorum;* a woman, though, belonged to the "order" of women.

32. Passages and allusions from Cereta's letter to Lucilia Vernacula, "Against Women Who Disparage Learned Women," trans. in *Her Immaculate Hand*, 85–86.

33. Yet she is sympathetic to the plight of women in general—she comforts them in grief and praises their capacity for loyalty—see letters nos. 47 and 64, in *Epistolae*, ed. Tomasini.

34. See *Her Immaculate Hand*, trans. of letter to Augustinus Aemilius, "Curse against the Ornamentation of Women," 77–80 at 79.

35. *Her Immaculate Hand*, trans. of letter to Biblius Sempronius, "Defense of the Liberal Instruction of Women," 81–84 at 83.

36. Costanza Varano, for example, saw the rejection of marriage and the choice of a life of studious solitude as particularly "fruitful" for a woman; see King, "Religious Retreat," 815. Olimpia Morata well understood that she was in some way denying her sex in undertaking a studious life when she wrote:

> I, a woman, have dropped the symbols of my sex,
> Yarn, shuttle, basket, thread,
> I love but the flowered Parnassus with the choirs of joy
> Other women seek after what they choose
> These only are my pride and my delight.

(Trans. from the Greek by Bainton, in *Women of the Reformation*, 1:25.) Both these women and others understood an unstated conflict between woman's conventional role and the life of the mind, and the uniqueness of their quest *as women* to participate in that life.

37. Nogarola, *Opera*, ed. Abel, 2:128.

38. Ibid., 2:123: "Memoria repeto cellulamillam tuam, quae undique sanctitatem redolet."

39. In his *Domus pudicicie;* prose exposition in King, "Goddess and Captive: Antonio Loschi's Poetic Tribute to Maddalena Scrovegni (1389), Study and Text," *Medievalia et humanistica* n.s. 10 (1980): 103–27 at 119–20, lines 33–37: "Sic michi mores tui, sic vita, sic etas atque habitus persuasere, et sacellum tuum quem unum locum in paternis penatibus aptum silencio, studiis, et orationibus elegisti, ita sese animo meo affixit, ut ab eo michi primum talis meditacio nata sit."

40. But none known to me matched the enthusiasm of Bartolommeo Goggio, whose *De laudibus mulierum* argued not merely the equality but the superiority of women to men in all regards; see Gundersheimer, "Bartolommeo Goggio."

41. Poliziano's letter to Fedele trans. in *Her Immaculate Hand*, 126–28.

42. Guiniforte Barzizza wrote to congratulate Varano on 2 June 1442, commenting on her worthy imitation of her maternal grandmother, Battista Montefeltro; *Gasparinii Barzizzii Bergomatis et Guiniforti filii opera*, ed. G. A. Furietti, 2 vols. (Rome, 1723), 135–36: "Gratulor inclytae illi Baptistae ex Monteferetrio maternae aviae tuae: quae cum humanitatis arctium peritissima judicetur, eloquentiae suae monumenta permulta confinxerit: nullum pulchrius, nullum certius, nullum majori sibi gloriae futurum optare potest, quam ut te neptem virtutis suae quasi simulachrum quoddam relinquat."

43. Contemporaries found it difficult to believe that women could write worthy works. Laura Cereta was accused of having presented her father's works as her own—and was proud of the accusation, since the quality of her own work was established, she felt, if it could be mistaken for that of a learned man (see her *Epistolae*, ed. Tomasini, no. 50). Ambrogio Miches wrote Cassandra Fedele that her learning would arouse wonder had it been attained by a man—let alone by a woman! (see her *Epistolae et orationes*, ed. Tomasini, 138: "[your learning] non solum in foemineo sexu, verum etiam in virile stupore forent"). Greeted by such responses, women may have felt that the attainment of recognition for learning entailed the abandonment of sexual identity. For the presentation in other areas of Renaissance literature of the image of the intelligent woman as androgynous or masculine, note the recent studies of S. Shepherd, *Amazons and Warrior Women: Varieties of Feminism in Seventeenth-Century Drama* (New York, 1981), and M. Tomalin, *The Fortunes of the Warrior Heroine in Italian Literature: An Index of Emancipation* (Ravenna, 1982).

44. *Concerning Famous Women*, trans. G. Guarino (New Brunswick, NJ, 1963), xxxiii–xxxiv; also *De mulieribus claris*, in *Tutte le opere di Giovanni Boccaccio*, ed. V. Branca (Verona, 2d ed., 1970), 10:18–21, text in Latin and Italian.

45. Letter of Quirini to Nogarola, trans. in *Her Immaculate Hand*, 111–16 at 113.

46. Fedele, *Epistolae et orationes*, ed. Tomasini, 142: "Ambigendum inscrutabili sapientia inauditum dedit seculo nostro miraculum. Virilem quippe animum muliebri sexui innasci et foeminas sexu quidem paulisper immutato virorum claros mores nancisci praestitit."

47. Trans. in *Her Immaculate Hand*, 127.

48. Ibid.

49. From the text published by A. Segarizzi in his "Niccolò Barbo, patrizio veneziano del secolo XV e le accuse contro Isotta Nogarola," *Giornale storico della letteratura italiana* 43 (1904): 39–54, at 53: "que sibi tantam ex dicendi facultate laudem acquisierit, ea agat, que minime cum tanta erudi-

tione et tanta sui existimatione conveniant, quamvis hoc a multis longe sapientissimis viris acceperim: nullam eloquentem esse castam, idque etiam multarum doctissimarum mulierum exemplo comprobari posse. . . . Nisi vero hoc nimium sane tetrum atque obscenum scelus sit aliquantulum a te comprobatum quod ante quam corpus suum assiduis connubiis divulgaret primo fuerit passa atque etiam omnino voluerit virginitatis sue specimen non ab alio nisi a fratre eripe hocque modo vinclo propiore ligari. Proh deum atque hominum fidem, 'quis celum terris non misceat et mare celo' [Juvenal, *Sat.*, 2.25] cum illa, que in tam spurcissima libidine modum sibi non inveniat, audeat se tantum in optimis litterarum studiis iactare." Nogarola learned, perhaps from this or other attacks, that the world of male learning was slow to recognize learning in women; for men considered learning in women, she wrote her uncle, "virus ac pestem publicam" (*Opera*, ed. Abel, 1:42). Cereta was also attacked by hostile critics—and she defended herself so valiantly and so frequently that her championship of learning in women emerges as a major theme of her *opera;* see Rabil, *Laura Cereta,* 12ff.

50. *De studiis et litteris*, trans. in *Vittorino da Feltre*, ed. Woodward, 126. Gregorio Correr, with great kindliness, urged Cecilia Gonzaga, in a similar vein, to give up her secular studies for sacred ones, so that she could translate into the vernacular sacred works for the instruction of "unlettered virgins"—an intellectual task of great merit but certainly not of the same seriousness as the composition of original Latin works; see his "Letter to the Virgin Cecilia Gonzaga, On fleeing this worldly life," trans. in *Her Immaculate Hand,* 91–105 at 103.

51. See particularly the letters to Nogarola by Paolo Maffei and Ludovico Foscarini, in her *Opera*, ed. Abel, vol. 2, nos. 54 and 67, respectively; the latter trans. in *Her Immaculate Hand,* 117–21.

52. For two instances in which men associate celibacy and freedom, see Gregorio Correr, *Soliloquium ad deum de vita sua,* in *Anecdota veneta,* ed. G. B. Contarini (Venice, 1757), 12–24, and Ermolao Barbaro (the Younger), *De coelibatu, De officio legati,* ed. V. Branca (Florence, 1969).

53. *Domus pudicicie;* prose exposition in King, "Goddess and Captive."

54. See *Her Immaculate Hand,* 126; *Aeneid,* 11.508–9.

55. Boccaccio, *De mulieribus claris;* note especially the cases of Zenobia and Pope Joan.

CONTRIBUTORS TO VOLUME 1

ALDO S. BERNARDO ("Petrarch, Dante, and the Medieval Tradition") is Distinguished Service Professor of Italian and Comparative Literature at the State University of New York at Binghamton. He is the author of *Petrarch, Scipio, and the "Africa"* (1962), *Petrarch, Laura, and the "Triumphs"* (1974), and other works on Petrarch. He has recently rendered Petrarch's *Epistolae familiares* into English.

JOHN F. D'AMICO ("Humanism in Rome") is Associate Professor of History at George Mason University. He is the author of *Renaissance Humanism in Papal Rome* (1983).

DENO J. GEANAKOPLOS ("Italian Humanism and the Byzantine Émigré Scholars") is Bradford Durfea Professor of Byzantine and Italian Renaissance History at Yale University. He is the author of *Greek Scholars in Venice* (1962), *Interaction of the "Sibling" Byzantine and Western Cultures in the Middle Ages and Italian Renaissance (330–1600)* (1976), *Byzantium: Church, Society, and Civilization Seen Through Contemporary Eyes* (1985), and other studies of the relation between Byzantine culture and Italian humanism.

MARGARET L. KING ("Humanism in Venice"; "Book-Lined Cells: Women and Humanism in the Early Italian Renaissance") is Professor of History at Brooklyn College and at the Graduate Center of the City University of New York. She is coeditor (with Albert Rabil, Jr.) of *Her Immaculate Hand: Selected Works By and About the Women Humanists of Quattrocento Italy* (1983) and author of *Venetian Humanism in an Age of Patrician Dominance* (1986), as well as of numerous articles on Venetian humanism and on women and humanism in Italy.

PAUL OSKAR KRISTELLER ("Renaissance Humanism and Classical Antiquity") is Frederick J. E. Woodbridge Professor of Philosophy Emeritus at Columbia University. His numerous books and articles largely determine the way in which Italian humanism is viewed today, and his *Iter Italicum* (3 vols. published, 3 more projected) continue to help define areas of research.

MARISTELLA LORCH ("Petrarch, Cicero, and the Classical Pagan Tradition"; "Lorenzo Valla") is Professor of Italian at Barnard College and Columbia University. She has published a critical edition of Valla's *De voluptate* (1970), collaborated in a translation of this treatise (1979) and, most recently, completed a commentary on it: *Valla's Defense of Life: A Theory of Pleasure* (1985).

ALBERT RABIL, JR. (Editor; "Petrarch, Augustine, and the Classical Christian Tradition"; "The Significance of 'Civic Humanism' in the Interpretation of the Italian Renaissance"; "Humanism in Milan") is Distinguished Teaching Professor of Humanities, State University of New York, College at Old Westbury. He is the author of *Erasmus and the New Testament* (1972), one of the translators of *Erasmus' Paraphrases of Romans and Galatians* (1983), and author and editor of *Knowledge, Goodness, and Power: The Debate over "Nobility" Among Quattrocento Italian Humanists*, 2 vols. (forthcoming).

EUGENE F. RICE, JR. ("The Renaissance Idea of Christian Antiquity: Humanist Patristic Scholarship") is William R. Shepherd Professor of History at Columbia University. He is the author of *The Renaissance Idea of Wisdom* (1958) and, most recently, of *Saint Jerome in the Renaissance* (1985). He is editor of *The Prefatory Epistles of Jacques Lefèvre d'Etaples* (1972).

DAVID B. RUDERMAN ("The Italian Renaissance and Jewish Thought") is Frederick P. Rose Professor of Jewish History at Yale University. He is the author of *The World of a Renaissance Jew: The Life and Thought of Abraham ben Mordecai Farissol* (1981) and of *The Perfect Kinship: Kabbalah, Magic, and Science in the Cultural Universe of a Jewish Physician* (1987).

MARIO SANTORO ("Humanism in Naples") is Ordinary Professor of Italian Literature at the University of Naples. He is editor of the journal *Esperienze letterarie* and president of the Istituto Nazionale di Studi sul Rinascimento Meridionale. The primary fields of his research have been Dante, humanism and the Renaissance, and eighteenth- and nineteenth-century Italian literature. His major works on humanism and the Renaissance are *Tristano Caracciolo e la cultura napoletana della Rinascenza* (1957), *Letture ariostesche* (1973), *La cultura umanistica nell'età aragonese* (1974), *Fortuna, ragione e prudenza nella civiltà letteraria del cinquecento* (2d ed. 1978), and *L'anello di Angelica* (1983).

CHARLES L. STINGER ("Humanism in Florence") is Professor of History at the State University of New York at Buffalo. He is the author of *Humanism and the Church Fathers: Ambrogio Traversari (1386–1439) and the Revival of Patristic Theology in Italy in the Early Italian Renaissance* (1977) and of *The Renaissance in Rome* (1985).

RONALD G. WITT ("Medieval Italian Culture and the Origins of Humanism as a Stylistic Ideal") is Professor of History at Duke University. He is the author of *Coluccio Salutati and His Public Letters* (1976) and of *Hercules at the Crossroads: The Life, Works, and Thought of Coluccio Salutati* (1983). He is completing a book-length study of the subject of his essay in this volume.

INDEX TO VOLUMES 1–3

References to volume numbers are set in italic type. Notes are cited only when they contain discussions of issues; otherwise, consult the Bibliography.